ESOTERIC HEALING

BOOKS BY ALICE A. BAILEY

ESOTERIC HEALING

VOLUME IV

A TREATISE ON THE SEVEN RAYS

By

ALICE A. BAILEY

LUCIS PUBLISHING COMPANY

New York

LUCIS PRESS, LTD.

London

First Printing, 1953
Sixth Printing, 1971 (First Paperback Edition)
Fourteenth Printing, 1998

ISBN 0-85330-121-2
Library of Congress Catalog Card Number: 53-19914

The publication of this book is financed by the Tibetan Book Fund which is established for the perpetuation of the teachings of the Tibetan and Alice A. Bailey.

This Fund is controlled by the Lucis Trust, a tax-exempt, religious, eductional corporation.

The Lucis Publishing Company is a non-profit organisation owned by the Lucis Trust. No royalties are paid on this book.

This title is also available in a
clothbound edition.

It has been translated into Danish, Dutch, French, German, Greek, Italian, Spanish, and Swedish. Translation into other languages is proceeding.

LUCIS PUBLISHING COMPANY
120 Wall Street
New York, NY 10005

LUCIS PRESS, LTD.
Suite 54
3 Whitehall Court
London SW1A 2EF

MANUFACTURED IN THE UNITED STATES OF AMERICA
BY FORT ORANGE PRESS, INC., Albany, NY

EXTRACT FROM A STATEMENT BY THE TIBETAN

Published August 1934

Suffice it to say, that I am a Tibetan disciple of a certain degree, and this tells you but little, for all are disciples from the humblest aspirant up to, and beyond, the Christ Himself. I live in a physical body like other men, on the borders of Tibet, and at times (from the exoteric standpoint) preside over a large group of Tibetan lamas, when my other duties permit. It is this fact that has caused it to be reported that I am an abbot of this particular lamasery. Those associated with me in the work of the Hierarchy (and all true disciples are associated in this work) know me by still another name and office. A.A.B. knows who I am and recognises me by two of my names.

I am a brother of yours, who has travelled a little longer upon the Path than has the average student, and has therefore incurred greater responsibilities. I am one who has wrestled and fought his way into a greater measure of light than has the aspirant who will read this article, and I must therefore act as a transmitter of the light, no matter what the cost. I am not an old man, as age counts among the teachers, yet I am not young or inexperienced. My work is to teach and spread the knowledge of the Ageless Wisdom wherever I can find a response, and I have been doing this for many years. I seek also to help the Master M. and the Master K.H. whenever opportunity offers, for I have been long connected with Them and with Their work. In all the above, I have told you much; yet at the same time I have told you nothing which would lead you to offer me that blind obedience and the foolish devotion which the emotional aspirant offers to the Guru and Master Whom he is as yet unable to contact. Nor will he make that desired contact until he has transmuted emotional devotion into unselfish service to humanity,—not to the Master.

The books that I have written are sent out with no claim for their acceptance. They may, or may not, be correct, true and useful. It is for you to ascertain their truth by right practice and by the exercise of the intuition. Neither I nor A.A.B. is the least interested in having them acclaimed as inspired writings, or in having anyone speak of them (with bated breath) as being the work of one of the Masters. If they present truth in such a way that it follows sequentially upon that already offered in the world teachings, if the information given raises the aspiration and the will-to-serve from the plane of the emotions to that of the mind (the plane whereon the Masters *can* be found) then they will have served their purpose. If the teaching conveyed calls forth a response from the illumined mind of the worker in the world, and brings a flashing forth of his intuition, then let that teaching be accepted. But not otherwise. If the statements meet with eventual corroboration, or are deemed true under the test of the Law of Correspondences, then that is well and good. But should this not be so, let not the student accept what is said.

TABLE OF CONTENTS

PART THREE

PART THREE

THE GREAT INVOCATION

From the point of Light within the Mind of God
    Let light stream forth into the minds of men.
      Let Light descend on Earth.

From the point of Love within the Heart of God
    Let love stream forth into the hearts of men.
      May Christ return to Earth.

From the centre where the Will of God is known
    Let purpose guide the little wills of men —
      The purpose which the Masters know and serve.

From the centre which we call the race of men
    Let the Plan of Love and Light work out
      And may it seal the door where evil dwells.

Let Light and Love and Power restore the Plan on Earth.

"The above Invocation or Prayer does not belong to any person or group but to all Humanity. The beauty and the strength of this Invocation lies in its simplicity, and in its expression of certain central truths which all men, innately and normally, accept—the truth of the existence of a basic Intelligence to Whom we vaguely give the name of God; the truth that behind all outer seeming, the motivating power of the universe is Love; the truth that a great Individuality came to earth, called by Christians, the Christ, and embodied that love so that we could understand; the truth that both love and intelligence are effects of what is called the Will of God; and finally the self-evident truth that only through *humanity* itself can the Divine Plan work out."

ALICE A. BAILEY

Introductory Remarks

THE ENTIRE SUBJECT OF HEALING is as old as the ages themselves, and has ever been the subject of investigation and experiment. But as to the right use of the healing faculty and forces, the knowledge is in its infancy. Only in this age and generation is it at last possible to impart the laws of magnetic healing, and to indicate the causes of those diseases—originating in the three inner bodies—which today devastate the human frame, cause endless suffering and pain, and usher man through the portal which leads to the world of bodiless existence. Only today is man at the point in the evolution of his consciousness where he can begin to realise the power of the subjective worlds, and the new and vast science of psychology is his response to this growing interest. Processes of adjustment, of elimination and of cure engage the minds of all thoughtful people as well as of all suffering people. We have much to do, and I ask therefore for patience on your part.

When one enters the realm of healing, one enters a world of much esoteric knowledge, and of an infinity of conclusions, and one is faced with the formulations of many minds, who, through the ages, have sought to heal and to help. The why and the wherefore of disease have been the subject of endless investigations and speculations, and much definite deduction has been made as to the cures of such complaints; there has been also much formulation of methods, of techniques, of formulae, of prescription, of varied manipulations and of

1

theories. All these serve to fill the mind with many ideas—some correct, some erroneous—and this makes it most difficult for new ideas to enter and for the student to assimilate the hitherto unknown.

Aspirants lose much by refusing to let go of that which the lower mind cherishes. When they do succeed in being entirely open minded and are ready to accept the new theories and hypotheses, they discover that the old and dearly held truth is not really lost, but only relegated to its rightful place in a larger scheme.

All initiates of the Ageless Wisdom are necessarily healers, though all may not heal the physical body. The reason for this is that all souls that have achieved any measure of true liberation are transmitters of spiritual energy. This automatically affects some aspect of the mechanism which is used by the souls they contact. When I employ the word "mechanism" in these instructions I refer to different aspects of the instrument, the body or form nature, through which all souls seek manifestation. I refer, therefore, to:

1. *The dense physical body,* which is the sumtotal of all the organisms which compose it; these possess the varying functions which enable the soul to express itself on the physical or objective plane as part of a greater and more inclusive organism. The physical body is the response apparatus of the indwelling spiritual man and serves to put that spiritual entity en rapport with the response apparatus of the planetary Logos, the Life in which we live and move and have our being.

2. *The etheric body,* which has one main objective. This is to vitalise and energise the physical body and thus integrate it into the energy body of the Earth and of the solar system. It is a web of energy streams, of lines of force and of light. It constitutes part of the vast net-

work of energies which underlies all forms whether great or small (microcosmic or macrocosmic). Along these lines of energy the cosmic forces flow, as the blood flows through the veins and arteries. This constant, individual —human, planetary and solar—circulation of life-forces through the etheric bodies of all forms is the basis of all manifested life, and the expression of the essential non-separateness of all life.

3. *The astral or desire body* (sometimes called the emotional body) is the effect of the interplay of desire and of sentient response upon the self at the centre, and the resultant effect—in that body—is experienced as emotion and as pain and pleasure and the other pairs of opposites. In these two bodies, the etheric and astral bodies, ninety percent of the causes of physical disease and troubles is to be found.

4. *The mental body,* or that much of the chitta or mind stuff which an individual human unit can use and impress, constitutes the fourth of the series of mechanisms at the disposal of the soul. At the same time let it not be forgotten that these four constitute one mechanism. Five percent of all modern disease originates in this body or state of consciousness, and here I wish to enunciate the truth that the constant reiteration by certain schools of healers that the mind is the cause of all sickness is not as yet a fact. A million years hence, when the focus of human attention has shifted from the emotional nature to the mind, and when men are essentially mental as today they are essentially emotional, *then* the causes of disease must be sought in the mind realm. They are to-day to be found (except in a few rare cases) in lack of vitality or in too much stimulation, and in the realm of feeling, of desires (thwarted or over-indulged) and in the moods, suppressions, or expressions of the deep-

seated longings, irritations, secret delights and the many hidden impulses which emanate from the desire life of the subject.

This urge to be and to have has first of all built, and is building, the outer physical response apparatus, and is today forcing a mechanism that has been constructed essentially for physical ends, to serve more subjective purposes. This again produces trouble, and only when man realises that within the outer physical sheath there exist other bodies which serve more subtle response purposes will we see the gradual readjustment and health of the physical body. With these more subtle sheaths we shall later deal.

You naturally ask here: What is the general plan which I shall seek to follow as I instruct you in the laws of healing, those laws which guide the initiates and must gradually supersede the more physical methods of the present art of healing? You naturally also seek to know what is the special technique which you—as healers—must learn to employ, both as regards yourselves and as regards those you seek to heal. I will briefly outline the teaching I shall endeavour to give and point out where you must lay the emphasis, as you commence the study of this subject.

I shall endeavour first of all to touch upon the causes of disease, for the occult student must ever begin in the world of origins and not in the world of effects.

In the second place, I shall elaborate the seven methods of healing which govern the "work of restitution" (as it is called in the occult terminology) as practiced by the initiates of the world. These determine the techniques which must be employed. You will note that these methods and techniques are conditioned by the rays (of which I have written elsewhere)* and that therefore the healer has to take into

---

* A Treatise on the Seven Rays, Volumes I and II.

consideration not only his own ray but also the ray of the patient. There are therefore seven ray techniques, and these require elucidation before they can be applied intelligently.

In the third place, I shall lay emphasis upon psychological healing and upon the need to deal with the patient in his inner life, for the basic law underlying all occult healing may be stated to be as follows:

LAW I

All disease is the result of inhibited soul life, and that is true of all forms in all kingdoms. The art of the healer consists in releasing the soul, so that its life can flow through the aggregate of organisms which constitute any particular form.

It is interesting to note that the attempt of the scientist to release the energy of the atom is of the same general nature as the work of the esotericist when he endeavours to release the energy of the soul. In this release the nature of the true art of healing is hidden. Herein lies an occult hint.

In the fourth place, we will consider the physical body, its diseases and ills, but only after we have studied that part of man which lies behind and surrounding the dense physical body. In that way we shall work from the world of inner causes to the world of outer happenings. We shall see that all that concerns the health of man originates from:

1. The sumtotal of forces, feelings, desires and occasional mental processes which characterises the three subtler bodies and determines the life and experience of the physical body.

2. The effect upon the physical body of the condition of humanity *as a whole*. A human being is an integral part of humanity, an organism in a greater organism. Conditions existing in the whole will be reflected in

the unit self, and many of the ills from which man suffers today are the effect upon him of conditions existing in the fourth kingdom in nature as a whole. For these he is not held responsible.

3. The effect upon his physical body of the planetary life, which is the expression of the life of the planetary Logos, Who is an evolving Entity. The implications of this are largely beyond our ken, but the effects are discernible.

I am not interested primarily in training individuals in order to make them more efficient healers. It is *group* healing at which I aim, and it is the work which is done in formation which interests me at this time. But no group of people can work as a unit unless they love and serve each other. The healing energy of the spiritual Hierarchy cannot flow through the group if there is disharmony and criticism. The first work, therefore, of any group of healers, is to establish themselves in love and to work towards group unity and understanding.

I would like to point out here the need for patience as a healing group integrates and the auras of the group members blend. It takes a little time for people to learn to work together in perfect *understanding* and *impersonality,* and at the same time to achieve, during their work, a one-pointedness which will produce the needed group rhythm—a rhythm of such unity and intensity that the work can synchronise internally. Aspirants and students as they work along these lines must train themselves to think as a group, and to give to the group (without a niggardly or reticent spirit) the best that is in them, and also the fruit of their meditation upon these matters.

I might also add that these instructions must be as concise as possible. I shall have to endeavour to put much truth and information into a brief space, so as to make each sentence convey some real idea and give some real light on the problems which confront a healing group. That which I have to say will fall into two parts: First, we will deal with the general work of healing and teaching, and this will involve the impartation by me of laws, of techniques and methods. Secondly, we will consider the healer and how he can perfect himself in the art of healing.

Is it not true that the prime requisite of all healers is a sympathetic rapport with the patient, so that the healer achieves insight into the trouble and establishes the confidence of the patient?

Two words I give you which embody the requirements of all true healers, and towards which you must work. They are *Magnetism* and *Radiation*. A healer must be magnetic above everything else, and he must attract to him:

a. The power of his own soul; this involves alignment through individual meditation.

b. Those whom he can help; this involves a decentralised attitude.

c. Those energies, when need arises, which will stimulate the patient to the desired activity. This involves occult knowledge and a trained mind.

The healer must understand also how to radiate, for the radiation of the soul will stimulate to activity the soul of the one to be healed and the healing process will be set in motion; the radiation of his mind will illumine the other mind and polarise the will of the patient; the radiation of his astral body, controlled and selfless, will impose a rhythm upon the agitation of the patient's astral body, and so enable the patient to take right action, whilst the radiation of the vital body, working through the splenic centre, will aid in organising the patient's force-body and so facilitate the work of healing. Therefore, the healer has the duty of rendering himself effective, and according to what he is, so will be the effect upon the patient. When a healer works magnetically and radiates his soul force to the patient, that patient is enabled more easily to achieve the end desired—which may be complete healing, or it may be the establishing of a state of mind which will enable the patient to live with himself and with his complaint, unhandicapped by the karmic limitations of the body. Or it may be enabling the patient to achieve (with joy and facility) the right liberation from the body and, through the portal of death, to pass to complete health.

Part One

The Basic Causes of Disease

THIS IS THE PROBLEM with which all medical practice down the ages has wrestled. In our present mechanistic age we have wandered far to the surface of things and away from the partially true point of view of earlier centuries which traced disease *back* of the "evil humours" bred and festering in the inner subjective life of the patient. In the evolution of knowledge on every hand we are now on the surface of things (note I do not use the word "superficial"), and the hour has struck in which knowledge can again re-enter the realm of the subjective and transmute itself into wisdom. There is today a dawning recognition on the part of the best minds in the medical and allied professions, that in the subjective and hidden attitudes of the mind and of the emotional nature, and in the life of inhibited or excessive sex expression, must be sought the causes of all disease.

From the beginning of our studies, I would like to point out that the ultimate cause of disease, even if known to me, would fail to be comprehended by you. The cause lies back in the history of the distant past of our planet, in the career (occultly understood) of the planetary Life, and that it has its roots in what is largely designated "cosmic evil." This is a perfectly meaningless phrase, but one that is symbolically descriptive of a *condition in consciousness* which is that of

9

certain of the "imperfect Gods." Given the initial premise that Deity itself is working towards a perfection past our comprehension, it may be inferred that there may exist for the Gods Themselves and for GOD (as the LIFE of the solar system), certain limitations and certain areas or states of consciousness which still await mastering. These limitations and relative imperfections may cause definite effects in Their bodies of manifestation—the various planets as expressions of Lives, and the solar system as the expression of a LIFE. Given also the hypothesis that these outer bodies of divinity, the planets, are the forms through which certain Deities express Themselves, it may be a true and logical deduction that all lives and forms within those bodies may be necessarily subject also to these limitations, and to the imperfections growing out of these unconquered areas of consciousness and these states of awareness, hitherto unrealised by the Deities, incarnated in planetary and solar form. Given the postulate that every form is a part of a still greater form, and that we do indeed "live and move and have our being" within the body of God (as St. Paul expresses it) we, as integral parts of the fourth kingdom in nature, share in this general limitation and imperfection.

More than this general premise is beyond our powers to grasp and to express, for the general mental equipment of the average aspirant and disciple is inadequate to the task. Such terms as "cosmic evil, divine imperfection, limited areas of consciousness, the freedom of pure spirit, divine mind," which are so freely bandied about by the mystical and occult thinkers of the time: What do they really mean? The affirmations of many schools of healing as to ultimate divine perfection, and the formulation of their beliefs in the real freedom of humanity from ordinary ills of the flesh, are they not frequently high sounding phrases, embodying an ideal, and based often on selfish desire? Do they not constitute utterly meaningless sentences in their mystical implications? How can it be otherwise, when only the perfected man has any real idea of what constitutes divinity?

It is surely better for us to admit that it is not possible for man to understand the deep-seated causes of that which can be seen emerging in the evolution of form life. Is it not wise to face the issue and the facts, as they exist for our present realisation, and understand that just as man can enter more intelligently into the mind of God than can the lesser mind of the animal, so there may exist other and greater Minds, functioning in other and higher kingdoms in nature which will surely see life more truly and more accurately than does mankind? It is possible, is it not, that the objective of evolution (as outlined and emphasised by man) may (in the last analysis) be only that partial fragment of a greater objective than he, with his finite understanding, can grasp. The whole intent, as it lies hid in the mind of God, may be very different to what man may conceive today, and cosmic evil and cosmic good, reduced to terminologies, may lose their significance altogether, and are only to be seen through the glamour and the illusion with which man surrounds all things. The best minds of this age are only just beginning to see the first dim ray of light which is piercing this glamour, and serving first of all to reveal the fact of illusion. Through the light thus cast, the following truth may stand revealed to those who have the expectant attitude and the open mind: *Deity itself is on the road towards perfection.* The implications of that statement are many.

In dealing with the causes of disease, we will take the position that the foundational and ultimate cosmic cause lies beyond our comprehension, and that only as the kingdom of God is revealed on earth shall we enter into some real understanding of the general widespread disease to be found upon our planet in all the four kingdoms in nature. A few basic statements can be made, however, which will be found true eventually in the macrocosmic sense, and can already be demonstrated to be true where the microcosm is intelligently concerned.

1. All disease (and this is a platitude) is caused by lack of harmony—a disharmony to be found existing between the form aspect and the life. That which brings together form and life, or rather, that which is the result of this intended union, we call the soul, the self where humanity is concerned, and the integrating principle where the subhuman kingdoms are concerned. Disease appears where there is a lack of alignment between these various factors, the soul and the form, the life and its expression, the subjective and the objective realities. Consequently, spirit and matter are *not* freely related to each other. This is one mode of interpreting Law I, and the entire thesis is intended to be an exposition of that Law.

2. This lack of harmony, producing what we call disease, runs through all the four kingdoms in nature, and causes those conditions which produce pain (where the sentiency is exquisite and developed) and everywhere congestion, corruption and death. Ponder on these words: Inharmony, Disease, Pain, Congestion, Corruption, Death, for they are descriptive of the general condition governing the conscious life of all forms, macrocosmic and microcosmic. They are not causes.

3. All these conditions, however, can be regarded as purificatory in their effects, and must be so regarded by humanity if the right attitude towards disease is to be assumed. This is oft forgotten by the fanatical healer and by the radical exponent of an idea, finitely grasped and in most cases only part of a greater idea.

4. Methods of healing and techniques of peculiar to humanity and are the result of tivity. They indicate his latent power as one who progresses towards freedom. They indicate discriminative ability to sense perfection, to vision the goal, and hence to work towards that ultimate liberation. His error at this time consists in:

a. His inability to see the true uses of pain.
b. His resentment at suffering.
c. His misunderstanding of the law of nonresistance.
d. His over-emphasis of the *form* nature.
e. His attitude to death, and his feeling that the disappearance of the life out of visual perception through the medium of form, and the consequent disintegration of that form, indicates disaster.

5. When human thought reverses the usual ideas as to disease, and accepts disease as a fact in nature, man will begin to work with the law of liberation, with right thought, leading to nonresistance. At present, by the power of his directed thought and his intense antagonism to disease, he only tends to energise the difficulty. When he reorients his thought to truth and the soul, physical plane ills will begin to disappear. This will become apparent as we study later the method of eradication. Disease exists. Forms in all kingdoms are full of inharmony and out of alignment with the indwelling life. Disease and corruption and the tendency towards dissolution are found everywhere. I am choosing my words with care.

6. Disease is not, therefore, the result of wrong human thought. It existed among the many forms of life long before the human family appeared on earth. If you seek verbal expression, and if you want to talk within the limits of the human mind, you can say with a measure of accuracy: God,

...anetary Deity, is guilty of wrong thinking. But you ...1 not be expressing the truth, but only a tiny fraction of ...he cause, as it appears to your feeble finite mind, through the medium of the general world glamour and illusion.

7. From one angle, disease is a process of liberation, and the enemy of that which is static and crystallised. Think not, from what I say, that therefore disease should be welcomed, and that the process of death should be cherished. Were that the case, one would cultivate disease and put a premium on suicide. Fortunately for humanity, the whole tendency of life is against disease, and the reaction of the form life upon the thought of man fosters the fear of death. This has been rightly so, for the instinct of self-preservation and the preservation of form integrity is a vital principle in matter, and the tendency to self-perpetuation of the life within the form is one of our greatest God-given capacities and will persist. But in the human family this must eventually give place to the use of death as the organised, freeing process in order to conserve force and give to the soul a better instrument of manifestation. For this liberty of action, mankind as a whole is not yet ready. The disciples and aspirants of the world should now, however, begin to grasp these newer principles of existence. The instinct to self-preservation governs the relation of spirit and matter, of life and form as long as the Deity Himself wills to incarnate within His body of manifestation—a planet, or a solar system. I have in the above statement given to you a hint as to one of the basic causes of disease, and to the endless fight between the imprisoned spirit and the imprisoning form. This fight uses for its method that innate quality which expresses itself as the urge to preserve and the urge to perpetuate—both the present form and the species.

8. The law of cause and effect, called Karma in the East, governs all this. Karma must be regarded in reality as the effect (in the form life of our planet) of causes, deep-seated and hidden in the mind of God. The causes that we may trace in relation to disease and death are in reality only the working out of certain basic principles which govern—rightly or wrongly, who shall say?—the life of God in form, and they must ever remain incomprehensible to man until such time as he takes the great initiation which is symbolised for us in the Transfiguration. All along in our studies, we shall be dealing with *secondary* causes and their effects, with the phenomenal results of those subjective effects which emanate from causes too far away for us to grasp. This should be admitted and grasped. This is the best man can do with his present mental apparatus. When the intuition rarely works, and the mind is seldom illumined, why should man arrogantly expect to understand everything? Let him work at the development of his intuition and at achieving illumination. Understanding may then come his way. He will have earned the right to divine knowledge. But the above recognition will suffice for our work and will enable us to lay down those laws and principles which will indicate the way humanity may gain release from the form consciousness and consequent immunity from the victory of death and those disease-dealing conditions which govern to-day our planetary manifestation.

We will divide our consideration of the causes of disease into three parts, eliminating from our quest for truth the quite understandable but equally futile desire to apprehend the mind of Deity.

    I. The psychological causes.
    II. Causes emanating from group life.
    III. Our karmic liabilities, the karmic causes.

In all this we shall but gain a general idea (all that is now possible) as to the presence of disease in the human family, and of that to be found also, in part, in the animal kingdom. When this general idea is grasped, we shall have a clearer understanding of our problem and can then proceed with our consideration of the methods which will enable us to handle the undesirable effects with greater facility. Students of the Art of Healing should likewise remember that there are three ways in which healing can be brought about, and that all three ways have their place and value, dependent upon the point in evolution of the subject being healed.

First, there is the application of those palliatives and ameliorating methods which gradually cure disease and eliminate undesirable conditions; they build up the form life and foster the vitality, so that disease can be thrown off. Of these methods the allopathic and the homeopathic schools and the various osteopathic and chiropractic and other therapeutic schools are good exponents. They have done much good and constructive work, and the debt of humanity to the wisdom, skill and unselfish attentions of the physicians is great. They are dealing all the time with urgent conditions and dangerous effects of causes which are not apparent on the surface. Under these methods, the patient is in the hands of an outside party, and should be passive, quiescent and negative.

Secondly, there is the appearance of the work and methods of the modern psychologist, who seeks to deal with subjective conditions and to straighten out those wrong attitudes of mind, those inhibitions, psychoses and complexes which bring about the outer states of disease, the morbid conditions and neurotic and mental disasters. Under this method, the patient is taught to cooperate as much as he can with the psychologist, so that he may arrive at a proper understanding of himself, and so learn to eradicate those inner compelling situations which are responsible for the outer results. He is trained to be positive and active, and this is a great step in the right direction. The tendency to combine psychology with the outer physical treatment is sound and right.

Thirdly, the highest and the newest method is that of calling into positive activity a man's own soul. The true and the future healing is brought about when the life of the soul can flow without any impediment and hindrance throughout every aspect of the form nature. It can then vitalise it with its potency, and can also eliminate those congestions and obstructions which are such a fruitful source of disease.

This gives you much to ponder upon. If we go slowly as regards the practical application of techniques and methods, it is because I seek to lay a sound foundation for that which I shall later impart.

The Training of the Healer

As regards the training of the healer, I will give from time to time the six rules which govern (or should govern) his activity. Bear in mind the two words which I earlier gave. They sum up the healer's story: MAGNETISM and RADIATION. They are different in their effects as we shall later see.

Rule One

The healer must seek to link his soul, his heart, his brain and his hands. Thus can he pour the vital healing force upon the patient. This is *magnetic work*. It cures disease, or may increase the so-called evil state, according to the knowledge of the healer.

The healer must seek to link his soul, his brain, his heart and auric emanation. Thus can his presence feed the soul life of the patient. This is *the work of radiation.* The hands are needed not. The soul displays its power. The patient's soul responds through the response of his aura to the radiation of the healer's aura, flooded with soul energy.

In considering the Causes of Disease, I find it necessary to speak a word in connection with conditions—external and internal. It will be apparent to the casual thinker that many diseases and many causes of death are due to environing conditions for which he is in no way responsible. These range all the way from purely external occurrences to hereditary predispositions. They might be listed as follows:

1. *Accidents,* which may be due to personal negligence, group happenings, the carelessness of other people, and the results of fighting, as in labour strikes or war. They can also be brought about by attacks from the animal or the snake world, accidental poisonings and many other causes.

2. *Infections* coming to a man from outside and not as the result of his own peculiar blood condition. Such infections are the various so-called infectious and contagious diseases, and prevalent epidemics. These may come to a man in the line of duty, through his daily contacts, or through a widespread condition of disease in his environment.

3. *Diseases due to malnutrition,* particularly when found in the young. This state of undernourishment predisposes the body to disease, lowers the resistance and the vitality, and offsets the "fighting powers" of the man, leading to premature death.

4. *Heredity.* There are, as you well know, certain forms of hereditary weaknesses, which either predispose a person to certain illnesses and consequent death, or produce in him those conditions which lead to a steady weak-

ening of his hold on life; there are also those tendencies which constitute a form of dangerous appetite, which lead to undesirable habits, a letting down of the morale, and are dangerous to the will of the person, rendering him futile to fight these predispositions. He succumbs to them and pays the price of such habits, which is disease and death.

These four types of disease and causes of death account for much that we see happening around us in people's lives, but they are not to be classed definitely under any of the psychological causes of disease, and will only be considered, and that very briefly, under the section dealing with group life and its predisposing causes of disease. Infectious diseases are there dealt with, but such situations as arise out of an automobile or railroad accident, for instance, are not to be considered as coming under the heading of causes producing disease. That the work of the healer may be involved in these cases is quite true, but the work to be done is somewhat different to that accomplished when dealing with those diseases which have their roots in some subtle body or other, or in the results of group disease, etc. The ills growing out of malnutrition and the wrong feeding of our modern life and civilisation will not here be considered. For these no child is individually responsible. I am concerned with the diseases arising in wrong internal conditions.

The responsibility of a child for his living conditions is practically nil, unless you admit karma as a predisposing factor, and its power to produce those re-adjustments which emerge out of the past and affect the present. I shall deal with this more fully under our third point, dealing with our karmic liabilities. I would only suggest here that the whole subject of disease could be treated from the angle of karma and be definite and conclusive in its value had there been right teaching on this abstruse subject from the time that it was given out in the West. But the truth as it has come to us from the East has been as much distorted by the Eastern theologian as the doctrines of the Atonement and of the Virgin Birth have been misinterpreted and taught by the Western theologian. The real truth bears little resemblance to our modern formulations. I am, therefore, seriously handicapped when dealing with the subject of disease from the angle of karma. It is difficult for me to convey to you anything of the truth as it really exists, owing to the pre-conceived ideas as to the ancient Law of Cause and Effect which are necessarily in your mind. When I say to you that the doctrine of Emergent Evolution and the modern theories of the work of a catalyst upon two substances which—when brought into relation with each other under the effect of the catalyst produce a third and different substance—carry in them much of the truth anent karma, will you understand? I question it. When I say to you that the emphasis given to the Law of Karma as it explains apparent injustices and stresses always the appearance of pain, disease, and suffering gives only a partial presentation of the basic cosmic truth, is your mind in any way clarified? When I point out that the Law of Karma, rightly understood and rightly wielded, can bring that which produces happiness, good, and freedom from pain more easily than it brings pain, with its chain of consequences, do you feel able to grasp the significance of what I am saying?

The world of glamour is at this time so strong and the sense of illusion so potent and vital that we fail to see these basic laws in their true significance.

The Law of Karma is not the Law of Retribution, as one would surmise as one reads the current books upon the subject; that is but one aspect of the working of the Law of Karma. The Law of Cause and Effect is not to be understood as we now interpret it. There is, to illustrate, a law called the Law of Gravitation, which has long imposed itself upon the minds of men; such a law exists, but it is only an aspect of a greater law, and its power can be, as we know, relatively offset, for each time that we see an aeroplane soaring overhead, we see a demonstration of the offsetting of this law by mechanical means, symbolising the ease with which it can be surmounted by human beings. If they could but realise it, they are learning the ancient technique of which the power to levitate is one of the easiest and simplest initial exercises.

The Law of Consequences is not the inevitable and set affair which modern thought surmises, but is related to the Laws of Thought far more closely than has been believed; towards an understanding of this, mental science has been groping. Its orientation and purposes are right and good and hopeful of results; its conclusions and modes of work are at present woefully at fault, and most misleading.

I have referred to this misunderstanding of the Law of Karma as I am anxious to have you set out on this study of the Laws of Healing with a free and open mind as far as may be, realising that your understanding of these laws is limited by:

1. Old theologies, with their static, distorted, and erroneous points of view. The teaching of theology is most misleading, but is, alas, generally accepted.

2. World thought, strongly tinged with the desire element, and with little in it of real thought. Men interpret these dimly sensed laws in terms of finality and from their little point of view. The idea of retribution runs through much of the teaching on Karma, for instance, because men seek a plausible explanation of things as

they appear to be, and are themselves fond of dealing out retribution. Yet there is far more general good karma than bad, little as you may think it when immersed in such a period as the present.

3. The world illusion and glamour, which prevents the average and ignorant man from seeing life as it truly is. Even the advanced man and the disciples are only beginning to get a fleeting and inadequate glance at a glorious reality.

4. Uncontrolled minds and unreleased and unawakened brain cells also hinder man from correct realisation. This fact is often unrecognised. The apparatus of realisation is as yet inadequate. This point needs emphasising.

5. National and racial temperaments, with their predisposing temperaments, and prejudices. These factors again prevent a just appreciation of these realities.

I have given enough here to indicate to you the stupidity of attempting to state that you understand these laws towards which you are groping and which you seek to understand. Nowhere in human thought is the darkness greater than in connection with the laws concerning disease and death.

It is necessary, therefore, to realise that, from the start, in all I have to say, under the heading *The Psychological Causes of Disease,* I am not dealing with those complaints or predispositions to disease which emerge out of the environment, or with those definitely physical taints which are inherited from parents who have carried in their bodies and transmitted to their children disease germs which they, in their turn, may have inherited from their parents. I would like to point out that these inherited diseases are far fewer than is at present surmised; of these, the predisposition to tuberculosis, to syphilis and to cancer are the most important where our present humanity is concerned; they are inherited and also can be imparted by contact. These I will deal with under our second major heading on the diseases emanating from the group.

CHAPTER I

The Psychological Causes of Disease

THE POINT I WOULD LIKE TO MAKE HERE, before proceeding further, is that I shall seek to avoid, as far as possible, all technicalities. Our theme is the esoteric consideration of disease and its forms; it seeks to elucidate the subject of and the vital causes of such diseases, and to indicate the general laws with which the healer must work and the six rules which he must impose upon himself—and to which he gives obedience, through discipline and understanding.

You will have noted that I listed the psychological causes under four headings:

1. Those arising out of the emotional-feeling nature.
2. Those which have their origin in the etheric body.
3. Those which are based on wrong thought.
4. The peculiar complaints and psychological troubles of disciples.

It may have interested you to see that I place the ills of the etheric body in the second place and not the first. The reason for this is that the *group ills and diseases* which have fastened upon the race, work primarily through the etheric body and find their way out into manifestation via the etheric bodies of all forms. But I have placed them second, even though they are in the last analysis the most numerous, owing to the fact that humanity cannot as yet deal with these en masse. The approach has to be through individuals, and men must clear their astral or emotional bodies of those conditions which pre-dispose them to disease, as individuals. At present, the race is astrally polarised. The emotional sentient nature is all-powerful in the masses. This leads to a relatively negative etheric body which is tuned in on the entire etheric substance of the planet. This substance, which underlies all forms, is simply a transferring and transmitting agency for vital energy to the outer dense physical body. Energy sweeps through this etheric substance, free from all control by the individual human being, and quite unrealised by him because his focus of attention is astral. From the astral or emotional state of consciousness, much concerning individual physical conditions can be deduced. We must, however, eliminate those ills which are group ills and which have swept into and through all mankind from the world of etheric force, leaving him in some way depleted, or overstimulated, or in such a condition that Death naturally supervenes. It might be stated as a basic generalisation that personal physical trouble has its seat at present in the emotional body, and that that vehicle of expression is the one predominant predisposing agent in the ill health of the individual, just as group ills and the sweep of epidemics of any kind through the masses are founded in some condition in the etheric substance of the planet. Those diseases which are general, national, racial and planetary find their way to an individual via his etheric body, but are not so personal in their implications. Upon this I will later enlarge. Today I but lay down the general proposition.

I would also like to point out that the diseases for the masses, for the average citizen, for the intelligentsia, and for the disciples of the world may, and do, differ widely—not so much in their expression as in their field of expression.

This is a point most difficult for the average healer to recognise; it is not easy or possible for him to grasp these distinctions and to gauge the point in evolution which a man may have reached. Some diseases must be dealt with from the mental plane, and will call in the mind of the healer; others require a concentration of emotional energy by the healing agent; and again, in other cases, the healer should seek to be only a transmitter of pranic energy to the etheric body of the patient, via his own etheric body. How many healers are really consciously aware of the focus of the consciousness or the life force in the patient with whom they may be concerned? How many realise anything of the type of healing which it is possible and necessary to apply to a disciple? How few realise that no disciple, for instance, can place himself in the hands of the average magnetic healer or radiatory worker, or psychological expert of any kind! A disciple dare not subject himself to the auric emanations of any chance healer, nor put himself in the power of the inexperienced academic psychologist, no matter how prominent he may be. He may, however, subject himself to the wise skill of the physical plane physician or surgeon, as—for him—the physical body is but an automaton. He can therefore avail himself of physical means for its benefiting. Much of the failure of the healing methods at present employed consists in the inability of the healer to:

1. Gauge the extent of the trouble, where it may be located basically, and in what body it principally arises and lies.
2. Know where the patient stands upon the ladder of evolution, and where, therefore, he must look first for the source of the difficulty.
3. Differentiate between the diseases which are due to inner personal conditions, or to inherited tendencies, or to group distribution.

4. To know whether the disease should be handled,

    a. Allopathically or homeopathically, for both can play their part at times, or through any of the other media of modern skill and science.

    b. Through radiation or magnetisation, or both.

    c. Through right inner psychological adjustment, aided by true insight on the part of the healing agent.

    d. Through calling in the power of a man's own soul—a thing that is not possible except to advanced people.

    e. Through definite occult means, such as forming a healing triangle of—

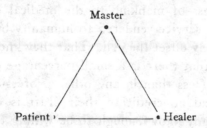

    This method involves much knowledge and a high point of spiritual attainment on the part of the healer;—it also presupposes the healer's link with a Master and the Master's group, plus the earned right to call upon that group for energy on behalf of the patient—a thing as yet rarely granted.

I would like first of all to point out that my purpose and intent is not to write a medical treatise. I shall not, therefore, deal with the anatomy of the body, nor shall I discuss the symptoms of diseases, except quite incidentally. I do not intend to elaborate symptoms or consider the many diseases with long names which distinguish the race at this time; all such information you can gather from the ordinary textbooks, if you so choose, and these you can study, if you care to do so. I find it personally not particularly satisfying. We will start with the premise that there is disease; that disease is an effect of inner causes; that man has made as vast strides in the understanding of the effect of these causes as they produce changes in the outer garment of man, as science has made in the understanding of the outer garment of God, the world of phenomenal nature.

The ameliorative and palliative and curative work of medicine and surgery are proved beyond all controversial discussion. The methods employed, such as the vivisection of animals, may rightly cause distress. In spite of all this the indebtedness of mankind to the medical profession is great, and the service rendered to humanity by the profession does largely offset the evil. That they know not everything is true; that there is a small percentage of physicians and surgeons (less than in any other profession) who are self-seeking and no credit to their craft is equally true; that they already know enough to be willing to admit how very much more there is to be known is also correct. But that it is a great and good and self-sacrificing group within the human family, is equally true. Forget this not.

I deal with the subjective aspect of man, and with the secondary causes which have their roots in man's inner bodies and in the subjective side of nature itself. The major primary causes, as I earlier explained, are impossible for you to grasp. They lie beyond the capacity of the concrete mind. I seek to make clear what man may do to free himself increasingly from the accumulation of the past, both individually and as a group, and in so doing to clear his physical body of the germs of disease. It must, however, be borne in mind that many diseases are of a group nature, and are consequently inherent in humanity itself. Just as the insect world devastates and destroys the vegetable kingdom, as any chance walker through the woods can note, so germs—individual and group—today devastate and destroy the human kingdom. They are agents of destruction and are performing a definite office and duty in the great scheme of things at present.

The intent is for men to die, as every man has to die, *at the demand of his own soul.* When man has reached a higher stage in evolution, with deliberation and definite choice of time, he will consciously withdraw from his physical body. It will be left silent and empty of the soul; devoid of light, yet sound and whole; it will then disintegrate, under the natural process, and its constituent atoms will pass back into "the pool of waiting units," until they are again required for the use of incarnating souls. Again, on the subjective side of life, the process is repeated, but many have already learnt to withdraw from the astral body without being subject to that "impact in the fog," which is the symbolic way of describing the death of a man upon the astral plane. He then withdraws on to the mental level, and leaves his astral carcass to swell the fog and increase its density.

I seek to point out, therefore, that my avoidance of medical technicalities will be deliberate, though we shall refer often to the physical body and to the diseases of which it is a prey.

Secondly, I seek today to give you another of the Laws of Healing, as well as one of the Rules for the Healer. Study these with care.

LAW II

Disease is the product of, and subject to, three influences. First, a man's past, wherein he pays the price of ancient error. Second, his inheritance, wherein he shares with all mankind those tainted streams of energy which are of group origin. Thirdly, he shares with all the natural forms that which the Lord of Life imposes on His body. These three influences are called "The Ancient Law of Evil Sharing." This must give place some day to that new Law of Ancient Dominating Good which lies behind all that God made. This law must be brought into activity by the spiritual will of man.

What is a law, my brother? It is the imposition (upon both the lesser and the more important) of the will and purpose of that which is superlatively great. Therefore, it lies beyond man's ken. Man has some day to learn that all the laws of nature have their higher, spiritual counterparts, and of these we shall shortly be in search. Our laws today are but secondary laws. They are the laws of group life and they govern the kingdoms of nature and find their expression (for the human kingdom) through the medium of the mind, of the emotional nature, and through a physical plane agent. It is not my intention in this present short treatise to elucidate the primary laws. I but state them, and at a future time (dependent upon certain factors yet undeveloped) I may deal with them.

In this treatise, the third part of it is stated to deal with the basic laws of Healing. These deal not with the Laws referred to above, but with the practical aspects of the healing art.

The second rule for the healer is as follows:

Rule Two

The healer must achieve magnetic purity through purity of life. He must attain that dispelling radiance which shows itself in every man when he has linked the centres in the head. When this magnetic field is established, the radiation too goes forth.

The significance of this will be somewhat apparent to the advanced esoteric student. As you know, the magnetic field is established when the powerful vibration of the centre in front of the pituitary body, and the centre around and above the pineal gland, swing into each other's orbit. The only controversial point in connection with the above rule (which we shall have later to consider) is how and in what manner magnetic purity is to be achieved, and how the two centres in the head can form together one magnetic field. Later, in our conclusion, which is intended to be intensely practical, I will touch upon these two points.

One of the things which should definitely emerge in our studies is the fact that disease is seldom of individual origin, unless a man misspends his life and definitely misuses his body (through drink or sexual dissipation), and that the bulk of the disease to be found in the world today is almost entirely of group origin, is inherited, is the result of infection, or the result of undernourishment. The last named cause is primarily an evil of civilisation; it is the result of economic maladjustment or the corruption of food. As I earlier pointed out, these latter causes of disease are not primarily the result of inner subtle forces, but are the pouring upwards, into the etheric body, of energies from the physical plane itself and from the outer world of forces.

Little attention has been paid by occult teachers to these forces which come from without, which originate upon the physical plane, and which affect the inner bodies. There are physical energy and streams of force entering into the etheric bodies of all forms, just as the world illusion and the miasmas of the astral plane oft have their causes in physical plane conditions. The energies entering into the centres of man from the subtler levels have oft been considered in occult books, but the forces which find their way into the centres from the world of physical plane life are seldom realised or discussed. This is a somewhat new thought which I offer for your consideration.

I have asked A.A.B. to insert a very brief synopsis of some of the points I have already made under the heading, What is Disease? I suggest the following:

1. All disease is disharmony and lack of alignment and control.
    a. Disease is found in all the four kingdoms in nature.
    b. Disease is purificatory in effect.
    c. Definite methods of healing are peculiar to humanity, and mental in origin.
2. Disease is a fact in nature.
    a. Antagonism to disease simply energises it.
    b. Disease is not the result of wrong human thought.
3. Disease is a process of liberation and the enemy of that which is static.
4. The law of cause and effect governs disease as it governs all else in manifestation.

We found also that healing is brought about in three ways:

1. Through the application of the methods of the many schools of medicine and surgery, and allied groups.
2. Through the use of psychology.
3. Through the activity of the soul.

I have also stated that the major causes of disease are three in number: they are psychological in nature; they are inherited through group contact; and they are karmic. Remember, however, that these are the secondary causes and with the first of these we will now deal.

1. Causes Arising in the Emotional-Desire Nature

In *A Treatise on White Magic,* I gave the world for the first time information as to the nature and the control of the astral body. This book is practically the first one ever given out to the public on this theme. Much has been given in the past on the subject of the physical body and its care, both by exoteric and esoteric science. Much of it is true, and some of it is illusion. It is illusion because it is based on false premises. Modern esotericists have dealt with the subject of the etheric body, and this too has been partially true and partially false, but it is more generally true from the occult point of view than it is exoterically. I may surprise you here if I tell you that *A Treatise on White Magic* is also true as far as it goes, but it is necessarily limited, and because of these limitations it is also partially incorrect. Does the above statement astonish you? Remember, how can it be entirely true when we consider the limitations of your power to comprehend? It is impossible for me to convey to you the truth, because there exist neither the terminology nor an adequate groundwork of knowledge on your part. This makes my task difficult. This teaching on healing is likewise the hardest I have yet undertaken, and this for two reasons. First (the real nature of) the phrase "subtler bodies" is somewhat meaningless, is it not? They are not bodies like the physical body. They can be regarded as centres or reservoirs of particular types of force, attached to each individual, and possessing their proper inlets and outlets. They are collections of atoms, vibrating at high speed and coloured (according to some schools of occultism) by certain definite hues; they emit a certain tone, and are at varying points of evolution. According to others, they are states of consciousness and some regard them as made in the likeness of a man. What is your definition, Brother of mine?

The astral body is, for the majority of mankind, the major determining factor to be considered. It is an outstanding cause of ill health. The reason for this is that it has a potent and predisposing effect upon the vital and etheric body. The physical body is an automaton of whichever inner body is the strongest. When you remember that the vital body is the recipient of the streams of energy, and is in fact composed and formed of such streams, and that the physical body is driven into activity by these streams, it is apparent that that stream which is the most potent is the one which will control the action of the physical body upon the physical plane. There are, however, two streams of energy which must be considered in studying the factors leading to physical plane actions. I would remind you in this connection that disease is an activity of the physical plane.

1. The stream of life itself, anchored in the heart, which determines the vitality of the man, his capacity for work, and the term of his existence.
2. The predominating stream of energy coming from the astral, mental or soul bodies. These control his expression upon the physical plane.

With the masses of people throughout the world, and those whom we call the vast unthinking public, the dominating factors are the stream of life and the stream of astral or desire energy. This can be either of a low or medium calibre.

With the thinking public, the dominating factors are these two streams, plus a steady inflowing and increasing tide of mental energy.

With the intelligentsia of the world and the aspirant (those ready for, or already on, the probationary path) we find the above three streams reaching a point of equilibrium, and thus producing an integrating or coordinating personality. These number amongst them also the mystics of the world and the creative workers, who are conscious of the inspiration and the spiritual contact which indicates a beginning of the inflow of soul energy.

With the disciples of the world, we find a group of men and women coming under the control of soul energy, whilst the other three energies are being increasingly subordinated to this higher type of control.

It should be borne in mind that there are two other types of energy with which to reckon, when considering intelligent man.

1. The energy which is composed of the fused and blended forces of a coordinated personality.
2. The energy of the physical plane itself, which is finally identified by the aspirant or disciple, and becomes so utterly negated that eventually it constitutes one of the major factors in the release of the centres.

Finally the time comes when the initiate works simply with three types of energy whilst expressing himself in incarnation: the energy of life itself, the negative energy of the personality, and the positive energy of the soul. Thus he is an expression in conscious manifestation of the three aspects of the Trinity.

Certain things should be established as occult facts in the consciousness of the healer before he is able to work constructively.

1. First of all, that there is nothing but energy and this energy manifests itself as many differing and varying

energies. Of these many energies, the universe is composed. Likewise man's bodies or vehicles of manifestation are without exception constituted of energy units. These we call atoms, and these atomic units are held together in body form by the coherent force of more potent energies.

2. The major focal point of energy to be found in human beings is that of the soul, but its potency as an agent of cohesion and of integration is as yet greater than its quality potency. In the earlier stages of human evolution, it is the *coherence* aspect that demonstrates. Later as man's response apparatus, or bodies, becomes more developed, the *quality* aspect of the soul begins to demonstrate increasingly.

3. Seen from the inner side where time is not, the human creature demonstrates as an amazing kaleidoscopic mutable phenomenon. Bodies, so called, or rather aggregates of atomic units, fade out and disappear, or flash again into manifestation. Streams of colours pass and repass; they twine or intertwine. Certain areas will then suddenly intensify their brightness and blaze forth with brilliance; or again they can be seen dying out and the phenomenon in certain areas will be colourless and apparently non-existent. But always there is a persistent over-shadowing light, from which a stream of lights pours down into the phenomenal man; this can be seen attaching itself in two major localities to the dense inner core of the physical man. These two points of attachment are to be found in the head and in the heart. There can also be seen, dimly at first but with increasing brightness, seven other pale disks of light which are the early evidence of the seven centres.

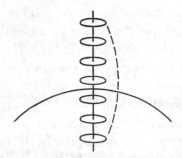

4. These centres, which constitute the quality aspects and the consciousness aspects, and whose function it is to colour the appearance or outer expression of man and use it as a response apparatus, are (during the evolutionary process) subject to three types of unfoldment.

   a. That unfoldment which takes place as a physical plane child grows from an infant to a man. By the time he is twenty-one, the centres should normally have reached the same quality of expression as they had attained when he passed out of life in a previous incarnation. The man then takes up life where he had previously left it off.

   b. The awakening of the centres through life experience. Occasionally only one centre may be dealt with in any one life; sometimes several are brought into greater functioning consciousness.

   c. There is, finally, the awakening of these centres through the process of initiation. This of course only happens when the man is consciously upon the Path.

5. The centres determine the man's point of evolution *as far as his phenomenal expression is concerned;* they work directly upon the physical body through the me-

dium of the endocrine system. This point should be borne in mind, for the future occult healer will approach his patient with this knowledge. He will then work through those centres and glands which govern the particular area of the body wherein the disease or discomfort is located. The time, however, for this has not yet come, for man's ignorance is great. Over-stimulation of the centres, and consequently of the glands, could easily be brought about, and the diseased condition might be stimulated also and increased, instead of dissipated or healed.

A. *Uncontrolled and Ill-Regulated Emotion.*

Given these basic facts, it can be seen how wrong emotional attitudes and a general unhealthy condition of the astral body must be potent factors in producing discomfort and disease. This is due to the fact that the vital or etheric bodies of the masses of humanity are governed primarily and swept into activity through the action of the astral body. Agitation in that body, any violent activity under stress of temper, intense worry or prolonged irritation will pour a stream of astral energy into and through the solar plexus centre, and will galvanise that centre into a condition of intense disturbance. This next affects the stomach, the pancreas, the gall duct and bladder. Few people (and I might well ask who is exempt at this particular time in the world's history) are free from indigestion, from undesirable gastric conditions, or from trouble connected with the gall bladder.

The tendency to criticism, to violent dislikes, and to hatreds based on criticism or a superiority complex, produces much of the acidity from which the majority of people suffer. I would like to add in passing that I am here generalising. So many people are prone to an inferiority complex in relation to themselves, but to a superiority complex where their relation to other people is concerned! Stomachic physical plane effects are closely tied up with the *desire aspect* of the physical body, which finds expression in the eating and drinking of that which is desired, leading subsequently to those attacks of biliousness to which so many are prone.

I offer these above illustrations to demonstrate the effect of the prevalent wrong attitudes to life and people which today distinguish mankind and produce the above mentioned conditions.

The ills which are based on criticism, upon hatred, and upon the capacity to judge each other (usually unkindly) work through from the throat centre to the solar plexus. This inter-relation existing between the centres is one that has never been properly considered. The centres in the etheric body pass varying kinds of energies amongst themselves, and a great deal of the energy transmitted from one centre to another is undesirable, flowing from the centres below the diaphragm to those above.

The physical body (etheric and dense) can be pictured as a house with two telephonic installations—one bringing in energies from without the house and the other being in the nature of a house telephone from room to room. The analogy is far more accurate than appears to the casual thinker. In every modern house, light and water and gas and telephonic interchange are brought. Light, the symbol of the soul; water, the symbol of the emotions; telephonic interchange, the symbol of mind with its intercommunication of knowledges; and gas, the symbol of the etheric nature.

It is interesting and saddening to note that that which at present goes out of the average house is the refuse that is undesirable—this is the correspondence to that which is selfish and sad and the demand for the satisfaction of personal needs and desires.

It can be seen, therefore, why I have so emphatically impressed the need of *harmlessness* upon all of you, for it is the scientific method, par excellence and esoterically speaking, of cleaning house and of purifying the centres. Its practice clears the clogged channels and permits the entrance of the higher energies.

The emotional causes of disease and the mental attitudes which produce physical discomfort are at this particular time those which are the most prevalent. When they are persisted in over a long period of time, and are carried over from life to life, they cause the more violent aspects of the conditions referred to above, and from them serious and destructive diseases can emerge, necessitating, for instance, the removal of the gall bladder or those operations incident to the appearance of chronic gastric ulcers. Other diseases grow from a constant pandering to the desire nature, though sexual diseases come under another category. It can be seen from the above how desirable it is that the true healer should combine in himself, not only a measure of esoteric knowledge, but—until he is an initiate—something of psychology, something of the work of a magnetic healer, and also be a trained medical man or surgeon.

Much of the healing now done is worse than useless, because the three above mentioned conditions are lacking. Most doctors, especially those who are called general practitioners, are good psychologists and they have also a sound knowledge of symptoms and of anatomy and of curative measures which are usually lacking in the average metaphysical healer. But they are entirely ignorant of one great field of knowledge—that concerning the energies which meet and war within the human frame and of the potencies which can be set in motion if certain esoteric truths are admitted in place. Until they work with the etheric body and study the science of the centres, they can make little further progress. The esoteric healer knows much about the inner forces and energies and has some understanding of the basic causes of the exoteric diseases, but his ignorance of man's mechanism is deplorable, and he fails to realise two things:

> First, that disease is sometimes the working out into manifestation of undesirable subjective conditions. These, when externalised and brought to the surface of the human body, can then be known, dealt with and eliminated. It is well to remember also that sometimes this working out and elimination may well bring about the death of that particular body. But the soul goes on. One short life counts for very little in the long cycle of the soul, and it is counted well worthwhile if a period of ill health (even if it eventuates in death) brings about the clearing away of wrong emotional and mental conditions.
>
> Second, disease is sometimes incident upon and part of the process of the withdrawal of the soul from its habitation. This we call death, and it can come quickly and unexpectedly when the soul withdraws with suddenness from its body. Or death can spread itself over a long period of time, and the soul may take several months or years for its slow and gradual emergence from the body, with the body dying by inches all the time.

There is not sufficient knowledge yet among healers to enable them to deal with wisdom in these matters. We might therefore conclude that:

1. Disease is a purificatory process, carried out in order to produce a purer expression, life aroma, influence and soul usefulness. When this is the case, a cure is possible.

2. Disease can be a gradual and slow process of dying and of thus releasing the soul. A cure then will not be possible, though paliative and ameliorative measures are needed and should most certainly be used. The length of the life can be prolonged, but a permanent and final cure is out of the question. This the average mental healer fails to realise. They make a horror out of death, whereas death is a beneficent friend.

3. Disease can be the sudden and final call to the body to relinquish the soul and set it free for other service.

In all these cases everything possible should be done from the standpoint of modern medical and surgical science and the allied sciences of which there are today so many. Much too can be done from the angle of mental and spiritual healing, aided by the science of psychology. Some day there must come cooperation in these various fields and a synthesising of their efforts.

I have earlier pointed out that the astral body is the prime motivating factor in the lives of the majority. This is caused by the fact that:

1. It is the body in which the bulk of human beings are today centering their consciousness.

2. It is the most developed of the bodies at this time, and therefore receives the bulk of the life energy as it comes down the life stream, from the soul, and likewise receives the energy of the stream of consciousness.

3. It is oriented, if I may so express it, outwards or towards
    the plane of physical experience. That orientation shifts
    at times and, temporarily in the case of the aspirant,
    turns inwards. Just as the centres in man, the "lotuses
    of life," are depicted as turned downwards and with
    the stalk upwards in the undeveloped man, but are
    turned upwards in the case of the developed, so there
    are conditions in the astral body analogous to this. In
    the case of the highly evolved man, of the initiate or
    the Master, the astral body is steadily oriented towards
    the soul. In the mystic, the aspirant and the disciple,
    the process of thus definitely changing the direction of
    the forces is going on and producing, therefore, a tem-
    porary chaos.

4. The astral body of man, being the latest to develop (the
    physical and the etheric being the first two in order of
    time) is still the most alive and potent. It reached its
    acme of development in late Atlantean days and its po-
    tency is still great, constituting the mass potency, the
    mass emphasis, and the mass polarisation. This is also
    augmented by energies coming from the animal king-
    dom, which is entirely astral in its point of attainment.

I would remind you here that the use of the word
"body" is most misleading and unfortunate. It produces
in the consciousness the idea of a defined form and a specific
shape. The astral body is an aggregate of forces, working
through into the consciousness in the form of desires, impulses, longings, wishes, determinations, incentives, and
projections, thus laying the basis for much of the truth
of the teachings of modern psychology. Psychologists have
discovered (or rather uncovered) the nature of some of
these forces, and their terminology in this connection is
frequently more truly occult and accurate than is that of

the orthodox esotericist and theosophist.

It may be of interest to you if I do two things. First of all, give you some technical information in connection with the working through of the forces from the astral plane into the physical body, and then give you the effects of that working through, as they take the form—owing to man's wrong use of them—of disease and the many varying disorders to which man is prone. With their cure we are not at this time concerned. I am here simply laying down the structure of fact upon which we can later base our conclusions. We shall, in this connection, only consider the average man. The problems of the disciple will be dealt with under Part I.4.

I pointed out earlier that the three major groups of diseases for the masses are—

1. Tuberculosis.
2. The social diseases, as they are called: the venereal diseases and syphilis.
3. Cancer.

To these we must add two other groups of disease which predominantly affect those who are a little above the average and whose general level of intelligence is higher than that of the mass; this includes also the aspirants of the world.

4. Heart diseases, but not what is called heart failure.
5. The nervous diseases so prevalent at this time.

These five groups of disease, and their various sub-divisions are responsible for the bulk of the physical ills which attack humanity. A right grasp of their preponderating causes will be of definite assistance to future medicine. How much will be accepted is at this time doubtful.

I would like to point out here that, as you well know, there are physical correspondences to the seven centres of forces located in the etheric body, and fed from the astral body. These we call the endocrine glands. These glands are effects of or testifying evidence to, the centres, and are in their turn initiating causes of lesser effects in the physical body. It will be of value if we here tabulate some of the things we know, and aid comprehension.

Centre	Gland	Physical Organs	Type of Force	Origin	Body
1. Head ... Brahmarandra. 1000-petalled lotus.	Pineal..	Upper brain. Right eye.	Spiritual will. Synthetic. Dynamic.	...Atma Monad via soul. Will.	Causal body. Jewel in the lotus.
	Occultist. Initiate. Master.		Dominant after 3rd Initiation.		
2. Centre between the eyes. Ajna centre.	Pituitary body.	Lower brain. Left eye. Nose. Nervous system.	Soul force.. Love. Magnetic. Light. Intuition. Vision.	Petals of egoic lotus, as a whole.	Buddhic vehicle. Causal body. Higher mental.
	Aspirant. Disciple. Mystic.		Dominant after 2nd Initiation.		
3. Heart ... Anahata.	Thymus ...	Heart Circulatory system. Blood. Also Vagus nerve.	Life force Group consciousness.	Love petals.	Higher mental. Causal body.
	All types of Spiritual People.		Dominant after 1st Initiation.		
4. Throat centre.	Thyroid	Breathing apparatus. Alimentary canal.	Creative energy. Sound. Self-consciousness.	Knowledge petals.	Mental body.
	Creative Artists.	*All advanced humanity.*		*The Intelligentsia.*	
5. Solar plexus.	Pancreas ...	Stomach Liver. Gall bladder. Nervous system.	Astral force. Emotion. Desire. Touch.	Astral centres.	Astral body.
	Average humanity.			*Ordinary people.*	
6. Sacral centre.	Gonads	Sex organs.	Life force Physical-plane force. Vital energy. Animal life.	Physical plane.	Etheric body.
			Low grade animal type of men.		
7. Base of spine. Muladhara.	Adrenals ..	Kidneys Spinal column.	Will energy. Universal life. Kundalini.	The Mother of the World.	

This tabulation is simply an outline and, like the tabulation of the principles and their correspondences, as given by H.P.B. in the third volume of *The Secret Doctrine,* its interpretation will be dependent upon the point of view of the student. We shall employ it later and add further columns to it and further correspondences. In all our considerations, what we have to say will have the following synthesis of structure behind it:

1. The soul.
2. The subtler bodies of the mind and the emotions, which are simply qualified energy centres.
3. The vital body with its seven major centres of force.
4. The endocrine system, which is an effect of the seven centres, and the determining controlling factor in the physical body of man.
5. The nervous system in its three divisions.
6. The blood stream.

All the subsidiary organs of man are effects; they are not pre-determining causes. The determining causes in man, and that which makes him what he is, are the glands. They are externalisations of the types of force pouring through the etheric centres from the subtler worlds of being. They express the point in evolution which the man has reached; they are vital and active or non-vital and inactive, according to the condition of the centres. They demonstrate a sufficiency, an oversufficiency or a deficiency, according to the condition of the etheric vortices.

Again, the process of control may be stated to be via the nervous system; the close interlocking directorate of the nervous system, the brain and the blood stream (as a carrier of the life principle) governs the activities of the man—conscious, sub-conscious, self-conscious, and finally, super-conscious. The three centres in supreme control today for the majority are:

1. The ajna centre, the centre between the eyebrows.
2. The solar plexus.
3. The sacral centre.

Eventually, when man will have "become that which he is" (that paradoxical esoteric phrase), the centres of control will be:

1. The head centre, the brahmarandra.
2. The heart centre.
3. The centre at the base of the spine.

Between the present and the future, the emphasis will be laid upon a constantly shifting triplicity, and each man will be different from his fellowmen as to emphasis, as to the conditions of his centres, as to their glandular correspondences in the physical body, and therefore as to the diseases and the ills, inhibitions, and difficulties to which his flesh will fall heir. It is in this connection that it becomes obvious that the work of the physician and of the psychologist must eventually go hand in hand. The three most important aspects of all diagnoses are:

1. *The psychological,* or the gauging of the inner bodies of man from the angle of their development, their integration and the total coordination of the personality, as these subtler aspects of the human being express themselves in consciousness.
2. *The work of the endocrinologist,* as he deals with the endocrine glands, viewing them as power stations through which energy—dynamic and illuminating—can pour through from the centres.
3. *The physician,* who, taking into consideration the conclusions of the two above experts, diagnoses the

disease, and treats it in collaboration with the other two.

These three may call in other experts and specialists in electro-therapy, osteopathy and chiropractic, but it is in the combination of the knowledge of the physician, the psychologist and the endocrinologist that the medical profession can take on a new expression of usefulness, and enter the new age equipped to deal with the people who will gradually assume the new types and a changing physical organism. Electricity, in relation to human ills, is as yet an infant science, but it has in it the germs of the new techniques and methods of healing. The work done by the chiropractors is good and needed but should, with osteopathy, constitute a definite subsidiary technique to that of the other three. The work of the chiropractors and of the osteopaths forms two halves of one whole, little as their practitioners may like to recognise it. The former group need a more careful and lengthy training, and a higher standard of technical knowledge should be required.

Medicine is entering slowly into a new usefulness. Once the cause of disease is shifted out of an organ or bodily system into a more subtle and vital realm, we shall see radical and needed changes, leading to simplification and not to a greater complexity and difficulty.

From the above remarks it will be seen that disease emerges into the physical body from the world of the unseen, and from the use, or misuse, of the subtler forces on the inner planes. It must be remembered, however, that disease—as it expresses itself in man—can be generally regarded as due to the following causes, and students would do well to have this most carefully in mind as they ponder on these matters:

1. Individual disease, due to interior conditions in a man's own equipment, to his mental state, or to an emotional

condition which can produce serious ills. This is inherited from the past.

2. Disease inherent in humanity as a whole. There are certain diseases to which all men are prone; the germs of these diseases are latent in the physical vehicles of the majority of men, only awaiting predisposing conditions in order to manifest. They might be regarded as group diseases.

3. Diseases which are, curiously enough, accidental. To these a man falls heir when, for instance, he succumbs to some infectious or contagious complaint.

4. Diseases inherent in the soil. Of these as yet but little is known. The soil of our earth, however, is very ancient, and is impregnated with disease germs which take their toll of the vegetable, animal and human kingdoms, manifesting differently in each, yet being due basically to the same causes.

5. Diseases which are the difficulties of mysticism. These are the peculiar ills and complaints which attack the disciples and aspirants of the world. These can be traced in every case to the pouring in of energy through centres which are not properly equipped, or adequately developed, to handle the force.

The above is a *generalisation* which may be found useful.

The method whereby these astral forces (which are, as we know, preeminently the determining life forces for the majority of men at this time) work out into manifestation is a relatively simple matter. In the astral vehicle of expression there are, as you may realise, the correspondences of the seven centres in the etheric body. These are essentially the seven major focal points of force, and each of them is expressive of one of the seven ray energies. Let me first of all make clear which centres express these seven ray types:

Centre	Ray	Quality	Origin
1. Head Centre	1st	The Divine Will.	Monadic
2. Ajna Centre	7th	Organisation. Direction.	Atmic
3. Heart Centre	2nd	Love-Wisdom. Group love.	Buddhic
4. Throat Centre	5th	Creativity.	Mental
5. Solar Plexus	6th	Emotion. Desire.	Astral
6. Sacral Centre	3rd	Reproduction.	Etheric
7. Base of Spine	4th	Harmony. Union through conflict.	Physical

Note: In the fourth kingdom, the human, it is the energy of the fourth ray which, cooperating with the first ray, eventually brings synthesis. There is a close relation between the highest centre (the head centre), and that at the base of the spine. This fourth type of energy thus expresses itself in cooperation with the first type because we are still Atlantean in our polarisation, and that civilisation was the fourth in order. It is very largely the work done in our fifth civilisation, our present Aryan race, which will, in cooperation with the fifth principle of the mind, bring a shift into a higher level of consciousness. This will produce a harmonising of all the centres through an act of the will, intellectually and intelligently applied, with the objective of producing harmony. This point warrants thought.

On the astral plane there will also be found in every astral body seven corresponding focal points through which energy can enter, raying forth then into the vital centres in the etheric physical body as seven differentiated types of force. These types of force produce both bad and good effects, according to the quality of the negative dense physical body. These differ according to the type of ray or force, and it may be interesting if I here indicate to you the good and the bad effects and the corresponding diseases.

Astral Force	Centre	Bad Aspect	Disease	Good Aspect
First ray. Will or Power.	Head	Self-pity. The dramatic I.	Cancer.	Sacrifice. Dedication of the I.
Second ray. Love-Wisdom.	Heart	Self-love. Personality.	Heart trouble. Stomach trouble.	Soul love. Group love.
Third ray. Activity.	Sacral	Sexuality. Over-activity.	Social diseases.	Parental love. Group life.
Fourth ray. Harmony.	Ajna	Selfishness. Dogmatism.	Insanities.	Mysticism.
Fifth ray. Knowledge.	Throat	Lower psychism.	Wrong metabolism. Certain cancers.	Creativity. Sensitivity. Inspiration.
Sixth ray. Devotion.	Solar plexus	Emotionalism.	Nervous diseases. Gastritis. Liver trouble.	Aspiration. Right direction.
Seventh ray. Organisation.	Base of the spine.	Self-interest. Pure selfishness. Black Magic.	Heart diseases. Tumors.	White Magic.

Please remember in studying this tabulation that it is a generalisation, and only a partial listing of the types of disease which can be the result of the inflow of energy. It is only intended to be suggestive; the complexity of the human equipment and the intricacy of the ray energies are such that no hard and fast rules can be laid down. The ray forces manifest differently, according to ray type and point in evolution. There is therefore no contradiction here to the previous tabulations. If you bear in mind that every human being is basically an expression of five ray forces:

1. The ray of the soul,
2. The ray of the personality,
3. The ray governing the mental body,
4. The ray governing the astral equipment,
5. The ray of the physical nature,

it will become apparent that for the average person two such tabulations would have to be drawn up.

1. There would be required the *positive* analysis of the astral forces as they express the personality.
2. An analysis of the soul forces as they are faintly indicated. A negative analysis concerning what is not present in the equipment can be of little value here.

It will again be necessary to have an analysis of the forces, playing through into the physical body from the astral plane, which are received directly from the soul and are therefore a combination of soul-force plus the highest type of astral energy. This would be in the nature of a synthetic analysis and would only be possible in the case of a disciple or an initiate. You will therefore eventually have for each person:

1. A positive analysis of the personality forces, primarily of the astral force as that is the predominating force pouring into the etheric centres.
2. A negative analysis of those aspects of soul energy which are *not* present.
3. A synthetic analysis, based on both the above, but combining also the record of *positive* soul expression.

In these tabulations and statements I have given you much food for thought.

B. *Desire, Inhibited or Rampant.*

It would be of value to you here if I made clear that one of the first things a student has to remember is that— for the majority of human beings, for the huge majority— the influences and impulses which emanate from the astral plane are a predisposing factor in all matters with which the individual concerns himself, apart from those conditions which (being imposed upon him from his environment and the period in which he lives) are, for him, unavoidable. The astral plane is a centre of dynamic emanating force, which is fundamentally *conditioning* in its effect because of the stage of the individual consciousness at which that majority finds itself. Men are swayed by the impulse of desire of a high or low calibre. This is, of course, a broad generalisation, for that basic condition is becoming steadily modified by impulses coming from the mental plane. This necessarily complicates the problem. Influences emanating from the soul are also becoming appreciably present, and still further complicate the problem of the advanced human being. This "problem of complication" (if I might so call it) constitutes a "hard saying" for the student to understand in relation to his own physical condition or to that of any one whom he may be seeking to help.

I should like here, in this connection, to give you the third of the Laws which govern the sacred art of healing.

LAW III

Diseases are an effect of the basic centralisation of a man's life energy. From the plane whereon those energies are focussed, proceed those determining conditions which produce ill health, and which, therefore, work out as disease or as freedom from disease.

It will be apparent to you, therefore, that a shift of the inner attention (the mental attitude) of the patient can and will produce either real freedom from physical ills or an intensification of those reactions which produce discomfort, disease or death.

In the three laws which I have given you and which you now have before you for consideration, it is obvious that the following facts emerge. These should form the basis of your reflection:

1. Disease is the result of the blocking of the free flow of the life of the SOUL.
2. It is the product, or the result, of three influences:
   a. Ancient error, emanating from the past history of the person involved.
   b. Human taints, inherited because one is a member of the human family.
   c. Planetary evil, imposed upon all forms on earth by the basic condition, and by time.
3. It is conditioned by the forces emanating from that plane whereon a man's consciousness is primarily centred.

To the above statements should be added a further fact, already mentioned, that:

4. There are five major groups of diseases, with their allied complaints and subsidiary diseases.
   a. Tuberculosis.
   b. The syphilitic diseases.
   c. Cancer.
   d. Heart difficulties.
   e. Nervous diseases.

I am not dividing what I have to say into organic and functional troubles, nor do I here refer to illnesses induced by epidemics or by accidents. I refer to those basic taints or predispositions that are the dubious heritage of humanity as a whole, and to those difficulties which are incident to those stages in evolutionary development which are characteristic of those upon the more advanced stages of the Path. It will be seen, therefore, that man comes into incarnation having inherited predispositions to disease which come:

1. From his own past; i.e., effects which are the result of causes initiated in earlier incarnations.
2. From the general racial heritage of humanity.
3. From the condition of the planetary life. These latter causes lift the whole problem out of the usual comprehension of the average man.

A human being is also predisposed to trouble if he has succeeded (as a result of a long evolutionary history) in awakening in some fashion, however slight, the centres above the diaphragm. The moment that that occurs he becomes subject, for a long cycle of lives, to difficulties connected with the heart or with the nervous system in its various branches. Frequently an advanced human being, such as an aspirant or a disciple, may have freed himself from the inherited taints, but will succumb to heart trouble, to nervous disorders, mental imbalance, and overstimulation. They are classified occasionally as the "diseases of the Mystics."

I would like to make it clear that it is not my intention to enter into the realm of physiological discussion, to elaborate the symptoms of disease, or to deal with the lesions, the pathological conditions, and the distressing details attendant upon the breakdown of any human organism. I am not going to write a treatise on anatomy or on the various sciences which have grown up from a study of the mechanism of the human being, connected as they are with the framework and structure, the organs, nerves, brain tissue and interrelated systems which compose that intricate piece of machinery, the human body. As far as the exoteric science is concerned, two things would successfully deter me:

1. The whole subject is marvellously dealt with in the many books which embody the literature of medicine and of surgery. There is little that I could add which would be of profit in such a discussion as this.

2. The readers of my words are not, with few exceptions, versed in the construction and constitution of the human body; and pathological details, the description of diseases, and the various unpleasant symptoms of human degeneration are unwholesome reading for the average man or woman. A little knowledge along these lines can be a most dangerous thing.

I seek to deal primarily with *causes,* with the inner *sources* of dis-ease and deal with those states of consciousness (I do not say states of mind only) which induce wrong functioning, and eventually wrong conditions.

The problem of the healer, therefore, is twofold: First, he must know whether the difficulty lies above or below the diaphragm; this takes him definitely into the realm of occult as well as of psychological knowledge. Secondly, he must have a clear grasp of the patient's inner emphasis; this last aids him in the diagnosis of the first.

This statement brings me to the formulation of the third Rule for Healers.

RULE THREE

Let the healer train himself to know the inner stage of thought or of desire of the one who seeks his help. He can thereby know the source from which the trouble comes. Let him relate the cause and the effect, and know the point exact through which relief must come.

I would like to call your attention to those last few words, and would emphasise to you the fact that disease primarily is an effort on the part of the natural physical body to seek relief and achieve release from inner pressures, from subjective inhibitions and hidden retentions. Primarily, from the point of view of esotericism, all physical disease is the result of:

1. Wrong stimulation, or overstimulation, or wrongfully placed stimulation and of inner tensions in some part of the mechanism.
2. Inhibitions, psychical starvation, and those accumulated subjective forces which dam the flow of the life forces.

You will see, therefore, that again (in the domain of health) all problems resolve themselves into the right use and the correct handling of force, in order to effect the free flow of energy.

The following questions will inevitably arise: From whence come these inherited taints? Is it possible to arrive at their source? The problem of the past, and the present effects of that past, is too vast for consideration, nor can any statements anent the situation possibly help humanity.

One generalisation I can, however, make, and even that may convey but little to your understanding.

Of the three major diseases which have been inherited from the past, it might be said that the syphilitic or so-called social diseases are remainders of the excesses indulged in in Lemurian times; they are of such ancient origin that the very soil is permeated with the germs of these diseases—a fact quite unknown to modern science. Down the ages, men have suffered from these groups of infections; they have died and been buried and in their millions have contributed their quota of infection to the earth. In Lemurian times, the emphasis of the life force was upon the physical body, upon its development, its use and control, and also upon its perpetuation or reproduction. It was in Lemurian times that troubles connected with the misuse of the sex life began; this was, in a peculiar sense, the essential primeval evil, and concerning this fact, ancient legends and hints are found throughout the earliest records and writings. There is much misinterpreted testimony to this effect, and when men can read the records more correctly and with right interpretation, they will understand the way out, because they will see more clearly the underlying causes.

Cancer is a gift to modern man from the Atlantean humanity, and the scourge of this disease was the major factor which devastated the inhabitants of old Atlantis. The roots of this dire evil are deep-seated in the emotional or desire nature, and are grounded in the astral body. Cancer is partially the result of a *reaction* to the diseases connected with the sex life which became so rampant in later Lemurian times and early Atlantean days. The people of those times, seeing the fearful evils and the extent of the disease which grew up out of the fertile Lemurian life, resulting from the promiscuous sex life on every hand, for the sake of self-preservation dammed back the natural flow of desire (the flow of life as it expresses itself through the centres of reproduction and procreation), and this in due time produced other evils. Cancer is primarily a disease of inhibition, just as the syphilitic diseases are those of over-expression and overuse of one aspect of the mechanism of man.

Today, owing to the vast reaches of time involved and to the untold generations of those who have died upon the earth, the "germs" (so-called by the unlearned thinker) of the dread complaint of cancer are to be found in the very soil on which we live, infecting the vegetable kingdom and also the human family. A correspondence to the syphilitic complaints of man is to be found in the mineral kingdom.

Tuberculosis, which was devastatingly rampant at a certain stage in Atlantean times, is nevertheless a disease which has been *generated* principally in our Aryan race, and one which we are bequeathing to the animal kingdom and are sharing with them. This is beginning to be realised. So close, however, is the relation between men and animals (particularly the domestic animals) that they today share with men practically all his ailments in some form or another, sometimes recognisable and sometimes not. Curiously enough, the cause of this great white scourge is to be found in the fact of the shift of the life emphasis away from the emotional nature into that of the mind nature, producing a temporary starvation of the emotional nature. It is largely a disease of depletion. Cancer, in its turn, was based similarly on a previous shift of the life force from the physical body into that of the emotional nature, producing an over-development of the cellular life, through overstimulation. I realise the difficulty of grasping these statements. I can only give you these unsubstantiated hints. Later discoveries alone can prove the truth of my suggestions. Let us here tabulate our conclusions:

Disease	*Race*	*Body*	*Kingdom*	*Organ*
Syphilitic	Lemurian	Physical	Mineral	Sex organs. Sacral centre.
Cancer	Atlantean	Astral	Vegetable	Solar plexus.
Tuberculosis	Aryan	Mental	Animal	Breathing apparatus. Throat centre.

In referring above to the centres I am referring to the centre for the distribution of the life force, wherein the emphasis for the mass will be found. From the above it will be apparent where the emphasis of the possible cure will have to lie. Already, and because it is the latest, and therefore the least deep-seated of the three major diseases inherited by modern man, we have learnt how to cure tuberculosis. It has been discovered (when the mind was intelligently applied to the problem) that sunshine and good food could cure, or at any rate arrest, the disease. It is an interesting item in the field of esoteric correspondence that just as the light of the soul, pouring into the mind, can be depended upon to solve any problem, so that light of the sun and its prophylactic rays can dispel the dread symptoms of tuberculosis.

Similarly, as the race develops right emotional control we shall see the gradual disappearance of the phenomena of cancer. I said *right* emotional control; inhibition and the suppression of the desire impulses by the force of the will is *not* right control. It is interesting also to note that though both men and women suffer from the disease of cancer, the *general* cause is not identical, though the *basic* cause (reaction from an over-expression of the sex life through the cultivation of the desire nature) remains the same. Women, owing to the risks they run in childbearing, through the turning of the life emphasis to the sex aspect of life, have revolted on a large scale (as did the Atlanteans) against this form of life expression, and it is along this line—the sex line—that their major inhibitions are found. They do not suffer so much from the general inhibition of the emotional-desire-feeling expression. Men *do* suffer from this latter inhibition and have a tradition or a marked tendency to greater emotional control in the handling of life than have women. Men do not require or acquire so marked a sex control. The general field of their inhibited life tendency is therefore of greater extent, and consequently (if statistics can be trusted) more men suffer from cancer than do women, though it is a dread disease, feared by all.

In the secret of right *transmutation* lies the cure of cancer, and this will eventually be realised. I am using this phrase not only symbolically but also technically and scientifically. This again will later be seen. In the secret of *right rhythmic living* and in a right proportional accent upon all phases of life will come (and it is rapidly coming) complete immunity from tuberculosis. In the secret of *right understanding of times and cycles,* and of periodic reproductive creation, will come the emergence of the race from the evils of the social diseases.

It will be apparent to you, therefore, that the syphilitic diseases will be the last to disappear, just as they were the first to devastate the race. Tuberculosis is disappearing. The attention of the experts is now being given to the cure of cancer.

I would like to add one or two comments which will be of general or rather modern interest. I have said that these taints to which humanity is prone are found in the soil, and that their presence there is largely due to the burial, down the ages, of millions of corpses. By the increased use of the processes of cremation, this condition will be steadily improved. Gradually, very gradually, the taint will thus die out. It is therefore highly desirable that there be as much propaganda as possible for the use of this method of disposing of the discarded physical vehicles of the souls who are passing out of incarnation. As the soil becomes less tainted, and as soul contact is established, we can hope to see a steady decrease in the number of those who succumb to the inherited taints. Curiously enough, the free use of salt sea bathing has a definite effect on the healthiness of the physical body. The water, incidentally absorbed through the medium of the skin and by the mouth, has a vitally prophylactic effect.

One of the major problems today to the psychologist, and in a lesser degree to the medical man, is the growth of homosexuality, both female and male. Specious arguments are brought forth in order to prove that this abnormal development (and the consequent interest in this morbid tendency) is due to the fact that the race is slowly becoming androgynous in its development, and that the future hermaphroditic man or woman is gradually making its appearance. This, again, is *not* true. Homosexuality is what you call a "left-over" from the sexual excesses of Lemurian times, an inherited taint, if you like. Egos who individualised and incarnated in that vast period of time are the ones who today demonstrate homosexual tendencies. In those days, so urgent was the sexual appetite, the normal processes of human intercourse did not satisfy the insatiable desire of the *advanced* man of the period. Soul force, flowing in through the processes of individualisation, served to stimulate the lowest centres. Hence, forbidden methods were practised. Those who thus practised them are today, in great numbers, in incarnation, and the ancient habits are too strong for them. They are now far enough advanced upon the evolutionary path so that the cure lies ready at this time —if they choose to employ it. They can, with relative ease, transfer the sex impulse to the throat centre, and thus become creative in the higher sense, employing the energy sensed and circulating in right and constructive ways. Many of them are beginning automatically to do this. However, it is well known that, among the so-called artistic types, homosexuality is very prevalent. I say "so-called" for the truly creative artist is *not* the victim of these ancient evil predisposing habits.

It might be pointed out here that homosexuality is of three kinds:

1. That which is the result of ancient evil habits. This is the major cause today and indicates:

   a. Individualisation upon this planet; for those who individualised upon the moon chain are not susceptible to these dangerous characteristics.

   b. A relatively advanced stage upon the evolutionary path which was achieved by the Lemurian egos who succumbed to this desire-satisfaction.

   c. A consequent study of sex magic, plus a constant insatiable physical and sexual urge.

2. Imitative homosexuality. A number of persons of all classes imitated their betters (if I might use so paradoxical a term) and so developed evil habits in sexual intercourse from which they might otherwise have remained free. This is one of the prevalent reasons today, among many men and women, and is based upon a too active imagination, plus a powerful physical or sex nature, and a prurient curiosity. This I say with advisement. This category accounts for many of our Sodomites and Lesbians.

3. A few rare, very rare, cases of hermaphroditism. These people, combining in themselves both aspects of the sex life, are faced with a very real problem. It is a problem which is greatly increased by human ignorance, human refusal to face facts, wrong early training and teaching,

and a widespread misunderstanding. These cases are to be found in small numbers everywhere, even though their numbers, in relation to the world population, is still negligible. But that they exist is of real interest to the medical profession and a subject of deep pity and commiseration to the humanitarian and the understanding psychologist. They face a difficult situation.

I have somewhat elaborated this matter as it is of use for you to know such facts and the information is of value to you. It serves to throw light upon a problem which an increasingly large number of people are called upon to face. Psychologists, social workers, physicians, and all those occupied with group training constantly meet with this problem, and it is just as well that some distinction is made between the types which must be considered, thus clarifying the issue.*

You will find in these instructions many hints which, though they may not be classified definitely as instructions in healing, yet fall into that category, for they will make those of you who read more efficient in understanding.

You will note also from the above how this taint, as might well be expected, has its roots in the astral or sentient body, the body of sensation. It is for this reason that I have included it. It would be an interesting experiment in analysis if these various well-known difficulties, diseases and complaints could be classified under their originating impulses. So few of them have a mental origin, in spite of all that Christian Science or Mental Science may say to the contrary. Perhaps I should say, rather, that they are not based on wrong human thought, though all evil can be aggravated and intensified by wrong thought. Many or perhaps most of the

---

* The Problem of Sex. Pages 268-307 of A Treatise on the Seven Rays, Vol. I.

complaints from which average man suffers are based upon astral causes or upon some clearly defined desire. A formulated desire is one that finds expression in some form of activity. Of these homosexuality is one of the clearest to define. The other diseases to which humanity is heir are sometimes not so easy to clarify and define. The man or woman is a victim but the cause producing the illness or difficulty—physical or psychological—lies hid in a long past which the victim (with his limited knowledge) is unable to investigate, nor can he arrive at the cause producing the effect. All that he can affirm is that, in all probability, desire was the initiating impulse. What human beings are today and what they suffer is the result of their long past, and the past presupposes long and well-established habits. Such habits are inevitably the result of one of two factors:

1. Desire, dominating and controlling action,

    or

2. Mental control which substitutes for desire a planned campaign which will run counter in many cases to the normally sensed, defined desire.

You will note from the above that it is my wish that you grasp the importance of the emotional sentient body and its power to initiate those secondary causes which, in this life, demonstrate as disease.

You will note consequently the emphasis I have laid upon the astral body as a promoter of wrong physical conditions, and the necessity for astral understanding and control on the part of the patient, if there is to be a true overcoming of disease. Will you understand me if I say that the true overcoming may mean an acceptance of the Way of Death as the way out, should it come normally, or of healing, if the causes which are the initial impulses are exhausted? Ponder on this.

In all the above, even in connection with what I have said concerning homosexuality, I have considered either rampant or inhibited desire, but I have only considered it in general terms and in a broad outline. Will you misunderstand if I point out to you that where desire is inhibited (which is the case with many aspirants today) all kinds of diseases—cancer, congestion of the lungs and certain liver complaints—become possible, as well as the dread malady of tuberculosis? The diseases of inhibition are numerous and serious, as you will note from the above enumeration. It should be noted that where desire is rampant and uncontrolled and no inhibition is present, such diseases as the syphilitic disorders, homosexuality and inflammations and fevers appear. According to the temperament so will be the types of disease, and the temperament is dependent upon the ray quality. People on the different rays are predisposed to certain disorders. The psychologists are right in their basic differentiation of human beings into the two major types—extroverts and introverts. These two types produce their own qualities of disease, which demonstrate as ill health through over-expression or inhibition.

We have considered our second point under the healing of diseases which arise in the emotional or desire nature. Our first point deals with uncontrolled emotion. I would remind you of our premise that we would only consider the ills to which advanced humanity, the aspirants and disciples of all degrees are prone. We will not deal (in this short treatise) with the whole gamut of diseases which affect humanity as a whole, or down the ages. The more advanced the aspirant, the greater probability there is that the diseases from which he suffers will be pronounced and powerfully demonstrating, on account of the inflow to a greater or less degree of the stimulating force of the soul. Subsidiary to the five major groups of diseases to which I earlier referred, and working out in connection with them in the human frame, are a group of symptoms which are loosely covered by the terms: fevers, tumors, congested areas, plus general debility and the auto-intoxication which lies behind so many symptoms. I would have you remember this with care and bear steadily in mind that I am here only generalising, but that this generalisation is basic and therefore of importance.

C. Diseases of Worry and Irritation.

The third category of complaints which arise in the emotional or astral body is synthesised esoterically under the term: diseases of irritation. These are the insidious poisons which lurk behind the phenomena of disease.

It might be said that all diseases can be covered by two definitions, from the standpoint of occultism:

1. Diseases which are the result of auto-intoxication. These are the most general.
2. Diseases which are the result of irritation. These are very common amongst disciples.

We hear much today about auto-intoxication, and many efforts are made to cure this by diet and the regulation of the life in terms of rhythmic living. All this is good and of help, but it does not constitute a basic cure, as its protagonists would lead us to believe. Irritation is a basic psychological complaint and has its roots in the intensification of the astral body, which definitely produces abnormal effects upon the nervous system. It is a disease of self-interest, of self-sufficiency, and of self-satisfaction. Again I would say, ponder on these terms, for these three aspects of irritation are of general discovery. We will therefore deal with irritation, "imperil," as it is called by exponents of the first ray, such as the Master M.

We have nearly completed our first section under the heading Psychological Causes of Disease, and have very briefly, yet I believe suggestively, considered those problems which arise from the overactivity and wrong condition of the astral body. All I can do in this short treatise is to generalise, because most of the statements I may make are, in any case, so new and revolutionary (from the standpoint of orthodox medicine) that it will take time for even this first inner structure of ideas and this somewhat new formulation of truth to make its impact upon the thinkers of the race. Then, if accepted as hypothetical possibilities by the open-minded among them, a long period of time must elapse before there has been enough investigation, leading to definitely formulated conclusions, which will make the ideas of popular recognition and use. In saying this, I am not reflecting critically upon the medical profession. The money-grasping specialist and the charlatan are rare; they of course exist, as do the corrupt and the undesirable in every profession. Where are they not to be found? The closed minds are many; but again, where are they not found? The pioneers along the new lines of thought and the man who has grasped some of the New Age concepts have often equally closed minds and see nothing but the new ways, modes and methods, and throw overboard all the old, losing much thereby. The medical profession has one of the greatest and most beautiful records in the world of its purpose and field of activity, and has developed some of the greatest of the soul qualities—self-sacrifice, compassion and service. But the ways and the techniques of the New Age are hard to grasp. Much of the old ways have to be given up and much sacrificed before the new art of healing becomes possible.

Until the fact of the subtler bodies is properly recognised by the world thinkers, and their existence is established through a right and true science of psychology and the development of the faculty of clairvoyance, the tracing of the causes of disease back to the subtler bodies is relatively meaningless. The best reaction which the most open-minded physician can (I say *can* and not *will*) produce or admit is that the psychological attitude, the mental state, and the emotional condition of the patient do either help or hinder. Many are already admitting that. That in itself is much.

When, therefore, I say that cancer, for instance, has its roots in an astral condition and began its career in Atlantean times, it means but little to the average man today. He does not realise that large numbers of people today are Atlantean in their consciousness.

I want briefly to touch upon the most common of all causes of trouble: Worry and Irritation. They are more prevalent at this time than ever before, and for the following reasons:

1. The world situation is such, the problems and uncertainty are such, that scarcely a person in the world at this time is exempt. Everyone is more or less involved in the planetary situation.

2. The intercommunication between people has increased so much, and men live so much in massed groups—large or small—that it is inevitable that they produce an effect upon each other as never before. "If one member suffers, all the members suffer with it" is a statement of truth, ancient but new in application and today realised for the first time.

3. The increased sensitivity of the human mechanism is also such that men "tune in" on each other's emotional conditions and mental attitudes in a new and more po-

tent manner. To their own engrossing concerns and worries are added those of their fellowmen with whom they may be en rapport.

4. Telepathically, and also with a developed sense of prevision, men are today adding the difficulties that belong to someone else, or to some other group of thinkers and of people, to *the difficulties that may be*. It is not sure that they *will be*.

These problems will demonstrate to you how intensely difficult it is for men to face up to life. It will be obvious that the problems of worry and irritation (called by the Master Morya "imperil") are many and must be considered.

Why are these difficulties of the astral body so "perilous" and so serious? Worry and Irritation are dangerous because:

1. They lower the vitality of the man to such a point that he becomes susceptible to disease. The scourge of influenza has its roots in fear and worry, and once the world settles down to freedom from the present "fearful" condition, we shall see the disease die out.

2. They are so highly infectious from the astral point of view that they lower in a peculiar manner the astral atmosphere, and thus make it hard for people—in the astral sense—to breathe freely.

3. Because the astral conditions of fear, worry and irritation are so widespread today that they might be regarded as *epidemic*, in a planetary sense.

4. Because irritation (I speak not here of worry) is inflammatory in its effects—and inflammation is hard to bear—and leads to much difficulty. It is interesting to note that certain forms of eye trouble are caused by this.

5. Because worry and irritation prevent true vision. They shut out the view. The man who is the victim of these conditions sees nothing but the cause of his complaints and is so submerged through self-pity, self-consideration, or in a focussed negative condition, that his vision is narrowed and his group hindered. Remember that there is group selfishness as well as individual selfishness.

I have cited sufficient reasons for the effects of Worry and Irritation to demonstrate to you the wideness of the difficulty. It is not much use at this time to talk of the remedy. One does not say to an influenza patient (when the worst throes of the disease are upon him), "There is nothing the matter. Pay no attention. Get up and go about your business." It is no use saying to men today, "Do not fear. Leave off worrying. All will be well." They will not believe you, for one thing—and that is fortunate, for it is not true. Things are not well and humanity and the planetary life are not well. This, the Hierarchy knows, and is working for the amelioration of the conditions. When the throes of the "planetary influenza" are over (and the patient will not die), then investigation can be made and effort produced which can prevent a recurrence. At present, all that can be done is to keep the patient quiet and also keep the fever down. This is the work of the New Group of World Servers and the intelligent men of goodwill. Their name is Legion.

2. Causes Arising in the Etheric Body

It will be wise for you to bear in mind that I am not here going to deal with those causes which, producing effects in the physical body, arise in the mind or in the astral body. Necessarily they pass through the etheric body. The etheric body is a transmitter of all energies to the physical body, and all types of force pass through it to different parts of the physical form, producing good and bad results, negative or positive results, as the case may be. This is a fact which we accept. I am here considering the diseases, problems and physical difficulties which arise in the etheric body itself and work out in its relations to the physical body. These are quite widespread and usual. It is essential that you keep these two lines of force-activity clearly differentiated in your mind. Both pass through and from the etheric body into the physical body, but only one of them originates in or is concerned with difficulties which have an etheric origin.

The etheric body is a body composed entirely of lines of force and of points where these lines of force cross each other and thus form (in crossing) centres of energy. Where many such lines of force cross each other, you have a larger centre of energy, and where great streams of energy meet and cross, as they do in the head and up the spine, you have seven major centres. There are seven such, plus twenty-one lesser centres and forty-nine smaller centres known to the esotericists. However, we will confine ourselves at this time to the etheric body as a whole and to the seven major centres. It might be of interest to you, nevertheless, to be told where the twenty-one minor centres are to be found. They can be located at the following points:

There are two of them in front of the ears close to where the jaw bones are connected.

There are two of them just above the two breasts.

There is one where the breast bones meet, close to the thyroid gland. This, with the two breast centres, makes a triangle of force.

There are two, one each in the palms of the hands.

There are two, one each in the soles of the feet.

There are two, just behind the eyes.

There are two also connected with the gonads.

There is one close to the liver.

There is one connected with the stomach; it is related, therefore, to the solar plexus, but is not identical with it.

There are two connected with the spleen. These form one centre in reality, but such a centre is formed by the two being superimposed one on the other.

There are two—one at the back of each knee.

There is one powerful centre which is closely connected with the vagus nerve. This is most potent and is regarded by some schools of occultism as a major centre; it is not in the spine, but is no great distance from the thymus gland.

There is one which is close to the solar plexus, and relates it to the centre at the base of the spine, thus making a triangle of the sacral centre, the solar plexus, and the centre at the base of the spine.

The two triangles referred to in this tabulation are of real importance. One is above and the other below the diaphragm.

It is of course apparent that where there is a free flow of force through the etheric body into the dense physical body there will be less likelihood of disease or sickness. There may, however, be increased tendency to difficulties arising from overstimulation and its consequent results of overactivity of the nervous system, with all the attendant problems. These forces, seeking inlet into the dense vehicle, are emanations from three directions (if I may use such a term):

1. From the personality vehicles—the astral and mental bodies.

2. From the soul, if contact, recognised or unrecognised, has been established.

3. From the environing world to which the vehicles of the soul and of the personality have acted as "doors of entrance." Incidentally, in connection with this last phrase, I would call your attention to a possible relation between these "doors of entrance" and the phrase "door of initiation."

In the case where these centres, through which the inflowing energy from these sources of supply flow, are quiescent, unawakened or only functioning partially or too slowly (as far as their vibratory rhythm is concerned), then you will have a condition of blocking. This will produce congestion in the etheric vehicle, and consequent and subsequent difficulties in the functioning of the physical body. One of the most common of these is congestion of the lungs which—though it may be exoterically traced to certain and definite physical causes—is in reality those causes, plus an inner condition of etheric congestion. It is the bringing together of the outer apparent cause and the inner true cause which is responsible for the outbreak of the trouble. When these two conditions are brought into conjunction with each other, and you have a physical handicap and an etheric situation which is undesirable, then you will have disease, illness, or weakness of some kind. Every outer congestion can always be traced to these two causes—an inner and an outer cause. In these cases, the outer cause is not an effect of the individual inner cause, which is interesting. You will note, therefore, that all ills are not purely subjective or psychological in origin as far as an individual is concerned, but are sometimes both exoteric and esoteric. Hence the complication of the problem.

The above statement opens up the whole question of the activity of the seven centres of force in the etheric body. These can be regarded as dormant or unawakened, awakening but only as yet sluggishly alive, or functioning normally, which means that some of the energies which produce the form of the centre are moving rhythmically, and are therefore receptive to inflow, while others are still entirely inactive and unresponsive. Other centres will be fully active, and therefore predominantly attractive to any inflowing forces; still others will be only partially so. For the majority of people, the centres below the diaphragm are more active than those above the diaphragm (I am referring here to the seven major centres and not to the twenty-one minor centres). For aspirants, centres below the diaphragm are active and the heart and throat centres are slowly coming into activity, while in the case of disciples, the ajna centre, plus those centres below it in the body, are rapidly awakening. In the initiate, the head centre is coming into vibrant activity, thus swinging all the centres into real and coordinated rhythm. Each patient or human being, being on some ray, responds differently; the time factor also differs; the pattern of the unfoldment varies, and the response to the inflowing forces is slightly differentiated.

All of this we will consider with due care when we deal with Chapter IX, which concerns itself with the seven modes of healing. I simply mention it here so as to lay the foundation for what must later be considered, and thus show you how the whole question of the relation of the etheric body to the physical body is connected with the problem of healing. It will be apparent, therefore, how important it is—before real healing can take place—-that the healer should know the point in evolution reached by the patient, and should also know his ray type, both personality and egoic. If to this you add some knowledge of his astrological inclinations and indications, a far more accurate diagnosis can be produced. The key to all release (either through the physical cure of disease or through death) lies in the understanding of the condition of the centres in the etheric body. These determine the rate of the bodily vibratory activity and the general responsiveness of the physical body. They even condition the activity and accuracy of the instinctual nature and its relation to the outer plane life and the "wholeness" and general health of the sympathetic nervous system.

A. Congestion.

Much real difficulty can be traced to congestion or to the lack of the free play of the forces. In this connection it might be pointed out that the etheric body is a mechanism for intake and for outlet. There is consequently a curious and intimate relation between it and such organs as the lungs, the stomach, and the kidneys. The symbology here present, when correctly understood, will tend to show that there is a deep underlying esoteric relation between:

1. The mind and the lungs. The process of breathing, with its stages of inhalation, the interlude, and exhalation, works out in connection with both aspects of force, mental and physical.
2. The desire nature and the stomach. Here again is the process of intake, of assimilation, and of elimination.
3. The etheric body itself and the kidneys, with the processes clearly defined in both cases of absorption, chemicalisation, and transmission.

There is no symbol so relatively accurate to the whole

creative process as the human frame.

Congestion in the etheric body, producing much distress in the physical body, can exist, therefore, at the point of intake from the astral body or from the astral plane (Note the phrasing and the difference.) or at the point of outlet, in relation to the centre to which the particular type of etheric force most easily flows and through which it most easily passes. Where there is no free play between the etheric body and the astral body, you will have trouble. Where there is no free play between the etheric body and the physical body, involving also the nerve ganglia and the endocrine system, you will also have trouble. The close relation between the seven major centres and the seven major glands of the physical system must never be forgotten. The two systems form one close interlocking directorate, with the glands and their functions determined by the condition of the etheric centres. These, in their turn, are conditioned by the point in evolution and gained experience of the incarnate soul, by the specific polarisation of the soul in incarnation, and by the rays (personality and soul) of the man. Forget not, that the five aspects of man (as he functions in the three worlds) are determined by certain ray forces; you have the ray of the soul, the ray of the personality, and the rays of the mental, the astral and the physical bodies. All these will, in the coming New Age, be definitely considered and discovered, and this knowledge will reveal to the healer the *probable* condition of the centres, the order of their awakening, and their individual and basic note or notes. The new medical science will be outstandingly built upon the science of the centres, and upon this knowledge all diagnosis and possible cure will be based. The endocrinologist is only beginning to glimpse possibilities, and much that he is now considering has in it the seeds of future truth. The "balancing of the glandular system" and the relation of the glands to the blood stream, and also to character and predispositions of many kinds, are considerations of real value and worth following. Much, however, remains to be discovered before it will be really safe to work with the glands, making them a major subject of attention (as some day will be the case in all forms of illness).

Throughout this short treatise I will give many hints which will serve to guide the open minded investigator in the right direction. Before passing on to the consideration of the relation of the etheric body, as a unit, to the physical body, I would like to point out that I place the complications of *congestion* first upon the list of diseases arising in the etheric body, because it is at this time—and will be for a couple of centuries—the major cause of difficulty for the bulk of humanity or of those people whom we esoterically call "solar-sacral" people. This is partly due to the age-long habits of suppression and of inhibition which the race, as a whole, has developed. It is this congestion at the point of intake and of outlet in the etheric body which is responsible for the impeding of the free flow of the life force, with the results of a rapid succumbing to diseases. Hence, also, you will see how carefully assigned breathing exercises, with their subtle effects of reorganising and readjusting the subtler bodies (particularly the etheric and astral bodies) will become more and more generally used. The widespread interest in breathing today evidences a subjective recognition of this fact, though not enough is yet known about methods and effects.

One other thing I would like to call to your attention is that the points of congestion may exist either in the astral body centre or in the etheric body, and this situation the healer will have to investigate.

B. Lack of Coordination and Integration.

We come now to a brief consideration of our second point of difficulty to be found in the etheric body, which in our tabulation we have called *lack of coordination or integration*. This is exceedingly prevalent today and is responsible for a good deal of trouble. The etheric body is the inner "substantial" form upon which the physical body is built or constructed. It is the inner scaffolding which underlies every part of the whole outer man; it is the framework which sustains the whole; it is that upon which the outer form is patterned; and it is the network of nadis (infinitely intricate) which constitutes the counterpart or the duplicate aspect of the entire nervous system which forms such an important part of the human mechanism. It is thus definitely, with the blood stream, the instrument of the life force. If, therefore, there is weakness in the relation between this inner structure and the outer form, it will be immediately apparent to you that real difficulty is bound to supervene. This difficulty will take three forms:

1. The physical form in its dense aspect is too loosely connected with the etheric form or counterpart. This leads to a devitalised and debilitated condition, which predisposes man to sickness or ill health.

2. The connection is poor in certain directions or aspects of the equipment. Through certain focal points or centres the life force cannot adequately flow, and therefore you have a definite weakness in some part of the physical body. For instance, impotence is such a difficulty and a tendency to laryngitis is another—to mention two widely different disorders.

3. The connection can also be so basically loose and poor that the soul has very little hold upon its vehicle

for outer manifestation, and obsession or possession is easily established. This is an extreme example of the difficulties incident to this condition. Others are certain forms of fainting or loss of consciousness and "petit mal."

There are also, as will be apparent, the exactly reverse conditions when the etheric body is so closely knit or integrated with the personality—whether it is of a highly evolved nature or simply an example of an ordinary etheric body—that every part of the physical body is in a constant condition of stimulation, of galvanic effort, with a resultant activity in the nervous system which—if not correctly regulated—can lead to a great deal of distress. It is to this that I refer in the third heading, *"Overstimulation of the Centres."* Too loose a connection or too close a connection leads to trouble, though the first kind of difficulty is usually more serious than the others. I have here given enough to show how interesting and how important a study of the etheric body may be. The whole theme of healing is "tied up" (to use a modern phrase which I find difficult) with the development, unfoldment and control of the seven major centres.

C. *Overstimulation of the Centres.*

There is much that I could add to what I have said on the cause of disease arising in the etheric body, but in Part II (when dealing with the section on certain basic requirements) I shall elaborate the theme much further. Congestion, lack of integration and over-stimulation of the centres, are obviously fundamental causes as far as the dense physical body is concerned, but they themselves are frequently effects of subtler causes, hidden in the life of the astral and mental bodies and, in the case of overstimulation, the result sometimes of soul contacts. The etheric body reacts normally, and by design, to all the conditions found in the subtler vehicles. It is essentially a transmitter and not an originator and it is only the limitations of the observer which lead him to ascribe the causes of bodily ills to the etheric body. It is a clearing house for all the forces reaching the physical body, provided the point in evolution has brought the various force centres to a condition wherein they are receptive to any particular type of force. Esoterically speaking, the centres can be in one of five conditions or states of being. These can be described in the following terms:

1. Closed, still and shut, and yet with signs of life, silent and full of deep inertia.
2. Opening, unsealed, and faintly tinged with colour; the life pulsates.
3. Quickened, alive, alert in two directions; the two small doors are open wide.
4. Radiant and reaching forth with vibrant note to all related centres.
5. Blended they are and each with each works rhythmically. The vital force flows through from all the planes. The world stands open wide.

Related to these five stages, wherein the etheric body expands and becomes *the vital livingness* of all expression upon the physical plane, are the five races of men, beginning with the Lemurian race, the five planes of human and superhuman expression, the five stages of consciousness and the various other groupings of five with which you meet in the esoteric philosophy. Incidentally it might be of value and of interest to point out that the five-pointed star is not only the sign and symbol of initiation and finally of perfected man, but it is also the basic symbol of the etheric

body and of the five centres which control perfected man—
the two head centres, the heart centre, the throat centre and
the centre at the base of the spine. When these centres
are fully awakened and functioning in right rhythm with
each other, the various quintuplets to which I have referred
above form an integral part of the consciousness of the
perfected man.

Though this particular piece of information is not definitely related to the Science of Healing, yet the entire subject is related to energy, and energy in some form or another is related to the causes and the effects of disease,
because disease is the undesirable effect of energy upon the
energy unit which we call the atom.

It should be remembered that the etheric body of the
human being is an integral part of the etheric body of the
planetary Logos and is, therefore, related to all forms
found within that body in any and all the kingdoms in nature.
It is part of the substance of the universe, coordinated with
planetary substance, and hence provides the scientific basis
for unity.

If you were to ask me what, in reality, lies behind all
disease, all frustrations, error and lack of divine expression in the three worlds, I would say it was *separativeness*
which produces the major difficulties arising in the etheric
body, plus the inability of the outer tangible form to respond
adequately to the inner and subtler impulses. Here is found
the cause (the secondary cause, as I pointed out above)
of the bulk of the trouble. The etheric body of the planet
does not yet freely transmit and circulate the forces which
are seeking entrance into the consciousness and the expression of man upon the physical plane. These forces emanate
from within himself as he functions on the subtler levels
of consciousness and from the soul; they come also from
associated and contacted groups, from the planetary life,

and eventually, in the last analysis, from the entire universe. Each of the centres can, when fully awakened and consciously and scientifically employed, serve as an open door through which awareness of that which lies beyond the individual human life can enter. The etheric body is fundamentally the most important response apparatus which man possesses, producing not only the right functioning of the five senses and consequently providing five major points of contact with the tangible world, but it also enables a man to register sensitively the subtler worlds, and, when energised and controlled by the soul, the spiritual realms stand wide open also.

The etheric body is a potent receiver of impressions, which are conveyed to the human consciousness through the medium of the awakened centres. There is, for instance, no true clairvoyance until either the solar plexus or the ajna centre is awakened. These transmitted impressions and information become the incentive whereby conscious activity is initiated. There are many words used to describe these forces and their actuating effects: such as impulses, incentives, influences, potencies, desires, aspirations, and many such terms which are only synonyms for force or energy and thus convey the same general idea. All of these words refer to forms of activity of the etheric body, but only as the physical body registers them and acts under their impression. The whole theme of motivating force is one of great interest.

The vastness of the subject is, however, so real that only little by little can humanity grasp the situation and come to the realisation that man is essentially (through his etheric body) an integral part of a great and vibrant Whole; only in time will he learn that, through the processes of evolution, can he hope to register all the different areas of divine expression. Only when the etheric body is swept into activity under the influence and through the "impressed forces" of the soul, the mind, and temporarily, of the astral body, can man become aware of all worlds, all phenomena, and all states of consciousness, and so achieve that omniscience which is the birthright of all the sons of God.

But, during the period wherein this state of being is in process of achievement, the lack of development, the failure to register, the life work of awakening and organising the various centres and of then correctly relating them to each other, produces much difficulty. It is this condition which is the fruitful source of those difficulties which, when carried down into the physical body, produce disease of various kinds, the many tensions and congestions, the overstimulation of the centres in one part of the etheric vehicle and their underdevelopment in another, plus the unequal unfoldment and wrong balance of the centres.

Much is said today in modern medical investigation anent the "imbalance" of the endocrine glands, and many physical difficulties are ascribed to this frequent imbalance. But behind this condition of the glandular system lies the basic imbalance of the centres themselves. Only when there is a right understanding of force and its reception and consequent use, will right balance be achieved and the human endocrine system control the physical man in the manner that is intended.

There is much need today for the study of the following problems:

1. The problem of the right reception of force through the appropriate centre. An instance of this might be found in the correct control of the solar plexus centre as the one in which astral sensitivity can be registered and properly handled.

2. The problem of the right relation of a particular centre to its related gland, permitting the free play of the force pouring through the centre to the allied glandular correspondence, thus conditioning its peculiar hormone and eventually conditioning the blood stream. If you grasp this sequence of contact, you will understand more clearly the occult significance of the words in the Old Testament that "the blood is the life." It is the vitality coming from the etheric body which works through into the blood stream, via the centre which is responsive to one of the seven peculiar types of force, and its allied gland. It will be apparent, therefore, that there is a close relation between:

a. The etheric body as a transmitter of a vast aggregate of energies and forces.

b. The endocrine system whose various glands are in reality the externalisation or materialisation of the centres, major and minor.

c. The heart, which is the centre of life as the brain is the centre of consciousness. From the heart, the blood circulates and is controlled. Thus these three great systems are related.

d. The entire glandular system to the nervous system through the medium of the network of nerves and the "nadis" which underlie this network. These nadis are the threads of life force which underlie every part of the body and particularly the nervous system in all its aspects.

To these problems and relationships another might be added. This is the interrelation which must be established between all the centres, permitting the free play of force in correct rhythm throughout the physical vehicle.

You have, therefore, certain great interlocking directorates which control or fail to control the physical body. Where there is lack of control it is due to the failure to establish right relations within the body, or to lack of development. These interlocking groups are:

1. That of the etheric body, which works primarily through its seven major centres but also through many other centres.

2. That of the endocrine system, which works primarily through the seven major glandular groups, but also through many other less important glands.

3. That of the nervous system (the sympathetic and the cerebro-spinal) with a peculiar emphasis laid upon the vagus nerve with its effect upon the heart and consequently upon the blood stream.

All these points have to be considered and correlated in any system of occult healing, and the technical matter to be covered is, in the last analysis, less intricate than the vast system built up by orthodox medicine and surgery. It is because of the lack of coordination of these three systems that the healing art is at this time failing to achieve all that it desires. It has done much, but must move another step onto the etheric plane before the real clue to disease and its cure can be ascertained.

For instance, lack of vitality and the common subnormal conditions with which we are so familiar, indicate the inertia of the etheric body and its lack of vitality. The results of this inertness of the vital body can be both physical and psychological, because the glands in the physical body will not function normally and, as is well known, they condition the physical expression of man as well as his emotional and mental states, in so far as those are able or not able to find expression through the medium of the physical vehicle. The glands do not condition the inner man or his states of consciousness, but they can and do prevent those inner states finding manifestation outwardly. In the reverse situation, too powerful an etheric body and the overstimulation of the centres concerned, may put too great a strain upon the nervous system and produce, as a consequence, definite nervous trouble, migraine, mental and emotional imbalance and, in some cases, lead to insanity.

I have elaborated this matter somewhat because the relation of the etheric body to the physical body and its receptivity to the inner energies most decidedly condition the man. It will be necessary for us to have this ever in mind as we study the causes of the diseases arising in the mental body, or due to the activity of the soul in the life of the disciple, or as we investigate the processes whereby a man is prepared for initiation. The etheric body must always, and invariably does, act as the transmitting agent of the inner energies to the outer plane, and the physical body has to learn to respond to and recognise that which is transmitted. The effectiveness of the transmission and the resultant physical activity depend always upon the centres, which, in their turn, condition the glands; these, later, determine the nature and the expressed consciousness of the man. If the centres are awakened and receptive, there will be found a physical apparatus which will be responsive to the forces flowing through. If the centres are asleep, and thus little force can be transmitted, you will find a physical apparatus which will be equally slow and unresponsive. If the centres below the diaphragm are awakened and those above are not, you will have a man whose consciousness will be focussed in the animal and the emotional natures, and much of his physical disease will lie below the diaphragm also. You will see, therefore, how intricate and complex this whole matter is—so complex that it will only be truly understood when human beings regain the lost power to "see the light" of the etheric body and of its seven major centres and, through a developed sense of touch in the hands and fingers, to ascertain the rate of vibration in the various centres. When these two means of knowledge are available, the entire subject of the etheric body will take on a new importance and be correctly understood.

3. Causes Arising in the Mental Body

I started this section of our study with the causes arising in the astral and etheric bodies because they are the major sources of trouble, owing to the fact that the bulk of humanity is astrally focussed, just as the bulk of the forms in the animal kingdom are etherically focussed. The forces pouring into the animal kingdom come predominantly from etheric levels and from the dense physical levels of life. The higher animals, however, owing to the development brought about through their contact with human beings, are becoming susceptible to forces coming from the astral plane, and they thus develop actions and reactions which are not purely instinctual.

Today, owing to the development of the mind in the Aryan race, certain difficulties may arise in the physical body. Their origin is not basically mental but primarily due to the fact that the mental body is the transmitter (when active and rightly aligned) of soul energy and this soul energy, pouring into the physical body, can produce certain conditions of overstimulation and difficulties connected with the nervous system. But it is the transmitted energy which causes the trouble and not the factor arising from the mind itself. I will elaborate this a little later.

A. Wrong Mental Attitudes.

I would like to deal, first of all, with the basic premise that disease and physical liabilities are not the result of wrong thought. They are far more likely to be the result of no thought at all, or are caused by the failure to follow those fundamental laws which govern the Mind of God. One interesting instance of this failure is the fact that man does not follow the basic Law of Rhythm, which governs all the processes of nature, and man is a part of nature. It is to this failure to work with the Law of Periodicity that we can trace much of the difficulty inherent in the use and the misuse of the sex urge. Instead of man being governed by the cyclic manifestation of the sex impulse, and his life, therefore, being ruled by a definite rhythm, there exists at this time no such thing, except in the cycles through which the female passes, and little attention is paid to these. The male, however, is not governed by any such cycles, and has broken in also on the rhythm to which the female body should be subordinated, and which—rightly understood— would determine the use of the sex relationship, including naturally the male impulse also. This failure to live by the Law of Periodicity and to subordinate the appetites to cyclic control is one of the major causes of disease; and as these laws are given form on the mental plane, one might legitimately say that their infringement has a mental basis. This might be the case if the race were working mentally, but it is not. It is in the modern world of today that there is beginning a widespread infringement of these mental laws, particularly of the Law of Cycles, which determines the tides, controls world events and should also condition the individual and so establish rhythmic life habits—one of the major predisposing incentives to good health.

By breaking this Law of Rhythm, man has disorganised the forces which, rightly used, tend to bring the body into a sound and healthy condition; by so doing, he has laid the foundation for that general debility and those inherent organic tendencies which predispose a man to ill health and which permit entrance into the system of those germs and bacteria which produce the outer forms of malignant disease. When humanity regains an understanding of the right use of time (which determines the Law of Rhythm on the physical plane), and can determine the proper cycles for the various manifestations of the life force upon the physical plane, then what was earlier an instinctual habit will become the intelligent usage of the future. This will constitute an entirely new science, and the rhythm of the natural processes and the establishing, as habits, the correct cycles of physical functioning, will bring about a new era of health and of sound physical conditions for the entire race. I used the word "establishing," for as the focus of racial attention shifts into the region of the higher values the physical vehicle will gain enormously, and good health—through right rhythmic living, plus correct thinking and soul contact —will become permanently established.

There are, therefore, very few ills to which flesh is heir which are mentally based. It is exceedingly difficult to establish what they are. There are two reasons for this statistical failure:

1. The fact that very few, relatively speaking of the race are mentally polarised and therefore thinking.
2. The fact that the bulk of diseases are etheric or astral.

Another factor producing this difficulty is that the thinking and the emotional reactions of man are so closely interrelated that it is not easy at this stage in evolution to separate feeling and thought, or to say that such or such ills arise in the astral or the mental body, or that certain ills are due to wrong feeling and others to wrong thinking. Speaking in terms of the entire human family, the thinking that is done in the world of today, is done by the relatively few. The rest are occupied with feeling, with sensuous perception and with the many and differing aspects of emotionalism such as irritability, worry, acute anxiety, aspiration towards some desired end or goal, depression, plus the dramatic life of the senses and of the "I in the centre" consciousness. Few live in the world of thought and fewer still in the world of reality. When they do, the result is inevitably a better average of health, because there is better integration, and as a result a freer play of the life forces throughout the vehicles of expression.

B. Mental Fanaticism. The Dominance of Thoughtforms.

I would point out here that the diseases and difficulties which arise from what I have called wrong mental attitudes, fanaticisms and frustrated idealisms and thwarted hopes, fall into three categories, and a study of these will show you that, in the last analysis, they are not of mental origin at all, but primarily are the result of emotionalism entering in.

1. Those incident to the imposed physical plane activity and work which find their incentive in these mental conditions. They lead, for instance, to furious activity and overwork, due to the determination not to be frustrated but to make the plan work. The result is frequently the breaking down of the nervous system, which could have been avoided had the mental condition been changed and right rhythm on the physical plane achieved. But it was the work of a physical nature which caused the trouble far more than the mental condition.

2. Those brought about by the state of rebellion which colours all the life, and the registering of violent emotional reactions. These may be based upon a mental realisation of the Plan, for instance, plus a recognition that those plans are not materialising, owing often to the inadequacy of the physical equipment; but the basic cause of the disease is the emotional rebellion, and therefore not the mental condition. Bitterness, disgust, hatred and a sense of frustration can and do produce many of the prevalent toxic conditions and a state of general poisoning and ill health from which many people habitually suffer. Their vision is bigger than their accomplishment, and this causes emotional suffering. The cure for this condition is to be found in the simple word *acceptance*. This is not a negative state of settling down to a submissive nonactive life, but it is a positive acceptance (in thought and in practical expression) of a condition which seems at present unavoidable. This leads to an avoidance of the waste of time in attempting the impossible and to right effort to carry forward that which is possible.

3. Those difficulties which are caused by the failure of the physical apparatus to measure up to the demands of the thought life of the individual. These are, naturally and usually, a part of the physical inheritance, and where this is the case there is normally nothing much to do, though where the aspiration is real and persistent, a great deal might be accomplished in bringing about improvement and laying the ground for better functioning in another life cycle.

It is necessary here that I should deal, as briefly as possible, with the problem of mental healing and with the teaching that all disease is the product of wrong thought. You are starting out to work, and I would have clear thinking on this point. The two problems which I have posited are closely related. We could express them in the form of two questions:

1. Is disease the result of thought?
2. Can the power of thought produce healing effects when used by an individual or a group?

In view of the fact that many diseases are, as I have told you, latent in the very material of the planet itself, it is obvious that human thought is not responsible for disease. It antedates the arrival of humanity upon the planet. There is disease in the mineral world, in the vegetable kingdom, and also among animals, even in their wild states and in their natural habitat, uncontaminated by man. Hence, man cannot be held responsible for this, nor is it the result of human wrong thinking. It provides no answer to the question to say that it must therefore be due to the wrong thinking of the planetary Logos or of the solar Logos. This is only a begging of the question and an evasion of the issue.

I would here remind you of the two definitions of the causes of disease which I earlier gave. Let me call them to your careful attention:

"All disease is the result of inhibited soul life. This is true of all forms in all kingdoms."
"Disease is the product of and subject to three influences. First, a man's past wherein he pays the price of ancient error. Second, his inheritance wherein he shares with all mankind those tainted streams of energy which are of group origin. Thirdly, he shares with all the natural forms that which the Lord of Life imposes on those forms. Those three influences are called the *Ancient Law of evil Sharing*. This must give place some day to that new *Law of Ancient Dominating Good*. This law will be brought into activity by the spiritual will of man."

If you analyse the four causes of disease here given, you will note that disease will eventually be controlled by the release of the soul in all forms, and that this will be done by the active use by man of his spiritual will. We could word this otherwise and say that when soul energy and the right use of the will (which in the individual is the reflection and the agent of the will energy of the soul) is released and rightly directed by the mind, then disease can be handled and brought eventually to an end. It is therefore by the imposition of a higher energy and of a higher rhythm upon the lower forces that disease can be controlled. Disease is therefore the result in the physical body of the failure to bring in these higher energies and rhythms, and that, in its turn, is dependent upon the point in evolution.

It is the dim sensing of this failure and the realisation of these facts that has brought so many groups to believe in the cure of disease by thought power and to ascribe the appearance of disease to wrong thinking. But in reality, humanity must some day learn that it is only the higher consciousness of the soul, working through the mind, that can finally solve this difficult problem.

We cannot consequently affirm that disease, as a general rule, has any relation to thought. It is simply the misuse of the forces of the etheric, the astral and of the dense physical levels. The majority of people are helpless to do anything about it, as the forces which constitute the physical body, for instance, and which pass through and play upon it, are inherited from a very ancient past, are a constituent part of the environment and of the group life into which they are integrated and which they share with all their fellowmen. Such force-matter is coloured with the results of ancient wrong rhythms, misused forces and inherited qualities. Soul energy, expressed through right thinking, can cure diseases to which man is prone. It is failure to think and to register and express the higher states of consciousness which leads to wrong rhythms. Consequently, I repeat that disease is not the result of thought.

C. *Frustrated Idealism.*

There are, however, certain diseases which appear in the physical mechanism and which are definitely rooted in the fact that activity (which is the result of thinking specifically) has been coloured and conditioned by the emotional life of the individual, and the emotional life is a fruitful source of disease and of establishing wrong rhythms. It is therefore the predominance of the astral force, and not of the mental energy, which really causes the physical trouble. I am not referring here to the diseases of the nervous system and of the brain, which are the result of overstimulation and of the impact of energy (often from the mind and the soul) upon an instrument unfitted to handle it. These we will consider later. I refer simply to the following sequence of events in the psychological life and the consequent resultant activities:

Disease is a form of activity.

1. Mental activity and energy produces (through the power of thought) certain registration of plans, idealisms and ambitions.

2. This energy, blended with astral energy, becomes dominated and controlled by astral reactions of an undesirable kind, such as worry over non-accomplishment, the failure to materialise the plans, etc. The life becomes consequently embittered.

3. Disease then appears in the physical body, according to the predisposing tendencies of the body and its inherent, inherited weaknesses.

You will note that, in reality, the mental body, and the power of thought, have in no case been the cause of trouble. It has been caused by the obliteration of the original thought and its stepping down to the level of emotionalism. When this stepping down and eventual control by astral forces does not take place, and the thought remains clear and untouched upon the mental plane, there may be trouble of another kind, due to a failure to "carry through" the thought into effective action upon the physical plane. This failure produces not only the cleavage in the personality so well known to the practicing psychologist, but also a cutting off of a much needed stream of energy. As a consequence, the physical body is devitalised and falls heir to bad health. When the thought can be carried through to the physical brain and there becomes a directing agent of the life force, you will usually have a condition of good health, and this has proved true whether the individual thought has been good or bad, rightly motivated or wrongly oriented. It is simply the effect of integration, because saints and sinners, the selfish and the unselfish and all kinds of people, can achieve integration and a thought-directed life.

The second question asks whether an individual or a group can heal by thought power.

Most certainly the generalisation can be made that an individual and a group can heal and that thought can play its potent part in the healing process, but not thought alone and unaided. Thought can be the *directing agency of forces* and energies which can disrupt and dispel disease, but the process must be aided by the power to visualise, by an ability to work with particular forces as is deemed advisable, by an understanding of the rays and their types of energies, and also by a capacity to handle *light substance,* as it is called. To these powers must be added the ability to be en rapport with the one to be healed, plus a loving heart. In fact, once these conditions are met, too much use of the thinking faculty and too potent a use of the mind processes can arrest and hinder the healing work. Thought has to condition the initial incentive, bringing the intelligence of the man to bear upon the problem of healing and a comprehension of the nature of the one to be healed; but once it has aided in focussing the attention of the healer and the healing group, it should become a steady but subconscious directive agent and nothing more than that.

The healing is accomplished, when possible, by the use of energy rightly directed and by detailed visualisation; love also plays a great part, as does the mind in the early stage. Perhaps I should say that a loving heart is one of the most potent of all the energies employed.

I have brought these two questions to your attention because I am anxious for your minds to be clear upon these problems before you start any group work in healing.

Thought neither cures disease nor causes it. Thought must be employed in the processes, but it is not the sole or the most important agent. It is on this point that many groups and healers go astray. The mind can direct energy and this energy can, in its turn, produce overstimulation of the brain and of the body cells and so cause nervous trouble and sometimes brain disease, but the mind itself and thinking, per se, cannot cause disease and trouble in the physical body. As the race learns to think clearly and definitely, and as the laws of thought begin to control the racial consciousness, disease—as we now know it—will be greatly lessened and more and more people will achieve integration. Where there is integration there is the free play of force and of energy throughout the material body. The problems of stimulation will, however, steadily increase with the growing sensitivity of the physical man and the developing focus of his consciousness in the mind nature. This will go on until man learns how to handle the higher energies and to recognise the need for a rhythmic life, paying attention to the Law of Periodicity.

In healing work, certain rules should be mastered and followed by the healer. I have given three important rules already. Briefly they are as follows, and I am dividing the first one into its component parts for the sake of clarity.

1. a. The healer must seek to link his soul, his heart, his brain, and his hands. Thus can he pour the vital force with healing power upon his patient. *This is magnetic work.*

   b. The healer must seek to link his soul, his brain, his heart and auric emanation. Thus can his presence feed the soul life of the patient. *This is the work of radiation.* The hands are needed not. The soul displays its power.

2. The healer must achieve magnetic purity, through purity of life. He must achieve that dispelling radiance which shows itself in every man once he has linked the centres in the head. When this magnetic field has been established, the radiance then goes forth.

3. Let the healer train himself to know the inner stage of thought or of desire of the one who seeks his help. He can thereby know the source from which the trouble comes. Let him relate the cause and the effect, and know the point exact through which relief must come.

I would here give you, as a group, another rule, making four major rules:

RULE FOUR

The healer and the healing group must keep the will in leash. It is not will that must be used, but love.

This last rule is of great importance. The concentrated will of any individual and the directed will of a united group should never be employed. The free will of the individual must never be subjected to the impact of a powerfully focussed group or individual; it is far too dangerous a procedure to be permitted. Will energy (particularly that of a number of people simultaneously playing upon the subtle and physical bodies of the one to be healed) can greatly increase the trouble instead of curing it. It can stimulate the disease itself to dangerous proportions and disrupt instead of cooperating with nature's healing forces, and can even eventually kill the person concerned by so increasing the disease that the patient's normal resistance can prove futile. I would ask you, therefore, in any group work of healing, to keep the will (and even keen desire) in abeyance. Only initiates of high degree are permitted to cure by the power of the will, focussed in the WORD OF POWER, and this only because they can test the capacity of the patient, the tension of the disease, and know also whether or no it is the will of the soul that the disease should be cured.

We have covered much ground of importance in this section and it will warrant your careful study. In the next one we will take up the peculiar problems of the disciple; I would ask you, in preparation for this, to study with attention, the teaching which I gave earlier on the diseases of the mystics.* Much said there need not be repeated by me, but should be incorporated in our teachings on healing. I suggest that you read them and know something of the problems themselves, both theoretically and from an understanding of yourself. You should be aware of some of these difficulties in your own experience, at least to some degree.

The Sacred Art of Healing

I do not intend, in this treatise, to deal with the pathology of disease, with its systems and their maleficent indi-

---

* A Treatise on the Seven Rays, Vol. II, Pages 520-625.

cations. These are fully covered in any ordinary medical treatise and textbook and I, my brothers, am no trained physician or medical authority, nor have I the time to be engrossed with the technicalities. What I am concerned with is to give the world some idea of the true and occult causes of disease and their hidden origins, and with the work of healing, as it is carried on and sanctioned by the Great White Lodge.

The work is, in reality, that of the judicious use of energy, applied with love and science. All that I tell you is the result of experiment. Such healing falls into two categories:

1. In *magnetic healing,* the healer, or the healing group, does two things:

    a. He attracts to the healing centre that type of energy which will counteract the disease.

    This is necessarily a vast subject and one of deep scientific import. Certain types of ray force can be used with certain types of disease, necessitating the use of certain specific centres for the distribution. These we shall consider and outline when we come to the section entitled *The Seven Modes of Healing.*

    b. He attracts to himself and absorbs those forces which are producing the disease, drawing it forth from the patient.

    This latter process necessitates a careful guarding of the healer from all contamination by the disease, so that the forces can find no place in his body. There must also be the supplying of fresh energy to the patient, in order to take the place of that which has been withdrawn. This process sets up a definite interplay between the healer and the patient. There is consequently some real danger in this work of occult healing, and for this reason the healers in training should bear in mind that they will work as a group and not as individuals. The free circulation of force produces good health in the individual or group. The free circulation of force between a healer or a healing group and the person to be healed can produce the cure of disease, provided it is the destiny of the man to be healed at any given time and his cooperation is given when possible, though this is not really essential. It facilitates more rapid results in many cases. In others, the patient's anxiety can negate the desired effects.

2. *In radiatory healing,* the process is simpler and safer for the healer simply gathers power into himself and then radiates it out on to the patient in the form of a steadily outflowing stream of radiant energy. This stream of energy should be directed to the centre nearest to the location of the disease.

In this work there is no risk to the healer, but if the element of will enters into his thought or the stream of energy projected is too strong, there may be danger to the patient. The impact of the force which is being radiated upon him may not only produce nervous tension, but may lead to an increase in the power of the disease and its intensification by stimulating the atoms and cells involved in the activity of the force responsible for the trouble. For this reason beginners must avoid any concentration upon the disease itself or the area in the physical body involved and carefully keep all thought in abeyance, once the preliminary work has been done, for energy ever follows thought and goes where the thought is focussed.

The healers have to determine the effectiveness of what they are attempting and the potency of their united group work and of the force which they can wield. They have also to discover their ability to keep the will in the background and to send the healing radiance out upon a stream of love-energy. Have ever in mind that love is energy and that it is a substance as real as dense matter. That substance can be used to drive out diseased tissue and provide a healthy substitute in place of the diseased material which has been eliminated.

They will, therefore, in the first cycle of work, attempt the radiatory method. It is simpler and far more easily mastered. Later, they can experiment with the method of magnetic healing.

You will now see the purpose of the rules anent the modes of healing which I gave early in this series of instructions. You will realise why, in this radiatory work, the linking process involves the soul, the brain and the entire aura or the magnetic field of individual or group activity. The mind is not mentioned or involved, and the brain acts solely as the focussing point of the love and the healing force to be projected into the stream of energy which issues from the ajna centre.

The healer will, therefore, keep all the forces focussed in the head, and his attention must be concentrated there also. The heart will be automatically involved, as he will be using the energy of love—at first entirely.

Let us now tabulate the rules under which all healing groups must work. I would like to interpolate here that it is not always necessary or possible to meet and work together in group formation. This work can be carried forward efficiently and potently, if the members work as a *subjective group;* each should then follow the instructions each day and as if he were working in his group in tangible form. This real linking is brought about by imagining himself as in the presence of his brothers. If they were to meet as a group upon the physical plane, it would be hard to prevent the dissipation of force through discussion, through the ordinary pleasantries of meeting, and through the physical interplay between personalities. It would be inevitable that there would be too much conversation, and the work done would not be adequately effective. From the physical standpoint, they work alone; from the true inner standpoint, they work in the closest cooperation.

Here are the first rules which I would have the student master:

Preliminary Rules for Radiatory Healing

1. By an act of the will, after making your own quick, conscious alignment, link up as a soul with the souls of your group brothers. Then link up with their minds, and then with their emotional natures. Do this by the use of the imagination, realising that energy follows thought and that the linking process is inevitable, if correctly done. You can then function as a group. Then forget about the group relation and concentrate upon the work to be done.

2. Within yourself, then, link soul and brain and gather together the forces of love that are to be found in your aura and focus yourself and all that you have to offer within the head, picturing yourself as a radiant centre of energy or a point of vivid light. This light is to be projected upon the patient through the ajna centre between the eyes.

3. Then say the following group mantram:

"With purity of motive, inspired by a loving heart, we offer ourselves for this work of healing. This offer we make as a group and to the one we seek to heal."

As you do this, visualise the linking process going on. See it as moving lines of living light substance, linking you to your brothers on the one hand, and to the patient on the other. See these lines going out from you to the heart centre of the group and to the patient. But work ever from the ajna centre until instructed to do differently. In this way, the ajna centre and the heart centre of all the persons involved will be closely interrelated. You see here where the value of visualisation comes in. It is in reality the etheric externalisation of the creative imagination. Think this last sentence out.

4. Then use thought, directed thought, for a brief moment and think of the one you seek to heal, linking up with him, and focussing your attention on him so that he becomes a reality in your consciousness and close to you. When you are aware what the physical difficulty is, then simply recall it to your mind and then dismiss it. Forget now the details of the work, such as the group, yourself and the difficulty of the patient, and concentrate upon the type of force you are going to handle, which is, in this case and for the present, second ray force, the force of love. What I am here giving out is an adaptation of the second ray method of healing, arranged for beginners.

5. Feel a deep love pouring into you. Regard it as substantial light which you can and will manipulate. Then send it out as a stream of radiant light from the ajna centre and direct it through the medium of your hands to the patient. In doing this, hold the hands before the eyes, palms outward and with the backs of the hands next to the eyes and about six inches away from the face. In this way, the stream which is issuing from the ajna centre, becomes divided into two and pours out through the two hands. It is thus directed on to the patient. Visualise it as pouring out

and sense the patient receiving it. As you do this, say aloud in a low voice:

"May the love of the One Soul, focussed in this group, radiate upon you, my brother, and permeate every part of your body—healing, soothing, strengthening; and dissipating all that hinders service and good health."

Say this slowly and deliberately, believing in the results. See that no thought-power or will-power enters into the stream of healing energy, but only a concentrated radiating love. The use of the visualising faculty and of the creative imagination, plus a sense of deep and steadfast love, will keep the mind and the will in abeyance.

I would emphasise the urgent necessity for *complete silence and reticence* in relation to all healing work. Never let it be known by anyone that you are working in this manner, and never mention to anyone the names of those you are seeking to aid. Do not discuss the patient under treatment even among yourselves. If this basic rule of silence is not kept, it will indicate that you are not yet ready for this work and should discontinue it. This injunction is far more important than you can realise; for speech and discussion not only tend to deflect and dissipate force, but violate a fundamental rule which all healers are trained to keep, and even the medical profession on the physical plane follows the same general procedure.

Three Major Laws of Health

There are three major laws of health and seven minor laws. These work out in the three worlds, which is all that concerns you at this time. In all teaching to be given in the immediate future, the main emphasis will eventually be laid upon the technique of the etheric body, for that is the next step forward. The three major laws are:

1. The law controlling the will to live, a manifestation of the first aspect of the Logos, will or power.

2. The law controlling equality of rhythm, a manifestation of the second aspect of the Logos, love or wisdom.

3. The law controlling crystallisation, a manifestation of the third aspect of the Logos, the activity or foundational aspect.

These three governing factors or laws manifest themselves through the three major divisions of the human entity.

1. *The will aspect* manifests through the organs of respiration. Another of its expressions is the faculty of sleep. In both of these you have a repetition or an analogy in the microcosm of Logoic manifestation and Logoic pralaya.

2. *The love aspect* shows itself through the heart, the circulatory system and the nervous system. This is in many ways most important for you to understand, for it controls paramountly the etheric body and its assimilation of prana or vitality. This prana works through both the blood and the nerves, for the life force uses the blood stream and psychic force works through the nervous system. These two departments of the human organism are those which cause the greatest amount of trouble at this time and will even more in the future. The race learns through suffering, and only dire need drives man to seek solution and relief. From the present standpoint of healing, man forms again a lesser trinity of importance:

a. The dense physical body, of which science and medicine know much.

b. The etheric body, which is the next field of endeavour, of experiment and of discovery.

c. The astral body which, simultaneously with the etheric, is the next object for scientific control. The science of psychology will work here.

3. *The activity aspect,* which manifests primarily through the organs of assimilation and elimination. I seek here to emphasise one point. Just as our solar system is developing the love aspect, which is the second aspect, and just as the human being is polarised in the astral body, which is the reflection of that second aspect, so the second of the three above mentioned departments of the human organism, the etheric, is the one of paramount importance. Up to date it has been the transmitter primarily of astral energy to the physical body. This is now in process of changing.

The whole trend of medical science should now be awake to the concrete facts of the dense physical body and moving towards the study of vitalisation and circulation, for these two are closely related. The nervous system is controlled principally today from the astral body, via the etheric, and the basis of all nervous trouble lies hidden in the emotional body wherein humanity at this time is polarised. The circulatory system of the physical body is controlled principally from the etheric body. When you have an etheric body that is not functioning properly and does not transmit prana sufficiently, and when you have an astral or emotional body that is not adequately or properly controlled, you have in these two the source of the majority of the diseases and nervous and mental conditions that are annually increasing. The reflex action of inadequate circulation upon the physical brain (again due to the etheric body) leads to mental strain and eventual collapse. From this you can see the importance of the etheric vehicle.

The first aspect, which has for its expression and field of control the organs of respiration and the faculty of sleep, when not functioning properly, produces death, insanity and some of the diseases of the brain.

The third aspect, when not functioning properly, causes stomach troubles, bowel complaints and the various diseases that are located beneath and below the solar plexus in the abdomen.

You see, therefore, how medical science must eventually seek solution in a simplification of methods and a return from a complexity of drugs and operations to an understanding of the right use of the energies which pour through from the inner man, via the etheric body, to the physical.

The following suggestions may help:

1. *By the development of goodwill,* which is the will of good intention and motive, will come the healing of diseases of the respiratory tract, lungs and throat, the stabilising of the cells of the brain, the cure of insanities and obsessions, and an attainment of equilibrium and of rhythm. Longevity will ensue, for death should be the recognition by the soul of work consummated and pralaya earned. It will only take place later at long and separated periods, and will be controlled by the will of the man. He will cease to breathe when he has finished his work, and then will send the atoms of his body into pralaya. That is the sleep of the physical, the end of manifestation, and the occult significance of this is not yet comprehended.

2. *By a comprehension of the laws of vitality*—and in this phrase are comprehended the laws governing prana, radiation and magnetism—will come the healing of the diseases in the blood, of the arteries and veins, of certain nervous complaints, lack of vitality, senile decay, poor circulation and similar ills. This too will result in the

prolongation of life. The laws of electrical energy will also be better understood in this connection.

3. *By the understanding of right methods of assimilation and elimination* will come the healing of diseases connected with the bodily tissues, the stomach and bowels and the male and female organs of generation. It will some day be understood that these latter are only another system of assimilation and elimination, centred this time in the feminine aspect or woman, for again remember that this is the second or love system. The order is thus:

a. The first system was masculine.
b. The present system, the second, is feminine.
c. The third system will be hermaphroditic.

E'en though the evolving human Hierarchy is masculine or positive, yet that is no guarantee that all that is found in the present system is masculine too. The fact is that the negative faculty or the feminine aspect dominates, even though this may be unrecognised by you. Let me demonstrate and give some indication by figures of this hypothesis:

1. In the first solar system there was one dominant evolution, and it consisted of one hundred thousand million monads.

2. In the present system, the second, there are two dominant evolutions, the human and the deva; there are—as earlier stated—sixty thousand million *human* monads. Add to this the feminine evolution of the *devas,* consisting of 140 thousand million, and you have the necessary two hundred thousand million. This elucidates my statement anent this being a feminine system.

3. In the third solar system, the total number in evolution will be the needed three hundred thousand million that perfection requires of the threefold Logos.

Our discussion has necessarily been sketchy, for all that I am here attempting to do is to give indications as to the lines along which the new art of healing must eventually run, and to give certain hints which will point the way to the cause of the prevalent diseases, and so enable the wise to negate effects. This brevity and this system of imparting knowledge through the medium of hints is essentially occult, and will be the only mode of dealing with this relatively dangerous subject until such time as a sound medical, surgical and neurological training of a technical nature is combined with an equally sound psychological understanding, plus a measure of spiritual vision. The ideal physician and surgeon is the man who is also a metaphysician; to the lack of this combination much of the present difficulty and confusion can be ascribed. The metaphysical healer today is so engrossed by that which is not the body that he is far less useful to the sick, diseased and damaged human being than is the practical physician. The average metaphysician, no matter by what label he calls himself, has a closed mind; he overemphasises the divine possibilities to the exclusion of the material or physical probabilities. Complete spiritual healing will be divinely possible ultimately; but this is not materially possible at certain given moments in time and space and with people at widely differing points on the ladder of evolution. Right timing and a sound knowledge of the working of the Law of Karma, plus a large measure of intuitive perception, are essential to the high art of spiritual healing. To this must be added the knowledge that the form nature and the physical body are not essentially the major considerations **or of** the vast importance that some may think.

Various cultists and healers usually take the position that it is of major importance that the physical vehicle be rendered free from disease and clutched away from the processes of death. It might, however, be desirable (and it often is) that the disease be permitted to do its work and death open the door to the escape of the soul from imprisonment. The time comes inevitably to all incarnated beings when the soul demands liberation from the body and from form life, and nature has her own wise ways of doing this. Disease and death must be recognised as liberating factors when they come as the result of right timing by the soul. It must be realised by students that the physical form is an aggregate of atoms, built into organisms and finally into a coherent body, and that this body is held together by the will of the soul. Withdraw that will on to its own plane or (as it is occultly expressed) "let the soul's eye turn in another direction" and, in this present cycle, disease and death will inevitably supervene. This is not mental error, or failure to recognise divinity, or succumbing to evil. It is, in reality, the resolution of the form nature into its component parts and basic essence. Disease is essentially an aspect of death. It is the process by which the material nature and the substantial form prepares itself for separation from the soul.

It must be borne in mind however that where there is illness or discomfort or disease which is not related to the final dissolution, the causes thereof are to be found in many factors; they can be found in the surroundings, for a number of diseases are environmental and epidemic; in the tuning in of the individual to streams of poison emanating from world hate, or from psychological complexes with some of which we have already dealt, and in the diseases (if I might so call them) which are indigenous to the matter of which humanity has chosen to construct its physical vehicle, isolating it and separating it from the general substance of manifestation, and thus creating a type of matter which is consecrated to the task of forming the outer expression of the inward reality. This constitutes, therefore, a unique and peculiar aspect of the universal substance, perfected to a certain point in the last solar system and of a necessarily higher order than the substance which vibrates creatively to the call of the three subhuman kingdoms in nature.

The Causes of Disease Summarised

In every occult consideration of disease it must be accepted as a basic proposition that all disease is a result of the misuse of force in some earlier life or in this. This is fundamental. In connection with this I would remind you of some statements I have earlier made on this matter.

1. Ninety per cent of the causes of disease are to be found in the etheric and astral bodies. Wrong use of mental energy and misapplied desire are paramount factors, yet with the bulk of humanity still in the Atlantean stages of consciousness, only five per cent of the prevalent diseases are due to mental causes. The percentage varies with the development of the race and its evolution. Disease is therefore the working out into manifestation of undesirable, subjective conditions—vital, emotional and mental.

2. Everything concerning the health of man can be approached from three angles:

   a. That of the personality life...of this we are learning much.

    b. That of humanity as a whole . . this is beginning to be appreciated.

    c. That of the planetary life . . . . of this we can know little.

3. All disease is caused by lack of harmony between form and life, between soul and personality; this lack of harmony runs through all the kingdoms in nature.

4. The bulk of diseases are of:

    a. Group origin.

    b. The result of infection.

    c. Malnutrition, physically, subjectively and occultly understood.

5. Diseases for the masses, for the average citizen, for the intelligentsia and for disciples differ widely and have differing fields of expression.

    a. The three major groups of diseases for the first two classes are:

        Tuberculosis.

        The social diseases.

        Cancer.

    b. The two major diseases for the intelligentsia and for disciples are:

        Heart complaints.

        Nervous diseases.

6. Disease is a fact in nature. When this is accepted, men will begin to work with the Law of Liberation, with right thought, leading to right attitudes and orientation, and with the principle of nonresistance. Of this nonresistance, the overpowering willingness to die which is so frequently a characteristic of the final stage immediately preceding death is the lowest manifestation. It is nonresistance which psychologically governs coma.

7. The Law of Cause and Effect, or of Karma, governs all disease. This embraces individual, group, national and total human karma.

If you will pause at this point and review what I have re-stated, and if you will reread and reflect upon the four Laws and the four Rules you will possess the needed groundwork upon which to proceed with our future studies, beginning with the diseases incident to the life of discipleship. Some of this I have already dealt with in the second volume of *A Treatise on the Seven Rays* (pages 520-625). There the approach was largely from the angle of the mystic, whereas I am here going to touch upon the problems of the accepted disciple.

4. Diseases Due to the Life of Discipleship

Earlier I told you that disease originated in the four following causes:

1. It is the result of blocking the free life of the soul.

2. It is caused by three influences or sources of contamination:

   a. Ancient mistakes, so-called sins and errors of the individual concerned, committed in this life or another earlier incarnation.

   b. Human taints and predispositions, inherited in common with all the rest of humanity.

   c. Planetary evil, incident to the point achieved by the planetary Logos and conditioned by planetary Karma.

3. It is conditioned by the forces emanating from the plane upon which the man's consciousness is primarily focussed.

4. The five major types of disease, with their allied and subsidiary effects, can and do produce results where the disciple is concerned; he is not immune until after the third initiation.

A. The Diseases of Mystics.

However, the disciple is seldom tubercular (except when karmically conditioned), nor is he prone to succumb to the social diseases except as they may affect him physically through his sacrificial life of service. Contagion can affect him but not seriously so. Cancer may claim him as a victim, but he is more liable to succumb to heart complaints and to nervous trouble of some kind or another. The straight mystic succumbs more to purely psychological situations connected with the integrated personality, and therefore incident to his being focussed largely on the astral plane. The disciple is more prone to mental difficulties and to those complaints which are concerned with energy and are due to fusion—either completed or in process—of soul and personality.

The first cause which I listed earlier in this treatise was summed up in the statement that disease is the result of the blocking of the free life and the inpouring energy of the soul. This blockage is brought about by the mystic when he succumbs to his own thoughtforms, created constantly in response to his mounting aspiration. These become barriers between him and the free life of the soul and block his contact and the consequent resulting inflow of soul energy.

The disciple reverses the entire situation and falls a victim (prior to the third initiation) to the terrific inflow of soul energy—the energy of the second aspect—coming to him from:

a. His own soul, with which centre of energy fusion is rapidly taking place.

b. His group or the Ashram with which he, as an accepted disciple, is affiliated.

c. His Master, with Whom he has spiritual relation and to Whose vibratory influence he is ever susceptible.

d. The Hierarchy, the energy of which can reach him through the medium of all the three above factors.

All these streams of energy have a definite effect upon the centres of the disciple, according to his ray and his specific polarisation in this incarnation. As each centre is related to one or other of the glands, and these in their turn condition the blood stream, and also have a specific effect upon the organic structure within the range of their vibratory influence (i.e. the stomach, close to the solar plexus, and the heart, close to the heart centre, etc.), you will see how it is possible that the major diseases from which a disciple can suffer (which are unique and confined primarily to advanced humanity) will be the result of overstimulation or the inflow of energy to one particular centre, producing excessive and localised trouble.

To these conditions the mystic is not so prone unless he is rapidly becoming the practical mystic or occultist. This is a definite transitional cycle between the mystical attitude and that more definite position which the occultist assumes. I shall not therefore deal with the diseases to which mystics fall heir, except that I would like to point out one interesting fact: The mystic is ever conscious of duality. He is the seeker in search of light, of the soul, of the beloved, of that higher something which he senses as existing and as that which can be found. He strives after recognition of and by the divine; he is the follower of the vision, a disciple of the Christ, and this conditions his thinking and his aspiration. He is a devotee and one who loves the apparently unattainable—the Other than himself.

Only when he becomes the occultist does the mystic learn that all the time the magnet which attracted him, and the dualism which coloured his life and thoughts and which gave motive to all he sought to do, was his true self, the one Reality. He recognises then that assimilation into and identification with that one reality enables duality to be transmuted into unity and the sense of search to be transformed into the effort to become what he essentially is—a Son of God, one with all Sons of God. Having accomplished that, he finds himself one with the ONE in Whom we live and move and have our being.

Next, I would point out that the lowest expression of the mystical condition, and one with which we are becoming increasingly familiar, is that which is called a "split personality"; when this condition is present, the personal lower self expresses itself through a basic condition of duality and two persons express themselves, apparently, instead of the integrated personality-soul. This necessarily creates a dangerous psychological condition and one which warrants trained scientific handling. That is largely lacking at this time, as so few trained psychologists and psychiatrists recognise the fact of the soul. I mention this as it is of value today, and will be increasingly so in the later years when it will be necessary to trace and comprehend the analogies existing in the human consciousness to great unexplored areas of awareness. The split personality and the mystic are two aspects of one whole—the aspect which is right, and along the line of high spiritual unfoldment, and the aspect which is a reflection and a distortion of that grade of development which precedes that of trained occultist. There are many conditions prevalent in humanity at this time which can be subjected to the same reasoning, and one of the modes of healing which will be worked out later is the discovery of the higher correspondences to the lower difficulties and diseases, and the recognition that they are but distortions of a great reality. This leads to the transference of the attention of the one under the care of the healer to that recognised higher aspect.

The whole Science of Integration is involved in this matter. This science, if properly understood, will open up an entirely new field of psychological approach to disease, whether physiological or nervous. A small beginning has already been made along this line by spiritually minded psychologists and educators. The system of helping people psychologically is definitely along these new lines, and might be expressed as follows: the average psychologist employs the method (when dealing with nervous cases, with those on the borderland, and with neurotically inclined people) of discovering the deep-seated complexes, the scars, the ancient shocks or the fears which lie behind the experience of the present and which have made the man what he is today. These conditioning factors can usually be traced back to the subconscious by the process of unearthing the past, of taking into consideration the present environment, of reckoning with heredity, and of studying the effects of education—either academic or based upon life itself. Then the factor which has been a major handicap, and which has turned the man into a psychological problem, is brought (with his assistance, if possible) to the surface of his consciousness, is then intelligently explained and related to the existing condition, and the man is consequently brought to an understanding of his personality, its problems and its impending opportunity.

The spiritual technique, however, is entirely different. The personality problem and the process of delving into the subconscious are ignored, because the conditions which are undesirable are regarded as the result of lack of soul contact and of soul control. The patient (if I might so call him) is taught to take his eyes, and consequently his attention, away from himself, his feelings, his complexes and his fixed ideas and undesirable thoughts, and to focus them upon the soul, the divine Reality within the form, and the Christ consciousness. This could well be called the process of scientific substitution of a fresh dynamic interest for that which has hitherto held the stage; it brings into functioning activity a cooperative factor whose energy sweeps through the lower life of the personality and carries away wrong psychological tendencies, undesirable complexes, leading to erroneous approaches to life. This eventually regenerates the mental or thought life, so that the man is conditioned by right thinking under the impulse or the illumination of the soul. This produces the "dynamic expulsive power of a new affection"; the old *idées fixes,* the old depressions and miseries, the hindering and handicapping ancient desires—these all disappear, and the man stands free as a soul and master of his life processes.

I have discussed these two conditions at length because it is essential that another law anent healing be understood before we proceed any further. The discussion about the split personality, the problems of the mystic and the new mode of approach to disease (from the soul angle and the realm of causes, instead of from the personality angle and the realm of effects) can clarify this law in your minds and indicate at least its reasonableness and its valuable application to human need.

LAW IV

Disease, both physical and psychological, has its roots in the good, the beautiful and the true. It is but a distorted

*reflection of divine possibilities. The thwarted soul, seeking
full expression of some divine characteristic or inner spiritual
reality, produces within the substance of its sheaths a point
of friction. Upon this point the eyes of the personality are
focussed, and this leads to disease.*

*The art of the healer is concerned with the lifting of
the downward focussed eyes unto the soul, the Healer within
the form. The spiritual or third eye then directs the healing
force, and all is well.*

B. Diseases of Disciples.

We will divide what we have to say anent the diseases
of disciples into two parts: the specific problems of all disciples, and the difficulties incident to soul contact.

We need here to remember that all disciples are susceptible to the major categories of disease. They are attempting to be one with all humanity, and this includes,
therefore, all the ills to which flesh is heir. They may
not, however, succumb to the frailties of the ordinary man,
and should remember that diseases of the heart and of the
nerves constitute their major problem. In this connection
it might be pointed out that the disciples are found in two
major groups: Those who live above the diaphragm and
who are, therefore, prone to heart diseases, to thyroid and
throat troubles, and those who are in process of transferring the energies of the centres below the diaphragm into
the centres above the diaphragm. Most of these at this
time are transferring solar plexus energies into the heart,
and the world agony is profoundly hastening the process.
Stomachic, liver and respiratory troubles accompany this
transference.

1. The Specific Problems of Disciples.

These special problems are, as you know, peculiar to
those who have lifted themselves in consciousness out
of the life of the personality into that of the soul. They

are primarily related to energy, its inflow, its assimilation or non-assimilation, and its rightly directed use. The other ills to which all flesh is heir at this time in human evolution (for it must be remembered that diseases vary according to the point in evolution and are also cyclic in their appearance), and to which disciples can and do succumb, are not dealt with here; suffice it to say that the three major diseases of humanity to which reference has been made take their toll of disciples, particularly in bringing about the liberation of the soul from its vehicle. They are, however—little as it may appear—controlled in these cases from soul levels, and the departure is planned to take place as a result of soul decision, and not as a result of the efficiency of the disease. The reason that these three major diseases, indigenous to the planetary life in which we live and move and have our being, have this power over disciples is that disciples are themselves an integral part of the planetary life, and in the earlier stages of their recognition of this unity they are prone to fall a ready prey to the disease. This is a fact little known or realised, but explains why disciples and advanced people are susceptible to these diseases.

We could divide these problems into four categories:

1. Those which are connected with the blood or with the life aspect, for "the blood is the life." These have specific effect upon the heart, but usually of a functional nature only. Organic disease of the heart arises in more deeply seated causes.

2. Those which are a direct effect of energy, playing upon and through the nervous system, via the directing brain.

3. Those which are related to the respiratory system and have an occult source.

4. Those which are specifically due to the receptivity or the non-receptivity, to the functioning or the non-func-

tioning, and to the influence of the centre. Necessarily, these fall into seven groups, affecting seven major areas of the body. For the average disciple, before there is complete soul control and monadic direction, the major directing agent, via the brain, is the vagus nerve, along which the energies (entering via the head centre) are distributed to the rest of the body. A definite science of the centres and their relation to kundalini has been built up by a certain powerful esoteric school in the orient. It has in it much truth, but also much error.

I have differentiated between problems and physical reactions and disease because the inflow, distribution and direction of energy do not necessarily produce disease. Always, however, during the novitiate which precedes all the initiations, they do produce difficulties and problems of some kind or another, either within the consciousness of the disciple or in his relation to those around him. Hence his environment is affected, and consequently his own reciprocal action.

It should be remembered in this connection that all disciples are energy centres in the body of humanity and are in process of becoming points of focussed, directed energy. Their function and activity always and inevitably produce effects, results, awakenings, disruptions and reorientations in the lives of those around them. In the early stages, they produce this unconsciously, and hence frequently the results on those they contact is not desirable, nor is the energy wisely directed, deflected or retained. Intelligent intent must lie behind all wise direction of energy. Later, when they are learning consciously to *be* and are becoming radiatory centres of healing force, consciously directed, this informing and then transmitted energy is more constructively employed along both psychological and physical lines. Nevertheless, in any case, the disciple be-

comes an effective influence and can never be what is esoterically called "unnoticed in his place and minus impact
on other souls." His influence, emanation and forceful
energy inevitably produce problems and difficulties for him;
these are based on the human relations which he has karmically established and the reactions of those he contacts,
either for good or for ill.

Essentially the influence of a disciple of the Great White
Lodge is fundamentally good and spiritually conditioning;
superficially and in its outer effects—particularly where
the disciple is concerned—difficult situations, apparent cleavages and the emergence of faults as well as virtues upon
the part of those affected make their appearance, and often
persist for many lives, until the person thus influenced
becomes what is called "occultly reconciled to the emanating
energy." Ponder on this. The adjustment has to come
from the side of those influenced, and not from the disciple.

Let us now consider the four problems from the psychological angle, not the physical:

a. *The problems arising from the awakened heart
centre of the disciple* are perhaps the commonest and frequently some of the most difficult to handle. These problems
are based on living relationships and the interplay of the
energy of love with the forces of desire. In the early stages,
this inflowing love-force establishes personality contacts
which veer between the stages of wild devotion and utmost
hate on the part of the person affected by the disciple's
energy. This produces constant turmoil in the disciple's
life, until he has become adjusted to the effects of his energy
distribution, and also frequent disruption of relationships
and frequent reconciliations. When the disciple is of sufficient importance to become the organising centre of a group,
or is in a position to begin to form, esoterically, his own
ashram (prior to taking some of the major initiations),

then the difficulty can be very real and most disturbing. There is, however, little that can be done by the disciple, except to attempt to regulate the outgoing energy of love. The problem remains fundamentally that of the one affected; the adjustments, as I have remarked above, have to be made from the other side, with the disciple standing ready to cooperate at the first indication of a willingness to recognise relationship and intention to cooperate in group service. This is a point which both parties—the disciple and the person reacting to his influence—need to consider. The disciple stands ready; the responsive party usually withdraws or approaches according to the urge of his soul or of his personality—probably the latter in the early stages. Eventually, however, he stands with the disciple in full cooperative understanding, and the trying time of difficulty is ended.

It is not possible for me to enter into explicit detail in considering these problems connected with the heart and the life energy of the disciple. They are conditioned by his ray, the initiation for which he is being prepared, and the quality, evolutionary status and the ray of those affected.

There are also difficulties and problems of a more subtle nature arising from the same cause, but not localised in certain definite human relationships. A disciple serves; he writes and speaks; his words and influence permeate into the masses of men, arousing them to activity of some kind— often good and spiritual, sometimes evil, antagonistic and dangerous. He has therefore to deal not only with his own reactions to the work he is doing, but also, in a general and specific sense, to deal with the masses whom he is beginning to affect. This is not an easy thing to do, particularly for an inexperienced worker with the Plan. He fluctuates between the mental plane, where he normally attempts to function, and the astral plane, where the masses of men are focussed, and this brings him into the realm of glamour and consequent danger. He goes out in consciousness towards those he seeks to help, but it is sometimes as a soul (and then he frequently overstimulates his hearers), and sometimes as a personality (and then he feeds and enhances their personality reactions).

As time goes on he learns—through the difficulties brought about by the necessary heart approach—to stand firm at the centre, sending forth the note, giving his message, distributing directed love energy, and influencing those around him, but he remains impersonal, a directing agency only and an understanding soul. This impersonality (which can be defined as a withdrawing of personality energy) produces its own problems, as all disciples well know; there is nothing, however, that they can do about it but wait for time to lead the other person forward into clear understanding of the significance and esoteric meaning of right human relations. The problem of workers with individuals and with groups is basically connected with the energy of the heart and with the vivifying force of its embodied life. In connection with this problem and its reactions upon the disciple, certain definite physical difficulties are apt to occur, and with these I will shortly deal.

It should also be pointed out that difficulties of rhythm are apt to occur, and problems connected with the cyclic life of the disciple. The heart and the blood are esoterically related, and symbolically define the pulsating life of the soul which demonstrates upon the physical plane in the outgoing and the withdrawing dual life of discipleship, each phase of which presents its own problems. Once a disciple has mastered the rhythm of his outer and inner life, and has organised his reactions so that he extracts the utmost meaning from them but is not conditioned by them, he then enters upon the relatively simple life of the initiate. Does that phrase astonish you? You need to remember that the initiate has freed himself, after the second initiation, from the complexities of emotional and astral control. Glamour can no longer overpower him. He can stand with steadfastness in spite of all that he may do and feel. He realises that the cyclic condition is related to the pairs of opposites and is part of the life manifestation of existence itself. In the process of learning this, he passes through great difficulties. He, as a soul, subjects himself to a life of outgoing, of magnetic influence and of extroversion. He may follow this immediately with a life of withdrawal, of apparent lack of interest in his relationships and environment, and with an intense introspective, introverted expression. Between these two extremes he may flounder distressingly—sometimes for many lives—until he learns to fuse and blend the two expressions. Then the dual life of the accepted disciple, in its various grades and stages, becomes clear to him; he knows what he is doing. Constantly and systematically, both outgoing and withdrawing, serving in the world and living the life of reflection, play their useful part.

Many psychological difficulties arise whilst this process is being mastered, leading to psychological cleavages, both deep-seated and superficial. The goal of all development is integration—integration as a personality, integration with the soul, integration into the Hierarchy, integration with the Whole, until complete unity and identification has been achieved. In order to master this science of integration whose basic goal is identity with the *One* Reality, the disciple progresses from one unification to another, making mistakes, arriving often at complete discouragement, identifying himself with that which is undesirable until, as soul-personality, he repudiates the earlier relationships; he pays the penalty again and again of misplaced fervour, distorted aspiration, the overpowering effect of glamour, and the many conditions of psychological and physical disarrangement which must arise whilst cleavages are being healed, right identification achieved and correct orientation established.

Whilst this basic, inescapable and necessary process is taking place, a definite work is going forward in the etheric body. The disciple is learning to lift the energies, gathered from the lower centres, into the solar plexus and from that centre into the heart centre, thus bringing about a re-focussing of the energies above the diaphragm instead of putting the emphasis below. This leads frequently to profound complications, because—from the personality angle—the solar plexus centre is the most potent, being the clearing house for the personality forces. It is that process of decentralisation and "elevation" of the lower consciousness to the higher which produces the main difficulties to which the disciple is subjected. It is this process also which is going on in the world as a whole today, causing the appalling disruption of human affairs, culture and civilisation. The entire focus of humanity's consciousness is being changed; the selfish life (characteristic of the man centred in his desires and consequently in the solar plexus centre) is giving place to the decentralised life of the man who is unselfish (centred in the Self or soul), aware of his relationships and responsibility to the Whole and not to the part. This sublimation of the lower life into the higher is one of deepest moment to the individual and to the race. Once the individual disciple, and humanity as well, symbolising the world disciple, have mastered the process of transference in this respect, we shall see the new order of individual service and of world service established, and therefore the coming in of the awaited new order.

Of all these processes, the circulation of the blood stream is the symbol, and the clue to the establishment of the world order lies hid in this symbology—free circulation of all that is needed to all parts of the great framework of humanity. The blood is the life, and free interchange, free sharing, free circulation of all that is required for right human living will characterise the world to be. Today these conditions do not exist, the body of humanity is diseased and its internal life disrupted. Instead of free circulation between all parts of the life aspect, there has been separation, blocked channels, congestion and stagnation. It has needed the terrific crisis of the present to arouse humanity to its diseased condition, to the extent of the evil which is now discovered to be so great, and the diseases of the "blood of humanity" (symbolically understood) so severe that only the most drastic measures—pain, agony, despair and terror—can suffice to establish a cure.

Healers would do well to remember this, and to have in mind that disciples and all good men and aspirants share in this universal disease of humanity which must take its toll psychologically or physically or both. The trouble is of ancient origin and of long established habit and inevitably affects the physical vehicle of the soul. Exemption from the effects of human ills is no indication of spiritual superiority. It might simply indicate what one of the Masters has called "the depths of spiritual selfishness and self-satisfaction." The initiate of the third degree can hold himself exempt, but this is only because he has completely freed himself from glamour and no aspect of the personality life has any further power over him. All the ray types are equally subjected to these particular problems. The seventh ray, however, is more susceptible to the problems, difficulties and diseases incident to the blood stream than are any of the other ray types. The reason is that this is the ray which has to do with the expression and manifestation of life upon the physical plane and with the organisation of the relationship between spirit and matter into form. It is concerned therefore today, as it seeks to create the new order, with free circulation and with a consequently intended freedom of humanity from the ills and problems of the past. This is of interest to remember, and students would find it helpful at this time, if they want to cooperate intelligently with the happenings of the day, to collect and study all that I have written about the seventh ray of ceremonial order and magic.

b. *Diseases of the nervous system*, due to the flow of energy to all parts of the body, directed by either the personality, some aspect of the personal lower self, or by the soul, via the brain, are many and become acute as the disciple nears initiation or becomes an initiate. Apart from the physiological ills which this produces, there are many other conditions brought about by this inflow of force. The disciple becomes, for instance, overstimulated, and therefore overactive; he becomes unbalanced, and when I say this I do not refer to mental imbalance (though that can happen), but to overdevelopment and overexpression in some part of his nature. He can become extravagantly overorganised through the medium of some overactive centre, or underorganised and inactive. He is therefore subject to the imbalance of the glandular system, with all its attendant difficulties. His overstimulation or his undevelopment, where the centres are concerned, normally affects the glands, and they in their turn produce character difficulties which necessarily, in their turn, produce environmental problems as well as personality handicaps.

It is then a vicious circle, and is all due to wrong direction of force and the inflow of force from one or other of the personality vehicles to its related centre (i.e., the astral force and its relation to the solar plexus), and then the appearance of the problems of health, of character and of influence. Over-radiatory activity, through the medium of some centre, attracts attention and the disciple becomes the victim of his own achievement. I shall deal with these at greater length when I take up the diseases which develop from the four categories.

These difficulties are of a most general kind but do affect primarily second and sixth ray disciples. The one because the second ray is the building ray, and is therefore concerned predominately with outer manifestation and with the utilisation of all the centres, and the other because it is primarily the ray of tension—a tension which can work out in the form of the most evil fanaticism or the most altruistic devotion. All the rays present the same problems, needless to say, but the second ray deals largely with the soul's activity through all the centres (those above and those below the diaphragm) but with the heart as the prime centre of attention. The sixth ray has a close relation to the solar plexus centre as the clearing house and the place of reorientation of the life force in the personality. Bear this constantly in mind.

c. *The problems connected with the respiratory or breathing system* are all related to the heart, and therefore concerned with the establishing of right rhythm and right contact with the environment. The drawing in of the life breath, the sharing of the air with all other human beings, denotes both an individual centre of life and participation also in the general life of all. To these problems of individual or separative existence and of its opposite, the Sacred Word, the OM, is intimately related. It might be said in the words of an occult manual on healing, given to advanced disciples, that

> "He who lives under the sound of the AUM knows himself. He who lives sounding the OM knows his brother. He who knows the SOUND knows all."

Then, in the cryptic and symbolic language of the initiate, the manual goes on:

> "The breath of life becomes the cause of death to the one who lives within a shell. He exists but he is not; the breath then leaves and spirals to the whole.

> "He who breathes forth the OM knows not himself alone. He knows the breath is prana, life, the fluid of connection. The ills of life are his because they are the lot of man—not generated in a shell, because the shell is not.

> "He who is the SOUND and sounding forth knows not disease, knows not the hand of death."

In these few words the whole problem of the third group of problems and diseases is summed up. They are concerned with the circulation of soul energy, which is the energy of love, and they are *not* concerned with the circulation of the life essence. These two basic energies, as they play upon the forces of the personality, bring about the bulk of the problems to which humanity falls heir. These are lack of love, lack of life, failure to sound forth correctly the note of the soul and of the ray, and failure to transmit. The secret of constituting a pure channel (to use mystic but not occult phraseology), is considered in the first group of problems; and the establishing of right relation by right sounding forth of the attractive note of the soul, is considered in the last two groups.

This third group of difficulties, problems and diseases are of course those of people upon all the rays, but first ray people have a definite predisposition to these specific troubles. At the same time, when they rightly utilise their latent powers, they can overcome by the right use of the OM, and finally of the SOUND, the incidental problems and difficulties far more easily than those on other rays. You have here a reference to the Lost Word of Masonry and to the SOUND of the Ineffable Name.

The sound of the AUM, the sound of the OM, and the SOUND itself, are all related to vibration and its differing and varied effects. The secret of the Law of Vibration is progressively revealed as people learn to sound forth the WORD in its three aspects. Students would do well to ponder on the distinction between the breath and the sound, between the process of breathing and the process of creating vibratory activity. They are related but distinct from each other. One is related to Time and the other to Space and (as the *Old Commentary* puts it) "the sound, the final and yet initiating sound, concerns that which is neither Time nor Space; it lies outside the manifested All, the Source of all that is and yet is naught" (or no-thing. A.A.B.).

For this reason, disciples on the fourth ray usually can develop by the power of the intuition an understanding of the OM. This ray of harmony through conflict (the conflict of the pairs of opposites) is necessarily concerned with the bringing in of that vibratory activity which will lead to unity, to harmony and to right relations, and to the release of the intuition.

d. *The problems incident to the activity or inactivity of the centres* are perhaps the most important from the standpoint of disease, because the centres govern the glandular system and the glands have a direct relation to the blood stream and they condition also the major and most important areas in the human body; they have both a physiological and a psychological effect upon the personality and its interior and exterior contacts and relations. The reaction is primarily physical but the effects are largely psychological, and it is therefore this fourth group upon which I shall principally enlarge, dealing with the diseases of disciples and giving some definite instructions upon the centres. This will indicate more clearly than elsewhere the causes of the many human ills and physical difficulties.

Before proceeding to our next point, try to grasp somewhat more fully the Laws of Healing and the Rules given thus far and repeated here to facilitate your endeavours.

LAW I

All disease is the result of inhibited soul life and this is true of all forms in all kingdoms. The art of the healer consists in releasing the soul so that its life can flow through the aggregate of organisms which constitute any particular form.

LAW II

Disease is the product of, and subject to, three influences: first, a man's past, wherein he pays the price of ancient error; second, his inheritance, wherein he shares with all mankind those tainted streams of energy which are of group origin; third, he shares with all the natural forms that which the Lord of Life imposes on His body. These three influences are called "The Ancient Law of Evil Sharing." This must give place some day to that new "Law of Ancient Dominating Good" which lies behind all that God made. This law must be brought into activity by the spiritual will of man.

LAW III

Diseases are an effect of the basic centralisation of a man's life energy. From the plane whereon those energies are focussed, proceed those determining conditions which produce ill health, and which, therefore, work out as disease or as freedom from disease.

LAW IV

Disease, both physical and psychological, has its roots in the good, the beautiful and the true. It is but a distorted reflection of divine possibilities. The thwarted soul, seeking full expression of some divine characteristic or inner spiritual reality, produces within the substance of its sheaths a point of friction. Upon this point the eyes of the personality are focussed, and this leads to disease. The art of the healer is concerned with the lifting of the downward focussed eyes unto the soul, the Healer within the form. The spiritual or third eye then directs the healing force, and all is well.

RULE ONE

The healer must seek to link his soul, his heart, his brain and his hands. Thus can he pour the vital healing force upon the patient. *This is magnetic work.* It cures disease, or increases the evil state, according to the knowledge of the healer.

The healer must seek to link his soul, his brain, his heart and auric emanation. Thus can his presence feed the soul life of the patient. *This is the work of radiation.* The hands are needed not. The soul displays its power. The patient's soul responds through the response of his aura to the radiation of the healer's aura, flooded with soul energy.

RULE TWO

The healer must achieve magnetic purity, through purity of life. He must attain that dispelling radiance which shows itself in every man when he links the centres in the head. When this magnetic field is established, the radiation too goes forth.

RULE THREE

Let the healer train himself to know the inner stage of thought or of desire of the one who seeks his help. He can thereby know the source from which the trouble comes. Let him relate the cause and the effect, and know the point exact through which the help must come.

RULE FOUR

The healer and the healing group must keep the will in leash. It is not will that must be used but love.

2. Difficulties Incident to Soul Contact.

Today we begin a study of the difficulties, the diseases and the psychological troubles (neurological and mental) of the aspirants and of the disciples of the world. These we shall study definitely from the angle of the seven centres, as well as considering the results of the forces and energies (I use these distinctive words advisedly) which pour through them. Much that I shall say will be open to question from the viewpoint of orthodox medicine, yet, at the same time, orthodox medicine has been steadily drifting towards the occult point of view. I shall not attempt to relate the esoteric attitude of healing, its propositions and methods, to the modern schools of therapy. The two are gradually approaching each other, in any case. The lay reader, for whom these teachings are intended, will get a clearer comprehension of my thesis if it is kept relatively free from the technical terms and the academic attitudes of the medical sciences. They would but serve to confuse, and my effort is to give a general picture of the underlying causes of outer physical ills. I seek to present certain aspects of occult therapy for which mankind is now ready, reminding you that the presentation is naturally inadequate and partial, and for that reason may appear incorrect and to be challenging to those who look ever for outlets for human credulity. That, however, concerns me not. Time will prove the accuracy of my statements.

The new medicine will deal with factors which are dimly
recognised at present and which are not, as yet, brought into
any real or factual relationship to man and his body. The
basic theory upon which the new medical teaching will rest
can best be summed up in the statement that there is in reality
nothing but energy to be considered, and the forces which
are resistant to or assimilative of higher or different types
of energy. Let me therefore start by giving you a new Law
to add to the four already communicated. The previous
Laws have been in the nature of abstract propositions, and
unless related to this fifth Law will remain somewhat vague
and meaningless.

LAW V

*There is naught but energy, for God is life. Two
energies meet in man, but other five are present. For each is
to be found a central point of contact. The conflict of these
energies with forces and of the forces twixt themselves produce the bodily ills of man. The conflict of the first and
second persists for ages until the mountain top is reached—
the first great mountain top. The fight between the forces
produces all disease, all ills and bodily pain, which seek release in death. The two, the five, and thus the seven, plus
that which they produce, possess the secret. This is the fifth
Law of Healing within the world of form.*

This Law can be resolved into certain basic statements
which can be tabulated as follows:

1. We live in a world of energies and are a constituent
   part of them ourselves.
2. The physical vehicle is a fusion of two energies and
   seven forces.
3. The first energy is that of the soul, the ray energy.
   It is the producer of conflict as the soul energy seeks
   to control the forces.

4. The second energy is that of the threefold personality—the personality ray as it is resistant to the higher energy.

5. The forces are the other energies or ray potencies which control the seven centres and are dominated either by the energy of the personality or by that of the soul.

6. Two conflicts, therefore, proceed between the two major energies and between the other energies, focussed through the seven centres.

7. It is the interplay of these energies which produces good health or bad.

There has been much teaching given anent the age-long struggle between personality and soul, but it has always been presented in the language of spiritual approach, of mysticism and of religion, or else in terms of character reaction, of abstract aspiration and of purity or non-purity. With these I shall not deal. My theme is the effects of this conflict in the physical body. I wish, therefore, to confine myself only to the physiological and psychological problems incident to the struggle which, in the main, make hard the lot of the disciple. It might be posited that:

A. All diseases and physical difficulties are caused by one or more of three things or conditions:

1. A developed soul contact, thus producing the vitalisation of all the centres in ordered rhythm, according to the soul ray. This necessarily produces stress and strain in the physical vehicle.

2. Personality life and focus, which attempts to negate this soul control, and which is largely expressed through the activity of the throat centre (predisposing an activity of the thyroid gland) and of the centres below the diaphragm.

3. A cycle in the life of the aspirant wherein personality control begins to weaken and in which the emphasis and consequent activity shifts into the centres above the diaphragm—again causing trouble and readjustment.

B. Certain objectives present themselves to the aspirant at various stages, and each involves progress, but at the same time certain attendant difficulties.

1. *The objective before the initiate* is to have every centre in the etheric body responsive to the ray energy of the soul and with all the other seven ray energies subsidiary to it. This process of stimulation, of readjustment, and the attainment of established control goes on until after the third initiation. Then, when that initiation has been taken, the physical vehicle is of a totally different calibre and quality, and the Rules and Laws of Health no longer apply.

2. *The objective before the disciple* is to promote control of the centres in the body, via the soul, through stimulation, elimination and eventual stabilisation. This inevitably produces difficulty, and the vitalisation or inspiration (either of these words would be appropriate), or their lack or deficiency, affect the bodily organs within the areas around the centres and affect all substances surrounding the centres.

3. *The objective before the aspirant* or the probationary disciple is to transfer the forces from the centres below the diaphragm, via the solar plexus centre, to the centres above the diaphragm. The energy of the base of the spine has to be transferred to the head; the energy of the sacral centre must be lifted to the throat, whilst the energy of the solar plexus must be transferred to the heart. This is done in response to the magnetic "pull" of the soul ray as it begins to dominate the personality ray. It is a long and painful

process, covering many lives and carrying, as the result, many physical ills.

4. *The objective before the average man* (unconsciously effective) is to respond fully to personality force, focussed primarily at the middle point, the solar plexus, and then steadily and intelligently to coordinate these forces so that an integrated personality is presented eventually to the soul for control and use.

5. *The objective before the primitive or undeveloped man* (again unconsciously effective) is to live a full animal and emotional life, thereby gaining experience of growth, of contact, and eventually of understanding. By this means the response apparatus of the soul in the three worlds is built.

I would also call attention to the thought which I have here interjected, that the objectives intrinsically in themselves have an effect upon that towards which man is striving. This is a thought warranting careful consideration.

These generalisations will be useful only if you remember that they are generalisations. No aspirant at any stage is perfectly clear cut in his endeavour until after the third initiation, nor is he entirely particularised in his life and effort. Men are at all imaginable stages of development, and many of these stages are intermediate to the five stages above mentioned. These all merge and blend into each other, and often constitute a formidable and confusing arena for thought and activity. It is only in the life of the undeveloped individual that clear simplicity is to be found. In between—from the stage of infancy of the race or of the man to that of the state of liberation from personality life—there is nothing but complexity, the overlapping of states of consciousness, difficulty, disease, psychological problems, illness and death.

This must obviously be so when the vast number of energies and forces which constitute man's being and form his environment are brought into relation with each other. Every human being is, in reality, like a miniature whirlpool in that great ocean of Being in which he lives and moves—ceaselessly in motion until such time as the soul "breathes upon the waters" (or forces) and the Angel of the Presence descends into the whirlpool. Then all becomes still. The waters stirred by the rhythm of life, and later stirred violently by the descent of the Angel, respond to the Angel's healing power and are changed "into a quiet pool into which the little ones can enter and find the healing which they need." So says the *Old Commentary*.

The Centres and the Glandular System

It will therefore be apparent to you that disease (when not of a group origin, or the result of planetary karma or based on accident) takes its rise in the activity or the non-activity of the centres. This is a statement of a basic truth, given in the simplest manner. The centres, as you know, govern the endocrine system which, in its turn, controls the seven major areas of the physical body and is responsible for the correct functioning of the entire organism, producing both physiological and psychological effects.

The importance of this glandular system cannot be over-estimated. It is a replica in miniature of the septenary constitution of the universe and the medium of expression and the instrument of contact for the seven ray forces, the seven Spirits before the Throne of God. Around this at present unrecognised truth the medicine and the healing methods of the future civilisation will be built.

The glands constitute a great relating system in the body; they bring all parts of the physical vehicle into relation with each other; they also relate the man to the etheric body—both individual and planetary—and likewise to the blood stream, the carrier of the life principle to all parts of the body. There are consequently four major agents of distribution to be found in the physical body. They are all complete in themselves, all contributory to both the functional and the organic life of the body, all closely inter-related and all producing both physiological and psychological results according to their potency, the response of the centres to the higher inflow, the point in evolution achieved, and the free expression, or the reverse, of the incoming energies. These four agents of distribution of energy are:

1. *The etheric vehicle itself.* This with its myriads of lines of force and of energy, the incoming and the outgoing energies, its responsiveness to energy impacts coming from the environment as well as from the inner spiritual man and the subtle bodies, underlies the entire physical body. In it are to be found the seven centres as focal points of reception and of distribution; they are the recipients of seven types of energy, and they distribute these seven energies through the entire little human system.

2. *The nervous system* and its various interlocking directorates. This is a relatively tangible network of energies and forces which are the outer expression of the inner, vital, dynamic network of the etheric body and the millions of nadis or the prototype of the nerves which underlie the more substantial body. These nerves and plexi and their many ramifications are the negative aspects of the positive energies which condition or are attempting to condition the man.

3. *The endocrine system.* This is the tangible and exoteric expression of the activity of the vital body and its seven centres. The seven centres of force are to be found in the same region where the seven major glands are located, and

each centre of force provides, according to the esoteric teaching, the power and the life of the corresponding gland which is, in fact, its externalisation.

Centres	Glands
Head centre	Pineal gland
Centre between eyebrows	Pituitary body
Throat centre	Thyroid gland
Heart centre	Thymus gland
Solar plexus centre	Pancreas
Sacral centre	The gonads
Centre at base of spine	Adrenal glands

These three systems are very closely related to each other and constitute an interlocking directorate of energies and forces which are essentially vital, galvanic, dynamic and creative. They are basically interdependent, and upon them the entire interior health of the physical organism depends. They are responsive first to one or other of the bodies (emotional or mental), then to the integrated personality and its ray, and finally to the soul ray as it begins to assume control. They are, in reality, responsible for the production of the physical body and—after birth—they condition its psychological quality, and this in its turn produces the developing physical man. They are the agents for the three divine aspects of all manifestation: life—quality—appearance.

4. *The blood stream.* This is the carrier of the life principle and of the combined energies and forces of the three above systems. This will be an idea of some novelty to the orthodox. The relationship of the circulatory system of the blood to the nervous system has not been as yet adequately developed in modern medicine. Much, however, has been done to relate the glandular system to the blood.

Only when these four interrelated systems are viewed as one integrated whole and as the four aspects of one vital circulatory system will the truth emerge. Only as they are acknowledged to be the four major distributing agents of the combined rays of the individual man will the true nature of material phenomena be grasped. It might be added here that:

1. The etheric vehicle from the circulatory angle, is governed by the Moon, as it veils Vulcan.
2. The nervous system is ruled by Venus.
3. The endocrine system is governed by Saturn.
4. The blood stream is governed by Neptune.

These four systems are in reality the manifestation of the four aspects of matter in its lowest or purely physical expression. There are other aspects of expression of the fundamental substance, but these are the four of greatest importance.

Each of these is essentially dual, and each duality corresponds to the ray of the soul or of the personality. Each is therefore both positive and negative; each can be described as a unit of resistant force and of dynamic energy; each is a combination of certain aspects of matter and substance—the matter being the relatively static aspect, and the substance the relatively fluid or quality-endowing agent. Their interplay, relationship and unified function are an expression of the One Life Principle, and when they have reached a point of perfected fusion or synthesis or coordinated activity there then appears that "life more abundantly" of which Christ spoke and of which we, as yet, know nothing. The four aspects of matter produce the correspondence also to the four divine attributes as well as to the three divine aspects.

The analogy of the basic dualism of all manifestation is also preserved, thus making the nine of initiation—the three, the four and the two. This correspondence to the initiatory process is, however, in the reverse direction, for it is initiation into the creative third aspect, the matter aspect and the world of intelligent activity. It is not initiation into the second or soul aspect, as is the case with the hierarchical initiations for which the disciple is preparing. It is the initiation of the soul into the experience of physical incarnation, into physical plane existence, and into the art of functioning as a human being. The door into this experience is the "Gate of Cancer." Initiation into the kingdom of God is entered through the "Gate of Capricorn." These four attributes and the three aspects of matter, plus their dual activity, are the correspondence to the four aspects of the personality and the Spiritual Triad and their dual active relationship. In this statement is hidden the key to liberation.

The Seven Major Centres

It would be of value here if we consider for a moment the nature of the centres themselves, summarising somewhat the teaching already given in my other books, and so presenting a clear picture of the energy body which underlies the dense physical vehicle.

There are many focal points of force within the body, but we shall deal only with the major seven which control in some degree or other all the remaining. In that way we shall not be confused. We shall consider the five centres found upon the spinal column and the two which are found in the head.

1. *The Head Centre*. This is located at the very top of the head. It is frequently called "the thousand-petalled lotus" or the Brahmarandra.

a. It corresponds to the central spiritual sun.

b. It is brought into functioning activity after the third initiation and is the organ for the distribution of monadic energy, of the will aspect of divinity.

c. It is related to the triple personality by the antahkarana, which disciples and initiates are in process of constructing and which reaches its full usefulness only after the destruction of the causal body at the fourth initiation.

d. It is the Shamballa centre in the physical body and the agent of the Father or of the first divine aspect.

e. It registers purpose, corresponds to the "electric fire" of the solar system, and is dynamic in quality.

f. Its dense physical externalisation is the pineal gland in the head. This remains active during infancy and until the will-to-be is sufficiently established so that the incarnating person is firmly anchored in physical incarnation. In the final stages of divine expression in man it again comes into activity and usefulness as the agent for the accomplishment on earth of the will energy of established Being.

g. It is the organ of synthesis because, after the third initiation and prior to the destruction of the causal body, it gathers into itself the energies of all the three aspects of manifested life. Where man is concerned, this means the energies of the Spiritual Triad, of the threefold egoic lotus and of the triple personality, thus again making the nine of initiation. The energies thus synchronised and focussed in, around and above the head are of great beauty and extensive radiation, plus dynamic effectiveness. They serve to relate the initiate to all parts of the planetary life, to the Great Council at Shamballa, and to the Lord of the World, the final Initiator—via the Buddha and one of the three Buddhas of Activity. The Buddha, in a most peculiar sense, relates the initiate to the second aspect of divinity—that of love—and therefore to the Hierarchy; the Buddhas of Activity relate him to the third aspect of divinity, that of active intelligence. Thus the energy of will, of consciousness and of creativity meet in him, providing the synthesis of the divine aspects.

h. This is the only one of the seven centres which at the time of perfected liberation retains the position of an inverted lotus, with the stem of the lotus (the antahkarana, in reality) reaching up into "the seventh Heaven," thus linking the initiate with the first major planetary centre, Shamballa. All the other centres start by being inverted, with all the petals turned downwards towards the base of the spine; all, in the process of evolution, gradually unfold their petals and then slowly turn upwards "towards the summit of the rod," as it is called in the *Old Commentary*. The above is a piece of information which is of small value, except in so far as it presents a truth, completes a picture, and gives the student a symbolic idea of that which is essentially a distributing agent of the will energy of Deity.

2. *The Ajna Centre.* This is the centre between the eyebrows and is found in the region of the head just above

the two eyes, where it "acts as a screen for the radiant beauty and the glory of the spiritual man."

a. It corresponds to the physical sun and is the expression of the personality, integrated and functioning—first of all as the disciple, and finally as the initiate. This is the true persona or mask.

b. It achieves this functioning activity fully by the time the third initiation is taken. I would remind you that this initiation is regarded by the Hierarchy as the first major initiation, a fact which I have already commmunicated. It is the organ for the distribution of the energy of the third aspect—the energy of active intelligence.

c. It is related to the personality by the creative thread of life, and is therefore closely connected with the throat centre (the centre of creative activity), just as the head centre is related to the centre at the base of the spine. An active interplay, once established between the ajna centre and the throat centre, produces a creative life and a manifested expression of the divine idea on the part of the initiate. In the same way, the active interplay between the head centre and the centre at the base of the spine produces the manifestation of the divine will or purpose. The forces of the ajna and the throat centres, when combined, produce the highest manifestation of "fire by friction," just as the energies of the head centre and the basic centre produce the individual "electric fire" which, when fully expressing itself, we call the kundalini fire.

d. It is the centre through which the fourth Creative Hierarchy on its own plane finds expression, and here also this Hierarchy and fourth kingdom in nature, the human family, are fused and blended. The head centre relates the monad and the personality. The ajna centre relates the Spiritual Triad (the expression of the monad in the formless worlds) to the personality. Ponder on this statement, because you have here—in the symbolism of the head centre, physically considered—the reflection of the spiritual will, atma, and spiritual love, buddhi. Here also comes in the teaching on the place of the eyes in the development of conscious expression, creatively carrying forward the divine purpose.

The Third Eye . . . . . . the head centre . . . . . . Will. Atma.
    The eye of the Father, the Monad.   SHAMBALLA.
    The first aspect of will or power and purpose.
    Related to *the pineal gland*.

The Right Eye . . . . . . the ajna centre . . . . . . Love. Buddhi.
    The eye of the Son, the Soul.   HIERARCHY.
    The second aspect of love-wisdom.
    Related to *the pituitary body*.

The Left Eye . . . . the throat centre . . . . Active Intelligence.
    The eye of the Mother, the personality.   HUMANITY.
    The third aspect of intelligence.
    Related to *the carotid gland*.

When these three eyes are functioning and all of them "seeing" simultaneously, you will then have insight into divine purpose (the initiate), intuitive vision of the plan (the disciple), and a spiritual direction of the resulting creative activity (the Master).

e. The ajna centre registers or focusses *the intention to create*. It is not the organ of creation in the same sense that the throat centre is, but it embodies the idea lying behind active creativity, the subsequent act of creation producing eventually the ideal form for the idea.

f. Its dense physical externalisation is the pituitary body; the two lobes of this gland correspond to the two multiple petals of the ajna centre. It expresses imagination and desire in their two highest forms, and these are the dynamic factors lying behind all creation.

g. It is the organ of idealism therefore, and—curiously enough—it is closely related to the sixth ray, just as the head centre is essentially related to the first ray. The sixth is peculiarly linked to the third ray and the third aspect of divinity as well as to the second ray and the second aspect. It fuses, anchors and expresses. This is a fact which I have not hitherto emphasised in my other writings. The ajna centre is the point in the head where the dualistic nature of manifestation in the three worlds is symbolised. It fuses the creative energies of the throat and the sublimated energies of desire or the true love of the heart.

h. This centre, having only two real petals, is not a true lotus in the same sense as are the other centres. Its petals are composed of 96 lesser petals or units of force $(48 + 48 = 96)$ but these do not assume the flower shape of the other lotuses. They spread out like the wings of an airplane to the right and left of the head, and are symbolic of the right hand path and the left hand path, of the way of matter and the way of spirit. They constitute symbolically, therefore, the two

arms of the Cross upon which the man is crucified—two streams of energy or light placed
athwart the stream of life descending from the
monad to the base of the spine and passing
through the head.

The idea of relativity is one that must ever be held
in mind as the student seeks to comprehend the centres,
interiorly related within the etheric body, related at the
same time to the subtler bodies, to the states of consciousness which are synonymous to states of being and of expression, to ray energies, to environing conditions, to the
three periodical vehicles (as H.P.B. calls the personality,
the threefold soul and the Spiritual Triad), to Shamballa
and to the totality of manifested Lives. The complexity
of the subject is extreme, but when the disciple or initiate
is functioning in the three worlds and the various energies
of the whole man are "grounded" in the earthbound man,
then the situation becomes clearer. I use the expression
"grounded" in its true and correct sense, and not as the
description of a man who has discarded his physical body
as the spiritualists use the term. Certain recognitions in
time and space become possible; certain effects can be noted,
certain ray influences appear more dominant than others;
certain "patterns of being" appear; an expression of a
spiritual Being at a certain point of conscious experience
emerges into clarity and can then be spiritually diagnosed.
Its aspects and attributes, its forces and energies, can be
determined at that time and for a particular created expression of life. This must be borne in mind, and the
thoughts of the student must not be permitted to rove too
far afield but must be concentrated upon the *appearance*
of the man (himself or another) and upon the emerging
quality. When that student is a disciple or an initiate, he
will be able also to study the *life* aspect.

Our study will, however, be somewhat different, for we shall attempt to discover the diseases and difficulties incident to the energy stimulation or the lack of stimulation of the centres, and so arrive at some of the effects which this energy inflow and conflict with forces will produce.

3. *The Throat Centre*. This centre is to be found at the back of the neck, reaching up into the medulla oblongata, thus involving the carotid gland, and down towards the shoulder blades. It is an exceedingly powerful and well developed centre where average humanity is concerned. It is interesting to note in this connection that

a. The throat centre is ruled by Saturn just as the two head centres are ruled respectively by Uranus (ruling the head centre) and Mercury (ruling the ajna centre). This is only where the disciple is concerned; the rulership changes after the third initiation or before the first. These three planets constitute a most interesting triangle of forces and in the following triplicities and their inevitable inter-relations you have—again only in the case of disciples—a most amazing picture story or symbol of the ninefold of initiation:

    1. The head centre
         The ajna centre
         The throat centre

    2. The third eye
         The right eye
         The left eye

    3. The pineal gland
         The pituitary body
         The carotid gland

thus presenting the mechanism through which the Spiritual Triad, the soul and the personality work.

The key to a right understanding of process lies in the relation of the three planets: Uranus, Mercury and Saturn, as they pour their energies through these nine "points of spiritual contact" upon the physical plane into the "grounded sphere of light and power which is the man in time and space."

b. This centre is related to the first initiation and develops great activity when that point in experience is achieved, as it has been achieved by the vast majority of men who are at this time the aspirants and the probationary disciples of the world. (Forget not that, technically speaking, the first major initiation from the hierarchical angle is the third. The first initiation is regarded by the Masters as signifying admission to the Path. It is called an initiation, by humanity, because in Lemurian days, it was then the first initiation, signifying entrance into complete physical control). It is the organ for the distribution of creative energy, of the energy of the third aspect by souls at the above point of evolution. There are three centres in the human being which are related to and the major expression of the third ray or aspect at certain differing stages of development upon the path:

1. The sacral centre for the undeveloped and the average man.
2. The throat centre for the aspirant and probationary disciple.
3. The ajna centre for disciples and initiates.

Here again you have a great triplicity of energies, containing great potencies today, owing to the fact that the expression of the third aspect of active intelligence has reached such heights through human development and consciousness.

c. It is related to the personality by the creative thread, to the soul by the thread of consciousness, and to the monad by the sutratma or life thread. It is not related to any of the divine aspects by the antahkarana because that thread which links monad and personality directly (and finally independently of the soul) simply anchors the monadic expression of life in the head, at the head centre. Then direct consciousness is established between the monad and the personality, and a great duality comes into being. Life, consciousness and form are then all focussed creatively and actively in the head, and their activity is directed from the head via the two head centres. The ajna centre only comes into creative activity when the antahkarana has been built. In the earlier stages it is the throat centre which is the creative agent, and in the earliest period of all the sacral centre is active. You have, however, one interesting thing to remember. The building of the antahkarana only becomes genuinely possible when the creative life of the aspirant shifts from the sacral centre into the throat and is becoming factual and expressive. Of this connecting "bridge," the neck itself is the symbol, as it relates the head—alone and isolated— to the dual torso, consisting of that which lies above the diaphragm and that which lies below—the symbol of the soul and the personality united, fused and blended into one. The head is the symbol of what Patanjali describes as the state of "isolated unity."

d. It is the centre through which the intelligence aspect of humanity focusses creatively. It is therefore the centre through which the creative energy of that great planetary centre called Humanity flows. The three major planetary centres are Shamballa, Hierarchy and Humanity. When perfection has been achieved, the Shamballa energy of will, power and purpose will pour freely through the head centre, the love-wisdom energies of the Hierarchy will flow through the heart centre, and the energy of humanity will focus through the throat centre, with the ajna centre acting as the agent of all three. Then will take place a new activity on the part of mankind. It is the task of relating the three superhuman kingdoms to the three subhuman kingdoms, and thus establishing the new heavens and the new earth. Then humanity will have reached the summit of its evolutionary goal on this Earth.

e. The throat centre is the organ specifically of the creative WORD. It registers the intention or creative purpose of the soul, transmitted to it by the inflow of energy from the ajna centre; the fusion of the two energies, thus brought about, will lead to some type of creative activity. This is the higher correspondence to the creativity of the sacral centre. In that centre the negative and the positive creative energies are embodied in the separate male and female organisms and are brought into relation in an act of creation, consciously undertaken, though as yet without much definite purpose.

f. The dense physical externalisation of this centre is the thyroid gland. This gland is regarded as of supreme importance in the well-being of the average human being of today. Its purpose is to guard health, to balance the bodily equilibrium in certain important aspects of the physical nature, and it symbolises the third aspect of intelligence and of substance impregnated with mind. It is in reality connected with the Holy Ghost, or the third divine aspect in manifestation, "overshadowing" (as the Bible expresses it), the Mother, the Virgin Mary. The parathyroids are symbolic of Mary and Joseph and the relation they hold to the overshadowing Holy Ghost. It will eventually be determined that there is a close physiological relation existing between the thyroid gland and the pineal gland, and between the parathyroids and the two lobes of the pituitary body, thus bringing into one related system the entire area of the throat and of the head.

g. Just as the head symbolises the essentially dualistic nature of the manifested God, so the throat centre symbolises the triple nature of the divine expression. The dualistic nature appears fused and blended in the head in the relation between the two centres and their two dense physical reflections. The three great energies which are brought into play during the divine creative activity are unified in activity by the full expression of the energy flowing through the throat centre, through the apparatus of speech and the two lungs. You have in this relation: Life or Breath, the Word or the Soul, and the throat centre of Substance in activity.

h. This lotus of the throat is inverted in the early stages of evolution, and its petals reach out towards the shoulders and include the two lungs or parts of them. During the life cycle of the soul, it slowly reverses itself, and its petals then reach out towards the two ears and include the medulla oblongata and the carotid gland. This gland is more closely related to the thyroid gland than it is to the two other glands in the head.

Thus it will be apparent to you how whole areas of the physical organism can be brought into active and correct functioning, can be vitalised and kept in good and true condition by the activity in some form or another of the centre nearest to the area of the body under consideration. It will also be apparent to you that deficiency and disease can result from the inactivity of a centre.

4. *The Heart Centre.* This is located between the shoulder blades and is—in this day and age—the centre which is receiving the most attention from Those Who are responsible for the unfoldment of the human consciousness. It might be truly said, brother of mine, that the rapid unfoldment of this lotus is one of the reasons why the world war could not be avoided. In one sense, it was a necessary happening (given the blind selfishness of the bulk of humanity) because it had become necessary to do away with all the old forms of government, of religion and of the crystallised social order. Humanity has now reached a point of group awareness and of group interplay of a deeply spiritual kind, and new forms were required through which this new spirit could function more adequately.

a. The heart centre corresponds to the "heart of the Sun," and therefore to the spiritual source of light and love.

b. It is brought into functioning activity after the second initiation. That initiation marks the completion of the process whereby the emotional nature (with its outstanding quality of desire) is brought under soul control, and the desire of the personal lower self has been transmuted into love. It is the organ for the distribution of hierarchical energy, poured out via the soul into the heart centre of all aspirants, disciples and initiates; in this way this energy is made available and brings about two results:

1. The regeneration of humanity through love.
2. The relationship, firmly established, between a rapidly developing humanity and the Hierarchy. In this way two great planetary centres—the Hierarchy and Humanity—are brought into a close contact and relationship.

As the Bible says: "the love of God is shed abroad" in the human heart, and its transforming, magnetic and radiatory power is essential for the reconstruction of the world and for the establishment of the new world order. Upon the unfoldment of the heart centre, and on an intelligent relation of mankind to the Hierarchy, with the consequent response of man to the energy of love, all disciples are asked at this time to ponder and reflect, for as a "man thinketh *in his heart,* so is he." Thinking in the heart becomes truly possible only when the mental faculties have been adequately developed and have reached a fairly high stage of unfoldment. Feeling in the heart is often confused with thinking. The ability to think in the heart is the result of the process of transmuting desire into love during the task of elevating the forces of the solar plexus into the heart centre. Heart thinking is also one of the indications that the higher aspect of the heart centre, the twelve-petalled lotus found at the very centre of the thousand-petalled lotus, has reached a point of real activity. Thinking as a result of correct feeling is then substituted for personal sensitivity. It gives us the first faint indications, likewise, of that state of being which is characteristic of the monad and which cannot be called consciousness— as we understand the term.

c. The heart centre becomes essentially related to the personality when the process of alignment with the soul is being mastered. This process is today being taught in all the newer and sounder esoteric schools, and has been emphasised in the Arcane School from the start; it is that procedure (distinguished by right orientation, concentration and meditation) which relates the personality to the soul, and thus to the Hierarchy. Relationship to the Hierarchy automatically takes place as this alignment goes forward and direct soul contact is thereby established. Personality consciousness is superseded by group consciousness, and the inflow of hierarchical energy follows as a natural consequence, for all souls are only aspects of the Hierarchy. It is this established relationship, with its subsequent interplay (magnetic and radiatory), which brings about the final destruction of the soul body or causal body as the relationship reaches its highest point of intensified recognition.

d. It is that centre, therefore. in the physical body through the medium of which the Hierarchy works; it is also the agent of the soul. When I here use the word "soul" I refer not only to the individual soul of man but to the soul also of the planetary Logos, both of which are the result of the union of spirit and matter, of the Father aspect and the Mother aspect. This is a great mystery which only initiation can reveal.

e. The heart centre registers the energy of love. It might here be stated that when the antahkarana has been finally constructed, the three aspects of the

Spiritual Triad will each find a point of contact within the etheric mechanism of the initiate who is functioning upon the physical plane. The initiate is now a fusion of soul and personality through which the full life of the monad can be poured.

1. The head centre becomes the point of contact for the spiritual will, Atma.
2. The heart centre becomes the agent for spiritual love, Buddhi.
3. The throat centre becomes the expression of the universal mind, Manas.

In the work of the initiate, as he works out the divine purpose according to the plan, the ajna centre becomes the directing agent or the distributor of the blended energies of the divine man. The heart centre corresponds to "solar fire" within the solar system, and is magnetic in quality and radiatory in activity. It is the organ of the energy which brings about inclusiveness.

f. Its dense physical externalisation is the thymus gland. Of this gland little is known at present, though much will be learned as investigators accept and experiment with the hypotheses which the occult sciences present, and as the heart centre develops and the thymus gland is returned to adult functioning activity. This is not as yet the case. The nature of its secretion is not yet established, and the effects of this gland are better known from their psychological angle than from the physical. Modern psychology, when allied to medicine, recognises that this gland when overactive will produce the irresponsible and amoral person. As the race of men learns the nature of responsibility we shall have the first indications of soul alignment, of personality decentralisation and of group awareness, and then— paralleling this development—we shall find the thymus gland becoming correctly active. At present, the general imbalance of the endocrine system militates against the safe and full functioning of the thymus gland in the adult. There is as yet an unrecognised relation existing between the pineal gland and the thymus gland, as well as between both of these and the centre at the base of the spine. As the Spiritual Triad becomes active through the medium of the personality, these three centres and their three externalisations will work in synthesis, governing and directing the whole man. As the pineal gland is returned to full adult functioning (as is not the case with adult man) the divine will-to-good will make itself felt and divine purpose be achieved; when the thymus gland similarly becomes active in the adult, goodwill will become apparent and the divine plan will begin to work out. This is the first step towards love, right human relations and peace. This goodwill is already making its presence felt in the world today, indicating the coming into activity of the heart centre, and proving that the heart centre in the head is beginning to unfold as a result of the growing activity of the heart centre up the spine.

g. It is the organ of fusion, just as the head centre is the organ of synthesis. As the heart centre becomes active, the individual aspirant is slowly drawn into an increasingly closer relation to his soul, and then two expansions of consciousness take place which are interpreted by him as events or happenings:

1. He is drawn into the Ashram of one of the Masters, according to his soul ray, and becomes an accepted disciple in the technical sense. The Master is Himself the heart centre of the Ashram and He can now reach His disciple, via the soul, because that disciple, through alignment and contact, has put his heart into close rapport with the soul. He then becomes responsive to the heart of all things which, as far as humanity is at present concerned, is the Hierarchy.

2. He is drawn into close service relationship with humanity. His growing sense of responsibility, due to heart activity, leads him to serve and work. Eventually he too becomes the heart of a group or of an organisation—small at first but becoming worldwide as his spiritual power develops and he thinks in terms of the group and of humanity. These two relationships on his part are reciprocal. Thus the love aspect of divinity becomes active in the three worlds, and love is anchored on earth and takes the place of emotion, of desire and of the material aspects of feeling. Note that phrase.

h. In the early stages of unfoldment, of both the individual and the race, the inverted heart lotus with its twelve petals reaches downwards towards the solar plexus centre. This last centre, since Atlantean days, has been reversed, and its petals are now reaching upwards towards the next centre up the spine, the heart centre, owing to the slowly mounting energies from the solar plexus centre which are seeking to escape from the "prison of the lower regions" through a process of transmutation.

As a result the heart centre is beginning slowly to unfold and also to reverse itself. The reversal of the "lotus centres" is always brought about as the result of a dual action—the pushing from below and the pull from above.

The reversal of the heart lotus and its upward unfolding is due to the following factors:

1. The growing potency of the hierarchical approach.
2. A rapidly establishing soul contact.
3. The response of the unfolding heart lotus to the pull of the Master's Ashram.
4. The surging upwards of the transmuted energies from below the diaphragm, via the solar plexus, in response to spiritual "pull".
5. The growing understanding by man as to the nature of love.

There are other factors but these are the ones you will most easily understand if you will regard them as symbolic and not too literally. Until the year, 1400 A.D., the relation of the solar plexus centre to the heart centre might be pictorially expressed as indicated in the diagram on page 715.

Eventually, at the close of the next root race, you will have the full expression of love and the lotuses up the spine will appear—all five of them—differing only in the number of petals found in each.

Finally at the close of the great world cycle when all the lotuses have reversed themselves, all will be opening and presenting free channels for the inflow and the transmission of the three major divine energies and the four lesser forces.

To this constant movement of the centres and to the constant inflow of energies we can trace much of the discomfort of humanity in its various bodies; it is the inability of the centres to respond or to unfold which in many cases produces disease and difficulty; it is the unbalanced unfoldment of the centres, their arrested development and their lack of response which creates problems in other cases; it is their premature unfoldment and their overactivity which in other cases brings about danger; it is the failure of the physical mechanism to measure up to the inner unfoldment which causes so much trouble. Thus again you can see the complexity of the subject. The *stage of theory* is a simple one, except in so far as it sets forces in motion which eventually lead to difficulty. The *stage of reaction* to response and of adjustment to the theory also institutes a cycle of intense difficulty and complexity, because it leads to a cycle of experiment and experience during which the disciple learns much and suffers much. Then as experience is gained, the *stage of spiritual expression* supervenes and freedom from danger and emancipation from difficulty and liberation from disease takes place. Simplicity is restored.

The Body, Phenomenal Appearance

Not much need be written here anent this, for the body nature and the form aspect have been the object of investigation and the subject of thought and discussion of thinking men for many centuries. Much at which they have arrived is basically correct. The modern investigator will admit the Law of Analogy as the basis of his premises and recognises, sometimes, that the Hermetic theory, "As above, so below," may throw much light on the present problems. The following postulates may serve to clarify:

1. Man, in his body nature, is a sumtotal, a unity.

2. This sumtotal is subdivided into many parts and organisms.

3. Yet these many subdivisions function in a unified man ner, and the body is a correlated whole.

4. Each of its parts differs in form and in function, but all are interdependent.

5. Each part and each organism is, in its turn, composed of molecules, cells and atoms, and these are held together in the form of the organism by the life of the sumtotal.

6. The sumtotal called man is roughly divided into five parts, some of greater importance than others, but all completing that living organism we call a human being.
   a. The head
   b. The upper torso, or that part which lies above the diaphragm.
   c. The lower torso, or that part lying below the diaphragm.
   d. The arms
   e. The legs

7. These organisms serve varied purposes, and upon their due functioning and proper adjustment the comfort of the whole depends.

8. Each of these has its own life, which is the sum total of the life of its atomic structure, and is also animated by the unified life of the whole, directed from the head by the intelligent will or energy of the spiritual man.

9. The important part of the body is that triple division, the head, upper and lower torso. A man can function and live without his arms and legs.

10. Each of these three parts is also triple from the physical side, making the analogy of the three parts of man's nature and the nine of perfected monadic life. There are other organs, but those enumerated are those which have an esoteric significance of greater value than the other parts.

   a. Within the head are:

      1. The five ventricles of the brain, or what we might call the brain as a unified organism.
      2. The three glands, carotid, pineal and pituitary.
      3. The two eyes.

   b. Within the upper body are:

      1. The throat
      2. The lungs
      3. The heart

   c. Within the lower body are:

      1. The spleen
      2. The stomach
      3. The sex organs

11. The sumtotal of the body is also triple:

   a. The skin and bony structure.

    b. The vascular or blood system.

    c. The threefold nervous system.

12. Each of these triplicities corresponds to the three parts of man's nature:

    a. Physical nature: The skin and bony structure are the analogy to the dense and etheric body of man.

    b. Soul nature: The blood vessels and circulatory system are the analogy to that all pervading soul which penetrates to all parts of the solar system, as the blood goes to all parts of the body.

    c. Spirit nature: The nervous system, as it energises and acts throughout the physical man is the correspondence to the energy of spirit.

13. In the head we have the analogy to the spirit aspect, the directing will, the monad, the One.

    a. The brain with its five ventricles is the analogy to the physical form which the spirit animates in connection with man, the fivefold sumtotal which is the medium through which the spirit on the physical plane has to express itself.

    b. The three glands in the head are closely related to the soul or psychic nature (higher and lower).

    c. The two eyes are the physical plane correspondences to the monad, who is will and love-wisdom, or atma-buddhi, according to the occult terminology.

14. In the upper body we have an analogy to the triple soul nature.

    a. The throat, corresponding to the third creative aspect or the body nature, the active intelligence of the soul.

    b. The heart, the love-wisdom of the soul, the buddhi or Christ principle.

c. The lungs, the analogy for the breath of life, is the correspondence to spirit.

15. In the lower torso again we have this triple system carried out.

a. The sex organs, the creative aspect, the fashioner of the body.

b. The stomach as the physical manifestation of the solar plexus is the analogy to the soul nature.

c. The spleen, the receiver of energy and therefore the physical plane expression of the centre which receives this energy, is the analogy to the energising spirit.

I realise well the technicalities which I have given here and their difficulty and apparent uselessness. It might be asked: Why should it be necessary to be so meticulous in enumerating the physical, psychological and systemic details of a purely academic nature when, by an act of the will and of divine power, and by the use of certain Words of Power, healing can be accomplished? These ideas are basically true, but are based upon a misapprehension—in time and space. *If* all healers were Masters of the Wisdom, *if* they were all clairvoyant, *if* they comprehended the Law of Karma and its working out in the life of the patient, *if* they had the full cooperation of the patient, and *if* they had the ability to add to all the above requirements the use of certain Words and Mantrams, then the academic knowledge would indeed be needless. But these requirements are not and can not be met. Healers, as a rule, have none of these powers. That they frequently heal (though not as often as they think they do) is true, but when successful they have succeeded in doing one or other of the following:

Healed the patient when his destiny and fate so willed it and his soul had therefore drawn its vehicle (the physical man) into the radiatory aura of a healer or a healing group. The probability is that the patient would have recovered in any case but that the process was hastened by the applied effort and attention, plus faith.

Interfered with the immediate design or pattern of the patient's life, and so postponed certain processes of spiritual tuition which were needed. This is very apt to be forgotten. It is too intricate a subject to be dealt with here, but I may be able to make it somewhat clearer as we deal with our final section.

Therefore (until there is full knowledge) it is vitally necessary that the structure of power and vitality and the network of energies and forces which compose the human organism should be studied. A mental grasp of the processes of healing is needed; and the reasons which make them seem difficult and complicated, unnecessary and wasteful of time, are as follows:

The inability of even the most advanced human mind to grasp themes and subjects *as a whole. The synthetic element is as yet lacking.* At present, the teaching and processes involved must be mastered step by step, detail by detail, precept by precept, application by application. But the future holds the promise clear, and the ability of the human eye to function synthetically, to grasp a landscape, for instance, in its broad and salient outlines and to do this simultaneously and in a flash of vision is the guarantee of the future technique of the race. One look by the illumined mind, one great radiation of love, and the healer or the healing group will know whether to heal, to aid the effort of the patient—a much slower process—or to refrain from healing.

The inertia of the average man or woman, which rebels against the effort needed to master the technical side of healing. It is so much easier to fall back on divinity (a divinity in reality latent but not expressive) and "let God do it." It is so much easier to recognise love and the outpouring of love than to master the processes whereby it can be made effective—or the nature of that which must be affected.

These are points requiring careful attention and consideration. They merit reflection. The synthetic power of the mind, aided by true love, will some day be the instrument of all true healers. In the meantime, for the sake of the future and in order to aid the formulation of the coming healing art—based on the understanding of energy, its inflow and circulation—this treatise will deal somewhat with the academic side. After all, the facts given are facts in existence and are truly present, as are those emotions which the average healer calls love.

The Seven Major Centres—(Continued)

Let us now continue with our consideration of the centres. We have dealt with the four above the diaphragm—the three centres through which the Spiritual Triad must eventually work, and the synthetic centre, the ajna centre, which finally expresses the integrated personality and becomes the direct agent of the soul. We now have three more centres to consider, all of them to be found below the diaphragm—the solar plexus centre, the sacral centre, and the centre at the base of the spine. The most important for all aspirants at this time is the solar plexus centre; the most active—generally speaking—in humanity as a whole, is still the sacral centre; the most quiescent centre in the body (from the angle of the spiritual man) is the basic centre.

5. *The Solar Plexus Centre.* This is located well below the shoulder blades in the spine and is exceedingly active. In Atlantean days, it was brought to a high stage of development, just as in Aryan days, the throat centre is being rapidly awakened. This centre is peculiarly related to two other centres: The heart and the ajna centre, and they form at this time an interesting triangle of energies in the human body and one which is receiving much attention from the Hierarchy. There is a down-flow of energy from the ajna centre to the heart from the soul, just in so far as the aspirant is in touch with his soul. This leads to three things:

A stimulation of the heart centre.

A responsive reaction from the heart which evokes a stimulation of the ajna centre and produces eventually the recognition of group consciousness by the personality.

The evocation of the heart centre in the head.

All this, however, is facilitated by the advanced development of the solar plexus in the aspirant, which has its own effect upon the heart and a reciprocal effect upon the ajna centre. There are, consequently, two important triangles to consider:

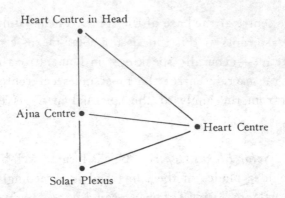

Just as there is, astrologically, a Science of Triangles, so there will later be developed a science of triangles in relation to the human system. But the time is not yet. I but give occasional indications of such a science upon which the intuition of disciples may play.

a. The solar plexus is a reflection in the personality of the "heart of the sun," just as the heart centre is. It is the central factor in the life of the personality for all humanity below the grade of probationary disciple. At that point the mind definitely begins to function, however faintly. It is the outlet—if such a word can be used—of the astral body into the outer world, and the instrument through which emotional energy flows. It is the organ of desire. It is of supreme importance in the life of the average man, and its control is a vital goal for the aspirant. He *must* transmute desire into aspiration.

b. The solar plexus came into full functioning in Atlantean times, during the period wherein the second great human race was developing. These lower centres are not so specifically related to initiations as are the centres above the diaphragm, for they are personality centres and have to be under the full control of the soul when initiations of a certain degree are taken.

c. The solar plexus centre is the great clearing-house for all energies below the diaphragm. This refers to the three major centres and the minor centres which were enumerated on page 72. The relation of this centre to the astral plane is (to use a peculiar but most expressive word) *acute*. It is the recipient of all emotional reactions and of desire impulses and energies and, because humanity is today becoming active in a group sense and is more inclusive than ever before in human history, the situation is one of acute and extreme difficulty. Mankind, through the individual and also through the collective solar plexus, is being subjected to almost unendurable pressure. Such are the tests of initiation! It is not my intention to deal here with the processes of attracting the lower energies, the mode of centralising them in the solar plexus, and there transmuting them and refining them to the point where transference into the heart centre becomes possible. Much of this is connected with the training given to accepted disciples, prior to the second initiation. It would be too intricate a matter to discuss, as well as carrying with it certain peculiar dangers for those not ready for the process; it is, however, one that—under *living* effort—goes forward almost automatically. The solar plexus is thus the most separative of all the centres (except the ajna centre, in the case of the man on the left-hand path) because it stands at the midway point, between the throat and the heart centres—above the diaphragm—and the sacral and basic centres—below the diaphragm. This is a consideration of major importance.

d. The solar plexus is the centre in the etheric vehicle through which humanity (average, unenlightened humanity) lives and moves and has its being. Humanity is conditioned by desire—good desire, selfish desire, wrong desire, and spiritual desire. It is the centre through which most of the energies flow which make a man progressive because he is ambitious, selfish because his personal desires are of importance, and fluidic because astrally polarised. Through it the "bright light generated in Atlantis" is poured, and the astral light is contacted. It is therefore the centre through which most mediums work and clairvoyants function. Later, these people will learn to work as intermediaries, consciously and intelligently using their powers; they will possess clear perception, and this will supersede clairvoyance. They will then be polarised in the ajna centre. It is consequently a most *disturbing* centre in the body, and is a basic cause of the majority of stomach complaints and troubles connected with the liver. The entire area immediately below the diaphragm is in a constant state of turmoil, where average man is concerned; this is due to individual and collective causes.

It is interesting to note here that just as the ajna centre (the synthesis of the personality forces, when highly developed) is a great directing and distributing agent, so the solar plexus centre (the synthesis of the average developed personality energies, prior to the process of integration) is a centre for collection, for a gathering-in of all the lower energies, and is finally a focal point for the direction and distribution of these collected energies—remitting them to their receptive higher centres:

1. The energies of the solar plexus centre itself have to be directed to the heart centre.
2. The energies of the sacral centre have to be transmitted to the throat centre.

3. The energies of the centre at the base of the spine have to be transferred to the head centre. After the third initiation, these basic energies are raised, controlled or distributed by an act of the will of the Spiritual Triad. Then "the light generated in Lemuria" (the sacral light) and "the light generated in Atlantis" (solar plexus light) will die out, and those two centres will simply be recipients of spiritual energies from on high; they will possess no direct, inherent light of their own; the light which they will transmit will come to them from collective sources on etheric planes.

The dense physical externalisation of this centre is the pancreas, with a secondary externalisation in the stomach. There is, in relation to the solar plexus centre, a curious relation which is symbolic both in form and in implication. You have

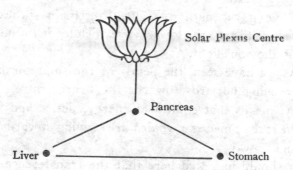

Solar Plexus Centre

Pancreas

Liver   Stomach

Here again appears the theme of a centre of spiritual force (for astral force is spiritual in essence) and its three manifestations. All these three dense materialisations are fed and nurtured by the forces and energies of the solar plexus centre. I have here given a very important fact to those who are interested in the study of medicine from the esoteric angle; rightly appreciated, it will lead to an understanding of the healing art. Control of the solar plexus centre, and the right reception and release of the energies focussed in that centre would bring about a major purification, an intensive strengthening and a vital protection of the three vital organs to be found in that area of the human physical mechanism.

As I have earlier pointed out, this centre is an organ of synthesis and gathers into itself all the lower energies at a certain point in the higher development of the human being. It is factually then an instrument (when rightly understood and rightly directed) for aiding in the integration of the personality life. The major problem of the man who is highly developed but not yet spiritually inclined is that of desire. What are his goals? To what are his aims directed? What is the nature of his realised ambitions? To what does he aspire? According to the nature of the forces and the energies which his thought life brings to bear upon the solar plexus centre, so will be his decision to move forward along the path of light, to remain statically self-centred, or to take the lower way which leads to the blotting out of the soul light.

As we have seen, the petals of the solar plexus centre are reaching upwards towards the heart centre. This, in reality, means that emotional energy, desire and ambition (in the race of men as a whole) are striving upwards towards the higher way.

It should be noted here that the transference of solar plexus energy *per se* is the task of all aspirants to the Path of Discipleship at this particular time, plus the gradual awakening of the heart centre. The first members of the human family to become group conscious are naturally the aspirants and the disciples, and these set the pace for the rest of humanity. This they achieve through the pressure of life itself and of circumstances, and not by the following of set rules or specific meditations. Later, prior to a certain major initiation, such rules and measures may be applied so as to give the initiate immediate and conscious control over the astral body and its focal point of entry into the physical organism, the solar plexus centre, and again at the time that certain major transferences are consciously made. Of these transferences there are three of primary importance:

1. From the three centres below the diaphragm into the heart, throat and ajna centres.
2. From the two centres above the diaphragm—the heart and throat centres—into the ajna centre and the thousand-petalled lotus of the head.
3. From the ajna centre into the head centre, signifying the complete unification of all the energies throughout the entire etheric body into one central focal point of distribution—under direct control of the Spiritual Triad.

The processes involved in these three great experiences (each preceded by much testing and experiment) naturally put a strain upon the physical body and are the cause of many of the ills to which disciples fall heir.

It will be obvious to you, for instance, that the transference of all the accumulated energies in the solar plexus centre into the heart centre will cause difficulty, very frequently of a serious nature; this is the reason why today so many advanced people die of heart disease. In the long cycle of the soul life and experience, this is of relatively small moment; in the short cycle of the individual disciple's life it is of great difficulty and oft of tragedy. Similarly, the transference of the energies of the five centres up the spine into the head centres will carry with it its own problems. The stimulation of the ajna centre by the focussing of these energies may lead to disastrous psychological problems. A man may become an ego-maniac temporarily (all is temporary in the long life of the soul!) and become such a human monster as Hitler and others of his ilk, though in lesser degree; there may be also violent conditions of epilepsy, or the eyesight may be affected and a man may become blind. All these points warrant careful thought.

6. *The Sacral Centre.* This centre is located in the lower part of the lumbar area and is a very powerful centre, controlling as it does the sex life. One of the interesting things about this centre is that it must always remain a powerful centre until two-thirds of mankind have taken initiation, for the generative processes must go on and remain active in order to provide bodies for incoming souls. But as the race progresses, this centre will be controlled and its activities will be carried forward intelligently and as the result of knowledge, of insight and of higher and subtler contacts, and not as the result of unlimited and uncontrolled desire, as is now the case. I cannot enlarge further upon this matter as the theme is too big. I can, however, bring to your attention what I have already written, and suggest that someone with the interest and the time should collect all I have said in all my books anent the subject of sex so that a pamphlet on the subject may be compiled.

a. The sacral centre corresponds to the physical sun, the source of vitality, and the life-giving agent on our planet.

b. The symbolism of the sacral centre is concerned primarily with the gestation period prior to birth, and in its right understanding can be traced and expanded the whole story of conception, of form-building, and this whether it is the physical form of a human being, the form of an idea, an organisation built around a central truth, the form of a planet or of a solar system. It is perhaps above everything else the centre through which the forces of IM-PERSONALITY must eventually express themselves, and the whole problem of dualism must be solved. This solution and interpretation of the symbol must come from the realm of the mind, thereby controlling the physical reaction and occupying itself with purposes and not with desire. Ponder on this. When it is thus understood, then we shall be reaching the point where a great transference can take place into the higher centre of creation, the throat centre.

c. The sacral centre is therefore closely related to matter, and there is a flow of energy between three points in the lower part of the human body:

1. The spleen, the organ of prana or of physical vitality coming from the sun.

2. The sacral centre, the predisposing agent towards physical generation.

3. The centre at the base of the spine which (until the will aspect is aroused in man) feeds the life-giving principle, the will-to-live, to all parts of the human frame.

These create a great triangle of force, concerned with matter, with substance, form-building, creation, vitality and persistence in form. This triangle is a reflection of a much higher one, composed of

1. The throat centre, corresponding to the sacral centre.

2. The pituitary body, corresponding to the splenic centre.

3. The pineal gland, corresponding to the basic centre.

In the relation of these two triangles lies the clue to the instinct of self-preservation, the survival of the subtle bodies after death, and the principle of immortality which is seated in the soul and functions when self-preservation and survival no longer hold sway. This constitutes a triplicity of ideas which requires most careful study and which—if I might so express it—gives the key to the spiritualistic movement.

d. The sacral centre is also connected with the ajna centre in the last analysis; the two together create a functioning duality which is productive of that subtle quality which we call *personality*. There is a wide field for investigation in the theme of personality as an integrated whole and in the quality of personality, which is the aroma, the influence, the effect and the radiation of a personality. I throw out these ideas to students, hoping that some research may follow which will relate this subject of the centres to the recognised facts of coordination, integration and their effects in producing greatness.

For those of you who are students of *The Secret Doctrine,* there is much to be unfolded anent the relation of the "lunar Lords," the Barhishad Pitris, to the solar Lord or Angel. The field of work of the former is the sacral centre, par excellence; that of the solar Angel is the throat centre.

e. The sacral centre registers the energy of the third aspect of divinity, just as the solar plexus centre registers that of the second aspect and the basic centre expresses the energy of the first aspect. Here again you have the lower centres reflecting the throat, heart and head centres and thus completing the higher and the lower manifestation of the divine Trinity in man. This centre was brought into full functioning activity in old Lemuria, the first human race; its energy is that of the Holy Spirit, overshadowing virgin substance. Here again we find also another divine reflection in the following:

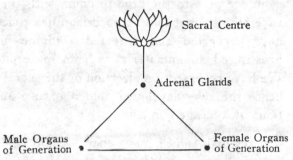

Eventually, in the Divine Hermaphrodite (later to appear) you will have another combination:

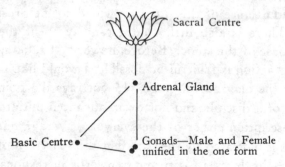

Again you will note, my brother, how the Science of Triangles governs the human frame in all its aspects, as well as the frame of a solar system. This is to be expected.

f. The dense physical externalisation of this centre is to be found in the gonads, the human organs of generation—viewing them as a basic unity, though temporarily separated in the present dualistic expression of the human being. It must be remembered that this separation fosters a powerful impulse towards fusion, and this urge to blend we call sex. Sex is, in reality, the instinct towards unity: first of all, a physical unity. It is the innate (though much misunderstood) principle of mysticism, which is the name we give to the urge to union with the divine. Like all else that undeveloped man has touched, we have perverted and distorted a divine idea and prostituted an immaterial urge to material desire. We have reversed the direction of the sacral energy, hence the over-developed animal nature and functions of average humanity.

There is necessarily much more that I could add to the above, but the theme would require much careful analysis, elucidation and wording that time permits not, or the established balance of this Treatise would not be preserved.

There is also little that I can say anent the centre at the base of the spine. Before, however, I take up whatever information is fruitful or possible, I would like to point out that the diagram on page 715 portrays the point in evolution of a disciple and not of an advanced initiate. It is not a description either of the everyday, average human being. This is indicated by the fact that the reflection of the heart centre in the head is turning upwards in response to an increased activity of the heart centre itself, and that the definition of the ajna centre is clear and exact, demonstrating an integrated, coordinated personality. This is not therefore the diagram of the centres of the ordinary or undeveloped person. It is impossible for such diagrams to do more than give some point of consummation, but it should be remembered that these points of consummation are not static attainments but are each of them preceded by phases and stages of activity which produce constantly changing results and varying aspects of the centres; these, in their turn, are succeeded by other cycles of movement, of change and of a renewed release of energies. *The effects* of the deep underlying causes themselves become *causes,* for in the cycle of manifestation there is nothing static or fixed or finally determined. This is a point of extreme importance. Be not therefore misled by apparent moments of achievement. They are but prefaces to change, for such is the Law of Being.

7. *The Centre at the Base of the Spine.* This centre is, above everything else, controlled and governed by the Law of Being, above referred to, and is established where spirit and matter meet and where matter, the Virgin Mary—under the influence of the Holy Spirit, the energy of the etheric vehicle—is translated "into Heaven," there (as the Christian phraseology puts it) "to be seated beside her Son in the house of the Father."

This centre is found at the very base of the spine, and *supports* all the other centres. It is relatively quiescent at this time, for it is only roused into full activity by an act of the will, directed and controlled by the initiate. It is responsive only to the will aspect, and the will-to-be in incarnation is the factor which at present controls its life and produces its effects as it feeds and directs the life principle in matter and form. Just as we are told that the life principle is "seated in the heart," so the will-to-be is seated in the base of the spine. There has been much idle and dangerous talk anent this centre, and the whole subject of the "kundalini fire" has proved an exciting and enticing tale by the pseudo-occultists of the world. The true occultist in training has naught to do with the kundalini fire—as usually understood. It is not possible for me to do more than make certain facts somewhat clearer to you, and yet at the same time I must refrain from indicating modes and methods of arousing the activity of this centre, on account of the extreme danger involved in any premature work on the basic centre. The best I can do is to make a series of statements which will be comprehended in the right way by those who know (and these are as yet few and far between), which will aid the thinking of those who are in training and give them a somewhat more complete picture, but which will protect the ignorant from disaster. I shall make these statements as clearly and briefly as possible, but shall give practically no explanatory matter with them.

1. This basic centre is the point where, under the evolutionary law, spirit and matter meet, and life is related to form.

2. It is therefore the centre where the essential dualism of the manifested divinity—man or planetary Logos—meet and produce form.

3. The nature of this divinity is only revealed when the second aspect has accomplished its work, through the medium of the third aspect, but under the directing will of the first aspect.

4. It is the centre where the "serpent of God" undergoes two transformations:
   a. The serpent of matter lies coiled.
   b. This serpent is transformed into the serpent of wisdom.
   c. The serpent of wisdom is translated and becomes the "dragon of living light."

5. These three stages are nurtured by the life and energy pouring down through the entire length of the spinal

column, via the etheric correspondence of the spinal cord, and—in time and space—this downpouring (plus the simultaneously uprising life) produces:

    a. The awakening in a gradual and orderly manner of the centres, according to ray types.

    b. The reversal of the centres so that the consciousness of the indwelling man is adequate to his environment.

    c. The synthesis of the life energies of all the centres, and adequacy to the demands of the initiate and the service of the Hierarchy and of Humanity.

6. The spinal column (from the angle of the esoteric sciences) houses a threefold thread. This is the externalisation of the antahkarana, composed of the antahkarana proper, the sutratma or life thread, and the creative thread. This threefold thread within the spinal column is therefore composed of three threads of energy which have channeled for themselves in the substance of the interior of the column a "threefold way of approach and of withdrawal." These are called in the Hindu terminology: the *ida,* the *pingala* and the *sushumna* paths, and they together form the path of life for the individual man and are awakened into activity sequentially and according to ray type and the point of evolution. The sushumna path is not used correctly and safely until the antahkarana has been built and the Monad and Personality are thereby related, even if it is only by the most tenuous thread. Then the Monad, the Father, the will aspect, can reach the personality in a direct manner, and can arouse the basic centre, and with it blend, unify and raise the three fires.

7. One of these paths is the one along which the energy which feeds matter is poured. Another is related to the path of consciousness and of sensitive psychic unfoldment. The third is the path of pure spirit. Thus in every living form the work of the Father, of the Mother and of the Son is carried on. Life-consciousness-form and life-quality-appearance are blended, and the response apparatus of the divine man is perfected, enabling him to contact and recognise the major divine aspects in the kingdoms in nature, in the planet and in the solar system—eventually.

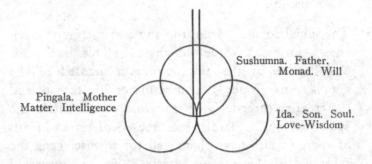

Sushumna. Father.
Monad. Will

Pingala. Mother
Matter. Intelligence

Ida. Son. Soul.
Love-Wisdom

Be not betrayed into placing these interlaced spheres of living energy on the right or the left of the spinal cord. Constantly a movement, an interplay and a reversal is going on. I can but portray the nature of a symbol which will indicate the special path of the three energies of the divine Trinity. I indicate *not a fact in location or place,* for it is this materialising and localising of the main concept which has produced so much danger. The initiate-student seeks to grasp the relation of the three basic energies, the three paths of living fire, their relation and inter-relation and their sequential polarisation. He seeks not to narrow the teaching down to points and lines and place until such time when these terms mean little to him and he knows more.

8. These three paths of life are the channels for electric fire, solar fire and fire by friction, and are related in their usage to the three stages of the path of evolution: the path of evolution in the material, earlier stages; the Path of Probation, and the early stages of the Path of Discipleship until the third initiation; and the Path of Initiation itself.

9. The Kundalini Fire, about which so much is taught and written in the East, and increasingly in the West, is in reality the union of these three fires, which are focussed by an act of the enlightened will, under the impulse of love, in the basic centre. This unified fire is then raised by the use of a Word of Power (sent forth by the will of the Monad) and by the united authority of the soul and personality, integrated and alive. The human being who can do this in full consciousness is therefore an initiate who has left the third initiation behind him. He, and he alone, can safely raise this triple fire from the base of the spine to the head centre.

10. As usually interpreted by the ignorant esotericist in the various occult groups, the kundalini fire is something which must be "raised," and when it is raised all the centres will then come into functioning activity and the channels up and down the spine will be cleared of all obstruction. This is a dangerous generalisation and a reversal of the facts. The kundalini fire will be raised and carried up into heaven *when* all the centres are awakened and the channels up the spine are unimpeded. This removal of all obstruction is the result of the livingness of the individual centres which,

through the potency of their life, themselves are effective in destroying all hindrances and obstructions. They can "burn up" all that hinders their radiation. What usually happens in those accidental cases (which do so much harm) is that the aspirant, through his ignorant curiosity and by an effort of the mind (not of the spiritual will, but purely as an expression of personality will), succeeds in arousing the lowest of the three fires, the fire of matter, fire by friction; this produces a premature burning and destroys the etheric web in the etheric body. These circular disks or webs are to be found between each pair of the centres up the spine and also in the head. They are normally dissipated as purity of life, the discipline of the emotions and the development of the spiritual will are carried forward.

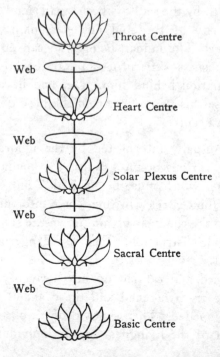

Throat Centre

Web

Heart Centre

Web

Solar Plexus Centre

Web

Sacral Centre

Web

Basic Centre

There are four of these webs. When the fourfold personality is highly developed and the ajna centre is awakening, then these webs slowly and gradually, normally and automatically disappear. The webs in the head are of much higher quality and bisect the skull horizontally and vertically. Thus they symbolise the Cross upon which a Son of God is crucified.

11. The three channels up the spine are responsive in their totality to the three major centres:

    a. To the solar plexus centre, providing thus the impulse of desire and feeding the physical life and the creative urge.

    b. To the heart centre, providing the impulse to love and to conscious contact with ever widening areas of divine expression.

    c. To the head centre, providing the dynamic impulse of the will to live.

    I do not indicate which channel is responsive to which centre, except in the case of the sushumna channel which is responsive *only* to the energy of the head centre and the directing will, centred in the 1000-petalled lotus. This can be safely stated, as the spiritual will is as yet undeveloped in those who seek to arouse kundalini. When it is aroused, they will know what they can safely do.

12. The three centres in the head are also related to this triple channel:

    a. The medulla oblongata area (the alta major centre) and the carotid gland.

    b. The ajna centre and the pituitary body.

    c. The 1000-petalled lotus and the pineal gland.

    Students will find it interesting to relate all these triplicities to the three major rays:

    a. The first ray of will or power,

    b. The second ray of love-wisdom,

    c. The third ray of active intelligence,

and also to the three human races which are endowed with the power to unfold the seed of these divine aspects: Lemuria, Atlantis and the Aryan race. These can be linked, *as seed,* to the two final races which will fuse and synthesise all the above powers, qualities, achievements and goals into one perfected planetary life.

Another synthesis is also possible and of importance:

    a. Path of Evolution.........centres below the diaphragm.

    b. Path of Discipleship........centres above the diaphragm.

    c. Path of Initiation.........centres in the head.

These groups and triplicities are all related in time and space to the triple spinal cord.

13. There is also—again in relation to all the above points of synthesis in the body—one consummating point of complete fusion. I give each of these in the sequence of their work of fusion:

    a. The solar plexus centre, fusing the centres below the diaphragm.

    b. The ajna centre, fusing centres both above and below the diaphragm.

    c. The base of the spine, fusing all six centres.

    d. The thousand-petalled lotus of the head, fusing all the seven energies.

Bear in mind, in connection with all the above, that we are dealing entirely with forces and energies, functioning through the etheric body; that we are dealing with the tertiary world of causes, which is responsible for the organic world of the dense physical manifestation. This physical manifestation is itself subject to the influence of the secondary world of conscious life, which in its turn is responsive in time and space to the dynamic world of purpose and of Being.

The key to the full life of the soul lies hidden in my words, but it takes the dedicated life and the illumined mind to profit by the knowledge conveyed, and to see behind the form of words the key thought which gives it life and—occultly speaking—generative warmth.

Have clearly in mind the concepts of stimulation or lack of stimulation, of interplay or of separativeness, of quiescence or of activity, for in these dualities are to be found the causes of health or of disease.

The Etheric Body, Nervous and Endocrine Systems

What I have to say here is based upon certain remarks in the previous pages wherein I pointed out that

1. The etheric body itself
2. The nervous system
3. The endocrine system

are closely "related to each other and constitute an interlocking directorate of energies and forces which are essentially vital, galvanic, dynamic and creative. . . . Upon them, the entire interior health of the body depends." To these three I then added the blood stream as the conveyor throughout the body of

1. The Life Principle,
2. The combined energies of the three above systems,

and pointed out that the great combination of forces which we call the pairs of opposites or the major dualities, govern the underlying causes of health and disease. In making these statements, I am endeavouring to reduce our entire theme to one of the utmost simplicity. In so doing, some of the truth is lost, but it is essential that certain broad generalisations are grasped by the student before he begins to study the exceptions and to deal with minutiae and the detail of bodily defects or their opposites.

It has become a truism with students of the occult that the etheric body conditions, controls and determines the life expression of the incarnated individual. It is a secondary truism that this etheric body is the conveyor of the forces of the personality, through the medium of the centres, and thereby galvanises the physical body into activity. These forces, routed through the centres, are those of the integrated personality as a whole, or are simply the forces of the astral or emotional body and the mind body; they also transmit the force of the personality ray or the energy of the soul ray, according to the point in evolution reached by the man. The physical body, therefore, is not a principle. *It is conditioned and does not condition*—a point oft forgotten. It is a victim of personality life or the triumphant expression of soul energy. It is for this reason that the science of psychology will, during the next two centuries, dominate modern medical science, except in the category of those diseases with which we will deal in our next section—those emanating from group life, such as tuberculosis, venereal diseases and cancer. Until the race is more definitely group conscious (something as yet far distant) it will not be possible to apply broad psychological generalisations to the diseases indigenous to our planet. We can, however, consider the handling of similar difficulties which arise in the individual unit; these are based on the conflict of the pairs of opposites and upon the lack of harmony to be found in the three major interlocking, directing systems.

You have, therefore, three systems to carry in your minds, and one carrier or conveying agent, plus the basic occult fact that certain great opposing energies, working within the body, produce what we call disease. To the above factors I would add another needed correlation. I would remind you that we are concerned with forms of life, and that all these forms are creative within themselves, and can create potentially more forms or can provide environments in which these forms can live. Please note this mode of expressing a fundamental truth. The basis of all the occult teaching as regards manifestation is that the building forces exist, and that this statement is true whether you are concerned with the Life of a solar system or only with the consciousness of that body in which the human being moves and lives—along sound or unsound lines; we are dealing with the world body in which a human being lives. Owing to this, we come up against another great natural Law which can be expressed simply as follows:

LAW VI

When the building energies of the soul are active in the body, then there is health, clean interplay and right activity. When the builders are the lunar lords and those who work under the control of the moon and at the behest of the lower personal self, then you have disease, ill health and death.

This is a profoundly simple rule, but it gives the clue to the causes of disease and to the reason for an established immortality; it will be understood with great clarity and comprehension in a few years' time and will then supersede those idealistic but factually unsound and untrue systems to which we give the name Unity, Mental Science and Christian Science. These systems present as immediate, demonstrable possibilities the stage of final liberation from the natural and material limitations which today control all forms; they ignore the time factor, and overlook the evolutionary process and also the point of development of the person concerned; their position is based on wishful thinking and on the innate desire of the average human being for comfort and physical harmony, and gloss the innate selfishness of their presentation of truth with the concept that all is to the eternal glory of God. Unquestionably, disease and physical limitations of any kind will vanish, but this will only happen when the soul of the individual controls and the lower personal self becomes as much an automaton of the soul as the physical body is at this time the automaton of the emotional nature, of the mind, and occasionally (and only very occasionally for the majority of people) of the soul.

Only when the soul, consciously and with the cooperation of the personality, builds the temple of the body, and then keeps it full of light, will disease disappear; this building is, however, a scientific process, and in the early stages of discipleship (which is the time wherein the soul begins to grasp its instrument, the personality) this leads inevitably to conflict, increased strain and frequently aggravated disease and disharmony. This dis-harmony and dis-ease lead to much necessary trouble and consequent undesirable effects. These effects will be overcome but—in the interim of adjustment—whilst they are registering and expressing themselves, there will be much distress, physical and psychological, and all the major and minor difficulties to which humanity seems heir.

In undeveloped humanity, the conflict (from the angle of consciousness) is practically nil; you have less susceptibility to the subtler diseases emanating from the three interlocking systems, but at the same time a much greater responsiveness to the three indigenous diseases, to infectious and contagious diseases, and to the great epidemics which sweep through nations and great planetary areas. As humanity develops, diseases become more personal (if I might express it in this manner) and are not so definitely related to the herd or mass condition. They arise within the persons themselves, and though they may be related to the mass diseases, they are based on individual causes.

When a man steps out of the general mass and steps upon the probationary path, and thus becomes a candidate for discipleship, then the diseases of the flesh and the inharmony of his entire threefold system, plus the conveying stream, constitute a *conscious problem* and one which the aspirant must himself tackle—thus revealing to him the need for conscious, creative building.

It is at this point that the doctrine of reincarnation becomes of supreme value; the disciple begins to institute those conditions, to create those forms and build those vehicles which, in another life, will prove more suitable for soul control and more adequate instruments with which to carry forward the perfecting process which the soul demands. Let me point out that the disciple does not concentrate upon the physical body at any time, or begin with any physical emphasis to work at the elimination of disease or disharmony. He begins with the psychology which the soul teaches and commences with the causes which are producing the effects upon the physical plane. *It is a slower process, but endures*. Much of the violent auto-suggestion of the systems allied to Christian Science and Unity are only temporary in their effects and are based upon a process of scientific suppression, plus a refusal to recognise existent factors. They are *not* based on truth. In a later life, the suppressed condition will again emerge in ever greater potency and will continue so to do until such time as it is ignored altogether and the life emphasis is laid on soul contact and the life expression is extroverted into service to others.

In connection with physical disease and its relation to the centres (regarding these as focal points for incoming energies from some source or another) it might be useful if certain broad generalisations were made here, remembering that to all of these there may be exceptions, particularly in the case of the health or the non-health of disciples.

1. Each of the seven major centres governs or conditions—from the material angle as well as from that of the soul and of the life principle—the area of the physical body in which it is found, including the multitude of lesser centres of energy and plexi of force which may be found therein.

2. The three great basic and manifesting divisions of divinity are to be found symbolically present in every centre:

   a. The life principle, the first aspect, discloses itself when the entire centre is esoterically unfolded or awakened. It is present all the time in latency, but it is not a dynamic factor producing monadic stimulation until the end of the great cycle of evolution.

   b. The quality or soul aspect is gradually disclosed in the process of evolutionary unfoldment and produces, in time and space, the definite effect which the centre has upon its environment. This quality is dependent upon the ray (either of the personality or the soul) which is the source of the incoming energy, or upon the ray governing the astral body in the case of the little evolved; it is also dependent upon the point in evolution and upon the radiatory influence of other centres.

   c. The appearance in the etheric body of a developed or a developing centre indicates the place of the man upon the ladder of evolution, his racial affiliations, and his conscious goal; this latter can range all the way from an emphasis upon the sex life, and consequent activity of the sacral centre, to the goal of the initiate, which brings the head centre into activity. All this produces a consequent effect upon the surrounding tissue, substance and organic forms within the radius of influence of the centre. The area of this influence is variable according to the activity of the centre and this is dependent upon the point of development reached by the individual and the preponderant type of energy to which the individual reacts.

3. The incoming energy is transmuted within the centre into forces. This involves a process of differentiation into secondary energies of the primary energy involved, and is an automatic happening; the rate of transmutation process, the strength of the resultant aggregation of forces, and the subsequent radiatory activity (producing conditioning results upon the dense physical body) are dependent upon the extent of the unfoldment of the particular centre involved and its awakened or unawakened state.

4. The outgoing forces from a centre play upon the etheric counterpart of the entire intricate network of nerves which constitute the nervous system. These counterparts of identical subjective correspondences are called in the Hindu philosophy, the "nadis"; they constitute an intricate and most extensive network of fluid energies which are an intangible, interior, paralleling system to that of the bodily nerves, which latter system is in fact an externalisation of the inner pattern of energies. There is as yet no word in the English language or in any European tongue for the ancient word "nadi," because the existence of this subjective system is not yet recognised, and only the materialistic concept of the nerves as a system built up in response to a tan-

gible environment yet holds sway in the West. The idea of these nerves being the dense physical result of an inner sensitive response apparatus is still undefined and unrecognised by modern Western science. When recognition is accorded to this subtle substance (composed of threads of energy) underlying the more tangible nerves, we shall have moved forward in our approach to the entire problem of health and disease, and the world of causes will be that much nearer. This network of nadis forms a definite life pattern which varies *according to the personality ray*.

5. The nadis, therefore, determine the nature and the quality of the nervous system with its extensive network of nerves and plexi covering the entire physical body. The nadis, and consequently the network of nerves, are related primarily to two aspects of man's physical equipment— the seven major centres in the etheric body (the substantial body which underlies the dense physical body), and the spinal column with the head. It must always be remembered that the etheric body is a physical body, though composed of subtler material than the one we can see and touch. It is made of substance or of that which "substands," or underlies, every part and particle of the dense physical vehicle. This is a point which will later receive attention from healers and from enlightened medical men in the New Age. When this relationship existing between the nadis and the nerves, and their joint relationship to the centres and spinal column is recognised, we shall see a great revolution in medical and psychiatric methods. Experience will tend to show that the more closely the interplay between these two—the nadis and the nerves—can be brought about, the more rapidly will the control of disease also be implemented.

6. The nadis in the physical body correspond to the life or spirit aspect; the nerves are the correspondence to the soul or quality aspect. That which demonstrates as their united externalisation is the endocrine system which corresponds to the form or matter aspect. These three—the nadis, the nervous system and the glands—are the material correspondences to the three divine aspects; they are esoterically responsive to these three aspects and they make the man upon the physical plane what he is. These three groups are themselves conditioned (via the seven centres, as we have earlier seen) by the astral or mental vehicles, or by the integrated personality, or by the soul which begins to use the personality as a transmitting and transmuting agency, and—at the close of the Path of Discipleship—by the monad, via the antahkarana, using that self-created path as a direct channel of communication to the seven centres and from there to the threefold system of nadis, nerves and glands.

7. These three major systems within the human being express through the medium of the physical body the condition or the state of development of the centres. The life, the quality and the energy which they represent are conveyed to every part of the physical vehicle via the blood stream. This, modern science is already recognising as a fact, indicating that the blood stream conveys certain elements released by the glands. It does not yet recognise the fact of the relationship of the glands to the centres, with the intermediate systems of nadis and nerves. The next great move in medicine will be to recognise the fact of the etheric body, the physical substance which underlies dense matter.

8. When the centres are awakened throughout the body, there will then be present a highly electric nervous system, responsive with immediacy to the energy carried by

the nadis; the result of this will be a well-balanced endocrine system. The vitality and life pouring through the entire body will then be of such potency that automatically the physical body will be resistant to disease, either innate, hereditary, or of group origin. In these words I express for you a future probability but not an immediate possibility. Man will some day have the three systems perfectly coordinated, psychically responsive to the inner pattern of nadis and centres, and consciously integrated with the soul, and later—via the antahkarana—with the Life principle.

9. Today as there is uneven development, with some centres unawakened, others overstimulated, and with the centres below the diaphragm overactive, you have consequently, whole areas of the body where the nadis are in an embryonic state, other areas where they are highly energised but with their flow arrested because some centre along the path of their activity is still unawakened or—if awakened—is still non-radiatory. These uneven conditions produce potent effects upon the nervous system and upon the glands, leading to overstimulation in some cases, subnormal conditions in others, lack of vitality, overactivity, and other undesirable reactions which inevitably produce disease. Such diseases either arise from within the body itself as the result of inherent (or should I say indigenous) or hereditary tendencies or predispositions, present in the bodily tissue; or they arise as the result of the radiation or the non-radiation of the centres, which work through the nadis; they can also arise as a result of external impacts or contact (such as infectious or contagious diseases and epidemics). These, the subject is unable to resist, owing to the lack of development of his centres.

10. To sum all up: Disease, physical disability of any kind (except of course those due to accidents and, to some

extent, to planetary conditions inducing epidemics of a peculiarly virulent nature such as war oft produces), and the many differing aspects of ill health can be directly traced to the condition of the centres, as they determine the activity or the non-activity of the nadis; these, in their turn, affect the nervous system, making the endocrine system what it is in the individual man, and the blood stream is responsible for this condition reaching every part of the body.

Effects Produced in Specific Areas

Let us now consider certain of the effects of the above facts, and their effect upon the areas governed by the centres and in which disease appears.

It will be apparent to you that as the energy pours through the centres, via the nadis and the nerves and potently affecting the glandular system and the blood stream, the areas of the body become vitally involved and responsive. This covers, of course, the head, the throat and the torso. The energy thus despatched penetrates to every part of the physical vehicle, to every organism and to every cell and atom. It is the working of the quality of energy upon the body which induces, stimulates, removes or palliates disease. I am not here referring to the three major indigenous diseases (if I may call them that)—cancer, syphilis and tuberculosis. With these I will deal later because they are planetary in scope, present in the substance of which all forms are made, and are responsible for producing a host of lesser diseases which are sometimes recognised as affiliates but are frequently not so known.

Those diseases which are loosely called mental diseases, and which are related to the brain, are little understood as yet. There was very little mental trouble in the last rootrace, the Atlantean; the mind nature was then quiescent and little stimulation was conveyed through mental levels via the head centre to the pineal gland and the brain. There was very little eye trouble either, and no nasal difficulties, for the ajna centre was unawakened and the third eye rapidly becoming inactive. The ajna centre is the organ of the integrated personality, the instrument of direction, and is closely related to the pituitary body and the two eyes, as well as to all the frontal areas of the head. In Atlantean days, personality integration was largely unknown, except in the case of disciples and initiates, and the goal of the initiate then, and the sign of his achievement, was this triple integration. Today, the goal is that of a still higher fusion—that of the soul and personality. Speaking in terms of energy, this involves the formation, activity and related interplay of the following triangles of force:

I. 1. The soul, the spiritual man on his own plane.
   2. The personality, the threefold integrated man in the three worlds.
   3. The head centre.

II. 1. The head centre, the point of the second fusion.
    2. The ajna centre, the point of the first fusion.
    3. The centre in the medulla oblongata, controlling the spine.

III. 1. The pineal gland, the externalisation of the head centre.
     2. The pituitary body, related to the ajna centre.
     3. The carotid gland, the externalisation of the third head centre.

All these triplicities, present within the circumference of the head, constitute the mechanism through which:

1. The soul controls its instrument, the personality.
2. The personality directs the activities of the physical body.

The spinal column (esoterically, the ida, pingala and sus-humna channels), the two eyes and the total brain tissue are receptive to, stimulated by, or nonreceptive to these ener-gies in the head. In the latter case, the entire area is in a quiescent state, spiritually speaking, and the focus of energy is elsewhere.

This deficiency or this stimulation, if unbalanced or if misapplied, will produce some definite type of trouble, fre-quently of a physiological nature as well as psychological, and in our Aryan times we shall see an increasing amount of diseases of the brain (a constantly increasing mental imbalance), and of eye difficulties, until the nature of the centres and the type of incoming force and their regulation are recognised and carefully and scientifically studied. Then we shall see the science of the regulation of energy, as it conditions the human being, developed. In the meantime, there is much difficulty everywhere, and mental diseases, neurotic conditions, insanities and, perhaps even more preva-lent, glandular imbalance, are on an expanding arc. To date, in the West, little is known as to the methods of con-trol or cure, and in the East, where some knowledge can be found, nothing is done, owing to the apathy there present.

The spinal column is primarily intended to be the chan-nel through which the energising of the centres and the dis-tribution of energy to the surrounding areas of the body is carried forward by the intelligent, integrated personality, acting under the *conscious* direction of the soul. I refer not here to the bony structure of the spinal column, but to the cord, its esoteric counterpart, and to the nerves which issue from the spine. Today this planned, directed esoteric con-trol of energy is not present, except in the case of those with the initiate consciousness and certain advanced dis-ciples. There are inhibitions, blockages, unawakened areas, deficiency of vitality, lack of free flow and consequent lack of development within the whole man; or else there is too much stimulation, a too rapid vibratory activity, a premature awakening of the centres, leading to the overactivity of the atoms and cells governed by any particular centre. All these conditions, along with others not mentioned, affect the nervous system, condition the glands and produce psychological difficulty and disease in some form or another. You have the following simple yet suggestive and symbolic diagram of the spinal column and the head, looking at both from the angle of the centres and the glands:

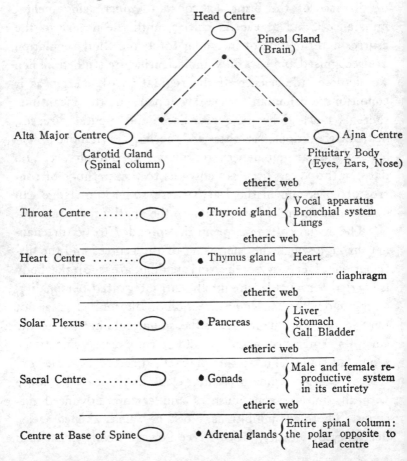

You will note that the spleen is not included in this diagram. Its function is a peculiar one, being the centre of vitality in relation to the planetary vitality and the radiation from the sun. It is not controlled in any way from the spinal column. It must be borne in mind that this diagram is simply an effort to relate in pictorial form the centres, the glands which they condition, and the organs which are affected by both. It is not intended to be a true picture of any physiological organic relations.

The centre at the base of the spine has a unique function. It is to the substance of the body, to the physical tissue and to all matter not included in the organs mentioned above, the source of life. In the perfected man, the two centres (the highest head centre and the basic centre) represent the great duality of spirit and matter, and they then control and govern, in perfect unison, the entire direction of the vehicle of the soul. Finally, you will have the spiritual aspect of the human being expressing itself perfectly through the related monad and personality (which is brought about by a third great major fusion). The material man is then responsive to these two, via the head centre (the monad) and the basic centre (the spiritually energised personality). These two centres will then be in complete rapport, expressing the full nature of the spiritual man.

It is essential that spiritual healers should get clearly in their minds the picture of the areas in the body which are governed by the head centres and the other centres, because within those areas are the various organs which react to disease. The health of these organs is largely dependent upon the centres, as they condition the glands and as the energy is distributed throughout the body. A full and balanced flow of energy from the centre into the area which it controls leads to resistance to so-called disease;

where there is lack of development and an unbalanced situation, where the centres are concerned, there will be no power to resist. The healing process in the New Age will start with definitely planned work with the centres, and the general trend of the healing art will then be—as you can easily see—preventive in nature rather than curative. The whole emphasis will be upon the energy centres, energy currents and the direction of energy to the organs within the radius of the influence of any particular centre. From a study of the glands (a study so much in its infancy that it hardly merits the word "embryonic") much will be later learned of their relationship to the centres, and much experimental work will be done. From the standpoint of the esotericist who admits the *fact* of the centres, the glands are, par excellence, the major determining factor in connection with the general health of an individual; they indicate not only his psychological development far more than is today grasped, but they have (as is suspected by the orthodox medical science) a most potent effect upon the whole organic system; their influence, via the blood stream, reaches into every part of the body and to the extremities. The glands are the result of the activity of the centres; they are first, last, and all the time *effects of inner predisposing causes,* and it is through the centres and their affiliated glands that the soul builds the apparatus upon the physical plane which we call the physical man.

Therefore, the group of related factors with which we have been dealing must be carefully studied and grasped by any practicing healer, for he will eventually have to work through his own centres in relation to the patient whose ills he is endeavouring to heal. He must remember, consequently, three factors: The centres, their related glands, and the group of organs for which these two are responsible. You have in the seven areas of the body, governed by the seven major centres and their affiliated glands, the appearance again of the basic trinity of manifestation:

1. Life or spirit . . . . . the energy centre.
2. Soul or quality . . . . the gland.
3. Form or matter . . . the organs in any particular area governed by any one centre.

This brings us to another law which the healer must ever have in mind.

LAW VII

When life or energy flows unimpeded and through right direction to its precipitation (the related gland), then the form responds and ill health disappears.

This is a basic law in healing and concerns the true art of relating spiritual energy with form life, and upon this the health and the vitality of the organs depend. Therefore we come to the next rule which the healer has to master. This is concisely expressed, and those phrases which convey instruction must be understood and applied intelligently.

RULE FIVE

Let the healer concentrate the needed energy within the needed centre.

Let that centre correspond to the centre which has need.

Let the two synchronise and together augment force.

Thus shall the waiting form be balanced in its work.

Thus shall the two and the one, under right direction, heal.

It will be obvious to you, therefore, that healers at the present time (I refer not here to the medical profession but to the multitude of the many schools of thought) have not yet got back to the basic factor, in spite of all their talk anent love being the healing force. They are in reality emphasising and dealing with the motive which impels the healer to ply his healing art. They are concerned with the instrumentality whereby contact can be made with the patient to be healed. That contact must ever be established in LOVE—fresh, compelling and selfless. But once that relation is established, the healer must grasp the fact that, as far as he is concerned, he must work scientifically; he must apply knowledge and—after right diagnosis, after right modern therapeutic methods, after due common sense, which includes the best that the tried science of medicine can give—he must then begin to work through his own centre, putting it en rapport with the centre in the patient which governs the distressed area or diseased organ.

As he thus works, the energy which loving intent and skilled knowledge has tapped and brought in is not permitted (during the healing process) to stimulate or affect the healer's own related glands or produce action in the connected area of his own body. The healer must learn to insulate himself from the energy to be used on behalf of the patient. He blends it with the energy of the patient's centre, governing the diseased area; the allied gland is then doubly energised (or lessened, as the case may be and diagnosis requires), and the blood stream releases into the diseased tissue that which is needed to cure or prevent the growth of the disease.

In this instruction I have given you much food for thought. I have emphasised an aspect of scientific esoteric healing which has not before been brought to the attention of students. I would have you grasp the general picture and get the outlines of process clear; I would have you study the relation between the healer and the patient as he passes out of the stage of just loving and sending out love or of seeing the patient in the light of love, and goes on to the scientific work of augmenting the patient's own spiritual energy. He thus enables him to effect his own cure, consciously or unconsciously.

You have, therefore, the healer, the patient and the reservoir of spiritual energy, plus the scientific process of bringing all three into a close and healing rapport. This is done via the centre concerned in the equipment of the patient, the corresponding centre in the equipment of the healer, and the direction (by an act of the will of the healer or of the healing group) of the united streams of required specific energy to the area diseased. This is usually done via the related gland, though it is not always so.

Ponder on these things and see, if you can, the simplicity of the process which is based on loving intent, which isolates the specific area in which the trouble exists, which identifies itself with the spiritual centre of energy in the patient, and which then applies and directs the fused and blended energies.

Effects of Under-Stimulation and Over-Stimulation of the Centres

We have been for some time studying the centres and their relation to the dense physical body. We have also noted the areas which are conditioned by these centres and the mediating work of the ductless glands. We have seen that two major predisposing causes of physical trouble, arising within the physical organism, are the understimulation or the overstimulation of the centres. There are also, as you will recall, three diseases which are inherent in substance itself, and which therefore create basic predispositions within the human body: cancer, syphilis and tuberculosis. With these three we are not at this time dealing. But the condition of the centres produces, basically, all the difficulties, permitting entrance to infections and germs which might not otherwise cause trouble, producing those situations where the diseases inherent in the form nature can be fostered, and making undesirable tendencies powerful. We might consequently lay down the premise (one which the medical profession will later accept in its entirety) that diseases which are self-engendered (if I may use so curious and inadequate a phrase), and which are not the result of contagion or infection or of accidents, are caused by the failure, the limitation, the deficiency or the excess, and by the overdevelopment or the underdevelopment, of the endocrine system. This ductless glandular system, via the hormones, affects every part of the physical organism—via the blood stream—and it may therefore be truly posited that when the ductless glands are perfectly balanced and functioning correctly, there will be no diseased areas in the body. The blood stream will then be kept also in perfect condition. The clue to perfect physical health as it is expressed by a Master of the Wisdom can consequently be directly traced to His full control of the centres, to their balanced state of energy reception and distribution, and to the effect which they produce upon the entire ductless glandular system. By this means every area of the body is properly supplied with the needed forces and is thus kept in perfect condition.

Coming midway between the centres and the corresponding endocrine glands, and acting as the agent for the distribution of energy, is the nervous system. Here, however, difficulty is usually to be found. There is a lack of adequate flow of energy; the energy distributed by its means to the body, via the centres, is unevenly distributed; some centres receive an undue supply; others receive an inadequate amount; some centres are still unawakened, and therefore are nonreceptive; others are prematurely developed and transmit too much force to the areas they govern. In esoteric medicine and its philosophical interpretation (which is in the last analysis the effective and practical application of the known facts) it is the cerebro-spinal aspect which conditions and governs the entire nervous system, for it is by means of this aspect and through its agency that the centres work and affect the bodily organism, supplying the body with the needed vital energy; thus the nervous system becomes eventually responsive, via·the seven centres, to the seven major energies or the seven ray forces.

In no human being, except a Master, are all the centres properly awakened and functioning in a balanced manner, nor are they properly related through intensive radiation; in no human being is the nervous system correctly responsive to the centres. There are two reasons for this, and both are related to the cerebro-spinal system:

1. The head centre is not yet awakened, or is only slowly being developed, as the disciple submits himself to training.
2. The flow of energy through the head to the centres up the spine is uneven, owing to the fact that the inflow is uneven, and that the etheric web—between the centres—permits as yet only a very little energy to flow through to all the centres.

It must be remembered that the life of the centres is founded, in the initial stage, upon the inherent life of the organism itself, with the focus of the emanating life to be found in the centre at the base of the spine. This is a point oft forgotten by esotericists. This basic centre is the one through which the life of matter itself works; this is the life or energy of the Holy Spirit aspect, the third aspect. Through its life each atom in the body is fed. This process of animating the substance of the physical form is started in the prenatal stage; after birth, this type of force is aided and paralleled by the inflow of planetary prana or vital energy from the planetary life itself, via the spleen.

This is the essential relating organ between the inherent life of matter itself, as present in the microcosm, and the inherent life in the planet.

As evolution proceeds, there is gradually added to this inherent force an inflow of "qualified" energy which is expressive of the consciousness aspect of divinity, and indicates to the esotericist the state of awareness of the man and also the ray type of his soul. This inflow comes from the second divine aspect, from the soul or the indwelling Christ. It might therefore be stated anent the two head centres that:

1. The ajna centre, or the personality centre, focussed between the eyebrows and conditioning the pituitary body, is related to the entire life of the integrated threefold organism. Through this organism the consciousness must perforce express itself, and the physical, emotional and mental vehicles demonstrate its point in evolution.

2. The head centre (called in the Hindu philosophy, the thousand-petalled lotus) conditions the pineal gland and is related to the life of the soul and—after the third initiation—to the life of the monad; it conveys to the centres the energy of the three major types of spiritual being of which the three forces of the personality are the reflections or physical counterparts.

Later, energy from the spirit aspect, the first or Father aspect, will become available and will pour down through the head centre to the ajna centre, combining personality energy and soul energy. Then, by an act of the will, it is projected down the spinal column, via the alta major centre, which conditions the carotid gland. As it passes down the spinal column it vitalises two aspects of the centres; when it reaches the basic centre, it combines with the latent energy of substance itself, and you have, therefore, the union of all three divine energies and the manifestation in man of the three divine aspects. These combined energies then rush up the central channel in the spinal column, and the third or highest receptive aspect of the centres is energised. All the centres are thus brought into full expression; all limitations are destroyed; every part of the body is vitalised and material perfection is produced, plus the full play of the enlightened consciousness and also of the life aspect.

The nervous system then comes under the complete control of the spiritual man, and the blood stream is purified and becomes an unimpeded and satisfactory channel for the circulation of that which the energised glands discharge. This is the esoteric significance of the Biblical words, "The blood is the life," and also of the words "saved by the blood of Christ." It is not by the blood of a Christ dying two thousand years ago upon the cross in Palestine that man is saved, but by the livingness of the blood of those in whom the Christ life and consciousness, and the quality of the Christ, is perfectly demonstrating and expressed. Then, when the nature of the indwelling Christ is fully, spontaneously and automatically expressing itself in and through the personality, the three fires of the creative process—the fire of matter, the fire of the soul, and the electric fire of spirit—are blended, and there is then a perfect manifestation on Earth of physical living, of the emotional and mental life, and also of the spiritual life of an incarnated Son of God, a Christ.

It is on this point of understanding that so many worthy people go astray, particularly in the mental science movements, in the Unity movement, and in Christian Science. Instead of focussing their effort on achieving the pure life of Christ in every day life, and acting as consecrated servers of their fellowmen and as channels for love, and becoming aware only of the consciousness of the whole, they are focussed on affirming a future perfection—mentally and vocally—in order to have good health and physical comfort. They regard it as their right and due, to be gained by affirmation, and forget the hard work necessary to bring about within themselves those conditions which will make the divine manifested Christ present. They need to bear in mind that good health will be normal and declarative if the inner consciousness is harmless (and the majority of these people are guilty of a superior spirit of criticism), if they are decentralised from the lower self in the three worlds, and if they are "focussed in heaven, thereby enabling the heavenly Son of Man Who is the Son of God to lead the heavenly life when far from the heavenly realm" —as an old Christian mystic, long forgotten, used to say. His words have been remembered by the Master M—and thus recalled to my attention.

Another school of thought, branding themselves untruthfully as occultists, are equally in error. They work, or rather profess to work, with the centres, only fortunately for them nature protects them often from themselves. They endeavour consciously to vitalise the centres, to burn away the protective web, and to raise the fires of matter before the fire of spirit has combined with the fire of the soul. They then fall victims to premature stimulation of the fires of substance before the balancing of the forces can take place. Disease, insanities, and many neurotic conditions, plus serious pathological conditions, then occur. Some of the glands become overactive; others are overlooked, and the entire glandular system and the dependent nervous system are in a state of complete imbalance.

Disciples need to learn to focus their attention upon the reality and upon the factors of primary spiritual importance. When they do this, the energies in the head, the correct use of the spinal area with its "beaded centres," and the awakening of the basic centre and its consequent fusion with the higher energies will be an automatic and perfectly safe happening.

The orderly rhythm of the glandular system and the free, safe use of the controlled nervous system will then be possible; the energies, projected from the centre, via the nadis, will be safely related and brought into a synthetic functioning within the body, and the disciple will experience not only a fully awakened consciousness, and a brain which is ever intelligently receptive, but a constant inflow of spiritual life. There will then be that perfect balance and perfect health which characterise a Master of the Wisdom.

Knowledge concerning the endocrine or ductless glands is as yet in an embryonic state. Much is known anent the glands connected with the sacral centre and about the thyroid gland, but to date, naturally, the medical profession does not admit that they are effects of the activity or the nonactivity of the centres, or that a line of least resistance exists between the sacral centre and the throat centre. Something is known (not much) about the pituitary body, but its extreme importance as it affects the psychological response of the person is not adequately grasped. Nothing is known, factually speaking, about the pineal or the thymus glands, and this because neither the head centre nor the heart centre is awakened in undeveloped man, or even in the average citizen. That there is a considerable wealth of knowledge anent the sacral centre (as the source of physical creation) and the conditioning effects of the thyroid gland is due to the fact that both these centres are awakened in the average man, and when the functioning is adequate and the necessary interplay is established, you then have a highly sexed individual who is also a creative artist along some artistic line. This is very frequently seen, as you well know. When the ajna centre and its externalisation, the pituitary body, are also active, and the relation between the three centres—sacral, throat and ajna centre—is awakened and beginning to function, and definite conscious relationship is being set up between it and the other centres (dependent upon ray, upon conscious objective and training), then you will have the practical mystic, the humanitarian and the occultist.

Students should remember that there is both an upward and a downward trend of energy within the entire structure of centres, where the aspirant and the disciple are concerned:

1. *The upward trend* ... producing Transmutation.

> From the sacral centre to the throat centre. Physical creation is transmuted into artistic creativity.
>
> From the solar centre to the heart centre. Individual, emotional consciousness is transmuted into group consciousness.
>
> From the base of the spine to the head centre. Material force is transmuted into spiritual energy.
>
> From any or all of the five spinal centres to the ajna centre. Uncoordinated living is transmuted into personality integration.
>
> From the six centres in relationship into the highest head centre. Personality activity is transmuted into spiritual living.

This is a wide generalisation, and the process is not carried forward in any sequential fashion or smoothly and in order as the tabulation above might suggest. The process involved is spread over many lives of unconscious transmutation in the earlier stages, and as a result of bitter experience and of conscious effort in the later stages, and becomes increasingly dynamic and effective as the various stages upon the Path are trodden by the aspirant. The five rays with which a disciple has to work (two major conditioning rays and three subsidiary rays) have a definite active effect; karmic adjustments provide opportunity or hindrance, and the intricacies of the entire process (within the relatively limited experience of the disciple) are so confusing whilst in process that all that he can do is to grasp the general outline as here given and not pay too much attention to the immediate factual detail.

2. *The downward trend* . . . producing Transformation.

Once the head centre is awakening and the disciple is consciously active in the work of directing the energies to the centres and thereby governing his personality life, there is a scientific undertaking of energising the centres in a certain ordered rhythm which is again determined by the rays, by circumstance and by karma; thus all the bodily energies are swung into correct spiritual activity. With the process involved we cannot here deal, beyond pointing out that this downward trend can be roughly regarded as falling into three stages:

1. The stage of energising the creative life, via the throat centre, thus bringing:
   a. The head centre and the throat centre,
   b. These two and the sacral centre,
   c. All three, consciously and simultaneously, into conscious relation.

This relation, when properly established, will solve the individual problem of sex, and without recourse to either inhibition or suppression, but by bringing about right control and making the disciple, at the same time, creative in a worldly sense, and therefore of use to his fellowmen.

2. The stage of energising the conscious life of relationship via the heart centre, thus bringing:

   a. The head centre and the heart centre,
   b. These two and the solar plexus centre,
   c. All three, simultaneously and consciously, into close cooperation.

This serves to establish right human relations, right group relations, and right spiritual relations throughout a man's entire life expression. Just as the stage of regulating the creative life has a paramount effect upon the physical body, so this stage affects the astral vehicle with great potency; emotional reactions are transformed into aspiration and service; selfish individual love is transformed into group love, and then divinity rules the life.

3. The stage of energising the entire man, via the basic centre thus bringing:

   a. The head centre and the basic centre,
   b. These two and the ajna centre,
   c. All the three, simultaneously and consciously, into rhythmic, coordinated expression. This is a final stage of great importance, and only takes place in its completeness at the time of the third initiation, that of the Transfiguration.

You can see, therefore, how three important words convey the purpose of the scientific unfoldment and the right direction of the centres:

Transmutation. Transformation. Transfiguration.

This process is wisely and safely carried out over a long period of time and—returning to our theme of health and of disease—when consummated, perfect physical health is the result; in the interim process of adjustment and of change, the reverse is frequently the case. The danger involved in a large number of physical ills can be traced to the condition of the centres, to their interplay or their lack of interplay, to an undeveloped condition, unawakened and sluggish, and to an overstimulation or an unbalanced activity. If one centre is prematurely awakened, it is frequently at the expense of other centres. The rude health of the savage or of the unskilled and unintelligent labourer or peasant (a state of being which is rapidly passing as the mind development and the process of evolution take effect) is largely due to the quiescent state of practically all the centres, with the exception of the sacral centre. The fact of their falling easy prey to the infectious diseases can also be traced to the same quiescence. As the emotional nature is developed and the mind begins to function, the centres then become more active. Definite trouble then ensues, largely because psychological conditions begin to appear. The man is no longer simply an animal. The wear and tear of the emotional life (the major predisposing factor in ill health) floods the lower nature with ill-directed energy (or should I say mis-directed?). The solar plexus centre then becomes unduly active and this activity falls into four stages:

1. The stage of its awakening, as the astral body becomes steadily more powerful.

2. The stage of its potency when, for lives, it is the conditioning centre in the etheric or vital body and the man is consequently entirely conditioned by his emotional-astral life.

3. The stage wherein the solar plexus centre becomes the clearing house for all the centres (major and minor) below the diaphragm.

4. The stage wherein the solar plexus energies are raised to the heart.

All these stages bring, temporarily, their own physical ills.

You will note that, beyond certain generalisations, I am not relating specific diseases to specific centres. I have indicated the areas conditioned by the centres, and far more powerfully conditioned than you have any means yet of ascertaining; I have said that fundamentally the ductless glands—as externalisations of the centres—are the determining factors in the health of the body, and that where there is imbalance, overdevelopment or underdevelopment you will have trouble; I have suggested that the medical profession in the New Age will deal increasingly with the theory of energy direction and its relation to the ductless glands, and that it will admit, at least hypothetically and for the purpose of experimentation, that the theory of the energy centres may be correct and that they are the primary conditioning factors, working through the ductless glands which, in their turn, guard the body, produce the necessary resistance, keep the blood stream supplied with the essentials to health and—when rightly interrelated—produce a balanced expression of the spiritual man throughout the entire physical body—physiological and psychological balance. When this desirable condition is not the case, then the ductless glands, through wrong relationship and incorrect and unbalanced development, are not adequate to the task; they cannot protect the body from disease, and are unable to pour into the blood stream what the physical vehicle needs. Owing to their inadequacy, the body is unable to resist infections, is in a constant state of ill health, and cannot cope with disease coming from without or latent within the organism of the body; this weakness often produces mortal disease.

Medicine in the next century will be built around certain major premises:

1. Preventive medicine will be the goal, producing the attempt to keep the body in proper balanced order.

2. Sound sanitation and the providing of healthy conditions will be regarded as essential.

3. The supply of the right chemical properties to the physical body will be studied—a science of chemistry which is yet in its infancy, though it is becoming a flourishing infant.

4. An understanding of the laws of vitality will be regarded as of prime importance, and of this the emphasis today on vitamins and the influence of the sun are wholesome indications.

5. The use of the mind will be regarded, above everything else, as a factor of major importance; the mind will be seen as the prime influence as regards the centres, for people will be taught to work on their centres through mental power and thus produce a right reaction from the endocrine system. This will necessarily involve the right directing of thought to a centre, or the withdrawal of attention from a centre, with consequent effect upon the glandular system. This will all be based upon the occult law that "Energy follows thought."

Owing to the fact that disciples have a greater development of mental power than the average man, and also to the fact that ray type is more easily ascertained, involving consequently a more correct determination of the condition of the glandular system, they will be the first to cooperate with the medical profession and to demonstrate the relation of the centres to the glands, and therefore to the body as a whole. Through concentration and right meditation, carried on in the head centre, and directed towards some one or other of the centres, disciples will demonstrate such definite changes in the ductless glands that the medical profession will be convinced of the importance and the factual existence of the centres and of their power, and also of the possibility of controlling the physical organism through the power of thought. This all lies in the future. I am but pointing the way and indicating a future technique whereby disease will be overcome. The various mental schools of thought, Unity and Christian Science, have been fantastic and fanciful in their claims and definitely unscientific in their approach. But they have had hold of at least one thread in the great process of right adjustment to life and to right relationships. They had the dream and the vision; they lacked perception and commonsense and ignored the evolutionary process.

Physiological science and psychological power, plus the cooperation of the trained disciple with the trained medical man (particularly with the open-minded endocrinologist), will eventually succeed in solving many human ills and will bring about the cure of the bulk of the diseases now troubling humanity.

We have, therefore, studied to some purpose our first section: *The Psychological Causes of Disease*. We have carried the idea down from the inner and more subtle causes of disease to the major physical conditioning factor, the ductless glands. We can now briefly consider certain far more occult causes and deal with those which emanate from the group life of humanity and from the karmic liabilities of mankind. Here we shall enter the realm of occult knowledge and of esoteric information, and this will be far more difficult for the orthodox thinker to accept.

CHAPTER II

Causes Emanating from Group Life

IN CONSIDERING DISEASE and its basic causes, we have dealt particularly with those which concern our Aryan race and modern humanity; these are largely astral in origin and might be described as Atlantean in nature. We have briefly considered also the various diseases which originate upon the mental plane; these are more strictly Aryan and involve also the ills to which disciples are prone. Infectious diseases and those which are fundamental in the planetary substance have a potent effect upon those races (still among us) which are the oldest on our planet, and which are related to the fast dying out Lemurian types; Negroes are specially prone to infectious epidemics.

I have not attempted in this treatise to deal pathologically with any of the diseases touched upon, nor have I paid attention to the physiology of the patient. That is entirely out of my province. I have, however, attempted to indicate the origins of some of the diseases, to call attention to the paramount importance of the glandular system, and to relate, as far as is just and wise, some of the oriental theories anent the centres and western wisdom. Later I shall point out some basic human conditions which must be changed if the true healing work is to be correctly applied, and then I hope to give some of the methods whereby healers can accomplish work which will be in line with the facts of the case and which will aid in the processes of restoration.

The problem of disease is today greatly enhanced, owing to the fact that in this race, the Aryan, which now dominates the planet, you have the first true appearance outwardly on the physical plane of the basic synthesis of humanity which will be—in its better form—so strikingly significant of the next major rootrace, the sixth. Inter-marriage between nations and races, the fusion of bloods for hundreds of years—due to migration, travel, education and mental unity—has led to there being no really pure racial types today. This is far more certainly the case than the most enlightened think, if the long, long history of mankind is considered. Sexual intercourse knows no impenetrable barriers, and people today have in them all the strains and the blood of all the races, and this (as a result of the world war, 1914-1945) will be increasingly the case. This development is definitely a part of the divine plan, no matter how undesirable it may appear to those who idealise purity of relationship, or how ruthless its application is at the present moment. Something intended is being brought about and it cannot be avoided The urge to mate becomes peculiarly strong when men are removed from their familiar settings and experience the novelty of complete loneliness, when the normal inhibitions and customs imposed by family relationships and national standards are removed, when danger of death is constantly faced and the larger value submerges the lesser values and the usual conventional attitudes, and when the physical organism has been trained and brought by scientific treatment and heavy feeding to the height of physical efficiency. I am speaking in terms of physical effectiveness and not of mental efficiency, which may or may not parallel the former.

The animal instincts are therefore potent; the centres below the diaphragm become peculiarly energised; the emotional demands enormously vitalise the solar plexus centre, and the centre at the base of the spine increases the activity of the adrenal glands as the will of the man is called into play to surmount danger; the will-to-live, with its adjunct, the will-to-perpetuate and to live in one's children, is powerfully fostered. To this must also be added, as a major adjunct of war, the will of Nature itself working (under certain divine laws) to offset the loss of life and the casualties of war by a fresh inflow of life into form, thus preserving the human race, providing the bodies for the next tide of egos and thus peopling the earth.

In saying this I seek only to explain the phenomena which can be noted at all times when war is present and which in the world war can be noted on a large scale. The armies of the world are everywhere and are spread over every country; racial transmigration is a universal factor, both from the angle of military necessity and from the plight of the civilians who find themselves in the path of war. This movement of millions of men everywhere is one of the paramount factors which will condition the new civilisation, and its importance is based upon the fact that in twenty-five years' time men and women will be a hybrid race whose fathers and mothers will be of every imaginable nation; white fathers will have had physical relation with women of every Asiatic or African origin, thus producing a fusion of blood which—if recognised and rightly handled and developed, from the educational angle and with understanding—will express in embryo the nature of the sixth rootrace, and which will be in fact HUMANITY without any racial or national barriers, with no so-called pure blood and exclusive castes, and with a new and virile sense of life because of the infusion of stronger stocks with the weaker or worn-out types and of the newer racial strains with the older and more developed. I hold no brief for the manner in which this is being brought about. It could have happened without war and through a conviction that all men are equal and human, and that the mixture of races would solve many problems; war, however, has hastened the process and the soldiers of all the armies of the world are having physical relations with women of all races, all civilisations and all colours. This must, whether regarded as right or wrong according to the code of ethics and standards of the observer, produce an entirely new situation with which the world of the future will have to cope; it must inevitably break down national prejudices and racial barriers—the first producing more effect than the latter during the initial stages. Inevitably a more homogeneous humanity will appear during the changes of the next one hundred years. Many attitudes and many customary reactions which today hold sway will vanish, and types and qualities and characteristics for which we have as yet no precedent will appear upon a large scale.

Whether the conservative and the so-called strictly "moral" people dislike this worldwide happening has no bearing on the case. It has happened and is happening daily and will materially bring about far-reaching changes. These inter-racial and mixed relationships have always happened upon a small and individual scale; they are now happening on a large scale. For the results of this due preparation must be made.

As is well known to you, there are certain diseases which are numerically dominant in the world today. They are:

1. Heart diseases of various kinds, particularly afflicting advanced humanity.

2. Insanities.

3. Cancer, so widely prevalent among every type of man today.

4. The social diseases—syphilitic in nature.

5. Tuberculosis.

In a subtle and occult manner, these diseases are due to two basic causes: One is the close interplay between people, living under modern conditions, and the massing of people into cities and towns; the other is the age of the soil upon which man lives (a fact little recognised or considered), for it is deeply impregnated with the germs and the residue incident to past ages. The immunity of man is an amazing matter, could you but realise it; he resists and throws off constantly and continuously every kind of disease—those which are the result of contact with others, those which are prevalent in the very atmosphere at every time, those which are latent within his own bodily organism, and those which are inherited and to which he has a constant predisposition. Man's fight for health is ceaseless and unending, ranging all the way from ordinary fatigue and tiredness (plus the universal tendency to take cold), to mortal disease, ending in death.

To the trained occult observer, it is as if humanity—as a whole—is walking partly in a dense shadow which engulfs the race, and some part of which involves an area of the body of every human being. One of the aims of the New Age will be "to lighten this shadow and bring people out into the fitness of true health." This same shadow penetrates also into the mineral kingdom, affects the vegetable kingdom, and involves also the animals; it is one of the major causes of all that can be considered under the name of "sin," which may surprise you. It is also the fertile seed of crime. This is a fact to be accepted, to be properly considered and dealt with rationally, sanely, intelligently and spiritually; it will require all the factors mentioned to lift humanity out of the darkness of disease into established and radiant health. Certain of the Masters are dealing with this problem in relation to the other kingdoms in nature, for there will be no true escape for man whilst his environment is still under the shadow of disease.

Much that I could tell you in this connection would sound fanciful and would call forth the scoffing amusement of the hardboiled scientist. The theories held by mankind as to the origin of diseases, and the recognition of bacteria and germs and similar intruding organisms are largely correct, but this is so only if you bear in mind that they are in reality effects of causes upon which the investigator has not touched and which are hidden in the very history of the planet itself and also in the racial history of the past—of which little or practically nothing is known. Surmise and conjecture rule here.

1. DISEASES OF HUMANITY, INHERITED FROM THE PAST

History, as studied today, goes back but a little way and although the enlightened historian and scientist may extend the story of humanity to millions of years, there is naught known about the races of men who lived those millions of years ago; naught is known of the civilisation which flourished in early Atlantean times twelve million years ago; naught is known at all of the still more ancient Lemurian civilisation which goes back more than fifteen million years; still less is known of that twilight period which existed twenty-one million years ago when men were scarcely human and when they were so closely related to the animal kingdom that we call them by the cumbersome name of "animal-man."

During the vast period between then and now, myriads of people have lived and loved and experienced; their bodies have been absorbed into the dust of the earth and each has contributed something which they have gained during life experience—something different, however, to that which they contribute to the life of the soul on its own plane. This something contributed has altered in some way the atoms and cells of the physical body, and that gained something has in due time been released again into the soil of the planet. Each soul, withdrawn from the body, has come to the earth repeatedly, and many millions are here today, particularly those who were present in later Atlantean times and who are, therefore, the flower and the highest product of that highly emotional race. They bring with them the predispositions and the innate tendencies with which their past history has endowed them.

It should therefore be borne in mind that the physical bodies in which humanity now dwells are constructed of very ancient matter and that the substance employed is tainted or conditioned by the history of the past. To this concept must be added two others: First, that incoming souls draw to themselves the type of material with which they must construct their outer sheaths, and that this will be responsive to some aspect of their subtler natures; if, for instance, physical desire conditions them, the material of their physical vehicle will be largely responsive to that particular urge. Secondly, each physical body carries within itself the seeds of inevitable retribution, if its functions are misused. The great original sin in Lemurian times was sexual in nature, and due largely not only to inherent tendencies, but to the extraordinarily dense population of its civilisation and to the close relation of the animal kingdom. The origin of the syphilitic diseases traces back to these times.

There is a beautiful idea in the minds of the ignorant that primitive races are free from that type of contamination and that the many sexual diseases and their results are predominantly the diseases of civilisation. This is not so from the occult angle of vision. True knowledge disproves it. In the infancy of the race, a great mismating, promiscuity and series of perversions took place, and in the language of some of the most ancient books in the Masters' Archives we read: "earth took its toll and earth to earth, polluted and impure, returned to earth; thus evil life entered the pristine cleanliness of the ancient mother. Deep in the soil the evil lies, emerging into form from time to time, and only fire and suffering can cleanse the mother of the evil which her children have given unto her."

The Lemurian race practically destroyed itself, owing to its misuse of the sacral centre, which was at that time the most active and the dominant centre. In Atlantean days it was the solar plexus centre which was the prime objective of the "entering fire." The work of the Hierarchy in Lemurian days was, as I have told you elsewhere, to teach infant humanity the nature, meaning and significance of the physical vehicle, just as in the next race, the emotional was fostered and the major object of attention, and in our race, it is the mind which is subjected to stimulation. The initiate in Lemurian times was one who had completely mastered the control of the body, and hatha-yoga was then the outstanding spiritual practice. This, in time, was superseded by laya-yoga, which brought all the centres in the etheric body (except the throat and head centres) into functioning activity. This is not the type of activity which is now possible, because it must be remembered that the Master in those days had not the development or the understanding of the Masters of today, the only exceptions being Those Who had come from other schemes and spheres to aid animal-man and primitive humanity.

A. Venereal and Syphilitic Diseases.

Paralleling all the activity of the Great White Lodge

(as was always the case and is the case today) was the activity of the dark forces. Their effects had to be brought about through the medium of the sacral centre, and thus a most vicious situation came about which weakened the stamina of the human body, which greatly increased the demands of the sex nature through the stimulation of the sacral centre, artificially brought about by the Black Lodge, and which produced many unholy alliances and widespread evil relations.

A great new law of nature was then imposed by the planetary Logos which has been expressed (very inadequately) by the words, "The soul that sinneth, it shall die." This law could be better expressed by saying, "He that misuses that which he hath built will see it fall from forces within itself."

As the centuries slipped away and the Lemurian race submitted to the evil impulses of the animal nature, gradually the earliest type of venereal disease made its appearance; eventually the entire race was riddled with it and died out, nature taking its toll and exacting its inexorable price. You might here ask how these early inhabitants of our planet could be held responsible for there is no sin where there is no sense of responsibility and no consciousness of wrong doing. The Hierarchy in those days had its own methods of teaching these infant peoples, just as the smallest child can be taught today to refrain from certain physical habits. Humanity then knew well what was evil, because the evidences of that evil were physically apparent and quite easily perceived. The penalty was obvious and the results immediate; the Teachers of the race saw to it that cause and effect were quickly to be noted.

At this time there also arose the first tendencies to marriage, as differentiated from promiscuity; the formation of family units became the subject of attention and

a goal for the most highly evolved. This was one of the
first tasks undertaken by the Hierarchy and the first effort
toward any form of group activity, conveying the first lesson
in responsibility. The family unit was not stable as it can
be now, but even its relatively brief tenure was a tremendous step forward; the segregation of the family unit and
the growth of the sense of responsibility has gone steadily
forward until it has culminated in our present system of
marriage and our stress in the Occident upon monogamy;
it has led to the western pride in family strains and pedi-
grees, our interest in genealogies and relationships, and the
complete horror of the occidental thinker over the syphilitic
diseases as they affect families and their offspring.

Two most interesting things are, however, happening
today. The family unit, on a worldwide scale, is being
broken up, owing to the fortunes of war and—on a smaller
scale—owing to the more modern views concerning marriage
and divorce. Secondly, definite and rapid cures for the sexual diseases are being discovered, and these may tend to
make people more reckless. When, however, they are perfected, they will in the long run safeguard the race and
will return bodies to the soil after death freed from the
plague which has contaminated the earth for endless ages.
There will thus be brought about a gradual purifying of the
soil. The growth of the practice of cremation will also aid
this process of purification. Destruction by fire and the intensity of the heat engendered by applied military methods
are also helping, and during the next one million years we
shall see syphilis (inherited from Lemuria) stamped out,
both in the human family and in the soil of the planet.

As the ages passed away, humanity entered into the
Atlantean stage of development. The conscious control of
the physical body dropped below the threshold of consciousness; the etheric body became consequently more potent (a

fact not oft considered), and the physical body reacted increasingly like an automaton to the impression and the direction of a steadily developing desire nature. Desire became something more than simply response to animal physical urges and to the primitive instincts, but was directed to objects and objectives extraneous to the body, towards material possessions and towards that which (when seen and coveted) could be appropriated. Just as the major sins of Lemurian times (if they could be called sins in any true sense, because of the low intelligence of the race) were through the misuse of sex, so the major sin of the Atlantean people was theft—widespread and general. The seeds of aggression and of personal acquisitiveness began to show themselves, culminating in the great war (as related in *The Secret Doctrine*) between the Lords of the Shining Countenance and the Lords of the Dark Face. To procure what they coveted and felt they needed, the most highly evolved of that race began to practice magic. It is not possible for me to outline to you the nature and practices of Atlantean magic with its control of elementals and of forms of life which have now been driven back into retreat and are inaccessible to humanity; neither can I indicate to you the particular methods used to acquire what was desired, the Words of Power employed and the carefully planned rituals which were followed by those who sought to enrich themselves and to take what they wanted, no matter what the cost to others. This magical work was the misdirected travesty of the White Magic so openly used in those days, prior to the great war between the Forces of Light and the Forces of Evil. Magic of the right kind was very familiar to the Atlantean people, and was used by those Members of the Hierarchy Who were entrusted with the guidance of the race and Who were combating rampant evil in high places. That same evil is again upon the warpath and is being fought by the men of goodwill, under the direction of the Great White Lodge. Heights of luxury were reached in Atlantis of which we, with all our boasted civilisation, know nothing and have never achieved. Some faint traces of it have come to us from legends and from ancient Egypt, from archeological discovery and old fairy tales. There was a recurrence of pure Atlantean mischief and wickedness in the decadent days of the Roman Empire. Life became tainted by the miasma of unadulterated selfishness and the very springs of life itself became polluted. Men only lived and breathed in order to be in possession of the utmost luxury and of a very plethora of things and of material goods. They were smothered by desire and plagued by the dream of never dying but of living on and on, acquiring more and more of all that they desired.

B. *Tuberculosis*.

It is in this situation that we find the origin of tuberculosis. It originated in the organs whereby men breathe and live, and was imposed—as a penalty—by the Great White Lodge; the Masters promulgated a new law for the Atlantean people when Lemurian vice and Atlantean cupidity were at their most ruthless height. This law can be translated into the following terms: "He who lives only for material goods, who sacrifices all virtue in order to gain that which cannot last, will die in life, will find breath failing him, and yet will refuse to think of death until the summons comes."

It is difficult for us in these days to appreciate or to comprehend the Atlantean state of consciousness. There was no mental process whatsoever except among the leaders of the race; there was only rampant, ruthless, insatiable desire. This action of the Great White Lodge forced two issues and confronted the race with two hitherto unrealised problems. The first was that psychological attitudes and states of consciousness can and do bring about physiological conditions, these being both good and bad. Secondly, for the first time the people faced with recognition the phenomenon of death—death which they themselves brought about in a new way and not just by physical means. This had to be dramatised for them in some definitely objective manner, for as yet the masses did not respond to verbal teaching but only to visual events. When, therefore, they saw a particularly predatory and rapacious person begin to suffer from a dire disease which seemed to arise from within himself and—whilst suffering—hold on to his love of life (as tubercular people do today), they were faced with another aspect or form of the original law (imposed in Lemurian times) which said: "The soul that sinneth, it shall die." Death had hitherto been accepted without questioning as the fate of all living things, but now, for the first time, mental relationship between individual action and death was recognised—as yet in a dim and feeble way— and a great step forward was made in the human consciousness. Instinct failed to handle this situation.

Death, brother of mine, is a great and universal heritage; all forms die, for such is the law of life, to speak in paradoxes. The time had arrived when the race could be taught the lesson that death can either be the ending of a cycle and an automatic response to the great Law of Cycles which continually institutes the new and ends the old, or it can be brought about by the misuse of the physical body, by misapplied energy and by the deliberate action of the man himself. The man who deliberately sins, and who is psychologically wrong in his attitudes and consequent actions, commits suicide just as truly as the man who deliberately blows out his brains. This is seldom realised, but the truth will become increasingly apparent.

The Biblical injunction to remember that the sins of the fathers will be visited upon the children is a literal statement anent the human heritage of disease from Lemuria and Atlantis. Syphilis and tuberculosis have been extensively prevalent in the first half of the Aryan race, in which we now find ourselves, and today they not only affect the organs of generation or the lungs (as they did in the early stages of their appearance), but now have involved the blood stream and consequently the entire organism of the human body.

Much has been done in the last fifty years to bring the great Atlantean disease of tuberculosis under control by simplicity of living, pure and ample food and good air. Much is being done to control, finally, the syphilitic diseases, and both will eventually be stamped out, not only by sound treatment and the discoveries of medical science, but because the race—as it becomes more mentally polarised—will itself deal with the problem from the angle of commonsense, will decide that the physical sins exact too heavy a penalty and that the possession of that which you have not earned or needed, and which consequently is not rightfully yours, is not worth while.

It is around these basic ideas that the world war (1914-1945) was fought. We call the unlawful possession of other people's land, territories, goods and chattels, aggression; but this is the same thing in principle as stealing, theft and rape. Today these evils are not only individual sins and faults, but can be national characteristics; the world war has brought the whole problem to the surface of the human consciousness and the ancient Atlantean struggle is being bitterly waged, with the probability that this time the Great White Lodge will triumph. That was not the case in the earlier conflict. Then the war was ended by the intervention of the planetary Logos Himself, and that ancient civilisation went down into the deeps and was engulfed in water—the symbol of purity, sanitation and universality, and therefore appropriate as an ending for what one of the Masters has called "a tubercularly oriented race." Death by drowning and death by obscure physical means which I am not at liberty to describe have both been tried in the effort to salvage humanity. Today, death by fire is the applied technique, and it promises to be successful. In contradistinction to the great Lemurian and Atlantean crises, humanity is now far more mentally alert, the causes of the trouble are recognised, motives are seen more clearly, and the will-to-good and to change past evil conditions is stronger than ever before. What is beginning to manifest now in the public consciousness is something utterly good and new.

The subjective reasons given to account for the appearance of these two most ancient racial diseases may well appear to the non-esotericist as possible but not probable and as fanciful and too general in nature. This cannot be helped. These two groups of diseases are of such exceedingly ancient origin that I have called them inherent in the planetary life itself and the heritage of all humanity, for in all, the breaking of certain laws will bring about these diseases. If I cared to do so, I could take you still further back into the realm of cosmic evil as it prevails in our solar system and affects the planetary Logos, Who is still numbered among "the imperfect Gods." The outer form of the planet through which He expresses Himself is impregnated to a certain depth with the seeds and germs of these two diseases; as immunity is built up, however, as methods of cure are developed, as preventive medicine comes into its own, and as man himself arrives at increasing mental and soul control of the animal and desire natures, these forms of human suffering will disappear, and (no matter what statistics may say) they are disappearing among the more controlled areas of the human family. As the life of God (expressing itself as individual divinity and universal divinity) pulsates more powerfully through the kingdoms of nature, these two penalties of evil-doing will inevitably no longer be required and will disappear for three reasons:

1. The orientation of humanity towards the light is steadily changing and "light dispels all evil." The light of knowledge and the recognition of causes will bring about those carefully planned conditions which will make the syphilitic diseases and tuberculosis things of the past.
2. The centres below the diaphragm will be subjected to a cleansing, lifting process; the life of the sacral centre will be controlled and the energy usually focussed there will be expended in creative living, through the medium of the throat centre; the solar plexus centre will have its energy lifted to the heart, and the trend of human selfishness will then die out.
3. Complete cures, implemented by science, will bring about a gradual fading out of contagion.

Another reason which will bring about the cessation of those practises and modes of living and desiring which account for these diseases is one little recognised as yet; it was referred to by the Christ when He spoke of the time when nothing secret would remain hidden and when all secrets would be shouted aloud from the housetops. The growth of telepathic registration and of the psychic powers such as clairvoyance and clairaudience will eventually tend to strip humanity of the privacy in which to sin. The powers whereby the Masters and the higher initiates can ascertain the psychic state and physical condition of humanity, its quality and consciousness, are already beginning to show themselves in advanced humanity. People will sin, commit evil deeds and satisfy inordinate desire, but they will be known to their fellowmen and nothing that they do will be carried out in secret. Some one or some group will be aware of the tendencies in the life of a man, and even of the incidents in which he satisfies some demand of his lower nature, and the fact of this possibility will act as a great deterrent—a far greater deterrent than you can imagine. Man is indeed his brother's keeper, and the keeping will take the form of knowledge and of "boycott and sanctions"—as it is called today in reference to the penalising of nations. I would have you ponder on these two modes of treating wrong doing. They will be practically automatically applied as a matter of good taste, right feeling and helpful intention by individuals and groups to other individuals and groups, and in this way crime and the tendency to evil doing will gradually be stamped out. It will be realised that all crime is founded upon some form of disease, or upon a glandular lack or overstimulation, based in turn upon the development or the underdevelopment of some one or other of the centres. An enlightened public opinion—informed as to man's constitution and aware of the great Law of Cause and Effect—will deal with the criminal through medical means, right environmental conditions, and the penalties of boycott and sanctions. I have no time to enlarge upon these matters, but these suggestions will give you food for thought.

C. Cancer.

We come now to a consideration of the rapidly increasing and typical Atlantean disease which we call cancer. We have spoken of one basic widespread disease related to the physical body; we have dealt superficially with another which is a product of the desire nature. Cancer, in our present cycle, the Aryan, is definitely a result of the activity of the lower concrete mind and of the stimulation of the etheric body which the mind can bring about. It is a major disease incident to stimulation, as far as the Aryan masses are concerned, just as heart disease is also a disease of stimulation, affecting very largely the advanced types of humanity who—through interest in business and leadership—often sacrifice their lives and pay the penalty of misused and over-concentrated energy by developing various forms of acute heart trouble.

Disciples and initiates are prone also to suffer from this disease, owing to the awakening into violent activity of the heart centre. In the one case, the life energy flowing through the heart is employed past all human tolerance in handling human affairs; in the other, the heart centre opens up and the strain put upon the organ of the heart is too great, and heart disease supervenes. A third cause of heart disease is due to the premature or deliberately planned lifting of the energy of the solar plexus to the heart, thus putting an unexpected strain upon it.

I am dealing naturally in broad generalisations; later evidence will go to show the types of activity which will evoke corresponding difficulty within the heart. Heart disease will increase greatly as we enter into the new root-race, particularly during the interim wherein the fact of the centres, their nature and qualities, is admitted and they consequently become the objective of trained attention. Energy follows thought, and this mental focussing upon the centres will inevitably produce overstimulation of all the centres, and this in spite of care and a carefully developed Science of the Centres. It is something which cannot be avoided, owing to the nervous and uneven unfoldment of man. Later, this stimulation will be regulated and controlled, and the heart will be subjected only to a general strain, along with all the other centres.

Cancer is a disease most definitely related to the centres, and it will be found that the centre in the area wherein the cancer exists is overactive, with a consequent increase of energy pouring through the related bodily substance. This energy and the overstimulation of a centre can be due not only to the activity of the centre and its consequent radiation, but also the suppression imposed by the mind upon any activity of a particular centre. This brings about a damming up of energy, and again we have the creation of too much concentrated energy in any particular area. One of the main sources of cancer as related to the sacral centre, and therefore to the sex organs, has been the well-intentioned suppression of the sex life, and of all thought connected with the sex life, by misguided aspirants; they are those who find the teaching—monastic and celibate—of the Middle Ages the line of least resistance. In that period of time, good people taught that sex was evil and wicked, something not to be mentioned, and a potent source of trouble. Normal reactions, instead of being controlled and transmuted into creative activity, were violently suppressed and all thoughts anent the sex life were refused expression. Nevertheless, energy follows the direction of thought, with the result that that particularly magnetic type of energy attracted an increasing number of cells and atoms to itself; therein is found the source of the tumours, growths and cancers so prevalent today. The same thing can be said about the violent inhibition imposed by an aspirant upon all emotional reactions and feelings. In their effort to control the astral body, these people resort to a process of direct inhibition and suppression. That suppression makes of the solar plexus centre a great reservoir of drastically retained energy. Transmutation of the emotions into aspiration and love and directed control is not present, and the existence of this vibrant reservoir of power brings about cancer of the stomach, of the liver, and sometimes of the entire area of the abdomen. I simply mention these causes (overactivity of a centre and the retention of energy, unexpressed and inhibited) as fruitful sources of cancer.

We come back in every case, as you can see, to the fact of the existence of the centres and their physiological effects. So much emphasis has been laid upon the qualities and characteristics which man will develop when the centres are all properly organised and directed, that the effects of the energy which they receive and distribute into the physical organism have been largely overlooked. Two factors in connection with the centres and the blood stream therefore warrant repetition and attention:

1. The blood stream is the agent of the glandular system as it, in its turn, is an effect of the centres; the blood stream carries to every part of the body those essential elements of which we know so little and which are responsible for making man psychologically what he is, and thus physically control his equipment.

2. The blood stream is also the life, and carries throughout the organism an aspect of the energy stored up by the centres which is not directly related to the endocrine system; it penetrates, by its radiation, into the blood stream and into all the veins, arteries and capillaries within the area controlled by the centre under consideration. This permeating energy of life itself, localised and qualified, can be either life-giving or death bestowing.

All diseases—except those due to accidents, wounds resulting in infections, and epidemics—can in the last analysis be traced to some condition of the centres, and therefore to energy running wild, to energy overactive and misdirected or insufficient and lacking altogether, or retained instead of used and transmuted into a higher corresponding centre of energy. The mystery of the blood still remains to be solved, and will receive increasing attention as time goes on. The anemias, so prevalent today, are also due to excess of energy.

I can only lay down general indications, state causes, and then leave to the intelligent investigators the task of studying effects, after accepting as a possible hypothesis the suggestions I have made. A proper study of the ductless glands (and later of the entire glandular structure of the body) and of the blood stream will establish them as the paramount source of physical difficulty; inevitably, though slowly and patiently, the investigators will be forced back upon the centres and will come to include in their calculations a subjective nervous system (the entire subjective system of nadis which underlie the nerves throughout the body), and will demonstrate that these factors are responsible for the major diseases and the many subsidiary diseases and obscure complaints which plague humanity. The open-minded investigator, however, who starts with an acceptance of the fact of the centres, regarding them as possibly present and eventually capable of demonstration, will make far more rapid progress; diseases will then be brought under control by a system of laya-yoga (the science of the centres) which will be the sublimated form of the laya-yoga of Atlantean days. Then the advanced student will control the centres by the power of thought. In the yoga of the future, through meditation and alignment and right practices, the centres will be brought under the direct control of the soul—a very different thing to the control of the centres by the mind and one for which the masses of men are not yet ready. To this the

Science of the Breath will be added—not breathing exercises as now taught, with often such dangerous results, but a breathing rhythm imposed by the mind through which the soul can work, and which will not require anything more than the simple rhythmic physical breath but which will re-organise the subtler bodies and bring the centres into ordered activity, according to ray and point in evolution.

I deal not with the pathology of these diseases. That has been well considered and dealt with by ordinary medicine. I seek only in this part of our discussions to emphasise the subjective causes and the objective effects. The two must be related. The activity—excessive or inadequate—of the centres is the subjective cause, but remains yet unrecognised except by esotericists. The causes (the apparent causes which are themselves the result of a true subjective cause) are initiated by the physical man himself, either in this life or an earlier one—a point which we will discuss later.

I have given you in the above much to consider, and as you ponder and think, as you study cases and types, as you watch the characteristics and qualities of those you know and which work out in some form of eventual disease, light will come.

It is only the necessity of indicating the major sources of diseases and not overlooking them, even if the subject is too esoteric for the average intelligence to grasp, that has led me to include our second point:

2. Diseases Arising From Obscure Planetary Conditions

It is obviously impossible for me to enlarge upon this subject, for it is not possible to give even a slight indication which could lead, at present, to any process of verification. What I say will have to be taken on trust and is dependent upon what I believe is recognised as my proved veracity and integrity. I shall, and can, say but little—only enough to indicate one fruitful cause of disease and one of such great age that it is inherent in the life of the planet itself. These diseases have no subjective or subtle origin; they are not the result of emotional conditions or of undesirable mental processes. They are not psychological in nature and therefore cannot be traced to any activity of the centres. They originate from within the planetary life itself and from its life aspect, having a direct emanatory effect upon the individual atoms of which the dense physical body is composed. This is a point of importance to remember. The source of any disease of this nature induced by the planet itself, is due primarily, therefore, to an external impact of certain vibratory emanations coming from the surface of the planet, engendered deep within the planet, and impinging upon the dense physical body. These radiations play upon the units of energy which, in their totality, constitute the atomic substance of the body; they are unconnected in any way with the blood stream or with the nervous system. They are consequently impossible to trace or isolate, because man is today so highly organised and integrated that these external impacts immediately evoke a response from the nervous system; the modern physician is at present unable to distinguish between the diseases arising from within the patient's own interior mechanism—tangible or intangible—and those which are in the nature of extraneous irritants, producing immediate effects upon the sensitive organism of man's body. I am not here referring to infectious or contagious difficulties.

Perhaps one point which I might helpfully emphasise is that it is this obscure planetary effect (obscure to us, at this time) upon the physical body which is the major cause of death where the purely animal form nature is concerned, or the forms of life present in the animal and vegetable kingdoms, and to a lesser and slower degree in the mineral kingdom likewise. Death, as far as the human being is concerned, is increasingly due to the *planned* intent and *planned* withdrawal of the soul, under the pressure of its own formulated intent. This is true to some degree of all who die, except those who are of so low a grade of intelligence that the soul is practically little more than an overshadowing agency. Of all who die, highly developed or not, the later stages of dissolution, effective after the conscious withdrawal of the soul (conscious on the part of the soul and becoming increasingly conscious on the part of the dying person), are taken over by this death-bestowing power of the planetary life itself.

In the case of the subhuman kingdoms in nature, death is the direct result of this obscure activity of the planet. The only idea as to its functioning which I can give you is that the soul of all non-human forms of life is an inherent aspect of the substance of which the planet is itself constructed; this soul can be withdrawn according to cycles, undetermined yet by science but fixed and certain in their working—apart from great planetary accidents or the direct action of the fourth kingdom in nature. This innate planetary power leads to the death of an animal and—in the larger sweep of evolution—to the extinction of a species; it leads also in time to the death of the forms of the vegetable kingdom and is also one of the causes which leads to the autumnal cycle in the year, producing the "sere, the yellow leaf," the loss of verdure in the grass, and those cyclic manifestations which indicate not alone death, upon a temporary and passing scale, but the complete cessation of vitality within a form. "Times of perishing" are cyclic manifestations of the "destroyer aspect" within the planet itself. These are necessarily difficult matters for you to grasp.

This radiatory activity of the planetary life, cyclic in nature and eternally present, is closely related to the influence of the first ray. It is that aspect of the Ray of Will or Power which produces the dissolution of the form, and the corruption and dissipation of the bodily vehicle until it has been again completely reabsorbed into the substance of the planet. A focussed use of the imagination will aid you in discovering how vitally constructive this agency of divinity can be. Death has been present upon our planet from the very night of time itself; forms have come and gone; death has overtaken plants and trees, animals and the forms of human beings for untold aeons, and yet our planet is not a charnel house as it well might be in the face of this fact, but is still a thing of beauty, unspoilt even by man. The processes of dying and of dissolution and the dissipation of forms goes on every moment without producing contagious contamination or the disfiguring of the surface of the earth. The results of dissolution are beneficent in effect. Ponder on this beneficent activity and on the beauty of the divine plan of death and disappearance.

With man, death takes on two aspects of activity; the human soul differs from the soul in the non-human forms in that it is itself a full and—on its own plane—an effective expression of the three divine aspects; it determines within certain limits—based on time conditions and spatial necessity —its entrance into human form and its exit therefrom. Once this exit has been made and the soul has withdrawn the thread of consciousness from the brain and its life thread from the heart, certain life processes still persist; they are now under the influence of the planetary life, however, and to these the physical elemental (the sumtotal of the living atoms of the body nature) is responsive. I would have you note the occult paradox that death is the result of living processes. Death, or the death-producing energy emanating from the planet, brings about the complete disruption of the bodily organism and its reduction to its essential elements—chemical and mineral, plus certain inorganic substances which are susceptible of absorption into the soil of the planet itself. Death, as the result of soul activity produces, therefore, the withdrawing from the body of the "light body and of the subtle bodies," leaving the dense form and its component parts to the benign processes of planetary control. This dual activity produces death—as we know it from the human angle.

It is necessary here to point out that this ability of the planetary Logos to extract the life essence innate in each atom, produces what might be called deterioration in the structure of the form at any point from whence this life essence is emitted. This brings about conditions which eventually become apparent visually; thus disease and the "tendency to die" become recognisable. Therefore, the withering of a flower, death from old age in an animal or a tree, and the many diseases of the human being are all brought about by the pull of the powerful life of the planet, speaking esoterically; this is an aspect of what is called, erroneously, the Law of Gravitation. This law is—again speaking esoterically—an aspect of the Law of Return, which governs the relation of a unit of life in form to its emanating source. "Dust thou art; unto dust thou shalt return" is a statement of occult law. In the curious evolution of words—as any good dictionary will show—the word "dust" comes from two roots, one meaning "wind" and the other "falling to pieces." The significance of both these meanings will be apparent and the sequence of ideas is arresting. With the withdrawing of the wind or breath, a falling to pieces eventuates, and this is a true and significant statement. As the greater life absorbs the lesser life, the disappearance of that which the life has informed takes place; this is true of all forms in the subhuman kingdoms as they respond to the drag or pull of the planetary life; it is true also of the human form as it reacts to the call of the soul to return its life principle to the soul, via the sutratma, and to return as consciousness to its registering source.

In this process and interaction, the form shows the results of being either the receiver of the tide of life from the planet or as the releaser of that life, under cyclic law, to its general reservoir of living energy. Upon these two reactions depends the health or the disease of the form in various stages and states of response and under the action of other contributing and conditioning factors. There are three major stages in the life cycle of all subhuman forms, and in the human form likewise when the soul is simply an overshadowing force and not an integrated energy:

1. The *stage of inflowing,* of vitalisation and of growth.
2. The *stage of resistance,* wherein the form preserves its own integrity for a temporary cycle, determined by its species and environment, thus resisting successfully any "pull" of the all-enveloping life and any reabsorption of its vitality.
3. The *stage of emission,* wherein the pull of the greater life of the planet draws out and absorbs the weakening lesser life. This weakening process is a part of a cyclic law, as the old adage "the days of a man are three score years and ten" hints. When the average of a general cyclic period is normally run, a point of weakening in the bodily tissue will surely and gradually arise. Disease or deterioration of some part of the form usually eventuates and death supervenes. The length of the cycles and their determining cause are a deep mystery and are specifically related to the various kingdoms in nature, and to the species and types and forms within those

aggregates of living processes. These cycles are known as yet only to the Masters and to those initiates to whom is given the task of promoting the evolutionary process within the subhuman kingdoms, and to the devas whose task it is to control the process.

As you well know, the great distinction between the human kingdom in the three worlds and the other kingdoms in nature is the factor of freewill. In the matter of death, this freewill has, in the last analysis, a definite relation to the soul; the will of the soul is either consciously or unconsciously followed, where the decision of death is concerned, and this idea carries with it many implications which students would do well to ponder.

We have arrived now at another major generalisation as to disease and death in relation to humanity:

LAW VIII

Disease and death are the result of two active forces. One is the will of the soul which says to its instrument: I draw the essence back. The other is the magnetic power of the planetary Life which says to the life within the atomic structure: The hour of reabsorption has arrived. Return to me. Thus, under cyclic law, do all forms act.

The reference here is to the normal dissolution of the form at the close of a cycle of reincarnation. As we well know, this cycle is determined in the case of man by major psychological factors which can hasten or prolong the "hour of the end," but only up to a certain point. The dictum of the soul and the fiat of the planetary Life are the final determining factors, except in the cases of war, accident, suicide or epidemics.

The power of absorption with which the planet is endowed is very great within certain limitations; it is these limitations, for instance, which promote epidemics as the aftermath of war. Such epidemics have a serious effect upon the human race after the war cycle is over and after the consequent epidemic has spent itself. Humanity, particularly in Eastern Europe, had not completely recovered from the epidemics, incident to the first part of the world war, when the second part took place. The psychological effects continue; the scars and the results of the second phase of that world war will persist for fifty years, even though—owing to man's greater scientific knowledge—the epidemic factor may be kept surprisingly within bounds. This, however, still remains uncertain. Time alone will demonstrate how successful humanity is in offsetting the penalties which outraged nature is apt to exact.

Much good will be brought about through the growing custom to cremate those forms which the indwelling life has vacated; when it is an universal custom, we shall see a definite minimising of disease, leading to longevity and increased vitality. The factor of resistance or the process whereby a form renders itself immune or non-responsive to the planetary pull and urge towards reabsorption requires the expenditure of much energy. When the life increases in potency within the form and there is less reaction to disease-conveying factors, the soul within the form will have fuller sway and greater beauty of expression and usefulness in service. This will be true some day of all the kingdoms in nature, and thus we shall have a steady radiance shining forth in the mounting glory of the Life of God.

3. Racial and National Diseases

It must be apparent to you by now that I am principally concerned with indicating factors which are the result of the past history of the race rather than with giving you a specific and detailed account of the diseases which are allied to the various nations. This, in fact, it would not be possible to do, owing to the overlapping and paralleling which goes on in every department of natural life. Above everything else, I seek to make clear what must be done along the line of preventive healing and what should be accomplished in the difficult task of offsetting conditions already prevalent on earth as the result of *past misuse of the natural powers*. There must therefore be brought about a healing of those conditions which are present upon our planet on a large scale, and consequently my emphasis will not be upon the specific and the individual. I am laying a foundation also for a discussion of our next theme—the relation of the Law of Karma to disease and death and to humanity as a whole.

In the consideration of racial and national diseases, I do not intend to point out that tuberculosis is distinctively a disease of the middle classes in every country, that diabetes is a major trouble among the rice-eating peoples of the world, and that cancer is rampant in Great Britain, whilst heart disease is a prime cause of death in the United States. Such generalisations are both as true and as false as statistics usually are, and nothing is gained by labouring these points. These difficulties will all be offset in due time through the growth of understanding, by the intuitive diagnosis of disease, and by the magnificent work of scientific and academic medicine, plus a truer comprehension of right living conditions.

I prefer rather to give still wider generalisations which will indicate causes and will not emphasise the consequences of these causes. I seek, therefore, to point out that:

1. *The soil of the planet* itself is a major cause of disease and of contamination. For untold aeons, the bodies of men and of animals have been laid away in the ground; that soil is consequently impregnated with the germs and

the results of disease and this in a far subtler form than is surmised. The germs of ancient known and unknown diseases are to be found in the layers of the soil and the subsoil; these can still produce virulent trouble if presented with proper conditions. Let me state that Nature never intended that bodies would be buried in the ground. The animals die and their bodies return to the dust, but return purified by the rays of the sun and by the breezes which blow and disperse. The sun can cause death as well as life, and the most virulent germs and bacteria cannot retain their potency if submitted to *the dry heat* of the sun's rays. Moisture and darkness foster disease as it emanates from and is nourished by bodies from whence the life aspect has been drawn. When, in all countries throughout the world, the rule is to submit dead forms to the "ordeal by fire," and when this has become a universal and persistent habit, we shall then see a great diminution of disease and a much healthier world.

2. *The psychological condition* of a race or of a nation, as we have seen, produces a tendency to disease and to a lowered resistance to the causes of disease; it can engender an ability to absorb evil contamination with facility. On this I need not further enlarge.

3. *Living conditions* in many lands also foster disease and ill health. Dark and crowded tenements, underground homes, undernourishment, wrong food, evil habits of life and various occupational diseases—all contribute their quota to the general ill health of humanity. These conditions are universally recognised and much has been done to offset them, but much remains to be done. One of the good effects of the world war will be to force the needed changes, the required rebuilding, and the scientific nourishment of the youth of the race. National physical

ills vary according to the predisposing occupations of the people; the diseases of an agricultural race will differ widely from those of a highly industrialised race; the physical predispositions of a sailor vary greatly from those of an office worker in one of our large cities. These items of information are again but the platitudes of the social worker in the many cities and lands. Certain diseases appear to be purely local; others seem universal in their effects; certain diseases are gradually dying out, and new diseases are appearing; certain forms of disease are forever with us; others seem to be cyclic in their appearance; some diseases are endemic whilst others are epidemic.

How can this vast array of disease and forms of bodily ills come to be? How is it that some races are prone to succumb to one form of physical ill whilst other races are resistant to it? Climatic conditions produce certain typical diseases which remain strictly local and are not found elsewhere in the world. Cancer, tuberculosis, syphilis, spinal meningitis, pneumonia and heart disease, as well as scrofula (using that term in its old sense to indicate certain forms of skin disease), are rampant throughout the world, taking their toll of millions; even though these diseases can be traced to certain great racial periods, they are now general in their effect. The clue to this can be found if students will remember that though the Atlantean racial period lies thousands of years away, a great majority of people today are basically Atlantean in their consciousness, and are therefore prone to the diseases of that civilisation.

If a full review of the health of the world were to be undertaken and presented to the thinking public—taken in normal conditions and not in war time—the question arises whether there are one hundred thousand perfectly healthy people to be found out of the billions now inhabiting the earth? I think not. If no actual and active disease is present, nevertheless the condition of the teeth, the hearing and the sight leave frequently much to be desired; inherited tendencies and active predispositions cause grave concern, and to all this must be added psychological difficulty, mental diseases and definite brain trouble. All this presents an appalling picture. Against the ills which it discloses, medicine is today battling; scientists are searching for alleviations and cures and for sound and lasting methods of eradication; research students are investigating the latent germs, and health experts are seeking new ways to meet the onslaught of disease. Sanitation, compulsory inoculation, frequent inspection, pure food laws, legal requirements and better housing conditions are all brought into this battle by the far-seeing humanitarian. Yet still disease is rampant; more hospitals are required and the death rate soars.

To these practical agencies, Mental Science, New Thought, Unity and Christian Science offer their aid, and seek quite honestly to bring the power of the mind to bear upon the problem. At the present stage, these agencies and groups largely are in the hands of fanatics and devoted, unintelligent people; they refuse all compromise and seem unable to recognise that the knowledge accumulated by medicine and by those who work scientifically with the human body is as God-given as their, as yet, unproved ideal. Later, the truths for which these groups stand will be added to the work of the psychologist and the physician; when this has been done, we shall see a great improvement. When the work of the doctor and the surgeon in relation to the physical body is recognised as essential and good, when the analysis and conclusions of the psychologist supplement their work, and when the power of right thought comes likewise as an aid, then and only then, shall we enter upon a new era of well-being.

To the various categories of trouble must also be added a whole group of diseases which are more strictly mental in their effect—the cleavages, the insanities, the obsessions, the mental breaks, the aberrations and the hallucinations. To the various healing agencies mentioned above should be added the work undertaken by Members of the spiritual Hierarchy and Their disciples; it takes soul power and knowledge, plus the wisdom of the other healing groups, to produce health among people, to empty our sanatariums, to rid humanity of the basic diseases, of lunacy and obsession, and to prevent crime. This is finally brought about by the right integration of the whole man, through a right comprehension of the nature of energy, and through a correct appreciation of the endocrine system, its glands and their subtle relationships.

At present there is little coherent and integrated work done *in unison* by the four groups:

1. Physicians and surgeons—orthodox and academic.
2. Psychologists, neurologists and psychiatrists.
3. Mental healers and New Thought workers, plus Unity thinkers and Christian Scientists.
4. Trained disciples and those who work with the souls of men.

When these four groups can be brought into close relation, and can work together for the release of humanity from disease, we shall then arrive at an understanding of the true wonder of the human being. We shall some day have hospitals in which the four phases of this one medical and remedial work will proceed side by side and in the fullest cooperation. Neither group can do a complete task without the others; all are interdependent.

It is the inability of these groups to recognise the good in the other groups striving for the physical well-being of humanity which makes it almost impossible for me to do more specific teaching and more direct talking on these matters. Have you any idea of the wall of antagonistic thinking and speech against which a new or pioneering idea has to batter itself? Have you ever seriously considered the aggregated and crystallised thoughtforms with which all such new ideas (and shall I call them hierarchical proposals) have to contend? Do you appreciate the dead weight of preconceived and ancient determinations which have to be moved before the Hierarchy can cause a new and needed concept to penetrate into the consciousness of the average thinking (or again should I say, unthinking?) public. The field of medicine is a most difficult field in which to work, for the subject is so intimate, and fear enters so strongly into the reactions of those who must be reached. The gulf between the old and established and the new and the spiritually demanded, needs much long and careful bridging. A great deal of the difficulty is, curiously enough, to be found fostered by the newer schools of thought. Orthodox medicine is slow, and rightly slow, in adopting new techniques and methods; it is at times too slow, but the case of the new mode of treatment or diagnosis must be rightly proven and statistically proven before it can be incorporated in the medical curriculum and method; the risks to the human subject are too great, and the good humanitarian physician will not make his patient the subject of experimentation. However, within the last few decades, medicine has advanced by leaps and bounds, the science of electricity and light therapy and many other modern techniques and methods have already been added to the various other sciences of which medicine avails itself. The demands of the intangible and the treatment of the nebulous—if such peculiar terms are in order—are being recognised increasingly and are known to play an orthodox and recognised part in the newer approaches to disease.

The approach of the mental schools and cults, as they erroneously call themselves, has not proceeded so helpfully. This is largely their fault. Schools of thought such as Mental Science, New Thought, Unity, Christian Science, Chiropractic enterprise, the efforts of the Naturopaths and many others, hurt their cause, owing to the large claims which they make and to their unceasing attacks upon orthodox medicine and other channels of proven helpfulness and upon the knowledge (acquired over centuries of experimentation) of the academic schools of medicine and surgery. They forget that many of their claims to success (and they are often irrefutable) can be classed under the general heading of faith cures, and this can be done correctly or incorrectly. Such cures have long been recognised by the academic thinker and known to be factual. These cults which are in fact the custodians of needed truths, need above everything else to change their approach and to learn the spiritual nature of compromise in these days of evolutionary unfoldment. Their ideas cannot come into full and desired usefulness apart from the already God-given knowledge which medicine down the ages has accumulated; they need also to keep a record of their numerous failures, as well as the successes which they loudly proclaim. I would here point out that these successes are in no way so numerous as those of orthodox medicine and of the beneficent work done by the clinics of our hospitals which—in spite of failures and often gross stupidity—greatly ameliorate the pains and ills of the masses of men. These cults omit to state, or even to recognise, that in cases of extreme illness or accident, the patient is physically unable to affirm or claim divine healing and is dependent upon the work of some healer who works with no knowledge of the karma of the patient. Many of their so-called cures (and this is the case also with orthodox medicine) are cures because the hour of the end has not yet arrived for the patient and he would have recovered in any case, though he often does so more rapidly, owing to the remedial measures of the trained physician.

In cases of serious accident, where the injured person will bleed, the cultist (no matter what his cult may be called) will perforce avail himself of the methods of the orthodox physician; he will apply a tourniquet, for instance, and take the measures which orthodox medicine enjoins, rather than stand by and see the injured person die because these methods are not used. When he is face to face with death, he will frequently turn to the tried and proved methods of help and will usually call in a physician rather than be charged with murder.

All the above is said in no spirit of disparagement, but in an effort to prove that the many schools of thought—orthodox, academic, ancient, material or spiritual, new, pioneering or mental—are interdependent; they need to be brought together into one great healing science. This will be a science which will heal the whole man and bring into play all the resources—physical, emotional, mental and spiritual—of which humanity is capable. Orthodox medicine is more open to cooperation with the newer cults than are the neophytes of the science of mental control of disease; they cannot, however, permit their patients to be turned into guinea pigs (is not that the term used in these cases, brother of mine?) for the satisfaction of the pioneering cultist and the proving of his theories—no matter how correct when applied in conjunction with what has already been proved. The middle way of compromise and of mutual cooperation is ever the wisest, and this is a lesson much needed today in every department of human thinking.

We shall now proceed to deal with our third and final section of thoughts around the basic causes of disease. The theme of *karma* has been little considered and I shall deal with it in a way larger than our particular subject perhaps warrants.

CHAPTER III

Our Karmic Liabilities

INTRODUCTORY REMARKS

WE HAVE REACHED NOW the concluding phase of our approach to the problem of disease. In our next part we shall deal with the attitudes and temperaments of the patient, taking into consideration his ray and also the state of mind of the healer; all these points are of prime importance when one comes to the consideration of the fine art of healing. It is, however, essential that ill health, acute disease, and death itself should find their place in the overall picture. A particular incarnation is not an isolated event in the life of the soul, but is a part and an aspect of a sequence of experiences which are intended to lead to one, clear, definite goal— the goal of free choice and a deliberate return out of matter to spirit and eventual liberation.

There has been much talk among esotericists (particularly in the Eastern presentation of the Path to Reality) anent liberation. The goal held before the neophyte is liberation, freedom, emancipation; this, by and large, is the keynote of life itself. The concept is a transitting out of the realm of the purely selfish and of personal liberation into something much wider and more important. This concept of liberation lies behind the modern use of the word "liberty" but is far wiser, better and deeper in its connotation. Liberty, in the minds of many, is freedom from the imposition of any man's rule, freedom to do as one wishes, to think as one determines and to live as one chooses. This is as it should be, provided that one's wishes, choices, thoughts and desires are free from selfishness and are dedicated to the good of the whole. This is, as yet, very seldom so.

Liberation is much more than all this; it is freedom from the past, freedom to move forward along certain predetermined lines (predetermined by the soul), freedom to express all the divinity of which one is capable as an individual, or which a nation can present to the world.

There have been in the history of the past two thousand years, four great symbolic happenings which have sequentially presented (to those who have eyes to see, ears to hear and minds to interpret) the theme of liberation—and not simply of liberty.

1. *The life of Christ Himself.* He, for the first time, presented the idea of the sacrifice of the unit, consciously and deliberately offered for the service of the whole. There had been other World Saviours, but the issues involved had not so clearly been expressed, because the mind of man had not been ready to grasp the implications. Service is the keynote of liberation. Christ was the ideal Server.

2. *The signing of the Magna Charta.* This document was signed at Runnymede, during the reign of King John on June 15th, 1215, A.D. Here the idea of liberation from authority was presented with the emphasis upon the personal liberty and rights of the individual. The growth and development of this basic idea, mental concept and formulated perception falls into four phases or chapters:

    a. The signing of the Magna Charta, emphasising personal liberty.

b. The founding of the French Republic with its emphasis upon human liberty.

c. The Declaration of Independence and the Bill of Rights, determining national policy.

d. The Atlantic Charter and the Four Freedoms, bringing the whole question into the international field, and guaranteeing to men and women everywhere in the world liberty and freedom to develop the divine reality within themselves.

The ideal has gradually become clarified so that today the mass of men everywhere know what are the basic essentials of happiness.

3. *The Emancipation of the Slaves.* The spiritual idea of human liberty, which had become a recognised ideal, became a demanding desire, and a great symbolic happening took place—the slaves were freed. Like all things which human beings enact, perfection is nonexistent. The Negro is not free in this land of the free, and America will have to clean house in this respect; to put it in clear concise words, the U.S.A. must see to it that the Constitution and the Bill of Rights are facts and not a dream. Only thus can the inevitable working of the Law of Karma (which is our theme today) be offset. The Negroes are Americans, as well as the New Englanders and all other stocks which are not indigenous in this country, and the Constitution is theirs also. As yet the privileges it confers are withheld by those who are the slaves of selfishness and fear.

4. *The Liberation of Humanity by the United Nations.* We are participating in a great spectacular and symbolic happening and are watching it in process. The liberation of the individual has moved onward through the symbolic liberation of a section of humanity (the rem-

nants of the first two races, the Lemurian and the Atlantean) to the liberation of millions of human beings, enslaved by the forces of evil, by millions of their fellow men. The ideal has worked through into a practical worldwide effort upon the physical plane and has demanded worldwide sacrifice. It has involved the entire three worlds of human evolution, and for this reason the Christ can now lead His forces and aid human beings to liberate mankind.

What has really been happening, therefore, in the lives of individuals, in the lives of nations and in the life of humanity? A tremendous move to put right most ancient evil, to offset consciously the Law of Cause and Effect by a recognition of the causes in the personal, national and international worlds which have produced the effects under which humanity today suffers.

The Law of Karma is today a great and incontrovertible fact in the consciousness of humanity everywhere. They may not call it by that name, but they are well aware that in all today's events the nations are reaping what they sowed. This great law—at one time a theory—is now a proven fact and a recognised factor in human thinking. The question "Why?" so frequently asked brings in the factor of cause and effect with constant inevitability. The concepts of heredity and of environment are efforts to explain existing human conditions; qualities, racial characteristics, national temperaments and ideals prove the fact of some initiating world of causes. Historical conditions, the relationships between nations, social taboos, religious convictions and tendencies can all be traced to originating causes— some of them most ancient. Everything that is happening in the world today and which is so potently affecting humanity—things of beauty and of horror, modes of living and civilisation and culture, prejudices and likings, scientific attainment and artistic expression and the many ways in which humanity throughout the planet colours existence—are aspects of effects, initiated somewhere, on some level at some time, by human beings, both individually and en masse.

Karma is therefore that which Man—the Heavenly Man in whom we live, humanity as a whole, mankind in groups as nations, and individual man—has instituted, carried forward, endorsed, omitted to do or has done right through the ages until the present moment. Today, the harvest is ripe and mankind is reaping what it has sown, preparatory to a fresh ploughing in the springtime of the New Age, with a fresh sowing of the seed which will (let us pray and hope) produce a better harvest.

The outstanding evidence of the Law of Cause and Effect is the Jewish race. *All nations prove this Law,* but I choose to refer to the Hebrew peoples because their history is so well known and their future and their destiny are subjects of worldwide, universal concern. The Jews have always had a symbolic significance; they sum up in themselves—as a nation, down the ages—the depths of human evil and the heights of human divinity. Their aggressive history as narrated in the Old Testament is on a par with present-day German accomplishment; yet Christ was a Jew and it was the Hebrew race which produced Him. Let this never be forgotten. The Jews were great aggressors; they despoiled the Egyptians and they took the Promised Land at the point of the sword, sparing neither man, woman nor child. Their religious history has been built around a materialistic Jehovah, possessive, greedy and endorsing and encouraging aggression. Their history is symbolic of the history of all aggressors, rationalising themselves into the belief that they are carrying out divine purpose, wresting away from people their property in a spirit of self-defense and finding some reason, adequate to them, to excuse the iniquity of their action. Palestine was taken by the Jews because it was "a land flowing with milk and honey,'" and the claim was made that the act was undertaken in obedience to divine command. Later, the symbolism gets most interesting. They divided into two halves: the Israelites with headquarters at Samaria, and the Jews (meaning two or three special tribes out of the twelve) locating around Jerusalem. Dualism ran through their religious beliefs; they were schooled by the Sadducees or the Pharisees, and these two groups were in constant conflict. Christ came as a member of the Jewish race and they renounced Him.

Today the law is working, and the Jews are paying the price, factually and symbolically, for all they have done in the past. They are demonstrating the far-reaching effects of the Law. Factually and symbolically, they stand for culture and civilisation; factually and symbolically, they *are* humanity; factually and symbolically, they stand as they have ever chosen to stand, for separation. They regard themselves as the chosen people and have an innate consciousness of that high destiny, forgetting their symbolic role and that it is Humanity which is the chosen people and not one small and unimportant fraction of the race. Factually and symbolically, they long for unity and cooperation, yet know not how to cooperate; factually and symbolically, they are the "Eternal Pilgrim"; they are mankind, wandering through the mazes of the three worlds of human evolution, and gazing with longing eyes towards a promised land; factually and symbolically, they resemble the mass of men, refusing to comprehend the underlying spiritual purpose of all material phenomena, rejecting the Christ within (as they did centuries ago the Christ within their borders), grasping for material good and steadily rejecting the things of the spirit. They demand the so-called restitution of Palestine, wresting it away from those who have inhabited it for many centuries; and by their continued emphasis upon material possession they lose sight of the true solution, which is that, symbolically and factually again, they must be assimilated into all the nations, and fused with all the races, thus demonstrating recognition of the One Humanity.

It is interesting to note that the Jews who inhabited southern Palestine, and whose chief city was Jerusalem, have succeeded in doing this and have fused with and been assimilated by the British, the Dutch and the French in a way that the Israelites, ruled from Samaria, have never done. I commend this to you for your consideration.

If the Jewish race would recall, therefore, their high symbolic destiny, and if the rest of humanity would see themselves in the Jewish people, and if both groups would emphasise the fact of human stock and cease thinking of themselves in terms of national and racial units, the karma of humanity would radically change from the retributive karma of the present to the recompensing good karma of the future.

Regarding this question from the long range vision (looking backward historically as well as forward hopefully), the problem is one to which the Jews themselves must make the larger contribution. They have never yet faced candidly and honestly (as a race) the problem of *why* the many nations, from the time of the Egyptians, have neither liked nor wanted them. It has always been the same down the centuries. Yet there must be some reason, inherent in the people themselves, when the reaction is so general and universal. Their approach to their direful problem has been one of supplication, or of distressed complaint, or of unhappy despair. Their demand has been for the Gentile nations to put the matter right, and many Gentiles have attempted to do so. Until, however, the Jews themselves face up to the situation and admit that there may be for them the working out of the retributive aspect of the Law of Cause and Effect, and until they endeavour to ascertain what it is in them, as a race, which has initiated their ancient and dire fate, this basic world issue will remain as it has been since the very night of time. That within the race there are and have been great, good, just and spiritual men is unalterably true. A generalisation is never a complete expression of the truth. But, viewing the problem of the Jews in time and space, in history and today, the points which I have made will bear careful consideration by the Jews.

What I have said in no way mitigates the guilt of those who have so sorely abused the Jews. You have a proverb, have you not? that "two blacks do not make a white." The behaviour of the nations towards the Jews, culminating in the atrocities of the second quarter of the twentieth century, have no excuse. The law must inevitably work. Though much that has happened to the Jews originated in their past history and in their pronounced attitude of separativeness and nonassimilability, and in their emphasis upon material good, yet the agents who have brought the evil karma upon them equally incur the retributive aspect of the same law; the situation has now assumed the form of a vicious circle of error and wrong doing, of retribution and revenge, and in view of this the time must come when together the nations will confer upon this problem, and together they will cooperate to bring to an end the wrong attitudes *on both sides*. All karma of evil nature is solved by the presentation of an accepting will, a cooperative love, a frank acknowledgment of responsibility and a skillful adjustment of united joint activity to bring about the good of humanity as a whole, and not just the good of an individual nation or people or race. The Jewish problem will not be solved by taking possession of Palestine, by plaint and demand and by financial manipulations. That would be but the prolongation of ancient wrong and material possessiveness. The problem will be solved by the willingness of the Jew to conform to the civilisation, the cultural background and the standards of living of the nation to which—by the fact of birth and education—he is related and with which he should assimilate. It will come by the relinquishment of pride of race and of the concept of selectivity; it will come by renouncing dogmas and customs which are intrinsically obsolete and which create points of constant irritation to the matrix within which the Jew finds himself; it will come when selfishness in business relations and the pronounced manipulative tendencies of the Hebrew people are exchanged for more selfless and honest forms of activity.

The Jew, owing to his rays and point of development, is outstandingly creative and artistic. This he must recognise and not seek as he now does to dominate in all fields, to grasp all opportunities away from other people, and so better himself and his own people at the expense of others. Release from the present situation will come when the Jew forgets that he is a Jew and becomes in his inmost consciousness an Italian, an American, a Britisher, a German or a Pole. This is not so at this time. The Jewish problem will be solved by intermarriage; that of the Negro will not. This will mean concession and compromise on the part of the orthodox Jews—not the concession of expediency but the concession of conviction.

Let me point out also that just as the Kabbalah and the Talmud are secondary lines of esoteric approach to truth, and materialistic in their technique (embodying much of the magical work of relating one grade of matter to the substance of another grade), so the Old Testament is emphatically a secondary Scripture, and spiritually does not rank with the Bhagavad-Gita, the ancient Scriptures of the East and the New Testament. Its emphasis is material and its effect is to impress a purely materialistic Jehovah upon world consciousness. The general theme of the Old Testament is the recovery of the highest expression of the divine wisdom *in the first solar system;* that system embodied the creative work of the third aspect of divinity—that of active intelligence, expressing itself through matter. *In this solar system,* the created world is intended to be the expression of the second aspect, of the love of God. This the Jew has never grasped, for the love expressed in the Old Testament is the separative, possessive love of Jehovah for a distinct unit within the fourth or human kingdom. St. Paul summed up the attitude which humanity should assume in the words: "There is neither Jew nor Gentile." The evil karma of the Jew today is intended to end his isolation, to bring him to the point of relinquishing material goals, of renouncing a nationality that has a tendency to be somewhat parasitic within the boundaries of other nations, and to express inclusive love, instead of separative unhappiness.

And what of the Gentile attitude? It is absolutely necessary that the nations meet the Jew more than half way when he arrives at altering—slowly and gradually—his nationalistic orthodoxy. It is essential that they cease from fear and persecution, from hatred and from placing barriers to cooperation. The growing anti-Semitic feeling in the world is inexcusable in the sight of God and man. I refer not here to the abominable cruelties of the obsessed German people. Behind that lies a history of Atlantean relationships into which it is needless for me to enter because I could not prove to you the truth of my statements. I refer to the history of the past two thousand years and to the everyday behaviour of Gentile people everywhere. There must be a definite effort upon the part of the nationals of every country to assimilate the Jews, to inter-marry with them, and to refuse to recognise as barriers old habits of thought and ancient bad relations. Men everywhere must regard it as a blot upon their national integrity if there is the appearance within their borders of the old duality— Jew and Gentile. *There is neither Jew nor Gentile; there is only Humanity.* This war (1914-1945) should be regarded as having brought to a conclusion the ancient enmity between Jew and Gentile, and the two groups have now the opportunity to originate a newer and happier measure of living and a truly cooperative relation on either side. The process of assimilation will be slow, for the situation is of so ancient a date that habits of thought, customary attitudes and separative customs are well established and hard to overcome. But the needed changes can be made if goodwill directs the spoken word, the written presentation and the mode of living together. The Hierarchy sees no distinction. The Head of the Hierarchy, though not in a Jewish body at this time, achieved the highest spiritual goal for humanity whilst in a Jewish vehicle. The Hierarchy is also sending into Jewish bodies certain disciples who will work with full intent at the changing of the situation. There are Jews today, a few in number, who do not think in terms of being Jews; who are not preoccupied with the Jewish problem to the exclusion of all else, and who are endeavouring to fuse all people into one humanity, thus bridging the gap.

Again, I say, that the Masters of the Wisdom see neither Jew nor Gentile, but only souls and sons of God.

In dealing with the subject of karma as a factor—decisive and lasting in both disease and health—one of the criticisms to which my approach is subjected is that I deal too much with generalities and that I give no specific and detailed analysis of particular diseases, particularly of the great basic diseases which today take such a toll of humanity and which are not fundamentally being curbed. I do not deal with their symptoms or their cure, and I indicate not techniques whereby they may be handled. This I feel is a criticism with which I should deal, so that you may proceed with your study under no misapprehension. This is an appropriate point at which to stop and meet this contention. Karma is necessarily a topic which is general and not specific; it is not yet accepted in the occult sense by the general public. It must be considered along broad lines until such time that the Law of Cause and Effect is accepted as a major conditioning factor in the human consciousness, not only on a large scale but in relation to individual lives. Of this Law, the public is yet, as a whole, ignorant.

It will be obvious to you that it is entirely needless for me to deal with the symptomatic aspect of diseases and with the facts that have been so ably ascertained by orthodox medical science. We have been for some time considering the causes of such diseases, and I propose to deal with occult methods of producing cures—where such cures are permissible under the Law of Karma and where the healer is willing to work in an occult manner. I have attempted to make clear to you that the fundamental cause is related to energy, to its presence in excess as it pours through the centres, or to its deficiency. Here lie the two main factors in the production of disease. It is essential that those of you who are interested in the study of disease and its healing should admit this and permit it to form the basis of your approach. I have indicated that medicine and medical treatments of the future will start with this fact as their prime determination. The factual nature of medical discovery is not disowned by me. I seek to carry the matter forward from that point, and it is no part of my programme to ignore the wise discoveries of modern medical science, nor am I on the side of those groups of people who run down and refuse to admit the findings of modern medicine. This I have earlier emphasised. I want to indicate the trend of future medical research, which will be to seek for the seat of the trouble in the realm of vitality (as it may be called by orthodox investigators), and which we would regard as in the realm of the etheric body. Let me here make a practical statement which might be regarded as the next Rule in this treatise:

RULE SIX

A careful diagnosis of the disease, based on the ascertained outer symptoms, will be simplified to this extent that, once the organ involved is known and thus isolated, the centre in the etheric body which is in closest relation to it will be subjected to methods of occult healing, though the ordinary, ameliorative, medical or surgical methods will not be withheld.

It is here that the fanatical cultist or healer of today so often goes astray. The old approach to medicine, with its physical investigation and its successful or unsuccessful diagnosis, will still be required until such time that physicians and surgeons have clairvoyant faculty, intuitive perception and spiritual insight, and also until they have worked out a technique for handling energy in relation to the patient. To this will some day be added correct astrological interpretation, immediate recognition of ray types, and then the application of the right healing techniques, as required by the ray which conditions the patient's life expression, plus his point in evolution.

I am handicapped greatly as a I seek to lay the foundation for this new approach to medicine. I am handicapped by the idealistic pronouncements of the pioneers in the new fields of nature healing, by the naturopaths, and by the premises of Christian Science and the Unity Schools. All that I can do (if you are to profit by my presentation) is to lay down certain broad and general assumptions which will govern the medical men of the future. But in the interim period between the old and the new eras, men will wander in a fog of speculation; a great conflict will be engineered between the fundamentalist schools and the speculators and the investigators of the new ideas, and temporarily the "noble middle path" of the Buddha will be forgotten.

There is present today, in the science of medicine, a situation paralleling that to be found in the realm of religion. The old approach suffices for the masses and is frequently successful both in its ameliorative and preventive aspects, and in its process of diagnosis. This is all that is possible at this time. In the same manner, the old religious presentation suffices to guide the unthinking masses along certain broad lines of controlled living, and to keep clearly in the consciousness of the average man certain uncontrovertible, spiritual facts. Both in the guidance and protection of the masses in their spiritual natures and in the guidance and protection of their physical vehicles, doctors and priests can be divided into various groups—some adhering to old proved techniques, some so fundamentalist in position that they refuse to investigate that which is new and unproven, and some so idealistic, speculative and fanatical that they rush ahead and enter into a world of speculative experiment which may or may not give them the key to the medicine of the future but which certainly puts their patients into the category of what you call "guinea pigs."

The surest and least speculative field in medical practice is that which is concerned with the *surgical relief* of the patient; it is founded on a sure knowledge of anatomy, its diagnosis of requirements can be intelligently controlled, and its practice (when in the hands of a sound and reputable surgeon) can and frequently does produce a cure or a real prolongation of life. However, even in that field little is known about the results of an operation as it may affect the etheric body and (consequently) the nervous system through the intermediate system of the "nadis" or the etheric counterpart of the nerves. I would instance the removal of some organ. Definite results must necessarily be present and a period of difficult adjustment must inevitably take place within the subtle mechanism of the patient. The area of the body which has received surgical treatment, and particularly the centre in closest relation to it, *must* be affected, for the circulatory flow of energy, emanating from the centre, will find itself "short circuited," if I could use such a phrase. This flow, which has hitherto passed through the area of surgical attention, must work its way to all parts of the body, via the "nadis"; these, as you know, underlie and feed the needed energy to the nervous system. Old channels for the flow of energy will have been removed, as the result of operative measures, major or minor. New channels or lines of force, bridging the "mutilated" area, will have to be established and a basic adjustment will have to be made within the vital mechanism of the patient. Along this line there is practically nothing as yet known. It is not even yet in the field of advanced research.

The new medicine cannot be scientifically formulated or intelligently presented until such time as the *fact* of the etheric body is accepted and *its existence, as a mechanism of energy supply and as the vital aspect of the outer form, is generally recognised.* The shift of the attention of the medical profession will then be away from the outer, tangible, physical effects and to the inner causes, as they are to be found in the centres and their related fields of activity.

Within the areas where a disease is manifested, certain esoteric facts anent the general subject have already been posited by me:

1. That disease, in its immediate cause, can be traced to the individual etheric body when the difficulty is purely local, or to the planetary etheric body (in particular the etheric body of the fourth kingdom in nature) where epidemics are involved, or to such a condition as war, affecting large masses of men.

2. That the etheric body has not hitherto been considered as an existent fact, from the angle of orthodox medicine, though there is a modern drift towards emphasis upon *vitality,* upon the vital qualities in food, and the giving of vitamin products in order to build up a vital response. This is the first indication of an unrealised need to increase the potency of the vital body.

3. That the condition of the etheric body predisposes the subject to disease or protects it from disease, making man resistant to the impact of deteriorating or epidemic factors, or failing to do so because of inherent etheric weakness.

4. That the etheric body is the mechanism of vital, pranic life, and "sub-stands" or underlies the outer, familiar equipment of the nervous system, which feeds and actuates all parts of the physical organism. The relationship existing between the centres, the nadis and the entire nervous system comprises the field of the new medicine and indicates the new major field of research.

5. That the main causes of all disease are two in nature:
   a. They are to be found, first of all, in the stimulation or the nonstimulation of the centres. This simply implies the overactivity or the underactivity of

any centre in any part of the body. Where the flow of energy is commensurate to the demands of the physical body at any particular stage of development, then there will be relative freedom from disease.

b. They are to be found, secondly, in the karmic effect of the three planetary diseases: Cancer, Tuberculosis, Syphilitic diseases. Some day medicine will realise that behind every single disease (irrespective of the results of accident or war) lie these three main tendencies in the human body. This is a basic and important statement.

6. That the etheric body is a focussing point for all the interior energies of the body, and therefore the energy transmitted will not be pure vital energy or simple planetary prana but will be qualified by forces coming from the astral or the emotional apparatus, from the mind or from the soul body. These "qualifications of force," indicating as they do the karma of the individual, are in the last analysis the major conditioning forces. They indicate the point of development of the individual and the areas of control in his personality. They therefore indicate the state of his karma. This lifts the whole subject of medicine into the psychological field and posits the entire problem of karmic effects and of ray types.

7. That these conditioning factors make the etheric body what it is in any one incarnation; these factors are, in their turn, the result of activities initiated and carried through in previous incarnations, and thus constitute the patient's karmic liabilities or his karmic freedoms.

8. That the basic energies pouring into the etheric body and conditioning the physical body will be of two major

types: the ray energy of the soul and the ray energy of the personality, qualified by the three minor forces or the rays of the mental nature, the astral body and the physical vehicle. This therefore involves five energies which are present in the etheric body which the physician of the future will have to consider.

9. That diagnoses, based upon the recognition of these subjective factors, are not in reality the involved and complicated matter they appear to be today to the student of the advanced occult theories. Medical men in the New Age will eventually know enough to relate these various ray forces to their appropriate centres; hence they will know which type of force is responsible for conditions—good or bad—in any particular area of the body. Some day, when more research and investigation have been carried forward, the science of medicine will be built upon the fact of the vital body and its constituent energies. It will then be discovered that this science will be far simpler and less complicated than present medical science. Today, medicine has reached such a point of complexity that specialists have perforce been needed who can deal with one area of the body and with its effect upon the entire physical vehicle. The average general practitioner cannot cope with the mass of detailed knowledge now gathered re the physical body, its various systems, their interrelation and their effect upon the many organisms which constitute the whole man. Surgery will remain occupied with the anatomical necessities of the human frame; medicine will shift its focus of attention, before long, to the etheric body and its incident circulatory systems of energy, its interlocking relationships and the flow between the seven centres, between the centres themselves and the areas which they control.

This will mark a tremendous advance in wise and useful approach; it will produce a basic simplification; it will lead to more correct methods of healing, particularly as clairvoyant vision is developed and becomes recognised by science, and known to be an extension of a normal sense.

10. As the true astrology comes into its own and is developed into a reputable science, the charts of the soul and of the personality can be related to each other; then the etheric body will be checked by correct astrological conclusions, and the physician will be on far surer ground than he now is. The astrology of the past concerned the life of the personality; the astrology of the future will indicate the purpose of the soul, and will completely revolutionise medicine (among other things). It must, however, be lifted out of the hands of those interested in predictional astrology, out of the hands of the thousands who at this time spend much time "casting" horoscopes (seeking to interpret their usually erroneous conclusions), and placed in the hands of trained mathematical scientists and in the hands of those who have given as much time to scientific training along astrological lines as is now given to training a reputable physician, a chemist or a biologist.

11. These astrological findings will not only be related to the personality and the soul charts, but will also enter the field of medicine, particularly in relation to the etheric body. Today, any astrological investigation done in the field of medicine has relation to physical disease within the physical body; in the future, it will concentrate upon the condition of the etheric vehicle. This is a new and imminent development in astrological research.

Another difficulty which I have to face (as I seek to present to you the medicine of the future) is that I think in terms of cycles and you think in terms of a few brief years. What I am in reality attempting to do is to indicate the lines along which medical research will trend during the next two hundred years. The effort of the present day approach is how to cure a person here and now; this is a natural reaction, and advanced thinkers seek to be able to do this at this time through the medium of so-called esoteric and mental modes of healing. Yet little is known of the make-up of the vital body and practically no background of research in this field exists. Modern medicine is of very ancient origin. Over the centuries it has grown and developed until modern skill, modern research, modern techniques and modern methods of healing and of cure are amazingly successful. This is oft forgotten in the emphasis laid by the adherents of new and untried schools upon the failures to cure, which they attribute to wrong methods and fail to allow for karmic limitations. The success of modern medicine is today so great that millions of people are kept alive—if not cured—who in earlier days and with less scientific aptitude would normally have died. In this developed skill and knowledge, and in this aptitude in the care of the physical mechanism, is today to be found a major world problem—the problem of the overpopulation of the planet, leading to the herd life of humanity and the consequent economic problem—to mention only one of the incidental difficulties of this success. This "unnatural" preservation of life is the cause of much suffering and is a fruitful source of war, being contrary to the karmic intent of the planetary Logos.

With this vast problem, I cannot here deal. I can only indicate it. It will be solved when the fear of death disappears and when humanity learns the significance of time and the meaning of cycles. It will be simplified when true astrological findings become possible, when man knows the hour of his departure from this outer plane, and masters the technique of "withdrawal" and the methods of abstracting himself *consciously* from the prison of the body. But much research has to take place first. The fact, however, that the problem is recognised and that speculation and investigation are rife, indicate that the time has come—karmically and from the angle of human evolutionary development— for a study of the etheric body, of the conditioning rays which govern its manifestation *in space,* and of astrology, which governs its manifestation *in time.*

It is for this reason that the world today is full of groups in revolt against orthodox medicine—wrongly in revolt, because in their fanatical enthusiasm for their particular approach to the problem of healing, they ignore the beneficent aspects of developed medical science. They thus attempt to throw overboard the contribution of the ages to man's knowledge of the human organism, its interrelations and its care, cure and preservation; they fail to profit from past wisdom, but prefer to set sail upon the sea of research in a spirit of revolt, full of prejudice and totally unequipped for the task in hand.

Naturopaths of many kinds, professors of methods of healing by electricity or light and colour, food dietitians with infallible cures for all diseases, the many who practice systems founded on the Abrams mode of diagnosis, and many advocates of the chiropractic methods, as well as the various healing systems which are completely divorced from medicine but which undertake to bring about cures, are all indicative of new and hopeful trends; they are nevertheless extremely experimental in nature, and are so fanatically endorsed, so exclusive of all recognised methods of healing aid (except their own), so violently opposed to all the findings of the past, and so unwilling to cooperate with orthodox medicine that, in many cases, they constitute a definite and real danger to the public. It is largely their own faulty approach which is responsible for this; their undoubted ignorance of the nature of the human body, their attack on existent medical practices (even of proven value), and their biassed belief in the infallibility of their experimental techniques, have brought them under the attack of the rigidly orthodox medical practitioners and of the fundamentalists within the ring-pass-not of academic medicine. Yet within the ranks of medicine are many enlightened men who would gladly cooperate if the small and vociferous cults would relinquish their exclusiveness and be willing to cooperate and accept that which the divine instinct in man down the ages has taught in connection with the healing of the human body. It will be through the collaboration of the new experimental schools and the older and proven methods that the medicine of the future will be developed. The value of all the many groups—good and indifferent—lies in the fact that they point the way towards new trends and indicate the lines along which the medicine of the future can enrich itself and become better adapted to man's need. They are too experimental as yet to be trustworthy, and are not yet scientifically proved. They are pioneering groups, and have a real contribution to make, but this will only be possible if they refuse to divorce themselves from the past and are willing to compromise in the present. Academic medicine is the result of the God-given gifts of the human mind; it is a proven divine expression and a most beneficent force in the world, in spite of human weakness, commercial exploitation and many mistakes. It is the same with religion. Both of these great sciences must eliminate the reactionary and fundamentalist positions, and then proceed with an open mind into the new ways of approach to divinity and of approach to physical well-being.

It might therefore be said that the main contribution which I am making at this time is to indicate the causes of disease and ill health which are not recognised by orthodox medicine, which deals with the effects of these subtle causes as they work out in the physical body and the nervous system. I am not dealing (as I have earlier warned you) with the symptoms of disease, with medical diagnosis or with systems of applied physical means to bring about cures or to ameliorate conditions. These have kept pace with man's growing capacity to discover and to know.

Let me reiterate that I am laying the foundation for an approach to the subject of the physical body in health and disease which will deal primarily with the etheric body. This should eventually lead to an accumulation of knowledge anent energy, its focal points and distribution in the etheric body, which will equal that already gained in the field of exact physical knowledge, and that exact knowledge is a fact.

The study of inherited disease indicates a faint recognition of man's karmic liabilities and karmic tendencies. A mistake lies however in the belief that these tendencies are to be found in the germs of life and of substance, brought together at the moment of conception, and therefore that the father or the mother is responsible for the transmission. Such is not the case. The subject in incarnation has—from the angle of the soul—definitely and consciously chosen his parents for what they can contribute to his *physical* make-up whilst in incarnation. The vital body is therefore of such a nature that the man is predisposed to a particular type of infection or of disease; the physical body is of such a nature that its line of least resistance permits of the appearance and control of that which the vital body makes possible; the incarnating soul produces, in its creative work and in its vital vehicle, a particular constitution to which the parents chosen contribute a definite tendency. The man is therefore nonresistant to certain types of disease. This is determined by the karma of the man.

It is well known to students of the esoteric sciences that the physical body is simply an automaton, responsive to and actuated by a subtler body of energies which are a true expression of the point in evolution. This point in evolution may be that of personality control, through one or other of its bodies, or of soul control. These are facts which the medical profession must grasp, and when it does a great step forward will have been made. Esoteric students are willing to recognise that the physical body is automatic in its response to emotional, mental or soul impression; so closely, however, is the etheric body interwoven with the physical vehicle that it is well nigh impossible to separate the two in consciousness; this will not be proven or possible until the science of etheric energy and the development of clairvoyant perception demonstrate the truth of what I say. This is again a needed repetition.

Medical science, through its study of the nervous system and its recognition of the power of thought over the physical body, is moving rapidly in a right direction. When it admits, in relation to the physical body, that "energy follows thought," and then begins to experiment with the concept of thought currents (as they are erroneously called) which are directed to certain areas of the etheric body— where the esotericists posit the existence of energy points or centres—much will then be discovered. Christian Science had a sound conception in its original basic concept of the mind as a permanently existent factor; its overemphasis upon the mind, its idealistic presentation of human nature, its expectancy of man's capacity to demonstrate today and immediately as a fully manifested son of God (with no intermediate or necessary unfoldments), and its contradictory position of using the energy of the mind for mainly physical requirements have soundly negated its basic tenets. Otherwise Man might have been permanently deluded. Had Christian Science fulfilled the original intention of the group of initiates who sought to influence humanity through its agency, and had it developed the idea correctly that energy follows thought, medical science would have greatly benefited.

Its presentation was both too high and too low, and a great opportunity was lost. Christian Science has failed from the angle of the Hierarchy, and its usefulness has been largely negated.

Healers and healing groups work as yet at a great disadvantage; but they can begin now to work, and their work is of a twofold nature:

1. They can, through the power of directed thought, pour energy into the centre which is the determining factor in that area of the physical body where the trouble lies. If, for instance, the patient is suffering from such a difficulty as gastric ulcer, the stimulation of the solar plexus centre may produce a cure, provided that the work done is *purely mental* and that the results expected are *purely physical*. Otherwise the emotional nature will share in the stimulation and real difficulty will arise.

2. They can stimulate a centre higher than the one controlling a particular area and thus—by the intensification of the higher centre—reduce the vitality of the lower. If, for instance, there is disease or trouble in connection with the organs of generation

(as for instance disease of the prostate gland), then the throat centre should receive attention. It is that centre which must eventually be the recipient of the energy of the lower creative aspect or correspondence. This is called "the technique of the withdrawal of the fire"; by its means what you call overstimulation in certain cases, or inflammation in others, can be stopped.

These two ways of using energy and thought control form the occult basis for the two fundamental methods used in directing energy in diseased areas. They produce, in the one case, an intensification of the life of the associated centre, with a consequent definite effect upon the diseased area; or they lessen the inflow of force in the other case, and thus weaken the quality of the disease. It will be apparent, therefore, that much must be known of the effects of these two basic and different techniques before a healer *dare* work. Otherwise he might greatly increase the trouble in the diseased area and even succeed (which frequently happens) in killing the patient.

There is another point which I would seek to emphasise. In all healing methods of an esoteric nature, it is essential that sound medical practices of an orthodox kind accompany the subtler modes of help. It is in the wise combination of the two approaches, and in the cooperative work of the orthodox physician and of the occult healer or healing group, that the soundest results will be produced.

Students who attempt to heal will therefore need to realise two things: the nature of the disease, as diagnosed by a good physician, and the centre which controls the area of the disease. The safest plan for the average student of healing or for a healing group is to work in cooperation with some reputable doctor and in relation to the centre which controls the diseased area. Initiates, in their healing work, deal with the higher correspondence of the controlling centre, working always through the analogous emotional and mental centres. This is *neither possible nor permissible* to the ordinary healing group. The higher the centres considered, involved and dealt with, the more potent the results, and therefore the greater care required.

The whole process is one of either stimulating activity or of withdrawing energy, of making more active an allied centre and thus abstracting attention from the centre governing the diseased area or organ, or of balancing the energies flowing between two centres and thus producing an equable and even interplay. The more the neophyte studies this subject of healing the more complex it will appear, until the time comes when he can work in collaboration with some physician who has the inner vision and can see the centres, or with patients who know within themselves their own destiny and can collaborate with some group which has sound occult knowledge, which can ascertain the patient's rays and which knows at least the nature of his disposition or his "indisposition," through consulting his natal chart.

You might ask, therefore, in view of all this, if it is possible for you to do definite healing work that will be effective, sound, right and permissible. The risks of over- or understimulation seem too great; the knowledge of the healer seems too small to permit experiment, and the karma of the patient is necessarily (for the average healer) not yet ascertainable.

To this I would reply that all work of a pioneering and experimental nature has always its own special risks. Many have been the casualties of science, and particularly of medical science, in the early days of modern medicine and surgery. But this never deterred the sincere investigator or slackened the growth of knowledge; in these days of pioneering in the field of occult healing, the same courage must be shown and the same risks assumed. The safeguard from the strictly legal and human angle will be that the patient will be in the hands of a reputable physician for diagnosis and medical care during the time that the occult healer is endeavouring to be of vital helpfulness.

The work of the healer and of the healing groups will therefore be supplementary to the orthodox care; results will have to be carefully watched and noted on both sides. Any group which is formed for healing should work under certain determined policies, and here are a few which I would suggest as essential to success in this transitional period:

1. The patient to be healed (or helped, if healing is not possible) should always be in the hands of a good and reputable doctor, and if not, should be encouraged to consult one.

2. The nature of the disease should be known to the group, and should be determined by careful, orthodox medical diagnosis.

3. The age of the patient, his birth date and some information anent his circumstances should also be known, so as to provide a focal point of interest, and a magnetic area should be constructed around the patient which will attract the thought-directed energy of the group.

4. The healer or the healing group should have a general grasp of the nature and the anatomy of the body, the placement of the various organs in the body and the position and nature of the centres governing the diseased area or areas. Charts giving this information should be studied.

5. The faculty of imagination and the power of visualisation should be emphasised in a healing group, and the

ability should be developed to send streams of energy to the patient and to the area in the patient's body where the trouble lies.

6. The healer or the healing group must remember that it is not mental energy only with which he works. He, for *himself,*

    a. Creates a thought of healing power.

    b. That created focal point of concentrated attention becomes the directing agent for the healing force or prana.

    c. This prana is neither mental nor astral in nature. It is pure planetary substance or living essence, and is that substance of which the vital body of the planet is made.

    d. The healer or the healing group appropriates as much of this substance as is possible, and by the power of their united thought they direct it to and through the centre involved. *Healing work is circulatory,* and this must not be forgotten. The pranic energy (thought-directed) is not sent to the centre and there permitted to accumulate. It is *passed through* the centre, first of all to the organ involved or the area where difficulty is to be found, and then is sent out to the body as a totality. It might be regarded as a system of *flushing,* with a purificatory and stimulating effect.

It is only possible in these early days of experiment and work along these lines to give certain simple rules. Out of the results achieved experience will come, and the healing group will learn gradually *how* to work, *when* to change its methods, and *what* to notice.

From the start of work along these lines, records should be kept. In this aspect of the work the patient will frequently cooperate. Dates, incidental phenomena, changes for the better or the worse should be noted, along with information as is possible anent the patient's general condition. For this reason, I recommend that in the early stages of this work healing be attempted only in connection with those who are well known to the members or who are put in the hands of the healing group by physicians or by those willing to give full information.

People who are so ill that they are not expected to live, or who are suffering from diseases which preclude ultimate recovery, should *not* be taken into the healing group for treatment, except with *ameliorative* results in mind. No neophyte knows enough of karma to work with confidence either at the task of health or of release by death. If, however, a patient gets worse whilst the group is working upon his case, he should not be dropped, but a definite and different technique can then be used to ease the path of death. In the next section I intend to touch upon the karma of death.

If you will bear in mind that work in connection with the etheric body (as an instrument of vitality) is today as little known as the science of modern medicine was known in the year 1200 A.D., you will be enabled to work without discouragement and without that undue expectation which today handicaps the neophyte. Assume consciously the position that nothing is as yet really known anent the centres, the areas of energy in the body, and thought direction; realise also that you are engaging upon a great research project. Nothing, literally nothing, has been done in relation to medicine and the science of the centres in any practical way, though certain books upon the relation of the centres to psychological research and equipment and the glandular or endocrine system have played tentatively with the subject. The field of research which I propose to you is an entirely new one. Those among you who enter it may not see the results of what you are attempting to do. Your impatience and your eagerness to help may handicap you; your ignorance may cause you to make mistakes. But, go on; persevere; keep careful records and preserve all correspondence. Then the results will be sure.

1. KARMIC LIABILITIES OF THE INDIVIDUAL

We have already studied (perhaps without realising its implications) our first point under this heading. This concerns the karmic liabilities of the individual, emerging from the subjective vehicles and from the personality as a whole.

As we discussed the psychological causes of disease as they arise in the subtle vehicles in the three worlds or from the disciple's tension as he endeavours to tread the Path, we were in reality concerned entirely with karma or the effect of the inner causes of events, equipment and circumstances upon the physical plane. We saw how the inner bodies, via the etheric body, conditioned the man's outer manifestation, and that disease or health was largely dependent upon them. They are the immediate karmic cause of physical plane existence. If the idea is then extended to include previous incarnations—as must inevitably be the case—then we arrive at the conclusion that the condition of these inner bodies, their limitations and their richness, their defects and their assets, and their general psychic and psychological tendencies are inherited from previous lives, and are therefore responsible for the present earthly situation. We have, consequently, simply pushed the causes of present day conditions still further back, and we could—if we so desired—enter a field of such intricacy and detail that nothing profitable would eventuate. The whole problem of the recovery of past incarnations is one of infinite possibility, and when I use this word "infinite" I immediately put the whole subject out of the control of the finite mind. We are then dealing with something which it is not possible to handle rationally.

Karma was, for infant humanity and for the undeveloped individual, a group matter. The man was a member of a group but without any thought as to the implications and the responsibilities entailed. Later, as the process of individualisation became more effective in character and purpose and more pronounced in temperament, karma became also more personal and definite, and the man in a position to make or work off more causes and effects. The personality not being thoroughly unfolded and integrated, the man was still involved in group life and the interrelations became more extensive. Later on, the personality became the conscious creator of its own causes and the conscious participator in the effects. Upon the Path, the karma of the chosen group, of the individual, and of those with whom the man chooses association through unity of spiritual purpose involves him, and another factor is added to the previous categories of karmic responsibility. Later still, karma in the three worlds is met, overcome and negated; at the same time karma connected with the initiating of causes through world service is added to that which the individual has already experienced, and he shares in the karmic responsibility of the Hierarchy itself. All these stages:

1. Elementary group karma—of the primitive man,
2. Individual karma of the self-conscious developing man,
3. Karma, related to the life of the disciple,
4. Hierarchical karma,

must be added to the well known *Karma of Retribution* with which the disciple is already familiar; to it must also be added national and racial karma, plus the educational karma which all disciples bring upon themselves when they are desirous of entering an Ashram to prepare for initiation.

There is also the *Karma of Reward* in contradistinction to that of *Retribution;* this is a type of karma oft forgotten, but one which will become better known in the coming world cycle. Humanity has worked off much evil karma, and the karma based on causes later to be initiated will not generate such dire effects as that of the past. Not all karma is bad, in spite of what man thinks. Much of it is necessarily punitive and distressing, owing to humanity's ignorance and low stage of development. When karmic retribution becomes acute and terrible, as it is in today's appalling world experience, it indicates that humanity has reached a point where consequences can be meted out on a large scale and with justice. Very little suffering is attached to karma where there is ignorance, leading to irresponsibility and complete lack of thought and there is attached to affairs but little true sense of guilt. There may be unhappy conditions and distressing circumstances, but the ability to respond to such conditions with commensurate pain is lacking; there is little mental reaction to the processes of karmic retribution. This should be borne in mind. The Aryan race is now, however, so developed mentally and on a large scale that karma is truly horrible and agonising and can express itself through world conditions. At the same time, the present widespread distress indicates the extent and success of human unfoldment and is a most hopeful and promising sign. In this idea, you have the clue as to why the good, the holy and the saintly servers of the race carry—in this world cycle—such a heavy load of karmic ill.

It is consequently quite impossible in the scope of this treatise to deal more fully with this subject of karma as it produces the many types of human ills, including disease— only one of its manifestations. The theme is too vast, too complicated and too widely diffusing in its effect. All that one can do is to posit the fact that past actions and reactions have established in previous lives such a karmic rhythm that today all the aspects of the lower nature are involved; and among the commonest and most ordinary effects, and one in which the great Law of Retribution takes effect, is that of disease. This is a point which healers and metaphysicians, so-called, should most carefully consider.

2. THE SEVEN RAY CAUSES OF KARMA

These carry the cause of all human difficulties, including ill health and disease—individual, national and racial—still further back to the very origin of creation itself. Karma demonstrates in those streams of energy and of primordial substance which pour into and through the created world, including the lower three worlds where work the lunar pitris and the elemental essences of all forms. This primordial karma (if I may so call it) is contributory to the existence of disease. We are told in the ancient books, to which the Masters have access, that the world is constructed of substance which is already tainted with the karma of a previous solar system.

It will be apparent to you that these streams of force, emanating from the Lords of the Seven Rays, are coloured, therefore, and "tainted"—if I may use such a word—by the limitations of these same great Beings; They are Gods, from our point of view, but in reality, Gods in the making, even though much nearer solar divinity than the most advanced human being is near to planetary divinity. They are the "imperfect Gods" spoken of in *The Secret Doctrine* and are the planetary Logoi of the sacred and non-sacred planets. If the great informing Lives of the planets within our solar system are imperfect, the effect of this imperfection must inevitably affect Their planetary creations, Their bodies of manifestation, and thus introduce a karmic condition over which the individual human being has absolutely no control, but within which he moves and which he shares. It is obviously impossible for me to elucidate this theme. All I can do or am permitted to do is to give you seven stanzas from one of the most ancient volumes in the world; it deals with the seven ray causes of imperfections in our planetary manifestations. To these should be added (if it were only possible) the stanzas which convey the significance of the defects emerging from astrological conditions and producing effects of a planetary nature and involving, therefore, the horoscope of our particular planetary Logos. But these are far too abstruse, elaborate and far-reaching in their theme, and can be studied and considered only when humanity has reached such a stage of intuitive development that men can "appreciate causes and effects as whole processes and can see both the beginning and the end in one flash of time in space." In these words the Master Serapis once summed up the matter when endeavouring to train a group of initiated disciples in this mode of approaching vast subjects.

The "Book of Karma" has in it the following stanzas, and these can serve as an introduction to those dealing with the Seven Ray causes of inharmony and disease. To the intuitive aspirant some meaning will emerge, but he must ever bear in mind that all that I am attempting to do is to put into words—unsatisfactory and quite inadequate—stanzas concerning the conditioning factors in the equipment of those great Beings Whose life force (which we call energy) creates all that is, colours and shapes all manifestations within the worlds, and adds its quota of force to the equipment of every single human being. Every man appropriates this energy to the measure of his need, and his need is the sign of his development. The stanzas I have selected are from *The Book of Imperfections*. Part Fourteen:

> "The seven imperfections issued forth and tainted substance from the highest sphere unto the lowest. The seven perfections followed next, and the two—that which is whole and sound and that which is known as detail and unwholesome in an awful sense—met upon the plane of physical life. (The etheric plane.—A.A.B.)
>
> And there they fought, swinging into the conflict all that they were and had, all that was seen and all that was unseen within the triple ring. (The three lower worlds.—A.A.B.)
>
> The seven imperfections entered the seven races of men, each in their own place; they coloured the seven points within each race. (The seven planetary centres, transmitting imperfect energy.—A.A.B.)
>
> The seven perfections hovered o'er each race, over each man within each race and over each point within each man.
>
> And thus the conflict grew from the outermost to the innermost, from the greatest One to the littlest ones. Seven the imperfections. Seven the perfect wholes; seven the ways to oust the dark of imperfection and demonstrate the clear cold light, the white electric light of perfect wholeness."

All that you can gain from the above, my brother, is a concept of agelong conflict, of seven great energies which manifest as dualities and which produce when anchored within one body (whether that of a planet, a man or an atom) an area or cycle of distress, as it is called; this distress produces the evolutionary urge and is itself *the cause* of manifestation, whilst *its effect* (which is karma) is the liberation ultimately of the perfect and the good. These things are not easy to comprehend. It must be remembered that the seven imperfections are related to the sevenfold nature of the One in Whom we live and move and have our being, and that these seven imperfect energies hold within themselves the perfect will-to-good, more potent in the long run than the will-to-harm.

These energies pour through the seven centres of the planetary body and are—as far as we are concerned—the seven ray energies. In relation to the will-to-harm which can and does demonstrate as disease in all the four kingdoms in nature, you have the reason why I instituted, among the esoteric students for whom I have made myself responsible, the development of harmlessness. It is the major agent for the offsetting of karma. I will here give you Law IX, and thus complete a group of laws which, when followed, will be found essential to the curing of disease and the maintenance of health.

LAW IX

Perfection calls imperfection to the surface. Good drives evil always from the form of man in time and space. The method used by the Perfect One and that employed by Good is harmlessness. This is not negativity but perfect poise, a completed point of view and divine understanding.

You will have noticed that what I have said in this connection removes the whole subject of disease into a distant world of origins—a world into which man is as yet unable to penetrate. It is for this reason that I have devoted so much time to the consideration of *the causes* of disease; more than half of what I have to say is to be found in this first part of our discussion. We have nearly concluded this, and face what many will regard as the more useful and practical part of the teaching anent this subject. It has never been my intention to deal with the pathology of disease or the symptoms of the many forms of ill health which ravage mankind. I seek mainly to lay the stress upon the subjective reasons for the majority of ills which attack the human frame. My purpose is, however, sound. The overemphasis which people put upon disease is bewildering to the soul, for it places the transient, constantly changing form-nature in a position of undue prominence, whereas—from the angle of the soul—the vicissitudes of the body are only of importance just in so far as they contribute to the enrichment of soul experience.

The factor that is of importance is the causes, initiated by man from life to life; these work out in the appearance of disease, in the emergence of some disastrous consequence in circumstance and in event, and in the general conditioning of some particular incarnation. It is with these causes that man must learn to deal, to recognise them, and to trace the conditioning energy to the appropriate effect, dealing primarily then with the task of negating the cause by the opposition of a trained will. Karma is not an inevitable, inescapable and dire happening. It can be offset; but this offsetting, particularly where disease is concerned, will include four lines of activity:

1. Determining the nature of the cause and the area in consciousness where it originated.
2. Developing those qualities which are the polar opposite of the effective cause.
3. Practising harmlessness so as to arrest the expression of the cause and to prevent any further implementing of the unfortunate condition.

4. Taking the necessary physical steps which will produce the conditions which the soul desires. These steps will include:

   a. A mental acquiescence and an acceptance of the *fact* of the effect—in the case which we are considering in relation to karma—disease.

   b. Wise action along the lines of orthodox medical procedure.

   c. The assistance of a healing group or a healer for aid in inner spiritual healing.

   d. Clear vision as to the outcome. This may lead to preparation for a more useful physical plane life or preparation for the great transition called death.

But behind all wise thinking and wise activity must be the acceptance of the existence of certain general conditions which work out as physical ill health during this world cycle, and not only for the human kingdom but also for the three sub-human kingdoms. The Law of Imperfection exists because the Great Realities (to be found in all the phenomenal world) are likewise in process of development and of evolutionary unfoldment. Therefore, until They, as spiritual Beings, have developed "sublime control"—as it is called—over the substance of Their phenomenal forms, those forms will fall short of divine perfection. Disease is only a form of transient imperfection, and death is just a method for refocussing energy, prior to a forward moving activity, leading steadily and always towards betterment.

The comprehension of the seven stanzas which I now propose to give you will lead eventually to the isolation of the seven psychological causes of disease, inherent in the substance of all forms in this world cycle, because all forms are infused with the life energy of the "imperfect Gods."

The seven Spirits, we are told in the Scriptures of the world, are "before the Throne of God"; this signifies that They are not yet in a position to mount the Throne, symbolically speaking, owing to the fact that They have not yet achieved complete divine expression. These Lords of the Seven Rays are greater and more advanced in the spiritual scale than are those great Lives who form the Council of the Lord of the World in Shamballa. They are the Representatives of the seven ray Energies Who inform the seven sacred planets but are not yet as divinely developed as They are. The problem of humanity in respect to imperfection is complicated, not only by the fact that the seven informing vitalising Energies are "tainted with imperfection," but also by the fact that the Lord of the World is Himself, from the angle of a Solar Logos for instance, far from perfect; this is the reason why our planet, the Earth, is *not* a sacred planet. We are told that Sanat Kumara is the divine prisoner of this planet, held here until the "last weary pilgrim has found his way home." This is His heavy karma even whilst it is an expression of His desire and of His joy; the "weary pilgrims" are the atoms (human or otherwise) in His body, and they are tainted with imperfection because of His imperfections; their complete "healing" will set the term for His release.

Bear in mind, therefore, that the stanzas—seven in number—now to be given, indicate the quality of the descending energies and the taints which these energies carry and convey to all forms which are vitalised by the life of our planetary Logos.

The Seven Ray Causes of Inharmony and Disease

I. "The Great One set Himself to follow by Himself alone His chosen path. He brooked no interference. He hardened in His courses. From plane to plane, this hardening proceeded; it grew and stiffened. His will was set, and crystal-like, brilliant, brittle and hard. The power to crystallise was His. He brought not will-to-live but will-to-die. Death was His gift to life. Infusion and diffusion pleased Him not. He loved and sought abstraction."

As far as we can understand the significance of this stanza in relation to our theme of disease, the imperfection of this divine energy produces a peculiar attitude which expresses itself in the power to crystallise, to harden, to bring about attrition and cause the great abstracting process which we call death. Other results are the many crystallising processes going on in the physical form, all atrophying processes, and old age.

II. "The Great One poured His life throughout all parts and every aspect of manifestation. From the centre to the periphery and from the periphery to the centre He rushed, carrying abundance of life, energising all forms of Himself, producing excess of movement, endless extension, abundant growth and undue haste. He knew not what He wanted because He wanted all, desired all, attracted all and gave to all too much."

The imperfection of this great energy with its building, vitalising and cohering potency, was and is the power to overstimulate, to produce accretion, to pile together, to build too many forms, to attract too many atoms and to bring about those conditions which lead to what has been called (esoterically) "the suffocation of the life"—another form of dying, but dying this time as a result of excessive vitality, affecting the blood stream, producing building within the forms already built, and frequently creating an etheric vehicle which is too potent for the outer exoteric physical form. Other results are, for instance, the appearance of tumors, of cancers, of growths, and the over-development of bodily aspects, overlarge organs and supernumerary bodily parts.

> III. "The Great One gathered here and there. He chose and He rejected. This power He refused and this power He accepted. He had no purpose linked to the six purposes of His six Brothers. He acquired a form and liked it not; threw it away and chose another. He had no settled point or plan but lived in glamour and liked it well. He smothered both the good and the bad, though using both. Excess in one direction could be seen and starvation in another. Both these extremes governed His choice of living substance, He threw together those that suited not each other, then saw the end was sorrow and deceit. Patterns He made, but purpose suited not. He gave up in despair."

The main effect of this imperfect "maneuvering" and manipulation, as it has been called, is largely astral in nature, producing consequent physical ill health and the undesirable effects which we have already studied in this treatise. It is because this third ray energy is the energy of substance itself that its imperfections demonstrate profusely in the human tendency to disease. Glamour results from the excessive use of this third ray energy for selfish and personal ends and manifests primarily upon the sixth or astral plane. As a result of this manipulation of desire, and the wild maneuvering for its satisfaction along material lines, you have such diseases as the gastric and intestinal disorders and the various stomach troubles which devastate civilised humanity—far more than the savage races. Certain brain disorders also are effects, and low vitality.

> IV. "The Great One fought and entered into combat. All that He met appeared to Him a subject for display of power. Within the fourth He found a field of battle and settled down to fight. He saw the right and knew the wrong and vibrated between the two, fighting first one and then the other, but missing all the time that midway point where battle is not known. There harmony, ease, rest and peaceful silence will be found. He weakened all the forms which used His strength and power. Yet all the time He sought for beauty; searched for loveliness; and yearned for peace. Despair overtook Him in His courses, and with despair the will-to-live could not survive. Yet all the time the loveliness was there."

Here we have a strong indication as to the reason why humanity (the fourth kingdom in nature) succumbs with such rapidity and such ease to disease. The conflicts to which humanity is so constantly summoned, both in group form and as individuals, lead—until understood and used as a means to triumph and progress—to a condition of constant devitalisation. Where this is present, resistance to disease fades out and practically all forms of ill health and bodily ills become possible. Diffusion of energy leads to a constant lessening of this resistance. As a result you have debility, quick and bad reaction to the disease indigenous in the planet itself, and a rapid taking on of infections and of contagious diseases. It is this energy which lies behind what we call epidemics, and influenza is one of its main expressions.

V. "The Great One arose in His wrath and separated Himself. He swept aside the great dualities and saw primarily the field of multiplicity. He produced cleavage on every hand. He wrought with potent thought for separative action. He established barriers with joy. He brooked no understanding; He knew no unity, for He was cold, austere, ascetic and forever cruel. He stood between the tender, loving centre of all lives and the outer court of writhing, living men. Yet He stood not at the midway point, and naught He did sufficed to heal the breach. He widened all cleavages, erected barriers, and sought to make still wider gaps."

It has been most difficult to describe the nature of the imperfection of the energy of the Lord of the fifth ray. In the activity of this energy which demonstrates primarily upon the fifth or mental plane will be found eventually the source of many psychological disorders and mental trouble. Cleavage is the outstanding characteristic—cleavage within the individual or between the individual and his group, rendering him anti-social. I have dealt with this in an earlier part of this treatise and need not further enlarge upon the difficulties here (In *Esoteric Psychology*, Vol. II of *A Treatise on the Seven Rays*). Other results are certain forms of insanities, brain lesions and those gaps in the relation of the physical body to the subtle bodies which show as imbecilities and psychological troubles. Another form of disease, emerging as a result of this fifth ray force is migraine, which is caused by a lack of relationship between the energy around the pineal gland and that around the pituitary body.

VI. "The Great One loved Himself in others and in all forms. On every hand, He saw objects of His devotion and ever they proved to be Himself. Into these others He ever poured Himself, asking response and never getting it. Surely and with certainty the outlines of the forms so loved were lost, grew dim and disappeared. The objects of His love slowly faded out. Only a world of shadows, of mist and fog remain. And as He looked upon Himself, He said: Lord of Glamour, that am I, and the Angel of Bewilderment. Naught is clear to me. I love yet all seems wrong! I know that love is right and the spirit of the universe. What then is wrong?"

Curiously enough, it is the potency of this sixth ray force (as it feeds desire) which is responsible for much of the ills and diseases of humanity which are based upon the misuse of the mission and function of sex. Desire, bewilderment, weakness, perversions and the one-pointed development of sexual and other satisfactions grow out of the misuse of this energy. The bewilderment growing out of desire leads to a violently demanded satisfaction and the taking of those steps—some right and some wrong—which lead to satisfaction. The results cover a wide field, all the way from sadistic cruelty and lust to those marriages which are based on physical desire and to those conditions which lead to the many forms of sexual disease. A clue to this whole world-wide problem lies in the words of an ancient writing which says that "the imperfection of the Lord of the Sixth Ray opened the door to an erroneous marriage between the poles."

VII. "The Great One gathered to Himself His forces and affirmed His intention to create. He created that which is outer and can be seen. He saw His creations and liked them not and so withdrew His attention; then the creations He had made died and disappeared. He had no lasting success and saw naught but failure as He travelled on the outer path of life. He comprehended not the need of forms. To some He gave an over-plus of life, to some too little; and so both kinds died and failed to show the beauty of the Lord Who gave them life but failed to give them understanding. He knew not then that love sustains."

The effects of this ray force are most peculiar and will be a great deal more prevalent than heretofore, as this ray is now coming into power. It is this energy which is largely responsible for infections and contagious diseases. The keynote of the work of the seventh ray is to bring together life and matter upon the physical plane. This, however, when viewed from the angle of imperfection, is a bringing together (if you can understand the implications) of Life, the lives and the general livingness of the creative process. This is symbolised by the promiscuity and the endless moving interplay of all life within all lives. The result is therefore the activity of all germs and bacteria within the medium which will best nurture them.

These are abstruse and difficult concepts, but they should be pondered upon, and deep reflection will lead to understanding. All disease and ill health are the result of the activity or the inactivity of one or other of the seven types of energy as they play upon the human body. All physical ills emerge out of the impact of these imperfect energies as they make their impact upon, enter into and pass through the centres in the body. All depends upon the condition of the seven centres in the human body; through these the impersonal energies play, carrying life, disease or death, stimulating the imperfections in the body or bringing healing to the body. All depends, as far as the human being is concerned, upon the condition of the physical body, the age of the soul and the karmic possibilities.

I would ask you not to misinterpret the significance of the word "imperfection" which I have used so constantly in relation to the great Beings Who express a divinity unattainable by humanity at any time upon this particular planet. You must bear in mind that this solar system is the second, and that in the first solar system the emphasis was laid upon intelligent materiality; the goal of the highest initiate was to attain complete control over matter, to unfold the mind principle and to evidence a definite materialism. In these so distant aeons *that* marked attainment, whereas in this solar system it marks defeat for humanity. This system, including all the planets along with our Earth, has a different goal, and the second divine aspect, that of love, has to be manifested, and manifested through the medium of matter impregnated with the qualities developed in system one. What was perfection at that time is not so now. Therefore, the Great Beings which are the sumtotal of all that is, are working through and in substance, which is already tinged or tainted with that which must be left behind and subjected to no further unfoldment.

These are the imperfections which we are considering—the seven aspects of intelligent materiality; it is here that disease has its seat and expression. We are told that the physical body is not a principle; in the last solar system it was. In this, the principles are different and it is in the clash between what is and what will be (what wills-to-be) that we have, upon the physical plane, the causes of disease and death. Ponder on these matters and bear in mind that you must see the picture upon a large scale, as large a scale as possible, if there is to be a true understanding of some of the causes of physical ills and disease.

CHAPTER IV

Some Questions Answered

MOST QUESTIONS ASKED by the neophyte would remain unasked if he had more patience and understood better what he was studying. Beginners need to await developments in themselves and expand their consciousness normally under instruction. However, the teacher may invite the asking of questions and for reasons:

1. Because where a group is involved and the members are very intelligent, through their questionings they could make much progress in learning to know and understand each other. Threads of intercourse could be set up which would link them more closely together.

2. Because through the questions, the teacher himself can enter into a closer rapport with the students' viewpoint. For example, myself, and the Western point of view as regards the healing art.

Forget not that I am an Oriental in the last analysis, and such is my background and training. I may know profoundly more about the healing art than you do and about the energies which constitute the human body, but your point of view, your terminologies, and your attitudes of mind are still somewhat foreign to me. Your questions would help me to understand your background and your limitations, and so enable me to aid you with greater intelligence.

3. Because asking of intelligent questions is the occult method of focussing the mind, of synthesising knowledge, and of becoming aware of the field of inquiry, and of possible expansions of consciousness.

On the Nature of Congestion.

How can I define *congestion* for you when the understanding of force and energy and their relation to each other in the human body is still as yet an embryonic study? To say that congestion is congealed force is misleading; to say that it is static energy means little; to say that it is irregular or non-rhythmic vibration hardly makes sense. My problem is lack of words and of correct terms in which to carry to you esoteric truth.

Congestion is perhaps best defined as the arresting of the free flow of the force through the centres or centre and throughout the body. It exists in two forms:

1. That congestion which produces its effect within the centre itself, and therefore and consequently, upon the gland. It is inhibited, either as it pours into the centre (when it does not affect the gland except in a negative sense), or as it leaves it (when its effect will be positive in some way or another). When the difficulty takes place as it pours into the centre, then the energy is thrown back upon its originating source—either the astral or mental bodies—and you have a psychological inhibition. There is no impetus from within to which the allied gland can respond. When the difficulty is in the outlet into the physical body, you will have no free flow of force, the gland related to the centre will be definitely affected, and either be overstimulated by the nonrhythmic flow or undernourished. This in turn affects the glandular secretion and later the blood stream.

2. That congestion which takes place as the energy or the life force flows throughout the physical body, and as it flows finds there certain forms of weakness, various diseased areas and regions where its flow is impeded or too rapidly circulated. The flow of energy can be arrested in certain areas and can nourish also diseased areas in the body, or can also cure and cleanse them. A temporary congestion can be of beneficent value as well as a malefic force. This may surprise you?

Again, I have to repeat how vast is the subject with which we are dealing, and all these earlier instructions and the answers which I give to the questions only serve to show how abstruse the matter is. But if you will have patience and will be willing to learn by absorption more than by analysis, you will later discover that you know much—intuitively and discriminately.

On Ascertaining the Location of Congestion.

There are three ways whereby the healer can ascertain the presence and the location of congestion and any other form of difficulty-producing objective disease:

1. There is, first of all, clairvoyance which enables the healer to see visually where the difficulty lies. This form of diagnosis is not always accurate and can be "coloured" by conditions present in the healer himself.
2. There is a form of direct perception, a process of "clear knowing," which is a soul faculty and infallible, once a person has been rightly trained in its use. It is a blend of mental and spiritual perception and is definite knowledge, or an intuition, if you like, which enables the healer unerringly to put his finger on the place of difficulty and to know its cause, its effect and its end.

3. There is also a more physical method, which is based on sensitivity in the lower nature, which enables the healer to register in his own body the same difficulty of which the patient is aware. This is called "occult transference" and should only be employed by those who know how to absorb and to dissipate. In this case, the healer can also feel the cause of the disease through the pouring in of energy to the etheric counterpart of the physical plane disease, or as an extreme emotionalism or sensitive response in the astral counterpart.

On the Dual Cause of Congestion.

Let me make one or two concise statements and then explain. First, subjective condition *alone* cannot cause an outer congestion. The soul has arranged to express itself through the medium of a body which has certain *predispositions*.

Second, the subjective *is* a causative factor when in collaboration with the inherited tendencies of the physical body; therefore, all congestion cannot be avoided, for the subjective life determines the condition and the physical body is predisposed to certain diseases. This is the will of the soul. Might I point out that at this stage of human evolution, no subjective conditions are ever right?

Third, an outer condition alone cannot be a causative factor. If I am right in my major premises (and this the new and coming science will prove), then the observations of the medical world will need to be readjusted to the facts. The causative factor exists in the meeting of the inner and the outer existing factors.

Let me make the matter a little clearer, for confusion may be caused by the idea that disease is the result of *two* causes—an inner cause and an outer cause. The subjective situation is the initiating cause. Some psychological factor, leading to a wrong use of energy, sets in motion those inner tendencies which find their way out, as vital determining factors, on to the physical plane. There they come into contact with the physical body or expression which has certain predispositions, certain inherited weaknesses, certain glandular deficiencies—all of which were part of the needed equipment whereby the soul determined that certain needed lessons should be mastered. The relation established between the outer and the inner forces is the basic cause (expressing itself in two causes) which produces some form of disease. It is again the negative and the positive aspects brought into a relation which produces a third factor: the manifestation of some form of disease.

If you speak of perfect physical conditions, I know of no such conditions or of any physical body or physical environment to which such a term could be applied. There must be both the inner psychological situation and cause, which is the subjective reality (on a tiny scale), and the outer physical condition, manifesting as a weakness or as imperfections; these, in their turn, are a tendency from a previous life, a predisposition, an hereditary lesion or a latent difficulty, based on earlier life interests or malpractice. Bring these two major determining factors together and—under the law—you will inevitably have some visible manifestation of physical disease or difficulty; this can be serious or relatively unimportant; it can be dangerous to life or capable of providing only temporary discomfort. No outer condition alone is adequate to produce disease, but the difficulty is that modern medicine does not yet permit the hypothesis of hidden cause except those superficial ones such as, for instance, that worry and intense anxiety can aggravate existing heart trouble. It does not yet permit of those factors which trace back to an earlier life. In the case of contagious diseases, the inner cause is of *group origin,* and has therefore an outer group effect and is an expression of group karma. The difficulty of the matter is consequently great.

There must be, as you perceive, two existing factors, and these, when related and stimulated, produce the appearance of disease. It should be remembered that the question of the soul's choosing of a body and the type of vehicle wherein certain types of lessons can be learned and certain educative experiences mastered, is a little-understood theme. In connection with this, I would remind you that disease is often a mode of clearance and ultimately beneficent in its effects. It is the working out into manifestation of an inner undesirable factor, and when the inner and the outer causes are brought out into the clear light of day they can be handled, understood and often dissipated and ended through the tribulation of disease and suffering. But this is a hard saying.

On Certain Types of Disease.

Arthritis and diabetes are both diseases which have their origin in the astral body, but if I might put it so inadequately, arthritis is primarily more objective than diabetes, being the result of the satisfaction of physical desire as it expresses itself through food, either in this life or the previous one. There would be little or no arthritis if the race ate with correctness and understood the proper food values and effects. Diabetes is more definitely the result of wrong *inner* desires, and is not so definitely the result of wrong *outer* desires. These may originate in this life, as I have said above, or be inherited from a previous existence. In this latter case, the incarnating soul chooses a family in which to be born, which will endow it with a body having a tendency or a natural predisposition to this disease.

There lies here a vast field of investigation; isolation must be made of the types which easily fall a prey to certain group diseases.

Syphilis and arthritis fall into the category of diseases which are largely based upon the satisfaction of physical desire. Cancer and diabetes are more definitely in the class of diseases which are connected with inner emotional desires and the violent suppressed wish-life of many. The infectious diseases, such as measles and scarlet fever, smallpox or cholera are, curiously enough, definitely group diseases and are definitely allied with the mental nature. This will surprise you but so it is.

A student with some insight into occult causes might suppose that when people are changing their focus of attention from the physical nature to the emotional, or from the emotional to the mental, that they become liable to acquire the ancient diseases, such as syphilis and cancer, which the Lemurians acquired. This is not so.

I would remind you that people do not incur these diseases because they made a shift in their consciousness, but through misuse of certain God-given powers. The shift in awareness and the disease are not remotely related to each other. I would remind you, as well, that today people are a blend of the three states of energy which we call physical, emotional and mental, which are the Lemurian, the Atlantean and the Aryan states of consciousness. Scarcely anyone today is a pure type, i.e., predominantly one or the other. They are usually a mixture of all three. You will find it difficult to find a person or a patient "changing his focus of attention from physical to emotional." He will be either emotional or mental, and at brief times, and from a purely physiological standpoint, physical. The clearest lines of demarcation are to be seen in the case of disciples who are definitely and consciously endeavouring to shift their focus of attention on to the mental plane. Nevertheless, they live predominantly in a region which we call kama-manasic, which means both astral and mental. It is an intermediate level of consciousness. Only broad generalisations are therefore possible. Such a generalisation is that syphilitic conditions are more generally physical in their origin than cancer. Clear lines of demarcation are *not* possible, and you must always remember that certain diseases may work out in a particular incarnation which have their origin in a very distant past; the seeds of the condition have lain dormant in the so-called permanent atom for ages. They may not be rooted in the tenor or quality of the present life at all. Suddenly they spring to life and influence the present incarnation, and incidentally, proffer opportunity for release.

On Fever.

Fever is simply indication of trouble and is a basic way of purification and of elimination. It is an indicator and not a disease in itself. Ponder on this, and apply it on all planes, for physical plane fever has its astral and mental counterparts. It is overexcessive energy which burns up and, in burning, relieves and cures (either through the subjugation of the germ or group of energies which caused it or by the releasing power of death). Where possible, and when the physical body is strong enough to stand the strain, it is well to let the fever have its way for a time, for it is nature's cure of certain undesirable conditions. Fevers not only give warning of the presence of that which causes distress, but have in themselves definite therapeutic value. But careful watching and balancing will be required— balancing against the energies of the body. Whilst the fever is rampant, the body is rendered relatively futile, and its normal activities are affected. As to the cure and the correct treatment of fevers, much is known by the orthodox medical profession, and this knowledge will suffice until such time as the causes of fevers are better understood and physicians can work with the cause and not with the effect.

Over-emotionalism is an astral correspondence of physical fever and indicates a rampant germ of desire which must be dealt with before the fever can subside. An over-active mind which is ill-regulated, very busy but futile in accomplishment, is the mental correspondence.

On the Cure of Cancer.

In all disease of malignant nature, there is a vital core or a living spot of energy which is absorbing, slowly or quickly, as the case may be, the life force in the man. In the early stages of such a disease as cancer, the vital core is not found until the malignant condition is established so potently that it is exceedingly difficult to do anything helpful. Yet the cure is only possible in these early developments and then the cure can be effected, but only again if the will of the patient is invoked. Little can be done in cancer cases unless there is the intelligent cooperation of the one to be healed, for the only method (which I may later elaborate) is to blend the directed will of the patient and of the healing group together into one functioning unit of force. When this has been done, then the invoked and concentrated energy will follow thought, under the ancient law, and so stimulate the area surrounding the cancer (that is, the healthy tissue) that the absorption of the weakened, diseased tissue by the stronger tissue can take place. If the energy is directed to the cancer itself, the cancerous condition will be stimulated and the trouble many times increased. The curing of cancer in the early stages falls therefore into two parts:

1. The stimulating of the healthy tissue.
2. The building in of new tissue to replace the diseased tissue which is being gradually absorbed and driven out.

Cancer always makes its appearance before there is transmutation of the emotional force, for the reason that there are few disciples (and therefore still fewer of the ordinary and majority of people) who have so transmuted emotion. This condition of freedom from emotion is so seldom to be found that—at this stage of the world's history—it may be said that it does not exist.

No one who is an integrated and actively functioning person is ever as prone to such a disease as cancer, or any disease, as is the emotional type; he is far more prone to heart trouble. A full active life prevents such a disease as cancer, but not always. As the forces of life run more slowly, as old age creeps on, cancer often appears, proving the truth of my primary contention. In days such as these, wherein cancer is the second great agent of destruction and mortality (and if I am right that cancer is a planetary disease), then almost anyone is liable to it. Fear is the great predisposing factor. Inertia and emotionalism are, likewise.

On Dementia Praecox.

What is dementia praecox? Does the phenomenon evidence a family group tradition? Is there any clue in the fact that it first manifests itself in early adolescence? Is the general practitioner correct in placing it in the category of hopeless cases? These and similar questions are constantly asked by students and practitioners of healing.

These forms of physical diseases which come under the general head of insanities are far more abstruse than is generally realised. From the standpoint of the esotericist, they fall into the following relatively simple categories:

1. Those where the difficulty is due to the breaking down of the brain tissue. Far more of these are definitely syphilitic in origin than is generally admitted, and I would remind you that, occultly speaking, that would naturally be the case, for the physical sex organs are a lower correspondence of the negative-positive relation existing in the brain between the two head centres and the pituitary and pineal glands.

2. Those where the difficulty is due to the overstimulation of the brain cells by some forms of energy which overbalance other forms and produce certain serious forms of insanity.

3. Those where there is no real physical difficulty, no lesions or diseased tissues, but simply a loose connection between the etheric body and the dense physical vehicle. Then obsession or possession can occur. Such cases are frequently (I might say, usually) regarded by the orthodox psychiatrist and medical man as forms of insanity; yet they are not truly so. If the afflicted person can be put again "in possession of himself" by some understanding psychologist, and this is entirely possible, then the trouble is ended. There is a pronounced tendency among the most forward-looking psychologists today, to handle these cases on the hypothesis which I have posited, and that is a definite improvement.

4. Those wherein certain hereditary forms of mental imbalance occur. These forms of imbalance are caused by happenings in other lives and are in the nature of punishment or retributive karma. To bring this about, the soul deliberately chooses for a physical vehicle that form which will have in it certain inherited taints, driven

thereto by the Lords of Karma when the soul is unable to grip its vehicle—as is the case in the unevolved; or with purpose and intent, when the body can be under soul direction because highly evolved. I am not listing these different forms of insanity or imbalance under the various headings, as the theme is too complicated, and often there are several predisposing factors, and often only indications of trouble which may never come to anything serious. I am only giving the categories, leaving to the research scholar the task of eventually listing symptoms and assigning due cause, after much experimental work. That time is only just arriving.

5. Those in which the mind is unduly fixed and static and controls the brain so unreasonably that there seems only one point of view, one attitude to life, and no fluidity and capability of adjustment. Such individuals may suffer, for instance, from what is called *idée fixe,* or they may be completely the victim of some obsessing mental thought. Such mental obsessions can range all the way from a mild fanaticism to religious mania, with its accompanying characteristics of sadism, ruthlessness and general morbidity.

Dementia praecox comes under the first and the fourth groupings and is a blend, usually, of the factors descriptive of both. It is inherited in every case and, if not apparently physically so, is then based on inherited astral conditions, which in their turn aid in determining the physical condition. It is syphilitic in origin (often carried over from another life) and is, in this particular life, quite incurable.

Its sexual basis is demonstrated by the fact that it manifests itself in early adolescence. The patient can, however, be greatly helped, in the early stages, if the symptoms are duly recognised and his thought life directed, and the dynamic effectiveness of new interests is employed. A spiritual motivation and like interests can sometimes retard the development of the disease; where this is the case and the matter is handled from early life onwards, the worst climaxes can be obviated. To the extent that the patient intelligently tries to help himself, and is protected also by the intelligent care of the physician, he can offset the trouble a great deal, and particularly as far as its repetition in another life is concerned.

Many of these problems are intrinsically tied up with the past, and until the laws which govern rebirth are given to the world it is difficult for me even to explain the processes governing physical inheritance, karmic results, and also what is called retributive karma. The recognition of the subtler forms of disease, and the aid of the psychologist in collaboration with orthodox medicine (which undoubtedly has its place, as, for instance, in the administration of glandular correctives), plus right hygienic handling from childhood onward, will accomplish much and gradually stamp out the mental and brain diseases which are today so numerous and so distressing.

On Euthanasia.

Some students are concerned over the organised effort to legalise euthanasia, and wonder about the placing of power of life and death in the hands of the physician. At the same time, they are aware that there is involved also the *humane* factor, in cases where no surcease can be given to prolonged suffering. To them I would say:

The problem which a consideration of the proposed practice of euthanasia involves will not exist when continuity of consciousness (which negates death) is achieved. That means that the time will come, in the racial development, when the soul will *know* that its term of physical life is over and will prepare itself to withdraw, in full consciousness, from the form. It will *know* that the service of the form is no longer required and that it must be discarded. It will *know* that its sense of awareness, being focussed in the mind nature, is strong enough and vital enough to carry it through the process and the episode of abstraction. When that consciousness has been developed in man, and the process has come to be recognised by the medical profession and the scientific students of the human mechanism, then the whole attitude to death and its processes, involving as they do pain and suffering, will be altered materially. Then the man whose time has come to die may avail himself of certain methods of release which, from the average point of view, might be regarded as involving euthanasia. Modes of abstraction will be studied and applied when death is near, and the process will be regarded as soul withdrawal, as a process of liberation and release. That time is not so far away as you might think.

Today, grave dangers attend the process of hastening withdrawal, and the legal safeguards will require most careful working out, and even then grave and serious issues might develop. But some hastening of the processes of death is in order and must be worked out. Primarily, however, the will-to-die of the patient is not based at this time on knowledge and on mental polarisation, or upon an achieved continuity of consciousness, but on emotional reactions and a shrinking from pain and from fear.

Where, however, there is terrible suffering and absolutely no hope of real help or of recovery, and where the patient is willing (or if too ill, the family is willing), then, under proper safeguards, something should be done. But this arranging of the time to go will not be based on emotion and upon compassion, but on the spiritual sciences and upon a right understanding of the spiritual possibilities of death.

On Germs.

How inadequately do words meet the need of truth. We use the word "germ" to indicate the source of some disease or the origin of some form. We talk of a germ or seed of life; we refer to the germ of an idea; we indicate that intangible point of energy which results later in some kind of manifested form. It may be a thoughtform, a human being, or a disease, yet the same word has to suffice for all three. How oft have I told you that all is energy and that there is naught else. A germ is a point of energy having within it certain living potentialities, causing certain effects upon the surrounding field of energy, and producing certain forms of expression which are recognisable upon the physical plane. But all that is referred to is, in the last analysis, some form of active energy that forms part of the energy available upon and within and around the planet Earth.

In relation to disease, a germ still remains a point of energy, but it might be regarded as energy which is not functioning correctly in relation to the particular form which has become susceptible to its activity or aware of its presence.

Germs are the first effect of an original cause. Some few form a part of the planetary evil, which means that they have a deep-seated and mental origin and one of such magnitude that the finite minds of men cannot yet grasp them. Such causes, for instance, may have their effects as a fierce and fiery and hot devotion to an idea or a person, or they may work out as an equally fierce and fiery fever in the physical body, and to this fever, according to its symptoms, a technical name will be given by the medical profession. The originating cause is the same, and the effects in the personality will differ according to the focus of the attention or where the emphasis of the life is laid. Ponder on this for I have given a hint here of real importance.

When I used these words, "the focus of attention," I did not refer to any mental attitude or to an attentive mind, but to the impact of life force in any given direction, any locality and any aspect of the human body, where the directed life energy goes. Germs are living organisms, great or small. They find their way into the human mechanism through the medium of the life force which, in its turn, uses the heart and the blood stream as its agents of distribution. In the same way, the energy of consciousness uses the nervous system and the brain as its distributing agency. Where there is inherent or inherited weakness, there the life force is not properly focussed, and there will be found some form of congestion, or some form of arrested development, or some form of predisposition to disease. When this is the case, germs can find a fruitful place in which to display their malignant activity. When the vitality is great and the life force has free and unimpeded circulation, then there will not be these predispositions, the germ cannot find a lodging, and there will not be the risk of infection.

For instance, scarlet fever is contagious, but not all those exposed to it succumb. The ability to throw off infection and immunity from contagious diseases is largely a matter of vitality (perhaps vitality in particular areas of the body where the focus of the attention and the emphasis of the life force may be found). It can also be based upon the activity of the blood corpuscles, which serves to keep the blood stream in good condition.

This focus and emphasis is the same in connection with animals, for it is not the focus of the mind but of the life energy within the physical body. This, when present and positive, protects. When it is negative and weak, it leaves the physical body (human and animal) open to the dangers of infection.

I cannot explain more fully than this, for the problem of origin and method remains an insoluble problem just as long as man remains equipped with his present mental approach and emotional reaction to pain and disease, and just as long as he places the same exaggerated emphasis upon *form* life. When a better sense of proportion has been developed, and men are beginning to think in terms of the soul and purposes and destiny, then disease, as we know it, will fall into two major categories:

1. Those which produce purification and necessitate a period of retuning and of rest for the body, preparatory to continued life on earth.

2. Those which produce the withdrawal or abstraction of the soul in its two aspects—livingness and consciousness.

On Inoculations.

"What is the standing or value of inoculation or vaccination from an occult or esoteric standpoint?" This question is often in the minds of healers as they ask the further question which is the real basis of their interest, "Does it affect the subtler bodies? How?"

There is no occult standard or value in inoculation, any more than there is an occult standard or value in giving a hypodermic injection. The entire question concerning serums and inoculations has been tremendously overemphasised by the so-called occult students. The human body, at the present time, is the recipient of such a vast amount of substance, extraneously precipitated into the interior of the body, that the whole subject is of vaster import, yet of lesser importance, than men think. Such is the paradox which I present to you. Wrong food of every kind, the inhalation of smoke down the centuries, the breathing in of tainted air, the taking of medicines and pills and tablets of every possible description, the rifling of the vegetable and mineral kingdoms in search of their ingredients, and the injection of mineral substances, of drugs and of serums, till one wonders sometimes at the remarkable assimilative powers of the human frame.

In all fairness, however, I would remind you that, as far as the physical well-being of man is concerned, these methods and techniques of the West have resulted in the production of a healthier race than in the East, in a very definite prolongation of human life, and in the elimination of many dire physical scourges which used to take their toll of man. This I, an Oriental, do admit. I have stated the situation thus in order to expand your view from the specific to the whole.

In relation to disease and inoculation, I would remind you that there are three groups of diseases which are not peculiar to man, but which are indigenous in the planet itself. These diseases are found in widely differing forms, in all the kingdoms in nature. These three families or groups of diseases are:

1. The great cancer group of diseases.
2. The syphilitic group.
3. Tuberculosis.

Most of the objections made by doctors with occult tendencies are based unconsciously on a feeling that there should be higher methods of controlling diseases in man than by injecting into the human body substance taken from the bodies of animals. That is most surely and definitely correct, and some day it will be demonstrated. Another reaction on their part is one of sensitive disgust, again largely unrecognised. A more vital objection should be based on the suffering entailed on the animals providing the vaccine and other substances.

The effect on the inner bodies is practically nil, and far less than the diseases themselves. Herein lies for the future a most interesting question. How far do diseased conditions in the human body carry through and affect the inner bodies from the structural angle? It is a question I do not intend to answer. The controlling of modern disease is being handled by modern medicine primarily in three ways: through the science of sanitation, through preventive medicine, and through inoculation. These are the lower correspondences to methods of activity emanating from the astral plane, from the etheric levels, and from the earth itself.

The science of sanitation, the use of water, and the growing knowledge of hydrotherapy are the precipitation on earth of certain inner activities on the astral plane of a most definite nature. From the angle of the aspirant, these methods are called purification.

The science of prevention (both of diseases and of death) is the precipitation on earth of certain modes of procedure on the etheric plane whereby forces are correctly used and certain destructive agencies are controlled and prevented from going the destructive way.

The science of inoculation is purely physical in origin and concerns only the animal body. This latter science will shortly be superseded by a higher technique, but the time is not yet.

On Glands.

"Is it possible by certain types of meditation to stimulate either one of the post or ante lobes of the pituitary body, when there is a minus functioning? Will a meditation designed to integrate the personality automatically adjust the trouble and bring about proper pituitary activity? Will this also adjust and balance the activity of the other important glands?"

You have here several questions; the whole matter is too vast for proper handling within the available time and limits.

I would say, however, very briefly, that the stimulation of either lobe of the pituitary body, and equally the stimulation of any of the glands by meditation, undertaken by neophytes, is a most dangerous undertaking. It can be done, but it is not an advisable proceeding except under the expert supervision of some of those who know more than you know and who can see more than you can see. The glands are the result of the activity or the inactivity of the centres or chakras in the body, and parallel their development. This development is dependent upon the ray and the point in evolution. The subject is vast and difficult, and I would have you all remember that constant dwelling upon the *physical* factors to be found in the personality equipment is *not* the way of the disciple. He must aim, as you suggest, at personality integration and at the goal of being a pure channel for the soul. Such an integration is the result, normally achieved, of

1. Character-building.
2. Soul contact through meditation.
3. Life expression through service.

The practice of these three, over a long period of years, will inevitably produce the desired results as far as the glandular equipment is concerned, and as far as the total mechanism can stand the pressure of the soul requirements, as they must be met in each specific life.

On the Vital Body.

"What are the principal factors that can be complied with in order to build a strong healthy vital body? Is it possible for a person with a rather weak vital body to strengthen it? May not a so-called weak vital body be a healthy one at the same time, the weakness manifesting in non-staying power and a slowness in recovery from fatigue?"

This question is concise and can be briefly answered. In fact it must be, or otherwise a long discussion will be necessary upon the subject of the vital body, and that is too vast a one with which to deal here, and the implications are too many. I have given you much in the various books I have written.

When you say a *weak* vital body I presume you mean one which is loosely coordinated with the physical vehicle and loosely connected, and which has therefore a weak hold upon the outer form, for it is the close integration of the etheric body with the physical form which is the cause of all its staying power. You are right in your belief that one can be perfectly healthy but have little resistance to fatigue.

The principal factors in re-establishing or making a better etheric control are:

1. Sunshine.
2. Careful diet, with the emphasis upon the proteins and vitamins.
3. The avoidance of fatigue and worry.

Against all the above, at this time, climate, world conditions, environment and our civilisation militate, and the individual has therefore to resign himself to a state of affairs which lies outside his individual control.

A normal, sane, regulated life is the best means for establishing a better measure of vitality. This is, I presume, what you mean. You need to remember, however, that where there is a devitalised etheric body, and conditions are such that a re-establishment of a vital control seems difficult or impossible, there must be recognition of karmic limitations and a willingness to submit to them and leave affairs to work themselves out. This particular life is not the only one there is. Frequently, therefore, in any particular incarnation, conditions cannot be changed, and are prolonged by inner rebellion and revolt. A disciple has to learn the lesson of going on, as the expression is, in spite of and not because of circumstances.

On Prana.

You can discover much on the nature of prana if you use the books which you possess and should possess. In my book *A Treatise on Cosmic Fire* and in A.A.B.'s book *The Light of the Soul,** the whole subject is considered.

Suffice it to say that:

1. There is nothing in manifestation except energy, taking form, using and actuating forms and dissipating forms.
2. This energy is divided into three types of so-called electrical phenomena, called in *The Secret Doctrine* and in *A Treatise on Cosmic Fire,* fire by friction, solar fire, and electrical fire.

---

* *A Treatise on Cosmic Fire* .... Pages 77-116.
   The Light of the Soul .... Pages 77, 217-225, 280-282.
                                        Pages 328-330, 332.

3. Prana is the name given to the energy which is drawn upon the physical plane from the etheric aspect of all phenomenal life. That etheric aspect of the divine energy is a synthesis of energies. If the energy in which an individual primarily lives and moves and has the focus of his being is, for instance, predominantly astral, then the major expression of energy in his equipment will be astral or emotional feeling energy. He will react all the time to physical energy or prana and to astral energy or the many sentient emotional forces. These work out pre-eminently through the spleen, the solar plexus and the throat, and affect in different ways the physical spleen, the stomach and the thyroid gland.

4. Interest in these two types of energy, when evidenced by an individual, is based on the fact that they are the two in which he himself is habitually immersed and to which he most easily and normally responds.

5. The current of energy used in healing will be a synthesis of the energies with which the healer normally works, with that type of energy predominating which is, for him, the paramount energy of his life. The average unintelligent healer is usually simply a transmitter of prana itself, which is the energy of the planet. This combines with the etheric physical energies of the patient, passing through the healer's body. These stimulate the patient sufficiently so that he is enabled to throw off the enfeebling disease. Some healers can work with that type of force and with emotional energy blended, and produce activity, therefore, not only in the patient's physical body but also in his astral body. This brings about serious difficulties at times and often hinders true physical healing, on account of the astral turmoil produced. On this matter, I cannot here enlarge, and there is no time for a longer elucidation at this time.

Mental healers (true mental healers who are rare indeed) blend soul energy with the two above mentioned forces and this produces a synthesis of the personality forces. Carried forward intelligently, this synthesis brings about the healing of the person through the production of definite organisation and alignment.

Soul healing supersedes the three above mentioned methods, and produces the pouring into and through the mechanism of the patient of pure soul energy. It was in this way that Christ worked, and there are few today to work this way. It must be held before you, however, as an objective.

Physical healing by prana is very common. It is often temporarily effective, but it concerns and deals only with effects and never touches causes. The disease can therefore be abated, but never cured. The power to heal mentally is on the increase and produces relatively permanent effects. But astral healing is rare and very seldom successful. The potency of the astral nature of the healer and also of the patient, and its usually unregulated condition, is too great for effective work, owing to the polarisation of humanity at this time and to the lack of correct emotional poise and control.

On Oriental and Occidental Bodies.

The question is also often in the minds of some healers whether there is a difference in the causes of disease and the effects as experienced in oriental or occidental bodies. To them I would say:

Humanity is one and the same all over the world, and both eastern and western bodies are prone to the same diseases and manifest the same symptoms; all suffer from tuberculosis, from cancer and the sexual taints; all die frequently from pneumonia and influenza. Through sanitation and other curative methods, carried out on a large scale, ancient diseases (inherited from old Atlantis) such as bubonic plague and cholera, are being slowly stamped out. They still crop out in the East owing to the strength of the ancient civilisations, the lack of food, of sanitation, and the dense crowding. They are also climatic diseases and perish in the colder air of the north. Certain diseases are the result of wrong diet, used over unnumbered centuries.

One of the main reasons for the apparent difference (if there is any) may lie also in the greater age of the oriental races. The diseases of old age, and those of youth or middle age, have their variations, and Asia and its peoples are very, very old. The body stock is wearing out fast. Yet the Japanese show no sign of that old age. India is far older than Europe, but the Chinese and Japanese stock is older still, yet they demonstrate no such sign of effete old age. The reason for this lies in the very different type of emotional body as found in the Aryan or Atlantean. The whole question is incalculably difficult.

I might answer your question, however, very briefly, by saying that there is no difference whatever in the basic causes of disease in the East and the West. They are the same for the whole human family.

On the Nervous System.

In the right understanding of the relationship of the etheric or vital body (with its major and minor centres and its network of nadis) to the nervous system of the human body, two great aspects of soul activity can be grasped.

First, that aspect of soul life which enables the soul to motivate and force into incarnation and activity the physical mechanism, the body, through the galvanising activity of what we call *Life*.

Second, that aspect of soul life which preserves the physical vehicle in health through the free play of the pranic currents. The above is an attempt to express a great truth in as simple a fashion as possible. The true significance of the above statement embodies the next great step in the field of true psychology and of healing. The whole subject is profoundly interesting. Some of it I have dealt with in the pages of *A Treatise on White Magic* * and you would find it of value to study the matter there outlined.

The general situation in this connection might be outlined very briefly as follows:

A human being is a combination of various types of force. There is the force or energy of matter itself which might be regarded as the energy aspect, in its totality, of the cells or atoms of the body. The word "cell" itself suggests, in its usual connotation, an imprisoned life, and life and energy are, for the esotericist, synonymous terms. This is the third aspect of divinity, expressing itself in humanity. There is also the dual energy which the soul embodies or transmits; this might be likened to two streams of energy, which merge and blend to form one stream when detached from the body, and which divide into two when they enter into matter and form. They bring to matter, or to the aggregated cell lives, the contribution of quality—consciousness and pure life. It might be stated also that:

a. The stream of life-energy finds its way to the heart, the physical heart, and there (via the physical permanent atom) it energises coherently the entire physical body, using the blood stream as its major agency and channel of contact and communication between this central pow-

---

* *A Treatise on White Magic, pages* 18-50.

erhouse of life and the periphery. As we well know, the blood is the life. This life activity is the factor which gathers together and holds in form all the living atoms and cells of the body. When that life thread is withdrawn by the soul at death, the living atoms separate, the body falls apart and disintegration ensues, with the atomic lives returning to the reservoir of power, to the bosom of living matter from whence they came.

b. The stream of energy which conveys the soul quality of intelligence, plus love-wisdom, and which constitutes what we understand as the consciousness, with its powers to contact, to sense and to rationalise, only penetrates as far as the physical brain. There this second aspect concentrates itself or anchors itself in the region of the pineal gland. From there in ever increasing potency, as the processes of incarnation and experience are pursued, the soul begins to control, galvanise into purposeful activity, and to use the physical body. Remember that, to the soul, the body is only its response apparatus on the physical plane and a medium of expression.

It might also be pointed out, as a third necessary statement, that the soul pours its consciously directed energy into the dense physical body through the medium of the etheric or vital body. This instrument is composed of:

1. Seven major centres of force and forty-nine minor centres. The major centres are found in the head and up the spinal column. The minor centres are to be found scattered all over the body.
2. The etheric network which is composed of streams of energy, connects all the centres into two systems— one major and one minor—and radiates out from these centres all over the entire body.

3. The nadis are infinitesimally small threads of energy or force fibres which radiate out from every part of the network and underlie every part of the triple nervous system. They are found in their millions, and produce the sensitive response apparatus through which we work and of which the mechanism of the five senses is one of the externalisations.

The controlling power station will be found to vary according to the point in evolution reached:

1. Low-grade humanity uses the solar plexus as the point where the basic energy is localised temporarily. There will also be found a slight activity in the ajna centre.
2. Average humanity works partly through the solar plexus centre but largely through the ajna centre and the throat centre.
3. High-grade human beings, the intelligentsia and world aspirants use the head centre, plus the ajna centre, the throat, heart, and solar plexus.

Finally it might be said that the physical apparatus which is the direct result of the inner activity of the centres, network and nadis, is the heart, the endocrine system and the brain. Into this general plan, very sketchily outlined above, all ancient medicine (particularly the Tibetan, the Chinese, and the Hindu), with our modern western science, fits. The correlation of the western and eastern techniques still remains to be made, and much will be gained thereby. Further than this I cannot here enlarge, but the above will suffice to show that the methods which you may discover in your reading (and their name is Legion) can all be brought into relation to this general scheme of energy processes in the human body.

On Diet.

No set diet could be entirely correct for a group of people on differing rays, of different temperaments and equipment and at various ages. Individuals are every one of them unlike on some points; they require to find out what it is that they, as individuals, need, in what manner their bodily requirements can best be met, and what type of substances can enable them best to serve. Each person must find this out for himself. There is no *group* diet. No enforced elimination of meat is required or strict vegetarian diet compulsory. There are phases of life and sometimes entire incarnations wherein an aspirant subjects himself to a discipline of food, just as there may be other phases or an entire life wherein a strict celibacy is temporarily enforced. But there are other life cycles and incarnations wherein the disciple's interest and his service lie in other directions. There are later incarnations where there is no constant thought about the physical body, and a man works free of the diet complex and lives without concentration upon the form life, eating that food which is available and upon which he can best sustain his life efficiency. In preparation for certain initiations, a vegetable diet has in the past been deemed essential. But this may not always be the case, and many disciples prematurely regard themselves as in preparation for initiation.

On the Spleen.

The spleen is the most important agent of the life force, but it is the life force inherent in matter itself, independently of form. It is therefore closely related to the planetary physical body. It is the externalisation of a very important centre.

There are three centres in the body (with allied externalisations) which are basically essential to life.

1. The heart centre and the physical heart itself. In these the life principle (the *Spirit* aspect) is located. Life and Spirit are one.
2. The head centre and the brain in which the consciousness principle (the *Soul* aspect) is located.
3. The pranic centre and the spleen, in which the life of matter itself (the *Matter* aspect) is located.

You must bear in mind that, as H.P.B. points out, the dense physical body is not a principle. It is atomic matter which is held in form by etheric substance, under the control of the soul. It is automatic in its response, and reacts to the outer world of impacts and inner impulses, but has no initiatory life of its own. It is composed of units of energy, as is all else in nature, and has its own individual life; its focus for the distribution of energy for this life is the spleen.

In the spleen, the negative life of matter and the living energy of the positive etheric body, are brought together. and then a "spark," as it is called, is made between the inner living bodies of man (through the medium of the etheric body) and the physical plane. It is a reflection on the lowest rung of the evolutionary ladder, as far as man is concerned, and corresponds to the relation of soul and body or—on a higher turn of the spiral—of spirit and matter.

On the Vagus Nerve.

There are two powerful centres connected with the vagus nerve: the heart centre and the centre at the base of the spine. These two, when brought under the control of the soul, functioning through the head centre (the brahmarandra), produce the raising of the kundalini fire. This, when taking place, swings the entire nervous system into a special form of rhythmic activity and responsiveness, and it is through the stimulation and the control of the vagus nerve that this is accomplished. It is not the vagus nerve which is instrumental in raising the kundalini fire, but the reverse situation. When the head, the heart and the centre at the base of the spine are in magnetic and dynamic rapport, producing a radiatory effect, then they affect the vagus nerve and the fires of the body are unified and raised, producing purification and the "opening of all doors."

On the Eye.

There is a certain school of scientific theorists who are working on the theory that the eye is the declarative factor in the human body and the rule or the key to its right understanding. They have already demonstrated much in connection with its declarative powers, where disease is concerned. They are on right lines. Nevertheless, the science with which they are working is so embryonic as yet that their conclusions are not fully demonstrated nor entirely reliable.

In the immediate future, when our planetary life is somewhat calmer, the whole subject of Vision and the registration by the eye of the inner worlds will receive an enormous impetus, and conditions—hitherto undreamed of—will be revealed. Man will enter into a new life and a higher era of understanding. The teaching concerning the iris of the eye is an indication of this.

Why not read up on the eye a little and note its occult correspondences to the created world, and to the whole problem of light? The eyes and the soul are closely related and—speaking in the language of occultism—the right eye is the representative of the soul, and therefore the agent of buddhi, whilst the left eye is the representative of the personality, and the agent of the lower concrete mind. You will find it interesting to read what can be found in *The Secret Doctrine* and other books (including mine) on this subject; it will compel the conclusion that here is a field of investigation hitherto unopened and a teaching which will warrant careful study for the sake of the group, if for no other reason.

On Psychological Causes of Disease.

Do "psychological causes of disease" register in brain symptoms before reflexing to other parts of the body? A sentence in *The Light of the Soul* has a bearing here:

> "The brain, for instance, is the 'shadow' or the external organ of the mind, and it will be found by the investigator that the contents of the brain cavity have a correspondence to the aspects of the human mechanism found upon the mental plane."

Bear in mind that the life force works through the heart, utilising the blood stream, whilst the consciousness aspect works through the brain, using the nervous system. This is the first and most important point to grasp.

Psychological causes of disease register in the brain or (if of a very low order) in the solar plexus. They do not, however, make their presence felt as symptoms of disease in these places where they thus register. They are energies or forces which—when brought into contact with the energies of the body—produce, as a result (and not before this point) those conditions to which we give the name of disease. The psychological causes are forms of energy, working out through the appropriate centres in the body, and these, in their turn, condition the glandular system.

The secretion or hormone, generated under this esoteric stimulation, finds its way into the blood stream, and the result of all this interaction can be either good health, as it expresses sound psychological causes, or poor health, as it expresses the reverse.

It is the internal relation between the subtler energies, working through certain centres, plus the related endocrine system, with its relation to the blood stream, that constitutes both the possibility of disease and its cure. But this recognition is still academically lacking. Much of the inherent psychology is grasped, but a gap still exists between the physical and the etheric bodies, and little recognition of the etheric body is yet academically accorded. There is yet no real understanding of the relation between the inner psyche and the outer form, via the etheric body. The study of the glands has somewhat helped, but medical science must go a step further and relate the glandular system to the inner centres.

On Problems of Melancholia.

These problems of melancholia are difficult to place and are due to a wide variety of causes. I will list them here, and the list may at some time serve you.

1. A sense of frustration, a thwarted wish-life, or a recognition of a basic life failure.
2. A sense of dramatics, and a desire to figure importantly on the little stage of a person's life. This can often be quite unrealised and have a truly subconscious origin, or it can be a carefully cultivated habit or attitude.
3. A devitalised condition, largely of an etheric nature, which robs life of all joy and desire and presents always a sense of futility. Many women passing through the menopause experience this.

4. A certain form of breakdown in the cells found in a particular area of the brain.

5. Based on fear of insanity and of death—a baseless fear which has never materialised but which does constitute an *idée fixe,* so that the person is the victim of a well developed thoughtform.

6. A tuning-in, through oversensitivity, on the suffering and massed pain of the world. Disciples can be temporarily overcome by this.

7. This condition is very seldom brought about by any form of obsession such as "an earthbound entity or a living vampire-like person." A very few such cases have been known, but they are too rare to be considered a factor.

8. Sometimes a person tunes in on a state of massed melancholia, such as can be found in our sanitariums or asylums. The condition has then nothing really to do with him, but being sensitive, he identifies himself with those who are suffering from acute melancholia.

9. Melancholia, as a symptom of disease (not of brain disease) is also fairly frequent and will disappear when the disease is under proper treatment.

A person may be suffering from a combination of such causes, as for instance a combination, let us say of the causes in 1, 2, 6.

On Full Moon and Psychoses.

One of the departments of esoteric medicine in the future will concern itself with the law of cycles, lunar and solar. It will then be demonstrated as a fact, what has always been suspected and is now generally recognised, that the period of the full moon has a definite effect upon unbalanced people, upon the dreaming state and frequently conditions quite drastically, the neurotic and erotic conditions so prevalent at this time.

The tremendous increase in insanity and imbalance today is due to three major causes:

1. The transitional period of today producing a clash between the Aquarian and the Piscean forces, has led to a condition which makes it very difficult for sensitive people to live normally at all. To express the idea in symbol: It is almost as if the race, after habituating itself to live on the earth, had now to accustom itself to live in water. I am talking from the standpoint of the form.

2. The intense spiritual and mental stimulation which is being applied today to the masses by the planetary Hierarchy. The intent is to bring to an end old forms of living, to create new forms through the process of adjustment, and thus bring in a new civilisation based on a more subjective *culture*. I would ask you to ponder on this last sentence.

3. The pouring in of more light from the astral plane (at present unrecognised) and also the tremendous increase of ordinary physical plane illumination. This produces oversensitivity. The work done by the prevailing use of electric light and the general glare in which humanity now lives, will exact its toll from the race until the human mechanism has adjusted itself to *light*. Remember that this general use of light is less than one hundred years old and is an occult effect with far reaching results.

I mention these three things because they are responsible for much of the predisposition to sensitivity of an abnormal kind. Occult students well know that at the time of the full moon certain high contacts are easier than at other times, but it is right here, my brother, that the difficulty lies.

At the time of the full moon (over a period of five days) the moon and the planet are the recipients of more reflected light from the sun than at any other time. For this there is a subjective cause. I can only explain it to you by a symbol which may convey truth to you or which may act as a blind. Symbolically speaking, the period of intensest meditation of our planetary Logos comes around at the full moon period each month; just as you have your daily meditation so He in His high place, has His cyclic point of contact. This produces the pouring in of radiance and the entering in of energy both subjective and objective. For all true students, therefore, their work on the mental plane is facilitated; they are enabled then to meditate more successfully and to attain realisation with greater ease. They definitely share in the achievement of the Lord of Shamballa.

The moon, as you know, is a shell, an ancient form through which the planetary Logos at one time sought expression. It is slowly disintegrating physically but not astrally as yet, and is therefore still closely linked with the astral body of the planetary Logos and therefore with the astral bodies of all people. Its influence is consequently more potent at the time of the full moon upon all who are unbalanced. This lack of equilibrium, which it really is, will eventually be found to exist between the astral body, the etheric body and the physical mechanism.

People who are definitely aspirants and people who are definitely mental, can profit by these full moon cycles; those who are definitely unbalanced, positively astral, and emotional, and frequently swept by uncontrolled desire, are hindered, overstimulated, and psychically upset by these same cycles. The veil of illusion is lit up at that time with a consequent result of hallucination, astral visions, psychic urges, and those misinterpretations of life, of over-emphasis upon aspects of life which we call phobias, lunacy, etc.

I would like to make a suggestion here, which is not possible for me to prove to you, but which the future will substantiate. The major diseases called mental, seldom have anything to do with the mind itself. They are:

1. Diseases of the brain.
2. Disorders of the solar plexus.
3. Astral domination.
4. Premature clairvoyance and clairaudience.
5. Obsession.
6. *Absence* of mind.
7. Soullessness.

This is, of course, a wide generalisation and has no reference to that category of diseases in which both mind and brain are involved. The diseases of mystics are also in a different category. These latter diseases involve the brain of course, indicate mental imbalance, produce various types of heart disease and the diverse neurotic tendencies with which the saints of the world were so often afflicted.

One thing I will add, however, for your encouragement. As the race, as a whole, becomes governed by the solar Lord, the sun god, the Soul, then the cycles of the moon will steadily lose their baleful effect and there will be a dying out of the various neurotic complaints and mental diseases today so prevalent. The time is not yet. It is not easy for me to give more information concerning the moon and its phases, as it constitutes one of the major mysteries to be revealed at the third initiation.

On Distribution of Force; Blood Transfusion.

Instead of two questions, you have several. Let me list them for you so that you will see what I mean, and for clarity in replying. Several of these questions are inferred and not definitely posited, but if I am to deal with them they must be put in the form of questions and even then the subject is so vast that there will not be time.

1. How can a more harmonious distribution of force be accomplished for the benefit of all?
2. Can you give us some more specific instructions and indicate to us some esoteric methods, suitable to our stage of development in connection with this problem of distribution?
3. Has the fact of blood transfusion . . . any correspondence in some process of the transfusion of subtle energies on the inner planes?
4. Are there some special means, besides what we are already trying to do, by which those of us who are on the second ray could more effectively transfuse our love quality into brothers on the first ray, and vice versa?
5. What is the interrelation and the cooperation among the ray lives and particularly between the first and second ray entities?
6. How can the example of the close cooperation and friendship between the Master M. and the Master K. H. be of practical help and inspiration to us?

You will see from the above how impossible it will be to deal with this wide range of subjects. I will, however, give you the briefest answers to some of them, or indicate the line along which your ideas may flow.

1. A harmonious distribution of forces varies in its arrangement and consequently in its outer effect not only

according to ray types but according to the age of the soul, and the individual status upon the Path. There is a difference in this arrangement in the subtle bodies of the probationary disciple and of the accepting disciple, and of the accepted disciple and for each grade upon the path of initiation. This arrangement is brought about in three ways or is subject to three forms of developing influences.

a. Through the life of aspiration, as registered in the physical brain consciousness.

b. Through the spontaneous awakening of the centres and in their right geometrical progression. This I have referred to in some of my books, but more cannot be given as it is one of the secrets of the first initiation. The rearranging and the readjustment proceeds during the whole period of the Path, technically understood.

c. Through the decentralisation of the whole inner conscious life. The server becomes:

1. The mystical extrovert.
2. The "one who steps aside from the centre."
3. The "one who lives upon the periphery of the heart."
4. The "one who hovers over the central lotus."
5. The "distant one who sees from far away, yet lives within the form of all that is."

A study of these descriptive phrases may give you the clue to the right distribution of energy.

2. The second question is somewhat answered in the above brief statement. I am doing what I can in my personal instructions * to all of you to bring about two things:

a. Clear the field of the personality life so that the higher energies can have freer play.

---

* *Discipleship in the New Age,* Vol. I and II.

b. Bring about those conditions and orientations which will produce harmony within, and consequently and equally, harmonious relations without. I would remind you, however, that the inner harmony of one brother in a group may not be adequate to produce harmony in another brother or in the group.

3. Blood transfusion is symbolic of two things: First, that the blood is the life, and secondly, that there is but one Life permeating all forms, and therefore transferable under right conditions. It is also a synthetic act of service. Ponder on this.

4. Your question gives me an opportunity to point out that even an understanding of, and interest in, the ray types (as represented for instance in a group) may itself lead to a subtle separative attitude. There is no necessity for any Son of God in incarnation upon the physical plane or in the three worlds to "transfuse" his ray quality into his brother. These ray qualities are shared by all alike, and a brother's own soul—differing in no way from another soul—will effect the needed transmutation or transfusion into the personality life. One may facilitate the process by providing those conditions of harmony and peace wherein a brother is faced with as few contrary attitudes as possible, and where the interplay of love may produce an effective stimulation. But this is not transfusion. What exists in you exists in all, and the love quality (above all other qualities) is the *dominant* characteristic of all rays.

5. This question is not only one of the mysteries of the occult sciences, but it is of far too vast a nature in its implications and too complicated a problem for me to deal with in this place.

6. The relationship of the two Masters you mention can be studied in two ways:

a. Through a consideration of the effective working relation which exists between the groups of disciples working under Them.

b. Through a study of those people (and they are many) who have a first ray personality and a second ray ego, or vice versa.

In the last analysis, my brother, we bring about the correct distribution of force, leading to harmonious relations, when we seek to live selflessly. For the probationer, this means an *imposed* selfless activity upon the physical plane. For the accepted disciple, it involves a life free from all selfish, self-centered emotion, and of these self-pity and self-dramatisation are outstanding examples; for the initiate it means a mental attitude which is devoid of selfish thought, and free from the dramatisations in thought of the ego.

On Suffering.

Suffering, in the last analysis, is only possible when the soul is identified with the body, or rather, when the spiritual aspect of the soul (in the body) is identified with the animal soul, which informs and vitalises the form and constitutes its temporary life. During unconsciousness, the animal soul is aware of pain and suffering, and those who nurse and watch know this well, but there is no real pain or true distress because the real man, the spiritual soul, has been driven away either by excessive pain (as in true unconsciousness) or by narcotics.

The suffering of the soul, when the personality goes astray, is only a symbolic form of words. There is no pain or true suffering, and frequently no knowledge of the happening, for the vibration is not high enough to penetrate into that high plane where dwells the soul. Where, however, there is such knowledge, the soul experiences, if I might so express it, a sense of lost opportunity, and therefore a sense of frustration, but it is not more than that, for the patience of the soul, as of the Hierarchy, is illimitable. Just because we speak symbolically and say the soul suffers, you must not interpret it in ordinary terms.

The suffering of Christ or of the planetary Logos or of God Himself, is not comprehensible in terms of personality reaction. We use the words, but they really mean "detached and isolated identification." Does that convey aught to you, my brother?

Wrong identification is the cause of pain and leads to suffering, distress and various effects. Right identification leads to understanding and comprehension of the psychological attitudes of the sufferer, but to no true pain or distress as we normally understand it.

On Planetary Energy.

The sumtotal of energy remains the same for as long as a planet persists, with its forms and life expression. It is part of the great storehouse of energy. It is the use and the effect of this energy, as it is appropriated by a form or forms of some kind, which we note as it is attracted from its own place to a place where normally it would not be functioning. There it creates situations and produces difficulties which are closely connected with a man's karma and destiny. There is a great abstracting energy which we call Death, whose influence at a given time proves more potent than the united influences of the body atoms and cells. It produces the tendency to withdraw and finally to abstract the soul energy which avails itself of these potencies in the process of discarding a vehicle on some plane or another. It might be said that the seeds of death (the germ of death) are latent in the planet and in the forms.

When powerful enough to be recognised, we call them *germs,* but this connotes a definite stage of almost tangible proof. When unduly potent, they produce acute disease and consequent death; when more feeble in effect, we call them illness and note their purificatory effect. These contaminations (as they can be called, though it is by no means a good name) are only such when that aggregate of energies which we call a man is brought in contact with these contaminating influences or types of ancient energies, and the reaction or the response is, from the angle of the comfort of the physical body, bad.

On Transmutation of Desire.

The point to be borne in mind is that desire dominates and controls action when the life force is focussed in the desire nature, as it predominantly is with the majority of people. But planned mental control is only possible when the life is focussed on the mental plane. When this is the case, desire will not require suppression, because the power of the focussed attention will be elsewhere and there will consequently be no furious desire to suppress. Suppression is an effort by the man focussed in the astral body to bring in the will aspect of the mind. But this he seldom does. The desire may pass off through the intense effort the man is making to achieve some mental consciousness, but no suppression takes place really, nor is the will evoked. When a man's life is run and controlled by the mind from mental levels, then transmutation does take place; transmutation (whereby the astral nature is changed and altered) may be of a spiritual nature or simply of an expedient nature. Desire may be transmuted into spiritual aspiration or into an attitude which is in conformity to the will of the mind which is expressing it. Hence the necessity for careful analysis of motive and of objectives.

On Karma.

I have already suggested to you that the entire question of karma is as yet imperfectly comprehended. A great Law of Cause and Effect exists, but one particular aspect of it has never been emphasised, and the knowledge of humanity on the subject of karma is very elementary. Karma has always been interpreted in terms of disaster, and consequences that are painful, of error, of penalty, and of evil happenings, both for the individual and for the group. Yet, such is the beauty of human nature, and much that is done is of such a fine quality and so selfless and so happily oriented, that the evil is frequently offset by the good. There is everywhere, little as it may be realised, an abundance of good karma of a potency (under the same Law) equal to that which is regarded as bad. Of this, small mention is ever made. This good karma brings into activity forces which may work out as healing energies in any specific case. Upon these energies for good, which have been earned and *are* operating, the healer can always count. This is my first point. Ponder upon it.

Karma *is* a determining factor, but unless a healer is an advanced initiate and so able to work effectively and intelligently on the causal levels whereon souls dwell, it is impossible for him to decide whether any specific case will yield to healing treatment or not. Therefore, the healer or practising disciple assumes in his mind the possibility of cure (which may be possible or not) and of the patient's good karma, and proceeds to apply all possible aid. This is my second point.

My third point is to suggest to you and to all engaged in the healing art that much of the so-called disaster, involved in disease and in death (particularly the latter) is to be found in a wrong attitude toward death, and to an overestimation of the beneficence of form life. The release of a soul through disease and death is not necessarily an unhappy occurrence. A new and better attitude to the phenomenon of death is essential, is possible and near. Upon this I need not here enlarge. But I do seek to give you a new slant on the subject of sickness and of death.

Will you be astonished also if I state that under the Law it is quite possible to "interfere with karma"? The great Laws can be transcended and frequently have been in the past, and increasingly will be in the future. The Law of Gravitation is frequently offset and daily transcended when an aeroplane is in flight. The energy of faith can set in motion superior energies which can negate or retard disease. The whole subject of faith, and its vital significance and potency, is as little understood as is the Law of Karma. This is a tremendous subject, and I cannot further enlarge upon it. But I have said enough to offer you food for thought.

As regards the lengthening of the span of life during the past century of scientific attainment, I would point out that true techniques and the possibilities of organised soul action are always parodied and falsely demonstrated on the physical plane by the earlier scientific activities which are right in motive but which are only a symbol, on the outer sphere of life, of coming and usually future soul action. The life span will eventually be shortened or lengthened at will by souls who consciously serve, and use the mechanism of the body as the instrument whereby the Plan is served. Frequently, today, lives are preserved in form— both in old age and in infancy—that could be well permitted liberation. They serve no useful purpose and cause much pain and suffering to forms which nature (left to herself) would not long use, and would extinguish. Note that word. Through our overemphasis on the value of form life, and through the universal fear of death—that great transition which we must all face—and through our uncertainty as to the fact of immortality, and also through our deep attachment to form, we arrest the natural processes and hold the life, which is struggling to be free, confined to bodies quite unfitted to the purposes of the soul. Misunderstand me not. I desire to say naught that could place a premium on suicide. But I do say, and I say with emphasis, that the Law of Karma is oft set aside when forms are preserved in coherent expression which should be discarded, for they serve no useful purpose. This preservation is, in the majority of cases, enforced by the subject's group and not by the subject himself—frequently an unconscious invalid, an old person whose response apparatus of contact and response is imperfect, or a baby who is not normal. These cases constitute definite instances of an offsetting of the Law of Karma.

The soul, through alignment, enters into a right use of time; or rather the brain, which is the only time-conscious factor in man, is no longer the dominant attribute; the mind, as the agent of the soul (whose consciousness is inclusive of the past, present, and the future), sees life and experience as it truly is. Death, therefore, is referred to as an episode, and as a transitional point in a vast series of transitions. When this attitude of the soul is grasped, our entire technique of living, and incidentally of dying, is utterly altered.

In conclusion, however, and in apparent but no real negation of all that I have said above, let me repeat that the healer will give of his best to the one he seeks to heal. Having no clairvoyant power in the majority of cases, and being time-conscious and under the influence of karma, he will do his utmost along the lines of his own training and in accordance with the instructions given in this treatise on healing. I suggest that you grasp that the objective before any healer at this time and at this given point in the evolutionary unfoldment of the race is the need, when so asked, to aid in the bringing about of health to the body and its sustained experience in life. You need also to realise that much that is believed, accepted and taught by the metaphysicians today is based on wrong premises, such as the nature of matter, the time equation, the value of form existence, and the fear of death. Seek to eliminate these attitudes from your consciousness, and you will arrive at a truer perspective as to the healing art.

Later, in a few years' time, we can probably begin to deal with specific cases. I seek, however, at this time to hold you to wide generalisations, and to basic laws and propositions, and not to cloud the issues with purely physical plane occurrences, temporary or chronic, or with death and destiny.

No request for real aid must ever be refused, however. A deaf ear must not be turned to trouble, either physical, mental or psychological. But I would call to your attention the fact that success in healing may not always mean release from disease and the so-called physical cure of the patient. It might simply involve, if physically successful, the postponement of the plan of the soul for the person. Success might mean the correction of wrong inner attitudes, of erroneous lines of thought, and at the same time leave the physical body as it was. It might mean the placing of the patient (through wise teaching and patience) en rapport with his soul and the consequent reorienting of the life to the eternal verities. It might consist in the proper preparation of the person for the tremendous purpose which we call Death, and thus bring about the relief of pain in this way.

The whole science of healing will shift eventually and increasingly into the realm of preventive medicine and the psychological adjustment of the individual within his group, and the providing of right living conditions, correct dieting and housing for the peoples. That, however, takes much time, and whilst the race is on its way to the newer modes of living, with their resultant effects of better health and a more correct comprehension of the laws of health, all who stand in the world as magnetic centres must proceed, according to the light that is in them, to work with people, in order to help them, to heal them, and to aid them in making needed adjustments. Nothing should stop your service along this line, not even the realisation of limitation and of ignorance. Do all you can to encourage and to sympathise, to point out undesirable attitudes, to end wrong ways of living, and change poor modes of psychological expression as far as you see them and to the best of your ability. Remember, nevertheless, that your best way may be far short of your future capacities, and remain ready ever to change your point of view when a higher and a better way is presented to you. Above everything else in life, give to all who seek your aid the fullest measure of *love,* for love releases, love adjusts and interprets, and love heals, on all three planes.

On Group Illnesses.

In the last analysis, most of the ills of the body are rooted in some response to group activity. It will be necessary for us to grasp the fact that the phrase "group life and activity" must include not only past heredity, or inherited group tendencies, but also may indicate present world contacts, which weaken or increase resistance far more than is generally believed possible. One of the causes of cancer, which was not so prevalent in the earlier and more leisured days of the racial life—for then the HERD instinct was not so powerful as it is today—is due to the increased stimulation of the body. This stimulation is caused by our close contact in our daily lives with each other through our massed group existence, particularly in our urban centres. If cells are living organisms (which they are), they respond to group life, to massed cell emanation and radiation. This constant stream of energy pouring from the aggregate of bodily cells in massed humanity may produce in certain types of people an overstimulation in some part of bodily cell structure. This usually occurs where there is a weakness in the etheric or vital body, which means that cell defenses are impaired and the result is frequently a cancer or a general cancerous condition. This is the fundamental cause, though modern investigation is occupied with secondary causes and effects of this etheric weakness. I shall consider this later in more detail. It will be obvious to you that when we begin to deal with the vital body and to consider it with greater understanding and knowledge, we shall be able to handle such diseases as cancer far more effectively.

On Using the Mind and the Imagination to Develop Group Consciousness.

When a member of a group, such as a group for healing, speaks of developing group consciousness, he refers to *his* particular group of brothers, and to *his* group as a unit of several souls. Forget not that such a unit is in itself a separative concept from the angle of the greater whole, but it serves a useful purpose in training the group members to think in those wider terms. It serves as a stepping stone away from the consciousness of the isolated personality.

If you can indeed feel, think and function as one complete unit—several personalities and one soul—it will then be relatively easy to extend the concept to a broader inclusiveness, to broaden your horizon and thus become in-clusive in a much wider sense.

The using of the mind to this end involves an aptitude to learn the distinction between analysis and criticism. This is a hard and well-nigh impossible thing for many to learn. Traces of illumination of this subject will show themselves if the group persists in all earnestness. The members have to learn to respond, as a group, to the same spiritual, mental and human ideas, and thus swing—as a "telepathic unit"—into one united train of thought. They have, as a group, to be preoccupied with the same things which are indicated by the soul of the group, and not by one person in the group, as is apt to be the case. They have to learn, as a group, to hold the mind steady in the light—the group mind, and not their individual minds.

In using the imagination to this end, you have to culti-vate the power to ignore the outer forms and to concentrate on the inner lines of light which unite brother to brother, group to group, and kingdom to kingdom in the expression of the Life of God Himself. It is the creative use of the imagination which produces an integrated group etheric body and which enables you to see this group body of force and light as one complete form and as one expression of the group intelligence, will and purpose—but not the will or purpose of the dominant mind or minds in the group. Thus these can work out on the physical plane in right expression. However, when the group members are primar-ily occupied with their own ideas, their plans, their prob-lems, and how they can use whatever light and knowledge may be received, they negate any possibility of such crea-tive use of the united imagination. To become entirely free from this will take much careful cultivation and self-surrender to the soul.

On Healing Energy.

The question is sometimes asked by beginners: "Can we clearly distinguish between the healing energy, as expressed by the soul and by the personality? Can we have some understanding of the part that love has to play in the art of healing?" I can answer with brevity.

When we come to work as a group with individuals whom we shall seek to aid, we shall then learn to use the various types of energy according to the need of the individual to be healed. It would serve a real group purpose if all of you would study what is said by Rama Prasad in his book, *Nature's Finer Forces,* and by Patanjali in *The Light of the Soul* on the subject of the pranas with which and within which we work; you should be somewhat familiar with the matter.

To answer the question specifically: An initiate or even a low-grade clairvoyant can easily distinguish between soul and personality healing energies, but the average intelligent aspirant as yet cannot. The initiate *knows* the source from which any type of healing energy may come. He senses its vibration and can follow it to its emanating source by an effort of the will, directed by the intuition. The clairvoyant can *see* the centre from which the healing energy can flow, and the centre then indicates the type and quality of the projected force. All energy is from the soul in the secondary instance, but in the primary sense all energy is simply life, functioning under direction of some kind.

As to the part love has to play in the healing process: Love is the life expression of God Himself; love is the coherent force which makes all things whole (I would have you ponder upon this phrase), and love is all that *is*. The main characteristic of the distinction between soul energy and personality force, as applied to healing, lies in the region of the application and the expression of love. Personality force is emotional, full of feeling, and—when in use—the personality is ever conscious of itself as the healer, and is the dramatic centre of the stage upon which are two players, the healer and the one to be healed. Soul energy functions unconsciously and is wielded by those who are in contact with their souls and who are consequently decentralised; they are "off the stage" themselves, if I might use that expression, and they are completely occupied with group love, group activity and group purpose.

Why then is it so extremely difficult, if not altogether impossible, for earnest would-be healers to work together, as a group, with the sacred science of healing? Because as individuals and as a group they are predominantly personal in their individual and inter-group relations. This may show itself in intense criticism of each other, or of oneself; in a vivid sureness of personal rectitude and sound judgment which does not permit those who hold it to see that there is perhaps a chance that they are not as correct in their ideas as they deem themselves to be; it may show itself in a deep satisfaction over personal subjective contacts. Any or all the above hindrances may be present and make the group demonstration a personality demonstration which negates constructive work, and any attempt only intensifies personality reactions and would greatly (and adversely) affect the personalities of those they might seek to help.

How, then, should they proceed? I would point out that any group member who, as an individual, is free from the above frailties of the personality and from these attitudes, nevertheless knows (and rightly rejoices) that he participates, as a group member, in the group quality. That is one of the incidental difficulties of group work. To participate and yet stand free from weakness; to recognise that the achievements or failures of the individual group members are entirely their own affair; to share and yet not be dominated by the powerful thoughts and ideas of the more potent members in the group is ever a problem. I point this out because, in this coming Age wherein group work will be greatly developed, it will be of value to understand group situations and problems, and then to go forward to the group work together with those who are yours to work with. You will then be the better and wiser for past experiences, and fused as a group through shared suffering and limitations and the gained ability of failure rightly met.

So let true love, silent, uncomplaining, non-critical and steadfast, be your goal and the quality of your group life. Then, when there is some definite work to do, you will work as a unit with hearts and minds as one.

On Instantaneous Healing.

Instantaneous healing may be of various kinds. We might cite the following from among several possibilities which account for the happening:

1. The healing which is the result of a definite practice, conscious or unconscious, of Hatha Yoga. This is brought about by a projection of purely physical magnetism, which, added to the quota of available physical magnetism at the patient's disposal within his own physical body, suffices to effect an immediate cure. The magnetism in the body of the patient, instead of being outgoing and radiating, becomes inverted and turns inward to make its contribution to the reservoir of physical force held in a static condition within the body. The more low grade human types produce this kind of healing with facility. This is equally so in relation to the patient and the healer. The case cited is a case in point. The healing was more easily brought about

by the "sheik" concerned because the wound (a bite in the arm—A.A.B.) was self-inflicted and before inflicting it, the patient (if I may so call him) held the outgoing force in abeyance by an act of the will, thus creating a reservoir of energy which was available to supplement that of the sheik which was, in its turn, released by a mantram. This is definitely *not* spiritual healing.

2. There is also that form of healing which can be instantaneous because the disease is largely psychological and hallucinatory. The healer is then in the position to enable the patient to throw off illusion and so stand free. The will of the healer when added to that of the patient, aids in the breaking of the illusion and of the glamorous thoughtform and the patient then stands free. This is a psychological healing and only one illustration of it.

3. Then there is a type of healing which is brought about in two ways, and this is the true spiritual healing:

> When the patient makes a sudden and frequently un-expected contact with his soul, and in which the soul energy is so great and so potent that it sweeps through the vehicles and definitely produces effects. Thus cures are brought about in some vehicle or another and frequently in the physical vehicle. The physical condition or disease retains, so oft, the un-divided attention of the consciousness of the human being involved, and the soul pours through to the point of concentrated attention. In this thought lies, for many of you, a clear hint.

> b. When the patient's evil physical karma is exhausted, and physical plane illness is not, at this particular time, his destiny. Then the healer can begin to bear upon the situation, if he is spiritual and full of wisdom, enough spiritual energy to ensure a cure.

I trust you will find these answers suggestive. Ponder deeply upon the implications.

On the Use of the Lord's Image.

Here we touch upon a point of real interest. The use of the Lord's image is frequently of vital importance, but—and it is here that I seek to lay the emphasis—it must be the image arrived at by oneself through the medium of the expansion of the Christ consciousness in one's own life, and by arriving at the stage of conscious discipleship. At that particular stage, when a man is definitely linked with a Master and His group, he is then, automatically and as an individual, linked with the Master of all Masters. He can then, via his own soul and the soul of his particular group, draw on the force of Maitreya Buddha. Why, think you, is there no good and true picture of the Blessed One, There are only a few speculations by the devotees of the early church and none by those who knew Him. The reason is a definite one. There is no true image of Him because it must be upon our hearts and not upon our canvases. We arrive at knowledge of Him because He is ours, as we are His. Do you understand that whereof I speak? He is the world Healer and Saviour. He works because He is the embodied soul of all Reality. He works today, as He worked in Palestine two thousand years ago, through *groups*. There He worked through the three beloved disciples, through the twelve apostles, through the chosen seventy, and the interested five hundred. Ponder on this fact, little emphasised. Now He works through His Masters and Their groups, and thereby greatly intensifies His efforts. He can and will work through all groups just in so far as they fit themselves for planned service, for the distribution of love, and come into conscious alignment with the greater potency of the inner groups.

You will find (fairly soon perhaps) that healing groups will employ mantrams of a definite kind, and that in those mantrams the name of the Blessed One will appear. But the mantram for His coming age is not yet for use. The world is not yet ready for the potency which it would release. Today, is there a more potent mantram than the oft spoken word: "For Christ's sake and for the glory of His Name"? But these words must be spoken with love and will behind them or else they are but an empty symbol and a sounding cymbal. Forget this not.

On the Christ.

Some aspirants and disciples may experience an almost constant recollection of the Christ; that is due to their increasing sensitivity to the inner planes and particularly to the fact that so much of the matter in the astral body of the advanced aspirant is taken from (and is therefore sensitive to) the highest subplane of the astral plane. It is also due to the fact that the Lord Maitreya with His workers is approaching nearer all the time to the physical plane. The focus of His attention in the year 1936 was, for the first time, predominantly on the first subplane of the astral plane. Hence the sensitives' correct and immediate response to His energy there expressed. He is coming nearer in His thought and activity. Should the peoples of the world respond to the presented opportunity, His forces and attention could penetrate more deeply and be predominantly on etheric levels with all that is implied in such a situation.

This, many sense subjectively and know; and great, therefore, is their opportunity and yours to constitute increasingly a channel for this force.

Remember that the work for which He comes and to which the attendant Hierarchy is pledged is to help Him in the "healing of the nations" as it is expressed in the Bible. This is a true statement of an imminent fact. This healing will be brought about if men of goodwill everywhere measure up to their opportunity; if the work of the Christ and of His helpers is brought more definitely to the attention of the general public, and if there is an inner relaxation in the world of men which will permit the devas to work. It is their readiness and their response to the near approach to the Christ which many consecrated servers are subjectively sensing, and which has somewhat perplexed them. The devas can only be sensed and felt; they cannot be approached by humanity as yet through the medium of the thought world and the use of the mechanism of thought in man. There is no danger involved for the server if he becomes aware of these deva forces and their activities, via the Christ and through their responsiveness to His work and imminent appearance.

On the Phrase "Mother of the World."

The various ways in which the phrase can be used can mean quite a number of differing things. It can mean:

1. The feminine aspect in manifestation, symbolised for us in many of the world religions as a virgin mother and in the Christian religion as the Virgin Mary. It is that substance which enables Deity to manifest.
2. Nature itself, the mother of all forms.
3. The moon also, who is the symbol of the generative, creative life which gives birth to forms and is therefore the symbol of the form nature.
4. The concentration of the feminine force in nature in some individual in female form who is then called the "World Mother." Such an individual has never existed in our particular planetary life, though the avatars of a previous solar system, expressing itself through

planetary life, always took this form. But not in this solar system. The tradition of such appearances is purely symbolic, inherited from the previous solar system from which we inherited the matter of which all manifested forms are made. This symbolism has come down from the far-off period of the Matriarchate, which had a religion that recalled the ancient ways of the earlier system and in which period of time Lilith symbolised the World Mother, until Eve took her place.

On the Sense of Futility.

In connection with the work of the healer with patients at the gate of death, he may experience a sense of futility. Is it possible to know just what he can do? Should he continue his effort to help the newly freed soul to go forward into the light? In the face of all his knowledge (and he may have much), and in spite of his yearning desire to aid the departing one, there seems naught to do but to step aside, with a sense of utter futility, whilst the loved one passes through the gate which leads to what, my brother? We can go up to the gates, but it seems as yet that we can go no further. Even the deep-seated belief in the persistence of the immortal soul proves inadequate, and only serves to comfort the serving healer personally, but suffices not to reveal to him what help he can give.

There is little I can say as we wait, at this significant time, for the coming revelation. That revelation is inevitable and sure, and such questions will not be raised two hundred years hence. To this emerging fact, the growing sensitivity of the race to the subtler angles of life, and the vast amount of investigation carried forward on every side, is the physical plane guarantee. This great truth and its guarantee is held steadily before us in the history of the "glorious resurrection of the Christ" and His after-death appearance, and in the powerful but little understood ritual of the sublime degree in Masonry, wherein the Master is raised.

Aid at the time of the "passing into the light" depends largely upon two things: First, the amount of close contact between the dying person and the one who watches, and the level upon which that contact is strongest. Secondly, upon the capacity of the watcher to detach and dissociate himself from his own feelings and to identify himself, through an act of pure unselfish will, with the dying person. None of this is really possible when the bond between the two is purely emotional or based upon a physical plane relation. The contact must be deeper and stronger than that. It must be a personal contact upon all planes. Where there is true soul and personality contact, there is then little problem. But this is rare to find. Nevertheless I have here given you a hint.

There should also be as little definite thought process as possible on the part of the watcher. All that is required and possible at present is simply to carry the dying person forward on an ever-deepening stream of love. Through the power of the creative imagination, and not through intellectual concepts (no matter how high), must the dying man be aided to discard the outer garment in which he has been encased and in which he has laboured during life. This involves an act of pure self-forgetfulness, of which few as yet are capable. Most people are swept by fear, or by a strong desire to hold the beloved person back, or are sidetracked in their aim by the activities involved in assuaging pain and deadening agony; they are dismayed also by the depths of their ignorance of the "technique of death" when faced with the emergency. They find themselves unable to see what lies beyond the doors of death, and are swept by the mental uncertainty which is part of the great illusion. There is as we know no sure touch in this process of dying. All is uncertainty and bewilderment. But this will end before long, and man will *know* and also *see*.

As regards those who have passed into the light, whom you want to help, follow them with your love, remembering that they are still the same people, minus the outer limiting shroud of body. Serve them, but seek not that they should serve your need of them. Go to them, but seek not to bring them back to you.

It is physical plane life that is the purgatory, and life experience that is the school of drastic discipline. Let us not fear death, or that which lies beyond it. The wise disciple labours in the field of service but looks forward steadily to the dawn of the "clear cold light" into which he will some day enter, and so close the chapter for a while upon the fever and the friction and the pain of earth existence. But there are other phases of life experience wherein the sense of futility and frustration meets the server in the world today.

From the angle of vision of a disciple, we might divide intelligent human beings into three groups, at the same time eliminating in our thought the dead weight of the unthinking masses who register desire but who as yet experience no sense of futility or frustration. They desire and are satisfied; or they desire and are thwarted or jealous or angry at those who appear to have that which they want and demand, and which appeals to the life of the senses. The three groups are:

1. Those *personalities,* integrated and intelligent, who are ambitious and pushing consciously forward, yet who meet with frustration. This frustration is due either to world conditions which are too strong for them, or to the imposition upon them of their own watchful souls

which throw obstructions in their way in order to lead
them into the light.

2. Those *mystically inclined* people and those rightly oriented visionaries who have not yet built in that mental
scaffolding which will enable them properly to materialise
their vision, through right thought processes. They
are many in number today, and their case is not an
easy one.

3. Those *disciples and aspirants* who are attempting to
work in the field of the world, yet who through karmic
limitation, misapplication of the law, or some basic personality weakness, never achieve in this life their goal,
and so are swept by an overwhelming sense of futility.

Beyond these three classes, acting as the opposite pole
to the struggling masses, are the integrated functioning
disciples of the world, who are achieving, and who are
too occupied and too one-pointed to waste much time over
feeling inferior or over mistakes and failures.

Therefore, by wisely placing the people who come to
you for help in one or other of these three categories (allow-
ing in your mind for the possibility of their passing into
another and higher one) you will be able to help them
more intelligently.

A large measure of the inferiority complex which affects so many people today is due most definitely to their
reaction to the inflowing spiritual influences. They *know*
themselves to be greater than their achievements; they
realise unconsciously and wordlessly their divinity, but the
limitation of circumstance and the hindrances of the body
nature are as yet too great for right response to opportunity and to reality. Look for these souls and aid them by
true understanding and by appreciation and cooperation,

and thus dispel the illusion of non-accomplishment which haunts their footsteps.

But exhibitionism and neurasthenic hallucinations have to be cured primarily through individual self-effort, through decentralisation, transference of interest, and unselfishness. Neurasthenic tendencies are likely to increase instead of decrease for some time yet, such is the strain under which man labours today. The present world condition forces him to find avenues of escape, and to revert to the curative power of his own creative imagination. Release comes through acceptance of the drama of the whole and not of the part, and through steady occupation in creative work on the physical plane.

Methods of training will later be used and are already coming into their elementary stages through the work of the psychologists of the world.

On Scientific Parallels.

Students seem to think that we, the teachers on the inner side, have read every book that may be written, particularly those embodying the new and advanced truths, and that we are also in touch with the personalities of those who are the dispensers of the growing body of new knowledge in the world. Such is not the case. How can I explain to you the true state of affairs? Only symbolically, I think.

As we look out over the world of the intellect and carry our thoughts from the points of living knowledge there to be found, we may become aware of areas of light (as we understand it) shining forth upon the physical plane. Such areas indicate the shining light of some worker in the field, of some disciple, or of some member of the New Group of World Servers. I know, for instance, that such areas are to be found (as regards the United States) in Baltimore, Chicago, Cleveland and Rochester. By a peculiar mode of shining this indicates to me that there is to be found a centre where the newer knowledges anent man's body are to be found. I know that there are other areas of light existing all over the world. My work and the work of all the teachers in this transition period is to stimulate them and fertilise their minds with ideas. Every theory they form in their search for truth, every book they write, and every conclusion they reach is not known to us. They must carry their own responsibility and fail or succeed in arriving at the truth through their own self-initiated effort.

H.P.B. prophesied the work now being done many years ago when she spoke of the recognition ultimately to be accorded by science to an universally diffused omnipresent Deity (the ether of space is an entity, she also tells us) and that the mystery of electricity, when solved, holds for us the solution of most of our problems. Many of the theories of modern science are laid down in *A Treatise on Cosmic Fire*, though scientists have not gone far enough yet to recognise this fact; there the electrical nature of man is posited. You would find it interesting and helpful to search out such passages. Science, however, gives no place to the electrical force of the soul, which is steadily growing in potency. A few of the scientists among the most advanced are beginning to do this. The next step ahead for science is the discovery of the soul, a discovery which will revolutionise, though not negate, the majority of their theories.

Individual students might aid in this if they took some of the basic postulates of a scientist whose researches appealed to them, and endeavoured to discover in my books, for instance, or in *The Secret Doctrine,* those paragraphs which will throw occult light upon what he says, or which may negate his hypothesis. Then they would be growing and using the analytical mind as a bridging factor between the world of human science and the occult sciences.

On Ions and Radiation.

Scientists have made statements to the effect that the air we breathe contains electrified particles positively or negatively charged, and they are able to produce artificially electrified air; that even an open flame in a fireplace ionises the air; that with suitable apparatus one may extract either the negative or the positive ions, and that patients exposed to the positively electrified ions developed feelings of fatigue, dizziness and headache, while if exposed to negatively charged ions a feeling of exhilaration was experienced; that positive ions increased the blood pressure and produced general discomfort, and negative ions lowered the pressure and brought a feeling of comfort and relaxation.

The question arises whether the healer's radiation has the effect of ionising the atmosphere surrounding the patient. I must point out that to answer such a question accurately would necessitate two things: the revelation of one of the mysteries for which mankind is not yet ready, and at the same time the giving of an answer which would be quite inexplicable to you, for there is no terminology adequate to the latent truth. In this truth is embodied the whole story of duality—which is the story of the relation of the negative and positive aspects of the living process. Certain things, however, I can point out:

1. The negative and positive ions with which the scientist deals are etheric in nature and, therefore, of the physical plane. These unseen particles of substance which can only be traced through their effects and through interference with their activities, are rapidly moving particles in relation to each other and, at the same time,

are themselves affected by a greater controlling factor which keeps them so moving.

2. In dealing with disease, the patient can only truly be helped when the positive radiation of the healer overcomes the negative condition of the patient.

3. The radiation of the healer has to permeate and overcome the resistance of the patient's disease—not of the patient, who may be mentally and emotionally negative to the healer, and therefore in a position to be helped. This is done through the more powerful radiation of the healer. The magnetism of the healer is then brought into play and, consciously and with intent, he can draw out and disperse those atoms of substance which are the seat and source of the patient's discomfort. A hint is here given of one of the future physical plane modes of dispersing a disease. The power of directing definitely the magnetic currents radiating from a source outside the physical body is not yet realised, but it will embody one of the new modes of healing.

The healing radiation, therefore, naturally affects the atmosphere around the patient. As yet, however, that radiation is uneven and not rightly directed. Some people radiate physical or animal magnetism; others astral or mental magnetism; still others radiate the energy of a fully integrated personality. A few radiate the magnetism of the soul, the major attractive energy in all forms. In the future the true healer must work through the radiation of the entire personality or of the soul. I say "or" advisedly, for there are few as yet who can work with soul energy, but many who could work as integrated personalities if they so desired. And when a man has achieved this power to radiate, what about the patient? How is he to be brought into a condition wherein he will respond accurately to magnetic radiation? If he is an astral type, as are so many, will he be able to respond to the magnetism of a mental healer? Can he be helped by the radiation of such a healer if he is himself a fully integrated human being? If you say to me that Christ healed all types, I would here suggest that I am not considering in this short treatise the laws of healing as they are wielded by a Master of the Wisdom or by an initiate. My book would otherwise be a futile effort. I am writing for interested aspirants and for those who can heal on some level below that of the soul, but who as yet know not how to do it. Later all this will be more fully elucidated.

On Vibration.

Some students make demand that I define what is the meaning of the word "vibration" and state exactly what a vibration is. If I tell you that vibration is an illusion, as sensory perception is known by the soul to be, do you comprehend (limited as all human beings are by the reactions of a series of vehicles, all of them instruments of perception)? If I tell you that vibratory reaction is due to our possessing a mechanism which is responsive to impact, I am answering your question in part, but if this is true, what does it mean to you and from whence comes the impact? If I give you the scientific definition (which you can discover in any good textbook on light, colour or sound), I am doing work that you can do yourself, and for that I have no time. In my books are several definitions of vibration, either by inference or defined, and these you might search for, and upon them you might meditate. If I elucidated for you here the relation between the Self and the not-Self, between awareness, that which is aware, and that of which it is aware, I am covering ground which a careful study of the Gita would aid you in comprehending.

Let simplicity be your guide and one-pointed love your major objective. Choose a field of service which has its definite limits (for all disciples are limited and cannot cover a planetary range in their thoughts), and work—mentally and physically—within those limits. The completion of some self-appointed task within the field of karmic limitation and of environment where your destiny has cast you is all that is required of you. What are you accomplishing really at this time? Let your service lie within the field of contact where you find yourself, and reach not out over the entire planet. Is there any greater or more important task than to fulfill your task and carry it to completion in the place where you are and with your chosen comrades?

Believe me when I assure you that I am not seeking to evade answering any questions, but if I can awaken you to the realisation of the necessity for "spiritual limitation" (as it is esoterically called when defining the career of a disciple within the limits of his task) and bring to your attention the need for achieving the goal you set yourself when you started to work, I shall have aided you far more than if I had defined vibration or pointed out to you just how much progress, through what process, you or others had made.

On the Future Schools of Healing.

These schools of healing are not to be developed in the near future, not before the close of this century. Only the preparatory work is now being done, and the stage set for future unfoldments. Things do not move so rapidly. There has to be a growing synthesis of the techniques of such schools, which embody:

1. Psychological adjustments and healing,
2. Magnetic healing,

3. The best of the allopathic and homeopathic techniques, with which we must not dispense,
4. Surgical healing in its modern forms,
5. Electro-therapeutics,
6. Water-therapy,
7. Healing by colour and sound, and radiation,
8. Preventive medicine,
9. The essential practices of osteopathy and chiropractic,
10. Scientific neurology and psychiatry,
11. The cure of obsessions and mental diseases,
12. The care of the eyes and ears,
13. Voice culture, which is a definitely healing agency,
14. Mental and faith healing,
15. Soul alignment and contact,

and many other processes and procedures which belong to the healing art. Some of the more ancient schools, such as the allopathic, call for a process of elimination in order to arrive at the vital and true contribution which they have to give. Others of a modern and tentative experimental kind must be lifted out of the hands of the fanatics; for until fanaticism with its blindness and lack of intelligent synthesis dies out (as it inevitably will as the sixth ray recedes and the Piscean Age passes out), the new schools cannot exist as they should; there must be a keener understanding of the underlying and fundamental good in all the schools and a better grasp of the principles which underlie the true healing art, before the schools, referred to in *Letters on Occult Meditation,* can come into being. When, as is the case today, some healer or school lays the entire emphasis upon some patent cure-all and despises all other systems of diet or method, it will not be possible to establish the true schools.

The period is coming in which we will pass through a cycle in which we will garner the fruit of the ages; in which we will skim (if I may so express it) the cream off the milk of human experience; and then, with the best that the past can confer upon us, we will inaugurate those new enterprises which will speed humanity upon its way. Among these new enterprises the healing art will be the foremost, because the most necessary.

We shall find that the work which is engaging our attention will fall into three categories; these will work out sequentially and not simultaneously.

1. The training in the principles of the healing art, as we

    a. Lay the foundation for later expansion in the New Age.

    b. Seek to preserve that which is good and useful in the shift of the emphasis from the outer external man to the more subtle etheric and vital body.

    c. Study this Treatise on the new healing which will meet with a measure of response, but which will only later enter into its true usefulness and mission.

2. Later, when a group can function together with impersonality as a unit and with true interplay of love, such a group can then begin to do some definite healing work, taking some case, for instance, of known physical illness, of obsession, or of mental difficulty and—working under soul direction or some initiated chela and in conformity with the teaching outlined in this Treatise—seek to cure and aid. The study of the art of dying is also to attract your attention and later that of the world at large.

3. Finally, there will come the forming of subsidiary groups to be taught and developed by the members of the pioneer healing groups, under soul instruction, or under

that of some initiated chela. These subsidiary groups will work under group direction for the healing of people. This will not be for some years yet, and not until the initiating group (or groups) can work with a measure of success and the group members have an intelligent grasp of the technique and principles involved in healing. The exoteric developments of the New Age healing will grow out of the above.

There is no school in existence today which should be retained. All of them embody some useful truth, principle or idea. I would point out that a synthetic group would still be a separative and separated entity, and no such group is our goal. *It is the synthesis of the life and of the knowledge which is desirable,* and not a synthesis of people. There will be eventually, let us hope, hundreds and thousands of groups all over the world who will express this new attitude to healing, who will be bound together by their common knowledge and aims, but who will all express this to the best of their ability in their own peculiar field, in their own peculiar way and with their own peculiar terminology. It is the subjective life unity that is of interest to the teachers on the inner side of life, and the production of a network of true healers all over the world.

A fresh start is now being made. We shall and do inherit the wonder of the past acquired knowledges and the use of much of it will persist; all that is needed is the elimination of the undesirable and the misunderstood interpretations of known facts, and the misapplied information, also the cessation of selfish interest, financial exploitation and greed. Modern surgery, modern sanitary methods, and modern medical science are full of wonder and usefulness.

Letter to a Scientist

My brother:

I have a few minutes to spare this morning after dictating to A.A.B. and will attempt to throw some forward light upon the questions which you have posited. I do not, as you will note, say that I will answer the questions.

The discoveries of science are as yet inadequate for the fulfilment of the prophecies I made in *A Treatise on the Seven Rays*. Towards the close of this century and when the world situation has clarified and the period of reconstruction is drawing to a close, discoveries will be made which will reveal some hitherto unrealised electrical potencies. I know not what other word to use for these electrical rays which will make their presence felt and lead to possibilities beyond the dreams of investigators today. The coming science of electricity will be as different next century as the modern usages of electricity differ from the understanding of the Victorian scientist.

In connection with your query anent the photography which concerns itself with departed souls, I would advise you that understanding of process will come from a study of the photographing of thoughtforms. A beginning was made in this connection by the great French scientist, d'Arsonval, of Paris. A.A.B. can tell you something of this if you do not already know. Light on the subject will come through this, through the perfecting of the plates of reception and their greatly increased sensitivity, and through the relating of electricity to photography. You may deem it well-nigh impossible to make plates of much greater sensitivity than those in use in the best equipped laboratories. But this is not so. Along this line of thought-photography and electrical equipment, will come the solution. It is the thought of those on the other side, and their ability to project thoughtforms of themselves, plus the providing of adequately sensitive plates or their equivalent, which will mark a new era in so-called "spirit photography." People frequently are so preoccupied with the tangible instrument on this side of the veil that they neglect the factor of what must be contributed from the other side by those who have passed over.

The work will be done from there, with the material aid which as yet has not been provided in the outer scientific field.

To bring this about, collaboration of a conscious medium (not a trance medium, but someone who is consciously clairvoyant and clairaudient) will be required. There are many such growing up among the children of today, and the next generation after them will provide still more. The separating veil will disappear through the testimony of the thousands of those who can see phenomena and hear sounds which lie outside the range of the tangible.

You say that the spirits state that they cannot stand electricity. What is meant is that they cannot stand electricity as it is at present applied. This is an instance of the inaccurate statements passed on by ignorant mediums or by those who on the other side have no more understanding of the laws of electricity than they probably had in the physical body. There is nothing but electricity in manifestation, the "mystery of electricity" to which H.P.B. referred in *The Secret Doctrine*. Everything in Nature is electrical in nature; life itself is electricity, but all that we have contacted and used today is that which is only physical and related to and inherent in the physical and etheric matter of all forms.

It must be remembered that the so-called "spirits" are functioning in the illusory astral body, while advanced "spirits" are only functioning as minds, and can therefore be reached solely by minds and in no other way. It will never be possible to photograph the mental vehicle; only the astral body will be susceptible of photographing. The grosser the person in the body, desire and appetite, the more easily will he be photographed after passing over (if any one wants to photograph him!), and the more advanced the person, the more difficult it will be to get a photograph.

As regards the use of radio as a means of communication with the "spirit world," the present electrical instruments are too slow in vibratory activity (if I may use such an unscientific term) to do the work; if astrally clothed "spirits" approach them, they are apt to have a shattering effect. Yet the first demonstration of existence after death, in such a way that it can be registered upon the physical plane, will come via the radio, because sound always precedes vision. Think on this. However, no radio now exists which is sufficiently sensitive to carry sound waves from the astral plane.

Future scientific discoveries, therefore, hold the secret. This is no evasion on my part, but a simple statement of fact. Electrical discovery is only in the initial stage and all that we have is simply a prelude to the real discovery. The magic of the radio would be completely unbelievable to the man of the eighteenth century. The discoveries and developments lying ahead in the twenty-first century will be equally unbelievable to the man of this century. A great discovery in relation to the use of light by the power and the directive agency of thought will come at the end of this century or the beginning of the next. Two small children—one living in this country (U.S.A.) and one in India—will work out a formula along scientific lines which will fill in some of the existing gaps in the scale of light vibration, carrying on from the high frequency rays and waves as you now have them. This will necessitate instruments hitherto undreamt of but really quite possible. They will be so sensitive that they will be set in motion by the power of the human eye under the focussed direction of thought. From then on tangible rapport with the spirit world will be possible. I cannot do more than give you the clue.

I am also handicapped by the complete ignorance of A.A.B. on these matters which involve electrical knowledge and terms. There is no seed thought in her mind on which I can work or from which I can expand the idea. She can explain what I mean if you ask her to do so. But even if she had a training such as you have, I could not explain clearly, as the discovery must first be made, and this will revolutionise all present ideas, even whilst growing out of them. An ordinary treatise on electricity such as is studied by electrical engineers would have been completely incomprehensible to even the most highly educated man two hundred years ago, or even one hundred, and so it is now. In the meantime, work with thought photography as a prelude to the coming science, for out of that and the gradual development of more sensitive modes of registering and recording subtle phenomena will come the new idea and possibilities. Does it mean anything to you when I say that electricity and photography are closely related because the human being is electrical in origin and nature? This must be demonstrated on the physical plane by the aid of the needed sensitive apparatus.

February 1944

Part Two

The Basic Requirements for Healing

W E ARE NOW ENTERING UPON a new section of our discussion on the Rays and Disease. It is essentially far
more practical in scope than the highly speculative section
(speculative to all of *you*) which we have just concluded.
Much that I have there told you is, for you, in the nature
of questionable truth (using this word "questionable" in
its real sense; i.e., as promoting questions). For the most
intuitive of you, it was at its best a "possibly accurate" hypothesis. I would here ask you to note this phrasing, paradoxical as it may appear. You have no direct means of
knowing how true it may be. A great deal of the mystery
of life and of living will clarify as more and more aspirants
in the world begin to function consciously in the realm
of causes. There is no questioning in the Hierarchy, except
upon those matters which touch upon the unpredictable
nature of human reactions. Even in connection with the
uncertain activities of mankind, the Masters can usually
gauge what will occur, but esoterically They refuse "to
ponder on the energies released upon the plane of earthly
living, for fear that counter-energies, issuing from the
Centre where They dwell may negate the truth of man's
freewill." I am here quoting one of the Masters, speaking
at a conference held in 1725.

What I have told you in the previous section is to me unquestionable truth and factually proven; to you it may be an adequate hypothesis or a questionable and nonacceptable interpretation of the underlying causes of disease.

Behind humanity lies a very ancient past, wherein so-called sins and errors, wrong-doing and wrong attitudes have piled up a very heavy karma which (fortunately for the race of men!) is being rapidly worked off at this time. The immense interest in disease which is displayed today, the focussing of all the resources of medical and surgical science on behalf of the fighting forces—(resources later to be mobilised in aid of the civilian populations of the devastated countries in both hemispheres)—the widespread research being carried on in our hospitals and centres of learning, and the rapid discoveries of science, plus a steady trend towards a much needed simplification, will before long bring about major changes in the approach to disease. These will lead to the eradication of many of the dreaded inherited diseases.

The inspiration and inflow of occult knowledge, via the disciples and initiates of the world, will bring about many alterations in technique; the coming revelation of new, yet most simple, laws of health, and the blending which will inevitably come of orthodox medicine, psychology and spiritual methods of healing, will produce an entirely new approach to the entire subject; the increasing use of *fire* as a means of purification (both in relation to the soil of the planet and to the human frame) will do much. Of this, the technique of inducing fever as a means of curing certain forms of disease, and the method (frequently employed by nature) of subjecting large areas of the soil to the impact of fire, will be developed into a new and most helpful science. This, however, will come later. I indicate simply faint trends in that direction. Man stands—in all fields of knowledge—at a climaxing point; this has been induced by the rapid unfoldment of the human consciousness, and it prefaces a great expansion of the understanding and a new insight into the conditioning causes which are responsible for much that today distresses man's physical body.

The new learning and the coming knowledge will arise as a result of an awakening intuition, of the presence upon earth of a very great number of advanced and developed souls, and the coming of the Hierarchy and Humanity into a closer relationship. The blending (slowly going forward) of the energies of those two planetary centres will bring about major changes and unfoldments, and this not only in the perceptive faculties of man but in the physical mechanism also. There will be a much greater resistance to the indigenous and inherited diseases and a real ability to resist infections; this will eliminate much pain and suffering. The reduction of the sum of human karma through the experience of this planetary war (1914-1945) will enable the souls seeking incarnation to create bodies free from tendencies to morbid developments. The Masters are entirely free from disease because they have entirely overcome the karma of the three worlds and are liberated.

The ability—developed during the past fifty years—to cope with the *planetary disease of tuberculosis* will, when extended into the densely populated areas of the Orient and to districts suffering hitherto from inadequate medical attention, stamp it out altogether. The *syphilitic diseases* are already being brought under rapid control through the use of the newly discovered drugs, though these are regarded as amelioratives only by the Masters, and as superficial in time and space. Such diseases will be slowly and correctly stamped out in toto as humanity shifts its consciousness on to the mental plane and away from the field of astral and sexual desire with their reflex action upon the automatic and responsive physical body. The *third great planetary disease, cancer,* is as yet basically uncontrollable, and the relative simplicity of surgery seems at present the only mode of possible cure. The mode of preventing the occurrence of cancer and the nature of its cause are still unknown, and the entire field is largely speculative and still subject to infinite research and investigation. Many minor ailments, infections and a wide range of allied physical ills will eventually be found traceable to one or other of these three basic diseases; they, in their turn, are related to a definite misuse of the energy of the three major rays. It might be stated that:

1. The syphilitic diseases are due to the misuse of third ray energy, that of the creative, intelligent energy of substance itself.
2. Tuberculosis is the result of the misuse of the energy of the second ray.
3. Cancer is a mysterious and subtle reaction to the energy of the first ray, the will-to-live, which is one of the aspects of this ray. It works out, therefore, in an overactivity and growth of the body cells whose will-to-live becomes destructive to the organism in which they are to be found.

I have here only given you a hint, and one that is not of wide usefulness at this time. A great deal of occult research remains to be done by the medical profession along these lines, but this will only be possible when the Science of the Rays is better understood and when the evidence substantiating the presence of five basic energies in every human being (the energies of his five conditioning rays) can be ascertained; men will learn some day to determine with ease their ray type, and the rays which govern their three-fold personality.

Along every line of man's expanding understanding, the opportunity for that which is new to make entrance and control is becoming increasingly evident. The door of adventure (in its highest sense) stands wide open, and nothing yet has ever succeeded in stopping humanity from passing through that door; down the ages man has passed through its portals and has entered into new and richer realms of investigation, of discovery and of subsequent practical application.

Today, the door which is opening will admit man into a world of meaning—a world which is the ante-chamber to the world of causes. Effect; Meaning; Cause. In these three words you have the key to the growth of man's consciousness. Most men live today in the world of effects, and have no idea that they are effects. Some few are now beginning to live in the world of meaning, whilst disciples and those functioning in the world of the Hierarchy are aware, or are steadily becoming aware, of the causes which produce the effects which meaning reveals. It is for this reason that we can now start considering the basic requirements which man must meet before he can move forward along the path of future enlightenment. This enlightenment will most necessarily remove all fear of death and deal with that subject which has for so long a time driven humanity into the depths of despair and of fear. I refer also to the required attitudes which those seeking healing, the surmounting of disease and the cure of bodily ills, must realise, and with which they must cope, principally along mental lines. These requirements will evoke the mental attention of both the healing agency and the patient. They have reference also to man as a whole.

It has generally been surmised that the main prerequisite to the art of healing is faith. But this is not so. Faith has little to do with it. Healing is dependent upon certain vital and basic factors into which faith enters not at all. The effort of the patient to achieve faith is frequently a great detriment to his freedom from the difficulties which lie between him and complete healing. When Christ so frequently emphasised faith (or rather that quality which is translated as faith in our Western Scriptures) He referred in reality to acceptance of law, to a recognition above all of karma, and to a knowledge of divine destiny. This, if grasped, will bring about a new attitude both to God and to circumstance. The prerequisites which I would like to emphasise might be enumerated as follows:

1. A recognition of the great Law of Cause and Effect, if possible. This is not always possible when dealing with the totally unenlightened.

2. Correct diagnosis of the disease by a competent physician, and later by a spiritual clairvoyant, when that capacity is developed by the initiate healer.

3. A belief in the law of immediate Karma. By that I mean an ability on the part of the patient or of the healer to know whether it is the destiny of the patient to be healed or else be helped to make the great transition.

4. A willingness to recognise that healing might be detrimental and basically undesirable from the standpoint of the soul. People are sometimes healed by the potency of the healer when it is *not* their destiny to resume active physical plane living.

5. The active cooperation of healer and patient—a cooperation based upon mutual understanding.

6. A determined acquiescence on the part of the patient to accept whatever may be the demonstrated will of the soul. It might be called an expression of divine indifference.

7. An effort upon the part of both healer and patient to express complete harmlessness. The value of this will repay careful thought. This has basically a reference to the relation of both parties to their associates.

8. An effort on the part of the patient (unless too ill) to adjust and put right those aspects of the nature and those characteristics which might militate against the right spiritual perception. This is one of the meanings hidden in the phrase, the "work of restitution," though not the most important meaning.

9. The deliberate eliminating of qualities, lines of thought and of desires which could hinder the inflow of spiritual force—a force which might integrate the soul more closely with the body in the three worlds and inaugurate a renewed life-expression, or which might integrate the soul with its emanating source and initiate renewed life on soul levels. This, therefore, affects the relation of the patient to his soul.

10. The capacity of both healer and patient to integrate into the soul group with which they are subjectively affiliated, to integrate in other cases both personality and soul, and, if they are at a needed point of development, both to integrate more closely into the Master's ashramic group.

These ten requirements may appear simple but are not so by any means. Superficially, they may appear to deal with character and quality and capacity; fundamentally, they concern the relation of soul and body, and deal with integration or abstraction. The objective underlying them in any case is to set up an unbroken rapport between the healer or the healing group and the patient who is receiving the scientific attention of the healing agent—group or individual.

One of the first things that any healing agent will have to do will be the drawing up of a simple outline of instruction which should govern the attitude of the one to be healed. These instructions must be simple, because where real illness is present it is not possible for the patient to make the simplest physical effort in order to institute any changed attitude. This is oft forgotten.

There are one or two things which I would like to make clear and which you must, in your turn, make clear to the patient.

1. Cure is not guaranteed. Patients must realise that continuance of life in the physical body is not the highest possible goal. It may be so if the service to be rendered is of real import, if obligations remain still to be carried out, and if other lessons must still be learned. Bodily existence is not, however, the summum bonum of existence. Freedom from the limitations of the physical body is of real beneficence. Patients must learn to recognise and accept the Law of Karma.

2. Fear is needless. One of the first objectives of the healing agent should be to aid the patient to achieve a happy, sane, expectant outlook upon his future— no matter what that future may bring.

It will be obvious too that there lies before you the opportunity to bring a new attitude to the whole problem of disease and healing and to train humanity in a better and happier sense of proportion where disease and health are concerned.

It will also be obvious to you that the word "restitution" concerns the high art of restoring to the patient that which he needs in order correctly to face life—life in a physical body and on the physical plane or the continuity of life on the other levels, unseen by the average man and regarded as problematical and intangible. Restitution may also involve the righting of wrongs by the patient, prior to receiving what he will regard as successful treatment, but it primarily concerns the effect of the healing group when it first establishes contact with the one to be healed. This must not be forgotten. Sometimes, when the patient's karma indicates it, the will-to-live must be restored to him; in other cases, the rejection of fear (fear of life or fear of death) must be induced, bringing with it the restoration of courage; the restoration of an affirmative attitude in all circumstances may be the quality needed, bringing with it the restitution of the willingness to take, with understanding and with joy, whatever the future may bring; it may also involve the restitution of harmonious relations with the patient's surroundings, with family and friends, and the consequent result of renewed correct adjustments, an uprising of a spirit of love and the negation of what may have been deepseated wrong thinking.

It will be apparent to you, therefore, that the process of following a healing ritual is only one phase of the work to be done, and that the relation of healer and patient is basically an educational one; it must be an education tempered by the physical condition of the sick person. You will find, as you work along these lines, that it will be necessary to have short expositions of the work to be done, of the restitutions which the patient must be prepared to make in order to facilitate the inflow of the healing force. He must be induced to "clean the slate" (if I may use such a symbolic phrase) if the work of healing is to be successful under the Law of Karma.

This phase of the preparatory work is not easy. With patients who may be grievously ill, it may not be possible. It will be found by all healing agencies that when working with those who are spiritually-minded and those whose lives have for a long time been based upon right effort and a correct "rendering unto Cæsar the things which are Cæsar's and unto God the things which are God's," that the work of healing will be greatly accelerated or, on the other hand, that the task of smoothing the way through the gates of death will be greatly simplified. After all, death is in itself a work of restitution. It involves the work of rendering back of substance to the three worlds of substance, and doing it willingly and gladly; it involves also the restoration of the human soul to the soul from whence it emanated, and doing this in the joy of reabsorption. You must all learn to look upon death as an act of restitution; when you can do this it will take on new light and true meaning and become an integral part—recognised and desired— of a constant living process.

If I were asked to say what is the major task of all healing groups, such as the Hierarchy seeks to see functioning in the future, I would say it is to prepare human beings for what we should regard as the restorative aspect of death, and thus give to that hitherto dreaded enemy of mankind a new and happier significance. You will find that if you work along these indicated lines of thought, the entire theme of death will constantly recur, and that the result of this will be new attitudes to dying and the inculcation of a happy expectancy where that inevitable and most familiar event occurs. Healing groups must prepare to deal with this basic condition of all living, and a major part of their work will be the elucidating of the principle of death. The soul, we are told, must return to the one who gave it. To date that has been an enforced and dreaded restitution, one which engenders fear and which leads men and women everywhere to clamour for the healing of the physcial body, overemphasising its importance and making them regard the prolongation of earthly existence as the most important factor in their lives. During the next cycle, these wrong attitudes must come to an end; death will become a normal and understood process—as normal as the process of birth, though evoking less pain and fear. This comment of mine is in the nature of a prophecy and should be noted as such.

I would, therefore, enjoin upon you the elementary fact that any healing group seeking to work along the new lines must (as a preliminary effort) seek to understand something about the factor of death to which is given the appellation of "the great restorative process" or "the great restitution." It concerns the art of wisely, correctly and with due timing, giving back the body to the source of its constituent elements and of restoring the soul to the source of its essential being. I am wording this with care because I seek to have you ponder most carefully and sanely upon the so-called enigma of death. It is an enigma to man, but not an enigma to disciples and knowers of the wisdom.

Healing groups and individual healers will find it necessary at times to confront their patients with the fact of death; one of the undertakings of disciples in my Ashram and in the Ashram of the Master K.H. is to interject the theme of death into their conversation with other seekers for truth, into their thinking and into their discussions with each other, and particularly with those they seek to heal. It will not be easy and it must not be done in a precipitate manner, but it is a subject which cannot and must not be avoided or evaded. Healing groups working out from an Ashram lay not the emphasis upon *bodily* healing, but upon timing and upon the cycles of work or of physical plane living, and the cycles of restitution or physical plane death.

This entire section with which we are now engaged, called The Basic Requirements, has reference in reality to the processes of dying, to the conditions of the material world or the three worlds of incarnated service. The *restitution* of the body to the general reservoir of substance, or to service in the outer world of daily physical living, the *restoration* of the soul to its source, the soul upon its own plane or—in reverse—to full responsibility within the body, are dealt with in this first point. The *elimination* of the life principle and the consciousness aspect is dealt with in the second point, and the theme is not that of character building, as some might surmise. I touched upon character and personal qualities in my opening remarks in this section because all true understanding of the basic principles of death and life is facilitated by right action, based on right thinking, which eventuates in right character building. I seek not, however, to enlarge upon these elementary prerequisites. The processes of integration as I seek to consider them here concern the integration of the soul into the threefold body, if karma so decides, or into the kingdom of souls, if karma decrees that what we call death lies ahead of the man.

We are therefore considering, in this second section, the problem of death or the art of dying. This is something which all seriously ill people must inevitably face, and for which those in good health should prepare themselves through correct thinking and sane anticipation. The morbid attitude of the majority of men to the subject of death, and their refusal to consider it when in good health, is something which must be altered and deliberately changed. Christ demonstrated to His disciples the correct attitude when referring to His coming and immediate decease at the hand

of His enemies; He chided them when they evidenced
sorrow, reminding them that He was going to His Father.
Being an initiate of high degree, He meant that He was,
occultly speaking, "making restitution to the Monad";
ordinary people and those below the grade of an initiate of
the third degree make "restitution to the soul." The fear
and the morbidness which the subject of death usually
evokes, and the unwillingness to face it with understanding
are due to the emphasis which people lay upon the fact of
the physical body and the facility with which they identify
themselves with it; it is based also upon an innate fear of
loneliness and the loss of the familiar. Yet the loneliness
which eventuates after death, when the man finds himself
without a physical vehicle, is as nothing compared to the
loneliness of birth. At birth, the soul finds itself in new
surroundings and immersed in a body which is at first totally
incompetent to take care of itself or to establish intelligent
contact with surrounding conditions for a long period of
time. The man comes into incarnation with no recollection as
to the identity or the significance to him of the group of souls
in bodies with which he finds himself in relationship; this
loneliness only disappears gradually as he makes his own
personality contacts, discovers those who are congenial to
him and eventually gathers around him those whom he
calls his friends. After death this is not so, for the man finds
on the other side of the veil those whom he knows and who
have been connected with him in physical plane life, and he
is never alone as human beings understand loneliness; he is
also conscious of those still in physical bodies; he can see
them, he can tune in on their emotions, and also upon
their thinking, for the physical brain, being nonexistent, no
longer acts as a deterrent. If people but knew more, birth
would be the experience which they would dread, and not

death, for birth establishes the soul in the true prison, and physical death is only the first step towards liberation.

Another fear which induces mankind to regard death as a calamity is one which theological religion has inculcated, particularly the Protestant fundamentalists and the Roman Catholic Church—the fear of hell, the imposition of penalties, usually out of all proportion to the errors of a lifetime, and the terrors imposed by an angry God. To these man is told he will have to submit, and from them there is no escape, except through the vicarious atonement. There is, as you well know, no angry God, no hell, and no vicarious atonement. There is only a great principle of love animating the entire universe; there is the Presence of the Christ, indicating to humanity the fact of the soul and that we are saved by the livingness of that soul, and the only hell is the earth itself, where we learn to work out our own salvation, actuated by the principle of love and light, and incited thereto by the example of the Christ and the inner urge of our own souls. This teaching anent hell is a remainder of the sadistic turn which was given to the thinking of the Christian Church in the Middle Ages and to the erroneous teaching to be found in the Old Testament anent Jehovah, the tribal God of the Jews. Jehovah is *not* God, the planetary Logos, the Eternal Heart of Love Whom Christ revealed. As these erroneous ideas die out, the concept of hell will fade from man's recollection and its place will be taken by an understanding of the law which makes each man work out his own salvation upon the physical plane, which leads him to right the wrongs which he may have perpetrated in his lives on Earth, and which enables him eventually to "clean his own slate."

I seek not here to impose upon you a theological discussion. I seek only to point out that the present fear of death must give place to an intelligent comprehension of the reality and to the substitution of a concept of continuity which will negate disturbance, and emphasise the idea of one life and one conscious Entity in many experiencing bodies.

It might be stated, in order to sum up my general proposition, that the fear and horror of death is founded upon the love of form—our own form, the forms of those we love and the form of our familiar surroundings and environment. Yet this type of love runs counter to all our teaching anent the spiritual realities. The hope of the future, and the hope of our release from this ill-founded fear, lie in the shifting of our emphasis to the fact of the eternal soul and to the necessity for that soul to live spiritually, constructively and divinely within the material vehicles. Into this concept again enters the thought of restitution. Wrong concepts are therefore forgotten; the idea of elimination also enters in so that right focus is attained. Integration demands consideration, so that absorption in the life of the soul will take the place of absorption in the life of the body. Sorrow, loneliness, unhappiness, decay, loss—all these are ideas which must disappear as the common reaction to the fact of death also vanishes. As men learn to live consciously as souls, as they also learn to focus themselves on soul levels and begin to regard the form or forms as simply modes of expression, all the old sorrowful ideas anent death will gradually disappear, and a new and more joyful approach to that great experience will take their place.

You will note that the various words I have chosen in considering the basic requirements have been so chosen for their specific meanings:

1. *The Work of Restitution* signifies the returning of the form to the basic reservoir of substance; or of the soul, the divine spiritual energy, returning to its source—either on soul or monadic levels, accordings to the point

in evolution. This restitution is predominantly the work of the human soul within the physical body and involves both the heart and the head centres.

2. *The Art of Elimination.* This refers to two activities of the inner spiritual man; i.e., the elimination of all control by the threefold lower man, and the process of refocussing itself upon the concrete levels of the mental plane as a point of radiant light. This concerns primarily the human soul.

3. *The Processes of Integration.* These deal with the work of the liberated spiritual man as he blends with the soul (the oversoul) upon the higher levels of the mental plane. The part returns to the whole, and the man comprehends the true meaning of the words of Krishna, "Having pervaded this whole universe with a fragment of myself, I remain." He, too, the conscious experiencing fragment which has pervaded the little universe of the form in the three worlds, still remains. He knows himself to be a part of the whole.

These three processes are Death.

It will be obvious to you that when humanity attains this outlook upon the fact of death or the art of dying, the entire attitude of the race of men will undergo beneficent change. This will be paralleled, as time elapses, by a rapport between men upon telepathic levels; men will be steadily growing in intelligence, and humanity will be increasingly focussed upon mental levels. This telepathic rapport will be a common and ordinary phenomenon of which modern spiritualism is the guarantee, though the distortion (and a very serious distortion) is largely based on humanity's wishful thinking, with very little true telepathy to be found in it. The telepathy which *is* present today between the medium (in or out of trance) and the bereaved relative or friend is *not* between the the one who has experienced the release of death and the one who is still in form. This should be remembered. In the interim where mind is not normally telepathic, there may be (though there very seldom is) the interposition of a mediumship based upon clairvoyance and clairaudience, but *not* upon trance. This will still necessitate a contact via a third party, and will be entirely astral; it will therefore be full of glamour and error. It will, however, be a step forward from the present mediumistic performances which simply ignore the man who is dead and give to the enquirer only what the medium reads in his aura—his recollection of the personal appearance, significant remembrances stored in the enquirer's consciousness, and wishful thinking anent advice demanded because the enquirer believes that because a man is dead he must be more wise than heretofore. When the medium at times succeeds in establishing true communication, it is because the enquirer and the dead person are mental types, and there is therefore a true telepathic rapport between them which the medium intercepts.

The race is progressing, developing and becoming increasingly mental. The relation between the dead and the living must and will be upon mental levels, prior to the processes of integration; the true severance of communication will come when the human soul is reabsorbed into the oversoul, prior to again reincarnating. The fact of communication up to that time will, however, completely destroy the fear of death. In the case of disciples working in a Master's Ashram, even this process of integration will constitute no barrier. In the next few pages I will give some teaching on what might be called the art of dying and so expand what I said in *A Treatise on White Magic*.

PRESENT ATTITUDES TO DEATH

I undertook to take up with you the processes of dying and to consider a little more fully the factor of death—the most familiar experience (could the physical brain but recall it and realise it) in the life of the reincarnating entity or soul. Let me make some comments as to the attitude of man to the experience of "restitution." This is a peculiarly occult word, largely used by the initiate when speaking of death. The outstanding attitude associated with death is one of fear. This fear is based upon the—at present—mental uncertainty as to the fact of immortality. Beyond the proven fact of some form of survival, established by the psychical research groups, immortality or the permanent existence of what we usually mean when we speak of the "I" remains as yet in the realm of wishful thinking or of belief. This belief can be founded on Christian premises, upon religious affirmation based on rationalising the matter, and on the more scientific approach which argues that economic necessity requires that that which has been so long in evolving and which is the culminating result of the evolutionary process cannot be lost. It is interesting to note that there is no evidence upon our planet of any higher evolutionary product than that of the human kingdom; even for the materialistic thinker, the uniqueness of man is to be found in his various stages of consciousness and in his capacity to present for investigation all stages of consciousness, from that of the illiterate savage, through all the intermediate stages of mental effectiveness up to the most advanced thinkers and geniuses, capable of creative art, scientific discovery and spiritual perception.

Putting it very simply, the question which the theme of death arouses is: Where is the "I," the occupying tenant of the body, when that body is relinquished and disintegrates? Is there, in the last analysis, an occupying tenant?

Human history records the endless search for assurance upon this subject; this search culminates today in the numerous societies which are occupying themselves with the attempt to prove immortality and to penetrate into those fastnesses of the spirit which apparently give sanctuary to that "I" which has been the actor on the physical plane and which has hitherto baffled the most earnest seeker. The incentive of fear lies behind this frantic search; it is an unfortunate fact that the majority of the people (apart from a few enlightened scientists and similar intelligent seekers) who engage in the usually questionable techniques of the seance room, are emotional types, easily convinced and only too ready to accept as evidence that which the more intelligent seeker would immediately repudiate.

Let me here make my position clear as regards the great spiritualistic movement which has done so much in the past to prove the fact of survival, and which has also, in certain of its phases, done so much to mislead and deceive mankind. Under this general term, I class also the various psychical research groups and exempt all sincere scientific work. None of these groups has as yet proven their case. The mystery and the foolishness of the average seance room, and the work of the mediums, have nevertheless demonstrated the presence of an inexplicable factor; the laboratories of the scientific research worker have scarcely proved even that. For every case of the definitely acceptable appearance of a discarnate person there are thousands of cases which can be explained upon the grounds of gullibility, telepathic rapport (with the bereaved person, but not with anyone who has passed over), the seeing of thoughtforms by the clairvoyant and the hearing of voices by the clairaudient, and also by trickery. Note that I refer to "acceptable appearances" of a returning spirit. There is enough evidence to warrant belief in survival and to prove its factual nature. Upon the grounds of the inexplicable phenomena of contact with the supposedly dead which have been noted, investigated and proven, and upon the character of the men who testify to the fact of these phenomena, we can affirm that something survives the "restitution" of the material body to the eternal reservoir of substance. It is on this premise that we proceed.

Today the phenomenon of death is becoming increasingly familiar. The world war has launched millions of men and women—civilians and those in the various branches of the armed forces of all the nations—into that unknown world which receives all those who discard the physical form. Conditions are at this time such that in spite of the ancient and deep-seated fear of death, there is emerging in the consciousness of mankind the realisation that there are many worse things than death; men have come to know that starvation, mutilation, permanent physical incapacity, mental disability as the result of war and the strain of war, the observation of pain and agony which cannot be relieved, are indeed worse than death; also, many know and believe (for such is the glory of the human spirit) that the relinquishing of the values for which men have fought and died down the ages and which are deemed essential to the life of the free human spirit is of greater significance than the process of death. This attitude, characteristic of the sensitive and the right thinking people at this time, is now emerging upon a large scale. This means the recognition, alongside of the ancient fear, of an unconquerable hope of better conditions to be found elsewhere, and this need not necessarily be wishful thinking but an indication of a latent subjective knowledge, slowly coming to the surface. Something is on its way as a result of human distress and human thinking; this is today sensed; this fact will be later demonstrated. Opposing this inner confidence and subjective realisation are old habits of thought, the developed materialistic attitude of the present, the fear of deception, and the antagonism of both the scientist and the religious man or churchman. The former rightly refuses to believe that which remains still unproven and seems also not to be susceptible of proof, whilst religious groups and organisations have no confidence in any presentation of truth which they have not formulated in their own terms. This lays an undue emphasis upon belief and thus stultifies all enthusiastic investigation. The discovery of the *fact* of immortality will come from the people; it will eventually then be accepted by the churches and proven by science, but this not until the aftermath of the war is over and this planetary disturbance has subsided.

The problem of death, needless to say, is founded upon the love of life which is the deepest instinct in human nature. The determination that nothing is lost under divine law is a recognition of science; eternal persistence in some form or another is universally held to be a truth. Out of the welter of theories, three major solutions have been proposed; these are well known to all thinking people. They are:

1. *The strictly materialistic solution,* which posits the experience and expression of conscious life as long as the physical, tangible form exists and persists, but also teaches that after death and the subsequent disintegration of the body there is no longer any conscious, functioning, self-identified person. The sense of the "I," the awareness of a personality in contradistinction to all other personalities, vanishes with the disappearance of the form; personality is believed to be only the sumtotal of the consciousness of the cells in the body. This theory relegates man to the same state as any of the other forms in the three other kingdoms in nature;

it is based on the nonsensitivity of the average human being to life, withdrawn from a tangible vehicle; it ignores all evidence to the contrary and says that because we cannot see (visually) and prove (tangibly) the persistence of the "I" or the immortal entity after death, it is nonexistent. This theory is not held by so many as it was in earlier years, particularly during the materialistic Victorian age.

2. *The theory of conditional immortality.* This theory is still held by certain fundamentalist and theologically narrow schools of thought and also by a few of the intelligentsia, primarily those of egoistic tendency. It posits that only those who reach a particular stage of spiritual awareness, or who accept a peculiar set of theological pronouncements, can receive the gift of personal immortality. The highly intellectual also argue at times that the crowning gift to humanity is a developed and cultured mind, and that those who possess this gift are likewise endowed with eternal persistence. One school dismisses those who are what they regard as spiritually recalcitrant or negative to the imposition of their particular theological certainties, either to complete annihilation as in the materialistic solution, or to a process of eternal punishment, thus at the same time arguing for a form of immortality. Owing to the innate kindness of the human heart, very few are vindictive or unthinking enough to regard this presentation as acceptable, and of course among those we must class the unthinking people who escape from mental responsibility into a blind belief in theological pronouncements. The Christian interpretation as given by the orthodox and the fundamentalist schools proves untenable when submitted to clear reasoning; among the arguments which negate its accuracy lies the fact that

Christianity posits a long future but no past; it is likewise a future entirely dependent upon the activities of this present life episode and accounts in no way for the distinctions and differences which distinguish humanity. It is only tenable upon the theory of an anthropomorphic Deity Whose will—as it works out in practice—gives a present that has no past but only a future; the injustice of this is widely recognised, but the inscrutable will of God must not be questioned. Millions still hold this belief, but it is not so strongly held as it was one hundred years ago.

3. *The theory of reincarnation,* so familiar to all my readers, is becoming increasingly popular in the Occident; it has always been accepted (though with many foolish additions and interpretations) in the Orient. This teaching has been as much distorted as have the teachings of the Christ or the Buddha or Shri Krishna by their narrow-minded and mentally limited theologians. The basic facts of a spiritual origin, of a descent into matter, of an ascent through the medium of constant incarnations in form until those forms are perfect expressions of the indwelling spiritual consciousness, and of a series of initiations at the close of the cycle of incarnation, are being more readily accepted and acknowledged than ever before.

Such are the major solutions of the problems of immortality and of the persistence of the human soul; they aim to answer the eternal questioning of the human heart as to Whence, Why, Whither and Where? Only the last of these proposed solutions offers a truly rational reply to all of them. Its acceptance has been delayed because, ever since the time of H. P. Blavatsky, who formulated this ancient truth for the modern world in the last quarter of the nineteenth century, it has been so unintelligently presented; it has been handicapped owing to the fact that the Eastern races have always held it, and—from the Western angle—they are heathen and the heathen "in their blindness bow down to wood and stone," to quote one of your fundamentalist hymns. How curious it is to realise that, to the man from Eastern countries, the religious people in ┼he West do likewise, and can be seen on their knees berore the Christian altars bearing statues of the Christ, of the Virgin Mary and of the Apostles.

The occultists of the world, through the theosophical societies and other occult bodies, so-called, have greatly damaged the presentation of the truth anent reincarnation through the unnecessary, unimportant, inaccurate and purely speculative details which they give out as truths anent the processes of death and the circumstances of man after death. These details are largely dependent upon the clairvoyant vision of astral psychics of prominence in the Theosophical Society. Yet in the Scriptures of the world these details are not given, and H.P.B. in *The Secret Doctrine* gave none. An instance of this inaccurate and foolish attempt to throw light upon the theory of rebirth can be seen in the time limits imposed upon departed human souls between incarnations on the physical plane and the return to physical rebirth—so many years of absence are proclaimed, dependent upon the age of the departed soul and its place upon the ladder of evolution. If, we are told, the soul is very advanced, absence from the physical plane is prolonged, whereas the reverse is the case. Advanced souls and those whose intellectual capacity is rapidly developing come back with great rapidity, owing to their sensitive response to the pull of obligations, interests and responsibilities already established upon the physical plane. People are apt to forget that time is the sequence of events and of states of consciousness as registered by the physical brain. Where no physical brain exists, what humanity understands by time is nonexistent. The removal of the barriers of the form, stage by stage, brings an increasing realisation of the Eternal Now. In the case of those who have passed through the door of death and who still continue to think in terms of time, it is due to glamour and to the persistence of a powerful thoughtform. It indicates polarisation upon the astral plane; this is the plane upon which leading Theosophical writers and psychics have worked, and upon which they have based their writings. They are quite sincere in what they say, but omit to recognise the illusory nature of all findings based on astral clairvoyance. The recognition of a pronounced time factor, and the constant emphasis laid upon timing, are characteristic of all highly developed people in incarnation and of those whose lower, concrete minds are powerful in calibre. Children and child-races on the one hand, and those highly advanced people whose abstract minds are functioning (through the medium of the interpretive lower mind), usually have no sense of time. The initiate uses the time factor in his relations and his dealings with those living upon the physical plane, but is detached within himself from all recognition of it elsewhere in the universe.

Therefore the use of the term "immortality" infers timelessness and teaches that this timelessness exists for that which is not perishable or conditioned by time. This is a statement requiring careful consideration. Man reincarnates under no time urge. He incarnates under the demands of karmic liability, under the pull of that which he, as a soul, has initiated, and because of a sensed need to fulfill instituted obligations; he incarnates also from a sense of responsibility and to meet requirements which an earlier breaking of the laws governing right human relations have imposed upon him. When these requirements, soul necessities, experiences and responsibilities have all been met, he enters permanently "into the clear cold light of love and life" and no longer needs (as far as he himself is concerned) the nursery stage of soul experience on earth. He is free from karmic impositions in the three worlds, but is still under the impulse of karmic necessity which exacts from him the last possible ounce of service that he is in a position to render to those still under the Law of Karmic Liability. You have, therefore, three aspects of the Law of Karma, as it affects the principle of rebirth:

1. *The Law of Karmic Liability,* governing life in the three worlds of human evolution, and which is ended altogether at the fourth initiation.

2. *The Law of Karmic Necessity.* This governs the life of the advanced disciple and the initiate from the time of the second initiation until a certain initiation higher than the fourth; these initiations enable him to pass on to the Way of the Higher Evolution.

3. *The Law of Karmic Transformation,* a mysterious phrase governing the processes undergone upon the Higher Way. These fit the initiate to pass off the cosmic physical plane altogether, and to function upon the cosmic mental plane. It is concerned with the release of those like Sanat Kumara, and His Associates in the Council Chamber at Shamballa, from the imposition of cosmic desire which demonstrates upon our cosmic physical plane as spiritual will. This should be to you an arresting thought. It will be obvious, however, that there is little that I can say upon this subject. The knowledge involved is not yet mine.

To turn now to another aspect of our theme. There are, speaking in the larger sense, three major death episodes.

There is, first of all, the constant recurrence of the fact of physical death. This is familiar to all of us through its extreme frequency, could we but realise it. This recognition would rapidly eliminate the present fear of death. There is then the "second death" spoken of in the Bible, which is in this present planetary cycle associated with the death of all astral control over the human being. In the larger sense, this second death is consummated at the fourth initiation, when even spiritual aspiration dies, being no more needed; the Will of the initiate is now fixed and immovable, and astral sensitivity is no longer required.

There is a curious counterpart to this experience upon a much lower level in the death of all astral emotion which takes place for the individual aspirant at the time of the second initiation. It is then a complete episode and is consciously registered. Between the second and the third initiations, the disciple has to demonstrate a continuity of non-response to astralism and emotionalism. The second death, to which I am here referring, has to do with the death or the disappearance of the causal body at the time of the fourth initiation; this marks the completion of the building of the antahkarana and the institution of direct, unimpeded continuity of relationship between the Monad and the personality.

The third death takes place when the initiate leaves behind him, finally and with no prospect of return, all relation with the cosmic physical plane. This death, necessarily, lies far ahead for all in the Hierarchy and is at present only possible and permissible for a few in the Council Chamber at Shamballa. It is not, however, a process through which Sanat Kumara will pass. He underwent this "transformation" many aeons ago, during the great cataclysm which inaugurated the Lemurian Age, and which was induced by His cosmic experience and the need for an inflow of energy from extra-planetary Beings.

I have given these brief summations so as to enlarge your general understanding of what the Masters call "the extension of death in space." Nevertheless, in the following pages we shall confine ourselves to the theme of the death of the physical body and of the subtler bodies in the three worlds; we shall deal also with the processes which bring about the reabsorption of the human soul into the spiritual soul upon its own plane, the higher mental plane; we shall consider the reassimilation of substance and the appropriation of matter in order again to reincarnate.

We shall therefore consider the three major processes to which I earlier referred; these cover three periods and lead, eventually, to other processes under the Law of Rebirth. They are:

1. *The Process of Restitution,* governing the period of withdrawal of the soul from the physical plane and from its two phenomenal aspects, the dense physical body and the etheric body. This concerns the Art of Dying.

2. *The Process of Elimination.* This governs that period of the life of the human soul after death and in the two other worlds of human evolution. It concerns the elimination of the astral-mental body by the soul, so that it is "ready to stand free in its own place."

3. *The Process of Integration,* dealing with the period wherein the liberated soul again becomes conscious of itself as the Angel of the Presence and is reabsorbed into the world of souls, thus entering into a state of reflection. Later, under the impact of

the Law of Karmic Liability or Necessity, the soul again prepares itself for another descent into form.

The field of experience (in which is death, as the average person knows it) is the three worlds of human evolution— the physical world, the world of emotion and desire, and the mental plane. This world is, in the last analysis two-fold, from the angle of death, and hence the phrase "the second death." This I have earlier applied to the death or destruction of the causal body, in which the spiritual soul has hitherto functioned. It can be applied, however, in a more literal sense, and may be referred to the second phase of the death process in the three worlds. It then concerns form only, and is related to those vehicles of expression which are found below the formless levels of the cosmic physical plane. These form levels are (as you know well, for the knowledge constitutes the a.b.c. of the occult theory) the levels on which the concrete, lower mind functions, the emotional nature reacts to the so-called astral plane, and the dual physical plane. The physical body con- sists of the dense physical body and the etheric vehicle. We have consequently, when considering the death of a human being, to employ the word death in relation to two phases in which it functions:

Phase One: The death of the physical-etheric body. This phase falls into two stages:

a. That in which the atoms which constitute the physi- cal body are restored to the source from whence they came. This source is the sumtotal of the mat- ter of the planet, constituting the dense physical body of the planetary Life.

b. That in which the etheric vehicle, composed of an aggregation of forces, returns these forces to the general reservoir of energy. *This dual phase covers the Process of Restitution.*

Phase Two: The "rejection" (as it is sometimes called) of the mental-emotional vehicles. These form, in reality, only one body; to it the early theosophists (correctly) gave the name of the "kama-manasic body" or the vehicle of desire-mind. I have said elsewhere that there is no such thing as the astral plane or the astral body. Just as the physical body is made up of matter which is not regarded as a principle, so the astral body—as far as the mind nature is concerned—is in the same category. This is a difficult matter for you to grasp, because desire and emotion are so real and so devastatingly important. But—speaking literally—from the angle of the mental plane, the astral body is "a figment of the imagination"; it is *not* a principle. The massed use of the imagination in the service of desire has nevertheless constructed an illusory glamorous world, the world of the astral plane. During physical incarnation, and when a man is not upon the Path of Discipleship, the astral plane is very real, with a vitality and a life all its own. After the first death (the death of the physical body) it still remains equally real. But its potency slowly dies out; the mental man comes to realise his own true state of consciousness (whether developed or undeveloped), and the second death becomes possible and takes place. *This phase covers the Process of Elimination.*

When these two phases of the Art of Dying are over, the discarnate soul stands free from the control of matter; it is purified (temporarily by the phases of Restitution and Elimination) from all contamination by substance. This is achieved, not through any activity of the soul in form, the human soul, but as a result of the activity of the soul on its own plane abstracting the fraction of itself which we call the human soul. It is primarily the work of the over-shadowing soul which effects this; it is not carried forward by the soul in the personality. The human soul, during this stage, is only responsive to the pull or the attractive force of the spiritual soul as it—with deliberate intent—extracts the human soul from its imprisoning sheaths. Later on, as the evolutionary processes proceed and the soul increasingly controls the personality, it will be the soul *within* the imprisoning sheaths which will bring about —consciously and with intention—the phases of dying. In the earlier stages, this release will be brought about with the aid of the overshadowing spiritual soul. Later on, when the man is living upon the physical plane as the soul, he will himself—with full continuity of consciousness—carry out the processes of abstraction, and will then (with directed purpose) "ascend to the place from whence he came." This is the reflection in the three worlds of the divine ascension of the perfected Son of God.

Some of the information I have already given anent the subject of Death in my other writings might well be ap-pended here. I have a definite purpose in suggesting this. Death is all around you at this time; the demand of the human spirit for light upon this matter has reached a crisis of potency; it is evoking the inevitable response from the Hierarchy. It is also my hope that students will do some-thing of major importance to aid in bringing forth the light upon the processes of death which humanity is today demanding.

ON DEATH

EXCERPTS FROM OTHER WRITINGS

"Why this blind power? Why Death? Why this decay

of forms? Why the negation of the power to hold? Why death, O Mighty Son of God?"

Faintly the answer comes: "I hold the keys of life and death. I bind and loose again. I the Destroyer am."

A Treatise on the Seven Rays, Vol. I, Page 63.

The intent of the Lord of the first Ray is to stand behind the other divine Aspects, and when They have achieved Their purpose, to shatter the forms They have built.

He is the controller of the death drama in all kingdoms—a destruction of forms which brings about release of power and permits "entrance into light through the gateway of death."

Page 64.

a. "Withhold thy hand until the time has come. Then give the gift of death, O Opener of the Door."

Page 65.

b. "Separate the robe from That which hides behind its many folds. Take off the veiling sheaths. Let God be seen. Take Christ from off the Cross."

Page 69.

The first step towards substantiating the fact of the soul is to establish the fact of survival, though this may not necessarily prove the fact of immortality. . . . That something survives the process of death, and that something persists after the disintegration of the physical body is steadily being proved. If that is not so, then we are the victims of a collective hallucination, and the brains and minds of thousands of people are untrue and deceiving, are diseased and distorted. Such a gigantic collective insanity is more difficult to credit than the alternative of an expanded consciousness.

Page 98-99.

a. The growth of etheric vision and the largely increased numbers of clairaudient and clairvoyant people is steadily revealing the existence of the astral plane and the etheric counterpart of the physical world. More and more people are becoming aware of this subjective realm: they see people walking around who are either the so-called "dead" or who, in sleep, have dropped the physical sheath.

Page 98.

b. The next two hundred years will see the abolition of death, as we now understand that great transition, and the establishing of the soul's existence. The soul will be known as an entity, as the motivating impulse and the spiritual centre back of all manifested forms . . . Our essential immortality will be demonstrated and realised to be a fact in nature.

Page 96.

Within the next few years the fact of persistence and of the eternity of existence will have advanced out of the realm of questioning into the realm of certainty. . . . There will be no question in anyone's mind that the discarding of the physical body will leave a man still a conscious living entity. He will be known to be perpetuating his existence in a realm lying behind the physical. He will be known to be still alive, awake and aware. This will be brought about by:

a. The development of a power within the physical eye of a human being . . will reveal the etheric body . . . men will be seen occupying that body.

b. The growth of the number of people who have the power to use the "reawakened third eye" will demonstrate immortality, for they will with facility see the man who has discarded his etheric body as well as his physical body.

c. A discovery in the field of photography will prove survival.

d. Through the use of the radio by those who have passed over will communication eventually be set up and reduced to a true science.

e. Man will eventually be keyed up to a perception and to a contact which will enable him to *see through,* which will reveal the nature of the fourth dimension, and will blend the subjective and objective worlds together into a new world. Death will lose its terrors and that particular fear will come to an end.

Page 183.

You must always bear in mind that the consciousness remains the same whether in physical incarnation or out of incarnation, and that development can be carried on with even greater ease than when limited and conditioned by the brain consciousness.

Discipleship in the New Age, Vol. I, Page 81.

The Law of Sacrifice and Death is the controlling factor on the physical plane. The destruction of the form, in order that the evolving life may progress, is one of the fundamental methods in evolution.

A Treatise on Cosmic Fire, Page 569.

a. The Law of Disintegration is an aspect of the Law of Death. This is the law that governs the destruction of the form in order that the indwelling life may shine forth in fullness. . . . This law breaks up the forms and the Law of Attraction draws back to primal sources the material of those forms.

Page 580.

b. The Law of Death controls in the three worlds.

Page 596.

c. The Law of Sacrifice is the Law of Death in the subtle bodies, whilst what we call death is the analogous thing in the physical body.

Page 596.

d. The Law of Death and Sacrifice governs the gradual disintegration of concrete forms and their sacrifice to the evolving life. . . .

Page 596.

e. When all the units or cells in the body of the planetary Logos have achieved, He too is set free from dense manifestation and physically dies.

Page 509.

The process of DEATH is occultly as follows:

a. The first stage is the withdrawal of the life force in the etheric vehicle from the dense physical body and the consequent "falling into corruption" and becoming "scattered to the elements." Objective man fades out and is no more seen by the physical eye, though still in his etheric body. When etheric vision is developed, the thought of death will assume very different proportions. When a man can be seen functioning in his etheric physical body by a majority of the race, the dropping of the dense body will be considered just as a release.

b. The second stage is the withdrawal of the life force from the etheric body, and its devitalisation. . . .

c. The third stage is the withdrawal of the life force from the astral or emotional form so that it disintegrates in a similar manner and the life is centralised elsewhere. It has gained an increase of vitality

through physical plane existence and added colour
through emotional experience.

d. The final stage for the human being is its withdrawal from the mental vehicle. The life forces
after this fourfold abstraction are centralised entirely in the soul. . . .

Pages 735-7.

The Law of Attraction breaks up the forms and
draws back to primal sources the material of those
forms, prior to rebuilding them anew. On the path of
evolution the effects of this law are well-known, not
only in the destruction of discarded vehicles, but in the
breaking up of the forms in which great ideals are
embodied. . . . All eventually break under the working
of this law.

Its workings are more apparent to the average
human mind in its manifestations at this time on the
physical plane. We can trace the connection between
the atmic (spiritual) and the physical plane—demonstrating on the lower plane as the Law of Sacrifice and
Death—but its effect can be seen on all five planes as
well. It is the law which destroys the final sheath that
separates the perfected soul.

Page 581.

When the "will to live" vanishes, then the "Sons of
Necessity" cease from objective manifestation. . . . When
the Thinker on his own plane withdraws his attention from
his little system within the three worlds and gathers within
himself all his forces, then physical plane existence comes
to an end and all returns within the causal consciousness.
. . . This demonstrates on the physical plane in the withdrawing from out of the top of the head of the radiant
etheric body and the consequent disintegration of the

physical. The framework goes and the dense physical form falls apart.

Page 85.

a. The etheric body is in reality a network of fine channels which are the component parts of one interlacing fine cord—one portion of this cord being the magnetic link which unites the physical and the astral bodies and which is snapped or broken after the withdrawal of the etheric body from the dense physical body at the time of death. (See Ecc: XII.6.)

Page 98.

b. Later "definite methods of demonstrating the fact that life persists after the death of the physical body will be followed and the etheric web will be recognised as a factor in the case."

Page 429.

Death is "initiation, or the entering into a state of liberation."

A Treatise on the Seven Rays, Vol. I, Page 197.

Death and the Etheric Body.

It is not our purpose to give facts for verification by science, or even to point the way to the next step onward for scientific investigators; that we may do so is but incidental and purely secondary. What we seek mainly is to give indications of the development and correspondence of the threefold whole that makes the solar system what it is—the vehicle through which a great cosmic ENTITY, the solar Logos, manifests active intelligence with the purpose in view of demonstrating perfectly the love side of His nature. Back of this design lies a yet more esoteric and ulterior purpose, hid in the Will Consciousness of the

Supreme Being, which perforce will be later demonstrated when the present objective is attained. The dual alternation of objective manifestation and of subjective obscuration, the periodic out-breathing, followed by the in-breathing of all that has been carried forward through evolution, embodies in the system one of the basic cosmic vibrations, and the keynote of that cosmic ENTITY whose body we are. The heart beats of the Logos (if it might be so inadequately expressed) are the source of all cyclic evolution, and hence the importance attached to that aspect of development called the "heart" or "love aspect," and the interest that is awakened by the study of rhythm. This is true, not only cosmically and macrocosmically, but likewise in the study of the human unit. Underlying all the physical sense attached to rhythm, vibration, cycles and heart-beat, lie their subjective analogies—love, feeling, emotion, desire, harmony, synthesis and ordered sequence—and back of these analogies lies the source of all, the identity of that Supreme Being Who thus expresses Himself.

Therefore the study of pralaya, or the withdrawal of the life from out of the etheric vehicle, will be the same whether one studies the withdrawal of the human etheric double, the withdrawal of the planetary etheric double, or the withdrawal of the etheric double of the solar system. The effect is the same and the consequences similar.

What is the result of this withdrawal, or rather, what causes that something which we call death or pralaya? As we are strictly pursuing the text book style in this treatise, we will continue our method of tabulation. The withdrawal of the etheric double of a man, a planet, and a system is brought about by the following causes:

a. *The cessation of desire.* This should be the result of all evolutionary process. True death, under the law, is brought about by the attainment of the objective, and hence by the cessation of aspiration. This, as the perfected cycle draws to its close, will be true of the individual human being, of the Heavenly Man, and of the Logos Himself.

b. By the slowing down and gradual cessation of the cyclic rhythm, *the adequate vibration is achieved* and the work accomplished. When the vibration or note is perfectly felt or sounded, it causes (at the point of synthesis with other vibrations) the utter shattering of the forms.

Motion is characterised, as we know, by three qualities:

1. Inertia
2. Mobility
3. Rhythm

These three are experienced in just the above sequence and presuppose a period of slow activity, succeeded by one of extreme movement. This middle period produces incidentally (as the true note and rate are sought) cycles of chaos, of experiment, of experience and of comprehension. Following on these two degrees of motion (which are characteristic of the atom, Man, of the Heavenly Man or group, and of the Logos or the Totality) comes a period of rhythm and stabilisation wherein the point of balance is achieved. By the force of balancing the pairs of opposites, and thus producing equilibrium, pralaya is the inevitable sequence.

c. *By the severing of the physical from the subtler body* on the inner planes, through the shattering of the web. This has a threefold effect:

First. The life that had animated the physical form (both dense and etheric) and which had its starting point in the permanent atom, and from thence "pervaded the moving and the unmoving" (in God, the Heavenly Man, and the human being, as well as in the atom of matter), is withdrawn entirely within the atom upon the plane of abstraction. This "plane of abstraction" is a different one for the entities involved:

    a. For the physical permanent atom, it is the atomic level.

    b. For man, it is the causal vehicle.

    c. For the Heavenly Man, it is the second plane of monadic life, His habitat.

    d. For the Logos, it is the plane of Adi.

All these mark the points for the disappearance of the unit into pralaya. We need here to remember that it is always pralaya when viewed from *below*. From the higher vision, that sees the subtler continuously overshadowing the dense when not in objective manifestation, pralaya is simply subjectivity, and is not that "which is not," but simply that which is esoteric.

Second. The etheric double of a man, a planetary Logos, and a solar Logos, being shattered, becomes non-polarised as regards its indweller, and permits therefore of escape. It is (to word it otherwise) no longer a source of attraction, nor a factual magnetic point. It becomes non-magnetic, and the great Law of Attraction ceases to control it; hence disintegration is the ensuing condition of the form. The Ego ceases to be attracted by its form on the physical plane, and proceeding to inbreathe, withdraws its life from out of the sheath. The cycle draws to a close, the experiment has been made, the objective (a relative one from life to life and from incarnation to incarnation) has been achieved, and there remains nothing more to desire; the Ego, or the thinking entity, loses interest, therefore, in form, and turns his attention inward. His polarisation changes, and the physical is eventually dropped.

The planetary Logos likewise in His greater cycle (the synthesis or the aggregate of the tiny cycles of the cells of His body) pursues the same course; He ceases to be attracted downward or outward, and turns His gaze within; He gathers inward the aggregate of the smaller lives within His body, the planet, and severs connection. Outer attraction ceases, and all gravitates towards the centre instead of scattering to the periphery of His body.

In the system the same process is followed by the solar Logos; from His high place of abstraction, He ceases to be attracted by His body of manifestation. He withdraws His interest and the pairs of opposites, the spirit and the matter of the vehicle, dissociate. With this dissociation the solar system, that "Son of Necessity," or of desire, ceases to be, and passes out of objective existence.

Third. This leads finally, to the scattering of the atoms of the etheric body into their primordial condition. The subjective life, the synthesis of will and love taking active form, is withdrawn. The partnership is dissolved. The form then breaks up; the magnetism that has held it in coherent shape is no longer present, and dissipation is complete. Matter persists, but the form no longer persists.

The work of the second Logos ends, and the divine incarnation of the Son is concluded. But the faculty or inherent quality of matter also persists, and at the end of each period of manifestation, matter (though distributed again into its primal form) is active intelligent matter plus the gain of objectivity, and the increased radiatory and latent activity which it has gained through experience. Let us illustrate: The matter of the solar system, when undifferentiated, was active intelligent matter, and that is all that can be predicated of it. This active intelligent matter was matter qualified by an earlier experience, and coloured by an earlier incarnation. Now this matter is in form, the solar system is not in pralaya but in objectivity—this objectivity having in view the addition of another quality to the logoic content, that of love and wisdom. Therefore, at the next solar pralaya, at the close of the one hundred years of Brahma, the matter of the solar system will be coloured by active intelligence and by active love. This means literally that the aggregate of solar atomic matter will eventually vibrate to another key than it did at the first dawn of manifestation.

We can work this out in connection with the planetary Logos and the human unit, for the analogy holds good. We have a correspondence on a tiny scale in the fact that each human life period sees a man taking a more evolved physical body of a greater responsiveness, tuned to a higher key, of more adequate refinement, and vibrating to a different measure. In these three thoughts lies much information, if they are carefully studied and logically extended.

d. *By the transmutation of the violet into the blue.* This we cannot enlarge on. We simply make the statement, and leave its working out to those students whose karma permits and whose intuition suffices.

e. *By the withdrawal of the life, the form should gradually dissipate.* The reflex action here is interesting to note, for the greater Builders and Devas who are the active agents during manifestation, and who hold the form in coherent shape, transmuting, applying and circulating the pranic emanations, likewise lose their attraction to the matter of the form, and turn their attention elsewhere. On the path of out-breathing (whether human, planetary or logoic) these building devas (on the same Ray as the unit desiring manifestation, or on a complementary Ray) are attracted by his will and desire, and perform their office of construction. On the path of in-breathing (whether human, planetary or logoic) they are no longer attracted, and the form begins to dissipate. They withdraw their interest, and the forces (likewise entities) who are the agents of destruction, carry on their necessary work of breaking up the form; they scatter it—as it is occultly expressed—to "the four winds of Heaven," or to the regions of the four breaths—a fourfold separation and distribution. A hint is here given for careful consideration.

Though no pictures have been drawn of death bed scenes nor of the dramatic escape of the palpitating etheric body from the centre in the head, as might have been anticipated, yet some of the rules and purposes governing this withdrawal have been mentioned. We have seen how the aim of each life (whether human, planetary or logoic) should be the effecting and the carrying out of a definite purpose. This purpose is the development of a more adequate form for the use of spirit; and when this purpose is achieved, then the indweller turns his attention away, and the form disintegrates, having served his need. This is not always the case in every human life, nor even in each planetary cycle. The mystery of the moon is the mystery of failure. This leads, when comprehended, to a life of dignity and offers an aim worthy of our best endeavour. When this angle of truth is universally recognised, as it will be when the intelligence of the race suffices, then evolution will proceed with certainty, and the failures be less numerous.

A Treatise on Cosmic Fire, Pages 128-133.

All severing of links produces severe reactions. Yet if you could but realise it, the severing of the outer physical plane links is the least severe and the most impermanent of all such events. Death itself is a part of the great illusion and only exists because of the veils which we have gathered around ourselves. All of us, as workers in the field of glamour (the new field in which humanity must learn *consciously* to work), have been honoured and trusted. Death comes to all, but for disciples there should be none of the usual glamour and distress. I would say to you, look not back at the past. In that direction lie glamour and distress. It is the usual direction and the line of least resistance for the majority. But such is not the way for you. Look not either to revelation or to the imparted illusory comfort of those who hover on the dividing line between the seen and the unseen. Again, that is not the way for you. You are not a distressed and bereaved disciple looking anxiously at the separating veil and hoping for some sign to come through which will convince you that all is well. . . .

Reach up to the heights of the soul, and having sought and found that pinnacle of peace and that altitude of joy whereon your soul immovably stands, then look into the world of *living* men—a threefold world in which all men— incarnate and discarnate—are to be found. Find there that which your soul can and will recognise. The glamours of one's own distress, the maya of the past, distort ever one's point of view. Only the soul stands clear from illusion, and only the soul sees things as they are. Mount, therefore, to the soul.

Discipleship in the New Age, Vol. I, page 463.

CHAPTER V

The Process of Restitution

THE THEME OF DEATH, which we are now considering, must be approached by us with as much of the spirit of normalcy and of scientific investigation as we can manage. The fear complex of humanity finds its point of entrance into man's consciousness through the act of dying; failure to survive is the basic fear; and yet it is the commonest phenomenon upon the planet. Bear that in mind. The act of dying is the great universal ritual which governs our entire planetary life, but only in the human family and faintly, very faintly, in the animal kingdom is the reaction to fear found. Could you but see the etheric world as Those on the inner side of life experience and see it, you would see (going on ceaselessly and without any pause) the great planetary act of restitution. You would see a great activity proceeding within the etheric world in which the anima mundi, the animal soul and the human soul are constantly restoring the substance of all physical forms to the great reservoir of essential substance. This essential substance is as much a vital, directed unity as the world soul of which one hears so much. This interplay of the principle of death with the principle of life produces the basic activity of creation. The impulsive, directive force is the mind of God, of the planetary Logos, as He pursues His divine purposes, carrying with Him in this process all the media through which He manifests.

The human fear of death is primarily caused because the orientation of the kingdom of souls, the fifth kingdom in nature, has been (until relatively late in the world's cycle) towards form expression and towards the necessity of seeking experience through matter, in order eventually freely to control it. The percentage of the souls of those who are oriented away from expression in the three worlds is relatively so small, in proportion to the total number of souls demanding experience in the three worlds, that, until the cycle or era which we call the Christian, it might be stated that death reigned triumphant. Today, however, we are on the eve of seeing a complete change in this condition, owing to the fact that humanity—on a much larger scale than ever known before—is achieving a needed reorientation; the higher values and the life of the soul, as entered upon through the insistence of the mind in its higher and lower aspects, is beginning to control. This will perforce bring in a new attitude towards death; it will be regarded as a natural and desirable process, cyclically undergone. Men will eventually understand the significance of Christ's words when He said, "Render unto Caesar the things that are Caesar's and unto God the things that are God's." In the incident where those words occur He was referring to the great act of restitution which we call death. Ponder that story and see the symbolism of the soul, contained within the universal soul, as the fish within the water, and holding a coin of metal, the symbol of matter.

In one of the ancient writings the following symbolic words occur—

Said the Father to the son: Go forth and take unto thyself that which is not thyself, and that which is not thine own, but which is Mine. Regard it as thine own and seek the cause of its appearance. Let it appear to be thyself. Discover thus the world of glamour, the world of deep illusion, the world of falsity. Then learn that thou hast taken that which is not the goal of soul endeavour.

And when that moment comes in each cycle and appearance of deception and of theft, a voice will then be heard. Obey that voice. It is the voice of that within thyself which hears My voice, a voice unheard by those who love to thieve. The order will go forth again and yet again: "Make restitution of the *stolen goods*. Learn they are not for thee." At greater intervals will come that voice again: "Make restitution of the *borrowed goods;* pay back thy debt."

And then, when all the lessons have been learnt, the voice once more will speak: "Restore with joy that which was Mine, was thine and now again is ours. Thou hast no longer need of form. Stand free."

The implication of the above words is clear.

Two major thoughts will serve to clarify the issue of death with which we are now concerned: First, the great dualism ever present in manifestation. Each of the dualities has its own expression, is governed by its own laws, and seeks its own objectives. But—in time and space—they merge their interests for the benefit of both, and together produce the appearance of a unity. Spirit-matter, life-appearance, energy-force—each have their own emanating aspect; they each have a relation to each other; each have a mutual temporary objective, and thus in unison produce the eternal flux, the cyclic ebb and flow of life in manifestation.

In this process of relationship between Father-Spirit and Mother-Matter the son comes into being, and during the child stage carries on his life processes within the aura of the mother, identified with her yet forever seeking to escape from her domination. As maturity is reached, the problem intensifies, and the "pull" of the Father begins slowly to offset the possessive attitude of the mother, until finally the hold of matter, or of the mother, over her son (the soul) is finally broken. The son, the Christ-child, released from the guardianship and clinging hands of the mother, comes to know the Father. I am talking to you in symbols.

Second: All the processes of incarnation, of life in form and of restitution (by the activity of the principle of death), of matter to matter, and soul to soul, are carried forward under the great universal Law of Attraction. Can you picture the time when the process of death, clearly recognised and welcomed by the man, could be described by him in the simple phrase, "The time has come when my soul's attractive force requires that I relinquish and restore my body to the place from whence it came"? Imagine the change in the human consciousness when death comes to be regarded as an act of simple and conscious relinquishing of form, temporarily taken for two specific objectives:

a. To gain control in the three worlds.
b. To give opportunity to the substance of the forms thus "stolen or borrowed or rightly appropriated," according to the stage of evolution, to reach a higher point of perfection through the impact upon it of life, via the soul.

These are significant thoughts. They have been expressed before, but have been discarded as symbolic, as comforting or as wishful thinking. I present them to you as factual in nature, as unavoidable in practice, and as familiar a technique and process as those activities, (rhythmic and cyclic in nature) which govern the average man's life—rising and retiring, eating and drinking, and all the periodic affairs which he is accustomed to pursue.

I dealt with the subject of death in *A Treatise on White Magic,* focussing therein primarily upon the physical processes of dying and doing so from the point of view of the onlooker or observer. I sought there to indicate what the attitude of the onlooker should be. Here I would like to present a somewhat different picture, indicating what is known by the departing soul. If this involves repetition of what you already know, there are however certain basic repetitions and statements I wish to make. Let me tabulate them with brevity. Will you regard them as foundational and factual.

1. The time for the departure of an incarnating soul has come. The soul has in the past:
   a. Appropriated a physical body of a certain calibre, adequate to the requirements and age of that soul.
   b. Energised that physical body through the medium of the etheric body, thus galvanising it into life activity for the duration of the soul's set term of physical enterprise.

2. Two major streams of energy enter the physical body and produce its activity, its quality and type of expression, plus the impression it makes upon its evironment.
   a. *The stream of dynamic life.* This is anchored in the heart. This stream of dynamic energy enters the body, via the head, and passes down to the heart, where it is focussed during the life cycle. A smaller stream of the universal energy or prana, distinctive from the individualised life force, enters the physical body, via the spleen. It then rises to the heart to

join the larger and more important life stream. The life stream energises and holds in coherency the integrated physical body. The stream of pranic energy vitalises the individual atoms and cells of which that body is composed.

b. *The stream of individual consciousness.* This is anchored in the head, is an aspect of the soul, reveals the type of consciousness which is, in its turn, indicative of the point attained in evolution. This stream of energy likewise functions in connection with a stream of personality force; and this force is characterised by desire (emotional or astral sentiency) and enters into the physical body, via the solar plexus centre. This relates the man to the entire astral plane, and therefore to the world of glamour. With undeveloped people and with the average type of man, the solar plexus is the focus of consciousness and the energy is registered by the focal point of consciousness in the head without any recognition whatsoever. It is for this reason that (at the time of death) the soul leaves the body, via the solar plexus and not via the head. In the case of the developed man, the mental type of individual, the aspirant, disciple or initiate, the thread of consciousness will withdraw from the body via the head.

3. The group soul of all forms in the animal kingdom—under the Law of Attraction—withdraws the life principle from any specific physical form via the solar plexus, which is the brain of the average animal. Highly developed and domesticated animals are beginning to utilise the brain to a greater or to a less degree, but the life principle and the sentient aspect, or animal consciousness, is still withdrawn via the solar plexus. You have,

therefore, in all stages of the evolutionary process, certain interesting triangles of energy.

a. In the case of the animals and of those human beings who are little more than animals, of imbeciles and certain men who appear to be born with no centralised point of individual consciousness, the following triplicity is of importance:

> The group soul
> The solar plexus
> The spleen or pranic centre.

b. In low grade, but nevertheless individualised human beings and with the average emotional type of person, the following triplicity must be noted:

> The soul
> The head centre
> The solar plexus.

c. For highly developed people and for those upon the Path of Discipleship you have the following triangle active at the time of death:

> The soul
> The head centre
> The ajna centre.

In connection with all these triplicities there exists a dual relationship to the life principle:

a. The heart in which is focussed the life of the soul in form.

b. The spleen through which passes constantly and rhythmically the universal life essence or prana.

The whole subject is of course most obscure, and for those on strictly human levels, as yet unverifiable. However, an acceptance of the above three points, hypothetical today, will help to clarify your minds concerning this entire theme of restitution with which we are occupied.

4. The next point needs no proving, for it is generally accepted. It is that desire governs the process of death, as it also governs the processes of life experience. We say constantly that when the will-to-live is lacking, death is the inevitable result. This will-to-live, whether it is the tenacity of the physical body, functioning as an elemental being or as the directed intention of the soul, is an aspect of desire, or rather, it is a reaction of the spiritual will upon the physical plane. There is therefore an interlocking relation between:

   a. The soul on its own plane.
   b. The astral body.
   c. The solar plexus centre.

This relationship has hitherto received little attention in connection with the Art of Dying. Nevertheless it warrants careful thought.

You will note that I am here dealing with the theme of death as it makes its presence felt through disease or through old age. I am not referring to death as it comes through war or accident, through murder or through suicide. These causes of death, and other causes, come under a totally different directive process; they may not even involve the karma of a man or his individual destiny, as in the case of war. Then vast numbers of people are killed. This has nothing to do with the Law of Cause and Effect as a factor in the soul career of any individual. It is not an act of restitution, planned by a particular soul as it works out its individual destiny. Death, through the destructive processes of war, is under the directive and cyclic intention of the planetary Logos, working through the Council Chamber at Shamballa. The Beings Who there direct world processes know that a time has come when the relation between planetary evil and the Forces of Light or of Good have reached a point of "explosive antagonism" (as it is called). This must be given free rein if the divine purpose is to work out unarrested. The explosion is therefore permitted; nevertheless, all the time a controlling factor is present, even though unrealised by man. Because these Beings (Who work out the will of God) are in no way identified with form life, they have consequently a just appreciation of the relative importance of life in form; the destruction of forms is, to Them, not death in the sense that we understand it, but simply and solely a process of liberation. It is the limited vision of those identified with form which has so consistently nurtured the fear of death. The cycle in which we now live has seen the greatest destruction of human forms in the entire history of our planet. *There has been no destruction of human beings.* I would have you note this statement. Because of this wholesale destruction, humanity has made a very rapid advance towards a more serene attitude in connection with death. This is not yet apparent but—in a few years' time—the new attitude will begin to be marked and the fear of death will begin to die out in the world. This will also be largely due to the increased sensitivity of the human response apparatus, leading to a turning inward or to a new orientation of the human mind, with unpredictable results.

The basis of all wars is fundamentally the sense of separateness. This fundamental individualism or pleased recognition of isolationism leads to all the secondary causes of war: greed, producing economic disaster; hatred, producing national and international friction; cruelty, producing pain and death. The roots of death are therefore deep-seated; it is the destruction of the cycle of separateness as an individual upon the physical plane which we call death in the usual sense; consequently death is a process of at-one-ment. Could you but see a little further into the matter, you would learn that death releases the individualised life into a less cramped and confined existence, and eventually— when the death process has been applied to all the three vehicles in the three worlds—into the life of universality. This is a point of inexpressible bliss.

The Law of Attraction governs the process of dying, as it governs all else in manifestation. It is the principle of coherency which, under the balanced integration of the whole body, preserves it intact, stabilises its rhythm and cyclic life processes and relates its varied parts to each other. It is the major coordinating principle within all forms, for it is the primary expression (within the soul) of the first aspect of divinity, the will aspect. This statement may surprise you, accustomed as you are to regard the Law of Attraction as an expression of the second aspect, love-wisdom. This attractive principle is found in all forms, from the tiny form of the atom to that form, the planet Earth, through which our planetary Logos expresses Himself. But if it is the principle of coherency and the cause of integration, it is also the medium through which "restitution" is brought about and by which the human soul is periodically re-absorbed into the overshadowing soul. This aspect of the Law of Attraction has, as yet, received little attention. The reason is that it concerns the highest expression of that Law, and is therefore related to the will aspect of Deity, as also the will aspect of the Monad. Only as the Shamballic force proceeds with its more direct work in the coming cycle, and men begin to discriminate (as they must and will) between self-will and the spiritual will, between determination, intention, plan, purpose, and fixed polarisation, will clarification come. The Law of Attraction has (as all else in manifestation) three phases or aspects, each related to the three divine aspects:

1. It relates life and form, spirit and matter—the third aspect.

2. It governs the coherent integrative process which produces forms—the second aspect.

3. It brings about the imbalance which results in the act of disintegration, thus overcoming form—as far as the human being is concerned—and brings this about in three phases to which we have given the names:

   a. *Restitution,* resulting in the dissolution of the body and the return of its elements, atoms and cells, to their originating source.

   b. *Elimination,* involving the same basic process in relation to the forces which have constituted the astral body and the mental vehicle.

   c. *Absorption,* the mode whereby the human soul is integrated into its originating source, the overshadowing, universal soul. This is an expression of the first aspect.

All these phases, rightly understood, illustrate or demonstrate the unique potency of the Law of Attraction and its relation to the Law of Synthesis, which governs the first divine aspect. Integration eventually produces synthesis. The many cyclic integrations which are carried forward in the great life cycle of an incarnating soul lead to the final synthesis of spirit and soul, which is the goal of the evolutionary process where humanity is concerned. After the third initiation, this results in the complete liberation of the man from the "pull" of substance in the three worlds and in his consequent ability to wield, with full understanding, the Law of Attraction in its various phases, as far as the creative process is involved. Other phases will then be later mastered.

One point must be borne in mind. The words "earth to earth and dust to dust," so familiar in the burial rituals of the Occident, refer to this act of restitution and connote the return of the physical body elements to the original reservoir of matter, and of the substance of the vital form to the general etheric reservoir; the words "the spirit shall return unto God who gave it" are a distorted reference to the absorption of the soul by the universal soul. The ordinary rituals, however, fail to emphasise that it is that individualised soul, in process of reabsorption, which institutes and orders, by an act of the spiritual will, that restitution. It is forgotten in the West that this "order to restore" has been given with great frequency down the ages by every soul within a physical form; in so doing, steadily and inevitably, the first divine aspect—the Monad on its own plane—is tightening its hold upon its body of manifestation, via its reflection, the soul. Thus the will aspect comes increasingly into play until, upon the Path of Discipleship, spiritual determination is brought to its highest point of development and, upon the Path of Initiation, the will begins to function consciously. It is worth remembering, is it not, that it is in the deliberate issuing of the command by the soul upon its own plane to its shadow in the three worlds that the soul learns to express the first and highest aspect of divinity, and this at first, and for a very long time, solely through the process of death. The difficulty at present is that relatively few people are soul-conscious, and consequently most men remain unaware of the "occult commands" of their own souls. As humanity becomes soul-conscious (and this will be one of the results of the agony of the present war), death will be seen as an "ordered" process, carried out in full consciousness and with understanding of cyclic purpose. This will naturally end the fear at present rampant, and will also arrest the tendency to suicide, evidenced increasingly in these difficult times. The sin of murder is in reality based upon the fact that it interferes with soul purpose, and not really upon the killing of a particular human physical body. That is also why war is not murder, as many well-meaning fanatics consider it; it is the destruction of forms with the beneficent intent (if one could scrutinise divine purpose) of the planetary Logos. However, it is the motives of the originators of war on the physical plane which make *them* evil. If war did not take place, the planetary life would, through what we call "acts of God," call back the souls of men on a large scale in line with His loving intention. When evil men precipitate a war, He brings good out of evil.

You can see, therefore, why the occult sciences lay the emphasis upon cyclic law, and why there is a growing interest in the Science of Cyclic Manifestation. Death appears frequently to be so purposeless; that is because the intention of the soul is not known; past development, through the process of incarnation, remains a hidden matter; ancient heredities and environments are ignored, and recognition of the voice of the soul is not yet generally developed. These are matters, however, which are on the very verge of recognition; revelation is on its way, and for that I am laying the foundation.

I am anxious for you to grasp the teaching I have already given before we proceed to that which is explanatory or new. Study it with care so that the theme of death can more surely and more sanely take shape in your mind. Seek to arrive at a new slant upon the subject and see law and purpose and the beauty of intention in what has hitherto been a terror and a major fear.

Later I shall endeavour to give you some glimpse of the death process as the soul registers it, when undertaking the act of restitution. To you, what I say may appear as speculative or hypothetical; in any case it will be a statement of which few of you will be in a position to prove the accuracy. But surely, brother of mine, it may be more sane and wholesome, more sound and beautiful, than the present darkness and sick hope, and the unhappy speculation and oft despair which overshadows every death bed at this time.

1. THE NATURE OF DEATH

EXCERPTS FROM OTHER WRITINGS

The whole must be seen as of more vital importance than the part, and this not as a dream, a vision, a theory, a process of wishful thinking, a hypothesis or an urge. It is realised as an innate necessity and as inevitable. It connotes death, but death as beauty, as joy, as spirit in action, as the consummation of all good.

A Treatise on the Seven Rays. Vol. V.

Death, if we could but realise it, is one of our most practised activities. We have died many times and shall die again and again. Death is essentially a matter of consciousness. We are conscious one moment on the physical plane, and a moment later we have withdrawn onto another plane and are actively conscious there. Just as long as our consciousness is identified with the form aspect, death will hold for us its ancient terror. Just as soon as we know ourselves to be souls, and find that we are capable of focussing our consciousness or sense of awareness in any form or on any plane at will, or in any direction within the form of God, we shall no longer know death.

A Treatise on White Magic, page 494.

Ponder, therefore, upon this doctrine of abstraction. It covers all life processes and will convey to you the eternally lovely secret of Death which is entrance into life.

A Treatise on the Seven Rays. Vol. V.

In this Rule, two main ideas are to be found, both of them connected with the first divine aspect: the thought of DEATH and the nature of the WILL. In the coming century, *death* and the *will* most inevitably will be seen to have new meanings to humanity and many of the old ideas will vanish. Death to the average thinking man is a point of catastrophic crisis. It is the cessation and the ending of all that has been loved, all that is familiar and to be desired; it is a crashing entrance into the unknown, into uncertainty, and the abrupt conclusion of all plans and projects. No matter how much true faith in the spiritual values may be present, no matter how clear the rationalising of the mind may be anent immortality, no matter how conclusive the evidence of persistence and eternity, there still remains a questioning, a recognition of the possibility of complete finality and negation, and an end of all activity, of all heart reaction, of all thought, emotion, desire, aspiration and the intentions which focus around the central core of man's being. The longing and the determination to persist and the sense of continuity still rest, even to the most determined believer, upon probability, upon an unstable foundation and upon the testimony of others—who have never in reality returned to tell the truth. The emphasis of all thought on this subject concerns the central "I" or the integrity of Deity.

You will note that in this Rule, the emphasis shifts from the "I" to the constituent parts which form the garment of the Self, and this is a point worth noting. The information given to the disciple is to work for the dissipation of this garment and for the return of the lesser lives to the general reservoir of living substance. The ocean of Being is nowhere referred to. Careful thought will here show that this ordered process of detachment, which the group life makes effective in the case of the individual, is one of the strongest arguments for the fact of continuity and for individual, identifiable persistence. Note these words. The focus of activity shifts from the active body to the active entity within that body, the master of his surroundings, the director of his possessions and the one who is the breath itself, despatching the lives to the reservoir of substance or recalling them at will to resume their relation to him.

A Treatise on the Seven Rays. Vol. V.

First of all that the Eternal Pilgrim, of his own free will and accord, chose "occultly" to die and took a body or series of bodies in order to raise or elevate the lives of the form nature which he embodied; in the process of so doing, he himself "died" in the sense that, for a free soul, death and the taking of a form and the consequent immersion of the life in the form, are synonymous terms.

Secondly, that in so doing, the soul is recapitulating on a small scale what the solar Logos and the planetary Logos have likewise done, and are doing. The great Lives come under the rule of these laws of the soul during the period of manifestation, even though They are not governed or controlled by the laws of the natural world, as we call it. Their consciousness remains unidentified with the world of phenomena, though ours is identified with it until such time that we come under the rule of the higher laws. By the occult "death" of these great Lives, all lesser lives can live and are proffered opportunity.

A Treatise on the Seven Rays. Vol. V.

The forces of death are abroad today, but it is the death of liberty, the death of free speech, the death of freedom in human action, the death of truth and of the higher spiritual values. *These* are the vital factors in the life of humanity. The death of the physical form is a negligible factor in relation to these and is easily righted again through the processes of rebirth and of fresh opportunity. . . . The destruction of the form in battle is of small importance to those who know that reincarnation is a basic law of nature and *that there is no death*.

June Message, 1940.

You say there are as yet only beliefs as to immortality, and no sure evidences. In the accumulation of testimony, in the inner assurances of the human heart, in the fact of belief in eternal persistence as an idea in the minds of men, lie sure indication. But indication will give place to conviction and knowledge before another hundred years has elapsed, for an event will take place and a revelation be given the race which will turn hope into certainty and belief into knowledge. In the meantime, let a new attitude to death be cultivated and a new science of death be inaugurated. Let it cease to be the one thing we cannot control and which inevitably defeats us, and let us begin to control our passing over to the other side, and to understand somewhat the technique of transition.

A Treatise on White Magic, page 500.

All I plead for is a sane approach to death; all I seek to make is a suggestion that when pain has worn itself out and weakness has supervened, the dying person be permitted to prepare himself, even if apparently unconscious, for the great transition. Forget not that it takes strength and a strong hold on the nervous apparatus to produce pain. Is it impossible to conceive of a time when the act of dying will be a triumphant finale to life? Is it impossible to vision the time when the hours spent on the death bed may be but a glorious prelude to a conscious exit? When the fact that the man is to discard the handicap of the physical sheath may be for him and those around him the long-waited-for and joyous consummation? Can you not visualise the time when, instead of tears and fears and the refusal to recognise the inevitable, the dying person and his friends would mutually agree on the hour, and that nothing but happiness would characterise the passing? That in the minds of those left behind the thought of sorrow will not enter and death beds shall be regarded as happier occasions than births and marriages? I tell you that, before so very long, this will be deeply so for the intelligent of the race, and little by little for all.

A Treatise on White Magic, page 499.

It is interesting here to note that death is governed by the Principle of Liberation and not by that of Limitation. Death is only recognised as a factor to be dealt with by self-conscious lives and is only misunderstood by human beings, who are the most glamoured and deluded of all incarnated lives.

A Treatise on White Magic, page 534.

When the nature of true Service is comprehended, it will be found that it is an aspect of that divine energy which works always under the destroyer aspect, for it destroys the forms in order to release. Service is a manifestation of the Principle of Liberation, and of this principle, death and service constitute two aspects. Service saves, liberates and releases, on various levels, the imprisoned consciousness. The same statements can be made of death. But unless service can be rendered from an intuitive understanding of all the facts in the case, interpreted intelligently, and applied in a spirit of love upon the physical plane, it fails to fulfill its mission adequately.

A Treatise on White Magic, page 537.

Fear of Death.

The fear of death is based upon:

a. A terror of the final rending processes in the act of death itself.

b. Horror of the unknown and the indefinable.

c. Doubt as to final immortality.

d. Unhappiness at leaving loved ones behind or of being left behind.

e. Ancient reactions to past violent deaths, lying deep in the consciousness.

f. Clinging to form life, because primarily identified with it in consciousness.

g. Old erroneous teaching as to Heaven and Hell, both equally unpleasant in prospect to certain types.

A Treatise on White Magic, page 300.

As time progresses and before the close of the next century, death will be finally seen to be nonexistent in the sense in which it is now understood. Continuity of consciousness will be so widely developed, and so many of the highest types of men will function simultaneously in the two worlds, that the old fear will go and the intercourse between the astral plane and the physical plane will be so firmly established and so scientifically controlled that the work of the trance mediums will rightly and mercifully come to an end. The ordinary common trance mediumship and materialisations under controls and Indian guides are just as much perversions of the intercourse between the two planes as are sex perversions and the distortions of the true relationship and intercourse between the sexes. I refer not here to the work of clairvoyants, no matter how poor, nor to the taking possession of the body by entities of high calibre, but of the unpleasant phenomena of the materialisation seance, of ectoplasm and the blind unintelligent work done by the old Atlantean degenerates and earthbound souls, the average Indian chief and guide. There is nothing to be learned from them, and much to be avoided.

The reign of the fear of death is well-nigh ended and we shall soon enter upon a period of knowledge and of certainty which will cut the ground from under all our fears. In dealing with the fear of death, there is little to be done except to raise the whole subject onto a more scientific level, and—in this scientific sense—teach people to die. There is a technique of dying just as there is of living, but this technique has been lost very largely in the West, and is almost lost except in a few centres of Knowers in the East. More of this can perhaps be dealt with later, but the thought of the needed approach to this subject can rest in the minds of students who read this, and perhaps as they study and read and think, material of interest will come their way which could be gradually assembled and published.

A Treatise on White Magic, pages 301-302.

Fear of death and depression constitute for man the Dweller on the Threshold in this age and cycle. Both of them indicate sentient reaction to psychological factors and cannot be dealt with by the use of another factor such as courage. They must be met by the omniscience of the soul, working through the mind—not by its omnipotence. In this is to be found an occult hint.

A Treatise on White Magic, page 309.

The instinct of self-preservation has its roots in an innate fear of death; through the presence of this fear, the race has fought its way to its present point of longevity and endurance.

A Treatise on White Magic, page 626.

Definition of Death.

Death itself is a part of the Great Illusion, and only exists because of the veils we have gathered around ourselves.

A Treatise on the Seven Rays, Vol. V.

But people are apt to forget that every night in the hours of sleep we die to the physical plane and are alive and functioning elsewhere. They forget that they have already achieved facility in leaving the physical body; because they cannot as yet bring back into the physical brain consciousness the recollection of that passing out, and of the subsequent interval of active living, they fail to relate death and sleep. Death is, after all, only a longer interval in the life of physical plane functioning; one has only "gone abroad" for a longer period. But the process of daily sleep and the process of occasional dying are identical, with the one difference that in sleep the magnetic thread or current of energy along which the life force streams is preserved intact, and constitutes the path of return to the body. In death, this life thread is broken or snapped. When this has happened, the conscious entity cannot return to the dense physical body, and that body, lacking the principle of coherence, then disintegrates.

A Treatise on White Magic, page 494.

The processes of abstraction are (as you may thus see) connected with the life aspect, are set in motion by an act of the spiritual will, and constitute the "resurrection principle which lies hidden in the work of the Destroyer," as an old esoteric saying expresses it. The lowest manifestation of this principle is to be seen in the process of what we call *death—which is in reality a means of abstracting the life principle,* informed by consciousness, from the form of the bodies in the three worlds.

Thus, the great synthesis emerges and destruction, death, and dissolution are, in reality, naught but life processes. Abstraction is indicative of process, progress and development. It is this aspect of the Law of Life (or the Law of Synthesis as it is called in certain larger connotations) with which the initiate specifically deals.

A Treatise on the Seven Rays, Vol. V.

Life is approached from the angle of the Observer, and not from that of a participator in actual experiment and experience in the three worlds (physical—emotional—mental) . . . if they are initiated disciples they are increasingly unaware of the activities and reactions of their personalities, because certain aspects of the lower nature are now so controlled and purified that they have dropped below the threshold of consciousness and have entered the world of instinct; therefore, there is no more awareness of them than a man asleep is conscious of the rhythmic functioning of his sleeping physical vehicle. This is a deep and largely unrealised truth. It is related to the entire process of death, and might be regarded as one of the definitions of death; it holds the clue to the mysterious words "the reservoir of life." Death is in reality unconsciousness of that which may be functioning in some form or another, but in a form of which the spiritual entity is totally unaware. The reservoir of life is the place of death, and this is the first lesson the disciple learns. . . .

A Treatise on the Seven Rays, Vol. V.

Purposes of Death.

Through death, a great at-one-ing process is carried

forward; in the "fall of a leaf" and its consequent identification with the soil on which it falls, we have a tiny illustration of this great and eternal process of at-one-ing, through becoming and dying as a result of becoming.

A Treatise on the Seven Rays, Vol. II, page 173.

I speak about Death as one who knows the matter from the outer world experience and the inner life expression: *There is no death.* There is, as you know, entrance into fuller life. There is freedom from the handicaps of the fleshly vehicle. The rending process so much dreaded does not exist, except in the cases of violent and sudden death, and then the only true disagreeables are an instant and overwhelming sense of imminent peril and destruction and something closely approaching an electric shock. No more. For the unevolved, death is literally a sleep and a forgetting, for the mind is not sufficiently awakened to react, and the storehouse of memory is as yet practically empty. For the average good citizen, death is a continuance of the living process in his consciousness and a carrying forward of the interests and tendencies of the life. His consciousness and his sense of awareness are the same and unaltered. He does not sense much difference, is well taken care of, and oft is unaware that he has passed through the episode of death. For the wicked and cruelly selfish, for the criminal and for those few who live for the material side only, there eventuates that condition which we call "earth-bound." The links they have forged with earth and the earthward bias of all their desires, force them to remain close to the earth and their last setting in the earth environment. They seek desperately and by every possible means to re-contact it and to re-enter. In a few cases, great personal love for those left behind, or the nonfulfillment of a recognised and urgent duty, holds the good and beautiful in a somewhat similar condition. For the aspirant, death is an immediate entrance into a sphere of service and of expression to which he is well accustomed and which he at once recognises as not new. In his sleeping hours he has developed a field of active service and of learning. He now simply functions in it for the entire twenty-four hours (talking in terms of physical plane time) instead of for his usual few hours of earthly sleep.

A Treatise on White Magic, pages 300-301.

True death, under the Law, is brought about by the attainment of the objective, and hence by the cessation of aspiration. The etheric double of a man, a planetary Logos, and a solar Logos, being shattered, becomes non-polarised as regards its indweller, and permits therefore of escape. It is (to word it otherwise) no longer a source of attraction, nor a focal magnetic point. It becomes non-magnetic, and the great Law of Attraction ceases to control it; hence disintegration is the ensuing condition of the form.

A Treatise on Cosmic Fire, pages 129-130.

"The Law demands the entrance of that which can effect a change."

Bearing in mind what I have elsewhere given, it is obvious that that which must find entrance is that vital concentrated will which, when set in motion in an individual, in a group, in a nation, in a kingdom of nature (a planetary centre), and in the planet as a whole, i.e., in all the planetary centres simultaneously, will cause a stirring, a changed measure, a new movement and momentum, an uprising and a consequent abstraction. The changes wrought in the centres when the death of the physical body is taking place have never yet been observed or recorded; they are, however, definitely present to the eye of the initiate and prove most interesting and informative. It is the recognition of the condition of the centres which enables the ini-

tiate to know—when in process of bestowing healing—
whether the physical healing of the body is permissible or
not. He can see, by looking, whether the will principle of
abstraction, to which I have been referring, is actively
present or not. The same process can be seen taking place in
organisations and in civilisations in which the form aspect is
being destroyed in order that the life may be abstracted and
later again rebuild for itself a more adequate form. It is the
same under the great processes of initiation, which are not
only processes of expanding the consciousness but are rooted
in the death or the abstraction process, leading to resurrection and ascension.

That which effects a change is a discharge (to use a
totally inadequate phrase) of directed and focussed will-
energy. This is so magnetic in quality that it draws to itself
the life of the centres, bringing about the dissolution of the
form but the release of the life. Death comes to the individual man in the ordinary sense of the term when the
will-to-live in a physical body goes and the will-to-abstract
takes its place. This we call death. In cases of death in
war, for instance, it is not then a case of the individual
will-to-withdraw, but an enforced participation in a great
group abstraction. From its own place, the soul of the
individual man recognises the end of a cycle of incarnation,
and recalls its life. This it does through a discharge of the
will-energy that is strong enough to bring about the change.
. . . Christ referred to this work of abstraction as regards
the third great planetary centre, Humanity, when He said
(and He was speaking as the Representative of the Hierarchy, the second planetary centre, into which all human
beings achieving initiation are "withdrawn" esoterically),
"I, if I be lifted up, will draw all men unto Me." A different word to this word of His will be spoken at the end of
the age when the Lord of the World will speak from Sham-

balla (the first planetary centre), will abstract the life principle from the Hierarchy, and all life and consciousness will then be focussed in the planetary head centre—the Great Council Chamber at Shamballa.

"The Law demands that the changes thus effected remove the form, bring quality to light, and lay the emphasis upon life."

Here the three great aspects—form, quality, and life—are brought into relation, and the point of the evolutionary objective is seen in its true light—LIFE. Note this phrasing. Form or appearance, having served its purpose, disappears. Death of the form takes place. Quality, the major divine attribute being developed in this planet, becomes dominant, is "conscious of itself"—as the ancient writings put it. It is identified and individual, but has no implementing form, except that of the greater whole in which it finds its place. Neither form nor quality (body nor consciousness) are paramount in the new state of being, only the life aspect, the spirit on its own plane becomes the dominating factor. Some faint dim light on the significance of this may come if you bear in mind that our seven planes are only the seven subplanes of the cosmic physical plane. The process of developing sensitivity in this sevenfold evolution has been undergone in order to enable the initiate to function upon the cosmic astral plane, when withdrawn or abstracted after the higher initiations. He is abstracted from our planetary life altogether. Only one factor could prevent this, and that might be his pledge to serve temporarily within the planetary ring-pass-not. Such members of the Hierarchy Who pledge Themselves to this work are stated to have Buddhic consciousness, and the line of Their descent (occultly understood) is from the Eternal Pilgrim, the Lord of the World, then the Buddha, and then the Christ. They remain identified through free choice with the "quality seen within the light" and, for the term of Their freely rendered service, work with the consciousness aspect in order to lay the emphasis later upon the life aspect. . . .

A Treatise on the Seven Rays, Vol. V.

The eighteen fires must die down; the lesser lives (embodying the principle of form, of desire and of thought, the sumtotal of creativity, based upon magnetic love) must return to the reservoir of life and naught be left but that which caused them to be, the central will which is known by the effects of its radiation or breath.

This dispersal, death or dissolution, is in reality a great effect produced by the central Cause, and the injunction is consequently: *"This they must bring about by the evocation of the Will."* . . . The disciple finds his group in the Master's Ashram and consciously and with full understanding masters death—the long-feared enemy of existence. He discovers that death is simply an effect produced by life and by his conscious will, and is a mode whereby he directs substance and controls matter. This becomes consciously possible because, having developed awareness of two divine aspects—creative activity and love—he is now focussed in the highest aspect and knows himself to be the WILL, the Life, the Father, the Monad, the One.

A Treatise on the Seven Rays, Vol. V.

A great upheaval in all the kingdoms in nature has characterised this day and generation; a stupendous destruction of all forms of divine life and in every kingdom has been the outstanding note of this upheaval. Our modern civilisation has received a death blow from which it will never recover, but which will be recognised some day as the "blow of release" and as the signal for that which is better, new and more suitable for the evolving spirit, to make its appearance. Great and penetrating energies and their evoked forces have met in conflict which has, figuratively speaking, elevated the mineral kingdom into the skies and which has brought down fire from heaven. I am talking to you factually and not just symbolically. The bodies of men, women and children, as well as animals, have been destroyed; the forms of the vegetable kingdom and the potencies of the mineral kingdom have been disintegrated, distributed and devastated. The coherent life of all the planetary forms has been temporarily rendered incoherent. As an ancient prophecy has put it: "No true united Sound goes out from form to form, from life to life. Only a cry of pain, a demand for restitution and an invocation for relief from agony, despair and fruitless effort goes out from here to There."

All this upheaval of the "soil" of the world—spiritual, psychological and physical—all this disruption of the forms and of the familiar contours of our planetary life, *had* to take place before there could come the emergence of the Hierarchy into the public consciousness; all this had to do its work upon the souls of men before the New Age could come in, bringing with it the Restoration of the Mysteries and the rehabilitation of the peoples of the Earth. The two go together. This is one of the major points which I am seeking to make. The disruption, disintegration and the completely chaotic conditions existing for the past five hundred years within all the kingdoms of nature have at last worked their way out into paralleling physical conditions. This is good and desirable; it marks the prelude to a better building of a better world, and the construction of more adequate forms of life and of more correct human attitudes, plus a sounder orientation to reality. The best is yet to be.

Everything is being rapidly brought to the surface—the good and the bad, the desirable and the undesirable, the past and the future (for the two are one); the plough of God has nearly accomplished its work; the sword of the spirit has severed an evil past from the radiant future, and both are seen as contributory in the Eye of God; our material civilisation will be seen as giving place rapidly to a more spiritual culture; our church organisations, with their limiting and confusing theologies, will soon give place to the Hierarchy with its emerging teaching—clear, factual, intuitive and nondogmatic.

A Treatise on the Seven Rays, Vol. V.

Intense desire for sentient existence or attachment. This is inherent in every form, is self-perpetuating and known even to the very wise.

When the life or Spirit withdraws itself, the form dies, occultly. When the thought of the ego or higher self is occupied with its own plane, there is no energy outgoing towards the matter of the three worlds, and so no form-building and form-attachment is there possible. This is in line with the occult truism that "energy follows thought," and is in line, too, with the teaching that the body of the Christ principle (the Buddhic vehicle) only begins to co-ordinate as the lower impulses fade out. . . . Attachment to form or the attraction of form for Spirit is the great involutionary impulse. Repulsion of form and consequent form disintegration is the great evolutionary urge.

The Light of the Soul, pages 137-8.

When the cause, desire, has produced its effect, the personality or form aspect of man, then as long as the will to live exists, so long will the form persist. It is kept in manifestation through mental vitality. This has been demonstrated time and again in the annals of medicine, for it has been proven that as long as the determination to live persists, so will be the probable duration of the physical plane life; but that the moment that will is withdrawn, or the interest of the dweller in the body is no longer centered upon personality manifestation, death ensues and the disintegration of that mind-image, the body, takes place.

The Light of the Soul, page 397.

There are two main lines of evolution, that which concerns matter and form, and that which concerns the soul, the consciousness aspect, the thinker in manifestation. For each of these the path of progress differs, and each pursues its course. As has been noted, for a long period of time the soul identifies itself with the form aspect and endeavours to follow the "Path of Death," for that is what the dark path is in fact to the thinker. Later, through strenuous effort, this identification ceases; the soul becomes aware of itself, and of its own path, or dharma, and follows then the way of light and of life. It should ever be borne in mind, however, that for the two aspects their own path is the right path, and that the impulses which lie hidden in the physical vehicle or in the astral body are not in themselves wrong. They become wrong from certain angles when twisted from their right use, and it was this realisation that led the disciple in the Book of Job to cry out and say, "I have perverted that which was right." The two lines of development are separate and distinct, and this every aspirant has to learn.

The Light of the Soul, pages 402-403.

The Art of Dying.

The soul, seated in the heart, is the life principle, the principle of self-determination, the central nucleus of positive energy by means of which all the atoms of the body are held in their right place and subordinated to the "will-to-be" of the soul. This principle of life utilises the blood stream as its mode of expression and as its controlling agency, and through the close relation of the endocrine system to the blood stream, we have the two aspects of soul activity brought together in order to make man a living, conscious, functioning entity, governed by the soul, and expressing the purpose of the soul in all the activities of daily living.

Death, therefore, is literally the withdrawal from the heart and from the head of these two streams of energy, producing consequently complete loss of consciousness and disintegration of the body. Death differs from sleep in that *both* streams of energy are withdrawn. In sleep, only the thread of energy which is anchored in the brain is withdrawn, and when this happens the man becomes unconscious. By this we mean that his consciousness or sense of awareness is focussed elsewhere. His attention is no longer directed towards things tangible and physical, but is turned upon another world of being and becomes centered in another apparatus or mechanism. In death, both the threads are withdrawn or unified in the life thread. Vitality ceases to penetrate through the medium of the blood stream and the heart fails to function, just as the brain fails to record, and thus silence settles down. The house is empty. Activity ceases, except that amazing and immediate activity which is the prerogative of matter itself and which expresses itself in the process of decomposition. From certain aspects. therefore, that process indicates man's unity with everything that is material; it demonstrates that he is a part of nature itself, and by nature we mean the body of the one Life in Whom "we live and move and have our being." In those three words—living, moving and being—we have the entire story. *Being* is awareness, self-consciousness and self-expression, and of this man's head and brain are the exoteric symbols. *Living* is energy, desire in form, coherence and adhesion to an idea, and of this the heart and the blood are the exoteric symbols. *Moving* indicates the integration and response of the existing, aware, living entity into the universal activity, and of this the stomach, pancreas and liver are the symbols.

It must be noted also that *death is, therefore, undertaken at the direction of the Ego, no matter how unaware a human being may be of that direction*. The process works automatically with the majority, for (when the soul withdraws its attention) the inevitable reaction on the physical plane is either death, by the abstraction of the dual threads of life and reason energy, or by the abstraction of the thread of energy which is qualified by mentality, leaving the life stream still functioning through the heart, but no intelligent awareness. The soul is engaged elsewhere and occupied on its own plane with its own affairs.

A Treatise on White Magic, pages 496-497.

Before I take up this subject in greater detail I would like to make some reference to the "web in the brain," which is intact for the majority but is non-existent for the illumined seer.

In the human body, as you know, we have an underlying, extensive vital body which is the counterpart of the physical, which is larger than the physical and which we call the etheric body or double. It is an energy body and is composed of force centres and nadis or force threads. These underlie or are the counterparts of the nervous apparatus— the nerves and the nerve ganglia. In two places in the human body there are orifices of exit, if I may use so cumbersome a phrase. One opening is in the solar plexus and the other is in the brain at the top of the head. Protecting both is a closely woven web of etheric matter, composed of interlacing strands of life energy.

During the process of death the pressure of the life energy beating against the web produces eventually a puncturing or opening. Out of this the life force pours as the potency of the abstracting influence of the soul increases. In the case of animals, of infants and of men and women who are polarised entirely in the physical and astral bodies, the door of exit is the solar plexus, and it is that web which is punctured, thus permitting the passing out. In the case of mental types, of the more highly evolved human units, it is the web at the top of the head in the region of the fontenelle which is ruptured, thus again permitting the exit of the thinking rational being.

In the process of death these are, therefore, the two main exits: the solar plexus for the astrally polarised, physically biased human being, and therefore of the vast majority, and the head centre for the mentally polarised and spiritually oriented human being. This is the first and most important factor to remember, and it will easily be seen how the trend of a life tendency and the focus of the life attention determine the mode of exit at death. It can be seen also that an effort to control the astral life and the emotional nature, and to orient one's self to the mental world and to spiritual things, has a momentous effect upon the phenomenal aspects of the death process.

If the student is thinking clearly, it will be apparent to him that one exit concerns the spiritual and highly evolved man, whilst the other concerns the low grade human being who has scarcely advanced beyond the animal stage. What then of the average man? A third exit is now in temporary use; just below the apex of the heart another etheric web is found covering an orifice of exit. We have, therefore, the following situation:

1. The exit in the head, used by the intellectual type, by the disciples and initiates of the world.

2. The exit in the heart, used by the kindly, well-meaning man or woman who is a good citizen, an intelligent friend and a philanthropic worker.

3. The exit in the region of the solar plexus, used by those whose animal nature is strong.

This is the first point in the new information which will slowly become common knowledge in the West during the next century. Much of it is already known by thinkers in the East and is in the nature of a first step towards a rational understanding of the death process.

A Treatise on White Magic, page 500.

In relation to the technique of dying, it is only possible for me at this time to make one or two suggestions. I deal not here with the attitude of the attendant watchers, I deal only with those points which will make for an easier passing over of the transient soul.

First, let there be silence in the chamber. This is, of course, frequently the case. It must be remembered that the dying person may usually be unconscious. This unconsciousness is apparent but not real. In nine hundred cases out of a thousand the brain awareness is there, with a full consciousness of happenings, but there is a complete paralysis of the will to express and complete inability to generate the energy which will indicate aliveness. When silence and understanding rule the sick room, the departing soul can hold possession of its instrument with clarity until the last minute, and can make due preparation.

Later, when more anent colour is known, only orange lights will be permitted in the sick room of a dying person, and these will only be installed with due ceremony when there is assuredly no possibility of recovery. Orange aids the focussing in the head, just as red stimulates the solar plexus and green has a definite effect upon the heart and life streams.

Certain types of music will be used when more in connection with sound is understood, but there is no music as yet which will facilitate the work of the soul in abstracting itself from the body, though certain notes on the organ will be found effective. At the exact moment of death, if a person's own note is sounded, it will coordinate the two streams of energy and eventually rupture the life thread, but the knowledge of this is too dangerous to transmit as yet and can only later be given. I would indicate the future and the lines along which future occult study will run.

It will be found also that pressure on certain nerve centres and on certain arteries will facilitate the work, and this science of dying is held in custody, as many students know, in Tibet. Pressure on the jugular vein and on certain big nerves in the region of the head and on a particular spot in the medulla oblongata will be found helpful and effective. A definite science of death will inevitably later be elaborated, but only when the fact of the soul is recognised and its relation to the body has been scientifically demonstrated.

Mantric phrases will also be employed and definitely built into the consciousness of the dying person by those around him, or employed deliberately and mentally by himself. The Christ demonstrated their use when He cried aloud, "Father, into Thy hands I commend My spirit." And we have another instance in the words, "Lord, now lettest Thou Thy servant depart in peace." The steady use of the Sacred Word, chanted in an undertone or on a particular key (to which the dying man will be found to respond), may later constitute also a part of the ritual of transition, accompanied by the anointing with oil, as preserved in the Catholic Church. Extreme Unction has an occult, scientific basis. The top of the head of the dying man should also symbolically point towards the East, and the feet and hands should be crossed. Sandalwood only should be burned in the room, and no incense of any other kind permitted, for sandalwood is the incense of the First or Destroyer Ray, and the soul is in process of destroying its habitation.

A Treatise on White Magic, page 505.

If there is one factor aspirants recognise, it is the need of freeing themselves from the Great Illusion. Arjuna knew this, yet succumbed to despair. Yet in his hour of need, Krishna failed him not, but laid down in the Gita the simple rules whereby depression and doubt can be overcome. They may be briefly summarised as follows:

a. Know thyself to be the undying One.
b. Control thy mind, for through that mind the undying One can be known.
c. Learn that the form is but the veil which hides the splendour of Divinity.
d. Realise that the One Life pervades all forms, so that there is no death, no distress, no separation.
e. Detach thyself therefore from the form side and come to Me, so dwelling in the place where Light and Life are found. Thus illusion ends.

A Treatise on White Magic, page 308.

A Master learns the meaning of each confining form; then He assumes control and wields the law upon the plane consistent with the form. He has then outgrown the form and discards it for other and higher forms. Thus, He has progressed always by means of the sacrifice and death of the form. Always, it is recognised as imprisoning, always it must be sacrificed and die so that the life within may speed ever on and up. The path of resurrection presupposes crucifixion and death, and then leads to the mount whence Ascension may be made.

Letters on Occult Meditation, page 261.

THE ACT OF RESTITUTION

In considering the consciousness of the departing soul (note that phrase) as it undertakes the act of restitution, I would again point out that I am dealing with a subject of which there is no tangible physical proof. Occasionally men are brought back again into physical plane existence when at the exact point of complete physical restitution. This can only be done as long as the conscious entity is still occupying the etheric vehicle, though the discarding of the dense physical body has to all intents and purposes been completed. Though the etheric body interpenetrates the entire physical body, it is much larger than that body, and the astral body and the mental nature can still remain etherically polarised even if the death of the physical body—the cessation of all heart activity and the concentration of the basic etheric focus in the region of the head, or the heart, or the solar plexus—has been effective and the withdrawal is already well under way.

The etheric forces are first of all withdrawn into the surrounding extension of the etheric ring-pass-not, prior to that final dissipation which leaves the man free to stand as a human soul within the ring-pass-not of his astral vehicle. You have here a somewhat new aspect of the death process. The withdrawal of the etheric body from occupation of the dense physical body has oft been posited and presented. But even when that has been accomplished, death is not yet complete; it still awaits a secondary activity of the will of the soul. This secondary activity will result in all the etheric forces dissolving into an emanating source which is the general reservoir of forces. Forget not that the etheric body has no distinctive life of its own. It is only an amalgamation of all the forces and energies which animated the physical body and which galvanised it into activity during the outer life cycle. Remember also that the five centres up the spine are not within the physical body, but are found at certain distinctive points in the paralleling etheric substance; they are (even in the case of the undeveloped man, and still more in the case of the average man) at least two inches away from the physical spine. The three head centres are also outside the dense physical body. The recollection of this will facilitate your understanding of the statement that the physical body is, *per se,* vacated when death is assumed by the watching authorities, but that, nevertheless, the man may not be truly dead. I would remind you also that this is equally true of the many minor centres as well as of the major centres, with which we are so familiar.

The last of the minor centres to "fade out into nothingness," in order to be resolved into the totality of etheric substance, are two which are closely related to and in the region of the lungs. It is on these two centres that the soul works if recalled into the dense physical body for some reason. It is when they swing into a returning or a fresh in-going activity that the breath of life returns to the vacated physical form. It is an unconscious realisation of this which constitutes the prompting cause of the process which is normally carried out in all cases of drowning or of asphyxiation. When a man has succumbed to disease and the physical body is consequently weakened, such restorative exercises are not possible and should not be employed. In cases of sudden death through accident, suicide, murder, unexpected heart attacks or through the processes of war, the shock is such that the somewhat leisurely process of soul withdrawal is entirely offset, and the vacating of the physical body and the complete dissolution of the etheric body are practically simultaneous. In normal cases of death from disease, the withdrawal is slow, and (where the malignancy of the disease has not caused too great deterioration of the physical organism involved) there is the possibility of a return for a shorter or a longer period of time. This frequently happens, especially when the will to live is strong or the life task remains as yet unaccomplished and is not correctly concluded.

There is another point upon which I wish to touch and which has relation to the eternal conflict being waged between the dualities of the dense physical body and the etheric vehicle. The physical elemental (which is the name given to the integrated life of the physical body) and the soul, as it seeks to withdraw and dissolve the sumtotal of the combined energies of the etheric body, are in violent conflict and the process is often fierce and long; it is this battle which is being waged during the long or short period of coma which characterises so many death beds. Coma, esoterically speaking, is of two kinds: there is the "coma of battle" which precedes true death; there is also the "coma of restoration" which takes place when the soul has withdrawn the consciousness thread or aspect, but not the life thread, in an effort to give the physical elemental time to regain its grip upon the organism and thus to restore health. As yet, modern science does not recognise the distinction between these two aspects of coma. Later, when etheric or clairvoyant vision is more common, the quality of the coma prevailing will be known, and the elements of hope or of despair will no longer control. The friends and relations of the unconscious person will know exactly whether they are watching a great and final withdrawal from present incarnation or simply looking on at a restorative process. In the latter case, the soul is still retaining its hold upon the physical body, via the centres, but is restraining temporarily all energising processes. The exceptions to this restraint are the heart centre, the spleen, and two minor centres connected with the breathing apparatus. These will remain normally energised, even if somewhat weakened in their activity; and through them control is retained. When true death is the soul's intention, then control over the spleen first of all takes place; then control over the two minor centres follows, and finally control over the heart centre supervenes and the man dies.

The above will give you some idea of the many points connected with dying that still remain to be discovered by orthodox medicine, and which will be revealed as the race of men reaches an increasing sensitivity.

I would ask you to remember that in all our present considerations we are dealing with the reactions and activities of the soul which is deliberately recalling its incarnated aspect because a life cycle has been concluded. The term of that life cycle may be long or short, according to the purposes involved; it may cover only a very few short years, or a century. Prior to the seventh year, the vitality of the physical elemental is largely the determining factor. The soul is then focussed in the etheric body, but is not fully utilising all the centres; it has simply a gently pulsating control and a gentle impulsive activity—sufficient to preserve consciousness, to vitalise the various physical processes, and to initiate the demonstration of character and of disposition. These become increasingly marked until the twenty-first year, when they stabilise into what we call the personality. In the case of disciples, the grip of the soul upon the etheric centres will be more powerful from the very start of the physical existence. By the time the fourteenth year is reached, the quality and the nature of the incarnated soul and its approximate age or experience are determined, the physical, astral and mental elementals are under control, and the soul, the indwelling spiritual man, already determines the life tendencies and choices.

In the case of the ordinary man, where death is intended, the battle between the physical elemental and the soul is a distinctive factor; it is occultly called a "Lemurian departure"; in the case of the average citizen, where the focus of the life is in the desire nature, the conflict is between the astral elemental and the soul, and this is given the name "the death of an Atlantean"; where disciples are concerned, the conflict will be more purely mental and is oft focussed around the will-to-serve and the determination to fulfill a particular aspect of the Plan and the will-to-return in full force to the ashramic centre. Where initiates are concerned, there is no conflict, but simply a conscious and deliberate withdrawal. Curiously enough, if there appears to be a conflict, it will be between the two elemental forces then remaining in the personality: the physical elemental and the mental life. There is no astral elemental to be found in the equipment of an initiate of high standing. Desire has been completely transcended as far as the individual's own nature is involved.

Factors Confronting the Withdrawing Soul

In physical death, therefore, and in the act of restitution, the withdrawing soul has to deal with the following factors:

1. The physical elemental, the integrated and coordinated life of the physical body, which is forever seeking to hold together under the attractive forces of all its component parts and their mutual interaction. This force works through a number of minor centres.

2. The etheric vehicle, which has a powerful coordinated life of its own, expressed through the seven

major centres which react under astral, mental and soul impulsive energy. It works also through certain of the minor centres which are not dedicated to a response to that aspect of the man's equipment which H.P.B. states is not a principle—the dense physical mechanism.

The minor centres are therefore to be found existing in two groups: Those responsive to the life of dense matter, to the mother aspect, and which are definitely upon the involutionary arc; these are an inheritance from the previous solar system wherein the entire man was controlled via these minor centres, with only a very few of the major centres dimly indicated in the case of initiates and advanced disciples of that time; secondly, those centres which are responsive to energies reaching them via the major centres; these then come under the control of the astral body and the mental apparatus. You will see consequently why, earlier in this treatise, I made the following reference to the minor centres. It might be of interest to you, nevertheless, to be told where the twenty-one minor centres are to be found. They can be located at the following points:

1. There are two in front of the ears, close to where the jaw bones are connected.
2. There are two just above the two breasts.
3. There is one where the breast bone connects, close to the thyroid gland. This, with the two breast centres, makes a triangle of force.
4. There are two, one each in the palms of the hands.
5. There are two, one each in the soles of the feet.
6. There are two, just behind the eyes.
7. There are two, also, connected with the gonads.
8. There is one close to the liver.

9.   There is one connected with the stomach; it is related, therefore, to the solar plexus, but is not identical with it.

10. There are two connected with the spleen. These form one centre in reality, but such a centre is formed by the two being superimposed one on the other.

11. There are two—one at the back of each knee.

12. There is one powerful centre which is closely connected with the vagus nerve. This is most potent and is regarded by some schools of occultism as a major centre; it is not in the spine, but is no great distance from the thymus gland.

13. There is one which is close to the solar plexus, and relates it to the centre at the base of the spine, thus making a triangle of the sacral centre, the solar plexus, and the centre at the base of the spine.

The two triangles referred to in this tabulation are of real importance. One is above and the other below the diaphragm.

Again, the death process can be seen as a dual activity and one which primarily concerns the etheric body. There is first of all the collecting and the withdrawing of the etheric substance, so that it no longer interpenetrates the dense physical organism, and its subsequent *densification* (a word I deliberately choose) in that area of the etheric body which has always surrounded, but not penetrated, the dense vehicle. This has been sometimes erroneously called the health aura, and it can be photographed more easily and successfully during the process of dying than at any other time, owing to the accumulation of the withdrawn forces for several inches external to the tangible body. It is at this point in the experience of the withdrawing soul that the "word of death" is spoken, and it is prior to this enunciation of this word that a return to physical living can be possible and the withdrawn etheric forces can again interpenetrate the body. Relationship with all the withdrawn forces is, up to this point, retained via the head or the heart or the solar plexus, as well as via the two minor chest centres.

All this time the consciousness of the dying man is focussed in either the emotional (or astral) body or the mental vehicle, according to the point in evolution. He is not unconscious as the onlooker might infer, but is fully aware within himself of what is occurring. If he is strongly focussed on physical plane life, and if that is the dominating desire of which he is the most aware, he may then intensify the conflict; you will then have the physical elemental battling furiously for existence, the desire nature fighting to retard the processes of death, and the soul, intent upon the work of abstraction and of restitution. This can and frequently does occasion a struggle which is quite apparent to the onlookers. As the race of men progresses and develops, this triple struggle will become much rarer; desire for physical plane existence will not appear so attractive, and the activity of the astral body will die out.

I wish you could get a picture (symbolically considered) of a man who is in full incarnation and rooted in his phase of experience, and of a man who is withdrawing from that experience. It connotes a repetition on a tiny scale of the great planetary processes of involution and evolution; it concerns those activities which produce a focussing or a polarisation in one of two directions; it resembles what might be regarded as a process of pouring in life and light into a vessel upon the physical plane, or an intensification of the radiation of that life and light of so potent a nature that under the evocative power of the soul they are both withdrawn and gathered up into the centre of life and light from whence they originally came. I have here given you (could you but recognise it) a definition of initiation, but one of a somewhat unusual phrasing. Perhaps some lines from the *Manual of Death* which is to be found in the hierarchical archives would prove explanatory to you, and might aid you in gaining a new perspective upon death. This manual has in it what are called the "Formulas preceding Pralaya." These deal with all the death or abstraction processes, covering the death of all forms, whether it be the death of an ant, a man or a planet. The formulas concern only the two aspects of life and light—the first conditioned by Sound and the second by the Word. The writing which I have in mind concerns the light, and the Word which abstracts it from the form or focusses it within the form.

"Bear in mind, O Chela, that within the known spheres naught is but light responsive to the WORD. Know that that light descends and concentrates itself; know that from its point of chosen focus, it lightens its own sphere; know too that light ascends and leaves in darkness that which it—in time and space— illumined. This descending and ascension men call life, existence and decease; this We Who tread the Lighted Way call death, experience and life.

Light which descends anchors itself upon the plane of temporary appearance. Seven threads it outward puts, and seven rays of light pulsate along these threads. Twenty-one lesser threads are radiated thence, causing the forty-nine fires to glow and burn. Upon the plane of manifested life, the word goes forth: Behold! A man is born.

As life proceeds, the quality of light appears; dim and murky it may be, or radiant, bright and shining. Thus do the points of light within the

Flame pass and repass; they come and go. This men call life; they call it true existence. They thus delude themselves yet serve the purpose of their souls and fit into the greater Plan.

And then a Word sounds forth. The descended, radiating point of light ascends, responsive to the dimly heard recalling note, attracted to its emanating source. This man calls death and this the soul calls life.

The Word retains the light in life; the Word abstracts the light, and only *That* is left which is the Word Itself. That Word is Light. That Light is Life, and Life is God."

The manifestation of the etheric body in time and space has in it what has been esoterically called "two moments of brilliance." These are, first, the moment prior to physical incarnation, when the descending light (carrying life) is focussed in all its intensity around the physical body and sets up a rapport with the innate light of matter itself, to be found in every atom of substance. This focussing light will be found to concentrate itself in seven areas of its ring-pass-not, thus creating seven major centres which will control its expression and its existence upon the outer plane, esoterically speaking. This is a moment of great radiance; it is almost as if a point of pulsating light burst into flame, and as if within that flame seven points of intensified light took shape. This is a high point in the experience of taking incarnation, and precedes physical birth by a very short period of time. It is that which brings on the birth hour. The next phase of the process, as seen by the clairvoyant, is the stage of interpenetration, during which "the seven become the twenty-one and then the many"; the light substance, the energy aspect of the soul, begins to permeate the physical body, and the creative work of the etheric or vital body is completed. The first recognition of this upon the physical plane is the "sound" uttered by the newborn infant. It climaxes the process. The act of creation by the soul is now complete; a new light shines forth in a dark place.

The second moment of brilliance comes in reverse of this process and heralds the period of restitution and the final abstraction of its own intrinsic energy by the soul. The prison house of the flesh is dissolved by the withdrawing of the light and life. The forty-nine fires within the physical organism die down; their heat and light are absorbed into the twenty-one minor points of light; these, in their turn, are absorbed by the major seven centres of energy. Then the "Word of Return" is uttered, and the consciousness aspect, the quality nature, the light and energy of the incarnating man, are withdrawn into the etheric body. The life principle withdraws, likewise, from the heart. There follows a brilliant flaring-up of pure electric light, and the "body of light" finally breaks all contact with the dense physical vehicle, focusses for a short period in the vital body, and then disappears. The act of restitution is accomplished. This entire process of the focussing of the spiritual elements in the etheric body, with the subsequent abstraction and consequent dissipation of the etheric body, would be greatly hastened by the substitution of cremation for burial.

Two Main Reasons for Cremation

Occultly speaking, cremation is needed for two main reasons. It hastens the release of the subtle vehicles (still enshrouding the soul) from the etheric body, thus bringing about the release in a few hours instead of a few days; it also is a much needed means for bringing about the purification of the astral plane and for arresting the "downward moving" tendency of desire which so greatly handicaps the incarnating soul. It can find no point of focus, because essentially fire repels the form-making aspect of desire and is a major expression of divinity with which the astral plane has no true relation, being created entirely by the human soul and not the divine soul. "Our God is a consuming fire" is the statement in the Bible which refers to the first divine aspect, the aspect of the destroyer, releasing the life. "God is love" connotes the second aspect and portrays God as incarnated existence. "God is a jealous God" is an expression indicating God as form, circumscribed and limited, self-centered and not outgoing. The destroying Sound; the attracting Word; the individualised Speech!

At the time of death, speech fades out as the Word sounds forth and restitution is enforced; later, the Word is no longer heard as the Sound obliterates or absorbs it, and there is then complete elimination of all that interferes with Sound. Silence then supervenes and the Sound itself is no longer heard; complete peace follows the act of final integration. Here, in esoteric phraseology, the entire process of death is described.

It is important to note that it is under the basic and fundamental Law of Attraction that the Art of Dying is carried forward, and that it is the love aspect, the second aspect of divinity, which does the attracting. I exclude cases of sudden death. There the activity is the result of the destroyer, or the first divine aspect. There the condition is different; individual karmic necessity may not be involved at all, and reasons of group conditioning and of great obscurity may lie behind such a happening. So obscure is the subject at this time that I shall not attempt to elucidate. You do not know enough about the Law of

Karma, about karmic group involvement, or about relationships and obligations established in past lives. When I say, for instance, that on occasion the "soul may leave the door of protection open so that the forces of death itself may enter anew, having no focal point behind the door" in order "more rapidly to obliterate past penalties due," you can see how obscure this whole matter can be.

In all that I am here writing, I am dealing simply with normal death processes—death which comes as the result of disease, old age, or the imposed will of the soul which has completed a designed cycle of experience and is using normal channels to attain projected ends. Death in these cases is *normal,* and this humanity needs to grasp with greater patience, understanding and hope.

Under the Law of Attraction, the soul, at the close of a life cycle, and with full intention, exerts its attractive power in such a manner that it offsets the attractive power inherent in matter itself. This is a clear definition of the basic cause of death. Where no soul contact has been consciously established, as in the case of the majority of people at this time, death comes as an unexpected or sadly anticipated event. Yet—*it is a true soul activity*. This is the first great spiritual concept to be proclaimed as the fear of death is combatted. Death is carried forward under this Law of Attraction, and consists in the steady and scientific abstraction of the vital body out of the dense physical body, leading eventually to an elimination of all soul contact in the three worlds.

Sequence of Events at Death

I feel that the best that I can do, in order to clarify this subject more completely, is to describe the sequence of events which happens at a death bed, reminding you that the points of final abstraction are three in number:

the head for disciples and initiates and also for advanced mental types; the heart for aspirants, for men of goodwill, and for all those who have achieved a measure of personality integrity and are attempting to fulfill, as far as in them lies, the law of love; and the solar plexus for the undeveloped and emotionally polarised persons. All I can do is to tabulate the stages of the process, leaving you to accept them as an interesting and possible hypothesis awaiting verification; to believe them unquestioningly because you have confidence in my knowledge, or to reject them as fantastic, unverifiable and of no moment anyway. I recommend the first of the three, for it will enable you to preserve your mental integrity, it will indicate an open mind, and at the same time it will protect you from gullibility and from narrow-mindedness. These stages, therefore, are:

1. *The soul sounds forth a "word of withdrawal"* from its own plane, and immediately an interior process and reaction is evoked within the man upon the physical plane.

   a. *Certain physiological events* take place at the seat of the disease, in connection with the heart, and affecting also the three great systems which so potently condition the physical man: the blood stream, the nervous system in its various expressions, and the endocrine system. With these effects I shall not deal. The pathology of death is well known and has received much study exoterically; much still remains to be discovered and will later be discovered. I am concerned, first of all, with the subjective reactions which (in the last analysis) bring about the pathological predisposition to death.

   b. *A vibration runs along the nadis.* The nadis are, as you well know, the etheric counterpart of the

entire nervous system, and they underlie every single nerve in the entire physical body. They are the
agents par excellence of the directing impulses of the
soul, reacting to the vibratory activity which emanates from the etheric counterpart of the brain.
They respond to the directing Word, react to the
"pull" of the soul, and then organise themselves for
abstraction.

c. *The blood stream becomes affected* in a peculiarly
occult manner. The "blood is the life," we are
told; it is interiorly changed as a result of the two
previous stages, but primarily as the result of an
activity hitherto undiscovered by modern science,
for which the glandular system is responsible. The
glands, in response to the call of death, inject into
the blood stream a substance which in turn affects
the heart. There the life thread is anchored, and
this substance in the blood is regarded as "death-
dealing" and is one of the basic causes of coma and
of loss of consciousness. It evokes a reflex action
in the brain. This substance and its effect will be
questioned as yet by orthodox medicine, but its presence will later be recognised.

d. *A psychic tremor is established* which has the effect
of loosening or breaking the connection between the
nadis and the nervous system; the etheric body is
thereby detached from its dense sheath, though still
interpenetrating every part of it.

2. *There is frequently a pause* at this point of a shorter
or longer period of time. This is allowed in order to
carry forward the loosening process as smoothly and
as painlessly as possible. This loosening of the nadis
starts in the eyes. This process of detachment often
shows itself in the relaxation and lack of fear which

dying persons so often show; they evidence a condition
of peace, and a willingness to go, plus an inability to
make a mental effort. It is as if the dying person, still
preserving his consciousness, gathers his resources together for the final abstraction. This is the stage in
which—the fear of death once and for all removed
from the racial mind—the friends and relatives of the
departing person will "make a festival" for him and
will rejoice with him because he is relinquishing the body.
At present this is not possible. Distress rules, and the
stage passes unrecognised and is not utilised, as it will
some day be.

3. *Next, the organised etheric body,* loosened from all
nervous relationship through the action of the nadis,
begins to gather itself together for the final departure.
It withdraws from the extremities towards the required
"door of exit" and focusses itself in the area around
that door for the final "pull" of the directing soul. All
has been proceeding under the Law of Attraction up to
this point—the magnetic, attractive will of the soul.
Now another "pull" or attractive impulse makes itself
felt. The dense physical body, the sumtotal of organs,
cells and atoms, is steadily being released from the integrating potency of the vital body by the action of the
nadis; it begins to respond to the attractive pull of matter itself. This has been called the "earth" pull and is
exerted by that mysterious entity whom we call the
"spirit of the earth"; this entity is on the involutionary
arc, and is to our planet what the physical elemental is
to the physical body of man. This physical plane life
force is essentially the life and light of atomic substance—the matter of which all forms are made. It is
to this reservoir of involutionary and material life that
the substance of all forms is restored. Restitution of

the commandeered matter of the form occupied by the soul during a life cycle consists in returning to this "Caesar" of the involutionary world what is his, whilst the soul returns to the God Who sent it forth.

It will therefore be apparent that a dual attractive process is at this stage going on:

a.   The vital body is being prepared for exit.
b.   The physical body is responding to dissolution.

It might be added that a third activity is also present. It is that of the conscious man, withdrawing his consciousness, steadily and gradually, into the astral and mental vehicles, preparatory to the complete abstraction of the etheric body when the right time comes. The man is becoming less and less attached to the physical plane and more withdrawn within himself. In the case of an advanced person, this process is consciously undertaken, and the man retains his vital interests and his awareness of relationship to others even whilst losing his grip on physical existence. In old age this detachment can be more easily noted than in death through disease, and frequently the soul or the living, interested, inner man can be seen losing his grip on physical and, therefore, illusory reality.

4.   *Again a pause ensues.* This is the point where the physical elemental can at times regain its hold upon the etheric body, if that is deemed desirable by the soul, if death is not part of the inner plan, or if the physical elemental is so powerful that it can prolong the process of dying. This elemental life will sometimes fight a battle lasting for days and weeks. When, however, death is inevitable, the pause at this point will be exceedingly brief, sometimes only for a matter of seconds. The physical elemental has lost its hold, and the etheric

body awaits the final "tug" from the soul, acting under the Law of Attraction.

5. *The etheric body emerges from the dense physical body* in gradual stages and at the chosen point of exit. When this emergence is complete, the vital body then assumes the vague outline of the form that it energised, and this under the influence of the thoughtform of himself which the man has built up over the years. This thoughtform exists in the case of every human being, and must be destroyed before the second stage of elimination is finally complete. We will touch upon this later. Though freed from the prison of the physical body, the etheric body is not yet freed from its influence. There is still a slight rapport between the two, and this keeps the spiritual man still close to the body just vacated. That is why clairvoyants often claim to see the etheric body hovering around the death bed or the coffin. Still interpenetrating the etheric body are the integrated energies which we call the astral body and the mental vehicle, and at the centre there is a point of light which indicates the presence of the soul.

6. *The etheric body is gradually dispersed* as the energies of which it is composed are reorganised and withdrawn, leaving only the pranic substance which is identified with the etheric vehicle of the planet itself. This process of dispersal is, as I have earlier said, greatly aided by cremation. In the case of the undeveloped person, the etheric body can linger for a long time in the neighbourhood of its outer disintegrating shell because the pull of the soul is not potent and the material aspect is. Where the person is advanced, and therefore detached in his thinking from the physical plane, the dissolution of the vital body can be exceedingly rapid. Once it is accomplished, the process of restitution is over; the man

is freed, temporarily at least, from all reaction to the attractive pull of physical matter; he stands in his subtle bodies, ready for the great act to which I have given the name "The Art of Elimination."

One thought emerges as we conclude this inadequate consideration of the death of the physical body in its two aspects: that thought is the integrity of the inner man. *He remains himself.* He is untouched and untrammelled; he is a free agent as far as the physical plane is concerned, and is responsive now to only three predisposing factors:

1. The quality of his astral-emotional equipment.
2. The mental condition in which he habitually lives.
3. The voice of the soul, often unfamiliar but sometimes well known and loved.

Individuality is not lost; the same person is still present upon the planet. Only that has disappeared which was an integral part of the tangible appearance of our planet. That which has been loved or hated, which has been useful to humanity or a liability, which has served the race or been an ineffectual member of it, still persists, is still in touch with the qualitative and mental processes of existence, and will forever remain—individual, qualified by ray type, part of the kingdom of souls, and a high initiate in his own right.

3. Two Questions of Importance

I have sought, in the preceding pages, to give an insight into the true nature of that which we call death. Death is the withdrawal, consciously or unconsciously, of the inner living entity from its outer shell, its inner vital correspondence, and finally it is the relinquishing of the subtle body or bodies, according to the point in evolution of the person. I have also sought to show the normality of this familiar process. The horror which attends death upon the battle-field or by accident consists in the shock which it precipitates within the area of the etheric body, necessitating a rapid rearrangement of its constituent forces and a sudden and unexpected reintegration of its component parts in response to definite action which has perforce to be taken by the man in his kama-manasic body. This action does not involve the replacing of the inner man again within the etheric vehicle, but requires a coming together of the dissipated aspects of that body under the Law of Attraction, in order that its final and complete dissolution can take place.

Before taking up our theme (which is the Art of Elimination), I want to answer two questions which seem to me of importance; they are frequently asked by earnest and intelligent students.

The first question is, in reality, the expression of disappointment in this series of instructions. It can be framed as follows: Why does not the Tibetan Teacher take up definite or basic diseases, and deal with their pathology, give their cures or suggested treatment, indicate their direct causes and give, in detail, the processes of recovery? Because, my brothers, there is little that I can add technically to what has already been ascertained by medical science anent the symptoms, the localities and the general trends in which diseased conditions are found. Observation, experimentation, trial and error, success and failure have given to modern man a wide and definitely accurate knowledge of the outer aspects and effects of disease. Time, and constant trained observation, have equally definitely indicated cures or ameliorative processes or preventive measures (such as vaccination for smallpox), and these have proved after many years to be helpful. Investigation and experiment and the steadily growing facilities which science provides are adding to man's capacity to help, to cure at times, to ameliorate frequently, and to lessen the reactions of pain. Medical science and surgical skill have advanced by leaps and bounds—so much so that what is today known and somewhat grasped is of so vast a nature and so intricate in its scientific and therapeutic aspects that they have given rise to specialists—to those who concentrate upon a particular field, and who therefore deal only with certain conditions of ill health and disease, thereby attaining much skill, knowledge and frequent success. All this is good, in spite of what cranks and people with a pet method of cure may say, or even those who have no use for the medical profession and prefer some cult or some of the newer approaches to the problem of health.

The reason that these newer approaches exist is that medical science has made such progress that it has now reached the limits of its purely physical area or field and is now on the verge of advancing into the realm of the intangible and is thus drawing nearer to the world of causes. It is for this reason that I have wasted no time with the details of disease, with enumerating or considering specific diseases, their symptoms or their treatment because that is fully covered in the textbooks available; they can likewise be seen in their many and various stages in our great hospitals.

I have, however, dealt with the latent causes of disease—such as tuberculosis, syphilis and cancer—inherent in the individual man, in humanity as a whole, and also in our planet. I have traced the psychological basis of disease and have indicated a practically new field wherein disease—particularly in its earlier stages—can be studied.

When the psychological basis of disease can be realised and its factual nature is admitted by the orthodox physician, the surgeon, the psychologist and the priest, then all will work together in this developing area of understanding, and what is today vaguely called "preventive medicine" will come into its own. I prefer to define this phase of medical application as the organisation of those methods whereby *disease will be avoided,* and the development of those techniques whereby correct psychological training will be given—from youth up—and by right emphasis upon the inner spiritual man, those conditions will be negated and those habits avoided which today lead inevitably to ill health, definitely symptomatic disease and eventual death.

In the above statement, I refer to no affirmative or speculative science such as Christian Science or those schools of thought which trace all disease to the power of thought. I am concerned with the immediate necessity of right psychological training, based upon a knowledge of the constitution of man, upon the science of the seven rays (the forces which condition man and make him what he is), and upon esoteric astrology; I am concerned with the application of the knowledges, hitherto regarded as peculiar and esoteric, which are slowly coming under general consideration, and which have made great progress during the past twenty-five years. I am not concerned with the abolition of medical treatment, nor am I concerned with endorsing the newer modes of treatment—all of which are still in the experimental stage and all of which have somewhat to contribute to medical science as a whole; out of the united contribution should come a richer and more fluid medical approach to the patient.

The picture I have outlined of the psychological background of all diseases will be long in painting; in the meantime, the contribution of medicine is indispensable. In spite of mistakes, faulty diagnosis and much error, humanity cannot do without its doctors, its surgeons and its hospitals. They are urgently needed, and will be for centuries to come. In this statement is no cause for discouragement. Humanity cannot be brought into a condition of perfect physical health immediately, though correct psychological training from infancy will do much in the course of a few decades. Wrong conditions have been long developing. Modern medicine must become far more open-minded, more ready to endorse (after due professional proof) that which is new, which is in the nature of innovation and which is unusual. The barriers erected by specialised medicine must come down, and the new schools must be sought, instructed and investigated, and finally be included in the orthodox ranks. The new schools, such as those concerned with electro-therapy, the chiropractic schools, the dieticians who claim to cure all diseases through right foods, and the rather eccentric naturopaths, plus many other cults and schools, must not be so arrogantly sure that they have the whole story, that their approach is the only one or that they have a universal cure-all which is unique and definitely sure. These groups, particularly the chiropractors, have definitely damaged their cause and crippled their effort by their loudly shouted surety (in a field which is yet experimental), and by their constant attack upon orthodox medicine. The latter, in its turn, has limited itself by its failure to recognise what is good and right in the newer schools; it has been antagonised by their clamour for recognition, and by their lack of scientific methods. The desire of orthodox medicine is to protect the general public. This they needs must do in order to avoid the disasters which fanatics and untried methods would bring about, but they have gone too far in this respect. The school of thought which I have sponsored in these instructions will also be challenged, and this for a long time. However, the mental and psychological effects of the world war will greatly hasten the recognition of the psychological basis for disease and other troubles; modern medicine, therefore, faces its major opportunity.

A combination of true medical science (as produced by man down the ages under the inspiration of his divine nature), of the newer aspects of treatment as formulated by the many emerging schools of thought, of practice and experiment, the recognition of the energies which condition man, working through the seven centres in his vital body, and of the astrological influences which equally condition him, *via the inner man,* will eventually produce the new medical approach which will keep man in good health, which will arrest disease in its earliest stages, and which will finally inaugurate that cycle in human affairs wherein disease and ill health will be exceptions and not the rule, as is the case today, and wherein death will be regarded as a happy and destined release and not, as is the case today, a dreaded enemy.

The second question is definitely concerned with the processes of death. It has been asked: What is the Tibetan's attitude towards cremation, and under what conditions should cremation be followed? It is a fortunate and happy thing that cremation is becoming increasingly the rule. Before so very long, burial in the ground will be against the law and cremation will be enforced, and this as a health and sanitation measure. Those unhealthy, psychic spots, called cemeteries, will eventually disappear, just as ancestor worship is passing out, both in the Orient—with its ancestor cults—and in the Occident—with its equally foolish cult of hereditary position.

By the use of fire, all forms are dissolved; the quicker the human physical vehicle is destroyed, the quicker is its hold upon the withdrawing soul broken. A great deal of nonsense has been told in current theosophical literature about the time equation in relation to the sequential destruction of the subtle bodies. It should be stated, however, that the moment that *true* death is scientifically established (by the orthodox doctor in charge of the case), and it has been ascertained that no spark of life remains in the physical body, cremation is then possible. This complete or true death eventuates when the thread of consciousness and the thread of life are completely withdrawn from the head and the heart. At the same time, reverence and an unhurried attitude have their rightful place in the process. The family of the dead person need a few hours in which to adjust themselves to the fact of the imminent disappearance of the outer and usually loved form; due care must also be given to the formalities required by the state or the municipality. This time element has reference mainly to those who are left behind, to the living and not to the dead. The claim that the etheric body must not be rushed into the cremating flames, and the belief that it must be left to drift around for a stated period of several days, have also no true basis at all. There is no etheric need for delay. When the inner man withdraws from his physical vehicle he withdraws simultaneously from the etheric body. It is true that the etheric body is apt to linger for a long time on the "field of emanation" when the physical body is interred, and it will frequently persist until complete disintegration of the dense body has taken place. The process of mummifying, as practised in Egypt, and of embalming, as practised in the West, have been responsible for the perpetuation of the etheric body, sometimes for centuries. This is particularly the case when the mummy or embalmed person was of an evil character during life; the hovering etheric body is then often "possessed" by an evil entity or evil force. This is the cause of the attacks and the disasters which often dog the steps of those who discover ancient tombs and their inhabitants, ancient mummies, and bring them and their possessions to light. Where cremation is the rule, there is not only the immediate destruction of the physical body and its restitution to the fount of substance, but the vital body is also promptly dissolved and its forces swept away by the current of flame into the reservoir of vital energies. Of that reservoir it has ever been an inherent part, either in form or in a formless condition. After death and cremation these forces still exist but are absorbed into the *analogous* whole. Ponder on this statement, for it will give you the clue to the creative work of the human spirit. If delay is necessary from family feeling or municipal requirements, cremation should follow death within thirty-six hours; where no reason for delay exists, cremation can be rightly permitted in twelve hours. It is wise, however, to wait twelve hours in order to ensure *true* death.

CHAPTER VI

The Art of Elimination

To TAKE UP AGAIN the thread of our instruction, we will now consider the activity of the inner spiritual man who has discarded his physical and etheric bodies and now stands within the shell of the subtle body—a body composed of astral or sentient substance and of mental substance. Owing to the strongly emotional and sentient polarisation of the average man, the idea has taken hold that man withdraws, after true death, first of all into his astral body, and then, later, into his mental vehicle. But this is not actually the case. A body constructed predominantly of astral matter is the basis of this idea. Few people are as yet so developed that the vehicle in which they find themselves after death is largely composed of mental substance. Only disciples and initiates who live mostly in their minds find themselves, after death, immediately upon the mental plane. Most people discover themselves upon the astral plane, clothed in a shell of astral matter and committed to a period of elimination within the illusory area of the astral plane.

As I have earlier told you, the astral plane has no factual existence, but is an illusory creation of the human family. From now on, however (through the defeat of the forces of evil and the disastrous setback suffered by the Black Lodge), the astral plane will slowly become a dying creation, and in the final period of human history (in the seventh rootrace), it will become nonexistent. Today this is not the case. The sentient substance which constitutes the astral plane is still being gathered into forms of illusion and still forms a barrier in the path of the soul seeking liberation. It still "holds prisoner" the many people who die whilst their major reaction to life is that of desire, of wishful thinking and of emotional sentiency. These are still the vast majority. In Atlantean days the astral plane came into being; the mental state of consciousness was then practically nonexistent, though the "sons of mind" had their place on what is today the higher levels of that plane. The mental permanent atom was also practically quiescent within each human form, and there was consequently no attractive "pull" from the mental plane, as is the case today. Many people are still Atlantean in consciousness, and when they pass out of the physical state of consciousness and discard their dual physical body, they are faced with the problem of elimination of the astral body, but they have little to do to release themselves from any mental prison of the soul. These are the undeveloped and average persons who, after the elimination of the kamic or desire body, have little else to do; there is no mental vehicle to draw them into a mental integration because there is no mentally focussed potency; the soul on the higher mental levels is as yet "in deep meditation" and quite unaware of its shadow in the three worlds.

The art of elimination falls, therefore, into three categories:

1. As practised by those people who are purely astral in quality and constitution. These we call "kamic" people.

2. As practised by those balanced people who are integrated personalities and who are called "kama-

manasic" individuals.

3. As practised by advanced people and disciples of all grades who are mainly mental in their "living focus." These are called "manasic" subjects.

The same basic rules control them all, but the emphasis differs in each case. I would have you bear in mind that where there is no physical brain and where the mind is undeveloped, the inner man finds himself practically *smothered* in an envelope of astral matter and is for a long time immersed in what we call the astral plane. The kama-manasic person has what is called the "freedom of the dual life," and finds himself possessed of a dual form which enables him to contact at will the higher levels of the astral plane and the lower levels of the mental plane. I would again remind you that there is no physical brain to register these contacts. Awareness of contact is dependent upon the innate activity of the inner man and his peculiar state of apprehension and of appreciation. The manasic person is possessed of a translucent mental vehicle with a light density which is in proportion to his freedom from desire and emotion.

These three types of people all use an eliminative process of a similar nature, but employ a different technique within the process. For the sake of clarity, it might be stated that:

1. *The kamic person* eliminates his astral body by means of attrition, and vacates it via the astral correspondence to the solar plexus centre. This attrition is brought about because all the innate desire and inherent emotion are, at this stage, related to the animal nature and the physical body—both of which are now nonexistent.

2. *The kama-manasic individual* uses two techniques. This would naturally be so because he eliminates, first of all, his astral body, and then his mental vehicle.

a. He eliminates the astral body by means of his growing desire for mental life. He withdraws gradually and steadily into the mind body, and the astral body esoterically "drops away" and finally disappears. This takes place usually unconsciously and may require quite a long time. Where, however, the man is above the average, and on the verge of becoming a manasic person, the disappearance is brought about suddenly and dynamically, and the man stands free in his mental body. This takes place consciously and rapidly.

b. He shatters the mental body by an act of the human will, and also because the soul is beginning to be slowly aware of its shadow. The inner man is therefore attracted towards the soul, though still only in a somewhat feeble manner. This process is relatively quick and is dependent upon the extent of the manasic influence.

3. *The manasic man,* focussed now in his mental body, has also two things to accomplish:

a. To dissolve and rid himself of any astral sediment which may be discolouring his translucent mental body. The so-called astral body is now practically nonexistent as a factor of expression. This he does by calling in increased light from the soul. It is soul light which, at this stage, dissolves the astral substance, just as it will be the combined light of the soul of humanity (as a whole) which will dissolve finally the astral plane—again so-called.

b. To destroy the mental body through the use of certain Words of Power. These Words are communicated to the disciple via the Ashram of his Master. They bring in soul power to a greatly enhanced extent, and produce consequently such an expansion of consciousness within the mental body that it is broken up and no longer constitutes a barrier to the inner man. He can now stand, a free son of mind, within the Ashram of his Master and "shall no more go out".

Activities Immediately After Death

Immediately after death, and particularly if cremation has taken place, the man, in his kama-manasic body, is as much aware and alert to his environment as he was upon the physical plane when alive. This phrasing permits latitude as to the extent of the awareness and of observation, for a similar latitude must be allowed for those on the physical plane. People are not all equally awake or equally conscious of circumstances or immediate experience. However, as most people are more conscious emotionally than they are physically, and live to a great extent focussed in their astral vehicles, the man is quite familiar with the state of consciousness in which he finds himself. Forget not that a plane is essentially a state of consciousness and *not* a locality, as so many esotericists seem to think. It is recognised by the focussed reaction of the self-conscious person who—constantly and distinctly aware of himself—is sentient to the theme of his environment and of his outgoing desires, or (where advanced people are concerned, functioning upon the more advanced levels of the astral plane) sentient of outgoing love and aspiration; the man is engrossed with what engrossed his attention and involved the kamic principle during his incarnated experience. May I again remind you that there is now no physical brain to respond to impacts generated by the inner man, and also that sex, as it is physically understood, is nonexistent. Spiritualists would do well to remember this and so grasp the foolishness as well as the impossibility of those spiritual marriages which certain schools of thought in the movement teach and practice. The man, in his astral body, is now free from the strictly animal impulses which, upon the physical plane, are both normal and right, but which now have no meaning to him in his kamic body.

Therefore, taking the average man, what are his first reactions and activities after the restitution of the physical body to the universal reservoir of substance? Let me enumerate some of these reactions:

1. He becomes consciously aware of himself. This involves a clarity of perception unknown to the average man whilst in physical incarnation.

2. Time (being the succession of events as registered by the physical brain) is now nonexistent as we understand the term, and—as the man turns his attention to his more clearly defined emotional self—there ensues *invariably* a moment of direct soul contact. This is due to the fact that even in the case of the most ignorant and undeveloped man, the moment of complete restitution does not pass unnoticed by the soul. It has a definite soul effect, something like a long and strong pull at a bell rope, if I might use so simple a simile. For a brief second the soul responds, and the nature of the response is such that the man, standing in his astral body, or rather in his kama-manasic vehicle, sees the experience of the past incarnation spread before him like a map. He records a sense of timelessness.

3. As a result of the recognition of these experiences, the man isolates those three which were the three major conditioning factors in the life which has gone and which also hold the keys to his future incarnation which he will next initiate. All else is forgotten, and all the lesser experiences fade out of his memory, leaving nothing in

his consciousness but what are esoterically called "the three seeds or germs of the future". These three seeds are in a peculiar manner related to the permanent physical and astral atoms, and thus produce the fivefold force which will create the forms later to appear. It might be said that:

a. *Seed One* determines later the nature of the physical environment in which the returning man will find his place. It is related to the quality of that future environment and thus conditions the needed field or area of contact.

b. *Seed Two* determines the quality of the etheric body as a vehicle through which the ray forces can make contact with the dense physical body. It delimits the etheric structure or vital web along which the incoming energies will circulate and is related in particular to the special one of the seven centres which will be the most active and alive during the coming incarnation.

c. *Seed Three* gives the key to the astral vehicle in which the man will be polarised in the next incarnation. Forget not, I am dealing here with the average man and not with the advanced human being, disciple or initiate. It is this seed which—through the forces it attracts—brings the man again into relation with those he previously loved or with whom he had close contact. It can be accepted as a fact that the group idea governs subjectively all incarnations, and that reincarnated man is brought into incarnation not only through his own desire for physical plane experience, but also under group impulse and in line with the group karma as well as with his own. This is a point which should receive more emphasis. Once this is truly grasped and understood, a great deal of the fear engendered by the thought of death would disappear. The familiar and the loved will still remain the familiar and the loved, because the relation has been closely established over many incarnations and—as the *Old Commentary* expresses it:

"These seeds of determining recognition are not unique to me and you, but also for the group; within the group they relate one to the other in time and space. Only in the lower three shall those related find their true existence. When soul knows soul and in the meeting-place within the Master's call, these seeds shall disappear."

It will be apparent, therefore, how necessary it is to train children to recognise and profit by experience, for this, once learnt, will greatly facilitate this third activity upon the astral plane after death.

4. Having completed this "isolating of experience," the man will then seek and automatically find those whom the third seed influence indicates as possessing a constant part in the group experience of which he is an element, consciously or unconsciously. The relation once again established (if those sought have not yet eliminated the physical body), the man acts as he would on earth in the company of his intimates and according to his temperament and point in evolution. If those who are closest to him and whom he deeply loves or hates are still in physical incarnation, he will also seek them out and—just again as he did on earth—he will remain in their neighbourhood, aware of their activities, though (unless highly evolved) they will not be aware of his. I can give no detail as to reciprocal give and take or to the modes and methods of contact. Each person differs; each temperament is largely unique. I only seek to make

clear certain basic lines of behaviour pursued by man
prior to the act or acts of elimination.

These four activities cover varying periods of time—from
the angle of "those who live below," though there is no time
recognised on the part of the man on the astral plane.
Gradually the lure and glamour (of a low or high order)
wears off, and the man enters into the stage where he
knows—because the mind is now more incisive and dominating—that he is ready for the second death and for the entire
elimination of the kamic body or of the kama-manasic
vehicle.

One of the things to remember here is that once restitution of the physical in its two aspects has taken place, the
inner man is, as I have earlier said, fully conscious. The
physical brain and the swirl of etheric forces (mostly somewhat disorganised in the case of the majority of men) are
no longer present. These are the two factors which have
led students to believe that the experiences of the man on
the inner planes of the three worlds are those of a vague
drifting, of a semi-conscious experience, or indicate a
repetitive life, except in the case of very advanced people or
disciples and initiates. But this is not the case. A man on
the inner planes is not only as conscious of himself as an
individual—with his own plans, life and affairs—as he was
on the physical plane, but he is also conscious in the same
manner of the surrounding states of consciousness. He may
be glamoured by astral existence or subject to the telepathic
impression of the varying thought currents emanating from
the mental plane, but he is also conscious of himself and of
his mind (or of the measure of manasic life developed) in a
far more potent manner than when he had to work through
the medium of the physical brain, when the focus of his
consciousness was that of the aspirant, but anchored in the

brain. His experience is far richer and fuller than he ever knew when in incarnation. If you will think this out for a little, you will realise that this necessarily would be so.

It may therefore be assumed that the Art of Elimination is practised more definitely and more effectively than was the restitution of the physical vehicle. Another point must also be considered. On the inner side, men *know* that the Law of Rebirth governs the experience-process of physical plane living, and they realise then that, prior to the elimination of the kamic, kama-manasic or manasic bodies, they are only passing through an interlude between incarnations and that they consequently face two great experiences:

1. A moment (long or short, according to the attained point in evolution) wherein contact will be made with the soul or with the solar angel.

2. After that contact, a relatively violent reorientation to earth life takes place, leading to what is called "the process of descent and calling," wherein the man:

   a. Prepares for physical incarnation again.
   b. Sounds his own true note into the substance of the three worlds.
   c. Revitalises the permanent atoms, which form a triangle of force within the causal body.
   d. Gathers together the needed substance to form his future bodies of manifestation.
   e. Colours them with the qualities and characteristics he has already achieved through life-experience.
   f. On the etheric plane arranges the substance of his vital body so that the seven centres take shape and can become the recipients of the inner forces.
   g. Makes a deliberate choice of those who will provide him with the needed dense physical covering, and then awaits the moment of incarnation. Esoteric

students would do well to remember that parents only donate the dense physical body. They contribute naught else save a body of a particular quality and nature which will provide the needed vehicle of contact with the environment demanded by the incarnating soul. They may also provide a measure of group relationship, where the soul experience is long and a true group relation has been established.

These two critical moments are consciously faced by the discarnate man and he knows what he is doing within the limits set by his point in evolution.

The Devachan Experience

I would also point out that this conscious undertaking of the art of elimination, and this awareness of process and purpose, in reality constitute the state of consciousness which has been called *devachan* by the orthodox theosophist. There has been a great deal of misunderstanding of this experience. The general idea has been that, after the process of ridding himself of the astral and mental bodies, the man enters into a sort of dream state wherein he reexperiences and reconsiders past events in the light of the future and undergoes a sort of rest period, a kind of digestive process, in preparation for the undertaking of renewed birth. This somewhat erroneous idea has arisen because the concept of time still governs theosophical presentations of truth. If, however, it is realised that time is not known apart from physical plane experience, the entire concept of devachan clarifies. From the moment of complete separation from the dense physical and etheric bodies, and as the eliminative process is undertaken, the man is *aware of past and present;* when elimination is complete and the hour of soul contact eventuates and the manasic vehicle is in process of destruction, he becomes immediately *aware of the future,* for prediction is an asset of the soul consciousness and in this the man temporarily shares. Therefore, past, present and future are seen as one; the recognition of the Eternal Now is gradually developed from incarnation to incarnation and during the continuous process of rebirth. This constitutes a state of consciousness (characteristic of the normal state of the advanced man) which can be called devachanic.

It is not my intention to elaborate the technique of the eliminative process. Humanity is at so many different stages —intermediate between the three already outlined—that it would be impossible to be definite or concise. Attrition is relatively easy to understand; the kamic body dies out because, there being no call from physical substance, evoking desire, there is nothing with which to feed this vehicle. The astral body comes into being through the reciprocal interplay between the physical plane, which is not a principle, and the principle of desire; in the process of taking rebirth, this principle is utilised with dynamic intent by the soul in the mental vehicle to reverse the call, and matter then responds to the call of the reincarnating man. Kamic man, after a long process of attrition, is left standing free within an embryonic mental vehicle, and this period of semi-mental life is exceedingly brief and is brought to an end by the soul who suddenly "directs his eye to the waiting one," and by the power of that directed potency instantaneously reorients the individual kamic man to the downward path of rebirth. The kama-manasic man practises a process of withdrawal and responds to the "pull" of a rapidly developing mental body. This withdrawal becomes increasingly rapid and dynamic until it reaches the state where the probationary disciple—under steadily growing soul contact—shatters the kama-manasic body, *as a unit,* by an act of the mental will,

implemented by the soul. You will note that the "devachanic" experience will necessarily be briefer in connection with
this majority than with the kamic minority, because the
devachanic technique of review and recognition of the implications of experience is slowly controlling the man on
the physical plane so that he brings the significance of meaning and learns constantly through experience whilst incarnating. Thus you will realise also that continuity of consciousness
is also being slowly developed, and the awarenesses of the
inner man begin to demonstrate on the physical plane,
through the medium of the physical brain at first, and then
independently of that material structure. I have here conveyed a definite hint on a subject which will receive wide
attention during the next two hundred years.

The manasic person, the integrated personality, works,
as we have seen, in two ways which are necessarily dependent
upon the integration achieved. This integration will be of
two kinds:

1. That of the integrated personality focussed in the
   mind and achieving a constantly growing rapport
   with the soul.
2. The disciple, whose integrated personality is now
   being rapidly integrated into and absorbed by the
   soul.

In this stage of mind development and of constant mental
control (based on the fact that the man's consciousness is
now definitely focussed and permanently centered in the
mental vehicle), the earlier processes of the destruction of
the astral body through attrition and by "dynamic negation"
are carried on whilst in physical incarnation. The incarnated
man refuses to be ruled by desire; what is left of the illusory
astral body is dominated now by the mind, and the urges
towards the satisfaction of desire are refused with full and

conscious deliberation, either because of the selfish ambitions and mental intentions of the integrated personality, or under the inspiration of soul intention which sub-
ordinates the mind to its purposes. When this point in
evolution is attained, the man can then dissolve the last
remaining vestiges of all desire by means of *illumination*. In
the early stages of purely manasic or mental life, this is done
through the illumination which knowledge brings and involves mainly the innate light of mental substance. Later,
when soul and mind are establishing a close rapport, the
light of the soul hastens and supplements the process. The
disciple now uses more occult methods, but upon these I
may not here enlarge. The destruction of the mental body
is no longer brought about by the destructive power of light
itself, but is hastened by means of certain sounds, emanating
from the plane of the spiritual will; these are recognised by
the disciple, and permission to use them in their proper
word-forms is given to him by some senior initiate within
the Ashram or by the Master Himself, towards the close
of the cycle of incarnation.

Tenth Law of Healing

I would like now to lay down certain postulates which
we shall need to consider in our study of Part Three where
we take up the Fundamental Laws of Healing. These Laws
and Rules, I have already given you, but I seek now to
elaborate.

We have studied at some length the immediate processes
which take place when the principle of life withdraws or is
withdrawn from the body. There is a distinction, based on
evolutionary development, in these two processes. We have
traced the withdrawal of the life principle, plus the consciousness, from the subtle bodies in the three worlds, and
have now reached the point where we are no longer dealing

with average man or with undeveloped man. We shall be concerned with the conscious activity of the soul in relation to its form aspect.

With the undeveloped or the average man, the soul plays a very small part in the death process, beyond the contribution of a simple soul determination to end the cycle of incarnated life, prior to another return to the physical plane. The "seeds of death" are inherent in the form nature and demonstrate as disease or as senility (using that word in its technical and not in its colloquial sense), and the soul pursues its own interests on its own plane until such time as the evolutionary process has brought about a situation wherein the integration or close relation between soul and form is so real that the soul is deeply and profoundly identified with its manifesting expression. It might be said that when this stage is reached, the soul is, for the first time, truly incarnated; it is truly "descending into manifestation" and the entire soul nature is thereby involved. This is a point little emphasised or realised.

In the earlier lives of the incarnating soul and for the majority of the cycles of life experience, the soul is very slightly concerned in what is going on. The redemption of the substance of which all forms are made goes forward under natural process and the "karma of matter" is the initial governing force; this is succeeded in time by the karma generated by the fusion of soul and form, though (in the earlier stages) very little responsibility is engendered by the soul. That which occurs within the threefold soul-sheath is necessarily the result of the innate tendencies of substance itself. However, as time goes on and incarnation follows upon incarnation, the effect of the indwelling soul quality gradually evokes conscience, and—through the medium of conscience, which is the exercise of the discriminative sense, developed as the mind assumes increasing control—an awakening and finally an awakened consciousness is evoked. This demonstrates in the first instance as the sense of responsibility; it is this which gradually establishes a growing identification of the soul with its vehicle, the lower triple man. The bodies become then steadily more refined; the seeds of death and of disease are not so potent; sensitivity to inner soul realisation grows until the time is reached when the initiate-disciple dies *by an act of his spiritual will or in response to group karma or to national or planetary karma.*

Disease and death are essentially conditions inherent in substance; just as long as a man identifies himself with the form aspect, so will he be conditioned by the Law of Dissolution. This law is a fundamental and natural law governing the life of the form in all the kingdoms of nature. When the disciple or the initiate is identifying himself with the soul, and when the antahkarana is built by means of the life principle, then the disciple passes out of the control of this universal, natural law and uses or discards the body at will— at the demand of the spiritual will or through recognition of the necessities of the Hierarchy or the purposes of Shamballa.

We come now to the enunciation of a new law which is substituted for the Law of Death and which has reference only to those upon the later stages of the Path of Discipleship and the stages upon the Path of Initiation.

LAW X

Hearken, O Chela, to the call which comes from the Son to the Mother, and then obey. The Word goes forth that form has served its purpose. The principle of mind (the fifth principle. A.A.B.) then organises itself, and then repeats the Word. The waiting form responds and drops away. The soul stands free.

Respond, O Rising One, to the call which comes within the sphere of obligation; recognise the call emerging from the Ashram or from the Council Chamber where waits the Lord of Life Himself. The Sound goes forth. Both soul and form together must renounce the principle of life and thus permit the Monad to stand free. The soul responds. The form then shatters the connection. Life is now liberated, owning the quality of conscious knowledge and the fruit of all experience. These are the gifts of soul and form combined.

I have wished to make clear in your minds the distinction between disease and death as experienced by the average man, and certain corresponding processes of conscious dissolution as practised by the advanced disciple or initiate. These later processes involve a slowly developing technique in which (in the earlier stages) the disciple is still the victim of disease-producing tendencies of the form, as of all forms in nature. This tendency produces subsequent death, through the stages of modified disease and peaceful, consequent death, on to the other stages where death is brought about by an act of the will—the time and the mode being determined by the soul and consciously recorded and registered in the brain. Pain is demonstrated in both cases, but upon the Path of Initiation pain is largely negated, not because the initiate endeavours to avoid pain, but because the sensitivity of the form to undesirable contacts disappears, and with it pain also disappears; pain is the guardian of the form and the protector of substance; it warns of danger; it indicates certain definite stages in the evolutionary process; it is related to the principle whereby the soul identifies itself with substance. When the identification ceases, pain and disease and also death lose their hold upon the disciple; the soul is no longer subject to their requirements, and the man is free because disease and death are qualities inherent in form, and subject to the vicissitudes of form life.

Death is to man exactly what the release of the atom appears to be; this the great scientific discovery of the release of atomic energy has demonstrated. The nucleus of the atom is split in two. (This wording is scientifically incorrect.) This event in the life experience of the atom releases a great light and a great potency; upon the astral plane, the phenomenon of death has a somewhat similar effect and has a close parallel in the phenomena brought about by the release of atomic energy. Every death, in all the kingdoms of nature, has to some extent this effect; it shatters and destroys substantial form and thus serves a constructive purpose; this result is largely astral or psychic and serves to dissipate some of the enveloping glamour. The wholesale destruction of forms which has been going on during the past few years of war has produced phenomenal changes upon the astral plane and has shattered an immense amount of the existing world glamour, and this is very, very good. These happenings should result in less opposition to the inflow of the new type of energy; it should facilitate the appearance of the ideas embodying the needed recognitions; the new concepts will now be seen, and their emergence into the realm of human thinking will be dependent upon the formulation of the new "lanes or channels of impression" whereby the minds of men can become sensitive to hierarchical plans and to the purposes of Shamballa.

This, however, is by the way. My proposition will serve to show you some of the relationships between death and constructive activity, and the wide usefulness of death as a process in reconstruction. It will convey to you the idea that this great Law of Death—as it governs substance in the three worlds—is a beneficent and corrective event. Without enlarging upon it, I would remind you that this Law of Death, which governs in such potency in the three worlds of human evolution, is a reflection of a cosmic purpose which governs the cosmic etheric planes of our solar system, the cosmic astral plane and the cosmic mental plane. The death-dealing energy emanates as an expression of the life principle of that greater LIFE which enfolds all the seven planetary systems which in Themselves express the Life of our solar system. When, in our thinking and in our effort to understand, we enter this realm of pure abstraction, it is time to call a halt and draw our minds back to the more practical ways of planetary living and to the laws governing the fourth kingdom in nature, the human.

We are now in a position (after this attempt to argue from the universal to the particular, which is ever the occult way), to take up, in Part Three, the last point which deals with the Basic Requirements, and must now consider the use of the death principle by the disciple or the initiate. I would have you note my way of expressing this concept. This is dealt with under the title of *The Processes of Integration.*

CHAPTER VII

The Processes of Integration

IN CONSIDERING THIS intelligently utilised event as it is employed by the soul, functioning consciously in the three worlds, we shall find it helpful to consider it under two main headings:

First: The processes whereby the cycle of incarnation is brought to an end through the complete integration of soul and personality. This we will approach from three points of view:

The significance of integration.
The state of mind of the soul.
The elimination of the thoughtform of the personality.

Second: The results of this:

Within the Ashram of the Master, as far as the disciple is concerned.

In the mode whereby the liberated disciple can now create a body for physical plane contact and for service in the three worlds—this time not under the Law of Necessity but under the Law of Service, as understood by the initiate.

You will by now have realised that we have discussed the fact of death as it has affected the physical body (a most familiar happening) and also the astral or mental sheaths—those aggregations of conditioned energy with which we are not so objectively familiar but which even psychology admits exist and which we believe must disintegrate or disappear with the death of the physical body. Has it, however, occurred to you that the major aspect of death with which a human being is ultimately concerned is the death of the personality? I am not here speaking in abstract terms, as do all esotericists when they work at the negation of quality or of the qualities which characterise the personal self. They speak of "killing out" this or that quality, of completely suppressing the "lower self," and similar phrases. Here I am speaking of the literal destruction, dissolution, dissipation or final dispersal of that beloved and well-known personal self.

It must be borne in mind that the life of a personality falls into the following stages:

1. Its slow and gradual construction over a long period of time. For many cycles of incarnations, a man is not a personality. He is just a member of the mass.

2. The conscious identification of the soul with the personality during this stage is practically nonexistent. The aspect of the soul which is concealed within the sheaths is for a long, long period dominated by the life of those sheaths, only making its presence felt through what is called "the voice of conscience." However, as time goes on, the active intelligent life of the person is gradually enhanced and coordinated by the energy which streams from the knowledge petals of the egoic lotus, or from the intelligent perceptive nature of the soul on its own plane. This produces eventually the integration of the three lower sheaths into one functioning whole. The man is then a personality.

3. The personality life of the now coordinated individual persists for a large number of lives, and also falls into three phases:

   a. The phase of a dominant aggressive personality life, basically conditioned by its ray type, selfish in nature and very individualistic.

   b. A transitional phase wherein a conflict rages between personality and soul. The soul begins to seek liberation from form life and yet—in the last analysis—the personality is dependent upon the life principle, conferred by the soul. Wording it otherwise, the conflict between the soul ray and the personality ray starts and the war is on between two focussed aspects of energy. This conflict terminates at the third initiation.

   c. The control by the soul is the final phase, leading to the death and destruction of the personality. This death begins when the personality, the Dweller on the Threshold, stands before the Angel of the Presence. The light of the solar Angel then obliterates the light of matter.

The "control" phase is conditioned by the complete identification of the personality with the soul; this is a reversal of the previous identification of the soul with the personality. This also is what we mean when speaking of the integration of these two; the two are now one. It was of this phase that St. Paul was speaking when he referred (in the Epistle to the Ephesians) to Christ making "out of two, one new man." It is primarily the phase of the final stages of the Probationary Path (where the work consciously begins) and its carrying forward to completion upon the Path of Discipleship. It is the stage of the practical and successful server; it is that wherein the entire focus and output of the life of the man is dedicated to the fulfillment of hierarchical intent. The man begins to work on and from levels not included in the three worlds of ordinary evolution, but which nevertheless have their effects and their planned objectives within those three worlds.

The Significance of Integration

The emphasis laid by most teachers and aspirants is upon the integration of the personality and its correct orientation towards the world of spiritual values. It should be remembered that this *is* an earlier stage and rightly so. The integration of the mind, the emotional nature and the brain is the major characteristic of all advanced human beings—the bad, the very bad, the good and the very good. It is, however, no sign of spiritual life, and is frequently quite the reverse. A "Hitler" or an ambitious person with a deeply selfish or cruelly directed life is a personality, with all the powers of his mind dedicated to evil purposes, with the emotional nature so constituted that it presents no obstacle to the furthering of these selfish intentions, and with a high-powered brain receptive to the plans and methods of the two vehicles, carrying out the behests of the personality.

I would point out that the majority of people are *not* personalities, no matter how glibly they may talk about their personalities. For example, the initial objective before the mass of aspirants and students is, first of all, to integrate the lower threefold man, so that they may become functioning personalities, prior to becoming functioning souls; the work is dedicated to the purpose of producing a conscious personality focus, whilst avoiding that cycle of incarnations wherein the personality is dedicated to lower and selfish ends. Students who are more advanced are dedicated to the purpose of producing a still higher integration of soul and personality, leading to that final integration which brings in the highest aspect of all, that of monadic life.

There are in the world today many truly integrated personalities. These, because soul and personality are integrated, can tread the Path of Accepted Discipleship. This is a most hopeful development, if you could but realise its implications and significance, and the question arises as to how the others who are as yet only in the process of re-orientation can develop an adequate personality integration. This they will never do if they overestimate themselves or depreciate themselves. Many are apt to regard themselves as personalities because of their natural self-will, or because they are occult students. They forget that an occult student is one who is in search of that which is hidden—in their case of that hidden, integrating thread which will enable them to blend the three bodies and thus truly merit the name of personality. Some of them cannot become personalities during this life, but they can develop the mental concept of its possibility and its nature; they need to remember that "as a man thinketh in his heart, so is he." It is not waste of time, but a very necessary process and *one through which every Member of the Hierarchy has passed.*

Study and meditation combined are the factors which all aspirants should employ if they seek to produce this needed integration and a consequent life of service. Thus the aspirant can test out both his point of integration and the extent of the serving quality produced by this integration. If aspirants would study their physical plane life with care, they would discover that they are either working automatically in response to physical plane conventional ideas of goodwill or of being kind, or they are working emotionally because they like to help, they like to be liked, they like to relieve suffering (owing to their hatred of the discomfort which suffering brings to them), they believe in following the steps of the Christ Who went about doing good, or because of a natural, deep-seated life tendency. This is a hopeful and finalising unfoldment.

Aspirants will eventually find out (when the physical and emotional phases of the integration are over) that there follows a phase of intelligent service, motivated in the first instance by mercy, then by conviction of its essentiality, then by a stage of definitely spiritual ambition, then by a submissive following of the example of the Hierarchy, and finally by the activity of the quality of pure love; this pure love increasingly expresses itself as the higher integration of soul and personality proceeds. All these phases of intention and of techniques are right in their own place, just as long as they have teaching value, and whilst the higher next phases remain vague and nebulous. They become wrong when they are perpetuated and carried on when the next stage is clearly seen but not followed. Ponder on this. It is of value to you to realise the true significance of these varying phases of integration, carried forward—as they are—under evolutionary law.

All these steps upon the way of integration lead to that culminating stage wherein the personality—rich in experience, powerful in expression, reoriented and dedicated—becomes simply the mediator of soul life between the Hierarchy and Humanity. Again—ponder on this.

The State of Mind of the Soul

And whilst all these phases, stages and realisations are taking place in the life of the personality, what is the attitude of the soul upon its own plane? A consideration of this involves, first of all, a recognition of the three aspects of mind which are to be found upon what we call the mental plane:

1. *The lower concrete mind,* which is the attitude of thought held by the tiny aspect of the soul which was initially "put down" into manifestation at the time of individualisation. This—during the long cycle of incarnations—has become increasingly sensitive to its overshadowing Self. This overshadowing Self says to its incarnated aspect: "Having pervaded this entire universe with a fragment of myself, I remain." The pull of that overshadowing "remaining Self" is what draws the little fragment back to its originating source.

2. *The Son of Mind,* the soul, the product of the thought of the Universal Mind, the thinking, perceiving, discriminating, analysing Identity or spiritual Entity. This aspect of the One Life is characterised by pure mind, pure reason, pure love and pure will. A "Lord of Sacrifice" Who, through incarnating experience, integration and expression, has undertaken the task of redeeming matter, and of raising substance into Heaven! These are familiar truths and ancient platitudes, but they still remain largely theory to you. You can test their theoretical nature by asking yourself: What am I doing, as a soul (if I function as a soul at all), to raise my matter aspect, my three vehicles and the substance out of which they are made, on to higher planes of expression?

3. *The higher abstract mind* which is to the soul what the lowest aspect of the soul, embodied in the knowledge petals, is to the concrete mind. This abstract mind is the lowest aspect of the Spiritual Triad.

Once integration has taken place between the personality and the soul, then the soul—in its own body and nature and on its own plane—can begin to attend to a higher integration or linking relation which it must eventually bring about between itself and the Spiritual Triad. Accomplish-

ment upon a lower level ever makes possible accomplishment
upon a higher. There is no true higher accomplishment
until, step by step, the lower reflected aspect is mastered,
used and recognised as an instrument for bringing about
still higher activities.

The state of mind of the soul during the processes of
lower integration can be briefly summarised as follows:

1. That of a complete disinterest during the earlier stages
   of the cycle of incarnation. Its "embedded aspect" (as
   it has been called) is quite adequate to the slow and
   tedious task of evolving the bodies, developing their
   characteristics and buying the bitter experience of blindness and ignorance. This period is by far the longest,
   and whilst it is proceeding the soul goes forward with
   its own life interest upon its own level of experience,
   upon its own ray and under the influence of the Master
   Who will eventually guide the thinking (through gladly
   accepted impression) of the developing personality.
   Forget not that this kingdom or this aggregate of souls
   is what the Christian calls the Kingdom of God and
   the occultist calls the spiritual Hierarchy of our planet.
   Remember also that the purpose of its aggregated life
   is to induce realisation in consciousness of the spiritual
   polarisation of the planetary LIFE.

2. As evolution proceeds, the three vehicles—now created
   and developed—become potent, and their vibration becomes strong enough to attract a measure of attention
   from the preoccupied soul. The first reaction is *irritation*. Occult irritation is not crossness, as human beings
   express it, but response to contact—a response which
   does not please. In other words, it is friction. You will,
   therefore, better understand the meaning of the statement that the last fetter which the Master casts off is

irritation. The personality no longer attracts attention; friction therefore ceases, and there is nothing left but a pure channel through which spiritual energy can pour. Irritation, as you understand it, takes place when your personal, self-will, self-esteem, ideas and plans are infringed upon by those of another person. It is not this form of irritation which the Master casts off.

The second reaction is that of a meditation process or the generation of power, later to be used in the three worlds to enhance soul energy within the form and to create the field of knowledge, peopled by the thought-forms into which the personality will later venture. The soul is therefore preparing for its own reorientation towards Life and its expression in the three worlds, and not to the gaining of life experience.

3. When the personality becomes dominant, the soul introduces a new factor into the life of its reflection, the incarnating soul. It mobilises and focusses the energy of the soul ray, and by an act of the will brings it into direct contact with the ray of the personality. This has a reflex action on the rays of the threefold lower man, stimulating them, awakening them, and conditioning the etheric body so that the centres, through which the personality rays are pouring, and the head centre which is responsive to the soul ray, can become more active. The ajna centre, through which the personality works, intensifies its activity, and two things occur:

a. The personality life becomes increasingly potent and the man develops into an intense individual.

b. The head centre begins to exert an influence upon the ajna centre, and slowly and gradually upon the centre at the base of the spine. Self-will grows as do all the qualities.

4. The soul is now in what esotericists call "a process of reversal." This produces a great interest in its reflection in the three worlds, and three things then happen:

   a. The lower concrete mind becomes subject to illumination from the soul.
   b. The energy of the soul ray increasingly pours into the personality, intensifying its conflict.
   c. The path of the man around the zodiac from Aries via Pisces to Taurus is reversed and he then proceeds anti-clockwise.

All these factors produce violent conflict upon the Probationary Path, which increases as the man steps upon the Path of Discipleship. The potency of the personality, dominant and being dominated, is that which induces an intense karmic activity. Events and circumstances pile fast and furiously into the experience of the disciple. His environment is of the highest quality available in the three worlds; his experience fluctuates between the extremes; he works off his karmic obligations and pays the penalty of past mistakes with great rapidity.

All this time, incarnation succeeds incarnation and the familiar process of death, intervening between cycles of experience, goes on. However, all the three deaths—physical, astral and mental—are carried out with a steadily awakening state of awareness, as the lower mind develops; the man no longer drifts—asleep and unknowing—out of the etheric, astral and mental vehicles, but each of them becomes as much an event as is physical death.

Finally the time comes when the disciple dies with deliberation and in full consciousness, and with real knowledge relinquishes his various vehicles. Steadily the soul takes control, and then the disciple brings about death through an act of the soul-will and knows exactly what he is doing.

The Elimination of the Personality Thoughtform

In dealing with this subject (and it can only be done very briefly) two things must be borne in mind:

1. That we are considering solely an idea in the mind of the soul and dealing with the basic fact of the illusion which has controlled the entire cycle of incarnation and so held the soul a prisoner to form. To the soul, the personality connotes two things:

    a. The soul's capacity for identification with form; this is first of all realised by the soul when the personality is beginning to react to a measure of real integration.

    b. An opportunity for initiation.

2. That the elimination of the thoughtform of the personality, which is consummated at the third initiation, is a great initiation for the soul on its own plane. For this reason, the third initiation is regarded as the first major initiation, since the two previous initiations have very little effect upon the soul and only affect the incarnated soul, the "fragment" of the whole.

These are facts which are little realised and seldom emphasised in any of the literature hitherto published. The emphasis up till now has been upon the initiations as they affect the disciple in the three worlds. But I am specifically dealing with the initiations as they affect or do not affect *the soul,* overshadowing its reflection, the personality, in the three worlds. What I have said, therefore, will have little meaning for the average reader.

From the angle of the personal self, regarding itself as the Dweller on the Threshold, the attitude or state of mind has been inadequately portrayed as one of complete obliteration in the light of the soul; the glory of the Presence, transmuted by the Angel, is such that the personality completely disappears, with its demands and its aspirations. Naught is left but the shell, the sheath, and the instrument through which the solar light can pour for the helping of humanity. This is true to a certain degree, but is only—in the last analysis—man's attempt to put into words the transmuting and the transfiguring effect of the third initiation, which cannot be done.

Infinitely more difficult is the attempt I am here making to depict the attitude and the reactions of the soul, the one self, the Master in the heart, as it recognises the stupendous fact of its own essential liberation and realises, once and for all, that it is now incapable of responding in any way to the lower vibrations of the three worlds, as transmitted to the soul by its instrument of contact, the personality form. That form is now incapable of such transmission.

The second reaction of the soul, once this realisation has been focussed and admitted, is that—having achieved freedom—that freedom now conveys its own demands:

1. For a life of service in the three worlds, so familiar and now so completely transcended.

2. An overshadowing sense of outgoing love towards those who are, as yet, seeking liberation.

3. A recognition of the essential triangle which has now become the centre of the conceptual life of the soul:

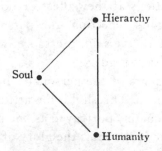

> The soul now vibrates between the two points or
> pairs of opposites and acts as an invocative and
> evocative centre.

None of the above realisations may be registered in the
brain consciousness or in the mind of the illumined personality. Theoretically, some dim vision of the inherent possibilities may be sensed, but the consciousness is no longer
that of the serving disciple in the three worlds, using mind,
emotions and physical body to carry out behest and hierarchical intent, as far as may be. That has disappeared with
the death of the personality consciousness. The consciousness is now that of the soul itself, aware of no separation,
instinctively active, spiritually obsessed by the plans of the
Kingdom of God, and completely free from the lure or the
faintest control of matter-form; the soul is, however, still
responsive to and immersed in substance-energy, and its
higher correspondence is still functioning on the levels of the
cosmic physical plane—the buddhic, atmic, monadic and
logoic planes.

What then must take place if the life of the soul is to
be full and complete and so thoroughly inclusive that the
three worlds form part of its area of awareness and its field
of service? The only way in which I can make clear to you
what the soul must do after the third initiation is to sum
it up in two ways:

First: The soul now becomes a conscious creator because the
third aspect—developed and mastered through experience in the three worlds during the long cycle of incarnations—has reached a point of perfected activity.
Putting it technically: the energy of the knowledge
petals and the energy of the love petals are now so actively fused and blended that two of the inner petals,
surrounding the jewel in the lotus, are no longer acting

as veils to that jewel. I am here speaking symbolically. Because of this happening, the death or the elimination of the personality is the first activity in the drama of conscious creation, and the first form created by the soul is a substitute for the personality. Thus an instrument for service in the three worlds is created. This time, however, it is an instrument with no life, no desire, no ambition and no power of thought of its own. It is only a sheath of substance, animated by soul life but— at the same time—responsive to and suited to the period, race and the environing conditions wherein the creating soul chooses to work. Think this statement out and emphasise the words "suited to."

Second: The soul then prepares itself for the coming fourth initiation. This is basically a monadic experience and results—as you know—in the disappearance or destruction of the soul vehicle or causal body, and the establishment, therefore, of a direct relation between the monad on its own plane and the newly created personality, via the antahkarana.

These two points are given to you for the first time in the sequential giving out of the occult teaching; hints have, however, prepared the way for these two facts. Information has also been given anent the mayavirupa through which the Master works and contacts the three worlds and which He deliberately creates in order to serve His purposes and plans. It is a definite substitute for the personality and can only be created when the old personality (built and developed during the cycle of incarnation) has been eliminated. I prefer the word "eliminated" to the word "destroyed." The *structure*—at the time of elimination—persists, but its separative life has gone.

If you will think clearly about this statement, you will see that a very complete integration is now possible. The personality life has been absorbed; the personality form is still left, but it persists without any real life of its own; this means that it can now be the recipient of energies and forces, needed by the working initiate or Master in order to carry on the work of salvaging humanity. Students would find it of value to study the three "appearances of the Christ" as recorded in the Gospel story:

1. His transfigured appearance upon the Mount of Transfiguration. That episode depicts symbolically the radiant soul, and also the three vacated bodies of the personality, and hints also at a future building of a vehicle of manifestation. St. Peter says, "Lord, let us here build three huts" or tabernacles.

2. His appearance as truth itself (silent yet present) before the bar or judgment seat of Pilate—repudiated by the world of men but recognised by the Hierarchy.

3. His radiant appearances after the resurrection initiation:

   a. To the woman at the sepulchre—symbolising His contact with Humanity.

   b. To the two disciples on the way to Emmaus—symbolising His contact with the Hierarchy.

   c. To the twelve disciples in the upper chamber—symbolising His contact with the Council Chamber of the Lord of the World at Shamballa.

You can thus see the factual nature of the results to which I earlier referred in this instruction. The disciple who has eliminated (in the technical sense as well as in the mystical sense) the hold of the personality has now the "freedom of the Ashram," as it is called; he can move at will among his fellow disciples and initiates. There will be nothing in his vibratory life or his quality which can disturb the rhythm of the Ashram; there will be nothing to call forth the "calming intervention" of the Master, as is frequently the case during the earlier stages of discipleship; nothing can now interfere with those higher contacts and spheres of influence which have hitherto been sealed to the disciple because of the intrusion of his own personality.

Part Three

The Fundamental Laws of Healing

W E HAVE NOW COMPLETED two sections of our consideration of the art of healing. We have dealt somewhat cursorily with the causes of disease and have noted that they emanate as a whole from three main sources: the psychological state of the patient, his karmic liabilities, and those which are incurred through his group relationship, environal, national or planetary. I then dealt with certain basic requirements of conditions and attitudes which must be established between the healer and the patient, and finally I took up the subject of death. I considered it as it affected the three transitory vehicles, emphasising its divine nature and its constructive purpose. We now reach the section in which the Laws of Healing and the Rules which should condition the healing process must be briefly considered.

We have found that there are ten laws and six rules. The tenth law will be found too abstruse for much elucidation; it concerns the life principle, of which we as yet know nothing, and is involved with monadic purpose. All occult teaching, which emanates directly from the Hierarchy, contains within it the living seed of that which will follow later. In *The Secret Doctrine*, for instance, H.P.B. (under my instruction) made occasional reference, very briefly and obscurely, to the antahkarana; she thus left the seed which,

521

when full grown, will indicate the requirements for those who—having achieved the higher initiations—can enter upon the Way of the Higher Evolution. In this tenth law, therefore, I embody also the seed for a much later approach to the problems of Life and Death.

I would here remind you that a law is in reality the effect of the life of a greater entity as it encloses a lesser within its living processes. It embodies that formulated purpose or organised will of an enfolding life, against which the expressed purpose or determined will of that which is enfolded is entirely helpless. You might argue, brother of mine, that this statement negates the freewill of the individual unit thus enclosed or enfolded. It assuredly does militate against the form aspect of manifestation—that aspect, for instance, of which a human being is pre-eminently conscious. Therefore, this relationship of the higher or greater and the lower or lesser, will equally and assuredly dominate and eventually render futile the lesser laws of the form nature, those which today are called the laws of nature.

Equally essentially, however, the soul within all forms is at war with those forms, and in its own integral life is conditioned by the higher laws which are the laws of its own being; these it freely obeys and follows, having no slightest wish to do otherwise. There is, therefore, no essential infringement of the freewill of the subject; there is only resistance from that which we call the "not-self" or the material aspect. This might be called the basic cause of all disease.

What we call the Laws of Nature were the highest phase of the divine life possible in the first solar system. They are primarily the laws inherent in the life aspect of the form, and have in them, therefore, the seeds of death. The Laws of the Soul, as they subordinate and render negative the Laws of Nature, are the highest laws to which humanity (the highest kingdom in nature at present) can respond, and these—when fulfilled—will conclude the purpose of the second solar system. The Laws of Life itself will finally supersede the Laws of the Soul and will completely offset and negate the Laws of Nature; these laws will be distinctive of the third solar system—the last personality expression of the solar Logos through the medium of the seven planetary Logoi with their varying forms and soul expressions.

Three Groups of Laws

We have, therefore, three groups of laws which govern the expression of the living purpose in this second solar system—one developed and another developing, with the third latent and relatively quiescent.

1. The Laws of Nature—the separative laws of the form nature.
2. The Laws of the Soul—the blending laws of group integrity.
3. The Laws of Life—the dynamic laws of Being itself.

It is with certain aspects of the Laws of the Soul that we shall now deal, for they concern the integrity and activity of the soul in form. This must be most carefully borne in mind. Disease is something which attacks the integrity or the harmony of the form nature which the inner spiritual man must use in order to make his contacts in the three worlds which constitute his environment when in incarnation. The ten laws which we shall consider might, therefore, be regarded as ten subsidiary laws of the fundamental *Law of Essential Integrity*. They constitute nine elaborations or aspects of that one law, and this you must have most carefully in mind. It is with these laws that the true healer must ever work.

The six rules deal only with the application of this realised integrity to the conditions and situation with which the healer is confronted. Integrity involves focus, tension and expression (simultaneously realised, consciously generated and dynamically used).

Qualities Required of the Healer

In the laws and rules which I have given, certain necessary characteristics of the healer are mentioned and certain needed requirements are indicated. These we should register first of all as they not only present qualities and attitudes which are essential to the successful practice of the healing art, but they indicate also why—up till the present time—there has been practically no successful or systematised healing of any patient under any of the current healing schools. There has been what I might call "accidental healing," due to the fact that the patient would have been healed anyway, for his hour to pass over had not yet arrived. Deliberate conscious healing, with full understanding, has only occurred when the healer was an initiate of high degree, patterning himself upon the life and the nature of the Christ.

Let us now look at the indicated qualities and attitudes. I will briefly enumerate and comment.

1. *The power to contact and work as a soul.* "The art of the healer consists in releasing the soul." Think for a moment what this power involves. The healer is not only in immediate and conscious touch with his own soul, but through that soul contact he can easily contact the soul of his patient.

2. *The power to command the spiritual will.* The particular law involved in the healing act must be "brought into activity by the spiritual will." This necessitates the capacity to make contact with the Spiritual Triad.

Therefore, the antahkarana must be somewhat in process of construction.

3. *The power to establish telepathic rapport.* The healer must "know the inner stage of thought and of desire" of his patient.

4. *He must have exact knowledge.* We read that he must "know the point exact through which relief must come." This is a most important point and one entirely overlooked by the so-called healers in such movements as Christian Science, Unity and others. Healing does not come through an intense affirmation of divinity, or by simply pouring out love and the expression of a vague mysticism. It comes through mastering an exact science of contact, of impression, of invocation, plus an understanding of the subtle apparatus of the etheric vehicle.

5. *The power to reverse, reorient and "exalt"* the consciousness of the patient. The healer has to "lift the downward focussed eyes unto the soul." This refers to the eyes of the patient. This statement implies limitation, because if the patient is not at the stage in evolution where this is possible, and at the point in evolution where he can contact his own soul, the work of the healer is rendered inevitably futile. The sphere of action, therefore, of the spiritual healer is strictly limited to those who have faith. Faith, however, is the "evidence of things not seen"; that evidence is largely lacking in the majority. Faith is not wishful thinking or an engineered hope. It is evidence of a well-grounded conviction.

6. *Power to direct soul energy* to the necessary area. "The spiritual or the third eye then directs the healing force." This presupposes a scientific technique on the healer's part and the right functioning of the mechanism of received and directed force within the head.

7. *Power to express magnetic purity and the needed radiance.* "The healer must achieve magnetic purity . . . and attain dispelling radiance." This involves great personal discipline in the daily life, and the *habit* of pure living. Purity inevitably and automatically results in radiance.

8. *Power to control the activity of the mechanism of the head.* The healer must have "linked the centres in the head." The true healer has established a magnetic area within his head which presents itself or expresses itself through a definitely recognisable radiation.

9. *Power over his own centres.* The healer has to "concentrate the needed energy within the needed centre." The centre in the patient's form which is nearest to the seat of the physical trouble has to be made receptive to the energy discharged into it by the corresponding centre in the healer's body. It will be obvious to you, therefore, how much knowledge and energy-control is required by the true healer.

10. *Power to utilise both exoteric and esoteric methods of healing.* The healer will employ "methods of occult healing though the ordinary medical and surgical methods will not be withheld." I have constantly emphasised the God-given nature of experimental medicine—which is a phrase qualifying medicine today, and qualifying still more metaphysical healing. There is no need to call in a spiritual healer for broken bones or for those difficulties which orthodox medicine has already mastered. However, the patient's general morale and condition can be justifiably helped whilst wise surgery and ameliorating medical knowledge are applied. This the usual so-called metaphysical healer is apt to ignore. Healers will be divided eventually into two groups:

a. Those comprising definitely trained spiritual healers.

b. Healers with less developed power but with enough radiation and magnetism to aid in the ordinary healing process. These will usually work under the guidance of the spiritual healer.

11. *Power to work magnetically.* "Thus he can pour the vital healing force upon the patient." This the healer does through a scientific coordination of his equipment, using the hands as a directing agent. In this way the disease can be healed, ameliorated or worsened, even to the point of death. The responsibility of the healer is therefore great.

12. *Power to work with radiation.* "Thus can his presence feed the soul life of the patient." This again is brought about through a system of coordination, but the agent of radiation is then the aura and not the hands.

13. *Power to practice at all times complete harmlessness.* "The method used by the Perfect One . . . is harmlessness." This, we are told, involves a positive expression of poise, an inclusive point of view, and divine understanding. How many healers combine these three qualities and also work through love?

14. *Power to control the will and work through love.* "The healer . . . must keep the will in leash." This is one of the most difficult qualities to be developed, for the will of the healer is frequently so potent in its determination to bring about a healing that it renders the effort to apply that healing process entirely futile. From the reverse angle, frequently the sentimental and mystical desire to love the patient negates all efforts to hold the will in leash. Remember, brother of mine, the spiritual will must be present as a quiet

deep pool of power behind all expression of the energy of love.

15. *Power eventually to wield the Law of Life.* Of this little can be said, for it can only be wielded by those who have developed or who are rapidly developing the consciousness of the Spiritual Triad—a very rare thing as yet.

In the study of these requirements there is no need for discouragement. Such a study will serve to set a needed goal for all healers in the New Age. It will also explain why the various healing systems which are practiced today throughout the world (particularly in the Anglo-American countries) have hitherto notably failed, in spite of their claims. None of them—if they kept properly certified records which would be scientifically accurate (and practically none of them do)—would register more than the tiniest percentage of cures based upon pure spiritual healing. The percentage cured is less than one in a million "cures." These cures would have recovered in any case in due time, if left to nature or to ordinary medical and surgical science.

But today, so great is the spiritual stimulation in the world, and so vast are the numbers responding to it, that the moving forward of a large group out of the ranks of average humanity on to the Path of Discipleship is inevitable. This moving forward will provide—during the next five hundred years—many healers who will fulfill to some degree the requirements which I have listed above.

The philosophies endorsed by the various systems such as Unity and Christian Science are basically sound and state the fundamental platitudes (the essential truths, nevertheless) which underlie all that I have said above. People, however, are not healed by the enunciation of platitudes, by the affirmation of divinity or by the statement of abstract theories. They will be healed when the right time comes because of the ability of the healer in the New Age to express in himself and in his daily life *the quality of divinity,* to be spiritually capable of invoking the soul of his patient, and also to be magnetically pure, and through the power of a particular type of radiated energy to stimulate the patient to heal himself—through the medium of his own inner mechanism. The healer in the New Age will possess the ability to make the following contacts with both ease and understanding:

1. With his own soul.
2. With the soul of the patient.
3. With the particular type of energy which is to be found either in the soul or the personality ray of the patient.
4. With any one of his own centres which is needed by him in order to act as a transmitting agency for energy to be sent into an area governed by some centre in the body of the patient.
5. With the centre in the patient's etheric body which controls the area where the disease is located.

This, as you can appreciate, connotes much technical knowledge. Added to this, the healer must also possess that spiritual perception which will enable him to intuit the "karma of the moment," as it is esoterically called, and therefore to know if a cure is permissible, practicable, or impossible. This is a form of knowledge which no healer in the world at this time possesses, no matter what his claim may be. Again I say, this is no cause for discouragement.

What is truly needed, and what will be brought about as the decades elapse, will be that disciples and men and women of spiritual orientation will enter the medical pro-

fession and perfect themselves in the techniques of orthodox medicine and in an exoteric knowledge of physical anatomy and of pathological symptoms, plus the orthodox
remedies and modes of handling disease. To this technical
knowledge and understanding they will add a measure of
esoteric learning, and they will then begin to combine, whilst
practising their profession, both the exoteric and the esoteric
wisdom which is theirs. This will at first be purely experimental, but out of the experience gained in utilising both
fields of knowledge a new medical science will emerge, based
upon two paramount recognised factors:

1. A cumulative mass of knowledge and information
   anent the dense physical vehicle. This has been
   accumulated by men of science down the ages and
   is largely proven and true.
2. A constantly growing understanding of the nature
   of the etheric body, of the centres, and of the transmission and circulation of certain controlled energies.

This combination of two aspects of truth will be greatly
facilitated by the increasing sensitivity and almost clairvoyant perception of developing humanity. One of the outstanding results of the recent world war will be found to
be a tremendously increased capacity for nervous reaction.
This nervous receptivity is at present abnormal and the results are sad. The reason for this is that the nervous apparatus of the average human being (and by that I mean his
nervous system, plus the nadis which underlie it) is not yet
adequate to the demands upon it. Time, however, will adjust
all this.

Both metaphysical healers and orthodox medical men
at this time are apt to repudiate each other with much vio-
lence. Taking it as a whole, the orthodox physician is less
rabid and exclusive than the modern metaphysician. They

know too well the limitations of their present medical attainments. But the so-called spiritual healer recognises at present no limitations, and this definitely constitutes a weakness. Both groups, in time, must become collaborators with each other and not opponents. Both have much to learn from each other, and both must recognise that the particular fields of knowledge for which they stand are equally a divine expression and indicate the ability of the human mind to search, to record, to discover and to formulate truth, so that others may benefit thereby.

I would recall to your attention the fact that both groups have much to do—the one in penetrating into the realm of the subtle and the intangible (and this is rapidly being done), and the other in descending from its vague abstractions and impractical generalisations in order to learn to recognise the *facts* anent the objective and the tangible; this is not as yet being done; metaphysical healing, so-called, is lost amidst a mist of words and high-sounding affirmations.

The sincerity of the majority of those who belong to these schools of thought is unquestioned; their motives are almost uniformly sincere and good. In both groups charlatans are to be found and also a small—a very small—minority of self-seeking and ignorant exploiters of men. Among them are numbered both physicians and metaphysicians who are commercially oriented; they are, however, a minority. In the sincere investigator and lover of humanity in both groups will be found the future hope of medical science as it seeks to meet the need of humanity—a humanity which is becoming increasingly sensitive and subjectively oriented.

CHAPTER VIII

The Laws and Rules Enumerated and Applied

Note: Certain of the Rules are related to certain of the Laws and will be considered by me in their rightful relationship. I have asked A.A.B. to give here a list of the ten laws and—where a rule is related to a particular law—to give it with that law. The rules are renumbered and do not follow in the order earlier given.

LAW I

All disease is the result of inhibited soul life. This is true of all forms in all kingdoms. The art of the healer consists in releasing the soul so that its life can flow through the aggregate of organisms which constitute any particular form.

LAW II

Disease is the product of and subject to three influences: first, a man's past, wherein he pays the price of ancient error; second, his inheritance, wherein he shares with all mankind those tainted streams of energy which are of group origin; third, he shares with all the natural forms that which the Lord of Life imposes on His body. These three influences are called the "Ancient Law of Evil Sharing." This must give place some day to that new "Law of Ancient Dominating Good" which lies behind all that God has made. This law must be brought into activity by the spiritual will of man.

RULE ONE

Let the healer train himself to know the inner stage of thought or of desire of the one who seeks his help. He can thereby know the source from whence the trouble comes. Let him relate the cause and the effect and know the point exact through which relief must come.

LAW III

Disease is an effect of the basic centralisation of a man's life energy. From the plane whereon those energies are focussed proceed those determining conditions which produce ill health. These therefore work out as disease or as freedom from disease.

LAW IV

Disease, both physical and psychological, has its roots in the good, the beautiful and the true. It is but a distorted reflection of divine possibilities. The thwarted soul, seeking full expression of some divine characteristic or inner spiritual reality, produces, within the substance of its sheaths, a point of friction. Upon this point the eyes of the personality are focussed and this leads to disease. The art of the healer is concerned with the lifting of the downward focussed eyes unto the soul, the true Healer within the form. The spiritual or third eye then directs the healing force and all is well.

RULE TWO

The healer must achieve magnetic purity, through purity of life. He must attain that dispelling radiance which shows itself in every man when he has linked the centres in the head. When this magnetic field is established, the radiation then goes forth.

LAW V

There is naught but energy, for God is Life. Two energies meet in man, but other five are present. For each is to be found a central point of contact. The conflict of these energies with forces and of forces twixt themselves produce the bodily ills of man. The conflict of the first and second persists for ages until the mountain top is reached— the first great mountain top. The fight between the forces produces all disease, all ills and bodily pain which seek release in death. The two, the five and thus the seven, plus that which they produce, possess the secret. This is the fifth Law of Healing within the world of form.

RULE THREE

Let the healer concentrate the needed energy within the needed centre. Let that centre correspond to the centre which has need. Let the two synchronise and together augment force. Thus shall the waiting form be balanced in its work. Thus shall the two and the one, under right direction, heal.

LAW VI

When the building energies of the soul are active in the body, then there is health, clean interplay and right activity. When the builders are the lunar lords and those who work under the control of the moon and at the behest of the lower personal self, then you have disease, ill health and death.

LAW VII

When life or energy flows unimpeded and through right direction to its precipitation (the related gland), then the form responds and ill health disappears.

RULE FOUR

A careful diagnosis of disease, based on the ascertained outer symptoms, will be simplified to this extent—that once the organ involved is known and thus isolated, the centre in the etheric body which is in closest relation to it will be subjected to methods of occult healing, though the ordinary, ameliorative, medical or surgical methods will not be withheld.

LAW VIII

Disease and death are the results of two active forces. One is the will of the soul, which says to its instrument:

I draw the essence back. The other is the magnetic power of the planetary life, which says to the life within the atomic structure: The hour of reabsorption has arrived. Return to me. Thus, under cyclic law, do all forms act.

RULE FIVE

The healer must seek to link his soul, his heart, his brain and his hands. Thus can he pour the vital healing force upon the patient. *This is magnetic work.* It cures disease or increases the evil state, according to the knowledge of the healer.

The healer must seek to link his soul, his brain, his heart and auric emanation. Thus can his presence feed the soul life of the patient. *This is the work of radiation.* The hands are needed not. The soul displays its power. The patient's soul responds through the response of his aura to the radiation of the healer's aura, flooded with soul energy.

LAW IX

Perfection calls imperfection to the surface. Good drives evil from the form of man in time and space. The method used by the Perfect One and that employed by Good is harmlessness. This is not negativity but perfect poise, a completed point of view and divine understanding.

RULE SIX

The healer or the healing group must keep the will in leash. It is not will that must be used, but love.

LAW X

Hearken, O Disciple, to the call which comes from the Son to the Mother, and then obey. The Word goes forth that form has served its purpose. The principle of mind then organises itself and then repeats that Word. The waiting form responds and drops away. The soul stands free.

Respond, O Rising One, to the call which comes within the sphere of obligation; recognise the call emerging from the Ashram or from the Council Chamber where waits the Lord of Life Himself. The Sound goes forth. Both soul and form together must renounce the principle of life and thus permit the Monad to stand free. The soul responds. The form then shatters the connection. Life is now liberated, owning the quality of conscious knowledge and the fruit of all experience. These are the gifts of soul and form combined.

Note: This last law is the enunciation of a new law which is substituted for the Law of Death, and which has reference only to those upon the later stages of the Path of Discipleship and the stages upon the Path of Initiation.

Application of the Laws and Rules

In the last few pages I greatly clarified the issue by indicating—even at the risk of somewhat discouraging you—certain of the essential requirements of the healer in the New Age, and also certain of the contacts which he will have to make with facility and promptness when attempting to heal. I likewise defined for you the nature of Law. This was preliminary to a consideration of the Laws to which the healer must conform and the Rules which he will automatically and intuitively obey. We might consider these Laws and Rules in relation to the healer and also in relation to each other, for several of the Rules are closely related to a Law which controls the healer.

From the definition of law, as given above, it will be apparent to you that in the last analysis disease, death, untruth, falsity and despair are inherent in the planet itself, because our planetary Logos (as I earlier stated when aiding H.P.B. in writing *The Secret Doctrine*) is an "imperfect God." After the present great world crisis, incident to our planetary Logos having moved forward upon the cosmic Path, and therefore having taken a cosmic initiation, His imperfections are demonstrably lessened; there will be less distress and disease on earth once the necessary planetary adjustments have been made. This you yourselves will not see take place, for adjustments on such a large scale take centuries to effect. What I have, therefore, to say upon the future healing of disease will not be of practical value for a long time to come, but the theory and the indications of possibility must be considered and discussed. Also, for a long time, medical practice and surgical knowledge will play their useful parts in preventive medicine, alleviative practices and curative processes. To these increasingly will be added many psychological methods of healing, and these will go hand in hand with the two above; to these again the services of the spiritual healers will be added. In this way, a rounded-out approach to the whole man will be steadily developed, and the need for this is today recognised by forward thinking physicians everywhere. Thus, and also through the method of trial and error, much will be learnt.

The healing processes I outline and indicate through these Laws and Rules are basically new. They are not based on affirmations, as in Christian Science and other mental healing cults; they are not posited on affirmed origins and on claiming results which will only be possible when the race has reached a far higher standard of perfection than is at present seen or that is immediately capable of development. As I have several times said in this treatise, there is nothing fundamentally wrong in the claims made by these groups and organisations anent the man who has arrived at soul expression and at realisation of the Christ consciousness. What is wrong is the claim that the ordinary man (obviously not at this advanced point in evolution) can perform these miracles of healing either in himself or for others. Very few people have as yet reached this point, and the healer in these cults and organisations who has done so is a rarity indeed. The healer in the New Age will recognise limitation and conditioning circumstances, plus destiny. This predisposes the development within him of knowledge-giving powers. He is also spiritually aware that the healing of the physical body is not always the highest spiritual good; the overestimation and serious, anxious care of the form life, of the physical vehicle, is *not* of major importance.

The healer in the New Age does not and will not work directly with the physical body at all; being an occultist, he will regard that body as not a principle. He works practically entirely with the etheric body and with the vital energies, leaving those energies to make their impact on the automaton of the physical body according to directed intent; they will then produce their effect according to the response of that body, conditioned as it will be by many factors. These energies, directed via the etheric body of the patient, or emanating from that body, may bring about a cure *if* the destiny of the patient permits, or they may so stimulate the area of the disease that the disease will be brought to a crisis and the patient will die. This often happens under the ministrations of cultist healers who are ignorant of the laws of healing and who base their activities on a realisation of a present (though usually unexpressed) divinity.

A much higher measure of spiritual perception and of mental understanding is required before the system I propose becomes effective. All that I give in my writings is largely of a pioneer nature, and this should be remembered.

Let us now study Law One; it has no Rule attached or related to it, as it is a basic statement, indicating the major underlying theory upon which the healer will work.

LAW I

All disease is the result of inhibited soul life. This is true of all forms in all kingdoms. The art of the healer consists in releasing the soul so that its life can flow through the aggregate of organisms which constitute any particular form.

This law indicates that, owing to the fact that the threefold lower man is not under control of his soul, disease can destroy him. Because the free flow of the energy pouring from the soul is inhibited and limited, disease can find place in the physical body. The physical organism is correctly supplied with the creative regenerating energy of the true man, the soul on its own plane. Where there is complete unobstructed inflow from the soul to the seven vitalising centres, you have the perfect health which the initiate of the fourth degree demonstrates, unless some disciplinary, experimental or initiating karma is being tried out in his case. However, as a general rule apart from these or planetary conditions, an initiate of high degree needs no healer; there is nothing in him requiring healing.

What must the healer do when, faced with a patient, he realises the inhibited condition which the disease evidences? Does he, under the law, work with the soul of the patient? Does he seek to get that soul (on its own plane) to affect definitely the man, superintending the transfer of energy from the soul to the mind, and from the mind to the astral body, and from thence to the etheric vehicle? By no means. In cases of real and serious illness, the condition of the patient is usually such that it is not possible for him to make the needed response to such attempted ministrations of the healer, either consciously or unconsciously. Any mental exertion is quite beyond his power, and he could not, therefore, cooperate with the effort of his soul to transfer energy; the activity of his astral body is usually concentrated in the formulation of a great desire to live and to get rid of the disease, *unless* the illness is so acute that the patient has reached the stage where he simply does not care and the will-to-live is rapidly leaving him. To these difficulties must be added the fact that very few people are so completely integrated that they can function as whole personalities, in response to soul stimulation. They are usually polarised in one or another of their three bodies, and this fact again presents a potent limiting condition to the healer. Again, and very frequently, the man is so intensely preoccupied with discomfort and pain present in the dense physical body, that the higher impressions which might come through from mind or soul bodies are quite unable to do so. What then must the trained and instructed healer do?

He must realise, first of all, that the etheric body is the factor of major importance and the main vehicle with which he must deal. He therefore concentrates upon that body of energy. This involves the necessity of ascertaining certain facts, and then making certain points of contact effectively useful.

The first fact to be ascertained is the potency with which the soul has gripped and is still gripping its personality. The healer is aware that because the patient is still alive, the soul is definitely present through the medium of the head and heart centres of the etheric body, thus anchoring both the consciousness and the life principles. If the patient is unconscious, the difficulties of the healer are greatly increased in some cases, though lightened in others. If the principle of consciousness is withdrawn from the head centre in the vital body, then the healer knows that death may supervene and his way is this much clearer, particularly if there is a dimming of the light of life in the heart. If consciousness is still powerfully present, he realises that there is still the possibility of cure, and can then, with greater confidence, proceed with the work to be done. In this statement, I am dealing with the average person. In the case of initiates, it is somewhat different, because they frequently remain fully conscious through the death process.

You will, therefore, realise the basic necessity for the healer in the New Age to be either clairvoyant or—far better still—to have true spiritual perception with its quality of infallibility. His first task is to investigate or "occultly see" the etheric body of the patient, and thus arrive at the following knowledge:

1. The potency with which the soul influences its etheric body. This is indicated by the point of light in the head centre and the area which it irradiates.

2. The condition of the etheric centre which controls or governs the area within which the physical trouble is to be found.

3. The relation of the centres above the diaphragm to those below, because this will give him a general indication of the point in evolution of the man to be healed.

Having ascertained these points to the best of his ability, he will then, under the law of "inhibited soul life," seek by the power of his own soul (working on the higher levels of the mental plane and through his head centre) to stimulate the point of soul life in the etheric body of the patient. He will do this with a view of attracting, if possible, a fuller inflow of the soul energy of the patient into the head centre, in order that the life thread may carry a fuller supply of life to the heart. In this manner, the patient's own "livingness" will bring about the desired cure; he will be healed apparently by nature itself, or by the natural and normal way of adequate vitality, and so enabled to throw off the disease.

When the healer, therefore, recognises and works with this law, the following points of contact are recognised and used:

1. The soul of the patient, anchored within his etheric body.

2. The soul of the healer, occupied with the stimulation of that point of soul contact, via the following triangle of energy:

This relates the vital body of the healer to that of the patient, via both their head centres and the heart of the patient, because there the life principle is focussed and is closely involved and affected by whatever occurs.

3. When this triangle of energy is functioning smoothly and a measure of response is coming from the head centre of the patient, evoking greater soul contact and producing a resultant inflow of soul energy into the head centre and from thence to the heart centre, then—by an act of the will and the use of an invocative mantram—the healer will seek to implement this increased flow of life, via the heart, to the diseased area, using the centre which controls that area of the physical body, whichever this may be. This has to be done with the greatest possible care, so that the flow is not too sudden, and therefore destructive in its effects; particular care has also to be evidenced in the cases of disease of the heart; embolisms, for instance, which prove fatal are frequently due to a violent expression on the part of the patient of the will-to-live, bringing on a flooding inflow of the life principle. This makes its impact too suddenly upon the heart, causing equally sudden movement in the blood stream, and thus of the embolism, producing death. I am putting this into entirely untechnical terms

and laying myself open to expert criticism, but I am doing so in order to convey to the lay reader a general idea of the risks involved, and thus produce caution in the enthusiast.

This law covers certain fundamental premises, and there is little more than I can profitably say anent its implications. Much will be learnt by accepting the premises and working upon their implications. What I have said is very far from being what I could have said, but I have here given the student a simple and working understanding of certain essential and basic concepts. We will now pass on to a consideration of the second Law and of Rule One.

LAW II

Disease is the product of and subject to three influences: first, a man's past, wherein he pays the price of ancient error; second, his inheritance, wherein he shares with all mankind those tainted streams of energy which are of group origin; third, he shares with all natural forms that which the Lord of Life imposes on His body. These three influences are called the "Ancient Law of Evil Sharing." This must give place some day to the new "Law of Ancient Dominating Good" which lies behind all that God has made. This law must be brought into activity by the spiritual will of man.

This Law is most comprehensive in its statements and really constitutes a summation of two laws, one of which is controlling at this time and one which will eventually control. Let us, for the sake of clarity, and because people usually read so carelessly, divide this law up into its various statements, and thus gain a better idea of its implications:

1. Disease is a product of and subject to three influences:

    a. A man's past, wherein he pays the price of ancient error.

    b. His inheritance, wherein he shares with all mankind those tainted streams of energy which are of group origin.

    c. His sharing with all natural forms that which the Lord of Life imposes on His body.

2. These three types of energy are called the "Ancient Law of Evil Sharing."

3. The "Law of Ancient Dominating Good" lies behind all that God has made.

4. This law will some day supersede the "Ancient Law of Evil Sharing."

5. It will be brought into activity by the spiritual will of man.

This law throws a man in his thinking back to the basic law of karma which, as you know, there is no avoiding, and which the modern healer in the present healing cults and organisations consistently overlooks. With these influences and predisposing causes we have already dealt, and there is no need further to elaborate them here, beyond remarking that one of the most helpful things for a patient to remember and for the healer to bear in mind is that disease has its roots in the past (a group past or an individual past) and may, in the last analysis, be a beneficent way of paying off ancient debts. This induces in the patient a constructive attitude of acquiescence—not an acquiescence which leads to nonaction, but one which produces a sense of responsibility for right action. This right action will lead either to full payment of the penalty through the well-known process of death or to the success of the steps taken to induce health. In the case of the healer, it will lead to a recognition of potent forces working through the patient and a willingness for the destined fate to take place; in both cases the feverish anxiety so often present will not intervene between the healer's intention and the patient, preventing sound happenings.

The second important thing is for the patient to remember, if his condition permits, that what he is enduring is the fate and the lot of the majority, and that he is not alone. A right handling of ill health is a major factor in breaking down separateness and a sense of aloneness and isolation; that is why the effects of bad health, when rightly handled, lead to a sweetening of the disposition and a broadening of the sympathies. Sharing and a sense of general participation has usually to be learnt the hard way—such again is the law.

In this law we have the clue to that which will ultimately sweep disease from the earth. Let me put it quite simply. When the majority of the inhabitants of the earth are being rapidly oriented towards good, towards righteousness, as the Bible expresses it, and when the bulk of human beings are inclined towards goodwill (the second major expression of soul contact and influence in the individual's life and in the life of mankind—the first being the sense of responsibility), then ill health will persistently, even if only gradually, disappear and die out and finally be nonexistent. Slowly, very slowly, this is already happening—not yet in the disappearance of disease, but in the bringing about of a more correct orientation. What this really means is that the channel of contact between the individual and his soul and the soul of humanity is becoming more direct and unimpeded. Alignment is being brought about. You can see again, therefore, why the emphasis in the life of the healer must be laid upon contact and alignment, and why so few succeed. There is little if any contact to be found among healers today, and little direct consciousness of the necessity, and no real understanding of the techniques to be followed.

It is wise to grasp this important point, for it will negate disappointment. Disease is not going to disappear miraculously and suddenly from a world in the immediate period, heralding the New Age. If it did, the implications would be that the Law of Karma no longer controlled, and this is not the case.

The final sentence of this second law gives a basic indication of the time period: the Law of Dominating Good will be brought into activity by the spiritual will of man. What does this mean? It means that only when truly large numbers of men are controlled by the Spiritual Triad, have built the antahkarana and can therefore use the spiritual will, can disease be stamped out and only good control. It will of course be a gradual process, and in the early stages almost imperceptible. Again, why is this? Because evil, crime and disease are the result of the great heresy of separateness, and because hate and not love controls. Forget not that he who loveth not his brother is a murderer—ever the symbol of hate. As yet, the sense of universality and of identity with all is not to be found, except in advanced disciples and initiates; the mass consciousness and the demonstration of the herd instinct must not be confounded with the sense of Oneness which marks the rightly oriented person. In the New Age, teaching anent the antahkarana and the constitution of man, principally from the angle of the "three periodical bodies," and not so much from that of the lower threefold man, will be emphasised, particularly in the higher schools of learning, thereby laying a sound foundation for the esoteric schools which will be slowly emerging. A new perspective upon humanity will be thereby attained. The nature of the spiritual will will be taught in contradistinction to that of the selfish personal will;

by its means tremendous new potencies will be released, and safely released, into daily life.

Up to the present time, even disciples have little idea of the exceeding power of the triadal will. It might be here affirmed that those healers who have triadal consciousness and can exercise the potency of the monadic life and will, via the Spiritual Triad, will always be successful healers; they will make no mistakes, for they will have accurate spiritual perception; this will give them knowledge as to the possibility of cure, and by the use of the will they can then work safely and with power on the head centre of the patient. They will necessarily confine their healing powers to those who live focussed in the head. They will stimulate the soul, there anchored, into effective activity, thus promoting a true self-healing.

You will note from all the above how relatively simple these Laws are when carefully considered, and how beautifully they are related to each other. The mastering and grasping of one facilitates the understanding of the next.

Forget not that the head centre is the one through which the will works, and with this in your mind, relate the information given you anent Law One in the early part of this instruction to that which I have here given you. If these laws are studied deeply by those who seek to learn to heal spiritually, and if the healer endeavours to make his life conform to the rules, a definite pattern of healing and an emerging technique will take shape in his mind and greatly increase his effective service. You will note also that I am not giving rules and laws which deal with specific diseases. This, I fear, will greatly disappoint many earnest workers. They would like me to indicate what should be done, for instance, to cure cancer of the liver, or pneumonia or gastric ulcer or forms of heart disease. This I do not intend to do. My work is far more basic than that. I am concerned with causes, and primarily with the etheric body as the distributor of energies or as the withholder of these energies when transformed into forces; I deal with the state of consciousness of the healer and with the theories which he should embrace, with his understanding of the relationship of the soul to its vehicles of expression (particularly, in the case of healing, to the vital body), and with the controlling fact of the centres found in every area of the body, either freely distributing energy and preserving the body in good health or—through undevelopment and inhibited activity—bringing about those conditions in which disease becomes possible and probable.

You can see, therefore, how the healing process is simplified when we recognise causes and realise that they are responsible for the functioning of the body on the outer plane. The healer has always to remember the following sequence of facts:

1. The fact of the soul, working through
2. The mind and the astral body, whose energies condition
3. The etheric vehicle, a vortex of energies focussed through numerous centres, both major and minor.
4. The seven major centres, controlling definite areas of the body via

    a. The nadis.
    b. The nerves.
    c. The endocrine system.
    d. The blood stream.

These four groups of conditioned aspects of the man concern life and consciousness, or the two major aspects of the soul when in manifestation upon the physical plane.

Orthodox medicine has been to date necessarily confined to the objective symptoms and their immediate apparent cause, and therefore to effects and not to real causes. The healing with which I am concerned is directed towards the reorganising and the revitalising of the etheric body, with the intent of getting behind the outer formal indications of wrong conditions to that vehicle of energies which—if correctly functioning and in right alignment—will preserve the physical body in good condition and keep it free from disease. The knowledge required by the healer in the New Age is therefore more basic and less detailed. He deals with areas and not with organs; he is concerned with energies and their distributing points, and not with the details of the physical body, with the construction of the organs and their malfunctioning. He will deal with the seven etheric centres, with the nadis through which they affect and stimulate (apart from radiation) the nervous system; he will watch with care the nervous system and the blood stream which the centres affect through radiation on to and through the hormones there to be found. But the keynote of all his work will be directed distribution, and the centre of his attention will be the channels of this distribution—the entire system of etheric centres.

I would beg you to reflect upon all this information with studious care. The keynote to good health, esoterically speaking, is *sharing* or *distribution,* just as it is the keynote to the general well-being of humanity. The economic ills of mankind closely correspond to disease in the individual. There is lack of a free flow of the necessities of life to the points of distribution; these points of distribution are idle; the direction of the distribution is faulty, and only through a sane and worldwide grasp of the New Age principle of sharing will human ills be cured; *only by the right distribution of energy will the ills of the physical body of individual man also be cured*. This is a fundamental (I would say *the* fundamental principle) of all spiritual healing. In the last analysis also this presupposes an eventual and scientific recognition of the etheric body of the planet, and consequently of man.

We come now to a consideration of Rule One.

RULE ONE

Let the healer train himself to know the inner stage of thought or of desire of the one who seeks his help. He can thereby know the source from whence the trouble comes. Let him relate the cause and the effect and know the point exact through which relief must come.

It will be apparent to you that the first rule which the healer has to master must necessarily be important. It is basic and essential in its implications if a cure is to be effected or if the healer is not to waste time in attempting the impossible. There are four injunctions in this rule:

1. The healer must train himself to know whether the patient is mentally or astrally (emotionally) focussed.
2. He can and must, therefore, ascertain the psychological basis of the existent trouble.
3. He will be able then to ascertain the location of the effect (the disease) through perception of the underlying cause.
4. This will enable him to know

   a. The area affected.
   b. The centre in the etheric body controlling that area.

You will also realise why I started my analysis of disease and healing by a presentation of the psychological causes.

This first rule is related to that entire section of the teaching and is, as you can see, intensely practical.

When the personality polarisation is known, two major facts emerge: the point of approach will be either through the head centre or the heart centre *if* the patient is highly developed—which presumably the healer can be supposed to know from character indications and the effectiveness of his life. Or the approach can be through the throat centre or the solar plexus centre *if* the patient is an ordinary and average advanced person; if he is quite undeveloped and relatively a low grade human being, the exact point through which relief will come will be the solar plexus centre or the sacral centre. It is interesting to note that when a man is so low in the evolutionary scale that he must be etherically reached via the sacral centre, he is often quite easily cured and will respond more rapidly to what is oft called "etheric manipulation" than will other types. One reason for this is that his mind and his emotions present no real obstacles, and all available energies can be directed unimpeded to the diseased area.

If the healer is clairvoyant, he can with facility ascertain the point of entry of the healing forces, because the "entering light" will then be the brightest, the light of the centre itself will convey the needed information. If he is a very advanced healer, he will not use any form of psychic perception but will react immediately upon contact to an impression so powerful, coming from the patient, that it cannot be denied and is probably entirely correct and to be depended upon. It must be remembered, however, that owing to the integrity of the human soul, and to the fact that every soul is in its own nature a Master, there will be always a margin of error where the healer is concerned, even if he is an initiate-healer; there will be evidence to him of a point where the spiritual man ('of which the patient is only a reflection) controls, and beyond which—except as a soul on an equal basis with the patient's soul—he cannot and dare not go. There are conditions, for instance, in which an advanced disciple or a high initiate (for definite purpose of vacating his physical vehicle) may be permitting the forces of disintegration, of limitation and of destruction to be breaking down and destroying his physical outer form. When this is the case, the healer may not be aware of the intention; he will, however, be aware of opposition and will be forced to desist from his efforts to heal.

When the patient is a strictly mental type, and the approach to the healing process must be through a highe1 centre, the head centre, the healer will be wise to gain the conscious cooperation of the patient so that their two wills will function in unison; this will entail a positive relationship between the two. When the patient is not so highly developed, the healer will have to strive for a spirit of hopeful acquiescence in the man; the emotional nature will be stronger in this case than in the more advanced type and the task of the healer consequently harder. He will have, very frequently, to combat anxiety, emotional reactions of diverse kinds, fear and forebodings. The psychological condition will therefore be fluid, and the healer will have much to do to aid the patient to preserve a constancy of emotional reaction and to become calm and quiescent. This quiet reaction has to be attained if the healing energies are to pass effectively to the right centre and its controlled area. This can be brought about by the establishing of a harmonious rapport between the healer and the patient, prior to any healing process. Healers in the New Age will also establish their own clientele, just as physicans do today, and so learn to know the constitution and the temperament of those they may be called upon to help; they will also educate them in certain healing processes and techniques in preparation for their use later, if needed; this time, however, still lies far ahead.

When the patient is an undeveloped human being and low down in the evolutionary scale, he will be controlled psychologically by the consecrated personality of the healer and by *the imposition of the healer's will* upon the etheric body of the patient. This does not mean the imposition of the energy of the will upon a negative person, thereby impelling the patient to action and imperilling even the very small measure of freewill which he possesses; it means the imposition of the authority of knowledge and of spiritual stabilisation upon the patient, thereby instilling confidence and a willingness to be obedient.

You have here the first steps which the healer must take in dealing with the patient and with the psyche, the lower psyche of the patient. They are three in number:

1. Gaining the cooperation of the personality of the advanced man; it is only the personality which requires healing.
2. Bringing about a condition of hopeful acquiescence on the part of the personality of the average man; he is not as yet capable of intelligent cooperation, but he can so handle himself that he reduces personality hindrances to a minimum.
3. Inducing *confident* obedience to the suggestions of the healer. This is all that the undeveloped man can do.

It will be obvious to you that broad generalisations such as the above do not cover every type of man and the many intermediate types and stages. The healer will need to be a true lover of his fellowmen and a trained psychologist as well; this means that he will have to practice as a soul and also as a perceptive mind.

Another point should here be noted. One problem which the healer will have to face with mental types will be the tendency to preserve all energies coming from the soul either in the head, or at least above the diaphragm; this does not mean that all the areas of the body below the diaphragm are not habitually supplied with the needed energies, but that there the functioning is largely automatic and the man is not in the habit of consciously directing energy to the centre and the area it controls, when below the diaphragm. It may be necessary to instruct him so to do, if he is attempting to collaborate with the healer and seeks to bring about a cure. His mental focus and the activity of the head centre will be a great help, provided he accepts instruction in the art of energy direction. This he can usually do if not too ill or too preoccupied with the preservation of a conscious contact with his body. When he is unable to focus his attention, either through pain or through lack of physical consciousness or profound weakness, the healer will have to work primarily as soul with soul, and trust that the rapport between the patient's soul and the etheric body will be adequate to promote a cure, if that is the destiny of the man.

Where the source of the trouble lies in the emotional or astral body, the task of the healer is not so easy; he has then to work, focussed as a soul in his head centre, but directing the needed energy and controlling the patient's emotional nature via his correctly oriented solar plexus centre. I refer here to the healer's solar plexus centre, which is one which he does not as a general rule employ as a point of focus or attention in his own life. The healer has a gained facility in the use of all his centres at will, regarding them as distributing points of directed energy. This directed energy, I would have you note, is *not* directed towards healing, but is the soul energy of the healer directed towards bringing some centre in the patient's body under control, owing to the emotionalism which the patient displays, and towards reorganising it as a centre for reception of the healing energies emanating from the patient's soul—a very different matter and one which must be most carefully borne in mind.

The healer, therefore, uses two centres, normally speaking: his own head centre and that centre in his own body which corresponds to the area which is diseased and its controlling centre. There has to be in every successful healing the establishing of a sympathetic relationship. As an ancient book in the Masters' Archives puts it: "Soul to soul, the two are one; point to point, together must they suffer; place to place, they find themselves allied, and thus the dual stream of energy results in cure."

One of the major difficulties with which the healer is faced, particularly if relatively inexperienced, is the result of this established sympathetic relation. There is apt to occur what we might call "transference." The healer takes on or takes over the condition of disease or discomfort, not in fact but symptomatically. This can incapacitate him or at least intercept the free activity of the healing process. It is a glamour and an illusion and is based on the healer's achieved capacity to identify himself with his patient; it also is founded on his anxiety and great desire to bring relief. The healer has become so preoccupied with the patient's need, and so decentralised from his own identified and positive consciousness, that inadvertently he has become negative and temporarily unprotected. The cure for this, if the healer discovers in himself this tendency, is to work through the heart centre as well as the head centre, and thus keep a steady flow of the positive energy of love pouring out towards the patient. This will insulate him from the disease, but not from the patient. He can do this by working through the heart centre within the *brahmarandra* (the head centre) and greatly increase the potency of his healing work; however, it presupposes a high degree of development on the healer's part. The average spiritual healer will have to link up head and heart centres by a definite act of the will. He will then realise that the love pouring from him to the patient will prevent any return of the undesirable emanations from the patient which have been flowing towards him; this because if such a flow existed, it would militate against the patient being healed.

The healer who responds to the inner urge to heal will face, as you can see, a very severe course of training before his own equipment—personality, etheric body and its centres—are brought into such submission to the soul that they offer no obstruction to the healing art. He has therefore to learn in connection with himself:

1. Rapid alignment between soul, mind, head centre and physical brain.
2. The use of the mind, illumined by the soul, in the psychological diagnosis of the causes of the disease which he proposes to handle.
3. Methods for establishing a sympathetic rapport with the patient.
4. Modes of protecting himself from any transference brought about through this rapport.
5. The establishing of a right relation with the patient of either cooperation, acquiescence or spiritual control.
6. Physical diagnosis and the locating of the area to which relief must come, via the controlling centre.
7. The art of cooperation with the patient's soul so that his etheric body focusses all its inflowing energies in order to bring relief to the diseased area. This involves the direct activity of the healer's etheric body in con-

nection with a renewed activity on the part of the patient's etheric body.

8. The technique of withdrawing his healing power when that of the patient is adequate to the undertaking.

I feel that I have here given you all that you need for immediate study and reflection. I have shown you that the healing art is not a vague mystical process, or wishful thinking and simple good intentions. I have indicated that it presupposes the mastering of the science of soul contact, first of all; the constant practice of alignment, and the comprehension of the Science of the Centres, or—literally—a modern form of Laya-Yoga. Healers in the future will undergo years of drastic training, and this need cause no surprise, for the ordinary medical profession calls for years of hard study and work. Many healers in the New Age will combine orthodox study and knowledge with the art of spiritual healing.

When trained healers, with perception, with a full working knowledge of the etheric body, with an understanding of the energies which compose it or which it does or can transmit, of the subtle constitution of man and of the methods of directing energies from one point and location to another, can work with full medical knowledge or in full collaboration with the orthodox physician or surgeon, then tremendous changes will be brought about. Great enlightenment will reach the race of man.

It is for this that we must prepare—not primarily for the healing of the physical body, but because of the expansion of the consciousness of the race that this new and esoteric study will bring about.

We have dealt with a number of fundamental realities which it is essential that all healers—endeavouring to work with the new type of esoteric healing—must master; what

I said, therefore, is of major importance. Each point made by me could form the basis of prolonged discussion, but (in this treatise) that is not possible, for I seek only to give indication of future possibilities. I seek also to foment distrust in the present approach of the metaphysical world to this subject of disease and its cure, and to undermine—if I may use so drastic an expression—the confidence of the public in the so-called New Age modes of healing, in the methods of the Christian Scientist, of Mental Science, and of all those schools of thought which deal with healing from the angle of affirmation—affirmation of man's divinity and the claim that that inherent and innate divinity guarantees his healing. This claim is a glamour and a delusion, as I have oft sought to show.

Today we deal with a law which (if properly understood) proves how inadequate is the approach of the modern metaphysician to this subject and—though it puts our instructions on healing on a sound basis—it postpones the era of truly occult healing quite definitely to a more distant time. This third law runs as follows:

LAW III

Disease is an effect of the basic centralisation of a man's life energy. From the plane whereon those energies are focussed proceed those determining conditions which produce ill health. These, therefore, work out as disease or as freedom from disease.

This law indicates that one of the primary determinations at which the healer must arrive is that of the level of consciousness from which the predominating energy in the etheric body emanates. I would remind you here that in *The Secret Doctrine,* H.P.B. states that a plane and a state of consciousness are synonymous terms, and entirely interchangeable; in all my writing I seek to emphasise not the level of matter or substance (a plane, as it is called), but the consciousness which expresses itself in that environing area of conscious substance.

We are assured in this ancient law that disease is an effect of the basic centralisation of a man's life energy. This life energy is not the same as the energy or force of consciousness, but consciousness is ever the directing factor in every expression of the indwelling life, for there is basically only one major energy—life energy. Where the consciousness of the man is focussed, there the life energy will gather its forces. If the consciousness is focussed on the mental plane or upon the astral plane, the life energy will not be so strongly focussed and anchored in the heart centre (the centre where the life principle is found), but only a part of its vital energy will find its way into the physical body, via the etheric vehicle. The greater part will be retained (to use an inadequate word) upon the plane where the consciousness is predominantly functioning or—to word it otherwise—it will be conditioned in expression by the state of consciousness, corresponding to that level of awareness or place of contact with the divine Whole or the divine Consciousness which the point in evolution of the man makes possible.

The task of the healer is therefore to find out where this focus of consciousness is to be found; this brings us back to a point I made anent the patient being essentially either a mental or an emotional type, and very, very rarely indeed purely physical in his consciousness. Where the consciousness is stabilised in that of the soul, there will be little disease present and the physical difficulties of the highly developed patient will then be associated with the impact of the soul energy upon an unready physical vehicle; at that stage only certain of the major diseases will affect him. He will not be susceptible to the little complaints and the

constant small infections which render the life of the average man or of the undeveloped man so trying and difficult.
He may suffer from heart trouble, from nervous diseases,
and from complaints affecting the upper part of the body
and those areas which are controlled by the centres above
the diaphragm; however, the difficulties brought about
through the minor etheric centres (of which there are many),
or by the centres below the diaphragm, will not usually be
present—unless (as can be the case in a very advanced disciple) he is deliberately taking on conditions engendered by
his world service for men.

As the majority of human beings are at this time centralised on the astral plane (or in the astral body), a clue
to one of the greatest sources of disease immediately becomes apparent. When the consciousness of the race shifts
on to the mental plane—and this is slowly taking place—
then the more widely known and prevalent diseases will
die out and only the diseases of mental types or the diseases
of disciples will remain to disturb the peace of individual
man. With these I have dealt in an earlier volume of this
treatise.*

Mental Science is right in its recognition that it is the
emotions of men (as expressed in that feeble imitation of
reality which they call thought) which are responsible for
much disease. They are right in their effort to make the
patient change his emotional attitudes and to react to life
and circumstances and people along a different line. But
they are hopelessly wrong in believing that that is sufficient;
in their ignoring of all scientific procedures connected with
the etheric body, they have nothing which relates the emotional nature to the physical vehicle, and therefore there
is a gap in their reasoning and a consequent fault in their

---

* *A Treatise on the Seven Rays,* Vol. II, page 520-625.

technique. This renders their activities futile, except from the character angle. When they do bring about a healing, it is because in any case the patient was predestined to recover, but they have served a useful purpose in correcting a character condition in which he was in constant danger of disease. They have not wrought a cure, and in claiming it both the healer and the patient are deceived. All deception is dangerous and hindering.

It might be of service here if I indicate along broad and general lines some of the types of disease which a centralisation of the life force upon the astral plane, for instance, could produce. I shall but list them; I will not deal with them in any detail for until the modern healer recognises *the fact of the etheric body,* and works scientifically and intelligently with it and its controlling centres of force, anything I could say of procedure would be futile. I am endeavouring at this time to promote certain basic acceptances—such as the fact of the existence of the etheric body.

1. Constant introspection, all forms of morbid suppression and a too drastically enforced silence where fundamental emotions are concerned can lead to serious liver trouble, to constant gastric difficulties and to cancer.

2. Where hatreds and deep dislike are present in the consciousness, or where the man lives in a constant state of irritation against a person or a group, or again where the sense of being abused is present, there is a real possibility that the blood stream will be affected; the man then will be susceptible to constant infections, to boils, to running sores and to the various blood conditions which are definitely septic in nature.

3. An irritable nature and one which is always in a state of fussiness, of bad temper, one which reacts furiously when things do not go as desired, may lead to disas-

trous explosions which can be diagnosed as brain difficulties and temporary insanities; they may lead to constant headaches which undermine the constitution and
bring about an inevitably debilitated condition.

4. A frustrated sex life or a state wherein an unmarried
person has had no normal expression of a natural and
universal process, and to whom therefore sex remains
a mystery (and at the same time a constant inner un-
recorded subject of thought) will lead:

a. To a condition of great devitalisation with a consequent and unavoidable ill health which attends that
type of person—the so-called obvious old maid or
bachelor. Needless to remark, there are many such
unmarried people who face life wholesomely and
do not come under this category.

b. To a constant effort to attract the attention of the
opposite sex until it reaches a point where it becomes
a nervous and most unwholesome tendency.

c. To the development of homosexual habits or to
those perversions which warp the life of many intelligent people.

d. To the tumours—malignant or otherwise—which attack the organs of generation and which frequently
make the subject an operative case.

There are other possible developments but upon them
I do not propose to dwell. I have here indicated enough
to show the danger of a sense of frustration and a
morbid (even if at the time an unrecognised) interest
in sex. This can evidence itself also in a dream life
which links the brain, the mind and the organs of generation closely together and proves the fact of astral
desire evoking the physical appetite; this demonstrates
my contention that the physical body automatically re-

sponds—even when unconscious in the hours of sleep—
to astral control. The cure, as you of course know, is a
full creative outer life, particularly one which is of
benefit to one's fellowmen and is not simply a transmutation of the sex urge into some form of creative
thinking which simply remains thinking, but takes no
shape or form on the outer plane of human life.

5. Self-pity, so prevalent a trouble, leads to acute indigestion, to intestinal trouble, to catarrh and head colds in
the average person, whilst in the more advanced man
it leads to chronic bronchial difficulties, gastric ulcers
and unhealthy conditions connected with the teeth and
the ears.

I could go on enumerating other emotional conditions which
produce disease in the person where these conditions are
present, but this will suffice to give the experimenting healer
a clue to certain possibilities which are responsible for
the physical difficulties with which he is called upon to deal.
He will have also (as I have pointed out elsewhere) to bear
in mind conditions which have been inherited from previous
incarnations or developed as a result of environing group,
national or planetary karma.

There is no rule connected with this law because we
are still dealing with the definition of causes producing the
objective disease; these have to be grasped and accepted
as working theories before the healer can efficiently deal
with the situation.

We come now to the consideration of a law which is so
inclusive in its significance and in its defining power that it
might be regarded as stating the reason for *all* disease of
any nature and at any time in the life history of the race
or of individual man. It is stated here and is only regarded
as Law IV because of the necessity for the main contentions

of the three preceding laws being admitted, considered and studied; also because it is the major law conditioning the appearance of disease in the fourth kingdom in nature, the human kingdom. It is essentially a law related to the fourth Creative Hierarchy, and it was definitely imposed and recognised as a law, governing humanity predominantly, by initiates working in the fourth rootrace, the Atlantean. Curiously enough also, when humanity can function with its consciousness centred upon the fourth or buddhic plane, disease will die out and the fourth Creative Hierarchy will finally be freed from that great limitation.

LAW IV

Disease, both physical and psychological, has its roots in the good, the beautiful and the true. It is but a distorted reflection of divine possibilities. The thwarted soul, seeking full expression of some divine characteristic or inner spiritual reality, produces—within the substance of its sheaths—a point of friction. Upon this point the eyes of the personality are focussed, and this leads to disease. The art of the healer is concerned with the lifting of the downward focussed eyes unto the soul, the true Healer within the form. The spiritual or third eye then directs the healing force, and all is well.

This law starts off with the statement of one of the paradoxes of the occult teaching: that good and evil are one and the same thing, though in reverse, or constituting the opposite sides of the one Reality.

Because man is a soul, and is spiritually determined to function as a soul, a state of friction is established between soul and personality; this friction is a major cause (if it is not *the* major cause) of all disease. Here is a clue to the understanding of the phrase, "fire by friction," the third aspect of the divine "fiery nature" of God, for "our God is a consuming fire." His nature, we are told also, is expressed through *electric fire,* through *solar fire* and through *fire by friction.* These three fires I dealt with at length in *A Treatise on Cosmic Fire* and hinted at earlier in *The Secret Doctrine.*

This law states that because man is divine, the urge to divinity produces resistance in the vehicles of expression; this resistance will localise itself in some area of the physical body and produce a point of friction; this friction, in its turn, produces a condition or an area of inflammation. This eventually leads to disease of some kind or another. It is possible, is it not, that you have here another clue—a clue to a problem which has caused so much concern in the metaphysical world: Why do advanced people, spiritual leaders and those oriented to the spiritual life, suffer so frequently from physical difficulties? It is probably because they are at the stage where the energy of the soul, pouring through the physical body, meets resistance from that body of a correspondingly intense kind. This friction set up is so acute that disease is promptly the result. This is not true of disciples who have taken the second initiation; their problem of ill health is otherwise developed.

Let us take this fourth law sentence by sentence and attempt somewhat to analyse the meaning:

> 1. *Disease, both physical and psychological, has its roots in the good, the beautiful and the true. This is but a distorted reflection of divine possibilities.*

I have shown that disease is fundamentally psychological in nature; there are, however, diseases which are inherent in the resistance of the dense physical body (and not only the subtler bodies) to the impact of the higher energies, or which are inherent in the planetary substance or matter of the Earth itself. Forget not that the physical body is constructed of such matter. This first clause of the fourth law tells us that three aspects of divinity produce disease. This sounds impossible upon first reading the statement, but a careful study will reveal its essential truthfulness. How can the good, the beautiful and the true, cause disease of any kind? Let us see.

a. *The Good*. What is the good? Is it not the expression of the will-to-good? Does not and should not this will-to-good work out on the physical plane in what we call goodwill among men? Is it not possible that the soul, seeking constantly (on its own plane) to conform to the Plan which implements the divine will-to-good, endeavours to impel its threefold expression, the personality, to express goodwill—doing this at the right stage of evolutionary unfoldment and when it is active and functioning? Yet, because of the resistance of the form nature, as yet inadequate to the desired divine expression, friction is immediately set up and disease eventuates. I think that even a brief consideration of the above questions will demonstrate to you how probable it is that the soul's inclination to "the good" can bring about resistance upon the physical plane so that the turmoil thus engendered in the consciousness of man can and does produce disease. This type of disease is responsible for many of the difficulties of advanced people, aspirants and disciples. This "friction" produces then a secondary reaction and leads to those psychological conditions to which we give the name "depression, an inferiority complex, and the sense of failure." This particular source of disease, "the Good," is one that primarily affects the mental types.

b. *The Beautiful*. Here you have a word qualifying the desire of all men for what they consider a desirable objective for their life pattern and that for which they choose to struggle. The beautiful, from the angle of a divine aspect, concerns the *quality* of life. I would refer you here to our initial definition in the first volume of this treatise of the words spirit-soul-body; we defined them as life-quality-appearance. Life is the energy in expression of the divine will-to-good; quality is the energy in expression of the soul, and this energy works at this time predominantly through the desire life and the determination of all men at every stage in evolution to possess, own and enjoy that which they regard as the beautiful. A definition of "the beautiful" and the range of man's desires are widely different and dependent upon the point in evolution; it is all dependent however, upon the outlook on life of the one who is desiring and the place where he stands upon the ladder of evolution. The inability of man to achieve at any time what he considers "the beautiful" determines his predisposition to disease, based upon the internal friction thus produced. At the present point in racial development, the majority of people are swept into diseased conditions as a result of the friction brought about by their striving after "the beautiful"—a striving enforced as an evolutionary urge because they *are* souls and under the influence of the quality of the second divine aspect.

c. *The True*. It has been said that the true or the truth is that much of the divine expression as any man can demonstrate at his particular point in evolution and at any given stage in his incarnated history. This expression of the truth presupposes that behind what he does manage to express there is much that he is unable to manifest; of this his soul remains persistently aware. This inability to live up to the highest ideal of which the man—at his particular level—is aware and can conceive, in his clearest and best moments, produces inevitably a point of friction, even if the man remains unaware of it. One of the major manifestations of this particular friction and the diseased condition which it brings about is rheumatism; this is widespread today and has been for centuries; from the medical standpoint, there is no ascertained or attributable cause for it, though there are many speculations and conclusions among the orthodox. It affects primarily the bony structure and is in reality the result of the inability of the soul to produce an expression of "the true" within the man, the instrument of the soul in the three worlds. The man, in his turn, no matter how low his position on the ladder of evolution, is conscious ever of the unattainable; he is constantly aware of an urge to betterment. These urges are not related to the expression of the will-to-good or to "the beautiful" (though he may be conscious of them also to a greater or less degree), but they are definitely related to the expression of something closer to the man's ideal as he sees it, and upon the physical plane. Friction, therefore, takes place and disease of some kind follows.

It is interesting to note that this inability to express "the true" or to "be the Truth" is the real cause of death among men who are below the stage of discipleship and who have not yet taken the first initiation. The soul tires of the frictional response of its instrument and determines to end the experiment of that particular incarnation. Death, therefore, supervenes as a result of the friction engendered.

In studying these ideas, it should be remembered that:

a. *The good* controls the man, via the head centre, and the friction engendered is due to the inactivity of the centre at the base of the spine. This centre controls the expression of the first divine aspect in a man by its interplay with the head centre. This interplay only takes place when the man has reached the stage of disciple or initiate.

b. *The beautiful* controls, via the heart centre, and friction is brought about by the failure of the solar plexus centre to respond. A condition of friction is therefore set up. The ending of this condition and the evocation of the right response from the solar plexus come when the forces of the solar plexus centre are raised and blended with the energy of the heart centre.

c. *The true,* as an expression of the divine, finds its point of centralisation in the throat centre; the failure of the personality to respond, and its inability to express the true, is to be seen in the relation of the sacral centre to the throat centre. This relation, when lacking, produces friction. There will be no real expression of "the true" until the forces of the creative centre below the diaphragm are raised to the creative centre of the throat. Then "the Word," which is man essentially, "will be made flesh" and a true expression of the soul upon the physical plane will be seen.

2. *The thwarted soul, seeking full expression of some divine characteristic or inner spiritual reality, produces within the substance of its sheaths a point of friction.*

Much of this statement I have covered above. I would, however, call your attention to the fact that in this sentence the emphasis is laid upon the fact that it is the soul which is responsible for producing the friction. In the analysis of the previous sentence, the emphasis was laid upon the personality, because its failure to respond produced the friction and consequent disease. Is it not possible that in this sentence we have the clue to the entire purpose of pain, of distress, and even of war? I would commend this to your careful and, if possible, illumined thinking.

3. *Upon this point, the eyes of the personality are focussed, and this leads to disease.*

We have here a most interesting hint as to the medium of force direction. The occult significance of the eye and the nature of its symbolism are little understood. The reference here has nothing to do in reality with eyes in the physical body. Here the words, "the eyes of the personality," refer to the focussed attention of the personality, emanating from the mental and astral bodies which are essentially the two eyes of the soul in incarnation. The use of these two windows or eyes of the soul leads to a concentration of energy (in this case strictly personality energy) in the etheric vehicle. This energy is then directed to the area of discomfort, and therefore to the point of friction. This friction is sustained and increased by the forces which are focussed upon it. People have little idea how much— objectively speaking—they increase the potency of the disease by the constantly directed thought which they expend upon it and by the attention they pay to that area wherein the trouble is located. Energies, mental and emotional, are brought to bear upon the diseased area, and the "eyes of the personality" are a potent factor in sustaining the disease.

In this sentence you have, moreover, a clear and unequivocal expression of the fact that mental and emotional conditions lead to disease. The activity of the soul and the impact of soul energy have to penetrate into the physical body, via the subtler bodies, and the point of friction (the outcome of resistance) is found first of all in the mental body, then is repeated even more potently in the astral body, and is reflected into the physical body; these (and this is

the a b c of occultism but is sometimes forgotten) constitute the personality, and the friction is necessarily to be
found throughout.

It might be of interest to you to correlate what I have
said in my other writing anent the eyes with the point made
above. As you well know, and as stated in *The Secret Doctrine*, the right eye is the "eye of buddhi" and the left eye
is the "eye of manas"—this (when in relation to buddhi)
referring to the higher mind and to man as he finally will
appear. In the average human being, and before reaching
perfection, the right eye transmits the energy of the astral
body when directed consciously towards an object of attention, and the left eye directs the energy of the lower mind.
In between these two directing eyes is to be found the ajna
centre, which is like a third eye or directing agent for the
blended and fused energies of the personality; related to
this third eye as it awakens and comes into functioning
activity is what we call "the eye of the soul"; this is a point
within the highest head centre. This eye of the soul can
and does transmit energy to the ajna centre and is itself the
agent (before the fourth initiation) of the energy of the
Spiritual Triad. This esoteric relationship is only set up
when the soul is dominating its instrument, the personality,
and is bringing all the lower activities upon the physical
plane under soul direction.

In the perfected man, there is to be found, therefore,
the following distributors or distributing agents of energy:

1. The eye of the soul . . agent of the Spiritual Triad . . Will.
2. The third eye . . . . . . agent of the soul . . . . Love.
3. The right eye . . . . . . distributor of buddhic energy.
4. The left eye . . . . . . conveyor of pure manasic energy.
5. The ajna centre . . . . focussing and directing point for
   all these energies.

In the disciple and the man who is beginning to function as a soul, you will have:

1. The third eye..distributor of soul energy.
2. The right eye..agent for astral energy.
3. The left eye...agent for lower mental energy.
4. The ajna centre.focussing point of these three energies.

In the average man, the situation will be as follows:

1. The right eye ....agent for astral energy.
2. The left eye ....agent for mental energy.
3. The ajna centre ....distributing station.

As occult knowledge increases a whole science of energy distribution will be built up around the eyes and their symbolic function, and their esoteric use will be understood. The time has not yet arrived for this, though already the power of the human eye when focussed on a person, for instance, is known to attract attention. One hint I can give you: the optic nerve is a symbol of the antahkarana, and the entire structure of the eye ball is one of the most beautiful symbols of the threefold deity and the threefold man.

> 4. *The art of the healer is concerned with the lifting of the downward focussed eyes unto the soul, the true healer within the form.*

In its most obvious and lowest connotation this phrase simply says that the healer must help the patient to look away from himself, that he must aid him to raise and re-orient the directed energy so that the "point of friction" is no longer the object of attention and a new preoccupation is presented. This has long been the attempted practice of all healers but it has a far more esoteric meaning than they have realised and one which I find it somewhat difficult to explain.

We have seen that the point of friction (responsible for the disease) has been caused by the good, the beautiful and the true in conflict with the forces of the lower man. This, we have also seen, is a fundamental law and one which he knows he must accept and with which he must intelligently work. How, therefore, can he apply this law and produce the results for which he is striving?

These downpouring energies of the soul enter the physical body, via the etheric vehicle, and are responsible for the frictional trouble and its consequence, disease; they have "descended into contact" via the sutratma and are anchored in three main centres, major centres, as you well know. From these, according to a man's nature, ray, development and weaknesses and limitations, they are distributed to the various areas of the physical body and either cause points of friction or manifest themselves as divine qualities. Where friction and resultant disease are present, and the patient is fortunate to have a trained occult healer available (either an initiate or an advanced disciple), these energies will be sent back—either with or without the cooperation of the patient—to their distributing points, the three higher centres, and this according to the type of energy which is producing the trouble. They cannot be sent out of the body altogether, via the head centre, for in that case the man would die; but they can be esoterically "driven to their point of emanation, from the point of friction, but not to their Source," as an ancient book on healing states.

The energy is sent from the infected area (to use an unsuitable word but we lack the correct words for these new sciences) into the point of friction and from thence to the centre which controls that area and by means of which soul energy entered the dense physical body. The healer is therefore working with the two aspects of the physical body simultaneously—the dense and the etheric. From that centre, the energy involved is gathered up and returned to one or other of the three major centres, or (if one of these higher centres is itself involved) the energy is gathered up and driven into the head centre and there retained. It must therefore be borne in mind that this phase of the healer's work falls into two parts:

1. The stage of esoteric "lifting up" or "driving forth." This itself falls into two phases:

    a. The phase of gathering the energy.
    b. The phase of refocussing it in its distributing centre.

2. The stage *after* the healer's work has been accomplished and the patient is either better or the work has not been successful. In this stage, the energy which has been "driven forth" is returned to the centre and the locality where the point of friction had been.

It will be obvious to you that this form of healing work is possible only to the highly trained person, and it is therefore needless for me to elaborate further on this technique. It is useful nevertheless to see at times the distant goals.

All that is at present possible in reference to this statement is to turn the patient's attention (if he is capable of responding to suggestions) towards the soul, and help him, with simplicity, to hold his consciousness as close to the soul as he can. This will aid in clearing the channels down which energy can flow, and also along which energy can be automatically withdrawn, because energy follows thought.

In the last analysis, true esoteric healing is a simple matter in comparison with the intricate and complex detail anent the human mechanism and its diseases with which the modern physician has to cope. The spiritual healer concerns himself with *the area* in which the disease is to be found, with its controlling *etheric centre* and its higher correspondence, and with the *three energies* coming from the soul which are responsible for producing the point or points of friction. The remainder of his work involves the use of the creative imagination, the power to visualise and a knowledge of scientific thinking, based upon the fundamental and universal law that "energy follows thought." This visualisation and this scientific thinking do not (where healing is concerned) involve the construction of thoughtforms. It involves the ability to move and direct energy currents.

> 5. *The third eye then directs the healing force, and all is well.*

The third eye referred to here is that of the healer and not that of the average patient; this the healer uses in conjunction with the eye of the soul. In the case of the healing of a very advanced person who is consciously able to cooperate, the third eye of the patient can also be active, and by this means two very potent streams of directed energy can penetrate into the area where the point of friction is located. In ordinary cases, however, and where no occult knowledge is present on the part of the patient, the healer does all the work, and this is desirable. The cooperation of the unskilled and those emotionally involved in their trouble is of no true assistance.

The few hints given in the analysis of the sentences composing Law IV will provide much food for thought, and we will now proceed to consider the rule connected with this law.

It should be remembered, as we study these laws and rules, that the laws are imposed upon the healer and provide the unalterable conditions under which he must work; he may not and cannot evade them. The rules, however, he imposes upon himself, and they constitute the conditions which he is advised to follow if he seeks success. Much depends upon his understanding of the rules and on his ability to interpret them correctly. They are a translation or an adaptation of the ancient rules which have, since time began, conditioned all occult healers, working under hierarchical impression. In the early days of their use they were submitted to and accepted by members of the Hierarchy at that time—the time or age of ancient Lemuria—and had then to be interpreted differently to the modern interpretation; the modern meaning is only now in process of emerging. It might be said that:

1. *In Lemurian times* these rules were accepted by members of the Hierarchy. Unless you were a member you could not ascertain them or work with them.

2. *In Atlantean times* they were externalised to the extent that disciples who were not yet initiates or who had taken only the first initiation were given them and permitted to use them. It is their Atlantean interpretation which largely colours the modern approach to their comprehension, but it is not adequate to the opportunity and the more mental type of human being.

3. Today, *in our Aryan race,* a new significance is emerging, and it is that significance and the new interpretation which I shall endeavour to impart.

Rule I was not subjected to the new interpretation because it was so obviously modern in its implications. In fact, the first rule was not part of the original ancient text from which these important rules have been taken, but is relatively very modern, being formulated early in the Christian era. It is a clear and concise rule and implies what should be the nature of the healer's thinking.

1. He must know the type of thought which conditions the patient.
2. He must be able to penetrate to the source of the difficulty, or to its psychological background; therefore, he must use thought power.
3. He must be able to relate cause and effect; the relating agent is ever the mind.

In old Lemuria and Atlantis the mind was practically entirely quiescent and not really functioning at all; it is only in this present race that the mental nature of man is becoming dominant, and therefore the new and modern interpretation of these rules (based on the mind principle) is now in order, and with this we shall proceed to deal.

RULE TWO

The healer must achieve magnetic purity, through purity of life. He must attain that dispelling radiance which shows itself in every man when he has linked the centres in the head. When this magnetic field is established the radiation then goes forth.

The East has ever emphasised magnetic purity but has totally ignored physical purity as the Occident understands it; the West has emphasised external physical purity but knows nothing about magnetic purity; this latter is largely based (somewhat erroneously though not entirely so) on the effect of the auric emanation and its purity or non-purity. The healer, in this rule, is advised to:

1. Achieve magnetic purity through purity of life.
2. Attain a dispelling radiance through linking the centres in the head.

3. Establish a radiatory field through the utilisation of this magnetic field.

Result: RADIATION.

The interesting part of this rule is its linking the two possible forms of spiritual healing—radiatory and magnetic—into one activity. The true healer automatically blends both modes of healing and uses both methods simultaneously and automatically because he works through the magnetic area, contained within the radius of influence of the three head centres, or within the triangle which is formed by so linking them.

In Lemurian days, the healer achieved his ends by the use of drastic physical disciplines, thus gaining the needed purity. The goal, as you know, of hierarchical effort in those days was to teach primitive man the uses and purpose of the physical body and its intelligent control; the man who mastered the body and was in control of it as a machinist is in control of a machine, was then regarded as an initiate. Today, it is the mastering of the personality which makes a man an initiate. Celibacy, careful modes of eating and a measure of bodily cleanliness, plus the rudiments of Hatha Yoga (embryonic physical, athletic control—muscular control primarily) were strictly emphasised. This achieved, so-called purity permitted the free flow of the pranic currents from the healer to the patient, via the sacral centre and the throat centre—the spiritual healer working through the throat centre, and the point of reception in the patient being the sacral centre; neither the heart nor the head centres were used. Prana, to define it for your purposes, is the vitality of the planet, its vital emanation; it is this prana which is distributed or transferred by a natural healer (one without any training, without much essential knowledge or with little, if any, spiritual orientation). He heals but does not know how or why; prana simply flows through him in the form of a strong current of animal vitality, usually from the splenic centre and not from any of the seven centres.

These drastic physical disciplines are often attempted today by well-intentioned aspirants; they practice celibacy, strict vegetarianism, relaxation exercises and many kinds of physical exercises, in the hope of bringing the body under control. These forms of discipline would be very good for the undeveloped and the lowest type of human being, but they are not the methods which should be employed by the average man or the practising aspirant. Concentration upon the physical body only serves to enhance its potency and to feed its appetites and bring to the surface of consciousness that which should be securely secluded below the threshold of consciousness. The true aspirant should be occupied with emotional, not physical, control and with the effort to focus himself upon the mental plane, prior to achieving a stabilised contact with the soul.

In Atlantean times, the shift of the attention from the dense physical body to the emotional vehicle began slowly to be made. The initiate of that time began to teach his disciples that the physical body was in reality only an automaton, and that it was the desire body, and the nature and quality of their habitual desires which should be considered if purity was to be attained. It was in this race, therefore, that personal magnetism first began slowly to show itself. The early and the primitive Lemurian was not in the least magnetic as we understand the word, but in Atlantean days a certain measure of magnetic radiation showed itself, though not to the extent which is now frequent and possible. The first dim outline of the halo could be seen around the heads of advanced Atlanteans. Magnetic purity became a possibility and a goal, but was dependent upon emotional

control and the purification of the desire nature; this produced automatically a much greater measure of purity in
the dense physical vehicle than the Lemurian initiate ever
achieved. Diseases of the body became more subtle and
complex, and the first psychological diseases appeared and
the various ills which are definitely based upon the emotions.
With this type of difficulty we have dealt in an earlier part
of this treatise. The healer in those days worked through
the solar plexus centre and (if an initiate) through the
heart. There was still no magnetic area or field of energy
in the head.

Today, in our Aryan race, magnetic purity is not dependent upon the physical disciplines; it is still—for the
mass of the people—dependent upon emotional disciplines,
but in the case of the true healer in the New Age it is dependent upon the "lighted magnetic area in the head." This
provides a field of activity for the soul, working through
the head centres and focussing itself in the magnetic field
which they enclose. When all the powers of the body and
the directed attention of the healer are centered in the
head, and when the astral body is quiescent and the mind
is active as a transmitter of soul energy to the three head
centres, you then have an established radiance, or energy
emanation which is a potent force in healing. The radiation
is intense, not so much from the familiar aspect of light,
but from the extent of its emanating rays of active energy
which can reach the patient and energise the needed centre.
All the centres in the body of the patient can be receptive
to this energy, and not just one, as in the previous two types
of healing.

When the karma or life-pattern of the patient permits,
these energy rays (emanating from the magnetic field in
the healer's head) become what is called a "dispelling radiance"; they can drive away the forces which create or

aggravate the disease. When this dispelling radiance is unable (because of the destiny of the patient) to bring about a physical cure, it can nevertheless be turned to the dispelling of subtler difficulties, such as fear in some form or other, emotional imbalance and certain psychological difficulties which greatly enhance the problem with which the patient is faced.

Healers would do well to remember that when the three centres in the head are linked up and the magnetic field is therefore set up and the radiance is present, the healer can then use the ajna centre as the directing agent for this "dispelling radiance." It is interesting to note that the two major centres in the head (corresponding to atma-buddhi, or the soul) are the head centre and the alta major centre, and that these correspond esoterically to the distributing agents of the right and the left eyes, as do the two glands in the head: the pineal gland and the pituitary body. You have, therefore, in the head three triangles, of which two are distributors of energy and the third is a distributor of force.

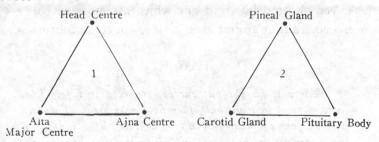

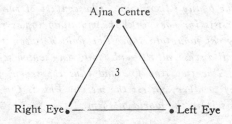

It is with these triangles that the trained healer eventually works and which he consciously employs. The time when this will be possible still lies very far ahead. At present the healer must work through visualisation and the power of the creative imagination. As he imagines, through visualisation, the relationship of these interlaced triangles, superimposing them the one upon the others, beginning with the first, he is doing a definite work of creative *placing,* then of creative *vitalising* and finally of creative *directing.* In these three words: placing, vitalising, directing, you have the results indicated as to what obedience to this rule will enable the healer to accomplish. The attention is placed; the magnetic field is spiritually vitalised; the generated vital radiance is then distributed and directed correctly through the medium of the third triangle. This sounds a somewhat complicated procedure but after a little practice this healing exercise of placing, vitalising and directing becomes an almost instantaneous and automatic accomplishment.

We come now to the consideration of a long and somewhat complicated law and one which attempts to cover so much ground that at first reading it is apt to be confusing.

LAW V

There is naught but energy, for God is Life. Two energies meet in man, but other five are present. For each is to be found a central point of contact. The conflict of these energies with forces and of forces twixt themselves produce the bodily ills of man. The conflict of the first and second persists for ages until the mountain top is reached— the first great mountain top. The fight between the forces produces all disease, all ills and bodily pain which seek release in death. The two, the five and thus the seven, plus that which they produce, possess the secret. This is the fifth law of healing within the world of form.

It has been impossible hitherto to give the subject-matter of this law because it is only today that teaching anent LIFE (and life as energy) has been possible. Also the teaching anent the five and the two energies which meet in man have only lately been given out by me, for the first time in any detail, although they were hinted at in *The Secret Doctrine*. I wonder sometimes if any of you realise the epoch-making importance of the teaching which I have given out anent the seven rays as manifesting energies. Speculations as to the nature of the divine Trinity have ever been present in the discussions and thinking of advanced men—and that since time began and the Hierarchy started its agelong task of influencing and stimulating the human consciousness—but information anent the seven Spirits before the Throne of the Trinity has not been so usual and only a few writers, ancient or modern, have touched upon the nature of these Beings. Now, with all that I have given you concerning the seven rays and the seven Ray Lords, much more can be discovered; these seven great Lives can be seen and known as the informing essences and the active energies in all that is manifested and tangible upon the physical plane as well as on all the planes of divine expression; in saying this, I include not only the cosmic physical plane (composed of our seven systemic planes) but the cosmic astral and the cosmic mental planes also.

In this rule the healer is expected to accept certain basic ideas which will serve to develop his understanding; certain broad and general axioms are laid down which will form a sound foundation for all future work. The main point to bear in mind is that this rule relates entirely to the physical plane (dense and etheric) and to the effects which the conflict between the energies and the forces produces within the physical body. The forces are those energies which are limited and imprisoned within a form of any kind—a body, a plane, an organ, a centre; the energies are those streams of directed energy which make impact upon these imprisoned forces (if I may so call them) from within a greater or more inclusive form, from a subtler plane, thus making contact with a grosser vibratory force. An energy is subtler and more potent than the force upon which it makes impact or establishes contact; the force is less potent but *is anchored*. In these last two words you have the key to the problem of the relationship of energies. *Free* energy, from the angle of the anchored point of contact, is in some ways less effective (within a limited sphere) than the energy already anchored there. It is essentially more potent but not effective. Ponder on this and let me illustrate my point. In the life of the aspirant, the energy of the solar plexus centre (from long use, centralisation and habit) is more potent in its effect upon the life of the aspirant than is the energy of the heart centre, which is only slowly, very slowly, coming into effective action. To illustrate further: the energies of the personality are far more potent in conditioning the life of the average man than is the energy of the soul, which for aeons has tried to grasp effectively its point of manifestation, the personality, but has failed until very late in the cycle of incarnations. Yet, in the last analysis, heart energy and soul energy are infinitely more potent than those of the solar plexus centre or the personality. For aeons, however, the energy of the heart centre and the energy of the soul have lacked responsive vehicles in the three worlds.

In a way, this simplifies the problem of the healer, because the first thing he has to decide is whether soul energy or personality energy is in control; that is a matter very simply discovered. The life trend of the patient, his mode of living or of service, the character he displays, are all indicative of the potencies which control his manifested expression. If the man is a true aspirant and is aiming consciously to tread the Path of Discipleship, he will aid the discovery by frank admission; however, if there is no response from the personality forces to the soul impact of the healer, the personality will remain unaware of the opportunity and quite unconscious of the impact. These conditions the healer can therefore easily ascertain.

This law is a long one and contains statements of major importance. It would be profitable for us, in the interests of our subject, to study them with the utmost care and so become aware of their significance and true meaning; this understanding must be from the standpoint of the initiate-consciousness, and not from the angle of vision of the average or unillumined man. We will, therefore, take each sentence by itself and seek its meaning. There are seven statements contained in this law, and much of their import is exoterically familiar to you, but can be restated in relation to the healing art.

1.   *There is naught but energy, for God is Life.*

This is a broad generalisation which may convey much to the initiate but assuredly conveys very little to the average thinker, to whom life means essentially and simply that which calls into manifestation a form, which sustains it in being and constantly demonstrates its presence by activity of some kind or another—an activity which demonstrates its livingness. We, however, erroneously apply the term *living* to the ability of a form to manifest and express its quality and nature. Yet livingness and quality exist apart from form and often come into major expression and usefulness through the application of the Law of Death.

The fact of divinity and of divine origin is proved by the fact of life. This is oft overlooked, and the emphasis is put upon the concept that life evokes and supports a form which anchors the life-essence and proves the reality of its existence.

It is the life of the One Source of all manifesting forms which creates relationships and essential qualities, and though this has been affirmed ceaselessly it still remains a meaningless platitude As men, however, begin to recognise God as energy and themselves as aspects of that energy, as they begin consciously to work with energies and recognise the distinction in time and space between energies and forces, and then as the soul comes into greater functioning activity, the fact of life will be recognised in a new and almost formidable manner. It should be remembered that the soul is a secondary energy, which proves the existence of the primary energy and is responsible for the appearance of the third form of energy—the tangible and the objective. Life will eventually be known as capable of being invoked by the soul in the interests of the form. Here lies a clue to our general theme.

Up till now the mechanism of approach to the life aspect—the antahkarana and the agent, the spiritual will—has not been understood in any useful sense. Today, the first faint hints as to the use of the antahkarana, and its purpose in relation to the personality and the Spiritual Triad, are being studied by a few students in the world, and their numbers will steadily increase as both personality and soul establish contact and fusion and more people take initiation. The *purpose,* consequently, for the very existence of the fourth kingdom in nature (as a transmitting agent for the higher spiritual energies to the three lower kingdoms) will begin to appear, and men, in group formation, will consciously begin this work of "saving"—in the esoteric sense, needless to say—these other grouped lives. The Macrocosm with its purpose and incentives will for the first time begin to reflect itself into the human kingdom in a new and more potent manner, and this in its turn will become the macrocosm of the three lesser states of conscious lives— the animal, the vegetable and the mineral kingdoms.

All this is a deep mystery, but has remained so only on account of the lack of development of the fourth kingdom. There had been a deviation from the original intent. Its function and field of service could, however, be realised and expressed only when this highest aspect, the will aspect, had been brought into conscious expression in mankind through the building and the utilisation of the antahkarana. Along the rainbow bridge the life aspect can flow, and it is to this that the Christ referred when He states that He had come so that there might be present upon the Earth, "life more abundantly." Always there has been life, but when the Christ consciousness is radiantly present (as is the case today, though on a small scale) and the numbers of those expressing it are vast indeed, the inference is that the antahkarana is firmly established; the rainbow bridge can then be traversed and crossed, and life in abundance and in a new and impelling sense, and a fresh impulsing sense can also flow through humanity into the subhuman kingdoms in nature. This is evidence of divinity, and outstanding testimony of man's divine origin, and the hope, the saving hope, of the world.

The energy and the forces constitute the sumtotal of all that *is*. This is another basic truism or platitude upon which the science of occultism is built and which the healing art must recognise. There is, in manifestation, nothing else of any kind whatsoever. Disease itself is a form of active energy, demonstrating in forces which destroy or produce death. Therefore, if our basic premise is correct, disease is also a form of divine expression, for what we know to be evil is also the reverse side of that which we call good. Shall we belittle the subject or cause a false impression if we regard evil (at least as far as disease is concerned) as misplaced or maladjusted good? Will you misunderstand if I say that disease is energy which is not functioning as desired or according to plan? Inpouring energies are brought into relation with forces, and good health, strong and adequate forms and vital activity result; the same inpouring energies can, however, be brought into relation with the same forces and a point of friction be set up, producing a diseased area, pain, suffering and perhaps death. The energies and the forces remain of the same essentially divine nature, but the relationship established has produced the problem. If this sentence is studied it will be obvious that a definition such as that can be used to cover all forms of difficulty, and that the ultimate producer of the situation (either good or evil) is the relationship aspect. This statement is of major importance in all your thinking.

2. *Two energies meet in man but other five are present. For each is to be found a central point of contact.*

The two energies which meet in man are the two aspects of the monad, of the One in manifestation; the monad manifests essentially as a duality; it expresses itself as will and love, as atma-buddhi and these two energies when brought into relation with the point of mind, with the third aspect of divinity, produce the soul and then the tangible manifested world; then there is demonstrated in the planet will, love, and mind or intelligence; or atma-buddhi-manas.

As the soul anchors itself as consciousness and life within the human being, that human being contributes the third something which is latent or karmically present in all substance, manas or mind; this is inherited or held in solution in substance from a previous solar system. In that system intelligence was unfolded and was retained within substance in order to form the basis of the evolutionary development of this, the second solar system. Forget not that the seven planes of our solar system constitute the seven subplanes of the cosmic physical plane and that, therefore, spirit is matter at its highest point of expression, and matter is spirit at its lowest. Life differentiates itself into will and love, into great impulsing energies which underlie the entire evolutionary process and motivate its inevitable consummation.

Atma-buddhi, as energies, anchor themselves in the soul vehicle, in the egoic lotus, and their fused activity evokes a response from the substance of the mental plane which then makes its own contribution. Its reaction produces what we call the higher mind, which is of so subtle a nature and so tenuous an emanation that it must perforce relate itself to the two higher aspects and become part of the Spiritual Triad. The vortex of forces established under the impact of the divine will, expressing divine purpose and unified with Being (as identity and not as a quality), produces the egoic lotus, the vehicle of that "identified soul" which has been swept into expression by the third result of the atmic-buddhic impact on the three worlds; the concrete mind and the human intellect come into expression. There is, therefore, a curious resemblance between the three divine aspects in manifestation and the spiritual man upon the mental plane. The correspondence is as follows:

The monad . . . . Abstract mind.
The soul . . . . Egoic lotus.
The personality . . . . . . Lower or concrete mind.

That vague abstraction, the monad, for aeons of time seems unrelated in any way to the soul and the personality; these two have been and are occupied with the task of establishing, in due time and under the evolutionary urge, a close fusion or at-one-ment. The abstract mind remains also for aeons of time something inconceivable and outside the modes of expression and of thinking of the man who is kama-manasic (or emotion and lower mind) and then finally soul and concrete mind (or the illuminator and the transmitter of illumination). These correspondences can be found most enlightening if due consideration is given to them.

In the human being you have, therefore, two major energies anchored; one unrealised, to which we give the name of the PRESENCE, the other realised, to which we give the name of the Angel of the PRESENCE. These are the soul (the solar angel) and the monad. One embodies the monadic ray and the other the soul ray, and both of these energies actively or subtly condition the personality.

The other five energies which are present are the ray of the mind or the conditioning force of the mental body; the ray of the emotional nature, and the ray of the physical body, plus a fourth ray which is that of the personality. The ray of the physical body esoterically "ascends upward towards juncture, whereas the others all move down," to quote an ancient writing. The ray of the personality is a consequence or result of the vast cycle of incarnations. You have therefore:

1. The monadic ray.
2. The soul ray.
      3. Ray of the mind.
      4. Ray of the emotions.
      5. Ray of the physical body.
6. Ray of the personality.
      7. The planetary ray.

The planetary ray is always the third Ray of Active Intelligence because it conditions our Earth and is of great potency, enabling the human being to "transact his business in the world of planetary physical life."

I have made only casual reference to these rays elsewhere and have said little anent the planetary ray; I have laid the emphasis upon another analysis of the conditioning rays, and in this analysis recognised only five rays for practical usefulness to the man. These are:

1. The soul ray.
2. The personality ray.
    3. The mental ray.
    4. The astral ray.
    5. The ray of the physical body.

However, with the creation and development of the antahkarana, the ray of the monad must also be brought into line, and then that which is its polar opposite, the planetary "livingness," the third ray, will have to be recognised. I have here imparted a point of much importance to you. All these energies play an active part in the life cycle of every man and cannot be totally ignored by the healer, even though the information may be relatively useless at this time.

   3. *The conflict of these energies with forces and of forces twixt themselves produce the bodily ills of man.*

You will note here that diseases are produced, according to this law, in two ways:

1. By the conflict of energies with forces.
2. By the conflict of the forces twixt themselves.

It will be apparent on the surface that this dual warfare is to be expected. Under the first category there is the warfare which takes place in the personality life when the soul definitely turns its attention to its vehicles and attempts to take control. The more determined the person is to submit his personality to soul control, the more intense will be the conflict, with consequent physical conditions of a serious kind as a result. Under this category would come the majority of the diseases of disciples and mystics, largely of a nervous nature and often affecting the heart or the blood stream. They will, in the majority of cases, be confined to the area above the diaphragm, and therefore to those areas conditioned by the head, the throat and the heart centres. A number of what we might call "borderline" cases come under this heading also, but these are confined to the transfer of energies (under soul impact) from the solar plexus centre to the heart, and the "line" involved is simply the diaphragm.

Under this first category also would come those difficulties which are brought about, for instance, when the energy of the astral body makes its impact upon the forces of the etheric vehicle, setting up an emotional turmoil, and thus producing serious solar plexus difficulty with resultant gastric, intestinal and liver disturbances. These are all the result of the conflict between energy and forces. All I can do at this point is to give indication of the type of problem which is related to one or other of these two categories; the subject is unsuitable for the brief handling which I purpose here to give.

Under the second category, which concerns the conflict between forces and forces, you have the etheric body involved, and the forces concerned are those to be found in the major and the minor centres, involving their relation to each other and their internal reaction to the impact of energies coming from without the etheric body. These forces and their interplay produce the common ills of man and control the disturbances in the physical organs and the areas of the physical body which are found around these centres.

These in reality constitute the major conditioning factors for the mass of human beings for long aeons or until such time as the soul "pays attention" to the appropriation in full control of its mechanism in the three worlds. These secondary difficulties, due to the interplay between the centres, fall into three categories, and these should be carefully noted:

1. The interplay between:

   a. The centres above the diaphragm, i.e., the head, the throat and the heart, and very occasionally the ajna centre.

   b. The centres below the diaphragm and their relation to each other.

2. The relation of certain centres to each other, such as takes place under the Law of Transmutation, or the process of lifting up of the forces from one centre to another:

   a. From the sacral centre to the throat centre.

   b. From the solar plexus centre to the heart centre.

   c. From the centre at the base of the spine to the head centre.

3. The impact of the "energy" (note the technical accuracy of my phrasing) of the centres above the diaphragm on those below the diaphragm.

   This is a reverse process to that which takes place when the forces below the diaphragm are raised to the centres above the diaphragm. In this third type of relation you have the exercise of the potency of magnetism, and in the other you have the expression of radiation. These two are closely allied at a certain stage of unfoldment.

Under all these relationships there are possibilities of difficulties, resulting in an undesirable effect upon the physical
organs found within the area involved. In the early stages
of the relation of the centres above the diaphragm to those
below, the man is usually quite unaware of what is going on
and is then simply the victim of the stimulation applied by
the centre emanating energy to the centre which receives its
impact; or he is the victim of devitalisation (producing
consequently many forms of physical ills) as the centres
respond to the stimulation. It is all a question of balance
or of equilibrium, and it is for this that the intelligent man
and the aspirant must strive.

We come now to a very ambiguous statement and one
that is purposely meant to be so:

4. *The conflict of the first and second persists for ages
   until the mountain top is reached—the first great
   mountain top.*

This refers vaguely (and again purposely so) to the
conflict between the energies above the diaphragm—which
normally come from the soul on its own plane—and the
forces below the diaphragm. This is a major and persistent
conflict; it begins when the solar plexus centre becomes
dominant and powerful, producing crises as in Atlantean
days. As the mass of men are still Atlantean in consciousness, being swayed mainly by their emotional natures, these
crises arise today. Eventually, and metaphysically speaking, the solar plexus centre begins to have a radiatory effect
in response to the magnetic "call" of the heart centre. When
the first initiation is taken the first great interplay is set up
between the two and the first coordinated activity is established. "That which is above is now related to that which
is below, but that which is below loses its identity in that
which is above," as the *Old Commentary* expresses it. The

mother is lost to sight because the Christ-Child assumed the place of interest. The soul is taking control and leading the aspirant from mountain top to mountain top.

At the first initiation, and increasingly at all initiations, energy is brought into a major conflict with the forces; soul energy sweeps into the etheric body and all the centres become "fighting areas," with one centre being emphasised more than the others. The nature of the battle is no longer that "twixt the forces and each other," but is now between the energies and the forces, and it is this which creates the acuteness of the tests for initiation; it is this which produces so many physical ills among those who have taken or are preparing to take the first and second initiations. And it accounts for the diseases of the saints!

A great science of the centres will some day emerge, and this will clarify the entire complex problem; the time, however, is not yet. At present, if this science were taught openly, the result would be that the thoughts of men would be turned to the fact of the centres and to the areas which they control, and not to the energies which pour through them. There would be an unwholesome and undesirable stimulation or devitalisation of the substance of the centres, with consequent acute disease. The law forever holds good that "energy follows thought," and that energy can be either radiatory or magnetic, but must not be statically contained within a centre. The true science of the centres will only be permitted free circulation when—and only when—men know the rudiments at least of thought direction and the control of energy impacts.

> 5. *The fight between the forces produces all disease, all ills and bodily pains which seek release through death.*

There is here an interesting distinction which should be noted. Death, when it comes, is the result of two things:

1. The fight between the forces, and not between energy and the forces. The area of conflict is the etheric body and the physical body, and no energies are coming in from without because the man is too ill.

2. The loss of the will-to-live. The patient has given in; the internal fight is too much for him; he can bring in no outside energy to combat the warring forces, and he has reached the point where he does not want to do so.

These two phases of the process of dying are indicative of the destiny of the patient, and should be immediately noted by the healer who (when he finds them present) will then apply his skill in aiding the man to die and will not attempt to effect a cure. The door of entry for the life-giving energies is sealed; nothing can enter to aid the healer in his work, and the conflict between the forces—of a general nature or confined to a bitter fight in a particular area—produces so much friction that there is no hope anywhere, except in death. In this sentence, it might be pointed out that *disease* refers to the point of friction or of acute trouble; *all ills* has reference to the general reaction of the man to the area of difficulty and to the general disability produced by the disease, whilst *bodily pain* refers to the discomfort of the area where the disease is located and which is indicative of its nature. All words in these laws and rules are most carefully chosen, and even if inadequate from the translator's point of view, are not redundant but express different meanings.

6. *The two, the five and then the seven, plus that which they produce, possess the secret.*

The enumeration is in the nature of a summation of what has been previously given, and its most superficial meaning and the one of the most use to the healer could be simply expressed as follows:

> The healer must bear in mind the fact of the two major energies which are present in every personality; the soul and the personality rays. He must then bear in mind that to these two he must add three conditioning rays, making the five above mentioned: the mind ray, the ray of the astral body and the ray of the physical body.

This enumeration will usually prove adequate for all ordinary or average people. If, however, the patient is a very advanced person, another form of enumeration will be in order; it will be necessary to add two more energies which will then be present in real potency: the ray of the monad and the ray of the planet, which is the third ray. This planetary ray when very active (as is the case with very advanced persons and those who have attained a high point of general integration) has a potent effect; planetary prana comes in powerfully on the planetary ray, and this can be used to bring about a cure. One reason why the general health of all very advanced people is usually good is that pranic energy from the planet has a free flow through the mechanism. It is this energy which the Master, working through a relatively perfect body, depends upon to keep it in good health. This is a somewhat new piece of information and one which—when recognised—will appear both simple and reasonable. "That which they produce" in this case, and to the healer, means the outer tangible form; there are other significances, but with these we need not here deal.

The "secret" referred to is the revelation of the manner in which good health may be preserved. It is not the secret

of how to cure the physical vehicle when "bodily ills" are
present. But there is a secret of good health which is known
to all initiates above the third initiation; and this they can
simply employ, if they so choose. However, they may not
so choose always unless they are working with other parts
of the Plan which have nothing to do with humanity. If they
are among those who are occupied with the unfolding consciousness in man and who are workers for and in the human
kingdom, they may know the secret but may, at the same
time, choose not to profit by it because of the need they feel
to be completely identified with mankind; they therefore
choose to share consciously all human experience and to die
along lines which are common to the rest of men. The entire
question of identification lies behind all manifestation; it
is identification with or of spirit and matter which is the
secret of divine appearance; one of the main causes of disease, as well you know, is the facility with which men identify themselves with the form aspect (with the many localised *forces*—localised within the personality ring-pass-not).
Man neglects to identify himself with the producer of the
form, the true spiritual man, and with the *energies* which
he seeks to direct, and which—later in the evolutionary
cycle—he is insistent upon directing.

There is also a secret meaning here which relates to the
seven rays as they express themselves in the human kingdom;
the knowledge of this secret enables a Master to control
epidemics and widespread diseases; with this you are not
at this time concerned. Incidentally, the relative freedom
from the plagues and epidemics which usually follow in the
wake of war has been partly due to the use of this sevenfold
knowledge by the Hierarchy, plus the scientific knowledge
of humanity itself.

In this connection also (and I mention it simply from
the angle of its interest) there are two hierarchical offi-

cials—the Mahachohan and His Representative upon the seventh ray—Who are today in possession of this secret in its entirety, and They are aided by five other Masters in applying the gained knowledge. These five Masters are working primarily with the deva evolution, and this is, as you know, connected with form, and in this particular case with the healing devas. These seven Members of the Hierarchy are aided in Their turn by one of the Buddhas of Activity, and also by the representative of the Spirit of the Earth. This again makes the two, the five, and then the seven—a different enumeration, and one which when brought together equals nine, which is the number of initiation. This numerical relationship brings man to the point where he is "initiated into the realm of perfection and knows no further aches or pains, and his mind is thus deflected from that which is below to that which is above."

I have mentioned this phase of mankind's relation to the subject of health so as to show you how subtle and esoteric are the matters with which we are dealing, and so give to the individual patient a sense of proportion, where his bodily ills or even his death are concerned.

7. *This is the fifth Law of Healing within the world of form.*

This fifth law is primarily concerned with the fifth principle of mind or manas; it is this principle which makes a human being what he is; it is this principle which makes him a prisoner within the form and upon the planet, and thus makes him vulnerable and open to attacks upon the form aspect; these constitute part of the agelong action of evil versus good. It is this fifth principle, when controlled and used by the Son of Mind, Who is a Son of God, which will enable the spiritual man to free himself from form of every kind, and therefore from disease and death.

It will be obvious that the healer, as he trains himself in the healing art, has to grasp clearly and candidly certain exceedingly simple yet esoteric facts:

1. That healing is simply and essentially the manipulation of energies.
2. That he must carefully differentiate between energies and forces.
3. That if he seeks real success, he must learn to place the patient as accurately as possible upon the correct rung of the ladder of evolution.
4. That knowledge of the centres is imperative.
5. That he himself must work as a soul through his personality.
6. That his relation to the patient (unless the latter is highly evolved) is a personality one.
7. That he must locate the centre controlling the area which involves the point of friction.
8. That, as with all else in the occult sciences, disease and healing are both of them aspects of the great "relationship" system which governs all manifestation.

If the healer will take these eight points and reflect and brood upon them, he will lay a sound foundation for all work to be done; their relative simplicity is such that it will be obvious that anyone can be a healer if he so chooses and is willing to conform to the requirements. The current idea that a person is a "born" healer, and therefore unique, in reality indicates only that it is one of his main directed interests. Therefore, because of this interest, his attention has been turned towards the healing art and consequently towards contact with patients; owing to the inevitable working of the law which governs thought, he discovers that energy follows his thought and flows through him to the patient. When he does this with deliberation, a healing will often follow. Any man or woman—given real interest and prompted by the incentive to serve—who thinks and loves, can be a healer, and it is time that people grasped that fact. The entire process of healing is thought-directed; it concerns the direction of energy currents or their abstraction, and this is another way of speaking about radiation and magnetism. Every initiate is a healer, and the more advanced the initiate the less is he occupied with the intricacies of centres and forces, energies and their direction. He heals automatically, as was the case with the initiate, Peter; of him we read that "the shadow of Peter passing by healed everyone of them."

The major difference to be seen in the interim (an interim of many, many thousands of years) between the type of healing mentioned above and the work of a less advanced healer, will be that those healers who are trained physicians and accredited medical men as well as spiritual healers will have a great advantage over the untrained healer, because their diagnosis of the disease will be more apt to be correct and their powers of visualisation will be greater, owing to their trained familiarity with the structure of the body and their knowledge of morbid pathology. It will be wise, for a very long time to come, for the spiritual healer to work always in collaboration with a trained physician. The healer will provide the required occult knowledge. The time when any nice, kindly and spiritually minded person sets up as a healer should be well-nigh over; any healing practice should be preceded by years of careful study anent the nature of energy, of the ray types, of the centres; a minimum of at least three years should be given to this; when to this is added the science of the trained medical man, graduating from our best medical colleges, you will then have a new and much better treatment of the human vehicle than is now the case. Then the healer's orthodox and occult knowledge, his visualising capacity and his power of thought direction will be real and practically effective.

The rule connected with Law V makes clear the need for this occult knowledge, for it states very definitely certain fundamental injunctions.

RULE THREE

> Let the healer concentrate the needed energy within the needed centre. Let the centre correspond to the centre which has need. Let the two synchronise and together augment force. Thus shall the waiting form be balanced in its work. Thus shall the two and the one, under right direction, heal.

This rule presupposes a knowledge of the centres, and this knowledge is, as you well know, still embryonic; all that is known in most cases is the location of a centre. This, however, especially with untrained healers, is sufficient. Too detailed a knowledge of the formation, condition and responsiveness of a centre would handicap the healer, for his thought would be deflected to the detail of the form and away from the energy and its movements.

The rule here requires that the healer, having aligned himself with the soul and "tapped" soul energy (thereby making himself a channel for spiritual force), directs this energy into that one of his own centres which corresponds to the centre conditioning the area of the point of friction. If the disease or physical trouble is stomachic, for instance, or related to the liver, the healer will direct his soul energy into the solar plexus centre, situated in the etheric spinal column. If the patient should be suffering from difficulty in the heart or the lungs the healer will use the heart centre, employing the throat centre for diseases of the bronchial tract, the throat, the mouth or the ears.

Two things, therefore, become of importance in connection with the healer himself:

1. He must know as accurately as possible his own point of development, for that will indicate to him capacity or non-capacity to work with any or with all the centres. In order to use any of his centres in the healing work, the healer must have awakened them in some measure and be able, consciously and by the power of thought, under the agency of the will, to focus energy in whichever centre he chooses. This does not mean that all the centres are awakened and truly functioning. It should, however, mean (if he is to heal at all) that he is not confined to the sole use of the centres below the diaphragm but that, by an effort of the spiritual will, thought can be channelled into the higher centres. Many aspirants can do this with greater facility than they believe.

2. The healer, as he channels energy into some centre, prior to directing it to a centre in the patient's body, must run no risk of his personal overstimulation. This is a very important point. So much disease and physical difficulty among ordinary people is abdominal, necessitating the constant use of the solar plexus centre by the healer; this could bring about a grave condition of overemotionalism and even acute astralism on the part of the healer. He would then be the victim of his good intentions and of his spiritual service, for the consequences would all the same be bad; energy is an impersonal force and a purely impersonal agency. Purity of intention, selfless service and goodwill are no true protection, in spite of the platitudes of the sentimental occultist. In fact, the presence of these desirable conditions only increases the difficulty, for soul energy will pour in with

great force. An understanding of the risks involved, a sane appraisal of possibility and a scientific and technical understanding of protective measures will be given to the healer towards the latter end of his training. For the present, and because the danger is not at this time so great (owing to lack of potency in people's thinking and their inability to direct thought) the major protective measure consists in the ability of the healer to hold his consciousness steady in the head centre with the "eye of direction" turned to the needed centre. This involves a dual focus, and for the ability to do this the healer must strive.

It is here that the healer distinguishes between the processes of radiation and magnetisation. Having concentrated soul energy in the appropriate centre, through the power of direction from the head (the seat of soul energy) and by the potency of thought, the process of radiation ends. This radiation has passed through two stages:

1. The stage wherein the soul radiated energy into the head centre.
2. The stage wherein the healer directs a ray of that energy from the head centre into the "needed centre"; it is there focussed and held steady.

From that appropriate centre the stage of synchronisation with the corresponding centre in the patient's body is established; this is done, not by the healer sending a ray into that centre, but because the potency of the healer's centre evokes response from that of the patient; it acts like a magnet, drawing forth a definite radiation from the patient. This radiation, esoterically, "lights up" the point of friction in the surrounding area and—were the healer clairvoyant— would thus enable him to see more clearly the seat of the trouble and, therefore, to arrive at a more accurate diagnosis. Ordinarily, the spiritual healer is depending upon the diagnosis of the medical man in attendance, if he is not one himself.

An interplay is now established between the healer and the patient and upon etheric levels. The energy of their two synchronised centres is now en rapport, and the healer has at this point to determine whether the treatment requires an expulsive technique or a stimulating one. He has therefore to ascertain whether the patient's centre is overstimulated and if some of the surplus energy should consequently be driven out or abstracted, or whether there is a condition of devitalisation and the energy of the centre involved requires a deliberate augmenting.

There is, however, a third possibility mentioned here which is slower, but in practically every case is more desirable; it is the attainment of that balance of energies (between the healer and the patient) which will hold the energy in the area of the point of friction and permit nature itself to bring about an unassisted cure. This is possible only when the rapport between the patient and the healer is complete. Then the sole task of the healer is to hold the situation steady, give the patient confidence in the powers inherent within him, and encourage a period of patient waiting. The cure then is more lasting, and there is no sense or period of psychic shock, which can be the case if sudden stimulation or drastic expulsion is employed.

We have noted here, as you see, three modes whereby the healer employs the force focussed, by direction, in his centres:

1. For the expulsion of surplus energy in an overstimulated centre.

2. For definite processes of stimulation of the patient's centres.

3. To preserve a state of equilibrium wherein natural healing can take place.

In the first case, the healer deliberately increases the potency of the energy stored in his centre, so that it becomes exceedingly magnetic and abstracts the oversupply of energy in the patient's centre; in the second case, the healer sends a powerful ray of his own energy into the corresponding centre in the patient's body. This is an act of radiation and is very effective; in the third case, an interplay is set up which preserves balance, and furthers steady and normal activity in the centre controlling the area of trouble.

You will note also how all these processes (and they are relatively simple when grasped) are dependent upon the decision of the healer. It is here that mistakes can be made, and the man who is seeking to work along the lines I indicate would be well-advised to move slowly and with due caution even at the expense of being ineffectual and unsuccessful. It is better to have no effect upon the patient and his condition than by the potency of one's unwise decision, the power of one's thought and the focus of one's direction, to hasten the patient's death by the sudden abstraction of needed energy or by the stimulation of a centre already overstimulated and overactive.

In the last analysis the aim in the three modes of aiding the patient by direct work with the centres involved, is to bring about a balanced and wholesome activity. This is more easily achieved in the case of an advanced person than in the case of the individual in whom the centre is normally inactive and unawakened and where the difficulty is more apt to be due to the action of some of the twenty-one minor centres situated in the body than to that of the seven major centres. In these cases, the patient can far more easily be helped by orthodox medicine and surgery than by any processes of spiritual healing. It is for this reason that the spiritual healer is only now becoming important and his work in any way possible. This is owing to the rapid spiritual development of humanity, which enables men, for the first time and on any substantial scale, to take advantage of these laws and rules.

In the last sentence in Rule Three, the meaning of the two and the one is that the combined energy within the healer—soul energy focussed in the head centre and the energy of the "needed centre," plus the energy of the centre which controls the point of friction in the patient's body—is responsible for the healing, providing it is the destiny of the patient to be healed.

LAW VI

When the building energies of the soul are active in the body, then there is health, clean interplay and right activity. When the builders are the lunar lords and those who work under the control of the moon and at the behest of the lower . personal self, then you have disease and ill health and death.

This is a most interesting law, because it deals basically with causes, primarily with causes over which the average person has no conscious control, and because it occultly gives a picture in miniature or microcosmically of the universal or macrocosmic situation. It deals with the entire problem of evil, or pain and suffering (the great mysteries of our little planet) in a few sentences, but they are sentences conveying vast implications. The very simplicity of this great natural law veils the far-reaching significances of its normal working. It says the following things quite simply, and I enumerate them because the breaking down of a paragraph into its clear and simple statements is a sound way to arrive at understanding:

1. When the soul controls the form involved, there is health.
2. The soul is the builder of the form, the constructive force in manifestation.
3. This is true of both the microcosm and the macrocosm.
4. The results are wholeness, right relation and correct activity.
5. When the soul is not in control, and the forces of the form nature are therefore the controlling factors, there will be ill health.
6. The builders of the form are the "lunar lords," the physical, astral and mental elementals.
7. These, in their triple totality, compose the personality.
8. They are occultly under the direction of the moon, the symbol of form, called often the "mother of the form."
9. The emanation coming from the moon has in it the seeds of death and disease, because the moon is a "dead planet."

It all comes back again, as you will note, to the source of the major energy controlling the body. Though the soul is the source of all life and consciousness, for aeons all the soul does is to preserve the form in life and in consciousness, until such time that it has reached the stage in evolution where it is a useful and suitable instrument (and will become increasingly so) for the soul to employ as a medium of expression and service. Karma determines then the quality and nature of the physical body. It can be healthy because it has not been misused in the particular life or lives conditioning a particular incarnation, or unhealthy because it is paying the price of error. Good health is not necessarily dependent upon conscious soul contact. That can and does produce good health, but it is also dependent, in the majority of average cases, upon the life and intentions of the personality—in this life and in previous lives; it is not until the will of the personality is towards spiritual betterment and a cleaner, purer life that the soul can be of real assistance.

This law carries also the implications of that basic relation which makes the threefold form of the man an integral part of the macrocosmic whole. All forms in all kingdoms are built by the lunar lords under an impulse emanating from the planetary Logos, working in cooperation with the Spirit of the Earth—the sumtotal of all the lunar lords and of the three types of energised substance which go to the creation of the physical, astral and mental bodies. The relation of the planetary Logos to this Spirit of the Earth (the relation of an evolutionary Being to an involutionary entity) is a reflection (distorted and under the influence of glamour) in the three worlds of the relation of the soul to the personality elemental. It is most useful for the healer to realise that in handling disease he is in reality handling involutionary lives and attempting to work with elementals. The natural trend of these elemental lives, all of them upon the involutionary arc, is to block and to frustrate his efforts and the efforts of the soul, and this—for them—is their way of evolution; it is that which will eventually bring them on to the evolutionary arc.

When the time comes that the soul can assume conscious control within and over the form, and can eventually create a form which is adequate to its spiritual needs, it will be because the elementals which are the sumtotal of the personality elemental have reached a point in their development where they are ready to move on to the path of return. The work of the soul is never the purely selfish one of having a medium of expression in the three worlds, as might sometimes appear to the casual and superficial thinker. That is entirely incidental from the angle of the soul; it is a needed activity, but it involves also the sacrificial work of salvaging substance and forwarding the evolution of matter. As the *Old Commentary* expresses it: "the Mother (substance-matter) is saved by the birth of her Son (the Christ within, the spiritual consciousness)." This is true of the macrocosm as well as of the microcosm.

Here lies the secret of planetary suffering and of death. Our planetary Logos (viewing the truth from the angle of the macrocosm) is, as you know, one of the "imperfect Gods" of *The Secret Doctrine,* although perfect past our human comprehension—the comprehension of a unit in one of the kingdoms which constitute His body of manifestation. There is still no true balance between spirit and matter, though the point of balance has almost been achieved; the involutionary forces are still potent and the spiritual energies are still frustrated, though far less so than earlier in human history; the next great human race, following on our present one, will see a point of balance reached which will usher in the so-called golden age. Points of friction will then be far fewer upon the planet and therefore in individual man; areas of frustration and of futile activity will die out. This can be seen working out in the body of an advanced person or an initiate to a great extent and for long periods in their incarnations; paralleling correspondences are as a general rule accurate.

This law gives an amazing picture, and one too which is full of hope, particularly if one considers certain facts which are present in the world today and compares them with conditions hundreds of years ago. The consciousness of humanity is awakened everywhere; the most undeveloped races are in process of achieving education, involving necessarily the discovery of the mind; goodwill is being recognised as necessary to world unfoldment, and men are finding that "no man liveth unto himself"—or any nation either; they are registering the fact that it is simply commonsense and the part of wisdom to better conditions for all men everywhere. This is a new attitude and a fresh and most hopeful approach. Men are learning to know and understand each other; nations are arriving at a closer contact with one another; statesmen of all nations are wrestling together and in joint conclave with the problem of bettering human living conditions; everywhere there is thought, there is appraisal, and there is the struggle for freedom and for the truer values. What is all this but the effort of the soul of humanity to kill out disease, restore unhealthy areas to health and eliminate points of friction? Is not this what the spiritual man who is ill is seeking to bring about in his own body, and what the healer is attempting to aid him to do?

In so doing, the "lunar lords" and the forces of substance must eventually yield to the energy of the soul, and are benefited, whether they are microcosmic forces or macrocosmic.

One of the things which frequently puzzle students is the statement that the dense physical body is not a principle. H.P.B. states this fact with emphasis; people are apt to think (unless they are theosophical fanatics) that he was incorrect or was intentionally misleading students. One of the points, little understood, is the nature of a principle. Yet only by understanding what a principle is can the beauty and accuracy of his statement be grasped. What, in the last analysis, is a principle? A principle is that which, macrocosmically speaking, is being developed upon each plane of our seven planes—the seven subplanes of the cosmic physical plane. It is the germ or the seed on each subplane which embodies some aspect of the divine unfolding consciousness;

it is that which is fundamentally related to some form of sensitivity; it is that to which the bodies, as they evolve, find that they can respond. A principle is a germ of awareness, carrying all the potentiality of full consciousness on some particular level of divine activity. It is that which makes knowledge and conscious response to environment possible; it is that which connotes a sequential and "unrolling" sensitive activity, resulting in divine understanding, possible and inevitable.

The physical body, and to a far less extent the astral and mental bodies, are automatic in their activity as aspects of a divine response apparatus, of a mechanism which enables the Heavenly Man, the planetary Logos and the spiritual man to register conscious response to that which is to be contacted under the divine plan and through the medium of a mechanism. At present, the physical body is the only one which is as yet so fully developed that it has in this planetary scheme of ours no further evolutionary development, except in so far as the spiritual man can affect it— and most of the effect is produced in the etheric body and not in the dense physical. This is a point little grasped but of major importance.

The dense physical body reached its high point of development and of interest (from the angle of mental attention and of hierarchical action) in the previous solar system. It was then the divine goal of the entire evolutionary process. This is not an easy point for humanity today to grasp. It is not possible or advisable for me to indicate the evolutionary stages through which this divine mechanism passed in preparation for the task to be undertaken in the present solar system. In this divine incarnation of our planetary Logos through the medium of this little planet, the Earth, the physical body is *not* a goal, but simply something which exists and must be accepted, and which must be adapted and incorporated into the general evolutionary plan. That plan has to do entirely with consciousness. The physical body is simply (no more and no less) the vehicle of consciousness upon the physical plane, but the emphasis of attention is the etheric body as an expression of the subtler vehicles and their state of embodied consciousness. The physical body is important because it has to house and respond to every type of conscious response, from that of the lowest type of human being up to and inclusive of the consciousness of an initiate of the third degree. The bodies and forms of the indwelling conscious life in the three subhuman kingdoms have an analogous but less difficult problem; I am here, however, considering only the physical body of a human being, which is not a principle because it is not in any way a goal; it is not the seed or germ of anything. Any changes wrought in the physical body are secondary to the goal of conscious response to the revelation of an emerging divinity. I have felt it necessary to emphasise this because of the confusion in men's minds anent the subject.

To sum up: the physical body is not a principle; it is not a main object of attention of the aspirant; it automatically responds to the slowly unfolding consciousness in all the kingdoms of nature; it constantly remains that which is worked upon and not that which has an innate influence of its own; it is not important in the active process, for it is a recipient and not that which initiates activity. That which is important is the unfolding consciousness, the response of the indwelling spiritual man to life, circumstances, events and environment. The physical body responds. When the physical body becomes, in error, the object of attention, retrogression is indicated; and this is why all profound attention to the physical disciplines, to vegetarianism, to diet and to fasting, and to the present modes of (so-called) mental and divine healing, are undesirable and not in line with the projected plan. Therefore undue consideration and excessive emphasis upon the physical body is reactionary and is like the worship of the golden calf by the children of Israel; it is reversion to that which at one time was of importance but today should be relegated to a minor position and below the threshold of consciousness.

I have dealt with this here because in Law VII the fact of the endocrine glands is brought to our attention, and it is necessary that we approach this subject from the right point of view. The endocrine glands are a tangible part of the physical body; they are therefore a part of that created manifestation which is not regarded as a principle. They are, however, effective and potent and may not be ignored. It is essential that students regard these glands as effects and not causes of events and happenings and conditions in the body. *The physical body*—no matter what its victims may believe and declare—*is always conditioned by inner causes; it is never, intrinsically, itself a cause.* It is, in this solar system and on our planet, automatic and affected by causes generated on the inner planes or by the action of the soul. Please note the importance of this statement. The physical body has no true life of its own, but is simply—in this cycle—responsive to impulses emanating from elsewhere. Its achievement and its triumph is that it *is* an automaton. If you can grasp this adequately, we can safely proceed to the consideration of Law VII and Rule Four.

LAW VII

When life or energy flows unimpeded and through right direction to its precipitation (the related gland), then the form responds and ill health disappears.

One of the interesting factors which students should note is *the doctrine of intermediaries* which is to be found in such rich abundance and is regarded as of such vital importance in all occult teaching. It has been emphasised (though erroneously interpreted) in the Christian teaching anent the Christ; Christianity has presented Him as acting as the intermediary between an angry God and a pitiful and ignorant humanity. Such was by no means the intent of His coming or of His work, but into the real meaning I need not enter here. I have dealt with this theme elsewhere in connection with the New World Religion.* It has been taught also in the esoteric presentation (and this is closely allied with the Christian doctrines) that the soul is the intermediary between the monad and the personality; the same idea is also found in many other religious presentations, i.e., the Buddha is shown as the intermediary between Shamballa and the Hierarchy, acting in this capacity once a year; the Hierarchy itself is the intermediary between Shamballa and Humanity; the etheric plane (and by this I mean the cosmic, planetary and individual etheric vehicles) is the intermediary between the higher planes and the dense physical body. The whole system of occult or esoteric revelation is based on this wonderful doctrine of interdependence, of a planned and arranged conscious linking, and of the transmission of energy from one aspect of divine manifestation to another; everywhere and through everything is circulation, transmission, and modes of passing energy from one form to another form, and always through an appropriate mechanism. This is true in the involutionary sense, in the evolutionary sense, and in a spiritual sense also; this latter is slightly different to the other two, as all initiates of the higher degrees know well. An entire thesis upon transmitting agencies could be written, and it would include, finally, the doctrine of Avatars. An Avatar is one

---

* *The Problems of Humanity*, Chapter VI.
  The Reappearance of the Christ, Chapter V.

who has a peculiar facility or capacity (besides a self-initiated task and a preordained destiny) to work with energies, transmitted via the etheric body of a planet or of the solar system; this, however, is a deep mystery. It was demonstrated in a peculiar manner, and in relation to cosmic energy, by the Christ Who, for the first time in planetary history, transmitted the cosmic energy of love *directly* to the physical plane of our planet, and also in a peculiar manner to the fourth kingdom in nature, the human. This should indicate to you that though the love energy is the second aspect of divinity, the Christ embodied and transmitted four qualities of this aspect to humanity, and consequently to the other kingdoms in nature—the only four which humanity could absorb. Only one of these four is as yet beginning to express itself—the quality of goodwill. The other three will later be revealed, and one is related in a peculiar sense to the healing quality of love. According to *The New Testament,* this quality was called by the Christ "virtue" (a somewhat inaccurate translation of the word originally used); Christ employed it when healing force had been taken from Him and He said "virtue has gone out of me."

I have called this to your attention because this truth is directly related to this seventh law. We have seen, in connection with all the healing processes, that the dense physical body is regarded esoterically as simply an automaton; it is only a recipient of transmitted energies. We have seen that the etheric body in or "substanding" every form is itself a structure for the transmission of energies coming from some source or another—the source being primarily the point where the life within the form lays its basic emphasis. For the average human being, this is usually the astral body, from which astral or emotional energy emanates and finds anchorage, prior to transmission into the etheric body. There will be, however, in the majority of cases, a greater or less admixture of mental energy. Later, soul energy, reinforced (if I may use such a word) by the purified mind and transmitted through the personality, will condition the etheric body and control, consequently, the activities of the physical vehicle.

This law brings to our attention the fact that the dense physical body, under the impact of subjective energies, in its turn produces a "structure for transmission" and automatically repeats the activity of the etheric body. It creates (in response to the inflow of energies from the etheric body, via the seven major centres) a dense physical interlocking structure, to which we have given the name "the endocrine glandular system." These glands—in their turn and in response to the inflowing energy from the etheric body—produce a secretion which is called a secretion of hormones, and this the glands transmit directly into the blood stream.

It is not my intention to be overtechnical in my consideration of this subject; I write for the lay reader, and not for the medical profession, who are frank to admit how little they know, as yet, anent this subject. The medical research worker knows little anent the relation of the endocrine glands to the blood and to the total physiology of the human being; he knows little anent the relation of the various glands to each other; these constitute an interlocking directorate of vital importance, linked and united, animated and directed by the seven etheric centres. This is a factor naturally overlooked by the orthodox scientist in this field, and until he recognises that which produces the endocrine glands he will remain totally at sea as to cause and true results. The glands are direct precipitations of the seven types of energy flowing through the seven etheric centres. They control all the areas of the body. In their creation you have a definite expression of the radiatory and the magnetic activity of all energies, for they are produced by radiation from the seven centres, but their effect—individual and combined—is magnetic. The radiation abstracts dense physical atoms and focusses them in the correct area in the physical body, so that they can act as distributors into the blood stream, and therefore into the dense physical body, of one aspect of the inflowing energy. I would have you note that only one aspect of the energy is thus distributed—that which corresponds to the third aspect of active intelligent substance; the other two latent aspects are distributed as pure energy, affecting areas but not affecting any localised focal point. A gland is such a localised focal point.

I am anxious for this subject of the glands and their relation to the centres to be correctly understood. The entire subject is closely related to the art of healing; one of the effects of the application of the healing energy (through the medium of any centre conditioning the area wherein the point of friction is located) is the stimulation of the related gland and its increased activity. The glands are intermediaries, in the last analysis, between the healer and the patient, between the centre and the dense physical body, and between the etheric body and its automaton, the receiving dense physical vehicle.

In continuing our consideration of the immediate transmitting agency of the centres into the blood stream (the endocrine glands) I would like to point out that the centres work through this endocrine system through direct impact, through a ray or stream of energy, emanating from the central point within the centre. Through this medium they condition and control entire areas of the body and they do this through those aspects of the centres which we symbolically call the "petals of the lotus." In a point at the very centre of the lotus the life force is focussed, and as it passes outward into the related gland, it takes on the quality of the energy for which the centre is responsible, because life force is essentially unqualified. The ray of life, if one may call it so, which is found at the heart of each centre, is identified monadically with its source, and possesses (when brought in contact with its petals) one major innate quality of attractive energy; all energy emanating from the one source in this solar system, is related to the energy which we call Love, and this energy is magnetic attraction. The petals of the lotus, and the area of surrounding energy which constitutes the form of the lotus, are qualified by one of the seven subsidiary types of energy; these emanate from the seven Rays which emerge out of the one Source, as Representatives of the manifold Creator.

Within the solar system, as you know, are to be found the seven sacred planets, which are the custodians or the expression of these seven rays, of these seven qualities of divinity; within our planet, the Earth (which is not a sacred planet), there are likewise seven centres which become, as evolution proceeds, the recipients of the seven ray qualities from the seven sacred planets, thus providing (within the solar ring-pass-not) a vast interlocking system of energies. Three of these centres, representing the three major rays, are well known to you:

1. Shamballa .... The ray of power or purpose.
   The first aspect.
   The energy of will.

2. The Hierarchy ..... The ray of love-wisdom.
   The second aspect.
   The energy of love.

3. Humanity .... The ray of active intelligence.
   The third aspect.
   The energy of mind or thought.

There are four other centres, and these, with the above three, constitute the seven centres, or the seven planetary focal points of energy, which condition the bodily manifestation of our planetary Logos. Through them the Lord of the World, working from His Own level on a cosmic plane and through His divine Personality, Sanat Kumara, carries out His purposes upon our planet.

Similarly, within the microcosm, man, the correspondences to these seven centres are to be found. Therein likewise are seven major centres, and they are the recipients of the energy emanating from the seven planetary centres, the custodians of the seven aspects of ray force; these seven energies—at various stages of potency—condition the man's expression in the three worlds, make him what he is at any given moment whilst in incarnation, and indicate (by their effect or lack of effect upon the centres) his point in evolution.

Two of these centres in the human being are to be found in the head, and the other five are to be found up the spinal column. This spinal column is the physical symbol of that essential alignment which is the immediate goal of directed relationships, carried forward in consciousness by the spiritual man and brought about as a result of right meditation.

Meditation is a technique of the mind which eventually produces correct, unimpeded relationship; this is another name for alignment. It is therefore the establishment of a direct channel, not only between the one source, the monad, and its expression, the purified and controlled personality, but also between the seven centres in the human etheric vehicle. This is—perhaps astonishingly to you—putting the results of meditation on the basis of physical, or rather of etheric, effects, and may be regarded by you as indicating the very lowest phase of such results. This is due to the fact that you lay the emphasis upon your mental reaction to the produced alignment, on the satisfaction you acquire from such an alignment, in which you register a new world or worlds of phenomena, and on the new concepts and ideas which consequently impinge upon your mind. But the true results (as divine and as esoterically desirable) are correct alignment, right relationship, and clear channels for the seven energies in the microcosmic system, thereby bringing about eventually a full expression of divinity. All the seven centres in the etheric vehicle of the Christ were rightly adjusted, correctly aligned, truly awakened and functioning, and properly receptive of all the seven streams of energy coming from the seven planetary centres; these put Him en rapport, therefore, and in full realised contact, with the One in Whom He lived and moved and had His being. The physiological result of this complete "esoteric surrender of the seven" (as it is sometimes called) to the incoming spiritual energies, in their right order and rhythm, was the appearance in the Christ of a perfect endocrine system. All His glands (both major and minor) were functioning correctly; this produced a "perfect man"—physically perfect, emotionally stable and mentally controlled. In modern terms, the "pattern of the behaviour" of the Christ—due to the perfection of His glandular system, as an effect of correctly awakened and energised centres—made Him an expression of divine perfection to the entire world; He was the first of our humanity to arrive at this point in evolution, and "the Eldest in a great family of brothers," as St. Paul expresses it. The current pictures of the Christ testify to their own complete inaccuracy, for they bear no witness to any glandular perfection; they are full of weakness and sweetness, but show little strength, alert power and aliveness. And the promise has gone forth that as He is, so may we be in this world.

This is a promise which lies behind the right understanding of the science of the centres; the factual reality of the centres will be proven to all men when the centres are gradually brought under control of the soul, are correctly and scientifically energised and brought to a condition of true "livingness," and begin to condition the entire area of the body in which a centre is found, and—between them—bringing every part of the human body under their radiatory and magnetic influence.

It is the centres which hold the body together and make it a coherent, energised and active whole. As you know, when death takes place, the consciousness thread withdraws from the head centre and the life thread withdraws from the heart centre. What has not been emphasised is that this dual withdrawal has an effect upon every centre in the body. The consciousness thread, anchored in the head centre, qualifies the petals of the lotus called in the oriental literature the "thousand-petalled lotus," and the petals of that lotus have a relationship and a definitely qualifying effect (both radiatory and magnetic) upon the petals in every one of the other major centres within the etheric body; the head centre preserves them in qualifying activity, and when this quality of conscious response is withdrawn from the head centre an immediate effect is felt in all the petals of all the centres; the qualifying energy is withdrawn, leaving the body via the head centre. The same general technique is true of the life thread which is anchored in the heart, after passing (in alliance with the consciousness thread) into and through the head centre. As long as the life thread is anchored in the heart it energises and preserves in livingness all the centres in the body, sending out its threads of life into a point which is found at the exact centre of the lotus, or at the heart of the centre. This is sometimes called "the jewel in the lotus," though the phrase is more frequently applied to the monadic point at the heart of the egoic lotus on its own plane. When death takes place and the life thread is gathered up by the soul and withdrawn from the heart into the head and from thence back into the soul body, it carries with it the life of each centre in the body; therefore, the body dies and disintegrates, and no longer forms a coherent, conscious, living whole.

Related to these centres, and reacting in strict unison with them, is the endocrine or glandular system, through which system—during incarnation—life or energy flows unimpeded and under right direction in the case of the highly developed man, or impeded and imperfectly directed in the case of the average or undeveloped human being; through this system of glandular control, the human form responds or does not respond to the surrounding world energies. In connection with our present theme of healing, a man can be sick and ill or well and strong, according to the state of the centres and their precipitation, the glands. It must ever be remembered that the centres are the major agency upon the physical plane through which the soul works, expresses life and quality, according to the point reached under the evolutionary process, and that the glandular system is simply an effect—inevitable and unavoidable— of the centres through which the soul is working. The glands therefore express fully the point in evolution of the man, and according to that point are responsible for defects and limitations or for assets and achieved perfections. The man's conduct and behaviour upon the physical plane is conditioned, controlled and determined by the nature of his glands, and these are conditioned, controlled and determined by the nature, the quality and the livingness of the centres; these, in their turn are conditioned, controlled and determined by the soul, in increasing effectiveness as evolution proceeds. Prior to soul control, they are conditioned, qualified and controlled by the astral body, and later by the mind. The goal of the evolutionary cycle is to bring about this control, this conditioning, and this determining process by the soul; human beings are today at every imaginable stage of development within this process.

I realise that much of the above is well known and in the nature of repetition. But I have felt it essential to repeat the story so that there may be a fresh clarity in your thinking.

It will be apparent to you also that the karmic process in any individual life must therefore work out through the medium of the glands, which condition the reaction of the person to circumstance and events. The results of all previous lives and of all activities carried on during those lives have been registered by the Lords of Karma; karmic law works in close cooperation with the lunar Lords, who build and construct the bodies which constitute the personality; later, the law works in an even closer cooperation with the soul purpose. The whole problem is necessarily most intricate and difficult. All I can do is to give certain indications.

It is with this system of centres and their externalised effects, the glands, that the healer has to work and which he has to take into most careful consideration; all stimulation which he may be able, for instance, to convey to a centre in the patient's body, or all abstraction of energy from a centre, will have a most definite effect upon the allied or related gland, and therefore upon the secretion which that gland is in the habit of pouring into the blood stream.

As again you know, the seven major centres and their allied glands are as follows:

1. The head centre . . . . The pineal gland.
2. The ajna centre . . . . The pituitary gland.
3. The throat centre . . . . The thyroid gland.
4. The heart centre . . . . The thymus gland.

5. The solar plexus centre . . . . . The pancreas.
6. The sacral centre . . . . The gonads.
7. The centre at base of spine . . . The adrenal glands.

There are also other centres and many other glands in the body, but these are the seven with which the healer works; the minor or subsidiary glands are conditioned by the centre controlling the area in which they are located. The healer, however, refuses to complicate his thinking with the multiplicity and detail of the other lesser glandular system and with the intricacies of lesser interior relationships. The above list gives also the centres and glands which basically determine the state of health—good, indifferent or bad—and the psychological equipment of a man. Students should bear in mind that the primary effect of the activity of the glands and of their secretions is psychological. A man is, upon the physical plane, emotionally and mentally what his glandular system makes him, and incidentally what they make him physically, because that is frequently determined by his psychological state of mind and emotions. The emphasis of the self-centred ordinary man is largely upon the physical vehicle, and he pays little or no attention to the balance or the imbalance of his endocrine system or setup (if I may use that word) from the angle of its determining his psychological effect upon his fellow men. It is not my intention to analyse the various glands, noting how they respond to the awakened or the unawakened condition of the centres, or how they limit or implement the responsiveness of the man to his environment or determine his interpretation of life and the passivity or the activity of his daily reactions to events and circumstance. A man, it may emphatically be stated, is what his glands make him, but they, in their turn, are only the effects of certain inner potent sources of energy. Again, as you see, I repeat this vital truth.

It is for this reason that medical science will eventually find the truth (and already they are sensing it) that it is impossible to fundamentally change the personality and the physical equipment of a man through treating the glands themselves; little real progress has been made along this line during the thirty or forty years during which the endocrinologists have considered and investigated this subject. Certain things have been found out; certain results of the activity or the inactivity of the glands have been noted; certain types of people have been recognised as illustrative of glandular activity or passivity; ameliorative measures have been applied and the action of a gland has been stimulated or retarded (with good or bad effects) through various methods and types of medication. Beyond this little is known, and the best minds in this particular field are conscious of the fact that they are face to face with a terra incognita. This situation will remain as it is until modern medical science recognises that the world of causes (as far as the endocrine glands are concerned) is the etheric body with its seven centres; they will then register the fact that all work in relation to the glands must be shifted away from the seven effects or precipitations of the centres on to the centres themselves.

The healer, therefore, ignores the gland involved and deals directly with the centre which conditions the "point of friction" and controls the area under its influence; this necessarily includes the gland which the centre has created, formed or precipitated and energised.

The concept in the mind of the healer should be, as this law indicates, that an unimpeded channel or a clear passage must be formed along which health-giving life may flow from the "needed centre" in the healer's etheric body to the allied centre in the body of the patient and from thence into the blood stream, via the related gland. Forget not, the truth remains eternally right that the "blood is the life"—even if as yet inexplicable in its implications from the angle of the esotericist as well as from the angle of medical science.

Healers have to learn to work with the life principle, and not with some vague energy which is set in motion by the power of thought or by the potency of love, as is the case presented today by the various healing systems of the world which mankind has evolved. This life principle is contacted and set in motion by the mode of clearing certain etheric channels within the etheric structure which underlies every part of the patient's body. This clearance is not brought about by thinking health or by affirming divinity or by eliminating "error" in the mental approach, but by the much more prosaic method of directing streams of energy, via certain centres, and thus affecting certain glands in the area of the physical body which is diseased and the seat of trouble, pain and distress.

That thought or correct thinking is involved is necessarily true; the healer has to think clearly before he can bring about the desired results, but the energy poured into the patient's vehicle is not mental energy, but one of the seven forms of pranic or life energy. This travels along the line of force or the channel which relates and links all the centres and connects those centres with the glands. Forget not that this constitutes an interlinking and interlocking directorate of the following systems, and that—from the point of view of the esotericist—these systems are symbols of great cosmic processes:

1. The etheric body, as a whole, with its channels and communicating lines of energy which underlie every part

of the human body.

2. The seven related centres, each specifically qualified and each in touch, via the etheric fibres or threads of force, with each and every centre.

3. The nadis, that system of slightly denser etheric channels or tiny threads of force which underlie the entire nervous system; they underlie every type of nerve and every type of nerve plexus.

4. The nervous system itself, which is found extending its radius of influence throughout the entire body of a man.

5. The endocrine or glandular system.

6. The blood stream, the recipient of streams of living energy from the endocrine system, via what are called the hormones.

7. The interrelated sumtotal, which is the divine manifestation of the spiritual man in any incarnation and at any point in evolution.

Therefore, two great streams of energy permeate and animate this entire aggregation of systems: the life stream and the consciousness stream. One works through the nervous system (the consciousness stream) and the other through the blood stream. Both are in fact so closely related and allied that, in action, it is not easy for the ordinary man to differentiate between them.

The healer, however, does not work with the consciousness aspect; he works entirely with the life aspect; the perfect healer (something at present nonexistent) works through the closed and sealed point within the centre (the very heart of the centre). There the point of life is to be found. From this point within the centre, life rays out into the petals of the lotus, and the combination of the life at the centre and the consciousness, inherent in the petals, is the source of the living, breathing, sensitive human being—from the physical angle—and this the healer must recognise.

Behind this livingness and this consciousness is the Being, the spiritual man, the actor, the one who feels (in varying degrees), and the thinker. The simplicity of the above statement is somewhat misleading, as there are other factors and relationships and other energies which must be considered, but it is nevertheless basically true, and upon this truth the healer can act.

It is interesting to point out that the Great Invocation now being distributed in the world is based upon this same fundamental concept of great systems, conditioning humanity as a whole, which can be energised by the inflow of streams of energy, bringing new life and health to the entire body of humanity via the planetary centres of divine livingness and consciousness.

Rule Four which accompanies Law VII is of major importance. This is because of its extreme simplicity, and because, if comprehended and followed, it forms a bridging rule between the subjective and the objective methods of handling disease. The law which we have just considered was also exceedingly simple and direct, and in its implications related to the subjective nature and the objective form. Students should not be deceived by simplicity and by plain, direct statements. There is a tendency to regard esoteric teaching as necessarily abstruse and indirect, requiring always the use of the "esoteric sense" (whatever is meant by that) in order to arrive at understanding. Yet the more advanced the teaching, very frequently the more simply is it expressed. Abstruseness is related to the ignorance of the student—not to the mode of presentation of the teacher. This rule runs as follows:

RULE FOUR

A careful diagnosis of disease, based on the ascertained outer symptoms, will be simplified to this extent—that once the organ involved is known and thus isolated, the centre in the etheric body which is in closest relation to it will be subjected to methods of occult healing, though the ordinary ameliorative, medical or surgical methods will not be withheld.

This rule requires little elucidation, for it is composed of clear, concise instructions. Let us list these instructions:

1. There must be careful diagnosis, based on the ascertained outer symptoms.
2. The organ which is the seat of the trouble must be located. Both these activities concern the dense physical body.
3. The centre in the etheric body closest to the area of the trouble will next receive attention.
4. Methods of occult healing are then employed, directed to the stimulation, or the reverse, of the centre involved.
5. Simultaneously, all outer orthodox methods are employed.

It is on this question of careful diagnosis that most modern so-called healers go astray. They do not know enough about the physical body, about the pathology of disease, about the primary or secondary symptoms, to determine the nature of the difficulty; this is because the usual healer has not had medical training, and at the same time he is not psychically equipped to arrive at a true diagnosis in an occult manner. He therefore falls back on the general assumption that the patient is sick, that the seat of the trouble appears to be in such or such an area of the physical body, that the patient complains of certain pains and aches, and that if the patient can be rendered acquiescent enough, if he can grasp (along with the healer) the fact of his divinity—and who can, my brother?—then if he has faith in the healer, he can assuredly be healed.

The outstanding thing usually to note is the ignorance of both the patient and the healer; the thing to be deplored is the assumption of the healer that, if a healing does follow, it is due entirely to the healing methods followed, whereas the patient would, in all probability, have recovered in any case. The healing may have been hastened by the factor of faith, and faith is simply the focussing of the patient's energy in line with the injunction of the healer, and a consequent "display" of that energy in the diseased area in obedience to the law that "energy follows thought." The "explosion" (if I may use so forcible a word) of the energy of faith on the part of the two people involved—the healer and the patient—occultly and occasionally produces sufficient energy stimulation to bring about a cure *where a cure in any case was inevitable*. It has simply been a hastening process. This is not, however, a true occult healing and no true occult healing methods were employed or involved. Psychologically, the same thing can be seen taking place in the case of a "conversion," as the Fundamentalist School of Christianity calls it. The faith of the person and the faith of the evangelist, plus the faith of the audience (where there is one) bring about a psychological healing along the line of resolving cleavages, or produce an at-one-ment, even if only of a temporary nature.

It must be increasingly borne in mind that there is nothing in the created world but energy in motion, and that every thought directs some aspects of that energy, though always within the sphere of influence of some greater thinking, directing energy. The healer's faith and the patient's faith are both examples of energy in motion, and at present usually the only energies employed in every case

of healing. Orthodox medicine also works with the same
energies, supplementing its orthodox methods with the patient's faith in the physician and in his scientific knowledge.

I am not here going to enlarge further on the injunction
to use medical and surgical methods whenever possible. I
have touched upon this subject several times in the course
of this teaching upon healing. It is essential that people
should realise that the ascertained knowledges of medicine
and surgery are just as much an expression of divine experience and understanding as the hopeful, assertive, yet fum-
bling methods of so-called divine healing—if not more so at
present. Though much of the orthodox methods remain
experimental, they are less so than the methods of the modern healers, and much of their scientific knowledge is proven
and real. It should be used, and confidence can be expressed
in it. The perfect healing combination is that of the medical
man and the spiritual healer, each working in his own field,
and both having faith in each other; this is not now the
case. There is no need to call in divine aid to set bones
which the surgeon is well equipped to do, or to clear up
infection which the physician knows well how to handle.
The healer can help and can hasten the healing process, but
the orthodox physician can also hasten the work of the
healer. Both groups need each other.

I realise that what I have said here will please neither
the spiritual healer nor the orthodox medical man. It is
time, however, that they learn to appreciate each other
and to work in cooperation. In the last analysis, the spiritual healer and the new modes of mental healing have
relatively little to contribute in comparison with the work
and the knowledge of the member of the orthodox profession. The debt of the world to its doctors and surgeons
is very great. The debt to healers is decidedly not so great;
they oft also poison the channel by bitterness and constant

criticism of the physician and of orthodox medicine. Surety of knowledge and experience prevents a similar attitude in the orthodox group, plus the realisation that even the spiritual healer will call in the doctor in times of emergency.

The law and the rule now to be considered will carry us into realms of real abstraction; it will not be easy for you to understand much of what I may say. This Law VIII takes us back to the very source of all phenomena as far as the human being is concerned—the will of the immortal soul to incarnate on earth or to withdraw from incarnation. It involves also the consideration of the factor of the Will in producing disease as the direct means of bringing about that withdrawal. So little is as yet understood anent the Will that it is particularly hard to explain.

LAW VIII

Disease and death are the result of two active forces. One is the will of the soul, which says to its instrument: "I draw the essence back." The other is the magnetic power of the planetary life, which says to the life within the atomic structure: "The hour of reabsorption has arrived. Return to me." Thus, under cyclic law, do all forms act.

Two aspects in the nature of the divine Will are called into play where disease and death are concerned: one is the will of the soul to bring an incarnation to an end; another is the will of the spirit of the earth (the basic elemental force) to draw back into itself the released and temporarily isolated substance of which the soul had availed itself during the cycle of incarnation.

The factor of time, the factor of the interplay between the point of will which is that of the soul, and the diffused ever present will of the elemental spirit of substance are involved, plus their cyclic relation. These we shall attempt to consider.

What I have here to say is of major importance and will throw a new and strange light upon the entire subject of disease. I will deal, first of all, with the second half of the law, which refers to the "magnetic power of the planetary life," which says to the life within the atomic structure: "The hour of reabsorption has arrived. Return to me."

To understand the reference, I would remind you that a human being is a spiritual entity, occupying or informing (which is the occult word I prefer) a dense physical vehicle. This dense physical body is part of the general structure of the entire planet, composed of living atoms which are under the control of, and are part of the life of the planetary entity. This dense physical vehicle is released into a temporary and directed freedom by the will of the informing soul, but remains at the same time an intrinsic part of the sumtotal of all atomic substance. This physical vehicle—having its own life and having a measure of intelligence which we call its instinctual nature—is called by esotericists the physical elemental. During incarnated life, it is the coherent force or agency by means of which the physical body preserves its particular form, under the impact of etheric livingness; this affects all the living atoms and brings them into relation with each other. The physical body is the great symbol (within the one Life) of the many of which it is constituted; it is the demonstrated fact of innate coherency, of unity, of synthesis and of relationship. Physical or planetary prana (the lowest form of pranic energy) is the life of the sumtotal of the atoms (of which all outer forms are composed) as they are brought into relation to the separated atomic structure of the dense physical body of an individual informing soul in any kingdom of nature—particularly, from our point of study, the human kingdom.

What is true in this connection of the individual or of

man, the microcosm, is true also of the planet, which—
like man—is a coherent whole. This wholeness is due to
the relation of two aspects of life: the life of the planetary
Logos and the life of the spirit of the earth, which is the
life of the sumtotal of all the atoms which compose all
forms. To this sumtotal of living substance, of elemental
life, man's dense physical body conforms and is therefore
the symbol. These two lives, functioning microcosmically
and also macrocosmically, create that living pranic energy
which circulates throughout the etheric bodies of all forms,
which produces coherency or a synthetic holding-together
and which can be discerned when the densest aspect of the
etheric body is seen, creating thus the health aura in plants,
trees, sea life, animals and man. Other energies and potencies circulate through and condition the etheric vehicle, but
I refer here only to the lowest physical aspect. This is indicative of the life of the elemental of our planet, the spirit
of the earth—a divine life, making its own progress upon
the involutionary arc of manifestation.

This spirit of the earth preserves its hold upon the
atomic structures of which all forms are made, including
the physical body of man; it gathers them together again
eventually and reabsorbs those elements of its life which
were temporarily isolated from it during any incarnated
experience of any soul in any of the kingdoms in nature.
These atoms, it must be noted, are imbued or conditioned
by two factors for which the spirit of the earth is solely
responsible:

1. The factor of the Karma of the life of the elemental
   of the planet. This is an involutionary, precipitating
   karma, entirely different to that of the planetary Logos,
   Who is a spiritual Life upon the evolutionary arc. This
   involutionary karma, therefore, conditions the life ex-

perience from the purely *physical* angle of all forms composed of atomic substance.

2. The factor of limitation. Apart from the karma, resulting in physical events, affecting all physical forms composed of this elemental essence, the physical vehicles of all lives in all the kingdoms of nature are also conditioned by the point in time of the cyclic influence of the planetary spirit and by its point in evolution. This involutionary spirit has not yet attained a point of perfection, but is progressing towards a specific goal which will be attained when the evolutionary arc of experience is reached. This lies very far ahead. Our planetary Logos, that great divine Life in Whom we live and move and have our being, is one of the "imperfect Gods" as yet, from the point of view of the goal set before all planetary Logoi. His body of expression, our planet, the Earth, is not yet a sacred planet. The spirit of the earth is yet very far from even the relative perfection of which a conscious human being is aware.

The point in evolution of the spirit of the earth affects every atom in his body—the body of an involutionary entity. The result of this imperfection, which is not that of the planetary Logos but that of the spirit of the earth, shows itself in the presence of disease in all forms in all the kingdoms of nature. Minerals are subject to disease and decay; even the "fatigue" of metals is a registered scientific fact; plants and animals all react to disease within the structure of their forms, and disease and death are inherent in the atom of which all organisms are composed. Man is not exempt. Disease, therefore, is not brought about by wrong thinking, as oft I have told you, or by any failure to affirm divinity. It is inherent in the form nature itself, being indicative of the imperfections from which the spirit of the earth suffers; it is the mode par excellence whereby this elemental life retains integrity and the capacity to reabsorb that which is his but which has been brought under other direction by the attractive potency of the life of that which informs every other kingdom in nature during a cycle of incarnation.

This will give you surely a new idea anent disease. Man creates, under soul impulsion and the will to incarnate, a form which is composed of substance already subjected to conditioning; it is already impregnated with the life impulses of the spirit of the earth. Man, in so doing, assumes responsibility for that elemental form but—at the same time—limits himself definitely by the nature of the atoms of which that form is composed. The atomic substance through which the spirit of the earth expresses itself has in it ever the "seeds of return," permitting a reabsorption. This substance is also composed of all grades and qualities of matter, from the very coarsest up to the very finest, as for instance the quality of the substance which makes the appearance of the Buddha or of the Christ possible. The Lord of the Earth, the planetary Logos, cannot find substance animated by the spirit of the earth of a quality and nature pure enough; He cannot, therefore, materialise or make an appearance, as can the Buddha or the Christ. Few of Those Who form the Council Chamber at Shamballa can find the needed or adequate substance by means of which to appear; They cannot take a dense physical body, and have to be content with an etheric vehicle.

There are therefore three types of life, affecting the dense appearance of a human being during his restricted manifestation or incarnation:

1. The life of the spiritual man himself, transmitted from the Monad, via the soul for the greater part of manifested existence.

2. The life of that sumtotal which is the elemental life of the fourth kingdom in nature, the human; this life is still an aspect (under the Law of Isolation or Limitation) of the life of the spirit of the earth.

3. The sumtotal of the life which is innate in atomic substance itself—the substance out of which all forms are made. This is the life of the spirit of the earth.

We are not here referring to the soul in an atom or the soul of any form, great or small; we are referring exclusively to the life or first aspect. This expresses itself as the will-to-be; it is only active, though ever present, during form life or the phase of created manifestation. It is here that the Will factor makes its appearance and the relation between will, form and incarnation is to be found.

One of the factors governing incarnation is the presence of what is called the will-to-live; when that is to be found, and when it is powerful in man, he is strongly anchored upon the physical plane; when that is not strongly present or is withdrawn, the man dies. Life in the physical body is preserved, technically and occultly, under the impulse of the powerful will-to-be of the incarnated spiritual man upon the magnetic power of the planetary life, inherent in every atom of the form nature; by means of these atoms— isolated and held by the Law of Attraction in form—he has come into being upon the physical plane. This magnetic power is the expression of the will (if such a word can be applied to the sense of coherency which distinguishes the spirit of the earth) of the planetary entity. It is a projection of his peculiar state of consciousness into an isolated form, created, occupied and indwelt by a soul, by a living man.

I have several times used the expression "isolated form," for it is this peculiar aspect of isolation which conditions the physical body of a man (or of any living form, for that matter), rendering it detached, coherent and temporarily living its own life in response to the imposition of the livingness of the incarnating soul. Temporarily, the united power of the segregated and isolated atoms—particularly the planetary structure of the spirit of the earth—is in abeyance as regards individual reaction to the planetary life. Only the coherent, magnetic qualities persist in any form of activity and in conjunction with the will-to-live of the spiritual man or of any ensouling entity. This creates a coherent form, held together by two aspects of livingness: that of the spirit of the earth and that of the spiritual man. Therefore—to use words in an effort to arrive at understanding—two aspects of life and two forms of will or purpose are brought together. The higher is evolutionary; the lower is involutionary in nature. It is this which creates the conflict. One type of energy is evolutionary and the other is involutionary. It is these conflicting forces which present the problem of dualism—a dualism of the higher and the lower at many differing and varying stages. The final phase of the conflict is fought out, or rather wrought out, when the Dweller on the Threshold and the Angel of the Presence face each other. It is in that consummating event that the pull or conflict between the involutionary life and the evolutionary life, between the inchoate, magnetic will of the elemental forces (inherent in the atoms of which all three bodies of the personality are made) and the will of the spiritual man, on the verge of liberation from the magnetic control of substance, is brought to the issue.

The spirit of the earth has its correspondence in the created expression of the spiritual man; it is to be found in the existence of the personality elemental; this personality elemental can be and frequently is an inchoate force, swayed entirely by desire, and no true personality integration is present; it can, however, be a highly organised and potent factor, producing what is called a high grade personality and an effective instrument for the spiritual man in the three worlds of his evolution. This is followed later by the conflicts upon the Path of Discipleship and the Path of Initiation. Then the livingness of the spiritual man, and his will to manifest divinely, dominate to such an extent that the death of the personality is brought about; this culminates at the time of the third initiation. At that experience the monadic will comes in with such dynamic potency that the will of the elemental lives of the threefold personality is completely negated.

But (to return to our theme) the atomic substance, impregnated with the life of the spirit of the earth and with the driving force of its inchoate will, demonstrates as magnetic power and is constantly in conflict, within the body of manifestation of the informing soul, with the life of the soul. This conflict or friction is the main cause of what you call disease.

Disease is inharmony; it is the fault of fire by friction; diseased areas are areas of friction wherein the atomic substance is temporarily asserting its own type of livingness and responding (sometimes to the point of death) to the magnetic pull of the will of the spirit of the earth. If that pull proves adequately strong, the friction within the atomic structure, localised in the area of some etheric centre, will be of such a nature that the quality of the disease increases, the life of the spiritual man is slowly or rapidly withdrawn; the desire for existence, the spiritual will-to-be is not then as strong as the will to be reabsorbed—the will of the atoms constituting the physical body; the man, therefore, dies, in the usual sense of the term.

The planetary life says, "The hour of reabsorption has arrived. Return to me." The urge to return is at present the dominant note in the substance of the bodies of humanity; it is responsible for the universal ill health which distinguishes the mass of human beings; this tendency has been dominant for centuries; the attitude is, however, slowly changing, and the time will eventually come when the atoms of the bodies, or the elemental forces, will be sent back along the path of reabsorption only at the will of the spiritual man and in response to his express command, and not in response to the magnetic power of the spirit of the earth.

We have seen—as we considered the Laws and Rules to date—that fundamentally, disease and death are due to the withdrawal of solar life (the energy of the soul, sometimes called solar fire) either from some particular area of the physical body or from the entire body. This fact should remind students of the need to distinguish between the force or life of the "lunar lords," inherent in every atom of which all organs and forms are made, and the energy of the soul which permeates the entire body as an integrating factor. Speaking symbolically, therefore, there are times in which the life of these lunar lords are so dominant that the life of the soul is overpowered in some particular area, and the consequent withdrawal of the solar life produces disease; or—putting it another way—the friction which ensues when the lunar lords are not compliant produces disease. Yet death is not indicative of a full victory of the lunar lords, but rather that under the plan of the soul, and because the life cycle is complete, the energy of the soul is entirely withdrawn, leaving the lunar lords alone. At times (because it is also in the planning of the soul) the lunar lords temporarily are the victors, though death does not follow; convalescence is significant of the gradual re-entry of soul energy and its subsequent control of the lunar lords. This aspect of soul energy is not that of those energies which represent and lead to the expression of soul quality. It is *life* energy, coming from the Monad which passes through the soul as a channel and medium of contact; its direct channel is, needless to say, the sutratma. It is not the antahkarana, or the creative thread or the thread of consciousness. These are frequently rendered inactive when acute disease is present, and the life aspect is weakening or rapidly or slowly withdrawing itself.

You can see, therefore, why it is that those who have succeeded in building the antahkarana, the rainbow bridge between the Monad and the personality, have established a contact (nonexistent in the average man) between the Monad, the Source of Life, and the personality—the expression of that Life in objectivity. The Monad then, and not the soul, controls the cycles of outward expression, and the initiate then dies at will and according to plan or the necessities of the work. This, of course, refers only to initiates of high degree. I felt these points to be interesting and also useful for you to know. Another point, growing out of all the above, indicates the all-inclusiveness of the divine Life, for the lunar lords are aspects of that Life as much as is the energy of the soul.

It is therefore of prime importance that cremation should be encouraged, and not the present method of burial. Cremation returns the life of the lunar lords more rapidly to the central reservoir of life than any other method, for "our God is a consuming Fire" and all fires have affinity with the central Fire.

Let us now study the rule which goes with Law VIII.

Rule Five

The healer must seek to link his soul, his heart, his brain and his hands. Thus can he pour the vital healing force upon the patient. *This is magnetic work.* It cures disease or increases the evil state, according to the knowledge of the healer.

The healer must seek to link his soul, his brain, his heart and auric emanation. Thus can his presence feed the soul life of the patient. *This is the work of radiation.* The hands are needed not. The soul displays its power. The patient's soul responds through the response of his aura to the radiation of the healer's aura, flooded with soul energy.

From just casually reading this Rule it will be obvious that its significance is vital to all successful healing work. It sums up the two modes of healing, based on two capacities of the healer, founded on two groups of related aspects in the healer's personality, and indicating two different points in evolution on the part of the healer. An analysis of this Rule will convey a still greater idea of its importance, for it indicates not only the lines along which the healer must train himself, but also certain interior relationships must be present, and these are dependent upon the point in evolution of the healer. Again, in one case the patient's physical body is the objective of the healing art, whilst in the other it is the patient's soul which feels the effect of the healing energy. In the first case the healer works with the prana or vital planetary fluid, and in the other with soul energy.

We can therefore, on the basis of this Rule, divide healers into two groups: one group wielding the vital etheric fluid which we call prana, and the second group working on a much higher level and employing an ability to draw down soul energy into the body (or rather, the personality) of the healer and—from the required centre—to send it forth again into the appropriate centre in the patient's body, but this time through the stimulation of the patient's aura controlled by the patient's soul. The two types of energy are of a widely different quality, for one is purely of the personality and is sometimes called *animal mag-*

netism, and the other is of the soul, involving a type of work called radiation.

It should be noted here that in reality we have three types of healers:

1. The healer who works purely through magnetism and brings to bear the healing vital life of the planetary etheric body as it uses his individual etheric body as a channel whereby prana can pour into the vital body of the patient.

2. The healer who works on a higher level, and necessarily therefore with a higher type of patient; he uses the energy of his own overshadowing soul in conjunction with the energy of his individualised soul, and thereby radiates it forth into the soul of the patient, via both of the auras.

3. The healer who can employ both techniques and whose range of contacts and possibilities of usefulness are far greater than the other two. He can employ with equal facility the energy of the soul or the vital pranic force, and has therefore mastered the two techniques which govern the two sets of related faculties. This class of healer is much rarer than the other two.

At present, in the modern world, there is no true system of spiritual healing taught to would-be healers. There is instead an effort to base the whole procedure, plus the techniques employed, on purely mental levels, on systems of affirmation, modes of prayer, stimulation of the patient's will-to-live, and occasionally the use of magnetic or hypnotic passes in relation to the etheric body; various forms of applied subjective thinking are taught, but no true formula for an intelligent and expected cure, only the vague faith of the healer and of the patient and a blind autosuggestion as to what the recognition and affirmation of divinity ought to produce.

True healing, however, is based on certain broad principles which require definite mental acceptance; the methods, nevertheless, which are employed are as definitely physical, using the etheric currents and the centres in the etheric body, as the laying on of hands and the establishing of relations which affect the physical body, and which are not at all of a mental nature and do not require to be appropriated and held by the mind of the patient. The etheric body is physical in nature, and this must not be forgotten and needs frequent reiteration. As we have earlier seen, there are three basic principles, affirmed and believed by the healer who is greatly aided if the patient accepts them also:

1. There is no reality in separation. The planetary etheric body is a whole, unbroken and continuous; of this etheric body, those of the healer and the patient are integral, intrinsic parts.
2. There is an unbreakable (though probably unrealised) relationship between the healer's etheric body and that of the patient, which can be used when once contact has been induced, for a definite circulation of energies.
3. The channels of relationship can be conductors of many different types of energy, transmitted by the healer to the patient. In this fact lies both hope and danger.

There are other principles, but in connection with this Rule these three are essential and explanatory. Much consequently depends upon the knowledge, the understanding and the perceptiveness of the healer. The danger in both radiatory healing and magnetic healing consists in the fact that where there is no *trained* healer, the amount of prana brought in or of soul energy distributed may produce death, as well as life. A healer may charge his etheric body with so much prana and project it so violently into the etheric body of the patient that he may do far more harm than good. Only long practice can teach the healer the right amount of energy to emit, and to learn this he would do well to use as little energy as possible, gradually increasing the quantity as he attains skill in action. Speaking in a broad and general way, and with the reminder that there are many exceptions to all rules, the magnetic healer will work with less developed people than will the spiritual healer using soul radiation, and he will deal primarily with those diseases which are found below the diaphragm. Spiritual healers work primarily with the upper part of the body, through the centres above the diaphragm and with the head centre, thereby controlling all centres in the entire body. Their work is most delicate and subtle and involves far greater risks. The true healer who is an initiate employs both methods with equal facility.

It is interesting, though not particularly useful to you, to point out that there are two other classes of healers who are sometimes found. They work quite differently to either of the methods mentioned above. They are:

1. Certain healers—few and far between—who have set up a relation with the spirit of the earth, the Ruler of all the lunar lords. Under certain formulas and given a certain amount of practice, these healers can invoke his aid and—in fact—command it. I do not advise any interested student to ponder overmuch along this line or to endeavour to set up a contact or to invoke his aid. Only initiates of high degree can deal safely with this powerful involutionary Elemental; they do so

only in connection with epidemics and international catastrophes such as the world war, in which thousands and thousands of bodies were involved. An individual not highly developed who endeavoured to establish rapport would probably only succeed in stimulating the lunar lords of his own little system to such an extent that his lower nature would be unduly energised— sometimes even to the point of death.

2. Other healers, not as few as in the above group but relatively few, work in cooperation with a healing deva. Such devas exist and have the power of bestowing life. They are to the involutionary lunar lords what the great Lives at Shamballa are to us. They are not a menace to humanity but are not readily reached, except at a certain stage upon the Path where, symbolically speaking, a door or point of contact exists between the two evolutions, for the devas are not upon the involutionary arc. Relations are established through affinity, but this can be brought about only by the deva, and not by the healer. If the healer is very advanced, his Master may instruct one of the serving devas to aid him. Only healers of great purity and of completely selfless motive can attract these angels, and when they do, the potency of their healing is much greater; they make fewer mistakes. They do not, for instance, attempt to heal patients for whom there is no healing possibility. The Angel of Death (and this time I am not speaking symbolically but am referring to an existing deva) will not permit a healing deva to collaborate; they are only permitted to approach where healing is indicated.

We might now take the sentences in this Rule and study their meaning, as there are more significances in them than appear upon the surface. The first sentence in each

paragraph of this Rule starts with an important injunction
to the healer:

> The healer must seek to link his soul, his heart, his
> brain and his hands. Thus can he pour the vital healing
> force upon the patient.

This is the technique of the lowest type of true spiritual
healer, and for this reason two of the aspects of the dense
physical body are included: the brain and the hands. The
healer works, therefore, through a triangle and two lines
of energy. The situation can be depicted in the following
diagram:

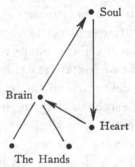

The triangle is completed when the healing work is done
and the energy is withdrawn from the hands to the brain
again and from thence returned by an act of the will to the
soul. When the healer (through practiced alignment) has
linked up with his soul, he then draws the soul energy down
into his heart centre, from whence he transfers it to the
brain, where it is definitely focussed. Using the ajna centre
as a distributing centre, he then uses his hands as the agency
through which the directed energy can reach that area in
the patient's body where the seat of the trouble is to be
found. He passes the energy into the patient's approximate
centre which governs the distressed area, from which it

permeates the surrounding part of the body, penetrating both to the centre of the trouble and to the limits of the distressed area.

There are two ways in which he uses his hands, and two methods which he employs:

1. *The laying on of hands.* This method is employed when the diseased area is strictly localised. The hands are laid on the centre in spine or head which may govern that area—the right hand being laid upon the spinal centre and the left hand on the part of the body immediately in front of the special area and over the part of the abdomen, chest or head in which the patient complains of distress. They are held in this position as long as the healer can hold the triangle of soul, heart and brain clearly in consciousness.

2. *The use of the hands in action.* Here the healer, having ascertained the difficulty and then located the needed centre up the spine or in the head, creates a circulation of energy (through the action of his hands) through the centre in the patient's body controlling the distressed area, and thence outwards through that area towards himself. He uses the right hand first, holding it momentarily over the diseased organ or area and slowly withdraws it towards himself; he follows this rapidly with the left hand which works in the same manner. Both hands, you will note, are now being used *positively*. No part or aspect of the healer's body or bodies is ever permitted to be negative, and the fiction that the right hand is positive and the left hand is negative will have to be discarded. If one hand was negative, the healer would be liable to absorb into himself those diseased atoms which, when successful, he draws out of the area of distress. These do not respond to the action of his

hands through the medium of the centre in the patient's body nearest to the seat of trouble, but are drawn out through the area which has responded to the disease.

In the first case, through the laying on of hands, of silent hands, of quiet hands, the energy flow is between the two hands, back and forth within the diseased area; the spinal centre is used all the time, and the activity set up, when successful, burns up and absorbs the forces causing the trouble without penetrating the body of the healer. In the second case, the forces are withdrawn by the action of the energy passing through the hands, applied one after the other in a regular time rhythm. They pass through the hands, but are unable to focus themselves there, owing to the concentration of the healing energies within the hands.

Healers on the second, third and fifth rays use more generally the mode of laying on of hands or *magnetic healing*. This term applies to the direct act of laying on of hands upon the patient's physical body, and not to the action of the hands in the second method, when the hands are immersed in the etheric body of the patient and are definitely working in etheric matter. Healers on the first, fourth and seventh rays use the mode of "hand immersion," as it is sometimes called. The sixth ray healer is rare and is successful only when highly developed; he will then use both methods interchangeably.

All spiritually advanced healers use both hands. Healers are, however, advised first of all to ascertain their ray, and then to perfect themselves in the type or mode of healing best suited to that ray; then, when adequately efficient and able to use facility and skill, they can add the mode of healing which is not so adaptable to their ray type. People on the sixth ray are advised to abstain from the healing art until they have arrived (consciously) at the initiate stage. When both modes of magnetic healing have been mastered, the healer may employ both alternately in the act of healing, or he may use the mode of magnetic passes first so as to set up a changed activity in the diseased area, and then finally use a definite laying on of hands.

At the close of the healing period the "sealing of the triangle" takes place. The energy, hitherto passing into the hands through the ajna centre from the brain, is withdrawn into the ajna centre, and from thence directed—by an act of the will—to the soul. The healing force is literally "turned off" and redirected; it is no longer available.

During the entire period of healing the healer says nothing. He is making no affirmation and uses no healing mantram. The process outlined here is that of the effect of energy or soul potency playing upon force. This is a point to be emphasised. The task of the healer is to preserve an attitude of intense concentration upon the triangle "existing in living lines of energy" (as it has been called) within his own fourfold aura—health aura, etheric body, astral body and mental body. This he must preserve intact and stable for the entire period of healing. Soul-heart-brain must be linked in such a "lighted" manner that a true clairvoyant would see a brilliant triangle in the healer's aura; the highest point of the triangle (that of the soul) he might fail to see unless he were himself highly developed, but he could not fail to see the signs of it in the inflowing energy to the heart and from the heart to the brain. The work done is *silent* work. There is therefore no loss of power at any time, as there always is through the spoken word or affirmation. It is not possible to hold the triangle geometrically correct and magnetically polarised if there is any sound made by the healer. This presupposes an advanced stage of alignment and of concentration and will indicate to you some of the lines along which the healer's training should go.

This mode of healing "cures disease or increases the evil state, according to the knowledge of the healer." In some respects (though this is a stage of healing which is not the highest) it is nevertheless the one most responsible because, in the case of radiatory healing, the soul of the patient is working in cooperation with the healer and it is the soul then which has the major responsibility. In magnetic healing, the healer needs to cooperate closely with the patient's physician or surgeon dealing with the case; he will supply the technical knowledge, and thus prevent the healer from making mistakes.

Where death is definitely indicated and the "signs of death" are noted by both the doctor and the healer, the healer has not need to stop his work. By continuing it, he may increase the evil condition, but will nevertheless be aiding the patient by hastening normally the act of dying. The old proverb is basically not true in all cases, that "where there is life there is hope." Life can and often is prolonged after the will of the soul is towards the withdrawal of the soul life; the life of the atoms of the lunar lords can be fostered for a long time, and this greatly distresses the spiritual man who is aware of the process and the intent of his soul. What is kept alive is the physical body, but the interest of the true man is no longer focussed there.

There inevitably comes a point, for instance in the case of malignant disease, where the physician knows that it simply is a question of time, and the spiritual healer can learn to recognise the same signs. Then, instead of the present silence on the part of both healer and doctor, where the patient is concerned, this remaining time will be employed (if the patient's faculties permit) with due preparation for the "beneficent and happy withdrawal" of the soul; the patient's family and friends will share in the preparation. In the early stages of the new world religion, this attitude towards death will be inculcated. An entirely new concept of death, with the emphasis upon conscious withdrawal, will be taught, and funeral services, or rather the crematory services, will be joyous events because their emphasis will be upon release and return.

The magnetic work, however, will cure if the patient's destiny indicates it, if the soul intends to prolong the life cycle unexpectedly in order to fulfill some duty, or if the patient is very far advanced spiritually and the Hierarchy requires his services for a longer term.

Let us now consider radiatory healing.

We shall now be dealing with a very different situation than that of the one we have just been considering. In radiatory healing, the patient (either consciously or unconsciously) is working with the healer and is cooperating with him. The basic premise in radiatory healing is that the patient is a person who has, at least to some degree, established rapport with his soul. This having been brought about, the healer knows that a channel of contact can be counted upon and that the *soul interest* can be evoked in its representative, the man upon the physical plane. He knows also that success in radiatory healing is dependent, to a great extent, upon the ability of his own soul to establish a firm relation with the soul of the patient. When the patient is conscious and able to cooperate, the work is greatly helped; according to the healer's capacity to avail himself of alignment and recognised contact will be the quality of the aid he will be able to give to the one who needs his assistance. When the patient is unconscious, even that provides no real hindrance, provided the healer can bring his soul and the patient's soul into relationship; in fact in some cases the unconsciousness of the patient can be a help, for too earnest, emphatic and impatient help can offset the work—quiet, silent and controlled—by the healer.

Once, however, the rapport is established, the work of the healer simply consists in holding the relationship steady; no interference must be permitted in the work being done by the patient's soul, set in motion by the aid of the healer. The Master Jesus on the Cross could not respond to any saving process (even had He desired to do so) because the soul body—as is always the case at the fourth initiation—was destroyed; there was nothing to respond to the evocative power of an outside person, interested or loving. As an adept and as one in whom monadic consciousness was firmly established, the powers then available to Jesus could not be used in the saving of His physical body. At the same time, it must be remembered that He would have no desire to save it, because He now possessed the power (demonstrated later in the Gospel story) to create a body at will in order to meet His needs. The subtle and subjective sin of the apostles was that they were not interested in evoking the living activity of the Master on His Own behalf (even though He would never do so; this they did not know), but were entirely preoccupied with their own grief. The evocation, had they attempted it, would have been useless, but the good that might have come to them and the revelation they might have received as to the deathlessness of the soul would have greatly illuminated them and might have produced a Christianity built around a living Christ and not around a dead Christ.

In radiatory healing, we are told that "the healer must seek to link his soul, his brain, his heart and auric emanation." You will note two points connected with this particular instruction which differ from that given in the case of magnetic healing:

1. The order of the triangle of energies created is different.
2. The means of contact are subtle and not tangible.

The energy released follows a direct line of contact with the brain, and the healer starts with a closed triangle and not with an open one, as in the case of magnetic healing. The triangle created is a simple one, and there is no physical contact and outlet as in magnetic healing:

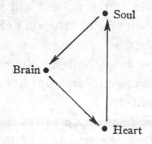

The brain of the healer is involved, but there is no physical contact of any kind with the patient. The result is a constant circulation of force from the soul back again to the soul. This causes necessarily an augmenting and an energising of the threefold personality of the healer, and therefore of his auric emanation. His aura would be seen by a clairvoyant as greatly extended, in rapid motion, and energised by light from his own soul, but with all its radiation turned in the direction of the patient. By this means the healing force of the healer stimulates all the three personality vehicles of the patient; the patient's soul is aided in the work it has to do. The healer will consequently find it necessary to stand at that side of the patient in which the trouble is located, so that the radiation of his aura can more easily penetrate. This is the easiest way, but not the most effective. Where the patient's vitality is strong, he should lie on the side, and the healer should stand behind the patient so that the energy pouring through, which the healer may be using and which is potently energising his aura with soul energy, may affect the patient's aura and thus facilitate the entry of the healing radiation, which the healer is contributing, to the centre or centres needed. Where the patient is very highly developed, the healer should stand at the patient's head. His personal effect is not then so great, but that does not matter because it is not needed; the soul of the patient will be adequate to the task. All that is needed is that the aura of the healer, blending with that of the patient, creates a zone of quiet rhythmic activity around the head centre. No physical contact by the hands is now required, and the healer must on no account touch the patient.

The situation is summed up for us in the words: "Thus can his presence feed the soul life of the patient. This is the work of radiation. The hands are needed not."

Speaking symbolically, it is almost as if a great vortex of power were set up by the contact between the two auras and by their high vibration; by its means the soul of the patient can work more easily. An initiate, if present, would see a golden stream of energy pouring straight down through the energised bodies of the patient's personality into the centre nearest to the area of trouble. Approach is made via the head centre directly to the point of difficulty, and towards this point the aura of the healer is also directed. The mental attitude of the patient is strengthened and clarified by the mental emanation of the healer's aura; his emotional reaction, often very powerful, is equally aided to attain dispassion and quiet, and the etheric and health auras have a definite effect upon the corresponding aspects of the patient's aura.

Radiatory healing is brought about by the mingling of the two auras, both of them responsive to soul contact; the soul aspect of both persons (under control of the soul) is then directed towards some area of the patient's physical body. This produces a tremendous effect upon the diseased area, and the centre in that same locality becomes exceedingly energised. The work of the healer during this process is one of intense quiescence. Having made his contact, he simply waits and has nothing more to do but to hold his soul alignment steady and permit nothing to disturb his personality vehicles. His task was accomplished when he made his own soul contact and then reached out and contacted the patient's soul. This he could do because he knows all souls are one; eventually the art of healing will be one of the demonstrating factors in proving the unity of all souls.

This rule, therefore, concludes with the words: "The patient's soul responds through the response of his aura to the radiation of the healer's aura, flooded with soul energy." It is consequently a question of the soul energy of both parties meeting on all three levels of human awareness. The expression "the soul" is here in the singular because unity (if only for a moment) has been reached. The soul of the patient recognises this unity by the "occult quickening" of his own aura and by its responsiveness to the entering radiations from the healer's aura. This flooding with soul energy through the medium of related auras is, all of it, directed as one unified effort towards the area of disease in the patient's body. You can see, therefore, that—consciously or unconsciously—the work can go forward and produce either healing or that "quickening of atoms which leads by soul direction unto release," as the *Old Commentary* calls the act of dying.

When it becomes evident that it is the patient's destiny to die, the technique of the healer alters somewhat. He then takes his place at the patient's head, and from that point deflects all his own radiations to the seat of the disease, causing necessarily a great acceleration of vibratory activity. The patient, in the meantime, consciously through brain recognition or unconsciously under soul direction, begins the process of withdrawing all consciousness from the body. This is why so many people are in a coma prior to death. When this act of the withdrawal of consciousness has been started, the work of the healer ends. He "shuts off" his soul contact and reassumes control of his aura as a medium of his own spiritual expression; it becomes no longer an instrument for healing by radiatory activity, and leaves the patient alone automatically to complete the withdrawal of the consciousness thread and the life thread, from the head and heart centres.

This is a broad and general outline of the processes followed in magnetic and radiatory healing. I have here given you the skeleton structure of the idea, but not the details; more can be inferred and given when we study the seven methods of healing with their ray implications.

This teaching has been given in such a manner that the student will have to hunt through its pages and gather together the facts needed, and thus formulate the first stage of the procedure of spiritual healing; unless he is himself a spiritual healer and ready to read between the lines and to distinguish between symbolism and fact, he will be misled and his work rendered useless. This is intended; for the healing art—when perfectly applied under correct formulas —can be dangerous. It must be remembered that although energy is thought, it is also, from a higher point of view, fire. The entire technique, procedure, and formulas will have to be discovered, subjected to experiment and the results noted before the true spiritual healing can take place;

by the time this investigation has been completed, it will be a safer matter than it is today.

In the meantime, much good can be accomplished and a great deal learnt if those interested read, study, meditate, carefully experiment, and thus gradually build up this much needed science as a co-partner in the medical science of modern times.

Let us now consider Law IX.

In Law IX and Rule Six we shall be dealing with such basic fundamentals that our problem will be to formulate the teaching in such a concise manner that vast themes may be briefly handled, and at the same time appear clear and simple. This law is in reality a definition of the Law of Evolution, but given from the spiritual angle. The Law of Evolution—as commonly understood—concerns the evolution of the form aspect as it is gradually fitted to be an exponent or an expression of soul energy, and later of monadic energy.

This law, which might be termed the Law of Perfection, deals with the interior energies which are responsible for the working of the Law of Evolution. It is the higher aspect or the determining cause of the lower; the laws subsidiary to the Law of Perfection are loosely called (by the neophyte) the spiritual laws, but of these he knows little and unifies them all in his mind under the general idea that they are an expression of the love aspect of Deity. That is essentially true, from the quality angle, if it is recognised at the same time that the love aspect is essentially pure reason and not an emotional sentiment expressing itself through kind actions.

The rule which accompanies this law deals with the relation of love and will, and is consequently of high importance to the initiate. I would remind you here that the only true healer is the initiate, and therefore the last two laws (Law IX and Law X) can only be truly understood by the initiated disciple. They are, however, profoundly interesting intellectually to the beginner, the enquirer and the aspirant, because (theoretically at least) he can grasp some of their meaning, though he is as yet quite incapable of "keeping the law"—spiritually understood.

LAW IX

Perfection calls imperfection to the surface. Good drives evil from the form of man in time and space. The method used by the Perfect One and that employed by Good, is harmlessness. This is not negativity, but perfect poise, a completed point of view, and divine understanding.

This law is profoundly simple and means exactly what it says. It can be interpreted in two ways:

1. It concerns the spiritual development of man through the medium of form, and the mode or law whereby the latent hold of matter—impregnated by selfishness and by all that is recognised as evil—is removed, and man stands free.

2. It can also be interpreted in terms of healer and patient. Oft the effect of the activity and knowledge of the true healer is to bring to the surface (in an acute form) the evil (disease) within the form. The result of this can either be the elimination of the disease and the securing of health, or the form will succumb to the increase of the difficulty and the probability is that the patient will die. It is therefore fortunate that the average healer is so futile that such a dire possibility is not present!

The method employed under the Law of Perfection is called "perfect harmlessness," and that was ever the method used by the Christ, the Perfect One. It is not the harmlessness enjoined so often by me as I speak to aspirants, but a harmlessness imposed by the spiritual man and by his natural destiny. It is an ignoring of the effect or the result upon the form nature. Frequently I have told you that the Hierarchy works only with the spiritual nature or with the soul of humanity, and that—to the Master—the form is regarded as relatively of no importance. Release from the three-fold form is ever regarded by the spiritual man as the greatest possible good, provided it comes to him under law, as the result of his spiritual destiny and of karmic decision; it must not come as an arbitrary act, or as an escape from life and its consequences upon the physical plane, or as self-imposed. Of this strange working of the Law of Perfection (strange to man's limited point of view), the war (1914- 1945) was a striking instance. Millions died; more millions suffered cruelly in their form nature, and many more millions underwent (and are still undergoing) the mental agony of insecurity, suspense and poverty. Nevertheless, two major results of a spiritual nature, working under the Law of Perfection, resulted:

1. Souls were released from a backward and decaying civilisation—for such is your vaunted civilisation from the angle of the Hierarchy—and will return in better bodies to a civilisation and a culture more in conformity with the needs of the spiritual man. The main reason why there has been such a complete destruction of the old forms (physical, emotional and mental) is that they constituted a complete imprisonment of the soul and negated all true growth for the masses of men.

2. From the rich to the poor, from the intelligent to the ignorant, one thing is now clearly grasped and will increasingly colour human thinking: happiness and

success are not dependent upon the possession of things or upon material good. That idea is the mistake of organised labour as it fights and strikes for more money in order to live more richly; it is also the mistake of the general public as it reacts to the action of labour, for it rebels against the curtailment of the steady inflow of *material* goods. Humanity has made this mistake for untold ages, and has erred grievously in its emphasis upon that which benefits the form. This is the good in the Russian position as it wars on capitalism and lays an emphasis upon education. However, its ruthlessness and cruelty and (above all else) its suppression of the rights of the individual citizen to certain of the essential freedoms may eventually negate the beauty and the hope of the initial idealism. Russia is right in her idealism, but terribly and basically wrong in her techniques. The United States and Great Britain are at a midway point. They have a vision but know not how to materialise it and make it true, for they favour not (and rightly) a totalitarian regime. The capitalistic spirit and the latent fascism of the United States are at this time a definite menace to world peace, and the capitalists are blocking the efforts of the men of goodwill. Great Britain is at present impotent, financially ruined, her old imperialistic policies entirely in the discard, and her people discouraged; she is therefore so preoccupied with the struggle to live (and she will live) that there is little time, interest or energy left to make the vision true.

There is, as you know, always a correspondence between the individual man and the world of men as a whole. Just as today practically every human being has something wrong with him physically—eyes, ears, teeth or bodily ills of some nature—so humanity is sick and awaiting healing. The healing will be brought about through the medium of the New Group of World Servers and by the men of goodwill, aided by the Hierarchy, from which planetary centre the healing energies will be drawn. Imperfection has been drawn to the surface; the evils to be eliminated are known to everybody, and this has all taken place under the influence of the Law of Perfection. I am dealing here with the general situation rather than with the individual relation between the healer and a patient. I do so for the simple reason that only an initiate of experience and of understanding can keep this law or obey this rule, and of such there are only a very few on earth today. The sickness of humanity as a race, and as a result of aeons of wrong living, of selfish purpose and of greed, has produced a mass of physical ills; today millions of children are born either openly diseased or with the seed of disease in them. When the evil which has made its presence felt, and when the imperfections which have been drawn to the surface have been cured or driven back to their own place, then—and only then— will physical disease come to an end or yield easily to treatment.

In considering the general subject of imperfection and of evil, we are dealing here with causes (and this the initiate must ever do); when these causes are themselves removed, then the effects will also disappear. Christian Science and Unity are therefore right in their general theory and premises, but totally wrong in their emphases and methods. In the long run, all the work they do today is relatively futile, except in so far that they preserve and enunciate the Law of Perfection, even though they do so in a muddled manner and their teaching is tainted with the universal selfishness.

You have oft been told that there are two modes of achievement; the long hard way of evolution, in which aeons are taken to arrive at relatively small results, or the short, still harder but much more rapid way of initiation. For ages it remained a question (a moot point, do you not call it?) whether the world of men would choose (and had better choose) the slow but safe method. It is a method in which imperfection is only very gradually eliminated, without much strain and with small effort on the part of man. It is a mode whereby good is only slowly realised and evil only slowly, very slowly, driven out. The will-to-good of Shamballa is, under the usual evolutionary system, only faintly present, and many, many aeons would still lie ahead of humanity before even the present point of human development could have been attained.

But something happened which had not been foreseen even by the Hierarchy. During the past two hundred years the entire picture has been altered. Individual men, in adequate numbers, achieved initiation and entered the Ashrams of the Masters, and through the decision of these successful aspirants, and subject to their continued activity, it was decided by them but for humanity that the rapid hard way was to be tried. Since that time three factors have been present:

1. The factor of tremendous progress in raising the consciousness of mankind, en masse, to much higher intellectual levels. To this the growth of education, the discoveries of science and the control of the material plane and of the air bear testimony.
2. The factor of worldwide distress, of economic disaster, of world wars, of natural cataclysms and of the myriad occurrences and difficulties which make individual life, national life and planetary life so hard these days. No one is exempt and there is no distinction shown.

3. The factor of the growth of knowledge anent the Hierarchy and, above all else, of the spiritual Plan. This has necessitated the presentation of a goal to man by the working aspirants and disciples, plus the outlining of the techniques of the Path whereby that goal can be reached. This has not been accomplished by the religious church groups throughout the world, but by members of the Ashrams. All that the churches have done is to preserve in the public mind the fact of God Transcendent, whilst ignoring the fact of God Immanent, to testify to the existence of the Christ whilst travestying His teaching, and to teach the fact of immortality, whilst ignoring the Law of Rebirth.

Humanity is, therefore, progressing rapidly upon the Upward Way, and two things can be looked for as a consequence: first, that the imperfections and evil (one latent and the other active though retreating) will become increasingly apparent to intelligent man, and secondly, that the mode of their elimination will also become known.

I deal not here with the nature of imperfection or the purpose of evil. Do I need to point out to any of my readers how inescapably both are present? I might point out that imperfection is inherent in the nature of matter itself and constitutes an inheritance from a previous solar system. I might indicate that evil emanates from that hierarchy of evil Forces which are the material correspondence to the spiritual Hierarchy; this is related to the fact that all our planes are composed of substance of the cosmic physical plane. It might also be stated that when the imperfection of matter is realised and corrected, and when the interest and emphasis of humanity is turned away from material conditions, then the Forces of Evil will have nothing in the three worlds (the three lower levels of the cosmic physical plane) upon which to work; there will be nothing they can influence, and no mode of influencing man will then exist as far as evil is concerned. I cannot expect you at this time to comprehend the meaning of my words. They are, however, related to the words in the Great Invocation which say, "and seal the door where evil dwells." There is a door into an evil realm and into blackness, just as there is a door into a world of goodness and light; the devil is to man who is dedicated and consecrated to evil what the Dweller on the Threshold is to the spiritual aspirant.

The main task of the spiritual Hierarchy has ever been to stand between the Forces of Evil and humanity, to bring imperfection into the light so that evil can "find no place" for action, and to keep the door open into the spiritual realm. This the Hierarchy has done, with small help from humanity; this situation is now changed and the world war was the symbol and the guarantee of that change; in it the Forces of Light, the massed United Nations, fought the Forces of Evil *upon the physical plane* and routed them. There has been a far greater spiritual significance to the war than has yet been realised. It marked a world turning point; it reoriented humanity towards the good; it drove back the Forces of Evil and made definitely clear (and this was new and needed) the true distinction between good and evil, and this not in a theological sense—as stated by the church commentators—but practically and obviously. It is evidenced by the disastrous economic situation and by the greed of prominent men in every country. The world of men (through the obviousness of the distinction between good and evil) has awakened to the fact of materialistic exploitation, to the lack of real freedom and to the rights, as yet unclaimed, of the individual. Man's ability to resist slavery has become apparent everywhere. That the strugglers towards freedom are employing wrong methods and are endeavouring oft to fight evil with evil is entirely true, but this indicates only transitional techniques and a temporary phase; it is temporary from the point of view of the Hierarchy (though possibly long from the angle of men in the three worlds), but it need not necessarily be long today.

So great has been the progress of man during the past two hundred years that the Council Chamber at Shamballa was forced to take notice. As a result of this attention by the Great Lives around Sanat Kumara and Their interest in the affairs of men, two things happened:

1. The will aspect of divinity made its first definite and direct contact with the human mind. The impact was direct and not deflected—as had hitherto been the case— to the Hierarchy and from thence to humanity. According to the type of man or group who responded or reacted to this contact, so were the results; they were very good or exceedingly bad. Great and good men appeared and enunciated the truths needed for the New Age, and of these Lincoln, Roosevelt, Browning, Briand and a host of lesser men could be cited. Evil and pernicious men also emerged, such as Hitler and the group he gathered around him, bringing much evil upon the Earth.
2. At the same time, the will-to-good from Shamballa evoked the latent goodwill in man, so that today and increasingly over the past one hundred years, goodness of heart, kindness in action, consideration for others and mass action to promote human welfare have spread over the Earth.

The emergence of imperfection and the planned effort of evil have been parallelled by the appearance of the New Group of World Servers and by the preparation which the Hierarchy is making towards its externalisation upon the physical plane. The Hierarchy is at this time exceedingly powerful; its Ashrams are full of initiates and disciples, and its periphery or magnetic field is drawing countless thousands of aspirants towards it. The war struck a mortal blow to material evil, and its hold on humanity is greatly weakened.

Confound not evil with the activities of the gangster or the criminal. Criminals and gangsters are the result of the emerging massed imperfections; they are the victims of ignorance, mishandling when children and misunderstanding down the ages of right human relations; the Law of Rebirth will eventually lead them on the way to good. Those men are truly evil who seek to enforce a return to the bad old ways, who endeavour to keep their fellowmen in slavery of some kind or another, who block the expression of one or all of the Four Freedoms, who gain material riches at the expense of the exploited, or who seek to hold for themselves and for gain the produce of the earth, and thus make the cost of life's necessities prohibitive to those not richly endowed. Those who thus work, think and plan are to be found in every nation, and are usually of prominence because of their riches and influence; however, they sin against light and not through ignorance; their goals are material and not spiritual. They are relatively few compared to the countless millions of men, but are exceedingly powerful; they are highly intelligent but unscrupulous, and it is through them that the Forces of Evil work, holding back progress, promoting poverty, breeding hatred and class distinctions, fostering racial differences for their own ends, and keeping ignorance in power. Their sin is great and it is hard for them to change, because power and the will-to-power (as it militates against the will-to-good) is a dominant all-controlling factor in their lives; these men are today working against the unity of the United Nations, through their greed, their determination to own the resources of the earth (such as oil, mineral wealth and food) and thus keep the people weak and with inadequate food. These men, who are found in every nation, thoroughly understand each other and are working together in great combines to exploit the riches of the earth at the expense of humanity.

Russia is today singularly free of such men, so I refer not here to that vast country, as many of her enemies might surmise. Russia is making great mistakes, but they are the mistakes of a fanatical ideologist or of a gangster who sins because of ignorance, through immaturity or in fury at the evil things with which he is surrounded. This is something totally different to the evil with which I have been dealing, and it will not last, because Russia will learn; these others do not learn.

I have used the above illustration so as to make my theme somewhat clearer. The whole problem of evil is, however, too vast to contemplate here, nor is it advisable or wise to discuss the source of evil (not of imperfection), the Black Lodge. Energy follows thought, and the spoken word can be potently evocative; therefore, until one is a member of the Great White Lodge, it is the part of wisdom to avoid consideration of forces potent enough intelligently to use the latent imperfection in humanity and to impose the vast evil of war, with all its results and far-reaching effects, upon humanity. The Black Lodge is the problem of the White Lodge, and not the problem of humanity; for aeons the Hierarchy has handled this problem, and is now in process of solving it. It is essentially, however, the main consideration and problem of Shamballa, for it is connected with the will aspect, and only the will-to-good will suffice to blot out and annihilate the will-to-evil. Goodwill will not suffice, though the united and invocative appeal of the men of goodwill throughout the world—increasingly voiced through the Great Invocation—will serve "to seal the door where evil dwells."

It is behind that door and in dealing with the forces there concealed (and mobilised) that the Hierarchy is effective; the methods and modes whereby They protect humanity from mobilised evil, and are gradually driving the evil back, would not be understood by you who have not yet passed through the door which leads to the Way of the Higher Evolution.

What shall I say concerning harmlessness? It is not easy for me to show or prove to you the effectiveness of the higher aspect, spiral or phase of harmlessness as employed by the Hierarchy, under the direction of the Perfect One, the Christ. The harmlessness with which I have earlier dealt has relation to the imperfections with which humanity is wrestling, and is difficult for you to apply in and under all circumstances, as well you know. The harmlessness to which I refer in connection with you is not negative, or sweet or kindly activity, as so many believe; it is a *state of mind* and one which in no way negates firm or even drastic action; it concerns motive and involves the determination that the motive behind all activity is goodwill. That motive might lead to positive and sometimes disagreeable action or speech, but as harmlessness and goodwill condition the mental approach, nothing can eventuate but good.

On a higher turn of the spiral, the Hierarchy also employs harmlessness, but it is related to the will-to-good and involves the use of dynamic, electric energy under intuitive direction; this type of energy is never brought into activity by man; it is energy which he cannot yet handle. This type of harmlessness is based on complete self-sacrifice, wherein the will-to-sacrifice, the will-to-good and the will-to-power (three phases of the will aspect, as expressed through the

Spiritual Triad) are all fused into one dynamic energy of a deeply spiritual nature. This energy is the epitome of complete or perfect harmlessness, where humanity and the subsidiary kingdoms in nature are concerned, but it is expulsive in its effect and dynamic in its annihilating impact, where the Forces of Evil are concerned.

A close but esoteric study of the three temptations of the Christ will reveal three major occasions when the Perfect One, expressing this higher harmlessness, forced the exponent of evil to retreat. This triple episode is symbolically related, but is factual in nature. Little thought has ever been given to what would have been the worldwide effect down the centuries if the Christ had not reacted as He did; speculation is of little use, but it might be stated that the entire course of history and of the evolutionary progress of humanity would have been altered, and in a dire and awful manner. But the dynamic harmlessness, the expression of the will-to-good and the demonstration of the will-to-power (forcing evil to leave Him) marked a most important crisis in the life of the Christ.

The Gospel story (with its resume of the five initiations) concerns the progress and triumph of the Master Jesus; the story of the three temptations indicated the taking of a still higher initiation, the sixth, by the Christ; this conferred on Him complete mastery over evil, and not mastery over imperfection; it was because He was the "Perfect One" that He could take this initiation.

I have given you much for mature consideration and thrown some light upon an initiation of which little, naturally, can be known. I would call your attention also to the three fundamental requirements for a successful approach to this initiation: perfect poise, a completed point of view, and divine understanding. You would find it of interest to see how these three qualities work out in relation to the three temptations; in so doing much light would be thrown on the life, nature and character of the Christ.

Under the Law of Perfection we are given the key to the civilisation and cycle of evolution which He inaugurated—the ideal of which is not lost, though the application of the teaching He gave has been neglected by the churches and by mankind. You will note also that one temptation takes place on the summit of a high mountain; from that elevation both time and space are totally negated, for the vision of Christ ranged from the past, through the present and on into the future. This state of awareness (I cannot call it consciousness, and awareness is almost as inaccurate a word) is only possible after the fifth initiation, reaching a high point of expression at the sixth initiation.

I would like to consider with you the nature of the three requirements presented as essential for a certain initiation, because they provide the link between Law IX and Rule Six. The rule is so clear and concise that it needs but little explanation, emphasising, as it does, energy which must be used and that which must not. It says:

Rule Six

The healer or the healing group must keep the will in leash. It is not will which must be used, but love.

These three basic requirements concern attainment on various planes of the universe; though I dealt with them in connection with the approach to the sixth initiation, they have—on a lower turn of the spiral—their correspondences, and are therefore of practical application by the initiated disciple, particularly one who has taken the third initiation. Let us take them, one by one, into our thinking:

Perfect Poise indicates complete control of the astral body, so that emotional upheavals are overcome, or at least are greatly minimised in the life of the disciple. It indicates also, on the higher turn of the spiral, an ability to function freely on buddhic levels, owing to complete liberation (and consequent poise) from all the influences and impulses which are motived from the three worlds. This type or quality of poise connotes—if you will think deeply—an abstract state of mind; nothing which is regarded as nonperfection can create disturbance. You can realise surely that, if you were entirely free from all emotional reactions, your clarity of mind and your ability to think clearly would be enormously increased, with all that that involves.

Naturally, the perfect poise of an initiated disciple and that of the initiated Master are different, for one concerns the effect of the three worlds or their non-effect, and the other concerns adaptability to the rhythm of the Spiritual Triad; nevertheless, the earlier type of poise must precede the later achievement, hence my consideration of the subject. This perfect poise (which is a possible achievement for you who read) is arrived at by ruling out the pulls, the urges, impulses and attractions of the astral or emotional nature, and also by the practice of what I have earlier mentioned: Divine Indifference.

A Completed Point of View. This necessarily and primarily refers to the universal outlook of the Monad, and therefore to an initiate of the higher degrees. It can, however, be interpreted on a lower rung of the ladder of evolution and refers to the function of the soul as an Observer in the three worlds and the completed all-round picture such an observer gradually attains. This is brought about by the development of the two qualities of detachment and discrimination. These two qualities, when expressed on the Way to the Higher Evolution, become Abstraction and the Will-to-good.

A completed point of view—as experienced on soul levels—indicates the removal of all barriers and the freedom of the disciple from the great heresy of separateness; he has therefore created an unclogged channel for the inflow of pure love. Perfect poise, viewed from the same level, has removed all impediments and those emotional factors which have hitherto blocked the channel, thus preparing the way for the Observer to see truly; the disciple then functions as a clear channel for love.

Divine Understanding must also be studied from two points of view. As a soul quality, it indicates a mind which can be held steady in the light, and can therefore reflect the pure reason (pure love) which qualifies the reflections of the Son of Mind, the soul on its own plane. On the higher Way of the Master, it relates to that identification which supersedes the individualistic consciousness; all barriers have gone, and the initiate sees things as they are; he knows the causes of which all phenomena are the ephemeral effects. This, consequently, enables Him to understand the Purpose, as it emanates from Shamballa, just as the lesser initiate understands the Plan as it is formulated by the Hierarchy.

All three of these divine attributes are, in some measure, essential in the development of the initiate-healer; he must work at their unfoldment as part of his necessary equipment; he must know that all reactions of an emotional nature create a wall or barrier between the free flow of healing force and the patient, and that the barrier is created by him and not by the patient. The emotions of the patient should have no effect upon the healer and should fail to deviate him from the intense concentration needed for his work; these emotions of the patient cannot in themselves create a barrier strong enough to deflect the healing force.

A completed point of view involves at least the attempt by the disciple to penetrate into the world of causes, and thus learn (if possible) what it is that is responsible for the disease of the patient. This need not involve penetration into previous incarnations, nor is that essential, in spite of what some modern and generally fraudulent healers may claim. There is usually enough psychological evidence, or indications of inherited tendencies, to give the healer his clue and to enable him to get a somewhat complete picture of the situation. It is obvious that this "penetration" into the causes of the trouble will only be possible if the healer *loves* enough; because he loves, he has achieved a poise which brings negation to the world of illusion and of glamour. Divine understanding is simply the application of the principle of pure love (pure reason) to all men and to all circumstances, plus right interpretation of the existing difficulties of the patient, or of those which may exist between patient and healer.

To these requirements I would like to add another factor: that of the doctor, physician or surgeon who is physically responsible for the patient. In the coming new era, the healer will work always with the scientific aid of the trained medical man; this is a factor which causes bewilderment, at present, to the average modern healer belonging to some cult or expressing some unorthodox phase of healing.

It will therefore be apparent how these three divine requirements (when stepped down for the use of the disciple in the modern world) indicate a line of training or of self-discipline to which all should apply themselves. When they have mastered even some of the earliest phases of this triple achievement, they will find that they can apply Rule Six with ease.

What is meant by the words "to keep the will in leash"? The will aspect here considered is not that of the will-to-good and its lower expression goodwill. The will-to-good signifies the stable, immovable orientation of the initiated disciple, whilst goodwill can be regarded as its expression in daily service. The will-to-good, as expressed by a higher initiate, is a dynamic energy having predominantly a *group* effect; for this reason, the higher initiates seldom concern themselves with the healing of an individual. Their work is too potent and too important to permit them to do so, and the will energy, embodying as it does divine Purpose, might prove destructive in its effects upon an individual. The patient would not be able to receive or absorb it. It is, however, assumed that goodwill colours the entire attitude and thinking of the healing disciple.

The will which must be kept in leash is the will of the personality which, in the case of the initiated disciple, is of a very high order. It also relates to the will of the soul, emanating from the petals of sacrifice in the egoic lotus. All true healers have to create a healing thoughtform, and through this they consciously or unconsciously work. It is this thoughtform which must be kept free from a too power-ful use of the will, for it can (unless held in leash, stepped down, modified or, if needed, eliminated altogether) destroy not only the thoughtform created by the healer, but it can also build a barrier between healer and patient; the initial rapport is thus broken. Only a Christ can heal by the use of the will, and He seldom in reality healed at all; in the cases where He is reported to have done so, His reason was to prove the possibility of healing; but—as you will note if you are familiar with the Gospel story—He gave no instructions to His disciples upon the art of healing. This is significant.

The self-will (no matter of how high a quality) of the healer, and his determined effort to heal the patient, create a tension in the healer which can seriously deflect the healing current of energy. When this type of will is present, as it frequently is in the inexperienced healer or the non-initiated healer, the healer is apt to absorb the patient's difficulty and will experience symptoms of the trouble and the pain. His willful determination to be of help acts like a boomerang and he suffers, whilst the patient is not really helped.

So the instruction is to use love, and here a major difficulty emerges. How can the healer use love, freed from its emotional or lower quality, and bring it through in its pure state for the healing of the patient? Only as the healer has cultivated the three requirements, and has therefore developed himself as a pure channel. He is apt to be so preoccupied with himself, with the definition of love, and with the determination to heal the patient that the three requirements are neglected. Then both he and the patient are wasting each other's time. He need not brood or worry about the nature of pure love, or endeavour too ardently to understand how pure reason and pure love are synonymous terms, or whether he can show sufficient love to effect a healing. Let him ponder on the three requirements, particularly the first, and let him fulfill within himself these three requirements as far as in him lies and his point in evolution permits. He will then become a pure channel and the hindrances to the inflow of pure love will be automatically removed for "as a man thinketh in his heart so is he"; then, without obstruction or difficulty, pure love will pour through him and the patient will be healed—if such is the law for him.

We come now to the final and the most mysterious law of all that I have given you. I called your attention to it earlier, and there pointed out that this "last law is an enunciation of a new law which is substituted for the Law of Death, and which has reference only to those found upon the later stages of the Path of Discipleship and the stages upon the Path of Initiation." By these later stages I refer to the period after the second initiation and prior to taking the third. This law does not apply in any way as long as the emotional nature can disturb the clear rhythm of the personality as it responds to the impact of soul energy, and later to monadic. There is not, therefore, a great deal that I can make clear to you as regards the full working of this law, but I can indicate certain most interesting ideas and correspondences; these will foster in you constructive speculative thinking, yet at the same time they embody proven facts for those of us who are initiated disciples of the Christ or of Sanat Kumara.

LAW X

Hearken, O Disciple, to the call which comes from the Son to the Mother, and then obey. The Word goes forth that form has served its purpose. The principle of mind then organises itself and then repeats the Word. The waiting form responds and drops away. The soul stands free.

Respond, O Rising One, to the call which comes within the sphere of obligation; recognise the call, emerging from the Ashram or from the Council Chamber where waits the Lord of Life Himself. The Sound goes forth. Both soul and form together must renounce the principle of life, and thus permit the Monad to stand free. The soul responds. The form then shatters the connection. Life is now liberated, owning the quality of conscious knowledge and the fruit of all experience. These are the gifts of soul and form combined.

This Law X is the forerunner of many new laws concerning the relation of soul to form or of spirit to matter; this one is given first for two reasons:

1. It can be applied by disciples and thus proven to be true to the mass of men, and above all, to the scientific world.
2. In the mass of testimony and in the type of death (called at this stage "transference") the fact of the Hierarchy and of Shamballa can be established.

There are three sources of the abstraction which we call "death" if we exclude accident (which may be incident to other people's karma), war (which involves planetary karma) and natural catastrophes (which are connected entirely with the body of manifestation of the One in Whom we live and move and have our being).

I might pause here at this thought and make somewhat clearer to you the distinction between this "unknown God," who expresses himself through the planet as a whole, and Sanat Kumara in His high place at Shamballa. Sanat Kumara is in Himself the essential Identity, responsible for the manifested worlds, but so great is His command of energies and forces—owing to His cosmic unfoldment—that He requires the entire planet through which to express all that He is. Having the full consciousness of the cosmic astral plane and of the cosmic mental plane, He can apply energies and forces—under cosmic law—which create, sustain and utilise, for the ends of His divine Purpose, the entire planet. He animates the planet with His life; He sustains the planet and all that is in or on it through His soul quality, which He imparts in varying measure to every form; He creates continuously the new forms needed to express the "life more abundantly" and the "increasing purpose of His will" which the progress of the ages makes cyclically possible. We live at this time in a cycle wherein His intense activity is utilising the technique of divine destruction for the release of the spiritual life, and He is simultaneously creating the new structure of civilisation which will express more fully the evolutionary attainment of the planet and the kingdoms in nature, leading eventually to the perfect expression of His divine life and purpose.

It would perhaps be wise if we took this tenth Law somewhat in detail, where possible, so as to arrive at the synthesis which it is intended to convey: we will thus gain some realisation that death itself is a part of the creative process of synthesising. It is essential that new ideas and a new approach to the entire problem of dying are inaugurated.

> *Hearken, O Disciple, to the call which comes from the Son to the Mother, and then obey.*

Even whilst we realise from the context that this refers to the discarding of the physical body, it is useful to remember that this form of wording can signify much more than that. It can be interpreted to mean the entire relation of soul and personality, and to involve the prompt obedience of the Mother (the personality) to the Son (the soul). Without his prompt obedience, involving as it does the recognition of the informing Voice, the personality will remain deaf to the call of the soul to relinquish the body. No habitual response has been developed. I would ask you to ponder on the implications.

I am, I know, recapitulating when I point out that the Mother aspect is the material aspect and the soul—on its own plane—is the Son. This injunction, therefore, concerns the relation of matter and soul, and thus lays the foundation for all the relationships which the disciple has to learn to recognise. Obedience is not here enforced;

it is contingent upon hearing; then obedience follows as the next development. This is an easier process, little as you may think it. This distinction, relative to the process of obedience, is interesting because the process of *learning by hearing* is always slow and is one of the qualities or aspects of the stage of orientation. *Learning by sight* is definitely connected with the Path of Discipleship, and any who wish to become wise and true workers must learn to distinguish between the hearers and those who see. A realisation of the difference would lead to basic changes in technique. In the one case, you are working with those who are definitely under the influence and control of the Mother, and who need to be trained to see. In the other, you are dealing with those who have heard and who are developing the spiritual correspondence of sight. They are therefore susceptible to the vision.

The Word goes forth that form has served its purpose.

This word, or this "spiritual proclamation" of the soul, may have a twofold purpose: it may produce death, or it may simply result in a withdrawal of the soul from its instrument, the threefold personality. This might consequently result in leaving the form uninformed and without any dweller in the body. When this happens the personality (and by this I mean the physical, astral and mental man) will continue to function. If it is of a high grade quality, very few people will realise that the soul is absent. This frequently happens in old age or serious illness, and it may persist for years. It sometimes happens where infants are concerned, and you then have either death or imbecility, as there has been no time to train the lower personality vehicles. A little thinking along the lines of this "forthgoing Word" will throw much light on circumstances which are regarded as baffling, and on states of consciousness which have hitherto constituted almost insoluble problems.

> *The principle of mind then organises itself*
> *and then repeats the Word. The waiting*
> *form responds and drops away.*

In the aspect of death here dealt with it is the mind which acts as the agent of authority, transmitting to the brain (where the thread of consciousness is located) the instructions to vacate. This is then passed on by the man in the body to the heart (where the life thread is anchored), and then—as you well know—the process of withdrawal begins. What transpires in those timeless moments prior to death no one as yet knows, for no one has returned to tell us. If they had done so, the question is: Would they have been believed? The probability is that they would not.

The first paragraph of this Law X deals with the passing out from the body (meaning the form aspect of the three-fold lower man) of the average intelligent aspirant, looking at this law from one of its lowest correspondences; however, under the same Law of Correspondences, the death of all men, from the lowest type of man up to and inclusive of the aspirant, is basically distinguished by the same identical process; the difference exists in the degree of consciousness evidenced—consciousness of process and intention. The result is the same in all cases:

> *The soul stands free.*

This moment of true freedom can be brief and fleeting as in the case of the undeveloped man, or it can be of long duration, according to the usefulness of the aspirant upon the inner planes; with this I have earlier dealt and have no need to repeat myself here. Progressively, as the urges and influences of the three lower levels of consciousness weaken their hold, the period of dissociation becomes longer and longer, and is characterised by a developing clarity of thought and by a recognition of essential being, and this in progressive stages. This clarity and progress may not be brought through into full realisation or expression when rebirth again takes place, for the limitations imposed by the dense physical body are excessive; nevertheless, each life sees a steady growth in sensitivity, and also the storing-up of esoteric information, using the word "esoteric" to signify all that does not concern normal form life or the average consciousness of man in the three worlds.

Esoteric living (as it develops) falls into three stages, broadly speaking; these are carried forward within the consciousness of the man and parallel the recognition and ordinary aspects of form life on the three levels of experience:

1. The stage of reception of concepts, of ideas and of principles, thus gradually asserting the existence of the abstract mind.

2. The stage of "light reception," or that period when spiritual insight is developed, when the vision is seen and accepted as true, and when the intuition or "buddhic perception" is unfolded. This carries with it the assertion as to the existence of the Hierarchy.

3. The stage of abstraction, or the period wherein complete orientation is brought about, the way into the Ashram is made clear, and the disciple begins to build the antahkarana between the personality and the Spiritual Triad. It is in this stage that the nature of the will is *dimly* seen, carrying with its recognition the implication that there is a "centre where the will of God is known."

Students are apt to think that death ends things, whereas from the angle of *termination* we are dealing with values which are persistent, with which there is no interference, nor can there be any, and which hold within themselves the seeds of immortality. I would have you ponder on this and know that everything that is of true spiritual value is persistent, ageless, immortal and eternal. Only that dies which is valueless, and—from the standpoint of humanity— that means those factors which emphasise and assume importance where the form is concerned. But those values which are based on principle and not upon the detail of appearance have in them that undying principle which leads a man from the "gates of nativity, through the gates of perception, to the gates of purpose"—as the *Old Commentary* expresses it.

I have endeavoured to show you how the first part of this Law X has a simple application to mankind, as well as an abstract and abstruse meaning for esotericists.

The last paragraph in this Law X cannot be interpreted in this same manner nor applied in this way; it concerns only the "passing over" or the "discarding of hindrances" by very advanced disciples and initiates. This is made clear by the use of the words, "O Rising One"—a term applied only to those who have taken the fourth initiation and who are therefore held by no aspect whatsoever of the form nature, even so high or transcendental a form as the soul in its own vehicle, the causal body or the egoic lotus. Yet again, facility in response to this law must be and is developed in the earlier stages of discipleship, where listening, responsiveness and occult obedience are developed and have their extensions in the higher levels of spiritual experience.

Here we must again consider words and phrases if we are to understand their true meaning.

> *Respond, O Rising One, to the call which comes within the sphere of obligation.*

What is this sphere of obligation to which the initiate of high standing must pay attention? The whole of life experience, from the sphere of nativity up to the highest limits of spiritual possibility, are covered by four words, applicable at various stages of evolution. They are: Instinct, Duty, Dharma, Obligation; an understanding of the differences serves to bring illumination, and consequently, right action.

1. *The sphere of instinct.* This refers to the fulfillment, under the influence of simple animal instinct, of the obligations which any assumed responsibility brings, even when assumed with no true understanding. An illustration of this is the instinctual care of a mother for her offspring or the relation of male and female. With this we need not deal in any detail, as it is well recognised and understood, at least by those who have passed out of the sphere of elementary instinctual obligations. To them no particular calls come, but this instinctual world of give and take is superseded by a higher sphere of responsibility eventually.

2. *The sphere of duty.* The call that comes from this sphere comes from a realm of consciousness which is more strictly human and not so predominantly animal as is the instinctual realm. It sweeps into its field of activity all classes of human beings and demands from them—life after life—the strict fulfillment of duty. The "doing of one's duty," for which one gets small praise and little appreciation, is the first step towards the unfoldment of that divine principle which we call the sense of responsibility, and which—when unfolded—indicates a steadily growing soul control. The fulfill-

ment of duty, the sense of responsibility, and the desire to serve are three aspects of one and the same thing: discipleship in its embryonic stage. This is a hard saying for those who are caught in the seemingly hopeless toils of duty fulfillment; it is hard for them to realise that this duty which seems to keep them chained to the humdrum, apparently meaningless and thankless duties of daily life, is a scientific process leading them to higher phases of experience, and eventually into the Master's Ashram.

3. *The sphere of dharma.* This is the outcome of the two previous stages; it is that in which the disciple recognises, for the first time with clarity, his part in the whole process of world events and his inescapable share in world development. Dharma is that aspect of karma which dignifies any particular world cycle and the lives of those implicated in its working out. The disciple begins to see that if he shoulders his phase or part in this cyclic dharma and works understandingly at its right fulfillment, he is beginning to comprehend group work (as the Masters comprehend it) and to do his just share in lifting the world karma, working out in cyclic dharma. Instinctual service, the fulfillment of all duty, and a sharing in group dharma are all blended in his consciousness and become one great act of living faithful service; he is then at the point of moving forward upon the Path of Discipleship, in which the Path of Probation is completely lost to sight.

These three aspects of living activity are the embryonic expression in the life of the disciple of the three divine aspects:

a. Instinctual living .... intelligent application.
b. Duty .... responsible love.

   c. Dharma ....will, expressed
                                      through the Plan.

4. *The sphere of obligation.* The initiate, having learnt the nature of the three other spheres of right action, and—through the activity of those spheres—having unfolded the divine aspects, passes now into the sphere of obligation. This sphere, which can be entered only after a large measure of liberation has been achieved, directs the reactions of the initiate in two phases of his life:

   a. In the Ashram, where he is governed by the Plan; this Plan is recognised by him as expressing his major obligation to life. I use the word "life" in its deepest esoteric sense.

   b. In Shamballa, where the emerging Purpose of Sanat-Kumara (of which the Plan is an interpretation in time and space) begins to have meaning and significance according to his point in evolution and his approach to the Way of the Higher Evolution.

In the Ashram, the life of the Spiritual Triad gradually supersedes the life of the soul-controlled personality. In the Council Chamber at Shamballa, the life of the Monad supersedes all other expressions of the essential Reality. More I may not say.

> *Recognise the call, emerging from the Ashram or from the Council Chamber where waits the Lord of Life Himself.*

Here again we come up against the whole underlying, evolutionary theme of Invocation and Evocation. Here, it is the two higher centres of the divine Existence which are invoking ceaselessly the lower centre; one of the factors governing the whole creative process is dependent upon the skill of the Great Lives in evoking response from the human and subhuman kingdoms or grouped lives within the three worlds of form life. Men are so pre-occupied with their own problems that they are apt to think that—in the long run—what happens is entirely due to their behaviour, conduct, and invocative powers. There is, however, another side to the picture; this involves the skill in action, the understanding hearts and the clear unimpeded will of both the Hierarchy and Shamballa.

It will be apparent to you, therefore, how essential it is that all disciples and initiates should know exactly where they stand on the Path, the final aspect of the ladder of evolution; otherwise, they will misinterpret the call and fail to recognise the source of the outgoing sound. How easily this can happen becomes apparent to every advanced teacher of occultism and esotericism when he perceives how easily unimportant people and beginners interpret calls and messages they hear or receive as coming to them from some high and elevated source, whereas they are in all probability hearing that which emanates from their own subconscious, from their own souls, or from some teacher (not a Master) who is attempting to help them.

The call referred to here, however, comes from the highest possible sources and must not be confused with the little voices of little men.

The SOUND *goes forth.*

It is not my intention here to deal with the creative sound, beyond calling to your attention the fact that it *is creative.* The Sound which was the first indication of the activity of the planetary Logos is not a word, but a full reverberating sound, holding within itself all other sounds, all chords and certain musical tones (which have been given the name of the "music of the spheres") and dissonances, unknown as yet to the modern ear. It is this Sound which the "Rising One" must learn to recognise, and to which he must respond not only by means of the sense of hearing and its higher correspondences, but through a response from every part and aspect of the form nature in the three worlds. I would remind you also that from the angle of the fourth initiation even the egoic vehicle, the soul body, is regarded and treated as a part of the form nature.

Though the "shattering of the Temple of Solomon" takes place at the time of the fourth initiation, those qualities of which it was composed have been absorbed into the vehicles which the initiate is using for all His contacts in the three worlds. He is now essentially the essence of all His bodies, and—from His point of view and technical understanding—it must be borne in mind that the entire mental plane is one of the three planes which constitute the cosmic dense physical plane; this is a point oft forgotten by students, who almost invariably place the soul body and the mental permanent atom *outside* the form limits and what they call the three worlds. Technically and from higher angles, this is not so, and this fact definitely changes and conditions the thinking and work of the initiate of the fourth and higher degrees. It accounts also for the need for the egoic body to disappear.

The Sound reverberates throughout the four higher subplanes of the cosmic physical plane; these are the higher correspondence of the four etheric levels of the physical plane in the three worlds—the three dense physical and the four etheric planes. It must be remembered, therefore, that our planes, with which we are so familiar, are the cosmic physical, and that the one we know the best is the densest of the seven—hence so much of our struggle and difficulty.

From "the silence which is sound, the reverberating note of Shamballa," the sound focusses itself either in the Spiritual Triad or in the Ashram, according to the status of the initiate and whether he is high in the ashramic circles, or still higher, in the circles through which radiates the light from the Council Chamber. In the first case, it will be the heart centre which responds to the sound, and from thence the whole body; in the second case, consciousness has been superseded by a still higher type of spiritual recognition, to which we have given the inadequate name of identification. Where the sound has been registered in the heart of the initiate, he has unfolded all possible types of knowledge which the form nature—soul and body—can make possible; when the registration is in the head, identification has produced such complete unity with all spiritual expressions of life, the word "more" (meaning increased) must perforce give way to the word "deep," in the sense of penetration. Having said this, brother of mine, how much have you comprehended?

It is at this point that the initiate is confronted for the first time with the Seven Paths, because each Path constitutes a mode of penetrating into realms of realisation beyond our planet altogether.

In order to do this, the initiate has to demonstrate his mastery of the Law of Differentiation and arrive at a knowledge of the Seven Paths through differentiating the seven sounds which make up the one Sound, but which are not related to the seven sounds which compose the threefold AUM.

> *Both soul and form together must renounce the principle of life, and thus permit the Monad to stand free. The soul responds. The form then shatters the connection.*

You can see here why I emphasised the fact that the initiate is the recipient of the essential quality or qualities which form has revealed and developed, and which the soul has absorbed. At this particular crisis, the initiate within the Ashram or "on His way of glory to the Place where dwells the Lord" (Shamballa) summarises or contains within himself all the essential good which was stored in the soul prior to its destruction at the fourth initiation. He epitomises in himself the knowledge and the wisdom of aeons of struggle and of patient endurance. Nothing further is to be gained by adhering either to the soul or to the form. He has taken all they had to give which throws light on the spiritual Law of Sacrifice. It is interesting to note how the soul becomes at this point simply the intermediary between the personality and the initiate of high degree. But now there is nothing more to relate, to report or to transmit, and—as the Sound reverberates— the soul disappears, as testimony of response. It is now but an empty shell, but its substance is of so high an order that it becomes an integral part of the buddhic level, and its function there is etheric. The principle of life is renounced and returns to the reservoir of universal life.

I would have you take notice of the importance of form activity. It is the *Form* which shatters the connection (the usually despised, belittled, frustrated form is that which performs the final act), bringing complete liberation. The "Lunar Lord" of the personality has achieved his goal, and those elements which have composed his three vehicles (physical, astral, mental), together with the life principle, will constitute the atomic substance of the first body of manifestation of some soul seeking incarnation for the first time. This is closely related to the abstruse subject of the permanent atoms. It marks a moment of high initiation for this Lunar Lord when he shatters the connection and severs all relation with the hitherto informing soul. He is no longer just a shadow, but has now those qualities which make him "substantial" (in the esoteric sense) and a new factor in time and space.

The remaining words of this law need no explanation and mark a fitting finish for this section of our studies:

> *Life is now liberated, owning the qualities of conscious knowledge and the fruit of all experience. These are the gifts of soul and form combined.*

CHAPTER IX

The Seven Modes of Healing

IT WILL BE OBVIOUS to you that even if the techniques or the seven modes of healing—relating as they do to the energies of the seven rays—were exactly imparted to you, it would be rare indeed to find a healer who was competent to use them in this interim period in world affairs. We are passing out of one age into another, and this necessarily creates difficulties which have hitherto not been recognised. This is the first time in human history wherein humanity is intelligent enough to register understanding of the implications of this happening, and far-sighted enough to be able to vision, imagine and plan for the new future. For another thing, the soul ray of the average aspirant is seldom in control to such an extent that it can bring adequate illumination and ray potency; until it is in control, these ray methods and techniques, determining the use and direction of the ray energies, are useless. This should not bring to you disappointment, but simply an attitude of expectancy, particularly where the younger students and readers are concerned. All things considered, this hiatus between expectancy and possibility is exceedingly good.

There has been so much given out during the past century along the lines of magical work, that more at this time would not be wise; so many mantrams and Words of Power have been communicated, and so wide a use of the

OM has prevailed, that a great deal of damage might be looked for as a result. Such damage has not, however, occurred. The relatively low point in evolution of the average student and experimenter has served as a protection, and little has been set in motion—either good or bad—by what they have attempted to do. Healings have frequently taken place (at least temporary healings), owing largely to the susceptibility of the patient to suggestion and his confidence in the healer. None of these healings can be traced esoterically to the scientific methods of occultism. In spite of this protection, or rather because of it, I am communicating no Ray Words at this time, such as the trained initiate employs when engaged in the healing work. These Words have to be accompanied by a trained use of the spiritual will, and (where the ordinary man and healer is concerned) even the lowest aspect of the will remains as yet undeveloped, and only self-will (which is determined, selfish desire) is expressed. It would therefore be a waste of my time to give instruction along these lines.

I have felt it necessary to explain this, so that there will be no undue expectancy that I shall impart the mysterious and the hitherto unknown. I seek only to lay the foundation for a future structure of knowledge, when it will be safe, wise and right to convey those "focussing Points," those "organising Words," and those "expressed Intentions" of the correctly trained occult healer. I seek to generate in you also a wise and searching expectancy which will use the little that I am able to impart, and the symbolic words I may dictate, and so prepare for a greater understanding later.

In the meantime there are certain things I can teach you which will be profitable. They may perchance enhance the visioned and realised difficulties, but may nevertheless prove useful in indicating the ground which must still be covered before the healer arrives at correct and sustained healing.

This section will be very short indeed, compared with the rest of this volume; it will consist simply of a series of summarised and condensed statements which will provide a textbook for the healer, a reference book for guidance to which he can refer. These statements will be under three classifications:

> I.   The Seven Ray Energies.
> II. The Rays of the Healer and the Patient.
> III. The Seven Healing Techniques.

These statements will complete Volume IV of *A Treatise on the Seven Rays* and will carry much information to the initiated disciple, and even in part to the intelligent aspirant; they should make their healing work more effectual, even though only the preliminary work and elementary rules are given. Needless to add, the healer has to perfect himself in this initial activity and—as he works—he may himself (alone and unaided) penetrate into the deeper meanings of this phase of the Ageless Wisdom.

I. The Seven Ray Energies

Fifteen Statements.

1. The seven rays embody and express the totality of energies which circulate throughout our planetary form.

2. These seven ray energies are the seven forces which unitedly compose the primary Ray of Love-Wisdom. This is the second ray of our solar system and the dominating ray in every planetary expression within the solar system. The seven rays are, all of them, subsidiary rays of this great cosmic ray.

3. No matter upon which ray the healer may be found, he must always work through the second subray of that ray—the ray of love-wisdom in each ray. By means of this, he becomes connected with or related to the governing soul and personality rays. The second ray has the capacity of all-inclusiveness.

4. The second ray and the second subray on all rays are themselves dual in expression. The healer must learn to work through the love aspect and not through the wisdom aspect. This takes much training in the practice of spiritual differentiation.

5. Those vehicles in the form nature which are on the line of 2-4-6 must be used by the healer when practicing the healing art. If he has no vehicles or bodies on this line of basic energy, he will not be able to heal. This is seldom realised. It is rare, however, to find an equipment lacking all second ray energy outlets.

6. Those healers who are on the second ray, or who are equipped with a powerful second ray vehicle, are usually great healers. The Christ, being the truest exponent of the second ray ever known on earth, was greatest of all the healing sons of God.

7. The ray of the soul conditions and determines the technique to be employed. The ray in the personality vehicles most closely related to the second ray (for which all the subrays act as channels) is the one through which the healing energy must flow.

8. The second subray of the soul ray determines the approach to the healing problem immediately confronting the healer; this energy is transmuted into healing force when passing through the appropriate personality vehicle. To be appropriate it must be on the line of 2-4-6.

9. The appropriate vehicle can be either the mental body or the emotional body. With the mass of men being centred in the astral nature, the healing will usually be most successful if the healer's channel of transmission is that body also.

10. A triangle of energies is therefore formed; it is composed of:
    a. The energy of the soul.
    b. The appropriate vehicle.
    c. The etheric body, through either the heart or the solar plexus centre.

11. Within the etheric body, a secondary triangle is formed for the circulation of energy between:
    a. The head centre, the centre of reception.
    b. The ajna centre, the centre for directed distribution.
    c. The centre which registers—as the line of least resistance—the energy of the soul ray, whichever of the seven rays that may be.

12. This secondary triangle is related to the primary triangle by an "act of deliberation." This is a part of the technique which I am withholding.

13. The healer who is sincere and experienced can (in default of the esoteric formula producing connection between the two triangles) do much to bring about some definite relation by a deliberate act of faith and by the firm statement of his *fixed intention*.

14. The greater triangle is that which affects the healer and makes him a transmitting agent; the lesser triangle is the one which produces the effect upon the patient and through which the healer—on the physical plane—works.

15. The procedure of the healer will therefore fall into three parts, prior to the conscious act of healing:

Process One.

   a. The healer will definitely and consciously link up with his own soul.

   b. He will then determine which of his personality vehicles is to be used; this will be based upon its reaction to energies, channeling along the line 2-4-6.

   c. By an act of the will he will then relate the soul energy, via the desired vehicle, with the appropriate centre in the etheric body; the heart or the solar plexus, always preferably the former.

Process two.

   a. He will next create the secondary triangle by focussing his attention in the centre of reception, the head centre.

   b. He will then connect this head centre, through the power of the creative imagination, with the centre between the eyebrows, and will hold the energy there because it is the directing agency.

   c. He will endeavour to gather into this ajna centre the energy of that centre within his etheric body which is related to his soul ray.

Process three.

He then, with deliberation, performs the act of linking the two triangles; once this is done, he is ready for the healing action.

II. THE RAYS OF HEALER AND OF PATIENT.

It will be apparent to the most superficial reader that the variation or the identity between the rays of the healer and his patient constitutes a factor of importance: many conditioning factors will be presented; there will also be present a contrast between the soul rays and the personality rays of both parties concerned. You may have, therefore, conditions in which:

1. The soul rays are identical and the personality rays are different.
2. The personality rays are the same but the soul rays are not.
3. The rays are similar in both cases.
4. The rays of neither soul nor personality are the same.
5. The soul ray is not known but the personality ray is apparent. The ray of the personality is easily ascertained, but there is often no indication as to the soul ray. This can apply to both healer and patient.
6. Nothing is known anent the rays of either party.

I am not bringing into this discussion any reference to the rays of the mental, astral or physical vehicles, though they have a definite and sometimes a decisive effect and the knowledge is most useful when known. The trained healer, when in possession of this knowledge, can use a secondary technique as an aid to the basic method, and use the appropriate lower vehicle (either his own or that of the patient) through which to pour a secondary stream of healing energy, thus enhancing the work of the primary stream. The addition of this secondary stream implies quite advanced knowledge on the part of the healer, or accurate information given by the patient. This is, as you may surmise, somewhat rare to find. People can, by careful study and the assembling of known analogous instances, ascertain with a fair degree of success the nature of the two major rays; it takes, however, an initiate of some standing to recognise and work through the rays of one of the lower bodies, and therefore be in a position to distribute the healing force through two centres simultaneously. We will not consequently consider more than the relation of the rays controlling the healer and the patient from the angle of soul and personality.

It is not possible for me to take each of the rays of both healer and patient and trace for you the appropriate technique; this will become clearer if you consider the great number of difficulties which are presented when both the rays of the two parties concerned are brought into relationship. In *Discipleship in the New Age* the rays are given of a large number of disciples. You might, as an experimental exercise, take these various rays, as assigned, and place each of these disciples in the part of either healer or patient, and see what centres would be employed in the case of some disease (each based in a different location in the human body), and then attempt to decide what method, mode or procedure the healer would be wise to follow. At the same time you should remember two things: first, that all these people are members of a second ray Ashram; also that they are disciples, and consequently their rays are apparent and obvious to the healer, which greatly helps. You could determine also what ray energy should be employed in the healing process, through what centre in yourself, as the healer, and the disciple as a patient, you should work and whether you are in a position to use a secondary technique. Then, having through the use of the imagination worked at an imaginary healing, look around among your friends and acquaintances for those whom you believe possess similar ray conditions and—if they are ailing or ill—seek to help them in the same way as you attempted to aid an imaginary patient; note then what happens. Avoid the use of a secondary technique, for you are more liable to be entirely wrong where the three lower vehicles are involved than with the two major expressions of life.

The rest of this subject can perhaps be clarified by certain statements which will become clearer as esoteric psychology emerges as a definite educational subject in the decades which lie ahead.

1. The healer should ascertain his rays, and then proceed with his work on the basis of that information. When that knowledge is not available, he should refrain from the attempt to heal.

2. When unable—from lack of this knowledge—to carry forward the healing work, let him confine himself to the task of acting as a channel for the energy of love to the patient.

3. The healer will find it easier in most cases to ascertain his rays, or one of them at least, than to know the rays of the patient.

   There are two reasons for this:

   a. The fact that he seeks to heal and help indicates a fair measure of advancement upon the spiritual way. Such advancement is required for correct finding of the ray quality. A little study of himself and of the possible rays present should in time show him the nature of the energies controlling him.

   b. The patient, if advanced, is liable not to seek his help, but will handle his own problem, through the soul and through the Ashram, if affiliated with one. If he is not advanced, the personality ray will be more easily ascertained than the soul ray, and will therefore provide the point of contact.

4. The healer, having to his satisfaction determined upon the rays or ray conditioning him, should then prepare himself for the healing task by a minimum of five hours of most careful preparation, related to his mind, the thinking apparatus. I mean not five hours of consecutive mental control and reflection, but a period of quiet thought, carried on—when possible—wherein the healer studies the patient and familiarises himself with:

    a. The problem of the disease and its particular nature.

    b. Its location in the physical body.

    c. The centre involved and (when he is an enlightened disciple) with its condition.

    d. The acuteness of the difficulty and the chance of a cure.

    e. The danger of death or not.

    f. The psychological condition of the patient.

    g. The rays of the patient, if feasible; these, if known, will condition his approach.

5. Thus prepared, the healer focusses his attention in his own ray. When he only possesses general and not specific knowledge of his own ray or rays and those of the patient, the healer may proceed upon the surmise that one or both are along the line of 1-3-5-7 or 2-4-6 and act upon that general assumption. To possess specific and particularised knowledge is useful, but where it exists not, and particular rays cannot be assigned, it is often possible to determine whether the general trend of the character is along the line of love or of the will, and then to act acordingly. The problem then is whether the relation between healer and

patient will be from personality to personality, from soul to soul, or from personality to soul and vice versa.

6. When the relation is that of personality to personality (and this will be the most usual), the energy with which the healer will work is simply that of planetary prana; the effect of this will be to stimulate the natural processes of the physical body and (in cooperation with nature and so in line with the patient's karma) so fortify his physical vehicle that he can cast off the disease or can be aided to face with confidence the processes of death, and with calm and intelligent understanding pass out to the subtler realms of being.

7. Where the relation is that of the soul of the healer to the personality of the patient, the healer will work with ray energy, pouring his own ray energy through the centre which is controlling the diseased area. When both the soul of the healer and that of the patient are working in cooperation there can be the blending of two energies or (where similar rays are present) the strengthening of one energy and a greatly hastened work of healing or of dissolution.

8. The healer must ever bear in mind that his task is either to heal—under the karmic law—or to aid in the processes of dissolution, bringing about, therefore, a higher form of healing.

9. Unless the healer is a higher initiate and can work in full awareness of circumstances and governing conditions, sudden healings and dramatically arrested disease will *not* occur. If they do occur, it will be due to three things:

   a. The destiny of the patient whose time has not yet come.

   b. The interposition of the patient's own soul, who is, in the last analysis, the agent of karma.

    c. The aid of the healer which proved adequate enough to give the patient the necessary confidence and added strength to bring about his own healing.

10. Nobody is ever brought back from the "gates of death" whose karma indicates that his time has come; the life cycle on the physical plane then ends unless he is a worker in an Ashram, a disciple of some standing whose work and presence is still needed on earth to complete his assigned task. Then the Master of the Ashram may add His knowledge and energy to that of the healer or to that of the patient, and bring about a temporary postponement of departure. Upon this the healer may not count, or the patient either, for they know not the full and warranting circumstances.

11. There are certain elementary requirements or conditions in which the healer should work and which are necessary. These are:

    a. Complete quiet in the sickroom, as far as possible.

    b. As few people in the patient's room as wisdom may dictate. The thinking and thoughtforms of the people present can either be distracting or distracted, and thereby deflect the healing currents; on the other hand, they can sometimes strongly aid the healer's work.

    c. The patient—again when possible—should lie on his back, or on his side so that centres up the spine are turned towards the healer. In some cases (and these the healer must himself determine) he should lie in such a position that the healer can hold his hands above the area of disease, though in no case must the healer touch the patient's body.

12. When quiet, peace and silence have been reached, the healer will proceed with the appropriate technique. The

quiet, peace and silence mentioned above refer not only to physical conditions, but to the emotional and mental states of the healer and the patient as well as of those present; this is not always easy to attain.

Where the healer has not the appropriate technique or does not understand the formulas given later in this instruction, he can assemble his own technique and rules after a close study of these healing instructions, which contain enough material and suggestions for such an action.

III. The Seven Healing Techniques

The techniques I shall have to give in the form of seven ancient symbolic statements or formulas, gathered out of the *Book of Rules for Initiated Disciples*. I dare not yet give the simple physical application of these ray techniques, as it would be too dangerous. When rightly used and understood they carry terrific force and—in the wrong hands—could work real damage. May I remind you here that the Black Lodge initiates likewise heal or produce death and disease, and employ very similar techniques; the difference lies in the fact that they can work only with the personality rays of both healer and patient, and because they are more potent *on the physical plane* than are the Members of the Great White Lodge, their work is frequently most effective. The spiritual healer, working with the energies of light whenever possible, is seldom as effective physically.

The members of the Black Lodge, or healers working under its influence, are, however, totally unable to work on a patient who is spiritually oriented to the slightest degree, and is therefore coming under the control of his soul; neither can they work through a healer who is spiritually oriented. When they attempt to do so they find themselves combatted by energy coming from the Ashram towards which either the healer or the patient is moving or with which he is affiliated, even if he has his place only upon the periphery. Where the average unthinking man is concerned, the danger of "black" interference is nil; the dark forces do not interest themselves in any unimportant person, save with those of potency and influence who can serve their ends. Also their evil work is only possible at the moment (or cycle) wherein the man is making decision as to whether he will move in spiritual living, remain static where he is, or turn with deliberation (which is exceedingly rare) to the path of pure selfishness. This path leads to the Black Lodge.

Some disciple in the early part of next century will take these techniques or magical statements, relating to the healing work, and interpret them and elucidate them. They are susceptible of three significances, the lowest of which the modern student may succeed in interpreting for himself if he reflects adequately and lives spiritually. Here are the seven statements.

THE SEVEN STATEMENTS

1. *The first ray technique.*

Let the dynamic force which rules the hearts of all within Shamballa come to my aid, for I am worthy of that aid. Let it descend unto the third, pass to the fifth and focus on the seventh. These words mean not what doth at sight appear. The third, the fifth, the seventh lie within the first and come from out the Central Sun of spiritual livingness. The highest then awakens within the one who knows and within the one who must be healed and thus the two are one. This is mystery deep. The blending of the healing force effects the work desired; it may bring death, that great release, and re-establish thus the fifth, the third, the first, but not the seventh.

This dynamic first ray energy is usually employed by the trained spiritual healer when it is apparent to him that the patient's hour has come and release approaches. In cases where the first ray is the soul ray of either healer or patient, this application of first ray energy must move from head centre to head centre, and from thence to the area of distress and to the centre allied with the location. This may cause (when healing is possible and karmically correct) a temporary increase of the trouble; this is owing to the fact that the incoming energy "expels dynamically" the very seed or roots of the disease. There may be a rise in temperature, or a collapse of some kind or another, and for this the healer, the patient and the attendant physician must be prepared and should take the needed physical steps for amelioration —steps as ordained by the orthodox medical profession, which will offset the purely physical reaction. Where the soul ray of the patient is not on the first ray, but the first ray is the ray of the personality, the healer must use great caution in applying first ray energy, and should proceed very slowly and gradually through the centre on the line of 1-3-5-7 which is nearest to the seat of trouble, passing the energy through that centre and thence to the centre (whichever that may be) found in the locality of the disease. If that particular centre happens to be on the line of 3-5-7, the healer will have to exercise special care, or else the dynamic first ray energy will destroy and not heal.

2. *The second ray technique.*

Let the healing energy descend, carrying its dual lines of life and its magnetic force. Let that magnetic living force withdraw and supplement that

which is present in the seventh, opposing four and six
to three and seven, but dealing not with five. The
circular, inclusive vortex—descending to the point—
disturbs, removes and then supplies and thus the
work is done.

The heart revolves; two hearts revolve as one;
the twelve within the vehicle, the twelve within the
head and the twelve upon the plane of soul endeavour, cooperate as one and thus the work is done.
Two energies achieve this consummation and the
three whose number is a twelve respond to the
greater twelve. The life is known and the years
prolonged.

If this ancient statement is read in the light of any knowledge you may have (and you probably have more than you
realise), particularly knowledge anent the centres, the
primary or easiest interpretation will appear.

3. *The third ray technique.*

The healer stands and weaves. He gathers from
the three, the five, the seven that which is needed
for the heart of life. He brings the energies together and makes them serve the third; he thus
creates a vortex into which the one distressed must
descend and with him goes the healer. And yet they
both remain in peace and calm Thus must the angel
of the Lord descend into the pool and bring the
healing life.

The "pool of waters" figures here and may cause much
questioning as to its significance. Its elementary interpretation relates in reality to the central and major cause of
much disease (as we have earlier seen), the emotional
nature, which it is the task of the third aspect of divinity

to control. Ponder on this, for much enlightenment may come.

The next healing technique is longer and far more abstruse. There is little of it that you will understand; it is entirely related, as far as our theme is concerned, to man himself and to the aphorism: "Man, *know* thyself."

4. *The fourth ray technique.*

> The healer knows the place where dissonance is found. He also knows the power of sound and the sound which must be heard. Knowing the note to which the fourth great group reacts and linking it to the great Creative Nine, he sounds the note which brings release, the note which will bring absorption into one. He educates the listening ear of him who must be healed; he likewise trains the listening ear of him who must go forth. He knows the manner of the sound which brings the healing touch; and also that which says: Depart. And thus the work is done.

This fourth technique is one that—in default of true ray knowledge—can be of general usefulness, because this fourth ray governs the fourth kingdom in nature, the human. The healer along this line of work (and such healers are practically nonexistent at this time because the fourth ray is not in incarnation) heals primarily through the use of the appropriate sound or sounds. In the early stages when this technique comes into demonstration, music will be largely used by the healer to bring about a cure or to facilitate the process of death or departure. It will, however, be music with one constantly recurring chord, which will embody the note of the fourth ray and of the human kingdom. Healing by the means of sound will be one of the first healing unfoldments to be noted at the close of the next century. More teaching along this line would be useless until the fourth ray again cycles into manifestation.

5. *The fifth ray technique.*

That which has been given must be used; that which emerges from within the given mode will find its place within the healer's plan. That which is hidden must be seen and from the three, great knowledge will emerge. For these the healer seeks. To these the healer adds the two which are as one, and so the fifth must play its part and the five must play its part and the five must function as if one. The energies descend, pass through and disappear, leaving the one who could respond with karma yet to dissipate and taking with them him who may not thus respond and so must likewise disappear.

The obvious and simplest meaning of the fifth ray mode of healing is that the healer, working scientifically and largely on concrete levels, employs all aids to bring about a cure, starting with appropriate physical care and passing on to subtler modes of healing. Again I would point out that physical aid can be as divinely used as the more mysterious methods which the metaphysical healer of the present time believes to be so profoundly more effective. Just as all modern knowledge, developed on the physical plane, through the personalities of men and women of insight and genius everywhere, is useful to the disciple and initiate, in time and space, so it is with the medical sciences. Just as right application of these varying sciences has to be made by the disciple or the initiate in order to bring about spiritual results, so must it be when the healer is at work.

All work becomes spiritual when rightly motivated, when wise discrimination is employed and soul power is added to the knowledge gained in the three worlds. The dynamic use of energy in one of its seven streams, added to the sane understanding and work of the modern physician, aided by the healer (who works as does a catalyst), can produce miracles when destiny so ordains. The metaphysical healer who works solely on the subtler levels is like the spiritual worker who fails so constantly to precipitate the needed financial assets on the physical plane. This is caused frequently by a subtle—though usually unrecognised—sense of superiority with which the average healer and the esotericist views his problem of materialisation of either physical health or money. Ponder on this and realise that fifth ray methods carry through to the physical plane; there they engender conflict and eventually produce a physical precipitation of the desired nature. In what I have said anent the fifth ray techniques, I have given more hints and information than in any of the others.

6. *The sixth ray technique.*

Cleaving the waters, let the power descend, the healer cries. He minds not how the waters may respond; they oft bring stormy waves and dire and dreadful happenings. The end is good. The trouble will be ended when the storm subsides and energy has fulfilled its charted destiny. Straight to the heart the power is forced to penetrate, and into every channel, nadi, nerve and spleen the power must seek a passage and a way and thus confront the enemy who has effected entrance and settled down to live. Ejection—ruthless, sudden and complete—is undertaken by the one who sees naught else but perfect functioning and brooks no interference. This perfect functioning opens thus the door to life eternal or to life on earth for yet a little while.

This technique is curiously potent and sudden when the healer is on the sixth ray; the results are drastic and full of pain, but the results are sure—healing or death, and oft the latter. The sixth ray healer is seldom disciplined or wise at this time, owing to this being the end of the sixth ray cycle. When again the sixth ray comes into manifestation, humanity will have progressed far along the Path and the present aggressive, too sure, fanatical sixth ray healer will not re-appear. Today they are the majority, and their work is not good; it is well-intentioned, but the technique is ignorantly applied and the end justifies not the assurance of the healer, leading to frequent deception of the patient.

7. *The seventh ray technique.*

> Energy and force must meet each other and thus the work is done. Colour and sound in ordered sequence must meet and blend and thus the work of magic can proceed. Substance and spirit must evoke each other and, passing through the centre of the one who seeks to aid, produce the new and good. The healer energises thus with life the failing life, driving it forth or anchoring it yet more deeply in the place of destiny. All seven must be used and through the seven there must pass the energies the need requires, creating the new man who has for ever been and will for ever be, and either here or there.

In this technique you have the clue to them all, for the work of the seventh ray healer is to bring together the life and the substance which will take the place of the substance which is diseased and bring new life to aid the recovery. The glory of life lies in consummation and in emergence. This is the prime task and the prime reward of all true healers. It is this technique of attraction and substitution which will be brought to a fine point of scientific expression in the coming new age wherein the seventh ray will dominate our planet, producing that which is new and needed and determining the coming culture, civilisation and science.

In conclusion I would like to tell you the reasons I am refraining from more detailed information and from a clear analysis of the wording of these ancient formulas of healing. Apart from the reason, earlier stated, that men are not yet ready to be given explicit instructions, for the time being anything I might say would appear to you puerile. That is the curious word which seems to be descriptive of possible immediate reaction. We are on the verge of entering a new era in scientific unfoldment, owing to the discovery of how to release the energy of the atom. Not even the scientists responsible for the discovery have the faintest idea of the far-reaching effects of this momentous happening. From the angle of our subject and the theme of this volume, an entirely new language related to energy and force is already in the making; the use of the discovery in the handling of disease will, in almost the immediate future (from the occult angle) be regarded as little short of miraculous.

This discovery of atomic liberation has been brought about by the activity of the first ray in relation to the incoming seventh ray and has its analogous situation in the liberation of the Master at the fifth initiation (when the door of the tomb bursts wide open) and in the act of dying, when the imprisoned soul finds release. In the light of future scientific happenings, these ancient techniques will become much clearer, and in the meantime any explanation of their true "energetic import" would be meaningless. The new and coming terminology will throw light on the ancient formulas, and in time you will see how much can be conveyed to the intelligent healer of that new generation by what seems to you both disappointing, without use or significance, and needlessly abstruse.

In this interim period between the past and that which is on its way, it is not easy for even a Master of the Wisdom to speak or teach, particularly in connection with the theme of healing. The physical body is not yet generally recognised as an electrical unit; its nature as pure atomic energy is not yet realised; the fact of the energy body, the etheric vehicle, is not at this time recognised in the teachings of the modern medical schools, though the fact has been discussed; the explosive nature of energy, when in contact with force, or of the soul in relation to substance, is completely unknown or veiled in mystical language. Until such time as the new scientific formulas and the new approach (which the discovery of the release of atomic energy has made possible) have become more generally understood, are a familiar subject of discussion and couched in familiar language, the coming science of healing must remain behind a veil of unsuitable language and hidden by inappropriate words.

This fact, as I have oft told you, handicaps all new presentations of truth; the language of the electrical engineer or of the automobile draftsman, for instance, would have been entirely meaningless to the average man a hundred years ago. So it is with the new themes and the great discoveries which are on their way and which will eventually affect every department of human life, including the Art of Healing.

I sign myself, because it has been given out who I am, as the Master *Djwhal Khul*.

THE TIBETAN

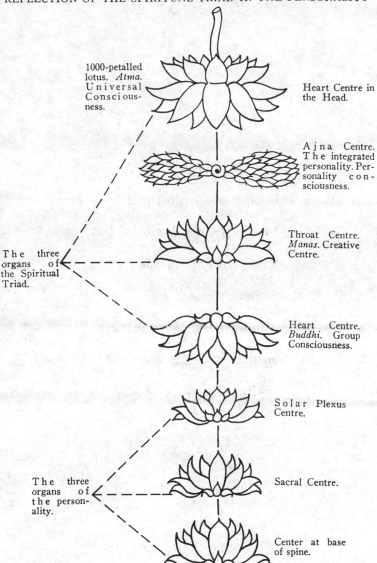

1000-petalled lotus. *Atma.* Universal Consciousness.

Heart Centre in the Head.

Ajna Centre. The integrated personality. Personality consciousness.

The three organs of the Spiritual Triad.

Throat Centre. *Manas.* Creative Centre.

Heart Centre. *Buddhi.* Group Consciousness.

Solar Plexus Centre.

The three organs of the personality.

Sacral Centre.

Center at base of spine.

The reflection of the Spiritual Triad in the personality is complete when the Ajna Centre is entirely under the control of the soul. There is no attempt in this diagram to picture the correct number of petals in each lotus.

See page 162

Training for new age

discipleship is provided

by the *Arcane School*.

The principles of the

Ageless Wisdom are

presented through esoteric

meditation, study and

service as a *way of life.*

INDEX

Abdomen—
  cancer, cause, 240
  diseases, cause, 108
Abrams method, contribution and limitation, 279–280
Absence of mind, 342
Absorption, definition, 434
Abstraction—
  developed from detachment, 674
  final, three points of departure, 472–473
  of its own intrinsic energy by soul, 470
  of life principle, 444–445
  plane of, 419–420
  stage, 683
  will principle of, 448
Acceptance of life, positive, results, 92
Acidity, causes, 38–39
Act of Restitution, 460–464
Adrenals, relations, 45
Affirmations, futility, 193, 212
After-death—
  consciousness. See Consciousness, after-death.
  experiences—
    activity of soul, 462–463, 467, 487, 489, 491, 497
    ashramic, 490
    astral, 488, 489, 490, 491, 494
    awareness of past, present, and future, 496–497
    death of astral body, 488, 489, 497
    destruction of mental body, 489–490, 499
    devachanic, 496–499
    dispersal of etheric body, 477–478
    etheric forces, return to general reservoir, 409, 460–461
    of average man, 491–493
    of disciples working in ashrams, 396
    preparation for reincarnation, 469–470, 495–496
    re-assimilation of substance and appropriation of matter, 497
    review, 491–492, 496, 498

seat of consciousness, 467, 478, 490, 494–495
seeking and finding loved and hated persons, 493
soul contact, 491, 495, 497
withdrawal from astral body, 487, 488–489, 494
withdrawal from etheric body, 470
withdrawal from mental body, 489
withdrawal of etheric body, 460, 462, 466, 475–476, 477
withdrawal of soul and re-absorption, 407, 409–410
techniques of elimination, 488–490
Alignment—
  constant practice, 557
  definition, 620
  for radiatory healing, 103, 653, 657
  in use of hands, 648, 651
  lack, results, 12
  lessons in, 556
  necessity, 545
  production, 329
  through meditation, 7
  use by soul, 241
  with soul, 158, 351
Allopathic—
  method, contribution, 373
  physicians, work, 16
Analogies, physical and higher nature of man, 163–166
Analogy of basic dualism of manifestation, 144
Analysis, distinction from criticism, 355
Ancient Law of Evil Sharing, 30, 544
Angel of Death, work, 647
Angel of the Presence—
  definition, 590
  conflict with Dweller on Threshold, 507, 639
  descent, 140
  self-consciousness, 407
  transmutation of glory, 515–516
  See also Soul.
Angels. See Devas.

717

Body—Continued
kama-manasic—
  destruction, 497
  rejection after death, 409
  See also Body, astral; Body, emotional.
mental—
  channel for healing force, 697
  definition, 3
  destruction by disciple, 489–490
  destruction by kama-manasic person, 489
  destruction by sounds, 499
  diseases, 88–114
  effect of death, 409, 415, 489–490
  functioning after death, 377–378
  functions, 88
  nature of, 612
  of manasic person, type, 488
  photographing, impossibility, 378
  purification, 489
  substance, 609
mental-emotional, rejection after death, 409
physical—
  activities, direction, 200
  animation, 209–210
  apparatus resulting from inner activity, 332–333
  appropriation by soul, 428
  atoms, diseases from planetary conditions, 243–249
  automatic response to astral control, 562–563
  change, 230–231
  concentration upon, results, 579–614
  control, 228, 230, 332
  coordination with etheric, 79–80
  death process, 408, 460, 470–476
  definition, 2
  discarded at will, 501, 502
  energising, 2, 331, 428–429
  factor of karma, 608
  forcing to extraneous uses, 4
  four major agents of energy distribution, 141–143
  functions, 332, 616, 617
  insensitivity to pain, 502
  isolated form, 638–639
  lunar lords, 609, 611
  nature of, 34, 39, 136, 190, 282, 335, 609, 611, 612–613, 614
  newer knowledge, 368
  phenomenal appearance, 163–168
  production and conditioning, 142
  relation to centres, 37–38
  relation to soul, 332

response to attractive pull of matter, 475
response to etheric energies, 87
stamina, weakening, 229
struggle with soul at death, 462, 464, 467, 476
substance, 609
tenant, 397–398
two aspects, simultaneous treatment, 574
vacating at death, 418–421, 429, 460–463, 464, 470
physical-etheric, death stages, 408
pituitary—
  expression, 149
  relationships, 45, 148, 149, 155, 200, 210
  stimulation, 325
soul. *See* Body, causal.
vital—
  building, 326–327
  deficient, traits, 326
  importance, 274, 276
  nature of, 34, 281
  See also Body, etheric.
Boils, causes, 561
Book of Imperfections, quotation, 294
Book of Rules for Initiated Disciples, 705
Borrowed goods, restitution, symbolic, 426
Bowel complaints, cause, 108
Brahmarandra. *See* Centre, head.
Brain—
  cells—
    breakdown, 339
    obstructing, 22
    over-stimulation, 316
    stabilisation, 108
  consciousness of time, 351
  diseases—
    causes, 108, 201, 562
    increase, 201
    not mental, 342
  effect of death-dealing substance in blood, 474
  etheric counterpart, reaction to, 474
  functions, 46–47, 85, 129
  lesions, 302
  link, 17, 648, 654–655
  nature of, 337
  physical, reflex action of inadequate circulation, 107
  tissue, breaking down, 316
  tissue, reaction to head centres, 201
  use in healing, 17, 23, 102, 648

Earth—Continued
  etheric—Continued
    body, recognition, importance, 550
    substance, nature of, 25
  life, re-orientation to before reincarnation, 495–496
  life source, 679
  non-sacred planet, 298
  planetary conditions, obscure, 242–249
  pull of matter, 475
  ray, 590, 597
  seven centres, 619
  surface, emanations causing disease, 243
Earthbound souls—
  frequenting seance rooms, 443
  status, 446
Economic ills, correspondence to disease, 549
Education of patient, 388–389
Ego. *See* Soul; Souls.
Ego-maniac, production, 176
Electric fire in microcosm, 145, 147
Electrical phenomena, types, 327
Electricity—
  future discoveries, 376, 377, 378–379
  in manifestation, 377
  mystery of, 368, 377
  relating to photography, 376
  type used today, 377
  use, 255, 377
Electro-therapy—
  contribution and limitation, 279–280
  use, 48, 373, 482
Elemental—
  astral, struggle with soul at death, 464
  involutionary, aid in healing, 646–647
  involutionary, conflict with spirit, 639–641
  personality, nature of, 639–641
  physical, definition, 462
  physical, struggle with soul at death, 462, 464, 467
  planetary, life, karma, 635
Elementals—
  of personality, 608, 609
  work with, 609
Elimination—
  of factors hindering inflow of spiritual force, 386
  organs, manifestation through, 107
  overcoming form, 434
  right methods, understanding, 109
  See also Art of Elimination.

Embalming, results, 484
Embolism, avoidance, 542
Emergent Evolution, doctrine, 20
Emotion—
  astral, death of, 406
  uncontrolled, effects, 38–52
Emotional—
  imbalance, cause, 87
  nature, starvation, 59
  reactions, inhibition, results, 239
  turmoil, cause and effects, 592
  upheavals, conquest, 672–673
Emotional-desire nature, diseases arising in, 33–71
Emotionalism—
  effect of full moon, 341–342
  non-response to, 406
Emotions—
  aggregation, 43–44
  cause of disease, 3–4
  control, 579–580, 708
  of patient, 674–675
  transformation, 216, 239–240, 315
  vehicle—
    cause, 3
    See also Body, astral; Body, emotional; Body, kama-manasic.
End of the age, 448
Endocrine system—
  aspects, 197
  control by thought power, 219–220
  deficiency, results, 208
  energy distribution, 141–142, 143
  hormones, 617
  nature of, 141–142
  relation to centres, 38, 45–46, 140
  relation to nadis and nerves, 197
  relationships, 45–46, 84, 140
  ruler, 143
  See also Glandular system; Glands.
Endocrinologist, work, 47, 48, 49–50, 219–220
Endocrinology, fallacy of gland treatment, 626
Energies—
  above diaphragm, conflict, 594
  affecting health, recognition, 483
  balancing in treatment, 605
  basic, pouring into physical body, 275–276
  below diaphragm, conflict, 594
  building, of soul, 191, 607
  in man, 136, 586
  interplay in man, results, 137
  of centres, lifting by disciple, 127
  of centres, synthesis, 183
  of etheric body, unification, 175

Index

Patient—Continued
  restoration, psychological, 388
  self-healing, 529, 547, 655, 656, 657, 701, 704
  soul—
    contact with, 524
    control, 643, 644
    interposition in sudden healing, 703
    life, stimulation, 18, 23, 541
    power, 27
  telepathic rapport with, 525
  treatment by etheric triangle, 697
  will, 7
Perfect One, method, 660
Perfection—
  and imperfection, 295
  bringing imperfection to surface, 660, 663
  material, of body, production, 211
Personal self, cause of disease, 191, 607
Personality—
  activity, transmutation, 214
  and initiate, intermediary, 691
  astral forces, 52
  cause of friction, 566, 569
  cleavage, 96
  conflict with soul, 507
  consciousness, death, 506, 507, 516, 517, 518, 640
  contact with Monad, 642
  control by soul, 200, 201, 507, 571
  control, weakening, results, 138
  coordinated, energy, 35
  coordinating, production, 35
  dead, incapable of transmission of lower vibrations, 516
  definitions, 642, 681
  development, results, 513
  direction of physical activities, 200
  elemental, nature of, 639–640
  elimination, 518
  energy, comparison with soul energy, 584
  equipment, physical factors, emphasis, 325
  factors affecting, 133
  force—
    characteristics, 356–357
    full response to, 139
    stream, 429
  forces, clearing-house, 127
  forces, synthesis, 172, 329
  functioning on physical plane after death, 681
  fusion with soul, 159, 200
  handicaps, causes, 129–130
  identification with soul, 507

integrated—
  after-death experiences, 487–496
  and functioning, 147
  definition, 487
  forces, 190
  growing rapport with soul, 498
  of disciple, 498
  of mystic, 115
  organ, 200
  use of nadis, nerves, and glands, 197
integration. *See* Integration, personality.
karmic law, 624
life, field, clearing, 344
life, stages, 506–507
link with Spiritual Triad, 683
linking with Monad, 153, 183
love, 356–357
lunar lord of, activity, 691–692
mastery, 578
negation of soul control, results, 137
obliteration, 515–516
polarisation, knowledge of, results, 551
production, 178
ray, causation, 590
ray, energy, 597
relation—
  of heart centre to, 158
  to ajna, 210
  to antahkarana, 153, 586
  to Monad, 153, 183, 406, 518
reorientation of life force, 120
representative, 337
responding to soul energy, rhythm, 678
spiritually energised, 203
split, 117
substitute created by Master, 518, 519
substitute created by soul, 518
thoughtform, elimination, 505, 515–520
vehicle, channel for flow of healing energy, 696, 697
will, 609, 676
work, mechanism, 151
Perversions due to frustration, 562
Petals. *See* Lotus petals.
Peter, healing, 601
Petit mal, cause, 80
Philosophy, esoteric, five groupings, 81–82
Phobias, effect of full moon, 342
Photographing health aura, 466
Physical apparatus resulting from inner activity, 232–233

Rhythm—Continued
  of living, result, **61**
  of personality, responding to soul energy, 678
  ordered, of centres, 137, 215
  orderly, of glandular system, 213
  physical, cause, 85
  right, establishment, 130
  study, 417
Rhythms, wrong, 94, 95
Right human relations, 125, 668
Rochester, N. Y., area of light, 367–368
Roman Catholic Church, doctrines, errors, 393
Roman Empire, decadence, 232
Roosevelt, Franklin D., work, 667
Rule for healers on—
  concentration of needed energy, 205, 602–607
  diagnosis, 271, 629–633
  linking, 17–18, 642–659
  magnetic purity, 30, 577–582
  self-training, 57, 550–558, 576–577
  will in leash, 98, 659, 672–678
Rules—
  application by healer, 576
  six, 524, 533–535
  source and application in past, 576
Russia—
  characterisation, 669
  vision and cruel techniques, 662

Sacred Word—
  chanting at death bed, 458
  See also Aum; Om; Word; Words.
Sadism, occurrence, 317, 393
Saints, diseases, 595
Salt water, value, 62
Salvation, each man's work, 393
Sanat Kumara, 298, 405, 406–407, 620, 667, 678, 680, 687
Sandalwood, ray and use, 459
Sanitation—
  in future, 219
  methods, 324, 375
  symbol, 235
  use, 330
Saturn—
  ruler of endocrine system, 143
  ruler of throat centre, 151, 152
Scarlet fever, nature of, 312, 321
School of pseudo-occultists, work, results, 212
Schools—
  esoteric, teaching, 158, 546–547
  healing, future, *372–373*

Science—
  modern, theories in *Treatise on Cosmic Fire,* 368
  next step ahead, 368
  of—
    centres, 557, 595
    cyclic manifestations, 436
    death, 440
    energy distribution, 572
    healing, 525
    integration, 118
    occultism, foundation, 586, 587
    soul contact, 557
    the Breath, 242
    the Centres, 557
Sciences, human and occult, bridge between, 369
Scientific unfoldment of disciple, 215–217
Scientist, basic postulates, occult light on, study, 368–369
Sea bathing, value, 62
Seance, materialisation, avoidance, 443
Secret Doctrine—
  narrative, 231
  quotation, 589
  references, 292, 337, 377, 521–522, 558, 565, 583
  study, 368
Seeds, three, of the future, 492–493
Seer, illuminated, 455
Self-consciousness of deceased man, 491, 494
Self-discipline of disciple, 675–676
Self-healing by patient, 529, 547, 655, 656, 657, 704
Self-improvement, 498 499
Self-interest, disease, 67
Self-pity, results, 563
Self-preparation for giving treatment, 702
Self-preservation, instinct, clue, 178
Self-satisfaction, disease resulting, 67
Self-sufficiency, disease resulting, 67
Self-training of healer, rule, 57, 550–558, 576–577
Self-will of healer, 677
Selfishness—
  group, 71
  human, end, 236
Selflessness, practical applications, 346
Senile decay, healing, 108
Senses, five, connection with nadis, 333
Sensitives, difficulties, 340
Sensitivity—
  astral, no longer required, 406